This book is for my children,
Steven, Bruce, David, and Suzanne,
and their mother, June.

I extend my special thanks to a world-class agent,
Geraldine B. Wallerstein.

And last, but certainly not least, I want to acknowledge
the enormous contribution of my editor,
Lucy Carson of Prometheus Books.

A Handbook for Booklovers

A Survey of Collectible Authors, Books, and Values

by

Joseph Raymond LeFontaine

PROMETHEUS BOOKS
Buffalo, New York

 Inquiries should be addressed to Prometheus Books, 700 East Amherst Street, Buffalo, New York 14215.

91 90 89 88 4 3 2 1

The publisher and the author assume no liability, implied or otherwise, in the use of the information presented in this book. Users should be aware that book values differ widely throughout North America and Europe and are subject to the laws of supply and demand. Always keep in mind that the value of any merchandise is that which a willing buyer will pay a willing seller.

Library of Congress Cataloging-in-Publication Data

LeFontaine, Joseph Raymond, 1927-
A handbook for booklovers: a survey of collectible authors, books, and values.

1. Book collecting—Handbooks, manuals, etc.
2. Books—Prices. I. Title.
Z987.L38 1988 002'.075 88-15128
ISBN 0-87975-491-5

A Handbook for Booklovers

Contents

Appendices

Introduction

A Handbook for Booklovers is for people who:

- have books and want to know whether or not they are collectible;
- want to acquire books that are collectible;
- want to know interesting, sometimes trivial facts about the authors and/or genres they most enjoy; and/or
- want to learn more about the collectible-books field in general.

If you fit into one or more of these categories, you are a booklover, or *bibliophile:* If you fit into one or both of the first two, then you are a book *collector* as well, even though you may not acknowledge being a collector because you perceive the mystique that surrounds the field, a mystique that is perhaps unconsciously perpetuated by many antiquarian booksellers who see themselves as scholars rather than as purveyors of used merchandise—in this case, books. *Collectibility* is a function of *value,* which can be in terms of either money, or pleasure, or a combination of both (see Chapter 3 for the definition of valuable).

A Handbook for Booklovers is not directed primarily at collectible-book scholars—whether neophyte or experienced—or members of the academic community (there are already plenty of books about books for experts). I hope scholars and academics will like it too, but more important, I want *everyone* to find it useful, understandable, and, above all, enjoyable.

This book is, for example, for the person who read John D. MacDonald's latest book and would like to know more about him. What other books did he write? What was his first book? Has he written any books using a pen name? Or for anyone asking the same questions about Danielle Steele, Mary Stewart, Robert B. Parker, Agatha Christie, or any one of a thousand other authors. Perhaps you are wondering if the name of the author of the latest best-selling espionage thriller is a pseudonym. If so, what is the author's true name? How many mystery lovers are aware that Ed McBain is a pseudonym for Evan Hunter, author of *The Blackboard Jungle*? Or that John LeCarre's real name is David John Cornwell?

How often have you picked up a book by an author you are unfamiliar with and, after reading it, decided you would like to read more by that author? And then run into a stone wall at the bookstore or library when you tried to find out what else that author may have written beyond what is currently on the shelf?

To go a step farther, most booksellers and libraries keep *Books in Print* on hand. However, *Books in Print* may show only a small portion of an author's total work. Like *Subject Guide to Books in Print* and *Paperback Books in Print*, it is only useful for those works that are still available from a publisher or bookstore. Out-of-print books, or those written under unknown pseudonyms, will remain a mystery.

On the face of it, it may appear that this book is for a specialized audience. That is not really true. Rather, it is a compendium of information that is normally difficult if not impossible to obtain, gathered together for the first time in one easy-to-use reference source.

This book is for all serious readers—those who buy or borrow a book a month, or perhaps one a week. Whether it's romance, mystery, western, juvenile, science fiction, or general Americana, each category has its devotees.

A Handbook for Booklovers provides the kind of information that is not available in other books on book collecting and presents enough factual data to enable any would-be collector, librarian, or bookseller to make knowledgeable choices. It offers a wealth of fascinating literary trivia, as well as useful information on thousands of collectible authors, book titles, and values.

How to Use This Book

Here are some suggestions for making the best use of this book. I'm sure you will find uses I haven't even contemplated. I hope so.

First, take a few minutes to read through the Table of Contents. This will give you an idea of just what I've included. Later, you can turn to those chapters that particularly interest or intrigue you and browse through them at a more leisurely pace. But before you do that, finish reading this section. It will enable you to make better use of the information and to better understand how it is presented and why it is presented that way.

Terminology

In order to gain the maximum benefit from the information I have compiled here, you will need to understand all the terms you come across. Some of these, such as *reprint*, or *edition*, are not unique to the collectible-books field, and you may already be familiar with them. Others, like *wraps*, or *points*, are specialized technical terms you may not have seen before. A third group is made up of terms like *pseudonym* and *N.p.* that have one meaning in common usage but whose definitions have been expanded or modified to meet the specific needs of *A Handbook for Booklovers.*

Chapter 3 lists terms and abbreviations that are commonly used in the field of collectible books.

Chapter Organization

Chapters 1 through 4 are straight text and are self-explanatory.

Chapters 5 through 18 are list chapters. Each opens with a brief note on what is included in that section, why it is interesting or important, and how to look up specific facts.

In Chapters 7 and 9 through 18, all books are listed by author in alphabetical order unless no author appears on the title page; then they are listed by the first main word in the title.

Finally, Chapters 9 through 18 are value chapters. All values in this book are for first editions in very good to fine condition, with their dust jackets if originally issued with one. It is reasonable to presume that all first editions by any of the authors listed will have value, but do not assume that all books by the same author will have comparable values. *Points* often need to be verified to properly identify many of these books. An out-of-print or rare-book specialist should be consulted for verification of edition and value.

Bibliographic Style

The bibliographic style used in *A Handbook for Booklovers* takes the form of: author, title, place of publication, publisher, date of publication, edition specifications (for example, wraps, illustrations, maps), and price. While every entry does not contain all of these facts, enough information is provided to make identification possible. Beyond this, a competent bookseller or librarian should be consulted.

All of the books described in *A Handbook for Booklovers* are collectible, and the primary sources for tracking down collectible books are out-of-print-/rare-book seller catalogs (see Appendix B for a partial list). In these catalogs, whose specialized function is to provide prospective buyers with estimated prices of the books they list, the information that appears on the *title page* is the controlling information—even if it conflicts with what is shown on the dust jacket or elsewhere. For example, if an author's name or the title is misspelled on the title page but nowhere else, the incorrect spelling is the one that is listed in the catalog, since the price given is for that specific copy and the error is one of the unique features that aids in its identification. (This is an example of a *point*—see Chapter 3 for the definition.)

Also, if additional details are known but do not appear on the title page (for instance, publisher name, or state or country of publication), they are supplied in parentheses, with "ca." if they are not documented. Many times these facts are not listed at all unless they are essential for determining a particular book's value. For example, place and date of publication are normally sufficient to permit identification of a collectible book—date being of most significance, closely followed by place. There are circumstances, however, when the publisher's name is also needed; for instance, when a first edition was published by more than one publisher in the same year. Or when the name of the publisher indicates other useful information, as in Avon or Pocket Books (paperback), or Grosset and Dunlap (reprint).

There are small but important differences between this bibliographic system and that used in conventional bibliographies, in which all available information is typically included whether it appears on the title page or not and is edited to a consistent style. Since the function of a conventional bibliography is to allow identification of a book without regard to its value so sources can be credited and interested readers can locate a copy at a library, bookstore, or through the publisher, as much specific information as possible is provided—including state or country if the city of publication is unclear, publisher name, etc. In conventional bibliographies, all verifiable information is supplied—the more the better—and parentheses are only used for details that are not documented (note how this varies from the function of parentheses in out-of-print-/rare-book seller catalogs).

Here's the critical difference between the kind of specialized bibliographic style followed in out-of-print-/rare-book seller catalogs and the more general conventional style: In the case of discrepancies, catalog editors consider the information on the *title page* the controlling information; conventional bibliography editors consult additional sources (for instance, the text of the book, or a reputable external source, such as a biographical dictionary) and define the controlling information by *frequency*.

The bibliographic style adopted in *A Handbook for Booklovers* combines the most useful features of the conventional system with those of the system used in out-of-print-/rare-book seller catalogs so that collectible-book buyers will be able to identify specific editions and estimate their values, while those who read simply for pleasure will be able to find something of general interest to them, as well.

Now that you have finished reading this section, you're on your own. Don't feel obligated to read this book from cover to cover if that's not your style. Skip around if you like! If you come across something you don't understand, you can always refer to the Table of Contents to find out where to look up the explanation.

The most important thing is, have fun! You may decide to turn a love of reading into the additional pleasure of collecting. If you do, the Appendices will get you started on the right track.

— 1 —

Collecting for Fun and Profit

Throughout this book you will find considerable general information that relates to book collecting for pleasure and intellectual reward; however, the aspect of intelligent investment must also be discussed.

What or who is a booklover? Are book *lovers* and book *collectors* one and the same? Yes and no.

A booklover is not necessarily a collector. There are most likely millions of people who own very few books but read many. That's what our libraries are for. There are also many people who, after having bought and read a paperback, either throw it away or pass it on to someone else. Though they love books and reading, they are not into retention. Sharing, yes. These are the people who are into a different kind of collecting. They collect pleasure, knowledge, thrills, fantasy, beauty, and whatever else strikes the right chord within them. Some read only certain kinds of books: historical romances, murder mysteries, romance novels, biographies, or what have you. Often, only books by certain authors within any one of the many genres interest them.

More significantly, this kind of booklover usually places no particular importance on whether the copy of the book being read is the first hardcover edition, or the seventeenth printing of the paperback edition. It isn't important if the copy is by the original publisher, or if it has been reprinted several times by several publishers through the years. Only the content, or the author, is of importance.

Book collectors, on the other hand, may not necessarily be booklovers. Happily, most are. I know of many book collectors who have read very few of the books in their collections. Some of them would be better termed book accumulators. There are many reasons for this. One reason is the perception that valuable books are good investments. Often this is true. Another reason is the prestige that some people associate with being known as a "book collector."

A person becomes a collector, whether he knows it or not, when books begin to accumulate in a less-than-haphazard pattern. Once you have several books by the same author or several books in the same genre, a pattern begins to emerge and, *voilà*, a collector is born. It is not necessary that any arbitrary "edition" standards be followed. If you're happy collecting Robert Ludlum novels without regard to whether they are all hardcover first editions, all paperback reprints, or a mix of both, that's marvelous. You're one kind of collector, and you should be proud to acknowledge it. However, for the most part, you must realize that the copies in your collection will probably never be worth as much as you originally paid for them. But that's not why you bought them in the first place, is it?

The traditional book collector focuses on different aspects from those I've mentioned. The serious collector is very much concerned with edition status. He wants only first editions of collectible books, and will go to great lengths to acquire them—often at great expense, as you will see when you read the chapters that provide values. The serious collector only wants copies that are in the finest condition obtainable, since condition is one of the most important factors in determining values. Since most collectible books are—to be blunt—used books, acquiring them can be quite a challenge.

One thing that all types of collectors have in common is the need for information about authors and their books and what those books are worth. Even if you are not concerned with edition status, you can find out if a used book you happen to acquire is worth a great deal more than you paid for it. If you are a traditional collector, you need to know proper values—you don't want to pay more than necessary, and when significant values are involved and your collection enlarges, you certainly will need appraisals for insurance or estate purposes.

It has always been fashionable to disparage the idea that anyone should collect books with the deliberate goal of making an eventual profit. Many dealers, particularly the older members of the book trade who style themselves as "antiquarian" or "rare" booksellers, are prone to this attitude. I've always felt that this is basically self-serving and that it is the result of two primary considerations: First is the fear that they will somehow be blamed if a purchase does not appreciate in value in a relatively short time; and second, that a price history for desirable books may remain capricious and in too many cases be elevated to an artificially high level, thus making it difficult, or at least time-consuming, to obtain a new and higher market value.

As in merchandising any goods that are not available in unlimited quantities, the laws of supply and demand operate in bookselling, too. In addition, collectible books, which for the most part are pre-owned, are subject to the yardstick of "condition." And, finally, a collector or investor must be aware of the simple economic rule that most dealers follow: Buy your books—or anything else, for that matter—for no more than half of what you hope to eventually sell them for—and, ideally, a great deal less. How *much* less becomes a function of many interrelated factors: the condition of the book, its scarcity in the marketplace and, of great importance—how quickly it can be resold. If a bookseller has a customer waiting for a particular book to turn up, the purchase price can be much higher and the profit smaller because the funds can be turned over quickly.

On the other hand, if the bookseller already has a comparable copy of the book in stock, or is aware that it is fairly common and readily available from other booksellers, the inclination would be to pay a much smaller percentage of its nominal value, or not to buy it at all.

How all this affects the collector or investor is, again, quite simple. Here is an example: A book is purchased for $100. A year or so later, for any number of reasons, it is brought back to be resold. Meanwhile, the fair market value has increased to $120, and the bookseller is willing to offer $60 to buy it back. Loss to the seller: $40. Not a very good investment—unless the collector or investor can sell it to another collector or a library willing to pay the current retail value. It is true that the book appreciated in value, but turning that paper profit into hard cash is quite another story.

What other options does a collector or investor have? One option is to wait until the value of the book at least doubles as a result of inflation, or increased scarcity or demand, or both. When the new value reaches $200, the book can be sold to a bookseller for $100 to break even. If the new value rises above $200, a profit is available.

Another option is to donate the book or collection to an institutional library and take a tax deduction. Since this avenue is subject to the vagaries of our tax laws, obtaining professional advice is suggested.

2

Collecting Guidelines

Collecting is sometimes a rather haphazard undertaking because of the lack of readily available reference sources. Someone who likes romance novels, for example, may decide that the works of a particular writer are of the greatest interest and make a concentrated effort to find additional works by that writer. Quite often, this effort may not go beyond a search of the shelves or racks of the nearest B. Dalton or Waldenbooks. Whatever is available becomes the stopping point.

Perhaps you would like to begin collecting specific authors, or specific genres, but you need some guidelines for focusing on an area that is of particular interest to you because of your vocation or normal inclination. For example, collecting mystery novels could ultimately provide a selection of thousands of books by hundreds of authors, costing many thousands of dollars but having the potential of eventually being worth many times the initial investment. Or, the focus could be narrower within this genre: only the first books of crime and mystery authors; only American or English authors; only police procedurals; or only specific authors, such as Ellery Queen, Rex Stout, or Erle Stanley Gardner. Any of these could be a lifelong endeavor.

The scope of collectible subjects is virtually infinite. Collections can be built around narratives of Indian captivities, nautical subjects, aviation, locks and keys, the occult, paper folding, biographies and autobiographies of writers, artists, statesmen, actors, industrialists, politicians, criminals—almost anything conceivable.

There is one very important thing that you should keep in mind: there are a great many authors whose books are *collectible* but not necessarily also *valuable*, although perhaps they will be sometime in the future. This is particularly true for many of our modern authors, whose books often become bestsellers. It is not unusual for a new book by any of these authors to sell several hundred thousand copies in hardcover and several million in paperback. Since one of the criteria for determining the value of a pre-owned copy of a book is availability, many, many years will have to pass before books published in such huge quantities will ever be worth more than a fraction of the original cover price.

This is not to say that you shouldn't collect these books. The pleasure they will provide does not depend on printing quantity—each copy stands by itself in that respect. But if you're a collector concerned about monetary value, you have to be realistic. And the reality is that any book that has made any bestseller list in modern times is not likely to be both collectible and valuable. Collectible, yes—valuable, no.

You should also bear in mind that in many cases an author's earlier books are both collectible and valuable, while later works by the same author may only be collectible. Why? Because earlier works are usually published in much smaller quantities than later works. This is especially true for those authors who are still living and publishing. So, if you note a value of several hundred dollars for an early title by any given author, don't assume that a copy of tomorrow's bestseller by that author is also going to be worth a large sum in the foreseeable future. Do, however, get a copy if you enjoy the writing or the genre.

The remainder of this chapter will provide a brief overview of the different categories of collectible books.

First Books by Collectible Authors—Chapter 7

Of all the collecting categories available, this is the one I would choose if investment were my motivation. As a general rule, an author's first book becomes the most difficult to obtain, particularly if the author has gone on to become a major literary figure, or if all his later books have become bestsellers. For anyone attempting to form a complete collection of an author's work, the first book is usually the "keystone" book, and its value may be disproportionate to any later book even if its literary merit is questionable.

The first edition of an author's first book is usually a small edition because the author has no track record for the publisher to use to estimate possible future sales. Quite often the first book may be in a genre very different from the one in which the author later achieves fame. For novelists, it may be a book of poetry—perhaps the only one the author will ever write—or a school textbook, a scholarly dissertation, or a how-to book. Perhaps a pseudonym was used because the author didn't want anyone to know, later, that his first book was a western novel written to put bread on the table.

The authors I have listed are but a fraction of all the authors who are collectible. The fact that any particular author's name does not appear here does not mean that that author's books—and particularly his first book—are not collectible. But I only have so much space, and to provide all the names and first-book titles would be an enormous undertaking requiring several volumes. Besides, I doubt anyone could even form a collection of all the books I have listed. If it were possible, it would be very expensive and would likely be worth many times the sum of its parts. It would also be a lifetime undertaking, even if money were no object.

Nevertheless, collections can be formed using less all-inclusive guidelines. Here are some suggestions based on selecting authors best known for writing in a specific genre:

Crime and mystery novelists
Western novelists
Children's book writers and juvenile novelists
Poets
Mainstream fiction novelists
Science fiction and fantasy novelists
Adventure or espionage novelists
Nonfiction books in any of dozens of fields
Historical romance novelists
Humorists
Horror novelists

Remember what I said earlier—the first book may not be in the same genre as the bulk of the later books.

Book Illustrators—Chapter 8

These are illustrators whose works enhance the value of the books in which they appear. However, most of them were also notable for their work in other fields, and if you wish to collect one or more illustrators, you can also find their work in other media, such as magazines, posters, catalogs, postcards, prints, and other printed paper ephemera.

Western Americana—Chapter 10

Americana is a generic term applied to nonfiction books that relate to the establishment, growth, and development of our country in particular, and all of the Americas in general. The field is vast, and is probably the most popular collecting field among private and institutional collectors like libraries, both private and public.

There are hundreds of possible subgenres within the whole genre. Western Americana is possibly the most popular of the subgenres, and it in turn can be divided into collecting specialties, any one of which could be a lifetime endeavor:

Cowboys
Indians
Rustlers
Law enforcement
Cattle ranching
Bandits and other desperados
Politics
Migration westward
Mining
Agriculture
Lumbering

This will give you some idea. There are many good bibliographies available in libraries that can supply you with thousands of titles.

General Americana—Chapter 11

This, of course, includes Western Americana, but the range of interests is infinitely larger. The list of books I have provided will at least give you some idea of the variety of subjects that it is possible to collect. Any of them could keep you busy for many years, and, if you're value-conscious, provide some good opportunities for enhancing the value of a collection.

Crime/Mystery/Adventure/Espionage—Chapter 12

This is one of the largest and most popular fiction genres and has been for a good many years. There are many prominent names here, beginning with Edgar Allan Poe and continuing through Arthur Conan Doyle and Agatha Christie, right up to current authors like Robert Ludlum and Joseph Wambaugh. This list will get you started. Here again, there are many special categories, such as police procedurals, locked-room mysteries, and series featuring cerebral sleuths like Hercult Poirot or detective-heroes like Sherlock Holmes and Travis McGee.

Western Fiction—Chapter 13

Though interest in western fiction slackened for many years, it appears to be on the rise again. Such authors as Louis L'Amour and James Michener have helped its resurgence in popularity. All of the names and titles I've listed here are collectible. You can consult bibliographies for additional authors.

Children's/Juvenile—Chapter 14

The collectibility of this genre is enhanced by many well-known illustrators. There are hundreds of children's book authors whose works are collectible. Those I have provided here are a beginning, and bibliographies can give you many more names. You will recognize many from your own childhood days, or your children's.

Mainstream Fiction—Chapter 15

Here is where we find all those authors who don't fit easily into any of the other genres. The biggest names of all: Norman Mailer, Ernest Hemingway, James Jones, John Updike, Herman Wouk, Jerome Weidman, and hundreds more. Look the list over and then check other bibliographies.

Literary Works/Poetry/Belles-Lettres—Chapter 16

This includes poetry, belles-lettres, essays, biographies and autobiographies, and other works in which the primary criteria are literary quality and importance of the subject. This list provides a representative sampling.

Science Fiction/Fantasy/Horror—Chapter 17

This is another large and important collecting category, popularized before the turn of the century by such writers as H. G. Wells, followed later by Edgar Rice Burroughs and contemporary writers like Isaac Asimov, Ray Bradbury, Frank Herbert, Rod Serling, Stephen King, and many, many others. I have listed some of the most important ones.

Miscellaneous Nonfiction—Chapter 18

This list excludes General and Western Americana and concentrates on various narrower categories, any one of which can provide years of collecting pleasure: animals, birds, fish, travel, whaling, hunting and fishing, jewelry, hobbies, sports, games and pastimes, actors and actresses, theater and cinema, carnivals and circuses, magic, astrology, astronomy, architecture, archaeology, anthropology —the list is endless.

3

Basic Terminology

As in any specialized field of activity, considerable jargon or esoteric terminology is used in the collectible-books field. Some knowledge of these trade terms is a must if you want to read booksellers' catalogs, which are the primary sources of collectible books—especially for those of you who do not live in or near a major urban area.

Terms and Abbreviations:

Advance copy — A copy of the first edition of a book, usually one of the first off the presses, and likely to be first issue. Distributed by the publisher for review purposes, sometimes they are specially bound, left unbound, or bound in wrappers.

Advts. — Advertisement pages that are bound into many books.

Americana — Any book, map, broadside, document, pamphlet, print, or other printed material dealing historically with the American scene. This includes Canada, the United States, and Mexico—all of North America.

Anonymous (Anon.) — A book that does not provide the name of the author.

Association copy — A book that bears an identifiable relationship to the author or some other famous person by the inclusion of a signature, photograph, or letter laid in, etc.

Auction price — The price realized for a book sold at auction. In the U.S. the major book auctions are held in New York, Chicago, Los Angeles, San Francisco, and a few smaller cities. As a rule, you can consider auction prices to be wholesale values since the auctions are largely attended by booksellers.

Author's copy — A book that has been the author's personal copy and is so inscribed and signed, or has his bookplate. This adds a premium to the normal value.

Autographed copy — Any book signed by the author.

Backstrip — The common term for the spine of a book—what you see when the book is standing between two other books on a shelf. Sometimes the backstrip is of a different material from the rest of the binding. Examples: boards with cloth backstrip; cloth with leather backstrip.

Belles-lettres — Literature regarded for its aesthetic value rather than for its informative content.

Bibliography (Biblio.) — An alphabetically arranged list of books about a special subject or author, usually providing considerably detailed information.

Bibliophile — A lover of books. What I hope you will become if you aren't one already.

Bibliophobe — A hater of books. Please, don't be one.

Bibliopole — A dealer in rare or unusual books.

Binding (Bndg.) — The cover of a book. May be any of a wide variety of materials.

Blind stamping — Any impression of lettering or ornament in the surface of a binding, without the addition of coloring or gilding.

Bookplate — A printed, and usually ornamental, label pasted on an endpaper or flyleaf to indicate ownership. This does not normally detract from a book's value, and may enhance it if it is that of a famous person and is signed. Most bookplates carry the words *ex libris*, which means "from the library of."

Books in Print A multivolume annual compilation of all the books available from publishers or distributors throughout North America, with separate alphabetical lists of titles and authors. A companion set called *Subject Guide to Books in Print* lists books alphabetically by subject, and there is also a set called *Paperback Books in Print* that only lists paperbacks.

Buckram A type of coarse linen or cotton used for bindings, especially by libraries.

Calf (calfbound) A binding of leather made from calf skin.

Case *See* Binding.

Cloth (Clo. or Cl.) The material used for binding most modern hardcover books.

Collate To check a book page by page to see that every page is present. This is very important for illustrated books in order to assure that no plates or illustrations have been removed.

Collectible *See* Valuable.

Colophon A final notice, usually at the back of a book, which gives the name of the printer or publisher and sometimes, in the case of a limited edition, the number of copies printed and details about paper and typeface used. Often important as a *point*. In modern books this information is often found on the copyright page. Sometimes an ornamental device is a part of the colophon.

Color plate (Clr. pl.) Colored illustrations in a book. May be hand or mechanically colored (*see also* Plates).

Compiler (Comp.) One who compiles a book by bringing its contents together from various sources, such as in an anthology, almanac, or directory.

Condition The physical state of a book or any printed item relative to its original state when it was first published. This is one of the most important factors affecting value aside from rarity, and one of the most troublesome.

Contemporary binding A binding that dates from the same time period in which the book was published. Not necessarily the original binding. At one time books were sold unbound, and the purchaser would then have the book bound in a style of his own choosing—perhaps so that all the books in his library would be in uniform bindings.

Copyright page The page carrying the copyright notice(s). Normally the back, or verso, of the title page. Often provides much information in addition to the copyright date, sometimes even including the true name of a pseudonymous author.

Covers bound in If a book is rebound because the original covers are damaged and beyond repair, the original covers may be bound into the new binding as evidence of the book's authenticity. This is quite common for books that were originally issued in wrappers but have been rebound in cloth or leather.

CWO Check with order.

Dampstained Staining or discoloration caused by moisture.

Desiderata A list of books or other collectibles wanted by a collector, library, or dealer. More commonly known as a Wants List.

Dust jacket (DJ) A printed or pictorial paper cover used to protect the binding of a book, normally issued with the book by the publisher. Printed dust jackets date from about 1832; plain jackets were used much earlier. If a book was issued with a printed dust jacket, it is considered incomplete without it. (This is an example of a *point.*) Some dealers refer to jackets as dust wrappers (DW).

Ed. Abbreviation for editor or edition.

Edition The form or version in which a text is published; also, the total quantity of books printed for a publisher at one time (*see also* First edition).

Endpapers The pages (which may be blank or printed) pasted to the inside covers of a book. A second set that is not pasted down may also be present; these are known as free endpapers or fly leaves.

Errata slip A printed slip containing corrections of printing errors in the book discovered after the printing was completed. The slip may be pasted (tipped) in or inserted loosely. Sometimes it is an important point in determining the first issue of a first edition, and, if missing, will adversely affect value.

Ex-lib (Ex-library) A book bearing library stamps or markings, a card pocket, etc. If the book has been legitimately disposed of by the library it will be marked "discard" on an endpaper or on the title page. Legitimate discards bring much lower prices than normal books no matter what the condition. Illegitimate discards should be completely avoided.

Facsimile An exact photograph or photocopy of a page, book, or catalog.

First edition (1st ed.) The first time an *edition* of a book is printed. The first edition may have several *issues* since the press can be stopped during the print run to make a correction to a plate. At that point all copies run with the error become the *first issue*, and copies run after the correction is made become the *second issue*. This can occur several times, creating several issues of the first edition. Each issue can be further divided into *states* for other changes, such as changing the type or color of the binding. Studying the descriptions in price guides, catalogs, and bibliographies will provide you with many examples of edition, issue, and state, and will explain the importance of *points* in their determination.

Folding map; folding plate (Fldg.) A map or illustration printed on a sheet larger than the book and folded to protect it. They are usually bound in, but sometimes a pocket will be provided on the inside of the book's cover. Missing maps or plates will lower a book's value considerably.

Foxed, foxing Reddish brown spotting (freckling) caused by iron oxide particles in the paper that have literally rusted. It may mar text and plates. Foxing should always be noted when describing condition, particularly if it affects either a text or a pictorial image.

Frayed *See* Rubbed.

Genre A distinctive class or category of literary composition.

Half-title The book title appearing on an otherwise blank page preceding the title page. Sometimes called the "bastard title."

Hinge The point in a binding where the covers join the backstrip. The terms "hinge cracking" or "hinges weak" indicate that the cover is beginning to separate from the body of the book. This condition should always be noted. Do not try to repair this condition yourself.

In print A book that is obtainable from a publisher (not necessarily the original one).

Issue — *See* First edition.

Jargon — The specialized or technical language of a trade or profession. The definition I find most apt is "a nonsensical, incoherent, or meaningless utterance."

Label — This has two meanings: a cover or backstrip label is a printed paper, cloth, or leather slip with the title and author's name that is pasted on an otherwise blank surface; label alone (pasted in) usually means a library or some other notice pasted to an endpaper.

Laid in — Indicates that some material, such as a letter, errata slip, photograph, newspaper review, etc., has been loosely inserted in a book (*see also* Tipped in).

Large paper copy — A book printed on paper larger than the regular trade edition and providing much wider margins; normally on better grade paper and nearly always a limited edition signed by the author, and sometimes the illustrator, as well.

Limited edition — Any edition consisting of a specific number of copies and having characteristics that distinguish it from the trade edition or other editions. Generally a limited edition is numbered to indicate which copy it is of the total number of copies issued. It may also be signed by the author and/or illustrator.

Literary — Of or relating to writers and books.

Mainstream — The prevailing direction of a movement, trend, or influence.

Mint — A book in the same condition as when first issued by the publisher. Some booksellers use the term "as new."

N.d. (no date) — A notation indicating that a book shows no date of publication on the title or copyright page. If the date of publication is known from other sources or there is only a copyright date, that date will often be placed in parentheses. Examples: Boston, n.d. (1866); or Boston, (1866).

N.p. (no place) A notation indicating that a book shows no place of publication. If the place of publication is known from other sources, it will be shown in parentheses. Examples: N.p. (Boston), n.d. (1866); or (Boston, 1866).

Original cloth (Orig. cl.) The original publisher's cloth binding.

Offsetting A term used to describe the effect when pictures or type have reproduced themselves on an adjacent page. Probably occurs when the ink is not completely dry when a book is assembled.

Out of print (O.P.) A book no longer available from any publisher. When a desirable book is out of print, its price begins to rise in the aftermarket. However, the mere fact that a book is out of print will not increase its value if none existed in the first place.

Paperback, paperbound *See* Wrappers.

Parts (Pts.) Some books were originally published (issued) in consecutive parts or serialized in a magazine in advance of regular book publication, with paper covers. Often they were bound together after all parts were issued. A complete set of the original parts of such books is often the most desirable form, as many collectors feel that this is the true first edition. Inasmuch as such sets are fragile and difficult to save, they can command very high prices. Many first works by Charles Dickens and Arthur Conan Doyle were first issued in parts.

Pictorial cloth (Pict. cl.) A cloth binding with a printed or blind-stamped pictorial design.

Picture label A large picture label pasted on the front cover of a book to provide a cover illustration.

Pirated edition An unauthorized reprint of a book, poem, print, item of music, etc.

Plates (Plts.) Another word for pictures, sometimes on a different paper from the text. Also may refer to the type from which a book is printed.

POB Post office box.

Point An identifying characteristic that helps to determine the edition, issue, or state of a book. There are numerous variations that can occur, such as typographical errors, broken typefaces, misspellings, changes of binding, deletions or additions, errata slips, etc.

Pp. Abbreviation for pages, as in 263 pp.

Ppd. Postpaid.

Presentation copy A book inscribed by an author to a particular person.

Pseudonym The assumed or pen name of an author. For example, Mark Twain is the pseudonym of Samuel Langhorne Clemens. Also, for the purposes of this book, any variation from the true name as it appears in Chapter 5.

Rare A book or other paper collectible that is extremely scarce. Usually all known copies are kept track of. Rarity in itself does not ensure a high price—demand and condition are also important.

Rebacked Indicates that the original backstrip has been replaced with a new one.

Rebound Indicates that the original binding has been replaced. Also called recasing.

Recto The right-hand page of a book.

Rubbed — A binding that shows evidence of wear and fraying. Another word for scuffed.

SASE — Self-addressed stamped envelope.

Scarce — An item that is difficult to find but is not necessarily also rare. An out-of-print book will become scarce if there is much demand for it.

Scout — One who locates scarce and rare books and other paper collectibles, buys them if the price is right, and sells them to dealers, libraries, and collectors.

Scuffed — *See* Rubbed.

Sewed — A method of binding thin books or pamphlets with wrappers by stitching them together with thread.

Shaken — A book with loose pages or signatures, or with the entire body of the book loose within its cover.

Signature — A section of a book consisting of 8, 12, 16, 32, or 64 pages that were originally cut and folded from a single printed sheet.

Slipcase — A cardboard, pasteboard, or leather protective case made to fit a book.

Spine — *See* Backstrip.

Started — Denotes a signature that has become loose when a book is not otherwise shaken, i.e., signature started.

State — *See* First edition.

Text — The main content of a book as distinguished from the forematter, index, etc.

Tipped in — Indicates that some material, such as extra plates, errata slips, etc., has been lightly glued into the book in an appropriate place (*see also* Laid in).

Title page (T.P.) — The key page at the front of the book, which usually contains the title, author's name, date and place of publication, publisher's name, and other information needed to identify a specific copy of a book.

Uncut — Indicates that the edges of pages in a book have not been trimmed to be even with each other (*see also* Unopened).

Unopened — Indicates that the untrimmed fore edges of a book are still joined, just as they came from the printer (*see also* Uncut). This is evidence that the book has not been read, and can increase the book's value if it is otherwise still in good condition. This is very seldom found in modern books. I once discovered an unopened book, published in the early 1920s, on the circulating shelf of a large public library. No one, in over 50 years, had wanted to read that book!

Valuable — *Objectively valuable book*: a book that can bring financial gain to its owner if it is sold (depending on the condition of the book, the law of supply and demand, and other factors). *Subjectively valuable book*: a book that can bring personal pleasure to its owner. Any book can be either objectively valuable, or subjectively valuable, or both.

Verso — The left-hand page of a book. The copyright page is usually a verso page (*see also* Recto).

Wants List — *See* Desiderata.

Water stained/damaged — Stains or discoloration caused by water. Difficult to remedy because it usually shrinks or warps pages and bindings.

Woodcut — A picture reproduced by carving a block of wood and inking it.

Wraps (Wrappers) — Stiff paper or pliable material used as a book or pamphlet cover (as in our modern paperback covers). Older books were quite commonly bound in wrappers, and tend to become rare because of their inherent fragility.

Book Sizes

Book sizes are often a puzzle to the average person. Modern hardcover books are typically the size known as *octavo,* or 8vo. Odd sized books can be measured by inches. The following table will serve as a guide to finding proper size descriptions.

32mo	4-5 inches tall.
16mo	Roughly 5-6 inches tall.
12mo	Approximately 6-7 inches tall, the usual modern paperback size.
8vo	Roughly 8 inches tall, the size of the ordinary hardbound novel.
4to	Approximately 10 inches tall, the size of the usual coffee-table book.
Folio	12 or more inches tall.
Elephant folio	A very large book, about the size of a newspaper page.

Care and Repair of Books

I'm not going to say too much about the repair of books beyond this: *don't.* If a book in a state of disrepair has any value at all, it deserves professional care in repairing it. There are many professional binding and repair services throughout the country, especially in major cities. Check the Yellow Pages and contact one of them.

As for care, treat ALL books as if they were valuable, because they are. This has nothing to do with monetary value, although that, too, is a consideration, and is all the more reason to be gentle and considerate—books are your friends. Store them upright on shelves, away from damp areas and direct sunlight. Don't use them as coasters for drinks. Don't turn down the corners of pages to mark your place. And don't write in them except for your name; better yet, use a bookplate. Above all, don't use ordinary cellophane tape to repair tears. Use the "magic" type tape on the reverse side of dust jackets if need be.

4

Dealing with Booksellers

This chapter provides a discussion of what to expect and what to watch out for when dealing with booksellers either in person or by mail. I have also included information on postal matters, such as standard abbreviations for the states and provinces of North America and for some of the more important counties of Great Britain.

You will find the names and addresses of hundreds of booksellers and book search services in Appendices A and B. The booksellers listed have been selected because they issue catalogs of collectible books. Some are specialists and some are generalists. Most do not charge for their catalogs; however, catalogs are expensive to prepare, print, and mail, so the first time you write to any of them to request a catalog, it would be a nice gesture on your part to enclose at least $1 to defray these costs. That dollar will be well spent, because catalogs can become a valuable source of reference information for you, particularly if they are specialized toward your own collecting interests. And of course, they are also the source of the books you need for your collection.

Dealing with Book Search Services

Many of the book search services I have listed are also booksellers who maintain stock and issue catalogs. However, many do not have any stock and only search for books on specific request, and will not purchase any book until they have sold it to their client. Some charge a small fee for their services in addition to a reasonable markup on the book(s) they locate. The fee itself will not normally be sufficient to cover the expense of the search, but it does help assure the search service that you are serious.

If you decide you want to use a search service, I would suggest that you write to a few of them and request information about their policies. If you also want to give them a specific search request at the same time, it will help both you and them if you provide as much information as you possibly can about the books you need. Be specific about the titles. If you will accept only first editions, say so. If you have a ceiling on how much you are willing to pay for a title, specify what it is. And don't give the same search request to several search services at the same time. This will not expedite matters for you, and the search services will probably catch on to what you are doing and perhaps refuse to do business with you in the future.

What to Be Aware of and Beware Of

Most booksellers and book search services are honest and reliable. It is customary to pay in advance for any book ordered from a catalog or quoted to you by a search service. However, it should be understood that any book you order should be returnable for a full and prompt refund if it does not meet the requirements you specified in your written request. This is particularly true with respect to condition.

Never order a book if the condition has not been described, even if it is an inexpensive paperback. Nothing can be more frustrating than to receive a book that has missing pages, even if it is free. This can happen not because the seller is dishonest, but because he was careless and did not check the book before offering or shipping it to you.

Needless to say, if you buy a book in a bookstore, or at a flea market or swap meet, you should check the book yourself.

You should also be aware that many booksellers are not as knowledgeable as they ought to be, and you must do your own homework when you order. The most common error that occurs is to accept a book that is represented as being a first edition but isn't. This can happen quite easily since many valuable books have *points* associated with them that go beyond the usual knowledge of place and date of publication and publisher's name, which may not really serve to adequately identify many first editions. Always keep a copy of any correspondence—especially your original request—so you can easily resolve this problem if it arises.

Some Hints and Courtesies

No matter what sort of collector you are or wish to become, there are some things you should bear in mind. You may have occasion to deal with collectors and booksellers in North America as well as many other countries. There are some very definite language and customs differences between English-speaking countries, to say nothing of those that exist between countries that have more radical differences. Use the glossary in Chapter 3 when needed. Here are some suggestions that may help prevent misunderstandings.

Legibility—People cannot respond to your letters, orders, or inquiries if they cannot read your writing. This is especially true if their native language is not the same as yours. TYPE your letters if at all possible. If you can't do that, HAND PRINT them as neatly and as legibly as you can. Take extra care with your name and address, as well as with the one on the envelope. Cursive writing should not be used no matter how many penmanship awards you won in school. This is also true for calligraphic writing when you write to non-English addresses. Do not assume that your correspondent speaks English just because you found the name and address in an English-language directory.

Forms of Signature—Always use your complete given name. If you must use initials, be courteous enough to indicate whether you are a Mr., Mrs., Miss, or Ms. If you are female, specify whether you prefer Mrs., Miss, or Ms., even if you use your first name, so your correspondent will know the proper salutation in a reply. Please be thoughtful about this.

Postal Costs—It is a thoughtful gesture when you correspond with someone in another country to enclose reply postage, especially if you are requesting a catalog. Overseas mail is expensive no matter where you live. You can purchase International Reply Coupons at your local Post Office. These can be exchanged by the recipient for the equivalent in his local postage, which can be used for a reply. Sending one or more of these coupons will always be appreciated.

POSTAL ABBREVIATIONS FOR THE UNITED STATES, CANADIAN PROVINCES, AND BRITISH COUNTIES

United States and American Territories

Alabama .... AL
Alaska .... AK
Arizona .... AZ
Arkansas .... AR
California .... CA
Colorado .... CO
Connecticut .... CT
Delaware .... DE
District of Columbia .... DC
Florida .... FL

Georgia . . . . GA
Guam . . . . GU
Hawaii . . . . HI
Idaho . . . . ID
Illinois IL
Indiana . . . . IN
Iowa . . . . IA
Kansas . . . . KS
Kentucky . . . . KY
Louisiana . . . . LA
Maine . . . . ME
Maryland . . . . MD
Massachusetts . . . . MA
Michigan . . . . MI
Minnesota . . . . MN
Mississippi . . . . MS
Missouri . . . . MO
Montana . . . . MT
Nebraska . . . . NB
Nevada . . . . NV
New Hampshire . . . . NH
New Jersey . . . . NJ
New Mexico . . . . NM
New York . . . . NY
North Carolina . . . . NC
North Dakota . . . . ND
Ohio . . . . OH
Oklahoma . . . . OK
Oregon . . . . OR
Pennsylvania . . . . PA
Puerto Rico . . . . PR
Rhode Island . . . . RI
South Carolina . . . . SC
South Dakota . . . . SD
Tennessee . . . . TN
Texas . . . . TX
Utah . . . . UT
Vermont . . . . VT
Virgin Islands VI
Virginia . . . . VA
Washington . . . . WA
West Virginia . . . . WV
Wisconsin . . . . WI
Wyoming . . . . WY

Canadian Provinces

Alberta . . . . AB
British Columbia . . . . BC
Labrador . . . . LB
Manitoba . . . . MB
New Brunswick . . . . NB
Newfoundland . . . . NF
Nova Scotia . . . . NS
Ontario . . . . ON
Northwest Territories . . . . NT
Prince Edward Island . . . . PE
Quebec . . . . PR
Saskatchewan . . . . SK
Yukon Territory . . . . YT

British Counties and Shires

Buckinghamshire . . . . BUCKS
Cambridgeshire . . . . CAMBS
Carmarthenshire . . . . CARMS
Glamorgan . . . . GLAM

Gloucestershire . . . . GLOS
Hampshire . . . . HANTS
Hertfordshire . . . . HERTS
Lancashire . . . . LANCS
Leicestershire . . . . LEICS
Lincolnshire . . . . LINCS
Middlesex . . . . MIDDX
Monmouthshire . . . . MON
Northamptonshire . . . NORTHANTS
Nottinghamshire . . . . NOTTS
Oxfordshire . . . . OXON
Pembrokeshire . . . . PEMBS
Shropshire . . . . SALOP
Staffordshire . . . . STAFFS
Warwickshire . . . . WARWICKS
Worcestershire . . . . WORCS
Yorkshire . . . . YORKS

5

True Names of Authors and Their Pseudonyms

This chapter contains the true names of authors who use one or more pseudonyms, or pen names. (For the purposes of this book, I am expanding the definition of the word *pseudonym* to include any variation on an author's full true name as it appears in this chapter.) Many of the other chapters will refer you back to this one for additional information because the use of pseudonyms has been so prevalent over the years. Indeed, some authors seldom or never published a book using their true name, for various reasons discussed in Chapter 6.

A good example is Frederick Schiller Faust, better known as Max Brand. Of his over two hundred published books, only three books of verse were published under his true name of Faust. The rest were published under one of at least thirteen different pseudonyms.

In selecting the authors to be included, I have chosen both living and deceased authors if they are generally considered collectible or of enduring reader interest. I have also selected a nearly equal number from the most popular genres; i.e., mystery, science fiction/fantasy, children's, western, romance/gothic, and mainstream novels.

If you want to know if a known author's name is the true name, or what pseudonym(s) that author may have used or still uses, refer to this chapter at the start. If the name is not listed here, consult the pseudonym list in Chapter 6 to find the true name, then refer back to the true name in this chapter to determine if the author used any other pseudonyms.

This chapter does not provide names of authors who do not use any pseudonyms. If you do not find a currently popular author's name in either Chapter 5 or Chapter 6, it probably means that the name is the true name and that the author has no known pseudonyms. In some cases it may be the pseudonym or true name of a new author who will perhaps be included in the next edition of this book.

When a name cannot be found in either Chapter 5 or Chapter 6, you should always check Chapter 7, which provides information on the first books of important and collectible authors who may or may not already be listed. If an author and first book is listed in Chapter 7, you can safely assume that other books by the same author are also of importance. You may well find books by that author listed in one of the value chapters (9 through 18).

TRUE NAMES	PSEUDONYMS
AARONS, EDWARD SIDNEY	Paul Ayres, Edward Ronns
ABBOTT, JACOB	Rollo Books
ABRAHAMS, DORIS CAROLINE	Caryl Brahms, Oliver Linden
ACLAND, ALICE	Anne Marreco
ADAMS, CLEVE FRANKLIN	Franklin Charles, John Spain
ADAMS, CLIFTON	Jonathan Grant, Matt Kinkaid, Clay Randall
ADAMS, HARRIET STRATEMEYER	Victor W. Appleton II, Frank W. Dixon, Franklin Dixon, Laura Lee Hope, Carolyn Keene
ADAMS, PETER ROBERT CHARLES	Perseus Adams
ADAMS, WILLIAM T.	Oliver Optic
AGATE, JAMES	Richard Prentis
AIKEN, CONRAD	Samuel Jeake
AINSWORTH, MARY D. SALTER	Mary D. Salter
ALBANESI, MADAME EFFIE ADELAIDE MARIA	Effie Rowlands
ALBERT, MARVIN H.	Nick Quarry, Anthony Rome
ALBRITTON, CAROL	Elizabeth Trehearne
ALCOTT, LOUISA MAY	A. M. Barnard
ALDEN, ISABELLA MACDONALD	Pansy
ALEXANDER, ROBERT WILLIAM	Joan Butler
ALLAN, MABEL ESTHER	Jean Estoril, Priscilla Hagon, Anne Pilgrim
ALLBEURY, THEODORE EDWARD LE BOUTHILLIER	Ted Allbeury, Richard Butler

TRUE NAMES	PSEUDONYMS
ALLEN, CHARLES GRANT BLAIRFINDIE	Cecil Power, Olive Pratt Rayner, Martin Leach Warborough
ALLEN, DON B.	T. D. Allen, Terry D. Allen
ALLEN, HENRY WILSON	Clay Fisher, Will Henry
ALLEN, JOHN E.	Bisonius, Paul M. Danforth
ALLEN, KENNETH S.	Alastair Scott
ALLIBONE, S. A.	Bibliophile
ALSOP, MARY O'HARA	Mary O'Hara, Mary Sture-Vasa
ALVAREZ-DEL RAY, RAMON FELIPE SAN JUAN MARIO SILVIO ENRICO	Lester Del Alvarez-Rey, Lester Del Rey, Edson McCann, Philip St. John, Erik Van Lhin, Kenneth Wright
AMBLER, ERIC	Eliot Reed
AMES, SARAH RACHEL	Sarah Gainham
AMIS, KINGSLEY WILLIAM	Robert Markham
AMY, WILLIAM LACEY	Luke Allan, Lacey Amy
ANDREWS, LUCILLA MATHEW	Diana Gordon, Joanna Marcus
ANGREMY, JEAN-PIERRE	Raymond Marlot, Pierre-Jean Remy
ANSLE, DOROTHY PHOEBE	Laura Conway, Hebe Elsna, Vicky Lancaster, Lyndon Snow
ARD, WILLIAM THOMAS	Ben Kerr, Mike Moran, Jonas Ward, Thomas Wills
ARMSTRONG, ANTHONY	A. A.
ARMSTRONG, CHARLOTTE	Jo Valentine
ARMSTRONG, DOUGLAS ALBERT	Albert Douglas
ARMSTRONG, RICHARD	Cam Renton
AROUET, FRANÇOIS-MARIE	Voltaire
ASHTON, WINIFRED	Clemence Dane
ASIMOV, ISAAC	Dr. A., Paul French
ATHANAS, WILLIAM VERNE	Ike Boone, Bill Colson, Bill Gordon, Anson Slaughter
ATHERTON, GERTRUDE FRANKLIN	Frank Lin
ATKEY, PHILIP	Pat Merriman, Barry Perowne
ATKINS, FRANK	Fenton Ash, Fred Ashley, Frank Aubrey
ATKINSON, NANCY	Nancy Benko
ATTHILL, ROBERT ANTHONY	Robin Atthill

TRUE NAMES	PSEUDONYMS
AUBREY-FLETCHER, HENRY LANCELOT	Henry Wade
AUCHINCLOSS, LOUIS	Andrew Lee
AUDEMARS, PIERRE	Peter Hodemart
AUSTIN, MARY	V. C. Andrews, Gordon Stairs
AVALLONE, MICHAEL ANGELO, JR.	James Blaine, Nick Carter, Troy Conway, Priscilla Dalton, Mark Dane, Jean-Anne de Pre, Dora Highland, Steve Michaels, Dorothea Nile, Ed Noone, Edwina Noone, Vance Stanton, Sidney Stuart, Max Walker
AVERILL, ESTHER HOLDEN	John Domino
AWDRY, RICHARD CHARLES	Richard Charles
BABA, MEHER	Merwan S. Irani
BAKER, BETTY DOREEN	Elizabeth Renier
BAKER, C.	Circuit Breaker
BAKER, RAY STANNARD	David Grayson
BALDWIN, GORDON CORTIS	Gordo Baldwin, Lew Gordon
BALL, ARMINE	Armine Von Tempski
BALL, DORIS BELL	Josephine Bell
BALLANTYNE, ROBERT MICHAEL	Comus
BALLARD, WILLIS TODHUNTER	Brian Agar, P. D. Ballard, Parker Bonner, Sam Bowie, Nick Carter, Hunter D'Allard, Harrison Hunt, John Hunter, Neil MacNeil, Clint Reno, John Shepherd, Clay Turner
BALLINGER, WILLIAM SANBORN	Bill S. Ballinger, Fredric Freyer, B. X. Sanborn
BALOGH, PENELOPE	Petronella Fox
BANGS, JOHN KENDRICK	T. Carlyle Smith
BANGS, ROBERT B.	Robert Babbitt
BANNER, CHARLA ANN LEIBENGUTH	Charla Ann Leibenguth
BANNISTER, PATRICIA V.	Patricia Veryan
BARBOUR, RALPH HENRY	Richard Stillman Powell
BARCLAY, FLORENCE LOUISA	Brandon Roy
BARDIN, JOHN FRANKLIN	Douglas Ashe, Gregory Tree

TRUE NAMES	PSEUDONYMS
BARKER, DUDLEY	Lionel Black, Tom Dudley-Gordon, Anthony Matthews
BARKER, E. M.	Nell Jordan
BARKER, SQUIRE OMAR	José Canusi, Dan Scott, Phil Squires
BARNARD, MARJORIE FAITH	M. Barnard Eldershaw
BARNE, MARION CATHERINE	Kitty Barne
BARNES, ARTHUR KELVIN	Dave Barnes, Kelvin Kent
BARNES, DJUNA	Lydia Steptoe
BARNSLEY, ALAN GABRIEL	Gabriel Fielding
BARR, ROBERT	Luke Sharp
BARRIE, J. M.	Gavin Ogilvy
BARRIE, SUSAN	Anita Charles, Pamela Kent
BARTLETT, ANNA	Amy Lothrop
BARTLETT, VERNON	Peter Oldfield
BARTON, EUSTACE ROBERT	Robert Eustace, Eustace Robert Rawlins
BASS, CLARA MAY	Claire May Overy
BASSETT, RONALD LESLIE	William Clive
BASSLER, THOMAS J.	T. J. Bass
BATES, H. E.	Flying Officer X
BATES, HIRAM GILMORE, III	Harry Bates, Anthony Gilmore, A. R. Holmes, H. G. Winter
BATTYE, GLADYS STARKEY	Margaret Lynn
BAUM, LYMAN FRANK	Floyd Akers, Laura Bancroft, L. Frank Baum, John Estes Cooke, Hugh Fitzgerald, Suzanne Metcalf, Schuyler Stanton, Edith Van Dyne
BAXTER, JOHN	Martin Loran
BAYBARS, TANER	Timothy Bayliss
BAYER, WILLIAM	Leonie St. John
BAYLEY, BARRINGTON JOHN	Alan Aumbry, P. F. Woods
BEARD, THOMAS FRANCIS	Frank Beard
BEATTY, PATRICIA	Jean Bartholomew
BEATY, BETTY	Karen Campbell, Catherine Ross
BEATY, DAVID	Paul Stanton
BECHKO, PEGGY ANNE	Bill Haller
BECK, LILY ADAMS	E. Barrington, Louis Moresby
BECKWITH, BURNHAM PUTNAM	John Putnam

TRUE NAMES	PSEUDONYMS
BELANEY, ARCHIBALD STANSFIELD	Grey Owl (Washaquonasin)
BELL, ERIC TEMPLE	John Taine
BELLEM, ROBERT LESLIE	Franklin Charles, John A. Saxon
BELLINGHAM, HELEN MARY DOROTHEA	Helen de Vere Beauclerk
BELLOC, HILAIRE	H. B.
BENNETT, ARNOLD	Jacob Tonson Gwendolyn
BENNETT, GEOFFREY MARTIN	Sea-Lion
BENNETT, GERTRUDE BARROWS	Francis Stevens
BENNETTS, PAMELA	Margaret James
BENTLEY, EDMUND CLERIHEW	E. C. Bentley, E. Clerihew
BENTLEY, PHYLISS	A Bachelor of Arts
BENTON, PEGGIE	Shifty Burke
BERGER, EVELYN MILLER	Evelyn Berger Brown
BERMAN, ED	Otto Premier Check, Professor R. L. Dogg, Super Santa
BERRY, BRYAN	Rolf Garner
BEVAN, ANEURIN	Celticus
BICKHAM, JACK MILES	Jeff Clinton, John Miles
BIDWELL, MARJORY ELIZABETH SARAH	Elizabeth Ford, Mary Ann Gibbs
BIERCE, AMBROSE	Dod Grile
BIGG, PATRICIA NINA	Patricia Ainsworth
BINDER, EARL ANDREW	Eando Binder
BINDER, OTTO OSCAR	Eando Binder, John Coleridge
BINGLEY, DAVID ERNEST	Bart Adams, Adam Bridger, Abe Canuck, Dave Carver, Henry Carver, Larry Chatham, Henry Chesham, Will Coltman, Ed Coniston, Luke Dorman, George Fallon, David Horsley, Bat Jefford, Syd Kingston, Eric Lynch, James Martell, Colin North, Ben Plummer, Caleb Prescott, Mark Remington, John Roberts, Steve Romney, Frank Silvester, Henry Starr, Link Tucker, Christopher Wigan, Roger Yorke
BIRNEY, HERMAN HOFFMAN	David Kent

TRUE NAMES	PSEUDONYMS
BIRO, BALINT STEPHEN	Val Biro
BISHOP, CLAIRE HUCHET	Claire Huchet
BISHOP, MORCHARD	Oliver Stoner
BLACKETT, VERONICA HEATH	Veronica Heath
BLAIR, ERIC ARTHUR	George Orwell
BLAIR, KATHRYN	Rosalind Brett, Celine Conway
BLAIR, WALTER	Mortimer Post
BLINDER, ELLIOT	Asa Elliot
BLISH, JAMES BENJAMIN	William Atheling, Jr.
BLIXEN, KAREN	Pierre Andrezel, Isak Dinesen
BLOCH, BARBARA	Phoebe Edwards
BLOCH, ROBERT	Collier Young
BLOCK, LAWRENCE	Chip Harrison, Paul Kavanagh
BLOOD, MARIE	Paige McKenzie
BLOOM, URSULA HARVEY	Sheila Burns, Mary Essex, Rachel Harvey, Deborah Mann, Lozania Prole, Sara Sloane
BLOOMFIELD, ANTHONY JOHN WESTGATE	John Westgate
BLUNDELL, HAROLD	George Bellairs
BLYTON, ENID MARY	Mary Pollock
BODINGTON, NANCY HERMIONE	Shelley Smith
BONFILS, MRS. CHARLES	Annie Laurie
BONHAM, BARBARA	Sara North
BONNER, GERALDINE	Hard Pan
BONSALL, CROSBY NEWELL	Crosby Newell
BOOTH, EDWIN	Don Blunt, Jack Hazard
BOOTH, ROSEMARY	Frances Murray
BORG, PHILIP ANTHONY JOHN	Phil Bexar, Jack Borg, John Q. Pickard
BORLAND, HAROLD GLEN	Hal Borland, Ward West
BORLAND, KATHRYN	Alice Abbott, Jane Land, Jane and Ross Land
BORNEMAN, ERNEST	Cameron McCabe
BOSTICCO, MARY	Isabelle Bey
BOSWORTH, ALLAN RUCKER	Alamo Boyd
BOUMA, JOHANAS L.	Steve Shannon

TRUE NAMES	PSEUDONYMS
BOUNDS, SYDNEY JAMES	Wes Saunders
BOURQUIN, PAUL HENRY JAMES	Richard Amberley
BOWDEN, JEAN	Jocelyn Barry, Jennifer Bland, Avon Curry, Belinda Dell
BOWEN, JOHN	Justin Blake
BOWEN-JUDD, SARA	Sara Woods
BOYD, WILLIAM C.	Boyd Ellanby
BRACKMAN, ARNOLD C.	Captain Moss Bunker
BRADBURY, RAY	Leonard Spaulding
BRADLEY, IAN	Duplex
BRADLEY, MARION ZIMMER	Lee Chapman, John Dexter, Miriam Gardner, Valerie Graves, Morgan Ives
BRAEME, CHARLOTTE M.	Bertha Clay
BRAMESCO, NORTON J.	Daedalus, Bram Norton
BRAND, MARY CHRISTIANNA MILNE	Mary Anne Ashe, Annabel Jones, Mary Roland, China Thompson
BRANDENBURG, ALIKI	Aliki
BRAWNER, H.	Geoffrey Coffin
BRENNAN, JOHN NEEDHAM HUGGARD	John Welcome
BRENT, MADELINE	A Pseudonym
BRENT, PETER LUDWIG	Ludovic Peters
BRENTANO, ELIZABETH	Bettina
BRETNOR, REGINALD	Grendel Briarton
BREUER, MILES JOHN	Simon Anthony, Lee Brett
BRIDGES, ROBERT	Droch
BRIGHT, ROBERT	Michael Douglas
BRONTE, ANN	Acton Bell
BRONTE, CHARLOTTE	Currer Bell
BRONTE, EMILY	Ellis Bell
BROOKS, EDWY SEARLES	Robert W. Comrade, Berkeley Gray, Victor Gunn, Carlton Ross
BROSSARD, CHANDLER	Daniel Harper
BROWN, MARGARET WISE	Timothy Hay, Golden MacDonald, Juniper Sage
BROWN, MORNA DORIS	E. X. Ferrars, Elizabeth Ferrars

TRUE NAMES	PSEUDONYMS
BROWN, ZENITH	Brenda Conrad, Leslie Ford, David Frome
BROWNE, CHARLES FARRAR	Artemus Ward
BROWNE, HABLOT K.	Phiz
BROWNJOHN, ALAN	John Berrington
BROXHOLME, JOHN	Duncan Kyle, James Meldrum
BRULLER, JEAN	Vercors
BRUNDAGE, JOHN HERBERT	John Herbert
BRUNNER, JOHN KILIAN HOUSTON	Gill Hunt, John Loxmith, Keith Woodcott
BRUTUS, DENNIS	John Bruin
BRYANS, ROBERT HARBISON	Robin Bryans, Donald Cameron, Robert Harbison
BRYANT, EDWARD WINSLOW	Lawrence Talbot
BRYNING, FRANCIS BERTRAM	Frank Bryning, F. Cornish
BUCHANAN, EILEEN MARIE DUELL	Marie Buchanan, Rhona Petrie
BUCK, PEARL S.	John Sedges
BUCK, WILLIAM RAY	William Buchanan
BUDRYS, ALGIRDAS JONAS	Algis Budrys, Frank Mason
BULLMORE, JEREMY	Justin Blake
BULLOCK, MICHAEL	Michael Hale
BULMER, HENRY KENNETH	Alan Burt Akers, Ken Blake, Ernest Corley, Arthur Frazier, Adam Hardy, Kenneth Johns, Philip Kent, Bruno Krauss, Neil Langholm, Karl Maras, Manning Norvil, Charles R. Pike, Andrew Quiller, Richard Silver, Tully Zetford
BULMER-THOMAS, IVOR	Ivor Thomas
BULWER-LYTTON, EDWARD ROBERT	Owen Meredith
BURGE, MILWARD RODON KENNEDY	John Frederick Burke, Jonathan Burke, Owen Burke, Robert Milward Burke, Evelyn Elder, Harriet Esmond, John Frederick, Jonathan George, Joanna Jones, Milward Kennedy, Robert Milward Kennedy, Sara Morris, Martin Sands

TRUE NAMES	PSEUDONYMS
BURNETT, WILLIAM RILEY	W. R. Burnett, John Monahan, James Updyke
BURROUGHS, EDGAR RICE	Norman Bean, John Tyler McCulloch
BURROUGHS, WILLIAM SEWARD	William Lee
BURROWES, MICHAEL ANTHONY BERNARD	Mike Burrowes
BURTON, ELIZABETH	Susan Kerby
BUSH, CHARLIE CHRISTMAS	Christopher Bush, Michael Home
BUTLER, GWENDOLINE	Jennie Melville
BUTLER, SAMUEL	Cellarius
BUTTERWORTH, MICHAEL	Sarah Kemp, Carola Salisbury
BUXTON, ANNE	Anne Maybury, Katherine Troy
BYRNE, JOHN KEYES	Hugh Leonard
CADELL, VIOLET ELIZABETH	Harriett Ainsworth
CAESER, R. D.	Dudley James
CAINE, THOMAS HENRY HALL	Hall Caine
CALDWELL, JANET MIRIAM TAYLOR HOLLAND	Taylor Caldwell, Max Reiner
CAMERON, LOU	Justin Adams, Julie Cameron
CAMPBELL, GABRIELLE MARGARET VERE	Marjorie Bowen, Robert Paye, George Preedy, Joseph Shearing, John Winch
CAMPBELL, GORDON	Tom Dudley-Gordon
CAMPBELL, WALTER STANLEY	Stanley Vestal
CAMPBELL, WILLIAM E.	Wilfred Campbell
CANADY, JOHN EDWIN	Matthew Head
CANAWAY, W. H.	Bill Canaway, William Hamilton, Hermes
CANNING, VICTOR	Alan Gould
CAPON, HARRY PAUL	Noel Kenton
CAREW-SLATER, HAROLD JAMES	James Carey
CARGILL, MORRIS	John Morris
CARNWORTH, LADY	Joan Alexander
CARR, ALBERT ZOTALKOFF	A. B. Carbury, A. H. Z. Carr
CARR, JOHN DICKSON	Carr Dickson, Carter Dickson, Roger Fairbairn

TRUE NAMES	PSEUDONYMS
CARR, MARGARET	Martin Carroll, Carole Kerr
CARR, TERRY GENE	Norman Edwards
CARRINGTON, CHARLES EDMUND	Charles Edmonds
CARTER, FELICITY WINIFRED	Emery Bonett, John and Emery Bonett
CARTER, FRANCES MONET	Frances Evans
CARTLAND, BARBARA HAMILTON	Barbara McCorquodale
CARTMILL, CLEVE	Michael Corbin
CATHER, WILLA	Willa Sibert
CATHERALL, ARTHUR	J. Baltimore, A. R. Channel, Dan Corby, Peter Hallard, Trevor Maine, Linda Peters, Margaret Ruthin
CAUTE, DAVID	John Salisbury
CAVANNA, BETTY	Betsy Allen, Elizabeth Headley
CEBULASH, MEL	Ben Farrell, Glen Harlan, Jared Jansen
CHACE, ISOBEL	Elizabeth Mary Teresa Hunter
CHALKE, H. D.	Hereth Blacker
CHALLANS, MARY	Mary Renault
CHANCE, JOHN NEWTON	J. Drummond, John Lymington, David C. Newton
CHAPMAN, JOHN	Johnny Appleseed
CHAPMAN-MORTIMER, WILLIAM CHARLES	Chapman Mortimer, Charles Mortimer
CHARBONNEAU, LOUIS HENRY	Carter Travis Young
CHARLIER, ROGER HENRI	Henry Rochard
CHARNOCK, JOAN PAGET	Joan Thomson
CHASE, VIRGINIA	Virginia Chase Perkins
CHERRY, CAROLYN JANICE	C. J. Cherryh
CHESTERTON, GILBERT KEITH	Arion, G. K. Chesterton, G. K. C.
CHEVALIER, PAUL EUGENE GEORGE	Eugene George
CHIBNALL, MARJORIE MC CALLUM	Marjorie Morgan
CHIPPERFIELD, JOSEPH EUGENE	John Eland Craig
CHITTY, SIR THOMAS WILLES	Thomas Hinde

TRUE NAMES	PSEUDONYMS
CLARK, ALFRED ALEXANDER GORDON	Cyril Hare
CLARK, CHARLES HEBER	Max Adeler
CLARK, MAVIS THORPE	Mavis Latham
CLARK, PATRICIA DENISE	Claire Lorrimer, Patricia Robins
CLARKE, BRENDA	Brenda Honeyman
CLARKE, DAVID WALDO	Dave Waldo
CLARKE, PAULINE	Helen Clare
CLARKE, REBECCA SOPHIA	Sophie May
CLAYTON, RICHARD HENRY MICHAEL	William Haggard
CLEMENS, SAMUEL LANGHORNE	Mark Twain
CLUTTERBUCK, RICHARD	Richard Jocelyn
CLYMER, ELEANOR	Janet Bell, Elizabeth Kinsey
CLYNE, DOUGLAS	Alisdair Sinclair
COAD, FREDERICK ROY	Sosthenes, I. M. Sutton
CODY, WILLIAM S.	Buffalo Bill
COFFMAN, VIRGINIA EDITH	Victor Cross, Jeanne Duval, Virginia C. Du Vaul, Anne Stanfield
COGHLAN, MARGARET M.	Peggie Coghlan, Jessica Stirling
COHEN, MORTON	John Moreton
COLES, CYRIL HENRY	Manning Coles, Francis Gaite
COLLIER, PRICE	Percy Collins
COLLIER, ZENA	Jane Collier, Zena Shumsky
COLLINS, MICHAEL DALE	Copeland
COLLOMS, BRENDA	Brenda Cross, Brenda Hughes
COMPTON, DAVID GUY	Guy Compton, Frances Lynch
CONARAIN, ALICE NINA	Elizabeth Hoy
CONE, MOLLY	Caroline Moore
CONLY, ROBERT LESLIE	Robert C. O'Brien
CONNELLY, CYRIL	Palinurus
CONNOR, WILLIAM	Cassandra
CONQUEST, GEORGE ROBERT ACWORTH	J. E. M. Arden
COOK, DOROTHY MARE	D. Y. Cameron, D. M. Carlisle, Elizabeth Clare
COOK, IDA	Mary Burchell, James Keene

TRUE NAMES	PSEUDONYMS
COOK, JOHN LENNOX	Lennox Cook
COOK, WILLIAM EVERETT	Wade Everett, James Keene, Frank Peace
COOKE, PHILIP ST. GEORGE, III	Peter Hertzog
COOKSON, CATHERINE ANN	Catherine Marchant
COOMBE, WILLIAM	Dr. Syntax
COOPER, COLIN SYMONS	Daniel Benson
COOPER, EDMUND	Richard Avery
COOPER, HENRY ST. JOHN	Mabel St. John
COPPEL, ALFRED	Sol Galaxan, Robert Cham Gilman, Derfla Leppoc, A. C. Marin
COPPER, BASIL	Lee Falk
CORCORAN, BARBARA	Paige Dixon
CORNWELL, DAVID JOHN MOORE	John Le Carre
CORYELL, J. RUSSELL	Nick Carter
COTTON, JOSE MARIO GARRY ORDONEZ EDMONDSON	G. C. Edmondson, Kelly P. Gast
COULSON, JOHN HUBERT ARTHUR	Emery Bonett, John and Emery Bonett
COULSON, JUANITA	John J. Wells
COULSON, ROBERT STRATTON	Thomas Stratton
COULTER, STEPHEN	James Mayo
COUNSELMAN, MARY ELIZABETH	Charles Dubois, Sanders McCrorey, John Starr
COUSINS, MARGARET	Avery Johns
COWEN, FRANCES	Eleanor Hyde
COX, ANTHONY BERKELEY	Anthony Berkeley, Francis Iles
COX, EDITH MURIEL	Muriel Goaman
COX, WILLIAM ROBERT	Mike Frederic, Joel Reeve, Roger G. Spellman, Jonas Ward
COX, WILLIAM TREVOR	William Trevor
CRAIG, EDWARD ANTHONY	Edward Carrick
CRAIG, MARY FRANCIS	M. S. Craig, Alexis Hill, Mary Francis Shura
CRANE, STEPHEN	Johnston Smith
CRAWFORD, JOHN RICHARD	J. Walker
CREASEY, JOHN	Gordon Ashe, M. E. Cooke, Margaret Cooke, Henry St. John Cooper,

TRUE NAMES	PSEUDONYMS
	Norman Deane, Elise Fecamps, Robert Caine Frazer, Patrick Gill, Michael Halliday, Charles Hogarth, Brian Hope, Colin Hughes, Kyle Hunt, Abel Mann, Peter Manton, J. J. Marric, James Marsden, Richard Martin, Rodney Mattheson, Anthony Morton, Ken Ranger, William K. Reilly, Tex Riley, Jimmy Wilde, Jeremy York
CRICHTON, DOUGLAS	Michael Douglas
CRISP, ANTHONY THOMAS	Tony Crisp, Mark Western
CROWE, LADY BETTINA	Peter Lum
CRUICKSHANK, CHARLES GREIG	Charles Greig
CUMBERLAND, MARTEN	Kevin O'Hara
CUNNINGHAM, CHET	Jess Cody, Cathy Cunningham, Lionel Derrick, Don Pendleton
CUNNINGHAM, EUGENE	Leigh Carder
CURTIS, JULIA ANN KEMBLE	Anne of Swansea, Julia Hatton
CURTIS, RICHARD	Ray Lilly, Morton Stultifer, Malanie Ward
CURTIS, SHARON	Laura London
CURTIS, THOMAS DALE	Laura London
DACE, LETITIA	Tish Dace
DANBY, MARY	Mary Calvert
DANEFF, STEPHEN CONSTANTINE	Stephen Constant
DANIEL, GLYN EDMUND	Dilwyn Rees
DANIEL, WILLIAM ROLAND	Sonia Anderson
DANIELL, ALBERT SCOTT	Richard Bowood, David Scott Daniell, John Lewesdon
DANIELS, DOROTHY	Danielle Dorsett, Angela Gray, Cynthia Kavanaugh, Helaine Ross, Suzanne Somers, Geraldine Thayer, Helen Gray Weston
DANNAY, FREDERIC	Daniel Nathan, Ellery Queen, Ellery Queen, Jr., Barnaby Ross
DAVIES, JOAN H.	Joan Drake
DAVIES, JOHN EVAN WESTON	Berkley Mather

TRUE NAMES	PSEUDONYMS
DAVIES, LESLIE PURNELL	Leslie Vardre
DAVIES, PAUL	P. C. W. Davies
DAVIS, FREDERICK CLYDE	Murdo Coombs, Stephen Ransome, Curtis Steele
DAVIS, JULIA	F. Draco
DAVIS, NORBERT	Harrison Hunt
DAVIS, ROBERT PRUNIER	Joe Brandon
DAY-LEWIS, CECIL	Nicholas Blake, C. D. Lewis, C. Day Lewis
DE FREES, MADELINE	Sister Mary Gilbert
DEGHY, GUY	Herald Froy, Lee Gibb
DEIGHTON, LEONARD CYRIL	Len Deighton
DE LA MARE, WALTER	Walter Ramal
DELANEY, MARY MURRAY	Mary D. Lane
DE LA PASTURE, EDMEE ELIZABETH MONICA	E. M. Delafield
DE LA RAMEE, LOUISE	Ouida
DELOUGHERY, GRACE L.	Grace L. Wiest
DEL VALLE-INCLAN, RAMON	Ramon Del-Valley Pena
DEMING, RICHARD	Max Franklin, Emily Moor, Nick Morino
DENISON, DULCIE WINIFRED CATHERINE	Dulcie Gray
DENNIS, GEOFFREY	Barum Browne
DENNISTON, ELINORE	Dennis Allan, Rae Foley
DENT, LESTER	Kenneth Robeson, Tim Ryan
DE REGNIERS, BEATRICE S.	Tamara Kitt
DE RENEVILLE, MARY MARGARET MOTLEY	Mary Motley
DERLETH, AUGUST WILLIAM	Stephen Grendon, Tally Mason
DE SCHANSCHIEFF, JULIET DYMOKE	Juliet Dymoke
DESMARAIS, OVIDE E.	Ovid Demaris
DEVINE, DAVID MC DONALD	Dominic Devine
DE VOTO, BERNARD AUGUSTINE	John August, Cady Lewes
DE WEESE, THOMAS EUGENE	Gene De Weese, Jean De Weese, Thomas Stratton

TRUE NAMES	PSEUDONYMS
DE WEESE-WEHEN, JOY	Jennifer Wade
DEWEY, THOMAS BLANCHARD	Tom Brandt, Cord Wainer
DEY, FREDERIC MERRILL VAN RENSSELAER	Nicholas Carter, Nick Carter, Marmaduke Dey, Frederic Ormond, Varick Vanardy
DICK, PHILIP K.	Richard Phillips
DICKENS, CHARLES	Boz
DICK-LAUDER, SIR GEORGE	George Lauder
DIENER, TERRIL	T. D. Allen, Terry D. Allen
DILCOCK, NOREEN	Jill Christian, Norrey Ford, Christian Walford
DI PRIMA, DIANE	Sybah Darrich
DISCH, THOMAS MICHAEL	Thom Demijohn, Leonie Hargrave, Cassandra Knye
DIXON, ROGER	John Christian, Charles Lewis
DODD, WAYNE D.	Donald Wayne
DODGE, MARY ABAGAIL	Gail Hamilton
DODGSON, CHARLES LUTWIDGE	Lewis Carroll
DONNELLY, AUSTIN S.	Bullen Bear
DONOVAN, JOHN	Hugh Hennessey
DOOLITTLE, HILDA	H. D.
DOUGLAS, NORMAN	Narmyx
DOYLE, CHARLES	Mike Doyle
DRACKETT, PHIL	Paul King
DRAGO, HARRY SINCLAIR	Stewart Cross, Kirk Deming, Will Ermine, Bliss Lomax, J. Wesley Putnam, Grant Sinclair
DRESSER, DAVIS	Asa Baker, Matthew Blood, Kathryn Culver, Don Davis, Hal Debrett, Brett Halliday, Anthony Scott, Anderson Wayne
DRUMMOND, JOHN	Lord Strange
DRURY, MAXINE COLE	Don Creighton
DUCHACEK, IVO D.	Ivo Duka
DUFAULT, JOSEPH ERNEST NEPHTALI	Will James
DUKE, MADELAINE	Alex Duncan
DUNBOYNE, LORD	Patrick Butler

TRUE NAMES	PSEUDONYMS
DUNCAN, ROBERT LIPSCOMB	James Hall Roberts
DUNCAN, WILLIAM MURDOCH	John Cassells, John Dallas, Neill Graham, Martin Locke, Peter Malloch, Lovat Marshall
DUNKERLEY, ELSIE JEANNETTE	Elsie Oxenham
DUNLOP, AGNES M. R.	Elisabeth Kyle, Jan Ralston
DUNMORE, JOHN	Jason Calder
DUNNE, PETER FINLEY	Martin Dooley
DUNNETT, DOROTHY	Dorothy Halliday
DUPIN, AMANDINE AURORE LUCIE	George Sand
DURRELL, LAWRENCE GEORGE	Charles Norden
DURST, PAUL	Peter Bannon, John Chelton, Jeff Cochran, John Shane
EAST, FRED	Roy Manning, Tom West
EBEL, SUZANNE	Suzanne Goodwin, Cecily Shelbourne
EBERT, ARTHUR FRANK	Frank Arthur
EDEN, DOROTHY	Mary Paradise
EDGINTON, HELEN MARION	May Edginton
EDSON, JOHN THOMAS	Rod Denver, Chuck Nolan
EDWARDS, LEO	Edward Edson Lee
EGLETON, CLIVE	Patrick Blake, John Tarrant
ELDERSHAW, ELISABETH	Elisabeth MacIntyre
ELDERSHAW, FLORA SYDNEY PATRICIA	M. Barnard Eldershaw
ELLERBECK, ROSEMARY ANNE L'ESTRANGE	Anna L'Estrange, Nicola Thorne, Katherine Yorke
ELLES, DORA AMY	Patricia Wentworth
ELLISON, JOAN AUDREY	Elspeth Robertson
ELLISON, VIRGINIA HOWELL	Virginia Tier Howard, Virginia T. H. Mussey, V. H. Soskin, Leong Gor Yun
ELMORE, ERNEST CARPENTER	John Bude
EMANUEL, VICTOR ROUSSEAU	H. M. Egbert, Victor Rousseau
ERNST, PAUL	Kenneth Robeson
ERNST, PAUL FREDERICK	Paul Frederick Stern

TRUE NAMES	PSEUDONYMS
ESTRIDGE, ROBIN	Philip Loraine
ETCHISON, BIRDIE L.	Leigh Hunter, Catherine Wood
EVANS, CONSTANCE MAY	Jane Gray, Mairi O'Nair
EVANS, JULIA	Polly Hobson
EVANS, MARIAN OR MARY ANN	George Eliot
EVELYN, JOHN MICHAEL	Michael Underwood
EVERETT-GREEN, EVELYN	Cecil Adair, Evelyn Dare, H. F. E.
EVERSON, WILLIAM	Antoninus, Brother Antoninus
EWENS, GWENDOLINE WILSON	Gladys Ashley, Gwendoline Wilson
FABRY, JOSEPH B.	Peter Fabrizius
FAIRBURN, ELEANOR	Caterine Carfax, Emma Gayle
FAIRMAN, PAUL W.	Adam Chase, Lester Del Rey, Ivar Jorgensen
FANTONI, BARRY	Sylvie Krin, E. J. Thribb
FARMER, PHILIP JOSE	Kilgore Trout
FARNDALE, W. A. J.	James Farndale
FARNILL, BARRIE	John Wellington
FARSON, DANIEL NEGLEY	Matilda Excellent, Negley Farson
FAST, HOWARD MELVIN	E. V. Cunningham, Walter Ericson
FAUST, FREDERICK SCHILLER	Frank Austin, George Owen Baxter, Max Brand, Walter C. Butler, George Challis, Peter Dawson, Martin Dexter, Evan Evans, John Frederick, Frederick Frost, David Manning, Peter Henry Morland, Hugh Owen, Nicholas Silver
FEARN, JOHN RUSSELL	Geoffrey Armstrong, Thornton Ayre, Hugo Blayn, Dennis Clive, John Cotton, Polton Cross, Astron Del Martia, Mark Denholm, Volsted Gridban, Timothy Hayes, Conrad G. Holt, Frank Jones, Paul Lorraine, Dom Passante, Laurence F. Rose, Doorn Sclanders, Joan Seager, Bryan Shaw, John Slate, Vargo Statten, K. Thomas, Earl Titan, Arthur Waterhouse, John Wernheim, Ephriam Winiki

TRUE NAMES	PSEUDONYMS
FEHRENBACH, T. R.	Thomas Freeman
FEILDING, DOROTHY	A. Fielding, A. E. Fielding
FEINBERG, BEA	Cynthia Freeman
FELLIG, ARTHUR	Weegee
FELTON, RONALD OLIVER	Ronald Welsh
FERNANDEZ, GLADYS CRAVEN	Happy Craven Fernandez
FETZER, HERMAN	Jake Falstaff
FICHTER, GEORGE S.	George Kensinger, Matt Warner, Marc Ziliox
FIELDING, A. W.	Xan Fielding
FINK, MERTON	Matthew Finch, Merton Finch
FINLEY, MARTHA F.	Martha Farquharson
FINNEY, WALTER BRADEN	Jack Finney
FINNIN, MARY	John Hogarth, Lawrence Vigil
FISCHER, BRUNO	Russell Gray
FISH, ROBERT L.	Robert L. Pike, Lawrence Roberts
FISHER, A. STANLEY	Michael Scarrott
FISHER, EDWARD	A. E. Fisher
FISHER, STEPHEN GOULD	Steve Fisher, Stephen Gould, Grant Lane
FLOREN, LEE	Brett Austin, Claudia Hall, Wade Hamilton, Matthew Whitman Harding, Felix Lee Horton, Grace Lang, Marguerite Nelson, Lew Smith, Maria Sandra Sterling, Jason Stuart, Lee Thomas, Len Turner, Will Watson, Dave Wilson
FOLSOM, FRANKLIN BREWSTER	Benjamin Brewster, Michael Gorham, Lyman Hopkins, Troy Nesbit
FOOT, MICHAEL	Cassius
FORBES, DELORIS FLORINE STANTON	D. E. Forbes, De Forbes, Forbes Rydell, Tobias Wells
FOSDICK, CHARLES AUSTIN	H. C. Castlemon, Harry Castlemon
FOULDS, ELFRIDA VIPONT	E. V. Foulds, Charles Vipont, Elfrida Vipont
FOWLER, J. K.	Rusticus
FOWLER, KENNETH ABRAMS	Clark Brooker

TRUE NAMES	PSEUDONYMS
FOX, GARDNER FRANCIS	Jeff Cooper, Jefferson Cooper, Jeffrey Gardner, James Kendricks, Elliott Kennedy, Simon Majors, Kevin Matthews, Bart Somers
FOX, NORMAN ARNOLD	Mark Sabin
FOXE, ARTHUR NORMAN	Ann Foda
FRAENKEL, HEINRICH	Assiac
FRANCIS, ANNE	Olivia Ellis
FRANCIS, DOROTHY BRENNER	Sue Alden, Ellen Goforth
FRANCK, FREDERICK	Dr. Frank Fredricks
FRANKAU, PAMELA	Eliot Naylor
FRANKEN, ROSE DOROTHY	Margaret Grant, Franken Meloney
FRANKLIN, BENJAMIN	Richard Saunders
FRAZEE, CHARLES STEVE	Dean Jennings
FREEDGOOD, MORTON	John Godey, Stanley Morton
FREELING, NICHOLAS	F. R. E. Nicholas
FREEMAN, GILLIAN	Eliot George
FREEMAN, KATHLEEN	Mary Fitt, Stuart Wick
FREEMAN, MARY ELEANOR WILKINS	Mary Wilkins
FREEMAN, RICHARD AUSTIN	Clifford Ashdown
FREEMANTLE, BRIAN HARRY	Richard Grant, John Maxwell
FREWER, GLYN	Mervyn Lewis
FREWIN, LESLIE	Paul Dupont
FREYBE, HEIDI HUBERTA	Martha Albrand, Katrin Holland, Christinne Lambert
FRIEDMAN, JACOB HORACE	Elias Friedman, John Friedman, Elias Pater
FRIEDMAN, ROSEMARY	Robert Tibber, Rosemary Tibber
FRY, CHRISTOPHER	Christopher Harris
FULLERTON, ALEXANDER	Anthony Fox
FULLERTON, GAIL	Gail J. Putney
FYFE, HORACE BROWNE	Andrew MacDuff
GALLUN, RAYMOND ZINKE	William Callahan
GALSWORTHY, JOHN	John Sinjohn
GANDLEY, KENNETH ROYCE	Oliver Jacks, Kenneth Royce

TRUE NAMES	PSEUDONYMS
GARDNER, ERLE STANLEY	A. A. Fair, Charles M. Green, Carleton Kendrake, Charles J. Kenny, Robert Park, Les Tillray
GARFIELD, BRIAN FRANCIS WYNNE	Bennett Garland, Alex Hawk, John Ives, Drew Mallory, Frank O'Brian, Jonas Ward, Brian Wynne, Frank Wynne
GARRETT, RANDALL PHILLIP	Gordon Aghill, Grandall Barretton, Alexander Blade, Alfred Blake, Andrew Blake, Walter Bupp, Ralph Burke, Gordon Garrett, David Gordon, Richard Greer, Larry Mark Harris, Laurence M. Janifer, Ivar Jorgensen, Darrel T. Langart, Clyde T. Mitchell, Mark Phillips, Robert Randall, Leonard G. Spencer, S. M. Tenneshaw, Gerald Vance, Barbara Wilson
GARVE, ANDREW	Paul Somers
GARVICE, CHARLES	Charles Gibson, Caroline Hart
GASTON, WILLIAM JAMES	Jack Bannatyne, Bill Gaston
GAULDEN, RAY	Wesley Ray
GAULT, WILLIAM CAMPBELL	Will Duke
GEACH, CHRISTINE	Elizabeth Dawson, Anne Lowing, Christine Wilson
GEISEL, THEODOR SEUSS	Theo Le Sieg, Seuss, Dr. Seuss
GELLIS, ROBERTA LEAH	Max Daniels, Priscilla Hamilton, Leah Jacobs
GEORGE, PETER BRYAN	Peter Bryant, Bryan Peters
GERD, JACOB STERN	Usco
GERMANO, PETER B.	Jack Bertin, Barry Cord, Jim Kane
GERSON, NOEL	Samuel Edwards
GESSNER, LYNNE	Merle Clark
GHOSE, AMAL	Lama Esohg
GIBSON, WALTER B.	Ishi Black, Douglas Brown, Maxwell Grant, Maborushi Kineji
GIESY, JOHN ULRICH	Charles Dustin
GIGGAL, KENNETH	Angus Ross
GILBERTSON, MILDRED	Nan Gilbert

TRUE NAMES	PSEUDONYMS
GILES, KENNETH	Charles Drummond, Edmund McGirr
GILKYSON, BERNICE KENYON	Bernice Kenyon
GILMAN, DOROTHY	Dorothy Gilman Butters
GILMER, ELIZABETH MERIWETHER	Dorothy Dix
GILMORE, JAMES R.	Edmuns Kirke
GIOVANNI, YOLANDE C.	Nicki Giovanni
GIPIUS, ZINAIDA	Zinaida Hippius, Zinaida Merezhkovski
GLASER, ELEANOR DOROTHY	Eleanor Dorothy Zonik
GLASER, KURT	Comstock Glaser
GLASKIN, G. M.	Neville Jackson
GLASSCO, JOHN	Sylvia Bayer, Jean De Saint-Luc, Miles Underwood
GLASSCOCK, ANNE	Michael Bonner
GLEN, DUNCAN	Simon Foster, Ronald Eadie Munro
GLIDDEN, FREDERICK DILLEY	Luke Short
GLIDDEN, JONATHAN H.	Peter Dawson
GLIEWE, UNADA G.	Unada
GLOUSTON, J. STORER	George Gissing
GLUT, DON F.	Johnny Jason, Mick Rogers
GODFREY, LIONEL	Elliott Kennedy, Scott Mitchell
GOLDMAN, WILLIAM	Harry Longbaugh
GOLDSTEIN, ARTHUR DAVID	Albert Ross
GOLDSTONE, LAWRENCE ARTHUR	A. Goldstone, Lawrence Treat
GOODEN, ARTHUR HARRY	Brett Rider
GOODRICH, SAMUEL GRISWOLD	Peter Parley
GORDON, CHARLES WILLIAM	Ralph Connor
GORDON, GORDON	The Gordons
GORDON, MILDRED	The Gordons
GORDON, RICHARD	Stuart Gordon, Alex Stuart, Alex R. Stuart
GOREY, EDWARD ST. JOHN	Edward Bluting, Mrs. Regera Dowdy, Redway Grode, O. Mude, Ogred Weary, Dreary Wodge
GORSLINE, MARIE	S. M. Carson, S. M. Gorsline
GOSLING, NIGEL	Alexander Bland

TRUE NAMES	PSEUDONYMS
GOTTSCHALK, LAURA RIDING	Laura Riding
GOULART, RONALD JOSEPH	Josephine Kains, Julian Kearney, Howard Lee, Kenneth Robeson, Frank S. Shawn, Con Steffanson
GOULDING, PETER GEOFFREY	Guy Viliers
GOVAN, CHRISTINE NOBLE	Mary Allerton, J. N. Darby
GOYDER, MARGOT	Margot Neville
GRABER, GEORGE ALEXANDER	Alexander Cordell
GRAHAM, ROGER PHILLIPS	Clinton Ames, Robert Arnette, Franklin Bahl, Alexander Blade, Craig Browning, Gregg Conrad, P. F. Costello, Inez McGowan, Rog Phillips, Melva Rogers, Chester Ruppert, William Carter Sawtelle, A. R. Steber, Gerald Vance, John Wiley, Peter Worth
GRANT, JOHN	Jonathan Gash
GRANT, NEIL	David Mountfield
GRAVES, ROBERT RANKE	Barbara Rich
GRAY, PEARL ZANE	Zane Gray, Zane Grey
GRAY, SIMON	Hamish Reade
GRAYLAND, VALERIE MERLE	Lee Belvedere, Valerie Spanner, Valerie Subond
GREEN, ELISABETH SARA	Liz Tresilian
GREEN, PETER	Denis Delaney
GREENE, SIGRID	Sigrid De Lima
GREENWOOD, EDWARD ALISTER	Ted Grenwood
GREENWOOD, GRACE	Sara Jane Lippincott
GREENWOOD, JULIA EILEEN COURTNEY	Francis Askham
GREENWOOD, THOMAS	Alain Verval
GREER, GERMAINE	Rose Blight
GREIG-SMITH, JENNIFER	Jennifer Ames, Ann Barclay, Maysie Greig, Mary Douglas Warren
GREVE, FELIX PAUL BERTHOLD FRIEDRICH	Frederick Philip Grove
GRIBBLE, LEONARD REGINALD	Sterry Browning, Landon Grant, Leo Grex, Louis Grey, Dexter Muir
GRIERSON, EDWARD DOBBYN	Brian Crowther, John P. Stevenson

TRUE NAMES	PSEUDONYMS
GRIFFIN, ROBERT JOHN THURLOW	Jonathan Griffin
GRIFFITH-JONES, GEORGE CHETWYND	Levin Carnac, George Griffith, Lara, Stanton March
GRIFFITHS, CHARLES	Charles Boardman, Ralph Bold
GRIMM, CHERRY BARBARA	Cherry Wilder
GRIMSTEAD, HETTIE	Marsha Manning
GROVES, SHEILA	Sheila Durrant
GRUBER, FRANK	Stephen Acre, Charles K. Boston, John K. Vedder
GUIRDHAM, ARTHUR	Francis Eaglesfield
GULICK, GROVER C.	Bull Gulick
GUTHRIE, THOMAS ANSTEY	F. Anstey, Hope Bandoff, William Monarch Jones
GUTHRIE, TOM	Tom Dudley-Gordon
GWINN, CHRISTINE MARGARET	Christine Kelway
HAAS, BENJAMIN LEOPOLD	John Benteen, Thorne Douglas, Richard Meade
HAAVIKKO, PAAVO JUHANI	Anders Lieksman
HAGBERG, DAVID J.	Sean Flannery, David James, Robert Pell, Eric Ramsey
HAINS, T. JENKINS	Mary Clew Garnett
HALDEMAN, JOE WILLIAM	Robert Graham
HALIBURTON, T. C.	Sam Slick
HALL, MARJORY	Carol Morse
HALL, NORAH E. L.	Aylmer Hall
HALL, OAKLEY MAXWELL	O. M. Hall, Jason Manor
HALLERAN, EUGENE EDWARDS	Evan Hall
HALLOWS, N. F.	Duplex
HALPERN, BARBARA STRACHEY	Barbara Strachey
HALSEY, HARLAN P.	Old Sleuth
HAMILTON, CHARLES HAROLD ST. JOHN	Martin Clifford, Martin Conquest, Owen Conquest, Frank Richards, Hilda Richards
HAMILTON, EDMOND	Brett Sterling
HAMMETT, SAMUEL DASHIELL	Peter Collinson

TRUE NAMES	PSEUDONYMS
HAMMOND, JOHN	Henry Johnson
HANLEY, CLIFFORD	Henry Calvin
HANLEY, JAMES	Patric Shone
HANSEN, JOSEPH	Rose Brock, James Colton
HANSHEW, THOMAS W.	Charlotte Mary Kingsley
HARBAGE, ALFRED BENNETT	Thomas Kyd
HARDING, LEE JOHN	Harold G. Nye
HARDISON, OSBORNE B.	H. O. Bennett
HARDWICK, MOLLIE	Mary Atkinson, John Drinkrow
HARKNETT, TERRY WILLIAMS	Frank Chandler, David Ford, George G. Gilman, Jane Harman, Joseph Hedges, William M. James, Charles R. Pike, William Pine, James Russell, Thomas H. Stone, William Terry
HARLING, ROBERT	Nicholas Drew
HARRIS, JOEL CHANDLER	Uncle Remus
HARRIS, JOHN	Mark Hebden, Max Hennessey
HARRIS, JOHN WYNDHAM PARKES LUCAS BEYNON	John Beynon, J. B. Harris, Johnson Harris, John Wyndham
HARRIS, LARRY MARK	Alfred Blake, Andrew Blake, Mark Phillips, Barbara Wilson
HARRIS, MARION ROSE	Henry Charles, Daphne Harriford, Keith Rogers, Rose Young
HARRISON, MICHAEL	Quentin Downes
HARTLEY, ELLEN R.	Ellen Raphael Knauff
HARVEY, JOHN B.	Jon Barton, William S. Brady, L. J. Coburn, J. B. Dancer, Jon Hart, William M. James, John J. McLaglen, James Mann, Thom Ryder, J. D. Sandon, Jonathan White
HARVEY, NIGEL	Hugh Willoughby
HASKIN, DOROTHY C.	Howard Clark
HASTINGS, PHYLISS DORA	John Bedford, Julia Mayfield
HASWELL, CHETWYND JOHN DRAKE	George Foster, Jock Haswell
HAUTZIG, ESTHER	Esther Rudomin
HAWES, LYNNE SALOP	Lynne Salop

TRUE NAMES	PSEUDONYMS
HAWKINS, SIR ANTHONY HOPE	Anthony Hope
HAWTHORNE, JULIAN	Judith Hollinshead
HAYES, JOSEPH ARNOLD	Joseph H. Arnold
HAYNES, DOROTHY K.	Dorothy Kate Gray
HEALEY, BENJAMIN JAMES	Ben Healey, J. O. Jeffreys, Jeremy Sturrock
HEARD, HENRY FITZGERALD	Gerald Heard
HEARNE, JOHN	John Morris
HEATHCOTT, MARY	Mary Raymond
HEAVEN, CONSTANCE	Constance Fecher, Christina Merlin
HECKELMANN, CHARLES NEWMAN	Cliff Campbell, Jackson Cole, Andrew Griffin, Charles Lawton, Charles Mann, Chuck Mann, Mat Rand, James Rourke, Charles Smith, Reeve Walker
HEILBRUN, CAROLYN GOLD	Amanda Cross
HEINLEIN, ROBERT	Anson MacDonald, Lyle Monroe, John Riverside, Caleb Saunders
HENNISSART, MARTHA	R. B. Dominic, Emma Lathen
HENSON, JAMES MAURY	Jim Henson
HERBERT, HENRY WILLIAM	Frank Forrester
HERON-ALLEN, EDWARD	Christopher Blayre, Nora Helen Wardell
HEUMAN, WILLIAM	George Kramer
HEWETT, ANITA	Anne Wellington
HEYER, GEORGETTE	Stella Martin
HIBBERT, ELEANOR ALICE	Eleanor Burford, Philippa Carr, Elbur Ford, Victoria Holt, Kathleen Kellow, Jean Plaidy, Ellalice Tate
HIBBS, JOHN	John Blyth
HIGHSMITH, PATRICIA	Claire Morgan
HILDICK, E. W.	Wallace Hildick
HILL, CHRISTOPHER	K. E. Holme
HILL, PAMELA	Sharon Fiske
HILL, REGINALD	Dick Morland, Patrick Ruell, Charles Underhill
HILL-LUTZ, GRACE LIVINGSTON	Grace Livingston Hill, Grace Livingston, Marcia Macdonald
HILTON, JAMES	Glen Trevor

TRUE NAMES	PSEUDONYMS
HINCKLEY, HELEN	Helen Jones
HITCHENS, JULIA CLARA CATHERINE DELORES BIRK OLSEN	Dolan Birkley, Noel Burke, D. B. Olsen
HOAR, ROGER SHERMAN	Ralph Milne Farley
HOCH, EDWARD DENTINGER	Irwin Booth, Stephen Dentinger, Pat McMahon, R. L. Stevens, Mr. X
HOCKING, MONA NAOMI ANNE MESSER	Mona Messer
HODDER-WILLIAMS, JOHN CHRISTOPHER GLAZEBROOK	James Brogan
HODGES, DORIS M.	Charlotte Hunt
HOFF, HARRY SUMMERFIELD	William Cooper
HOFFMAN, LEE	Georgia York
HOGAN, ROBERT RAY	Clay Ringold
HOGARTH, GRACE	Grace Allen, Amelia Gay, Allen Weston
HOLDING, JAMES	Ellery Queen, Jr.
HOLLAND, J. G.	Timothy Titcomb
HOLLAND, CECELIA ANASTASIA	Elizabeth Eliot Carter
HOLLAND, ISABELLE	Francesca Hunt
HOLLAND, SHEILA	Sheila Coates, Laura Hardy, Charlotte Lamb, Sheila Lancaster
HOLLEY, MARIETTA	Josiah Allen's Wife
HOLMAN, CLARENCE HUGH	Clarence Hunt
HOOVER, HELEN	Jennifer Price
HOPE-SIMPSON, JACYNTH	Helen Dudley
HOPKINS, ROBERT SYDNEY	Robert Rostand
HOPKINS, SAM	Lightnin' Hopkins
HOPKINSON, SIR HENRY THOMAS	Tom Hopkinson, Thomas Pemberton, Thomas Pembroke, Vindicator
HOPLEY-WOOLRICH, CORNELL GEORGE	George Hopley, William Irish, Cornell Woolrich
HOPSON, WILLIAM L.	John Sims
HORNE, GEOFFREY	Gil North
HORNUNG, ERNEST WILLIAM	E. W. H., E. W. Hornung
HORTON, MILES	Thomas Pembroke
HOSKEN, CLIFFORD JAMES WHEELER	Richard Keverne

TRUE NAMES	PSEUDONYMS
HOSKINS, ROBERT	Grace Corren, John Gregory, Susan Jennifer, Michael Kerr
HOSSENT, HARRY	David Savage
HOUGH, RICHARD ALEXANDER	Bruce Carter, Elizabeth Churchill, Pat Strong
HOUGH, STANLEY BENNETT	Rex Gordon, Bennett Stanley
HOWARD, ROBERT E.	Patrick Irvin
HOWARTH, PAMELA	Pamela Barrow
HOWARTH, PATRICK	C. D. E. Francis
HOWAT, GERALD	Gerald Henderson-Howat
HOWE, DORIS	Mary Munro, Newlyn Nash
HOWE, MURIEL	Newlyn Nash, Barbara Redmayne
HUBBARD, ELBERT	Fra Elbertus, Cal Hubbard
HUBBARD, GEORGE BARRON	Amos Moore
HUBBARD, LAFAYETTE RON	L. Ron Hubbard, Rene LaFayette, Kurt Von Rachen
HUEFFER, FORD MADOX	Ford Madox Ford
HUGHES, WALTER LLEWELLYN	Hugh Walters
HUMPHRIES, ELSIE MARY	Mary Forrester
HUMPHRIES, SYDNEY VERNON	Michael Vane
HUMPHRYS, LESLIE GEORGE	Bruno Condray, Geoffrey Humphrys
HUNT, HOWARD	Robert Deitrich
HUNTER, ELIZABETH MARY TERESA	Isobel Chace
HUNTER, EVAN	Curt Cannon, Hunt Collins, Ezra Hannon, Ed McBain, Richard Marsten
HURLEY, JOHN J.	Duffy Carpenter, S. S. Rafferty
HUTCHIN, KENNETH CHARLES	Kenneth Challice, A Family Doctor, Kenneth Travers
HYLAND, ANN	Laurence Ross, Trailrider
HYNDMAN, JANE LEE	Lee Wyndham
HYNE, CHARLES JOHN CUTCLIFFE WRIGHT	Weatherby Chesney
IAMS, SAMUEL H., JR.	Jack Iams
INNES, RALPH HAMMOND	Ralph Hammond

TRUE NAMES	PSEUDONYMS
IRVING, WASHINGTON	Geoffrey Crayon, Diedrich Knickerbocker, Launcelot Langstaff, Jonathan Oldstyle
IRWIN, CONSTANCE	C. H. Frick
ISAACS, ALAN	Alec Valentine
JACKSON, HELEN HUNT	H. H., Saxe Holm
JACKSON, MRS. SCHUYLER B.	Barbara Rich, Laura Riding
JACOB, NAOMI ELLINGTON	Ellington Gray
JACOB, PIERS ANTHONY DILLINGHAM	Piers Anthony
JACOBS, SOPHIA YARNALL	Sophia Yarnall
JAKES, JOHN WILLIAM	Alan Payne, Jay Scotland
JAMESON, MARGARET STROM	James Hill, William Lamb
JANAS, FRANKIE-LEE	Zachary Ball, Francesca Greer, Sallee O'Brien
JARRETT, CORA	Faraday Keene
JARROLD, ERNEST	Mickey Finn
JARVIS, FREDERICK G. H.	Fritz Gordon
JAY, GERALDINE MARY	Geraldine Halls, Charlotte Jay
JEFFREY, GRAHAM	Brother Graham
JEFFRIES, GRAHAM MONTAGUE	Peter Bourne, Bruce Graeme, David Graeme
JEFFRIES, RODERIC	Peter Alding, Jeffrey Ashford, Hastings Draper, Roderic Graeme, Graham Hastings
JELLY, GEORGE OLIVER	Alfred Fosse, Hilya Harsch
JENKINS, WILLIAM FITZGERALD	Murray Leinster
JENKS, GEORGE C.	W. B. Lawson
JERVIS, MARGUERITE FLORENCE	Marguerite Barclay, Countess Helene Barcynska, Oliver Sandys
JESSE, F. TENNYSON	Beamish Tinker
JOHNS, WILLIAM EARL	William Earle
JOHNSON, ANNABELL JONES	A. E. Johnson
JOHNSON, EDGAR RAYMOND	A. E. Johnson
JOHNSON, FORREST B.	Frosty Johnson
JOHNSON, PAULA JANICE	Jan Johnson

TRUE NAMES	PSEUDONYMS
JOHNSON, RYERSON	Matthew Blood
JOHNSTON, NORMA	Nicole St. John
JOHNSTON, VELDA	Veronica Jason
JONES, JUDITH PATERSON	Judith Paterson, Judith Paterson-Jones
JONES, LEROI	Imamu Amiri Baraki
JORDAN, ROBERT FURNEAUX	Robert Player
JOSCELYN, ARCHIE LYNN	A. A. Archer, Al Cody, Tex Holt, Evelyn McKenna
JOSKE, ANNE NEVILLE GOYDER	Margot Neville
JOSLIN, SESYLE	Josephine Gibson, G. B. Kirtland
KALER, JAMES OTIS	James Otis
KANE, FRANK	Frank Boyd
KANE, HENRY	Anthony McCall
KARP, DAVID	Adam Singer, Wallace Ware
KAYE, BARRINGTON	Tom Kaye
KEEVIL, HENRY JOHN	Clay Allison, Burt Alvord, Bill Bonney, Alison Clay, Virgil Earp, Wes Harding, Frank McLowery, Burt Mossman, Mark Reno, Johnny Ringo, Will Travis
KELLAR, JOHN W.	Cholly Knickerbocker
KELLER, DAVID HENRY	Henry Cecil
KELLY, TIM	R. H. Bibelot
KELTON, ELMER	Alex Hawk, Lee McElroy
KENDRICK, BAYNARD HARDWICK	Richard Hayward
KENNEDY, JOSEPH CHARLES	X. J. Kennedy
KENT, ARTHUR	James Bradwell, M. Dubois, Paul Granados, Alexander Karol, Alex Stamper, Bret Vane
KENT, ROCKWELL	Hogarth, Jr.
KENTON, WARREN	Zev Ben Shimon Halevi
KENYON, MICHAEL	Daniel Forbes
KERMOND, EVELYN CAROLYN CONWAY	E. Carolyn Conway
KEROUAC, JEAN-LOUIS LEBRID	Jean-Louis Incogniteau, Jack Kerouac

TRUE NAMES	PSEUDONYMS
KERR, JAMES LENNOX	Peter Dawlish
KETCHUM, PHILIP L.	Miriam Leslie, Mack Saunders
KIEFER, WARREN	Middleton Kiefer
KIMBRO, JOHN M.	Kym Allyson, Ann Ashton, Charlotte Bramwell, Jean Kimbro, Katheryn Kimbrough
KING, FRANCIS	Frank Cauldwell
KINGSLEY, CHARLES	Parson Lot
KININMONTH, CHRISTOPHER	Christopher Brennan
KIRKLAND, CAROLINE	Mary Clavers
KLASS, PHILIP	William Tenn
KNIBBS, HENRY HERBERT	Henry K. Herbert
KNIGHT, ALANNA	Margaret Hope
KNIGHT, FRANCIS EDGAR	Frank Knight, Cedric Salter
KNOTT, WILLIAM S.	Bill J. Carol, Tabor Evans, Bill Knott, Will C. Knott
KNOWLES, MABEL WINIFRED	Lester Lurgan, Bryan Smith, May Wynne
KNOX, WILLIAM	Michael Kirk, Bill Knox, Robert MacLeod, Noah Webster
KOESTLER, ARTHUR	Vigil
KONIGSBERG, HANS	Hans Koning
KOONTZ, DEAN RAY	David Axton, Brian Cofffey, K. R. Dwyer
KORNBLUTH, CYRIL M.	Simon Eisner, Cyril M. Judd, Jordan Park
KORTNER, PETER	Peter Hofer
KORZENIOWSKI, TEODOR	Joseph Conrad
KOS, ERIC	Erich Kosch
KOSINSKI, JERZY	Joseph Novak
KOUYOUMDJIAN, DIKRAN	Michael Arlen
KRULL, KATHLEEN	Kathryn Kenny, Kevin Kenny
KUEHNELT-LEDDIHN, ERIK	Francis Stuart Campbell, O'Leary, T. Vitezovic
KULSKI, W. W.	W. W. Coole, W. M. Knight-Patterson
KURLAND, MICHAEL JOSEPH	Jennifer Plum
KURNITZ, HARRY	Marco Page

TRUE NAMES	PSEUDONYMS
KUSKIN, KARLA	Nicholas Charles
KUTTNER, HENRY	Will Garth, Lewis Padgett
KYLE, ELIZABETH	Jan Ralston
LAFFIN, JOHN	Mark Napier, Dirk Sabre
LAKE, KENNETH ROBERT	Robert Boyer, Arthur King, Mentor, Ken Roberts, Fred Souter, Xeno
LAMB, CHARLES	Elia
LAMB, GEOFFREY FREDERICK	Balaam
LAMBERT, DEREK	Richard Falkirk
LAMBOT, ISOBEL MARY	Daniel Ingham, Mary Turner
LAMBURN, RICHMAL CROMPTON	Richmal Crompton
LA MOORE, LOUIS DEARBORN	Tex Burns, Louis L'Amour, Jim Mayo
LAMPMAN, EVELYN SIBLEY	Lynn Bronson
LANDAU, MARK A.	Mark Aldanov
LANDE, LAWRENCE MONTAGNE	Alain Verval
LANG, ANDREW	A. Huge Longway
LANGE, JOHN FREDERICK, JR.	John Norman
LARDNER, RING	Jack Keefe, Old Wilmer
LASSALLE, CAROLINE	Emma Cave
LATHAN, JEAN LEE	Julian Lee
LATIMER, JONATHAN WYATT	Peter Coffin
LATIS, MARY J.	R. B. Dominic, Emma Lathen
LATNER, HELEN	Helen Stambler
LAUNAY, ANDRE	Droo Launay
LAWRENCE, LOUISE DE KIRILINE	Louise De Kiriline
LAWRENSON, HELEN	Helen Brown Norden
LAZARUS, MARGUERITE	Marguerite Gascoigne, Anna Gilbert
LAZEROWITZ, ALICE AMBROSE	Alice Ambrose
LEE, AUSTIN	John Austwick, Julian Callender
LEE, ELSIE	Elsie Cromwell, Norman Daniels, Jane Gordon, Lee Sheridan
LEE, MANFRED BENNINGTON	Ellery Queen, Ellery Queen, Jr., Barnaby Ross

TRUE NAMES	PSEUDONYMS
LEE, NORMAN	Raymond Armstrong, Mark Corrigan, Robertson Hobart
LEE, WAYNE CYRIL	Lee Sheldon
LEEMING, JILL	Jill Chaney
LE FONTAINE, JOSEPH RAYMOND HERVE	Herve Aruba, Dan Cingfox, Evreh Eniatnof El Dnomyar, Sebastian Largo Gregory, Joseph Herve, Raymond Hervey, Raymond LaFontaine, J. R. LeFontaine, Ray LeFontaine, Charlotte Raymond, Joseph Raymond
LEHMAN, PAUL EVAN	Paul Evan
LEHNUS, OPAL HULL	Opal I. Hull
LEISK, DAVID JOHNSON	Crockett Johnson
LENT, BLAIR	Ernest Small
LEON, HENRY CECIL	Henry Cecil
LESSER, MILTON	Adam Chase, Andrew Frazer, Stephen Marlowe, Jason Ridgeway, C. H. Thames
LEVER, CHARLES	Cornelius O'Dowd
LEVIN, JANE WHITBREAD	Jane Whitbread
LEWIS, ALFRED HENRY	Dan Quin
LEWIS, CLIVE STAPLES	N. W. Clerk, Clive Hamilton, C. S. Lewis
LEWIS, D. B. WYNDHAM	Timothy Shy
LEWIS, HARRY SINCLAIR	Tom Graham
LEWIS, J. R.	Roy Lewis
LEWIS, LESLEY	Lesley Lawrence
LEXAU, JOAN M.	Joan L. Nodset
LEY, ROBERT ARTHUR	Martin Luther, Arthur Sellings
LIGHTNER, ALICE MARTHA	Alice L. Hope
LINDARS, FREDERICK C.	Barnabas Lindars
LINDSAY, JACK	Richard Preston
LINDSAY, RACHEL	Roberta Leigh, Janey Scott
LINEBARGER, PAUL MYRON ANTHONY	Felix C. Forrest, Carmichael Smith, Cordwainer Smith
LININGTON, BARBARA ELIZABETH	Anne Blaisdell, Lesley Egan, Egan O'Neill, Dell Shannon

TRUE NAMES	PSEUDONYMS
LIPKIND, WILLIAM	Will
LIPPINCOTT, SARA JANE	Grace Greenwood
LIVINGSTONE, HARRISON EDWARD	John Fairfield
LOCKE, DAVID	Petroleum V. Nasby
LOCKRIDGE, FRANCES AND RICHARD	The Lockridges
LITTLE, CONSTANCE	Conyth Little
LITTLE, FRANCIS	Frances C. Macauley
LITTLE, GWENYTH	Conyth Little
LODER, JOHN DE VERE	Cornelius Cofyn
LOFTS, NORAH	Juliet Astley, Peter Curtis
LOGUE, CHRISTOPHER	Count Palmiro Vicarion
LONDON, JOHN GRIFFITH	Jack London
LONG, FRANK BELKNAP	Lyda Belknap Long
LONGRIGG, ROGER ERSKINE	Ivor Drummond, Rosalind Erskine
LONGSTREET, STEPHEN	Thomas Burton, Paul Haggard, David Ormsbee, Henri Weiner
LONIGAN, GEORGE THOMAS	Aesop
LOOMIS, NOEL MILLER	Sam Allison, Benjamin Miller, Frank Miller, Silas Water
LORD, DOUGLAS	Doreen Ireland
LORING, EMILIE	Josephine Story
LOTHROP, HARRIET MULFORD	Margaret Sidney
LOVESEY, PETER	Peter Lear
LOW, LOIS DOROTHEA	Zoe Cass, Dorothy Mackie Low, Lois Paxton
LOWELL, JAMES RUSSELL	Hosea Biglow
LOWNDES, MARIE ADELAIDE BELLOC	Philip Curtin
LOWNDES, ROBERT AUGUSTINE WARD	Arthur Cooke, S. D. Gottesman, Carol Grey, Carl Groener, Mallory Kent, Paul Dennis Lavond, John MacDougal, Wilfred Owen Morley, Richard Morrison, Robert Morrison, Michael Sherman, Peter Michael Sherman, Lawrence Woods
LOWRY, JOAN	Joanna Catlow

TRUE NAMES	PSEUDONYMS
LUCAS, E. V.	E. V. L., V. V. V.
LUCEY, JAMES D.	Matthew Pierce
LUCIE-SMITH, EDWARD	Peter Kershaw
LUDLUM, ROBERT	Jonathan Ryder, Michael Shepherd
LUTYENS, MARY	Esther Wyndham
LUTZ, GILES ALFRED	James B. Chaffin, Wade Everett, Alex Hawk, Hunter
LYLE-SMYTHE, ALAN	Alan Caillou
LYNDS, DENNIS	William Arden, Nick Carter, Michael Collins, John Crowe, Carl Dekker, Maxwell Grant, Mark Sadler
LYNNE, JAMES BROOM	James Quartermain
MC ALLISTER, ALISTER	Lynn Brock, Anthony Wharton
MACARTHUR, DAVID WILSON	David Wilson
MACAULEY, FRANCES C.	Frances Little
MC CAIG, ROBERT JESSE	Edith Engren
MC CARTHY, SHAUN LLOYD	Theo Callas, Desmond Cory
MC CLARY, THOMAS CALVERT	Calvin Peregoy
MC CLOY, HELEN WORRELL CLARKSON	Helen Clarkson
MC COMAS, JESSE FRANCIS	Webb Marlowe
MC CONNELL, JAMES DOUGLAS RUTHERFORD	Douglas Rutherford
MACCORMACK, SABINE G.	Sabine Oswalt
MC CUE, LILLIAN BUENO	Lillian De La Torre
MC CUTCHAN, DONALD PHILIP	Robert Conington Galway, Duncan MacNeil, T. I. G. Wigg
MC CUTCHEON, GEORGE BARR	Richard Greaves
MC CUTCHEON, HUGH	Hugh Davie-Martin
MACDIARMID, HUGH	C. M. Grieve
MACDONALD, JOHN DANN	John Wade Farrell, Scott O'Hara, Peter Reed
MACDONALD, PHILIP	Oliver Fleming, Anthony Lawless, Martin Porlock
M'DONNELL, BODKIN M.	Crom A Boo
MACDOWELL, KATHERINE	Sherwood Bonner

TRUE NAMES	PSEUDONYMS
MC ELFRESH, ELIZABETH ADELINE	John Cleveland, Jane Scott, Elizabeth Wesley
MC EVOY, MARJORIE	Marjorie Harte
MC GAUGHY, DUDLEY DEAN	Dudley Dean
MACGIBBON, JEAN	Jean Howard
MACGILL, MRS. PATRICK MARGARET	Margaret Gibbons
MC GIVERN, MAUREEN DALY	Maureen Daly
MC GIVERN, WILLIAM PETER	Bill Peters
MACGREGOR, JAMES MURDOCH	J. T. McIntosh, H. J. Murdoch
MACGREGOR, JOHN	Rob Roy
MACHEN, ARTHUR	Leolinus Siluriensis
MC ILWAIN, DAVID	Will Daemer, Charles Eric Maine, Whit Masterson, Wade Miller, Richard Rayner, Bob Wade, Robert Wade, Dale Wilmer
MC INTOSH, KINN HAMILTON	Catherine Aird
MACKAY, ALBERIGH	Ali Baba
MACKAY, JAMES ALEXANDER	Ian Angus, William Finlay, Bruce Garden, Peter Whittington
MACKAY, MARY	Marie Corelli
MACKIE, DORIS	Susan Inglis
MACKINLAY, LEILA ANTOINETTE STERLING	Brenda Grey
MACKINTOSH, ELIZABETH	Gordon Daviot, Josephine Tey
MC LAURIN, ANNE	Anne Laurin
MACLEAN, ALISTAIR STUART	Ian Stuart
MAC LEOD, CHARLOTTE MATILDA	Alisa Craig, Matilda Hughes
MACLEOD, ELLEN JANE	Ella Anderson
MACLEOD, JEAN S.	Catherine Airlie
MC NEILE, HERMAN CYRIL	Sapper
MAC PHERSON, A. D. L.	Sara Seale
MC SHANE, MARK	Marc Lovell
MADDISON, ANGELA MARY	Angela Banner
MAINWARING, DANIEL	Geoffrey Homes
MAIR, GEORGE BROWN	Robertson MacDonall

TRUE NAMES	PSEUDONYMS
MAJOR, CHARLES	Edward Caskoden
MALERICH, EDWARD P.	Edward Easton
MALLESON, LUCY BEATRICE	Anthony Gilbert, J. Kilmeny Keith, Anne Meredith
MALLOWAN, DAME AGATHA MARY CLARISSA	Agatha Christie, Agatha Christie Mallowan, Mary Westmacott
MALZBERG, BARRY NORMAN	Mike Barry, Francine de Natale, Claudine Dumas, Mel Johnson, Lee W. Mason, K. M. O'Donnell, Gerrold Watkins
MANFRED, FREDERICK FEIKEMA	Feike Feikema
MANLEY-TUCKER, AUDRIE	Linden Howard
MANN, EDWARD BEVERLY	Peter Field, Zachary Strong
MANN, THOMAS	Paul Thomas
MANNING, ADELAIDE FRANCES OKE	Manning Coles, Francis Gaite
MANNING, ROSEMARY	Mary Voyle
MANTLE, WINIFRED LANGFORD	Anne Fellowes, Frances Lanf, Jane Langford
MARQUIS, DON	Lantern, Sundial
MARRISON, LESLIE WILLIAM	D. M. Dowley
MARSH, JOHN	John Harley, Grace Richmond, Lilian Woodward
MARSHALL, EDISON TESLA	Hall Hunter
MARSHALL, ELIZABETH SOUTHERLAND	Ellizabeth Sutherland
MARSHALL, EVELYN	Lesley Bourne, Jean Marsh
MARSHALL, MARGARET LENORE	Margaret L. Wiley
MARTIN, PATRICIA MILES	Miska Miles
MARTIN, RHONA	Rhona M. Neighbour
MARTIN, ROBERT BERNARD	Robert Bernard
MASON, DOUGLAS RANKINE	R. M. Douglas, John Rankine
MASON, FRANCIS VAN WYCK	Geoffrey Coffin, Frank W. Mason, Ward Weaver
MASON, PHILIP	Philip Woodruff
MATHER, ANNE	Caroline Fleming
MATTHEWS, PATRICIA ANNE	P. A. Brisco, Patty Brisco, Laura Wylie

TRUE NAMES	PSEUDONYMS
MAUGHAM, ROBERT CECIL ROMER	David Griffin, Robin Maugham
MAXWELL, PATRICIA ANNE	Jennifer Blake, Maxine Patrick, Patricia Ponder, Elizabeth Trehearne
MAY, WINIFRED JEAN	Wynne May
MAYNE, WILLIAM	Martin Cobalt, Dudley James, Dynely James, Charles Molin
MEADE, ELIZABETH THOMASINA	L. T. Meade
MEADOWCROFT, ERNEST	Arnold Williams
MEAKER, MARIJANE	M. E. Kerr
MEARS, LEONARD F.	Marshall Grover, Marshall McCoy, Johnny Nelson
MEEK, PAULINE PALMER	Agnessan McRoberts
MEEK, STERNER ST. PAUL	Sterner St. Paul
MEIGS, CORNELIA LYNDE	Adair Aldon
MERCER, CECIL WILLIAM	Dornford Yates
MERRIL, JOSEPHINE JUDITH	Cyril Judd
MERTZ, BARBARA LOUISE GROSS	Barbara Michaels, Elizabeth Peters
MERWIN, SAMUEL KIMBALL, JR.	Elizabeth Deare Bennett, Jacques Jean Ferrat, Matt Lee, Carter Sprague
MEYNELL, LAURENCE WALTER	Valerie Baxter, Robert Eton, Geoffrey Ludlow, A. Stephen Tring
MIDDLETON, HARRY	Middleton Kiefer
MILLAR, KENNETH	John Macdonald, John Ross Macdonald, Ross Macdonald
MILLARD, JOSEPH JOHN	Joe Millard
MILLER, BILL	Will Daemer, Whit Masterson, Wade Miller, Dale Wilmer
MILLER, CINCINNATUS HEINE	Joaquin Miller
MILLER, HARRIETT MANN	Olive Thorne Miller
MILLER, JOHN GORDON	Jon Miller
MILLER, R. S.	Fran Huston
MILNE, ALAN ALEXANDER	A. A. Milne
MILSOM, CHARLES HENRY	William Weston
MINER, JANE CLAYPOOL	Jane Claypool, Veronica Ladd
MINES, SAMUEL	Peter Field
MITCHELL, DONALD G.	Ik Marvel

TRUE NAMES	PSEUDONYMS
MITCHELL, GLADYS MAUDE WINIFRED	Stephen Hockaby, Malcolm Torrie
MITCHELL, LANGDON E.	John Philip Varley
MODELL, MERRIAM	Evelyn Piper
MOLESWORTH, MARY LOUISA	Ennis Graham
MONRO-HIGGS, GERTRUDE	Gavin Monro
MONTGOMERY, ROBERT BRUCE	Edmund Crispin
MONTGOMERY, RUTHERFORD GEORGE	A. A. Avery, Al Avery, Art Elder, Everitt Proctor
MOORCOCK, MICHAEL	Bill Barclay, E. P. Bradbury, James Colvin
MOORE, BRIAN	Michael Bryan
MOORE, CATHERINE LUCILLE	Lewis Padgett
MOREAU, DAVID MERLIN	David Merlin
MORETON, DOUGLAS ARTHUR	Arthur Douglas
MORGAN, MARY PENOYRE	Mary Penoyre
MORLAND, NIGEL	Mary Dane, John Donavan, Norman Forrest, Roger Garnett, Vincent McCall, Neal Shepherd
MORRISSEY, JOSEPH LAWRENCE	Henry Richards, Richard Saxon
MORTIMER, JOHN	Geoffrey Lincoln
MORTIMER, PENELOPE	Penelope Dimont
MOSS, ROBERT	Nancy Moss, Roberta Moss
MUDDOCK, JOYCE EMMERSON PRESTON	Dick Donovan, J. E. Muddock
MUGGESON, MARGARET ELIZABETH	Margaret Dickinson, Everatt Jackson
MUIR, AUGUSTUS	Austin Moore
MUNRO, H. H.	Saki
MUNRO, LEAF	Mun
MUNRO, NEIL	Hugh Faulis
MUNRO, RONALD EADIE	Duncan Glen
MURFREE, MARY NOAILLES	Charles Egbert Craddock
MURPHY, LAWRENCE AUGUSTUS	Stephen C. Lawrence, C. L. Murphy
MURRY, COLIN MIDDLETON	Richard Cowper
MUSSI, MARY	Josephine Edgar, Mary Howard
MUSTO, BARRY	Robert Simon

TRUE NAMES	PSEUDONYMS
NABOKOV, VLADIMIR	Vladimir Nabokoff
NAKASHIMA, GEORGE KATSUTOSHI	Sundarananda
NELSON, RADELL FARADAY	Jeffrey Lord, R. N. Nelson, Ray Nelson
NESBIT, EDITH	E. Bland, Fabian Bland
NETTELL, RICHARD	Richard Kenneggy
NEVILLE, BARBARA ALISON	Edward Candy
NEVIN, EVELYN C.	Evelyn Ferguson
NEWLIN, MARGARET RUDD	Margaret Rudd
NEWMAN, BERNARD	Don Betteridge
NEWMAN, MONA ALICE JEAN	Barbara Fitzgerald, Barbara Newman, Jean Stewart
NEWTON, DWIGHT BENNETT	Dwight Bennett, Clement Hardin, Ford Logan, Hank Mitchum, Dan Temple
NICHOLSON, MARGARET BETA	Margaret York
NICKSON, ARTHUR THOMAS	Arthur Hodson, Roy Peters, John Saunders, Matt Winstan
NICOLE, CHRISTOPHER ROBIN	Leslie Arlen, Robin Cade, Peter Grange, Mark Logan, C. R. Nicholson, Christina Nicholson, Robin Nicholson, Alison York, Andrew York
NISOT, ELIZABETH	William Penmare
NOLAN, FREDERICK	Frederick H. Christian
NORTON, ALICE MARY	Andrew North, Andre Norton, Allen Weston
NORTON, OLIVE MARION	Hilary Neal, Bess Norton, Kate Norway
NORWAY, NEVIL SHUTE	Nevil Shute
NORWOOD, VICTOR GEORGE CHARLES	Coy Banton, Sane V. Baxter, Jim Bowie, Clay Brand, Victor Brand, Paul Clevinger, Walt Cody, Shayne Colter, Wes Corteen, Clint Dangerfield, Johnny Dark, Vince Destry, Doone Fargo, Mark Fenton, Wade Fisher, G. Gearing-Thomas, Mark Hampton, Hank Jansen, Nat Karta, Whip McCord, Brett Rand, Brad Regan, Shane Russell, Rhondo Shane, Victor Shane, Jim Tressidy
NOWLAN, PHILIP FRANCIS	Frank Phillips

TRUE NAMES	PSEUDONYMS
NUNN, WILLIAM CURTIS	Will Curtis, Ananias Twist
NUTT, CHARLES	Charles Beaumont, Keith Grantland
NYE, NELSON CORAL	Clem Colt, Drake C. Denver
O'CONNOR, PATRICK JOSEPH	Padraic Fiacc
O'CONNOR, RICHARD	Frank Archer, John Burke, Patrick Wayland
O'DANIEL, JANET	Lillian Janet
OFFUTT, ANDREW JEFFERSON V.	John Cleve
OGNALL, LEOPOLD HORACE	Harry Carmichael, Hartley Howard
O'GORMAN, EDWARD CHARLES	Ned O'Gorman
OLCHEWITZ, M.	Jules Verne
O'LEARY, LIAM	Liam O'Laoghaire
OLSEN, ALFRED JOHN, JR.	Bob Olsen
OLSEN, THEODORE VICTOR	T. V. Olsen, Joshua Stark, Christopher Storm, Cass Willoughby
O'MALLEY, LADY MARY DOLLING	Ann Bridge
O'NEAL, ELIZABETH	Zibby O'Neal
OPPENHEIM, EDWARD PHILLIPS	Anthony Partridge
ORCZY, EMMA MAGDELENA ROSALIA MARIA JOSEFA BARBARA	Baroness Orczy
ORGEL, DORIS	Doris Adelberg
ORLEY, JOHN	Allen Tate
O'ROURKE, FRANK	Kevin Connor, Frank O'Malley, Patrick O'Malley
OURSLER, CHARLES FULTON	Anthony Abbott
OVERHOLSER, WAYNE D.	John S. Daniels
OVSTEDAL, BARBARA	Barbara Douglas, Rosalind Laker, Barbara Paul
OWEN, JACK	Jack Dykes
PAGE, P. K.	Judith Cape
PALMER, CHARLES STUART	Jay Stewart
PALMER, JOHN LESLIE	Francis Beeding, Christopher Haddon, David Pilgrim

TRUE NAMES	PSEUDONYMS
PALMER, MADELYN	Geoffrey Peters
PALMER, RAYMOND A.	Henry Gade, G. H. Irwin, Frank Patton, J. W. Pelkie, Wallace Quitman, A. R. Steber, Morris J. Steel
PANGBORN, EDGAR	Bruce Harrison
PANOWSKI, EILEEN JANET THOMPSON	Eileen Thompson
PAPPAS, GEORGE S.	Justificus
PARES, MARION STAPYLTON	Judith Campbell, Anthony Grant
PARGETER, EDITH MARY	Ellis Peters
PARISH, MARGARET CECILE	Peggy Parish
PARKER, MARION DOMINICA HOPE	Sister Marion Dominic, Marion Hope
PARKINSON, ROGER	Matthew Holden
PARRY, HUGH JONES	James Cross
PATCHETT, MARY ELWYN OSBORNE	David Bruce
PATON WALSH, GILLIAN	Jill Paton Walsh
PATTEN, LEWIS BYFORD	Lewis Ford, Len Leighton, Joseph Wayne
PATTERSON, HENRY	Martin Fallon, James Graham, Jack Higgins, Hugh Marlowe, Harry Patterson
PATTERSON, PETER	Peter Terson
PATTINSON, NANCY EVELYN	Nan Asquith
PAUL, ELLIOT HAROLD	Brett Rutledge
PAULDING, JAMES KIRK	Bull-Us, Launcelot Langstaff
PAWLEY, MARTIN	Rupert Spade
PAYNE, DONALD GORDON	Ian Cameron, Donald Gordon
PEARSON, KATHARINE	Katharine Gordon
PEDLER, CHRISTOPHER MAGNUS HOWARD	Kit Pedler
PENDELTON, DONALD EUGENE	Dan Britain, Stephen Gregory
PENDOWER, JACQUES	Kathleen Carstairs, Tom Curtis, Penn Dower, T. C. H. Jacobs, Marilyn Pender, Anne Penn
PERRY, RITCHIE JOHN ALLEN	John Allen
PESHKOV, ALEXI MAXIMOVITCH	Maxim Gorki, Maxim Gorky

TRUE NAMES	PSEUDONYMS
PETERS, MAUREEN	Veronica Black, Catherine Darby, Belinda Grey, Levanah Lloyd, Judith Rothman, Sharon Whitby
PEYTON, KATHLEEN M.	Kathleen Herald, K. Peyton, K. M. Peyton
PFLAUM-CONNOR, SUSANNA	Susanna Whitney Pflaum
PHILIPP, ELLIOT ELIAS	Philip Embey, Anthony Havil, Victor Tempest
PHILIPS, JUDSON PENTECOST	Hugh Pentecost
PHILLIFENT, JOHN THOMAS	John Rackham
PHILLIPS, HUBERT	Caliban
PHILLIPS, JAMES ATLEE	Philip Atlee
PHILLPOTTS, ADELAIDE	Mary Adelaide, Eden Ross
PHILLPOTTS, EDEN	Harrington Hext
PICKLES, MABLE ELIZABETH	Elizabeth Burgoyne
PILCHER, ROSAMUNDE	Jane Fraser
PITCAIRN, J. J.	Clifford Ashdown
PLATH, SYLVIA	Victoria Lucas
PLUMMER, CLARE EMSLEY	Clare Emsley
PLUNKETT, EDWARD JOHN MORETON DRAK	Lord Dunsany
POCOCK, HENRY ROGER ASHWELL	Robert Pocock
POE, EDGAR ALLAN	Hans Pfaal, Quarles
POHL, FREDERIK	Edson McCann, James MacCreigh, Jordan Park
POLAND, DOROTHY	Allison Farely, Jane Hammond
POLITELLA, DARIO	Tony Granite, David Stewart
POLLAND, MADELEINE ANGELA	Frances Adrian
POLLEY, JUDITH ANNE	Judith Hagar, Helen Kent, Valentina Luellen
PONSONBY, DORIS ALMON	Doris Rybot, Sarah Tempest
POORE, BENJAMIN PERLEY	Perley
PORGES, ARTHUR	Peter Arthur, Pat Rogers
PORTER, ELEANOR HODGMAN	Eleanor Stuart
PORTER, GENEVA GRACE STRATTON	Gene Stratton Porter

TRUE NAMES	PSEUDONYMS
PORTER, HAROLD EVERETT	Holworthy Hall
PORTER, WILLIAM SYDNEY OR SIDNEY	O. Henry
POSNER, RICHARD	Jonathan Craig, Iris Foster, Beatrice Murray, Paul Todd, Dick Wine
POSTL, KARL	Charles Sealsfield
POTTER, JOANNA	Caroline Harvey, Joanna Trollope
POTTER, MARGARET EDITH	Anne Betteridge, Anne Melville, Margaret Newman
POUND, EZRA	Alfred Venison
POURNELLE, JERRY EUGENE	Wade Curtis
POWE, BRUCE	Ellis Portal
POWELL, ERIC	Peter Rusholm
POWELL-SMITH, VINCENT	Francis Elphinstone, Justicar
PRATHER, RICHARD SCOTT	David Knight, Douglas Ring
PRATT, MURRAY FLETCHER	George U. Fletcher
PRAZ, MARIO	Alcibiade, Giano Di Guisa
PRESBERG, MIRIAM	Miriam Gilbert
PRICE, BEVERLY JOAN	Beverly Randell
PRITCHARD, JOHN WALLACE	Ian Wallace
PRONZINI, BILL	Jack Foxx, William Jeffrey, Alex Saxon
PUECHNER, RAY	Ray Peekner, Charles B. Victor
PULLEIN-THOMPSON, JOANNA MAXWELL	Joanna Maxwell Cannan
PUMILLA, JOSEPH F.	M. M. Moamrath, Joe Pumilla
PUTLAND-VAN SOMEREN, ELIZABETH	Liesje Van Someren
QUIBELL, AGATHA HUNT	A. H. Pearce
QUILLER-COUCH, SIR ARTHUR	Q
RADFORD, EDWIN ISAAC	E. and M. A. Radford
RADFORD, MONA AUGUSTA	E. and M. A. Radford
RAE, HUGH CRAWFORD	Robert Crawford, R. B. Houston, Morgan McGrath, Stuart Stern, Jessica Stirling

TRUE NAMES	PSEUDONYMS
RAND, ANN	Anne Binkley
RANDOLPH, GEORGIANA ANN	Craig Rice, Daphne Sanders, Michael Venning
RAPHAEL, CHAIM	Jocelyn Davey
RATHBONE, ST. GEORGE HENRY	Harrison Adams, Hugh Allen, Oliver Lee Clifton, Duke Duncan, Aleck Forbes, Lieutenant Keene, Marline Manly, Mark Merrick, Warne Miller, M. D., Harry St. George, Colonel J. M. Travers
RAUBENHEIMER, GEORGE HARDING	George Harding
RAWORTH, THOMAS MOORE	Tom Raworth
RAWSON, CLAYTON	The Great Merlini, Stuart Towne
RAYER, FRANCIS GEORGE	George Longdon, Milward Scott, Roland Worchester
RAYMOND, RENE BARBAZON	James Hadley Chase, James L. Docherty, Ambrose Grant, Raymond Marshall
RAYNER, CLAIRE BERENICE	Sheila Brandon, Ann Lyton, Ruth Martin
READ, JOHN HILTON	Jan Read
REED, LILLIAN	Kit Reed
REEMAN, DOUGLAS	Alexander Kent
REES, JOAN	Susan Strong
REESE, JOHN	John Carpenter, Cody Kennedy, Jr.
REEVES, JOYCE	Janice Gard, Joyce Gard
REID, WHITLAW	Agate
REILLY, HELEN	Kieran Abbey
REITCHI, JOHN GEORGE	Jack Ritchie
RENIER, ELIZABETH	Betty Doreen Baker
REPP, EDWARD EARL	John Cody, Peter Field
RESSLER, LILLIAN	Lillian Janet
REYNOLDS, DALLAS MC CORD	Todd Harding, Mack Reynolds, Maxine Reynolds
RHAMEY, BEN	H. H. Hollis
RICE, ALICE CALDWELL	Alice Caldwell Hegan
RICHARDSON, ROBERT SHIRLEY	Philip Latham

TRUE NAMES	PSEUDONYMS
RICHELSON, GERALDINE	Ed Lea
RICHMOND, ROALDUS FREDERICK	Roe Richmond
RICKARD, ROBERT J. M.	Bob Richard, Bob Rickard
RIDDLE, BETSEY	Baroness Betsy Riddle Von Hutten
RIEFE, ALAN	Barbara Riefe
RIFKIN, SHEPPARD	Jake Logan, Dale Michaels
RIGONI, ORLANDO	Leslie Ames, Carolyn Bell, James Wesley
RIGSBY, VECHEL HOWARD	Mark Howard, Vechel Howard
RILEY, JAMES WHITCOMB	Benjamin F. Johnson
RITCHIE, CLAIRE	Sharon Heath
RITCHIE, EDWIN	Voltaire Lewis
RIVETT, EDITH CAROLINE	Carol Carnac, E. C. R. Lorac
ROAN, TOM	Adam Rebel
ROARK, GARLAND	George Garland
ROBERTS, IRENE	Roberta Carr, Elizabeth Harle, I. M. Roberts, Ivor Roberts, Iris Rowland, Irene Shaw
ROBERTS, JANET LOUISE	Louisa Bronte, Rebecca Danton, Janette Radcliffe
ROBERTSON, CONSTANCE NOYES	Dana Scott
ROBERTSON, FRANK CHESTER	Robert Crane, Frank Chester Field
ROBERTSON, JAMES LOGIE	Hugh Haliburton
ROBERTSON, KEITH CARLTON	Carlton Keith
ROBINS, DENISE NAOMI	Denise Chesterton, Ashley French, Harriet Gray, Hervey Hamilton, Julia Kane, Francesca Wright
ROBINSON, DEREK	Dirk Robson
ROBINSON, JOAN MARY GALE	Joan Gale Thomas
ROBY, MARY LINN	Pamela D'Arcy, Georgina Grey, Elizabeth Welles, Mary Wilson
ROCKLIN, ROSS LOUIS	Ross Rocklynne
RODDA, CHARLES	Eliot Reed
RODELL, MARIE FREID	Marion Randolph
RODGER, THOMAS ALEXANDER	Alec Rodger
ROE, F. GORDON	Uncle Gordon
ROE, IVAN	Richard Savage

TRUE NAMES	PSEUDONYMS
ROHEN, EDWARD	Bruton Connors
ROLFE, FREDERICK	Baron Frederick Corvo
ROLLINS, KATHLEEN	Hal Debrett
ROLVAAG, OLLE EDVART	Paal Morck
ROOS, AUDREY	Kelley Roos
ROOS, WILLIAM	William Rand, Kelley Roos
ROSS, WILLIAM	Clarissa Ross, Dana Ross, Marilyn Ross
ROSS, ZOLA HELEN	Helen Arre, Bert Iles, Z. H. Ross
ROSSI, JEAN BAPTISTE	Sebastian Japrisot
ROSSITER, JOHN	Jonathan Ross
ROSTEN, LEO	Leonard Q. Ross
ROTH, HOLLY	K. G. Ballard, P. J. Merrill
ROTSLER, WILLIAM	William Arrow, John Ryder Hall
ROWLAND, DONALD SYDNEY	Annette Adams, Jack Bassett, Hazel Baxter, Karla Benton, Helen Berry, Lewis Brant, Alison Bray, William Brayce, Fenton Brockley, Oliver Bronson, Chuck Buchanan, Rod Caley, Roger Carlton, Janita Cleve, Sharon Court, Vera Craig, Wesley Craille, John Delaney, John Dryden, Freda Fenton, Charles Field, Graham Garner, Burt Kroll, Helen Langley, Henry Lansing, Harvey Lant, Irene Lynn, Stuart McHugh, Hank Madison, Chuck Mason, G. J. Morgan, Glebe Morgan, Edna Murray, Lorna Page, Olive Patterson, Alvin Porter, Alex Random, W. J. Rimmer, Donna Rix, Matt Rockwell, Charles Roscoe, Minerva Rosetti, Norford Scott, Valerie Scott, Bart Segundo, Bart Shane, Frank Shaul, Clinton Spurr, Roland Starr, J. D. Stevens, Mark Suffling, Kay Talbot, Will Travers, Sarah Vine, Elaine Vinson, Rick Walters, Neil Webb
RUBEL, JAMES LYON	Timothy Hayes, Mason MacRae
RUMBOLD-GIBBS, HENRY ST. JOHN CLAIR	Henry Gibbs, Simon Harvester

TRUE NAMES	PSEUDONYMS
RUNDLE, ANNE	Georgianna Bell, Marianne Lamont, Alexandra Manners, Joanne Marshall, Jeanne Sanders, Jeanne Summers
RURIC, PETER	Paul Cain
RUSKIN, JOHN	A Graduate of Oxford
RUSSELL, GEORGE WILLIAM	A. E.
RUSSELL, COUNTESS MARY ANNETTE VON ARNIM BEAUCHAMP	Alice Cholmondeley, Elizabeth
RUSSELL, WILLIAM	Inspector F., Inspector Robert Warneford, RN, Waters
RYAN, MARAH ELLIS	Ellis Martin
RYAN, PAUL WILLIAM	Robert Finnegan, Mike Quin
RYDELL, HELEN	Forbes Rydell
RYDELL, WENDY	Wendell Rydell
RYDER, M. L.	Michael Lawson
SAIDY, FAREED MILHEM	Fred M. Siady
SAINT, DORA JESSIE	Miss Read
SALMON, ANNIE ELIZABETH	Elizabeth Asheley
SAMPSON, RICHARD HENRY	Richard Hull
SANCTUARY, BRENDA	Bridget Campbell
SANDBURG, CARL A.	Militant
SANDERS, DOROTHY LUCIE	Lucy Walker
SANDERS, RUTH	Ruth Manning-Sanders
SAROYAN, WILLIAM	Sirak Goryan
SAUNDERS, HILARY ADAM ST. GEORGE	Francis Beeding, Barum Browne, Cornelius Cofyn, David Pilgrim
SAUNDERS, JEAN	Jean Innes, Rowena Summers
SAWYER, JOHN	Nancy Buckingham, Nancy John, Erica Quest
SAWYER, NANCY	Nancy Buckingham, Nancy John, Erica Quest
SAYER, NANCY MARGETTS	Nancy Bradfield
SAYERS, JAMES DENSON	Denver Bardwell, Dan James
SCHACHNER, NATHAN	Chan Corbett, Walter Glamis

TRUE NAMES	PSEUDONYMS
SCHLEIN, MIRIAM	Lavinia Stanhope
SCHLER, RAOUL STEPHEN	Rex Burns
SCHMIDT, JAMES NORMAN	James Norman
SCHOEPFLIN, HAROLD VINCENT	Harl Vincent
SCHOFIELD, SYLVIA ANNE	Max Mundy
SCHONFIELD, HUGH JOSEPH	Hubert Fielding, Hegesippus
SCHREIBER, HERMANN O. L.	Lujo Basserman
SEAMAN, ELIZABETH C.	Nellie Bly
SEARLS, HENRY HUNT, JR.	Hank Searls
SEBENTHAL, ROBERTA ELIZABETH	Paul Kruger
SEBLEY, FRANCES RAE	Rae Jeffs
SEED, CECILE EUGENIE	Jenny Seed
SEIFERT, ELIZABETH	Ellen Ashley
SELDES, GILBERT	Foster Johns
SELTZER, CHARLES ALDEN	Hiram Hopkins
SENARENS, LUIS PHILIP	Captain Howard
SESYLE, JOSLIN	Josephine Gibson, G. B. Kirtland
SETH, RONALD	Robert Chartham
SETON, ERNEST THOMPSON	Wolf Thompson
SEWELL, BROCARD	Joseph Jerome
SHAFFER, ANTHONY JOSHUA	Peter Anthony
SHAFFER, PETER LEVIN	Peter Anthony
SHAGINYAN, MARIETTA SERGEYEVNA	Jimmy Dollar
SHAPPIRO, HERBERT ARTHUR	Burt Arthur, Herbert Arthur
SHARKEY, JOHN MICHAEL	Mike Johnson, Jack Sharkey
SHAVER, RICHARD SHARPE	Wes Amherst, Edwin Benson, Peter Dexter, Richard Dorset, Richard English, G. H. Irwin, Paul Lohrman, Frank Patton, Stan Raycraft
SHAW, BYNUM G.	Bob Gillette
SHAW, FELICITY	Anne Morice
SHAW, GEORGE BERNARD	Corns Di Bassetto
SHAW, HENRY WHEELER	Josh Billings
SHELDON, ALICE HASTINGS	Racoona Sheldon, James Tiptree, Jr.
SHELLABARGER, SAMUEL	John Estevan, Peter Loring

TRUE NAMES	PSEUDONYMS
SHEPHERD, DONALD LEE	Barbara Kevern
SHIEL, MATTHEW PHIPPS	Gordon Holmes
SHILLABER, BENJAMIN P.	Mrs. Partington
SHIRAS, WILMAR HOUSE	Jane Howes
SHIRREFFS, GORDON DONALD	Jackson Flynn, Stewart Gordon, Art MacLean
SHULTZE, CARL E.	Bunny
SIHANOUK, SAMDECH NORDOM	Nordom Sihanouk
SILVERBERG, ROBERT	Walter Chapman, Ivar Jorgensen, Calvin M. Knox, David Osborne, Robert Randall, Lee Sebastian, S. M. Tenneshaw
SIMON, S. J.	Caryl Brahms
SIMONS, JAMES MARCUS	Jim Simons
SIMS, GEORGE R.	Dragonet
SINCLAIR, OLGA ELLEN	Ellen Clare
SINCLAIR, UPTON	Frederick Garrison
SINCLAIR-COWAN, BERTHA MUZZY	B. M. Bower
SINTAVSKY, ANDREY	Abram Tertz
SKINNER, JUNE O'GRADY	D. M. Carleon, Rohan O'Grady
SLADEK, JOHN THOMAS	Thom Demijohn, Cassandra Knye
SLAUGHTER, FRANK GILL	G. Arnold Haygood, C. V. Terry
SLAVITT, DAVID	Henry Sutton
SLESAR, HENRY	O. H. Leslie
SMITH, CHARLES H.	Bill Arp
SMITH, DODIE	C. L. Anthony
SMITH, ERNEST BRAMAH	Ernest Bramah
SMITH, EVELYN E.	Delphine C. Lyons
SMITH, FREDERICK E.	David Farrell
SMITH, GEORGE HENRY	M. J. Deer, Jan Hudson, Jerry Jason, Clancy O'Brien, Diana Summers
SMITH, HELEN ZENNA	Evadne Price
SMITH, NORMAN EDWARD MACE	Neil Sheraton, Norman Shore
SMITH, SARAH	Hesba Stretton

TRUE NAMES	PSEUDONYMS
SNEDEKER, CAROLINE DALE	Caroline Dale Owen
SNOW, CHARLES HORACE	H. C. Averill, Charles Ballew, Robert Cole, James Dillard, Allen Forrest, Russ Hardy, John Harlow, Ranger Lee, Gary Marshall, Wade Smith, Dan Wardle, Chester Wills
SOHL, GERALD ALLAN	Nathan Butler, Jerry Sohl, Sean Mei Sullivan
SOUSTER, RAYMOND	John Holmes
SOUTHERN, TERRY	Maxwell Kenton
SPALDING, RUTH	Marion Jay
SPEICHER, HELEN ROSS	Alice Abbott, Jane Land, Jane and Ross Land
SPENCE, WILLIAM JOHN DUNCAN	Jim Bowden, Kirk Ford, Floyd Rogers, Bill Spence, Duncan Spence
SPICER, BART	Jay Barbette
SPICER, BETTY COE	Jay Barbette
SPILLANE, FRANK MORRISON	Mickey Spillane
SPRIGG, CHRISTOPHER ST. JOHN	Christopher Caudwell
STABLEFORD, BRIAN MICHAEL	Brian Craig
STAPLES, REGINALD	James Sinclair, Robert Tyler Stevens
STEEGMULLER, FRANCIS	David Keith, Byron Steel
STEELE, HARWOOD ELMES ROBERT	Howard Steele
STEELE, MARY QUINTARD	Wilson Gage
STEELE & SWIFT	Isaac Bickerstaff
STEEN, MARGUERITE	Lennox Dryden, Jane Nicholson
STEIN, AARON MARC	George Bagby, Hampton Stone
STEIN, BENJAMIN	Ben Stein
STEVENSON, FLORENCE	Zandra Colt, Lucia Curzon, Zabrina Faire
STEWART, ALFRED WALTER	J. J. Connington
STEWART, DOROTHY MARY	Mary Elgin
STEWART, JOHN INNES MACKINTOSH	Michael Innes
STINE, GEORGE HARRY	Lee Correy
STINE, HENRY EUGENE	Hank Stine

TRUE NAMES	PSEUDONYMS
STIRLING, JESSICA	Peggie Coghlan
STOCKTON, FRANCIS RICHARD	Frank R. Stockton
STOKER, ALAN	Evan Evans
STORR, CATHERINE	Irene Adler, Helen Lourie
STOUTENBERG, ADRIEN	Lace Kendall
STRAKER, J. F.	Jan Rosse
STRATEMEYER, EDWARD	Captain Ralph Bonehill, Arthur M. Winfield
STRATTON, REBECCA	Lucy Gillen
STREET, CECIL JOHN CHARLES	Miles Burton, F. O. O., John Rhode, C. J. C. Street
STREIB, DAN	J. Faragut Jones, Jonathan Schofield
STROTHER, DAVID H.	Porte Crayon
STUART, VIVIAN	William Stuart Long
STUBBS, HARRY CLEMENT	Hal Clement
STYLES, FRANK SHOWELL	Glyn Carr
SUDDABY, DONALD	Alan Griff
SUMMERS, ETHEL SNELSON	Essie Summers
SUMMERTON, MARGARET	Jan Roffman
SWAN, ANNIE S.	David Lyall
SWATRIDGE, CHARLES	Theresa Charles
SWATRIDGE, IRENE MAUDE	Fay Chandos, Theresa Charles, Leslie Lance, Irene Mossop, Virginia Storm, Jan Tempest
SWETENHAM, MRS. ANTHONY	V. H. Drummond, Violet Hilda Drummond
SWINNERTON, FRANK	Simon Pure
SYMONS, DOROTHY GERALDINE	Georgina Groves
TANN, JENNIFER	Geoffrey Booth
TAYLOR, CONSTANCE LINDSAY	Guy Cullingford
TAYLOR, LOIS DWIGHT	Caroline Arnett, Lynn Avery, Nancy Dudley, Allan Dwight, Anne Eliot, Anne Lattin
TAYLOR, MARGARET STEWART	Margaret Collier
TAYLOR, PHOEBE ATWOOD	Alice Tilton
TELLER, NEVILLE	Edmund Owen

TRUE NAMES	PSEUDONYMS
TENNANT, EMMA CHRISTINA	Catherine Aydy
TERHUNE, MARY VIRGINIA	Marion Harland
THACKERY, WILLIAM MAKEPEACE	Michael Angelo Titmarsh, Theophile Wagstaff
THAYER, EMMA REDINGTON	Lee Thayer
THIMBLETHORPE, JUNE SYLVIA	Sylvia Thorpe
THIRKELL, ANGELA	Leslie Parker
THOMAS, EDWARD	Edward Eastway
THOMAS, ROSS	Oliver Bleeck
THOMAS, SARA	Sara Jackson
THOMPSON, ARTHUR LEONARD BELL	Francis Clifford
THOMPSON, EDWARD ANTHONY	Anthony Lejeune
THOMPSON, GEORGE SELDEN	George Selden
THOMSON, DAISY HICKS	Jonathan H. Thomsom
THOMSON, DERICK S.	Ruaraidh MacThomas
THORNE, SABINA	Sabina Thorne Johnson
TILLET, DOROTHY STOCKBRIDGE	Dorothy Stockbridge, John Stephen Strange
TINNE, DOROTHEA	Dorothea Strover, E. D. Tinne
TIPPETTE, GILES	Wilson Young
TIRBUTT, HONORIA	Emma Page
TITUS, EVE	Nancy Lord
TODD, BARBARA EUPHAN	Barbara Bower, Euphan
TOMALIN, RUTH	Ruth Leaver
TOMPKINS, JULIA	Marguerite Neilson
TOOMBS, JOHN	Joselyn De White, Fortune Kent, Jonathan Scofield, Jocelyn Wilde
TORDAY, URSULA	Paula Allardyce, Charity Blackstock, Lee Blackstock, Charlotte Keppel
TRALINS, S. ROBERT	Ray Z. Bixby, Norman A. King, Keith Miles, Sean O'Shea, Rex O'Toole, Cynthia Sydney, Leland Tracy, Richard Trainor, Ruy Traube, Dorothy Verdon
TRANTER, NIGEL GODWIN	Nye Tredgold
TREVOR, ELLESTON	Mansell Black, Trevor Burgess, T. Dudley-Smith, Roger Fitzalan,

TRUE NAMES	PSEUDONYMS
	Adam Hall, Howard North, Simon Rattray, Warwick Scott, Caesar Smith
TRIMBLE, LOUIS PRESTON	Stuart Brock, Gerry Travis
TRIMMER, ERIC J.	Eric Jameson, Dr. Philip Lawson
TRIPP, MILES BARTON	Michael Brett
TROUBETSKOI, PRINCESS	Amelie Rives
TUBB, EDWIN CHARLES	Chuck Adams, Jud Cary, J. F. Clarkson, James S. Farrow, James R. Fenner, Charles S. Graham, Charles Grey, Volsted Gridban, Gill Hunt, E. F. Jackson, Gregory Kern, King Lang, Mike Lantry, P. Lawrence, Chet Lawson, Arthur MacLean, Carl Maddox, M. L. Powers, Paul Schofield, Brian Shaw, Roy Sheldon, John Stevens, Edward Thomson, E. C. Tubb
TUCCI, NICCOLO	Bartolomeo Stravolgi
TUCKER, GEORGE	Joseph Atterley
TULLETT, DENIS	John Sutton
TURNER, JUDITH	Judith Saxton
TURNER, PHILIP WILLIAM	Stephen Chance
TURNER, W. PRICE	Bill Turner
TUTE, WARREN	Andrew Warren
TYLER-WHITTLE, MICHAEL	Mark Oliver, Tyler Whittle
ULLMAN, ALLAN	Sandy Alan
UNGERER, JEAN THOMAS	Tomi Ungerer
UNWIN, DAVID STORR	David Severn
UPCHURCH, BOYD BRADFIELD	John Boyd
UTTLEY, ALICE JANE	Alison Uttley
VALLENTINE, B. B.	Fitznoodle
VANCE, JOHN HOLBROOK	Peter Held, John Holbrook, Ellery Queen, Jack Vance, John Van See, Alan Wade
VANCE, WILLIAM E.	George Cassidy

TRUE NAMES	PSEUDONYMS
VAN SILLER, HILDA	Van Siller
VENABLES, TERRY	P. B. Yuill
VERRILL, ALPHEUS HYATT	Ray Ainsbury
VIAN, BORIS	Vernon Sullivan
VIAUD, L. M. JULIEN	Pierre Loti
VICKERS, ROY C.	David Durham, Sefton Kyle, John Spencer
VICTOR, METTA FULLER	Seeley Regester
VIDAL, EUGENE LUTHER GORE	Edgar Box
VINING, ELIZABETH GRAY	Elizabeth Janet Gray
VINSON, REX THOMAS	Vincent King
VOELKER, JOHN DONALDSON	Robert Traver
VON HOFMANNSTAHL, HUGO	Loris, Loris Melikow, Theophil Morren
VULLIAMY, COLWYN EDWARD	Anthony Rolls
WADDELL, EVELYN MARGARET	Lyn Cook
WADE, ROBERT	Will Daemer, Whit Masterson, Wade Miller
WADE, ROSALIND	Catharine Carr
WAINWRIGHT, GORDON RAY	Ray Gordon
WAINWRIGHT, JOHN	Jack Ripley
WALDO, EDWARD HAMILTON	Frederick R. Ewing, Ellery Queen, Theodore Sturgeon
WALKER, EMILY KATHLEEN	Sarah Devon, Anne Durham, Louise Ellis, Jane Lester, Jill Murray, Quenna Tilbury, Kathleen Treves, Kay Winchester
WALL, JOHN W.	Sarban
WALLACE, BRUCE	Thirsty McQuill
WALLACE-CLARKE, GEORGE	George Jaffa
WALLIS, G. C.	John Stanton
WALLIS, GEORGE C.	B. Wallis, B. and G. C. Wallis
WALSH, JAMES MORGAN	H. Haverstock Hill, Stephen Maddock, George M. White
WALSH, SHEILA	Sophie Leyton
WARD, ARTHUR HENRY SARSFIELD	Michael Furey, Sax Rohmer

TRUE NAMES	PSEUDONYMS
WARD, LESLIE	Spy
WARD, NATHANIEL	Theodore De La Guard
WARD-THOMAS, EVELYN BRIDGET PATRICIA	Evelyn Anthony
WARE, EUGENE FITCH	Ironquill
WARNER, GEOFFREY JOHN	Geoffrey Johns
WARNER, SUSAN BOGERT	Elizabeth Wetherell
WARRINER, THURMAN	Simon Troy
WATERHOUSE, KEITH	Herald Froy, Lee Gibb
WATKINS-PITCHFORD, DENYS JAMES	BB
WATSON, JOHN MACLAREN	Ian MacLaren
WATSON, JULIA	Jane De Vere, Julia Fitzgerald, Julia Hamilton
WATTS, PETER CHRISTOPHER	Matt Chisholm, Cy James, Luke Jones, Duncan Mackinlock, Tom Owen
WAUGH, HILLARY BALDWIN	Elissa Grandower, H. Baldwin Taylor, Harry Walker
WAY, ELIZABETH FENWICK	E. P. Fenwick, Elizabeth Fenwick
WEBB, CHARLES HENRY	John Paul
WEBB, JACK	John Farr, Tex Grady
WEBB, JEAN FRANCIS	Ethel Hamill, Roberta Morrison, Lee Davis Willoughby
WEBB, RICHARD WILSON	Q. Patrick, Patrick Quentin, Jonathan Stagge
WEBSTER, ALICE JANE CHANDLER	Jean Webster
WEEKS, LADY CONSTANCE AVARD	Constance Tomkinson
WEINSTEIN, NATHAN WELLENSTEIN	Nathaneal West
WEISS, EHRICH	Harry Houdini
WELLMAN, MANLY WADE	Gans T. Field
WELLS, CAROLYN	Rowland Wright
WELLS, HERBERT GEORGE	H. G. Wells
WERT, LYNETTE L.	Lynn Le Mon
WEST, BENJAMIN	Isaac Bickerstaff
WEST, JOYCE	Manu Gilbert

TRUE NAMES	PSEUDONYMS
WEST, MORRIS	Michael East, Julian Morris
WESTLAKE, DONALD EDWIN	Curt Clark, Tucker Coe, Timothy J. Culver, Richard Stark
WHEELER, HUGH CALLINGHAM	Q. Patrick, Patrick Quentin, Jonathan Stagge
WHITAKER, RODNEY	Benat Le Cagat, J-L. Moran, Nicholas Seare, Trevanian, Rod Whitaker
WHITE, JUDE GILLIAM	Jude Deveraux
WHITE, PHYLLIS DOROTHY	P. D. James, Phyllis Dorothy James
WHITE, TERENCE HANBURY	James Aston
WHITE, THEODORE EDWIN	Ron Archer, Norman Edwards, Ted White
WHITE, WILLIAM ANTHONY PARKER	Anthony Boucher, Theo Durrant, H. H., Holmes
WHITFIELD, RAOUL	Ramon Decolta
WHITSON, JOHN HARVEY	Lieutenant A. K. Sims
WHITTINGTON, HARRY	Ashley Carter, Robert Hart Davis, Tabor Evans, Whit Harrison, Kel Holland, Harriet Kathryn Myers, Blaine Stevens, Clay Stuart, Hondo Wells, Harry White, Hallam Whitney, Carter Wick
WIBBERLEY, LEONARD PATRICK O'CONNOR	Leonard Holton, Patrick O'Connor, Christopher Webb
WILBY, BASIL LEE	Gareth Knight
WILCOX, COLIN	Carter Wick
WILDE, OSCAR FINGAL	Sebastian Melmoth
WILDING, PHILIP	Logan Stuart
WILLIAMS, CAROL	Carol Fenner
WILLIAMS, DOROTHY JEANNE	Megan Castell, Jeanne Crecy, Jeanne Foster, Kristin Michaels, Deirdre Rowen, J. R. Williams
WILLIAMS, GEORGE VALENTINE	Douglas Valentine
WILLIAMS, GORDON	Terry Venables, P. B. Yuill
WILLIAMS, JAY	Michael Delving
WILLIAMS, MARGARET WETHERBY	Margaret Erskine

TRUE NAMES	PSEUDONYMS
WILLIAMSON, ALICE MURIEL	Charles De Crespigny, Dona Teresa De Savallo, M. P. Revere, Alice Stuyvesant, Mrs. Harcourt Williamson
WILLIAMSON, CHARLES NORRIS	Charles De Crespigny, Dona Teresa De Savallo, M. P. Revere, Alice Stuyvesant, Mrs. Harcourt Williamson
WILLIAMSON, JOHN STEWART	Will Stewart, Jack Williamson
WILLIS, EDWARD HENRY	Ted Willis
WILLIS, SARA PAYSON	Fanny Fern
WILSON, MRS. HARRY LEON	Rose Cecil O'Neill
WILSON, JOHN ANTHONY BURGESS	Anthony Burgess, Joseph Kell
WILSON, JOYCE MURIEL	Joyce Stranger
WILSON, RICHARD GARRATT	Dick Wilson
WILSON, SANDRA	Sandra Heath
WINTERTON, PAUL	Roger Bax, Andrew Garve, Paul Somers
WODEHOUSE, PELHAM GRENVILLE	Pellham Grenville, C. P. West, J. Walker Williams, Basil Windham, P. G. Wodehouse
WOJTYLA, KAROL	Pope John Paul II
WOLCOTT, JOHN	Peter Pindar
WOLLHEIM, DONALD ALLEN	David Grinnell
WOOD, EDGAR ALLARDYCE	Kerry Wood
WOODS, HELEN	Helen Ferguson, Anna Kavan
WOODWORTH, FRED	Kent Winslow, I. R. Ybarra
WOOLSEY, SARAH CHAUNCY	Susan Coolidge
WORBOYS, ANNETTE ISOBEL	Annette Eyre, Vicky Maxwell, Anne Eyre Worboys
WORMSER, RICHARD EDWARD	Ed Friend
WRIGHT, PATRICIA	Mary Napier
WRIGHT, SYDNEY FOWLER	Sydney Fowler, Alan Seymour, S. Fowler Wright
WRIGHT, WILLARD HUNTINGTON	Van Dine, S. S.
WYND, OSWALD MORRIS	Gavin Black
YARDLEY, ALICE	Angela Young

TRUE NAMES	PSEUDONYMS
YATES, ALAN GEOFFREY	Carter Brown, Peter Carter Brown, Peter Carter-Brown
YIN, LESLIE CHARLES BOWYER	Leslie Charteris
YORINKS, ARTHUR	Alan Yaffe
YOUD, CHRISTOPHER SAMUEL	John Christopher, Hilary Ford, William Godfrey, Peter Graaf, Peter Nichols, Anthony Rye, C. S. Youd
YOUNG, GORDON RAY	Hugh Richmond
YOUNG, JANET RANDALL	Janet Randall, Jan Young
ZACHARY, HUGH	Ginny Forman, Ginny Gorman, Elizabeth Hughes, Zach Hughes, Peter Kanto, Derral Pilgrim, Olivia Rangely, Marcus Van Heller, Elizabeth Zachary
ZIEGLER, RICHARD	Robert Ziller
ZINBERG, LEONARD S.	Steve April, Ed Lacy, Len Zinberg
ZOLOTOW, CHARLOTTE	Sara Abbot, Charlotte Bookman
ZWEIG, STEFAN	Stephen Branch

— 6 —

Pseudonyms of Authors and Their True Names

This chapter is cross-indexed to Chapter 5, and provides the names of many additional authors who only use a single pseudonym. After locating any given name here, a quick check in Chapter 5 under the author's true name will provide all other pseudonyms that author may have used—if any.

PSEUDONYMS	TRUE NAMES
A., Dr.	ASIMOV, ISAAC
A. A.	ARMSTRONG, ANTHONY
A. E.	RUSSELL, GEORGE WILLIAM
A Bachelor of Arts	BENTLEY, PHYLISS
Abbey, Kieran	REILLY, HELEN
Abbot, Sara	ZOLOTOW, CHARLOTTE
Abbott, Alice	BORLAND, KATHRYN
Abbott, Alice	SPEICHER, HELEN ROSS
Abbott, Anthony	OURSLER, CHARLES FULTON
Acre, Stephen	GRUBER, FRANK
Adair, Cecil	EVERETT-GREEN, EVELYN
Adams, Annette	ROWLAND, DONALD SYDNEY
Adams, Bart	BINGLEY, DAVID ERNEST
Adams, Chuck	TUBB, EDWIN CHARLES
Adams, Harrison	RATHBONE, ST. GEORGE HENRY
Adams, Justin	CAMERON, LOU
Adams, Perseus	ADAMS, PETER ROBERT CHARLES
Adelaide, Mary	PHILLPOTTS, ADELAIDE
Adelberg, Doris	ORGEL, DORIS

PSEUDONYMS	TRUE NAMES
Adeler, Max	CLARK, CHARLES HEBER
Adler, Irene	STORR, CATHERINE
Adrian, Frances	POLLAND, MADELEINE ANGELA
Aesop	LONIGAN, GEORGE THOMAS
Agar, Brian	BALLARD, WILLIS TODHUNTER
Agate	REID, WHITLAW
Aghill, Gordon	GARRETT, RANDALL PHILLIP
Ainsbury, Ray	VERRILL, ALPHEUS HYATT
Ainsworth, Harriett	CADELL, VIOLET ELIZABETH
Ainsworth, Patricia	BIGG, PATRICIA NINA
Aird, Catherine	MC INTOSH, KINN HAMILTON
Airlie, Catherine	MACLEOD, JEAN S.
Akers, Alan Burt	BULMER, HENRY KENNETH
Akers, Floyd	BAUM, LYMAN FRANK
Alan, Sandy	ULLMAN, ALLAN
Albrand, Martha	FREYBE, HEIDI HUBERTA
Alcibiade	PRAZ, MARIO
Aldanov, Mark	LANDAU, MARK A.
Alden, Sue	FRANCIS, DOROTHY BRENNER
Alding, Peter	JEFFRIES, RODERIC
Aldon, Adair	MEIGS, CORNELIA LYNDE
Alexander, Joan	CARNWORTH, LADY
Aliki	BRANDENBERG, ALIKI
Allan, Dennis	DENNISTON, ELINORE
Allan, Luke	AMY, WILLIAM LACEY
Allardyce, Paula	TORDAY, URSULA
Allbeury, Ted	ALLBEURY, THEODORE EDWARD LE BOUTHILLIER
Allen, Betsy	CAVANNA, BETTY
Allen, Grace	HOGARTH, GRACE
Allen, Hugh	RATHBONE, ST. GEORGE HENRY
Allen, John	PERRY, RITCHIE JOHN ALLEN
Allen, T. D.	ALLEN, DON B.
Allen, T. D.	DIENER, TERRIL
Allen, Terry D.	ALLEN, DON B.
Allen, Terry D.	DIENER, TERRIL

PSEUDONYMS	TRUE NAMES
Allerton, Mary	GOVAN, CHRISTINE NOBLE
Allison, Clay	KEEVIL, HENRY JOHN
Allison, Sam	LOOMIS, NOEL MILLER
Allyson, Kym	KIMBRO, JOHN M.
Alvord, Burt	KEEVIL, HENRY JOHN
Amberley, Richard	BOURQUIN, PAUL HENRY JAMES
Ambrose, Alice	LAZEROWITZ, ALICE AMBROSE
Ames, Clinton	GRAHAM, ROGER PHILLIPS
Ames, Jennifer	GREIG-SMITH, JENNIFER
Ames, Leslie	RIGONI, ORLANDO
Amherst, Wes	SHAVER, RICHARD SHARPE
Amy, Lacey	AMY, WILLIAM LACEY
Anderson, Ella	MACLEOD, ELLEN JANE
Anderson, Sonia	DANIEL, WILLIAM ROLAND
Andrews, V. C.	AUSTIN, MARY
Andrézel, Pierre	BLIXEN, KAREN
Angus, Ian	MACKAY, JAMES ALEXANDER
Anne of Swansea	CURTIS, JULIA ANN KEMBLE
Anstey, F.	GUTHRIE, THOMAS ANSTEY
Anthony, C. L.	SMITH, DODIE
Anthony, Evelyn	WARD-THOMAS, EVELYN BRIDGET PATRICIA
Anthony, Peter	SHAFFER, ANTHONY JOSHUA
Anthony, Peter	SHAFFER, PETER LEVIN
Anthony, Piers	JACOB, PIERS ANTHONY DILLINGHAM
Anthony, Simon	BREUER, MILES JOHN
Antoninus	EVERSON, WILLIAM
Anvil, Christopher	CROSBY, HARRY C.
Appleseed, Johnny	CHAPMAN, JOHN
Appleton, Victor W., II	ADAMS, HARRIET STRATEMEYER
April, Steve	ZINBERG, LEONARD S.
Archer, A. A.	JOSCELYN, ARCHIE LYNN
Archer, Frank	O'CONNOR, RICHARD
Archer, Ron	WHITE, THEODORE EDWIN
Arden, J. E. M.	CONQUEST, GEORGE ROBERT ACWORTH
Arden, William	LYNDS, DENNIS

PSEUDONYMS	TRUE NAMES
Arion	CHESTERTON, GILBERT KEITH
Arlen, Leslie	NICOLE, CHRISTOPHER ROBIN
Arlen, Michael	KOUYOUMDJIAN, DIKRAN
Armstrong, Geoffrey	FEARN, JOHN RUSSELL
Armstrong, Raymond	LEE, NORMAN
Arnett, Caroline	TAYLOR, LOIS DWIGHT
Arnette, Robert	GRAHAM, ROGER PHILLIPS
Arnold, Joseph H.	HAYES, JOSEPH ARNOLD
Arp, Bill	SMITH, CHARLES H.
Arre, Helen	ROSS, ZOLA HELEN
Arrow, William	ROTSLER, WILLIAM
Arthur, Bert	SHAPPIRO, HERBERT ARTHUR
Arthur, Frank	EBERT, ARTHUR FRANK
Arthur, Herbert	SHAPPIRO, HERBERT ARTHUR
Arthur, Peter	PORGES, ARTHUR
Aruba, Hervé	LE FONTAINE, JOSEPH RAYMOND HERVE
Ash, Fenton	ATKINS, FRANK
Ash, Pauline	WALKER, EMILY KATHLEEN
Ashdown, Clifford	FREEMAN, RICHARD AUSTIN
Ashdown, Clifford	PITCAIRN, J. J.
Ashe, Douglas	BARDIN, JOHN FRANKLIN
Ashe, Gordon	CREASEY, JOHN
Ashe, Mary Anne	BRAND, MARY CHRISTIANNA MILNE
Ashford, Jeffrey	JEFFRIES, RODERIC
Ashley, Elizabeth	SALMON, ANNIE ELIZABETH
Ashley, Ellen	SEIFERT, ELIZABETH
Ashley, Fred	ATKINS, FRANK
Ashley, Gladys	EWENS, GWENDOLINE WILSON
Ashton, Ann	KIMBRO, JOHN M.
Ashton, Sharon	VAN SLYKE, HELEN LENORE
Askham, Francis	GREENWOOD, JULIA EILEEN COURTNEY
Asquith, Nan	PATTINSON, NANCY EVELYN
Assiac	FRAENKEL, HEINRICH
Astley, Juliet	LOFTS, NORAH
Aston, James	WHITE, TERENCE HANBURY
Atheling, William, Jr.	BLISH, JAMES BENJAMIN

PSEUDONYMS	TRUE NAMES
Atkinson, Mary	HARDWICK, MOLLIE
Atlee, Philip	PHILLIPS, JAMES ATLEE
Atterley, Joseph	TUCKER, GEORGE
Atthill, Robin	ATTHILL, ROBERT ANTHONY
Aubrey, Frank	ATKINS, FRANK
August, John	DE VOTO, BERNARD AUGUSTINE
Aumbry, Alan	BAYLEY, BARRINGTON JOHN
Austin, Brett	FLOREN, LEE
Austin, Frank	FAUST, FREDERICK SCHILLER
Austwick, John	LEE, AUSTIN
Averill, H. C.	SNOW, CHARLES HORACE
Avery, A. A.	MONTGOMERY, RUTHERFORD GEORGE
Avery, Al	MONTGOMERY, RUTHERFORD GEORGE
Avery, Lynn	TAYLOR, LOIS DWIGHT
Avery, Richard	COOPER, EDMUND
Axton, David	KOONTZ, DEAN RAY
Aydy, Catherine	TENNANT, EMMA CHRISTINA
Ayre, Thornton	FEARN, JOHN RUSSELL
Ayres, Paul	AARONS, EDWARD SIDNEY
Baba, Ali	MACKAY, ALBERIGH
Babbitt, Robert	BANGS, ROBERT B.
Bagby, George	STEIN, AARON MARC
Bahl, Franklin	GRAHAM, ROGER PHILLIPS
Baker, Asa	DRESSER, DAVIS
Baker, Betty Doreen	RENIER, ELIZABETH
Balaam	LAMB, GEOFFREY FREDERICK
Baldwin, Gordo	BALDWIN, GORDON CORTIS
Ball, Zachary	JANAS, FRANKIE-LEE
Ballantine, Bill	BALLANTINE, WILLIAM OLIVER
Ballard, K. G.	ROTH, HOLLY
Ballard, P. D.	BALLARD, WILLIS TODHUNTER
Ballew, Charles	SNOW, CHARLES HORACE
Ballinger, Bill S.	BALLINGER, WILLIAM SANBORN
Baltimore, J.	CATHERALL, ARTHUR

PSEUDONYMS	TRUE NAMES
Bancroft, Laura	BAUM, LYMAN FRANK
Bandoff, Hope	GUTHRIE, THOMAS ANSTEY
Bannatyne, Jack	GASTON, WILLIAM JAMES
Banner, Angela	MADDISON, ANGELA MARY
Bannon, Peter	DURST, PAUL
Banton, Coy	NORWOOD, VICTOR GEORGE CHARLES
Baraki, Imamu Amiri	JONES, LEROI
Barbette, Jay	SPICER, BART
Barbette, Jay	SPICER, BETTY COE
Barclay, Ann	GREIG-SMITH, JENNIFER
Barclay, Bill	MOORCOCK, MICHAEL
Barclay, Marguerite	JERVIS, MARGUERITE FLORENCE
Barcynska, Countess Helene	JERVIS, MARGUERITE FLORENCE
Bardwell, Denver	SAYERS, JAMES DENSON
Barlay, Bennett	CROSSEN, KENDELL FOSTER
Barnard, A. M.	ALCOTT, LOUISA MAY
Barne, Kitty	BARNE, MARION CATHERINE
Barnes, Dave	BARNES, ARTHUR KELVIN
Barretton, Grandall	GARRETT, RANDALL PHILLIP
Barrington, E.	BECK, LILY ADAMS
Barrow, Pamela	HOWARTH, PAMELA
Barry, Jocelyn	BOWDEN, JEAN
Barry, Mike	MALZBERG, BARRY NORMAN
Bartholomew, Jean	BEATTY, PATRICIA
Barton, Jon	HARVEY, JOHN B.
Bass, T. J.	BASSLER, THOMAS J.
Basserman, Lujo	SCHREIBER, HERMANN O. L.
Bassett, Jack	ROWLAND, DONALD SYDNEY
Bates, Harry	BATES, HIRAM GILMORE, III
Baum, L. Frank	BAUM, LYMAN FRANK
Bax, Roger	WINTERTON, PAUL
Baxter, George Owen	FAUST, FREDERICK SCHILLER
Baxter, Hazel	ROWLAND, DONALD SYDNEY
Baxter, Sane V.	NORWOOD, VICTOR GEORGE CHARLES
Baxter, Valerie	MEYNELL, LAURENCE WALTER
Bayer, Sylvia	GLASSCO, JOHN

PSEUDONYMS	TRUE NAMES
Bayliss, Timothy	BAYBARS, TANER
BB	WATKINS-PITCHFORD, DENYS JAMES
Bean, Norman	BURROUGHS, EDGAR RICE
Beard, Frank	BEARD, THOMAS FRANCIS
Beaumont, Charles	NUTT, CHARLES
Bedford, John	HASTINGS, PHYLISS DORA
Beeding, Francis	PALMER, JOHN LESLIE
Beeding, Francis	SAUNDERS, HILARY ADAM ST. GEORGE
Bell, Acton	BRONTE, ANNE
Bell, Carolyn	RIGONI, ORLANDO
Bell, Currer	BRONTE, CHARLOTTE
Bell, Ellis	BRONTE, EMILY
Bell, Georgianna	RUNDLE, ANNE
Bell, Janet	CLYMER, ELEANOR
Bell, Josephine	BALL, DORIS BELL
Bellairs, George	BLUNDELL, HAROLD
Belvedere, Lee	GRAYLAND, VALERIE MERLE
Benko, Nancy	ATKINSON, NANCY
Bennett, Dwight	NEWTON, DWIGHT BENNETT
Bennett, Elizabeth Deare	MERWIN, SAMUEL KIMBALL, JR.
Bennett, H. O.	HARDISON, OSBORNE B.
Ben Shimon Halevi, Zev	KENTON, WARREN
Benson, Daniel	COOPER, COLIN SYMONS
Benson, Edwin	SHAVER, RICHARD SHARPE
Benteen, John	HAAS, BENJAMIN LEOPOLD
Bentley, E. C.	BENTLEY, EDMUND CLERIHEW
Benton, Karla	ROWLAND, DONALD SYDNEY
Berkeley, Anthony	COX, ANTHONY BERKELEY
Bernard, Robert	MARTIN, ROBERT BERNARD
Berrington, John	BROWNJOHN, ALAN
Berry, Helen	ROWLAND, DONALD SYDNEY
Bertin, Jack	GERMANO, PETER B.
Betteridge, Anne	POTTER, MARGARET EDITH
Betteridge, Don	NEWMAN, BERNARD
Bettina	BRENTANO, ELIZABETH
Bexar, Phil	BORG, PHILIP ANTHONY JOHN

PSEUDONYMS	**TRUE NAMES**
Bey, Isabelle	BOSTICCO, MARY
Beynon, John	HARRIS, JOHN WYNDHAM PARKES LUCAS BENYON
Bibelot, R. H.	KELLY, TIM
Bibliophile	ALLIBONE, S. A.
Bickerstaff, Isaac	STEELE & SWIFT
Bickerstaff, Isaac	WEST, BENJAMIN
Biglow, Hosea	LOWELL, JAMES RUSSELL
Billings, Josh	SHAW, HENRY WHEELER
Binder, Eando	BINDER, EARL ANDREW
Binder, Eando	BINDER, OTTO OSCAR
Binkley, Anne	RAND, ANN
Birkley, Dolan	HITCHENS, JULIA CLARA CATHERINE DOLORES BIRK OLSEN
Biro, Val	BIRO, BALINT STEPHEN
Bisonius	ALLEN, JOHN E.
Bixby, Ray Z.	TRALINS, S. ROBERT
Black, Gavin	WYND, OSWALD MORRIS
Black, Ishi	GIBSON, WALTER B.
Black, Lionel	BARKER, DUDLEY
Black, Mansell	TREVOR, ELLESTON
Black, Veronica	PETERS, MAUREEN
Blacker, Hereth	CHALKE, H. D.
Blackstock, Charity	TORDAY, URSULA
Blackstock, Lee	TORDAY, URSULA
Blade, Alexander	GARRETT, RANDALL PHILLIP
Blade, Alexander	GRAHAM, ROGER PHILLIPS
Blaine, James	AVALLONE, MICHAEL ANGELO, JR.
Blaisdell, Anne	LININGTON, BARBARA ELIZABETH
Blake, Alfred	GARRETT, RANDALL PHILLIP
Blake, Alfred	HARRIS, LARRY MARK
Blake, Andrew	GARRETT, RANDALL PHILLIP
Blake, Andrew	HARRIS, LARRY MARK
Blake, Jennifer	MAXWELL, PATRICIA ANNE
Blake, Justin	BOWEN, JOHN
Blake, Justin	BULLMORE, JEREMY

PSEUDONYMS	TRUE NAMES
Blake, Ken	BULMER, HENRY KENNETH
Blake, Nicholas	DAY-LEWIS, CECIL
Blake, Patrick	EGLETON, CLIVE
Bland, Alexander	GOSLING, NIGEL
Bland, E.	NESBIT, EDITH
Bland, Fabian	NESBIT, EDITH
Bland, Jennifer	BOWDEN, JEAN
Blayn, Hugo	FEARN, JOHN RUSSELL
Blayre, Christopher	HERON-ALLEN, EDWARD
Bleeck, Oliver	THOMAS, ROSS
Blight, Rose	GREER, GERMAINE
Blood, Matthew	DRESSER, DAVIS
Blood, Matthew	JOHNSON, RYERSON
Blunt, Don	BOOTH, EDWIN
Bluting, Edward	GOREY, EDWARD ST. JOHN
Bly, Nellie	SEAMAN, ELIZABETH C.
Blyth, John	HIBBS, JOHN
Boardman, Charles	GRIFFITHS, CHARLES
Bold, Ralph	GRIFFITHS, CHARLES
Bonehill, Captain Ralph	STRATEMEYER, EDWARD
Bonett, Emery	CARTER, FELICITY WINIFRED
Bonett, Emery	COULSON, JOHN HUBERT ARTHUR
Bonett, John and Emery	CARTER, FELICITY WINIFRED
Bonett, John and Emery	COULSON, JOHN HUBERT ARTHUR
Bonner, Michael	GLASSCOCK, ANNE
Bonner, Parker	BALLARD, WILLIS TODHUNTER
Bonner, Sherwood	MACDOWELL, KATHERINE
Bonney, Bill	KEEVIL, HENRY JOHN
Bookman, Charlotte	ZOLOTOW, CHARLOTTE
Boone, Ike	ATHANAS, WILLIAM VERNE
Booth, Geoffrey	TANN, JENNIFER
Booth, Irwin	HOCH, EDWARD DENTINGER
Borg, Jack	BORG, PHILIP ANTHONY JOHN
Borland, Hal	BORLAND, HAROLD GLEN
Boston, Charles K.	GRUBER, FRANK
Boucher, Anthony	WHITE, WILLIAM ANTHONY PARKER

PSEUDONYMS	TRUE NAMES
Bourne, Lesley	MARSHALL, EVELYN
Bourne, Peter	JEFFRIES, GRAHAM MONTAGUE
Bowden, Jim	SPENCE, WILLIAM JOHN DUNCAN
Bowen, Marjorie	CAMPBELL, GABRIELLE MARGARET VERE
Bower, B. M.	SINCLAIR-COWAN, BERTHA MUZZY
Bower, Barbara	TODD, BARBARA EUPHAN
Bowie, Jim	NORWOOD, VICTOR GEORGE CHARLES
Bowie, Sam	BALLARD, WILLIS TODHUNTER
Bowood, Richard	DANIELL, ALBERT SCOTT
Box, Edgar	VIDAL, EUGENE LUTHER GORE
Boyd, Alamo	BOSWORTH, ALLAN RUCKER
Boyd, Frank	KANE, FRANK
Boyd, John	UPCHURCH, BOYD BRADFIELD
Boyer, Robert	LAKE, KENNETH ROBERT
Boz	DICKENS, CHARLES
Bradbury, E. P.	MOORCOCK, MICHAEL
Bradfield, Nancy	SAYER, NANCY MARGETTS
Bradwell, James	KENT, ARTHUR
Brady, William S.	HARVEY, JOHN B.
Brahms, Caryl	ABRAHAMS, DORIS CAROLINE
Brahms, Caryl	SIMON, S. J.
Bramah, Ernest	SMITH, ERNEST BRAMAH
Bramwell, Charlotte	KIMBRO, JOHN M.
Branch, Stephen	ZWEIG, STEFAN
Brand, Clay	NORWOOD, VICTOR GEORGE CHARLES
Brand, Max	FAUST, FREDERICK SCHILLER
Brand, Victor	NORWOOD, VICTOR GEORGE CHARLES
Brandon, Joe	DAVIS, ROBERT PRUNIER
Brandon, Sheila	RAYNER, CLAIRE BERENICE
Brandt,Tom	DEWEY, THOMAS BLANCHARD
Brant, Lewis	ROWLAND, DONALD SYDNEY
Bray, Alison	ROWLAND, DONALD SYDNEY
Brayce, William	ROWLAND, DONALD SYDNEY
Brennan, Christopher	KININMONTH, CHRISTOPHER
Brent, Madeline	A PSEUDONYM

PSEUDONYMS	TRUE NAMES
Brett, Lee	BREUER, MILES JOHN
Brett, Michael	TRIPP, MILES BARTON
Brett, Rosalind	BLAIR, KATHRYN
Brewster, Benjamin	FOLSOM, FRANKLIN BREWSTER
Briarton, Grendel	BRETNOR, REGINALD
Bridge, Ann	O'MALLEY, LADY MARY DOLLING
Bridger, Adam	BINGLEY, DAVID ERNEST
Brisco, P. A.	MATTHEWS, PATRICIA ANNE
Brisco, Patty	MATTHEWS, PATRICIA ANNE
Britain, Dan	PENDLETON, DONALD EUGENE
Brock, Lynn	MC ALLISTER, ALISTER
Brock, Rose	HANSEN, JOSEPH
Brock, Stuart	TRIMBLE, LOUIS PRESTON
Brockley, Fenton	ROWLAND, DONALD SYDNEY
Brogan, James	HODDER-WILLIAMS, JOHN CHRISTOPHER GLAZEBROOK
Bronson, Chuck	ROWLAND, DONALD SYDNEY
Bronson, Lynn	LAMPMAN, EVELYN SIBLEY
Bronte, Louisa	ROBERTS, JANET LOUISE
Brooker, Clark	FOWLER, KENNETH ABRAMS
Brother Antoninus	EVERSON, WILLIAM
Brother Graham	JEFFREY, GRAHAM
Brown, Carter	YATES, ALAN GEOFFREY
Brown, Douglas	GIBSON, WALTER B.
Brown, Evelyn Berger	BERGER, EVELYN MILLER
Brown, Peter Carter	YATES, ALAN GEOFFREY
Brown, Rosalie	BROWN, BILL AND ROSALIE MOORE
Browne, Barum	DENNIS, GEOFFREY
Browne, Barum	SAUNDERS, HILARY ADAM ST. GEORGE
Browning, Craig	GRAHAM, ROGER PHILLIPS
Browning, Sterry	GRIBBLE, LEONARD REGINALD
Bruce, David	PATCHETT, MARY ELWYN OSBORNE
Bruce, Leo	CROFT-COOKE, RUPERT
Bruin, John	BRUTUS, DENNIS
Bruton, Connors	ROHEN, EDWARD
Bryan, Michael	MOORE, BRIAN

PSEUDONYMS	TRUE NAMES
Bryans, Robin	BRYANS, ROBERT HARRISON
Bryant, Peter	GEORGE, PETER BRYAN
Bryning, Frank	BRYNING, FRANCIS BERTRAM
Buchanan, Chuck	ROWLAND, DONALD SYDNEY
Buchanan, Marie	BUCHANAN, EILEEN MARIE DUELL
Buchanan, William	BUCK, WILLIAM RAY
Buckingham, Nancy	SAWYER, JOHN
Buckingham, Nancy	SAWYER, NANCY
Bude, John	ELMORE, ERNEST CARPENTER
Budrys, Algis	BUDRYS, ALGIRDAS JONAS
Buffalo Bill	CODY, WILLIAM S.
Bullen Bear	DONNELLY, AUSTIN S.
Bull-Us	PAULDING, JAMES KIRK
Bunker, Captain Moss	BRACKMAN, ARNOLD C.
Bunny	SHULTZE, CARL E.
Bupp, Walter	GARRETT, RANDALL PHILLIP
Burchell, Mary	COOK, IDA
Burford, Eleanor	HIBBERT, ELEANOR ALICE
Burgess, Anthony	WILSON, JOHN ANTHONY BURGESS
Burgess, Trevor	TREVOR, ELLESTON
Burgoyne, Elizabeth	PICKLES, MABLE ELIZABETH
Burke, John	O'CONNOR, RICHARD
Burke, John Frederick	BURGE, MILWARD RODON KENNEDY
Burke, Jonathan	BURGE, MILWARD RODON KENNEDY
Burke, Noel	HITCHENS, JULIA CLARA CATHERINE DOLORES BIRK OLSEN
Burke, Owen	BURGE, MILWARD RODON KENNEDY
Burke, Ralph	GARRETT, RANDALL PHILLIP
Burke, Robert Milward	BURGE, MILWARD RODON KENNEDY
Burke, Shifty	BENTON, PEGGIE
Burnett, W. R.	BURNETT, WILLIAM RILEY
Burns, Rex	SCHLER, RAOUL STEPHEN
Burns, Sheila	BLOOM, URSULA HARVEY
Burns, Tex	LA MOORE, LOUIS DEARBORN
Burrowes, Mike	BURROWES, MICHAEL ANTHONY BERNARD

PSEUDONYMS	TRUE NAMES
Burton, Miles	STREET, CECIL JOHN CHARLES
Burton, Thomas	LONGSTREET, STEPHEN
Bush, Christopher	BUSH, CHARLIE CHRISTOPHER
Butler, Joan	ALEXANDER, ROBERT WILLIAM
Butler, Nathan	SOHL, GERALD ALLAN
Butler, Patrick	DUNBOYNE, LORD
Butler, Richard	ALLBEURY, THEODORE EDWARD LE BOUTHILLIER
Butler, Walter C.	FAUST, FREDERICK SCHILLER
Butters, Dorothy Gilman	GILMAN, DOROTHY
Cade, Robin	NICOLE, CHRISTOPHER ROBIN
Caillou, Alan	LYLE-SMYTHE, ALAN
Cain, Paul	RURIC, PETER
Caine, Hall	CAINE, THOMAS HENRY HALL
Calder, Jason	DUNMORE, JOHN
Caldwell, Taylor	CALDWELL, JANET MIRIAM TAYLOR HOLLAND
Caley, Rod	ROWLAND, DONALD SYDNEY
Caliban	PHILLIPS, HUBERT
Callahan, William	GALLUN, RAYMOND ZINKE
Callas, Theo	MC CARTHY, SHAUN LLOYD
Callender, Julian	LEE, AUSTIN
Calvert, Mary	DANBY, MARY
Calvin, Henry	HANLEY, CLIFFORD
Cameron, D. Y.	COOK, DOROTHY MARE
Cameron, Donald	BRYANS, ROBERT HARBISON
Cameron, Ian	PAYNE, DONALD GORDON
Cameron, Julie	CAMERON, LOU
Campbell, Bridget	SANCTUARY, BRENDA
Campbell, Cliff	HECKELMANN, CHARLES NEWMAN
Campbell, Francis Stuart	KUEHNELT-LEDDIHN, ERIK
Campbell, Judith	PARES, MARION STAPLYTON
Campbell, Karen	BEATY, BETTY
Campbell, Wilfred	CAMPBELL, WILLIAM E.
Canaway, Bill	CANAWAY, W. H

PSEUDONYMS	TRUE NAMES
Candy, Edward	NEVILLE, BARBARA ALISON
Cannan, Joanna Maxwell	PULLEIN-THOMPSON, JOANNA MAXWELL
Cannon, Curt	HUNTER, EVAN
Canuck, Abe	BINGLEY, DAVID ERNEST
Canusi, José	BARKER, SQUIRE OMAR
Cape, Judith	PAGE, P. K.
Carbury, A. B.	CARR, ALBERT ZOTALKOFF
Carder, Leigh	CUNNINGHAM, EUGENE
Carey, James	CAREW-SLATER, HAROLD JAMES
Carfax, Caterine	FAIRBURN, ELEANOR
Carleon, D. M.	SKINNER, JUNE O'GRADY
Carlisle, D. M.	COOK, DOROTHY MARE
Carlton, Roger	ROWLAND, DONALD SYDNEY
Carmichael, Harry	OGNALL, LEOPOLD HORACE
Carnac, Carol	RIVETT, EDITH CAROLINE
Carnac, Levin	GRIFFITH-JONES, GEORGE CHETWYND
Carol, Bill J.	KNOTT, WILLIAM S.
Carpenter, Duffy	HURLEY, JOHN J.
Carpenter, John	REESE, JOHN
Carr, A. H. Z	CARR, ALBERT ZOTALKOFF
Carr, Catharine	WADE, ROSALIND
Carr, Glyn	STYLES, FRANK SHOWELL
Carr, Philippa	HIBBERT, ELEANOR ALICE
Carr, Roberta	ROBERTS, IRENE
Carrick, Edward	CRAIG, EDWARD ANTHONY
Carroll, Lewis	DODGSON, CHARLES LUTWIDGE
Carroll, Martin	CARR, MARGARET
Carson, S. M.	GORSLINE, MARIE
Carstairs, Kathleen	PENDOWER, JACQUES
Carter, Ashley	WHITTINGTON, HARRY
Carter, Avis Murton	ALLE, KENNETH S.
Carter, Bruce	HOUGH, RICHARD ALEXANDER
Carter, Elizabeth Eliot	HOLLAND, CECELIA ANASTASIA
Carter, Nicholas	DEY, FREDERIC MERRILL VAN RENSSELAER

PSEUDONYMS	TRUE NAMES
Carter, Nick	AVALLONE, MICHAEL ANGELO, JR.
Carter, Nick	BALLARD, WILLIS TODHUNTER
Carter, Nick	CORYELL, J. RUSSELL
Carter, Nick	DEY, FREDERIC MERRILL VAN RENSSELAER
Carter, Nick	LYNDS, DENNIS
Carter-Brown, Peter	YATES, ALAN GEOFFREY
Carver, Dave	BINGLEY, DAVID ERNEST
Carver, Henry	BINGLEY, DAVID ERNEST
Cary, Jud	TUBB, EDWIN CHARLES
Caskoden, Edward	MAJOR, CHARLES
Cass, Zoe	LOW, LOIS DOROTHEA
Cassandra	CONNOR, WILLIAM
Cassells, John	DUNCAN, WILLIAM MURDOCH
Cassidy, George	VANCE, WILLIAM E.
Cassius	FOOT, MICHAEL
Castell, Megan	WILLIAMS, DOROTHY JEANNE
Castlemon, H. C.	FOSDICK, CHARLES AUSTIN
Castlemon, Harry	FOSDICK, CHARLES AUSTIN
Catlow, Joanna	LOWRY, JOAN
Caudwell, Christopher	SPRIGG, CHRISTOPHER ST. JOHN
Cauldwell, Frank	KING, FRANCIS
Cave, Emma	LASSALLE, CAROLINE
Cecil, Henry	KELLER, DAVID HENRY
Cecil, Henry	LEON, HENRY CECIL
Cellarius	BUTLER, SAMUEL
Celticus	BEVAN, ANEURIN
Chaber, M. E.	CROSSEN, KENDELL FOSTER
Chace, Isobel	HUNTER, ELIZABETH MARY TERESA
Chaffin, James B.	LUTZ, GILES ALFRED
Challice, Kenneth	HUTCHIN, KENNETH CHARLES
Challis, George	FAUST, FREDERICK SCHILLER
Chance, Stephen	TURNER, PHILIP WILLIAM
Chandler, Frank	HARKNETT, TERRY WILLIAMS
Chandos, Fay	SWATRIDGE, IRENE MAUDE
Chaney, Jill	LEEMING, JILL

PSEUDONYMS	TRUE NAMES
Channel, A. R.	CATHERALL, ARTHUR
Chapman, Lee	BRADLEY, MARION ZIMMER
Chapman, Walter	SILVERBERG, ROBERT
Charles, Anita	BARRIE, SUSAN
Charles, Franklin	ADAMS, CLEVE FRANKLIN
Charles, Franklin	BELLEM, ROBERT LESLIE
Charles, Henry	HARRIS, MARION ROSE
Charles, Nicholas	KUSKIN, KARLA
Charles, Richard	AWDRY, RICHARD CHARLES
Charles, Theresa	SWATRIDGE, CHARLES
Charles, Theresa	SWATRIDGE, IRENE MAUDE
Charteris, Leslie	YIN, LESLIE CHARLES BOWYER
Chartham, Robert	SETH, RONALD
Chase, Adam	FAIRMAN, PAUL W.
Chase, Adam	LESSER, MILTON
Chase, James Hadley	RAYMOND, RENE BARBAZON
Chatham, Larry	BINGLEY, DAVID ERNEST
Check, Otto Premier	BERMAN, ED
Chelton, John	DURST, PAUL
Cherryh, C. J.	CHERRY, CAROLYN JANICE
Chesham, Henry	BINGLEY, DAVID ERNEST
Chesney, Weatherby	HYNE, CHARLES JOHN CUTCLIFFE WRIGHT
Chesterton, Denise	ROBINS, DENISE NAOMI
Chesterton, G. K.	CHESTERTON, GILBERT KEITH
Chisholm, Matt	WATTS, PETER CHRISTOPHER
Cholmondeley, Alice	RUSSELL, COUNTESS MARY ANNETTE VON ARNIM BEAUCHAMP
Christian, Frederick H.	NOLAN, FREDERICK
Christian, Jill	DILCOCK, NOREEN
Christian, John	DIXON, ROGER
Christie, Agatha	MALLOWAN, DAME AGATHA MARY CLARISSA
Christopher, John	YOUD, CHRISTOPHER SAMUEL
Churchill, Elizabeth	HOUGH, RICHARD ALEXANDER
Cingfox, Dan	LE FONTAINE, JOSEPH RAYMOND HERVE

PSEUDONYMS	TRUE NAMES
Circuit Breaker	BAKER, C.
Clare, Elizabeth	COOK, DOROTHY MARE
Clare, Ellen	SINCLAIR, OLGA ELLEN
Clare, Helen	CLARKE, PAULINE
Clark, Curt	WESTLAKE, DONALD EDWIN
Clark, Howard	HASKIN, DOROTHY C.
Clark, Merle	GESSNER, LYNNE
Clarkson, Helen	MC CLOY, HELEN WORRELL CLARKSON
Clarkson, J. F.	TUBB, EDWIN CHARLES
Clavers, Mary	KIRKLAND, CAROLINE
Clay, Alison	KEEVIL, HENRY JOHN
Clay, Bertha	BRAEME, CHARLOTTE M.
Claypool, Jane	MINER, JANE CLAYPOOL
Clement, Hal	STUBBS, HARRY CLEMENT
Clerihew, E. C.	BENTLEY, EDMUND CLERIHEW
Clerk, N. W.	LEWIS, CLIVE STAPLES
Cleve, Janita	ROWLAND, DONALD SYDNEY
Cleve, John	OFFUTT, ANDREW JEFFERSON V.
Cleveland, John	MC ELFRESH, ELIZABETH ADELINE
Clevinger, Paul	NORWOOD, VICTOR GEORGE CHARLES
Clifford, Francis	THOMPSON, ARTHUR LEONARD BELL
Clifford, Martin	HAMILTON, CHARLES HAROLD ST. JOHN
Clifton, Oliver Lee	RATHBONE, ST. GEORGE HENRY
Clinton, Jeff	BICKHAM, JACK MILES
Clive, Dennis	FEARN, JOHN RUSSELL
Clive, William	BASSETT, RONALD LESLIE
Coates, Sheila	HOLLAND, SHEILA
Cobalt, Martin	MAYNE, WILLIAM
Coburn, L. J.	HARVEY, JOHN B.
Cochran, Jeff	DURST, PAUL
Cody, Al	JOSCELYN, ARCHIE LYNN
Cody, Jess	CUNNINGHAM, CHET
Cody, John	REPP, EDWARD EARL
Cody, Walt	NORWOOD, VICTOR GEORGE CHARLES
Coe, Tucker	WESTLAKE, DONALD EDWIN
Coffey, Brian	KOONTZ, DEAN RAY

PSEUDONYMS	TRUE NAMES
Coffin, Geoffrey	BRAWNER, H.
Coffin, Geoffrey	MASON, FRANCIS VAN WYCK
Coffin, Peter	LATIMER, JONATHAN WYATT
Cofyn, Cornelius	LODER, JOHN DE VERE
Cofyn, Cornelius	SAUNDERS, HILARY ADAM ST. GEORGE
Coghlan, Peggie	COGHLAN, MARGARET M.
Coghlan, Peggie	STIRLING, JESSICA
Cole, Jackson	HECKELMANN, CHARLES NEWMAN
Cole, Robert	SNOW, CHARLES HORACE
Coleridge, John	BINDER, OTTO OSCAR
Coles, Manning	COLES, CYRIL HENRY
Coles, Manning	MANNING, ADELAIDE FRANCES OKE
Collier, Jane	COLLIER, ZENA
Collier, Margaret	TAYLOR, MARGARET STEWART
Collins, Hunt	HUNTER, EVAN
Collins, Michael	LYNDS, DENNIS
Collins, Percy	COLLIER, PRICE
Collinson, Peter	HAMMETT, SAMUEL DASHIELL
Colson, Bill	ATHANAS, WILLIAM VERNE
Colt, Clem	NYE, NELSON CORAL
Colt, Zandra	STEVENSON, FLORENCE
Colter, Shayne	NORWOOD, VICTOR GEORGE CHARLES
Coltman, Will	BINGLEY, DAVID ERNEST
Colton, James	HANSEN, JOSEPH
Colvin, James	MOORCOCK, MICHAEL
Compton, Guy	COMPTON, DAVID GUY
Comrade, Robert W.	BROOKS, EDWY SEARLES
Comus	BALLANTYNE, ROBERT MICHAEL
Condray, Bruno	HUMPHRYS, LESLIE GEORGE
Coniston, Ed	BINGLEY, DAVID ERNEST
Connington, J. J.	STEWART, ALFRED WALTER
Connor, Kevin	O'ROURKE, FRANK
Connor, Ralph	GORDON, CHARLES WILLIAM
Connors, Bruton	ROHEN, EDWARD
Conquest, Martin	HAMILTON, CHARLES HAROLD ST. JOHN
Conquest, Owen	HAMILTON, CHARLES HAROLD ST. JOHN

PSEUDONYMS	TRUE NAMES
Conrad, Brenda	BROWN, ZENITH
Conrad, Gregg	GRAHAM, ROGER PHILLIPS
Conrad, Joseph	KORZENIOWSKI, TEODOR
Constant, Stephen	DANEFF, STEPHEN CONSTANTINE
Conway, Celine	BLAIR, KATHRYN
Conway, E. Carolyn	KERMOND, EVELYN CAROLYN CONWAY
Conway, Laura	ANSLE, DOROTHY PHOEBE
Conway, Troy	AVALLONE, MICHAEL ANGELO, JR.
Cook, Lennox	COOK, JOHN LENNOX
Cook, Lyn	WADDELL, EVELYN MARGARET
Cooke, Arthur	LOWNDES, ROBERT AUGUSTINE WARD
Cooke, John Estes	BAUM, LYMAN FRANK
Cooke, M. E.	CREASEY, JOHN
Cooke, Margaret	CREASEY, JOHN
Coole, W. W	KULSKI, W. W.
Coolidge, Susan	WOOLSEY, SARAH CHAUNCY
Coombs, Murdo	DAVIS, FREDERICK CLYDE
Cooper, Henry St. John	CREASEY, JOHN
Cooper, Jeff	FOX, GARDNER FRANCIS
Cooper, Jefferson	FOX, GARDNER FRANCIS
Cooper, William	HOFF, HARRY SUMMERFIELD
Copeland	COLLINS, MICHAEL DALE
Corbett, Chan	SCHACHNER, NATHAN
Corbin, Michael	CARTMILL, CLEVE
Corby, Dan	CATHERALL, ARTHUR
Cord, Barry	GERMANO, PETER B.
Cordell, Alexander	GRABER, GEORGE ALEXANDER
Corelli, Marie	MACKAY, MARY
Corley, Ernest	BULMER, HENRY KENNETH
Cornish, F.	BRYNING, FRANCIS BERTRAM
Corren, Grace	HOSKINS, ROBERT
Correy, Lee	STINE, GEORGE HARRY
Corrigan, Mark	LEE, NORMAN
Corteen, Wes	NORWOOD, VICTOR GEORGE CHARLES
Corvo, Baron Frederick	ROLFE, FREDERICK
Cory, Desmond	MC CARTHY, SHAUN LLOYD

PSEUDONYMS	TRUE NAMES
Costello, P. F.	GRAHAM, ROGER PHILLIPS
Cotton, John	FEARN, JOHN RUSSELL
Cough, J. R.	YEUR, VICTOR OLIVER
Court, Sharon	ROWLAND, DONALD SYDNEY
Cowper, Richard	MURRY, COLIN MIDDLETON
Craddock, Charles Egbert	MURFREE, MARY NOAILLES
Craig, Alisa	MAC LEOD, CHARLOTTE MATILDA
Craig, Brian	STABLEFORD, BRIAN MICHAEL
Craig, John Eland	CHIPPERFIELD, JOSEPH EUGENE
Craig, Jonathan	POSNER, RICHARD
Craig, M. S.	CRAIG, MARY FRANCIS
Craig, Vera	ROWLAND, DONALD SYDNEY
Craille, Wesley	ROWLAND, DONALD SYDNEY
Crane, Robert	ROBERTSON, FRANK CHESTER
Crawford, Robert	RAE, HUGH CRAWFORD
Crayon, Geoffrey	IRVING, WASHINGTON
Crecy, Jeanne	WILLIAMS, DOROTHY JEANNE
Creighton, Don	DRURY, MAXINE COLE
Crisp, Tony	CRISP, ANTHONY THOMAS
Crispin, Edmund	MONTGOMERY, ROBERT BRUCE
Crom A Boo	M'DONNELL, BODKIN M.
Crompton, Richmal	LAMBURN, RICHMAL CROMPTON
Cromwell, Elsie	LEE, ELSIE
Cross, Amanda	HEILBRUN, CAROLYN GOLD
Cross, Brenda	COLLOMS, BRENDA
Cross, James	PARRY, HUGH JONES
Cross, Polton	FEARN, JOHN RUSSELL
Cross, Stewart	DRAGO, HARRY SINCLAIR
Cross, Victor	COFFMAN, VIRGINIA EDITH
Crowe, John	LYNDS, DENNIS
Crowfield, Christopher	STOWE, HARRIET BEECHER
Crowther, Brian	GRIERSON, EDWARD DOBBYN
Crumarums	CRUMB, R.
Cullingford, Guy	TAYLOR, CONSTANCE LINDSAY
Culver, Kathryn	DRESSER, DAVIS
Culver, Timothy J.	WESTLAKE, DONALD EDWIN

PSEUDONYMS	TRUE NAMES
Cum, R.	CRUMB, R.
Cunningham, Cathy	CUNNINGHAM, CHET
Cunningham, E. V.	FAST, HOWARD MELVIN
Curry, Avon	BOWDEN, JEAN
Curtin, Philip	LOWNDES, MARIE ADELAIDE BELLOC
Curtis, Peter	LOFTS, NORAH
Curtis, Tom	PENDOWER, JACQUES
Curtis, Wade	POURNELLE, JERRY EUGENE
Curtis, Will	NUNN, WILLIAM CURTIS
Curzon, Lucia	STEVENSON, FLORENCE
Dace, Tish	DACE, LETITIA
Daedalus	BRAMESCO, NORTON J.
Daemer, Will	MC ILWAIN, DAVID
Daemer, Will	MILLER, BILL
Daemer, Will	WADE, ROBERT
D'Allard, Hunter	BALLARD, WILLIS TODHUNTER
Dallas, John	DUNCAN, WILLIAM MURDOCH
Dalton, Priscilla	AVALLONE, MICHAEL ANGELO, JR.
Daly, Maureen	MC GIVERN, MAUREEN DALY
Dancer, J. B.	HARVEY, JOHN B.
Dane, Clemence	ASHTON, WINIFRED
Dane, Mark	AVALLONE, MICHAEL ANGELO, JR.
Dane, Mary	MORLAND, NIGEL
Danforth, Paul M.	ALLEN, JOHN E.
Dangerfield, Clint	NORWOOD, VICTOR GEORGE CHARLES
Daniell, David Scott	DANIELL, ALBERT SCOTT
Daniels, John S.	OVERHOLSER, WAYNE D.
Daniels, Max	GELLIS, ROBERTA LEAH
Daniels, Norman	LEE, ELSIE
Danton, Rebecca	ROBERTS, JANET LOUISE
Darby, Catherine	PETERS, MAUREEN
Darby, J. N.	GOVAN, CHRISTINE NOBLE
D'Arcy, Pamela	ROBY, MARY LINN
Dare, Evelyn	EVERETT-GREEN, EVELYN

PSEUDONYMS	TRUE NAMES
Dark, Johnny	NORWOOD, VICTOR GEORGE CHARLES
Darrich, Sybah	DI PRIMA, DIANE
Davey, Jocelyn	RAPHAEL, CHAIM
Davie-Martin, Hugh	MC CUTCHEON, HUGH
Davies, P. C. W	DAVIES, PAUL
Daviot, Gordon	MACKINTOSH, ELIZABETH
Davis, Don	DRESSER, DAVIS
Davis, Robert Hart	WHITTINGTON, HARRY
Dawlish, Peter	KERR, JAMES LENNOX
Dawson, Elizabeth	GEACH, CHRISTINE
Dawson, Peter	FAUST, FREDERICK SCHILLLER
Dawson, Peter	GLIDDEN, JONATHAN H.
Dean, Dudley	MC GAUGHY, DUDLEY DEAN
Deane, Norman	CREASEY, JOHN
Debrett, Hal	DRESSER, DAVIS
Debrett, Hal	ROLLINS, KATHLEEN
Decolta, Ramon	WHITFIELD, RAOUL
De Crespigny, Charles	WILLIAMSON, ALICE MURIEL
De Crespigny, Charles	WILLIAMSON, CHARLES NORRIS
Deer, M. J.	SMITH, GEORGE HENRY
Deighton, Len	DEIGHTON, LEONARD CYRIL
Deitrich, Robert	HUNT, HOWARD
De Kiriline, Louise	LAWRENCE, LOUISE DE KIRILINE
Dekker, Carl	LYNDS, DENNIS
Delafield, E. M.	DE LA PASTURE, EDMEE ELIZABETH MONICA
De La Guard, Theodore	WARD, NATHANIEL
Del Alvarez-Rey, Lester	ALVAREZ-DEL RAY, RAMON FELIPE SAN JUAN MARIO SILVIO ENRICO
Delaney, Denis	GREEN, PETER
Delaney, John	ROWLAND, DONALD SYDNEY
De La Torre, Lillian	MC CUE, LILLIAN BUENO
De Lima, Sigrid	GREENE, SIGRID
Dell, Belinda	BOWDEN, JEAN
Del Martia, Astron	FEARN, JOHN RUSSELL

PSEUDONYMS	TRUE NAMES
Del Rey, Lester	ALVAREZ-DEL REY, RAMON FELIPE SAN JUAN MARIO SILVIO ENRICO
Del Rey, Lester	FAIRMAN, PAUL W.
Del Valley-Pena, Ramon	DEL VALLE-INCLAN, RAMON
Delving, Michael	WILLIAMS, JAY
Demaris, Ovid	DESMARAIS, OVIDE E.
Demijohn, Thom	DISCH, THOMAS MICHAEL
Demijohn, Thom	SLADEK, JOHN THOMAS
Deming, Kirk	DRAGO, HARRY SINCLAIR
De Natale, Francine	MALZBERG, BARRY NORMAN
Denholm, Mark	FEARN, JOHN RUSSELL
Dentinger, Stephen	HOCH, EDWARD DENTINGER
Denver, Drake C.	NYE, NELSON CORAL
Denver, Rod	EDSON, JOHN THOMAS
De Pre, Jean-Anne	AVALLONE, MICHAEL ANGELO, JR.
Derrick, Lionel	CUNNINGHAM, CHET
De Saint-Luc, Jean	GLASSCO, JOHN
De Savallo, Dona Teresa	WILLIAMSON, ALICE MURIEL
De Savallo, Dona Teresa	WILLIAMSON, CHARLES NORRIS
Destry, Vince	NORWOOD, VICTOR GEORGE CHARLES
Deveraux, Jude	WHITE, JUDE GILLIAM
De Vere, Jane	WATSON, JULIA
De Vere Beauclerk, Helen	BELLINGHAM, HELEN MARY DOROTHEA
Devine, Dominic	DEVINE, DAVID MC DONALD
Devon, Sarah	WALKER, EMILY KATHLEEN
De Weese, Gene	DE WEESE, THOMAS EUGENE
De Weese, Jean	DE WEESE, THOMAS EUGENE
De White, Joselyn	TOOMBS, JOHN
Dexter, John	BRADLEY, MARION ZIMMER
Dexter, Martin	FAUST, FREDERICK SCHILLER
Dexter, Peter	SHAVER, RICHARD SHARPE
Dey, Marmaduke	DEY, FREDERIC MERRILL VAN RENSSELAER
Di Bassetto, Corns	SHAW, GEORGE BERNARD
Dickinson, Margaret	MUGGESON, MARGARET ELIZABETH
Dickson, Carr	CARR, JOHN DICKSON

PSEUDONYMS	TRUE NAMES
Dickson, Carter	CARR, JOHN DICKSON
Di Guisa, Giano	PRAZ, MARIO
Dillard, James	SNOW, CHARLES HORACE
Dimont, Penelope	MORTIMER, PENELOPE
Dinesen, Isak	BLIXEN, KAREN
Dix, Dorothy	GILMER, ELIZABETH MERIWETHER
Dixon, Frank W.	ADAMS, HARRIET STRATEMEYER
Dixon, Franklin	ADAMS, HARRIET STRATEMEYER
Dixon, Paige	CORCORAN, BARBARA
Docherty, James L.	RAYMOND, RENE BARBAZON
Dogg, Professor R. L.	BERMAN, ED
Dollar, Jimmy	SHAGINYAN, MARIETTA SERGEYEVNA
Dominic, Sister Mary	PARKER, MARION DOMINICA HOPE
Dominic, R. B.	HENNISSART, MARTHA
Dominic, R. B.	LATIS, MARY J.
Domino, John	AVERILL, ESTHER HOLDEN
Donalds, Gordon	SHIRREFFS, GORDON DONALD
Donavan, John	MORLAND, NIGEL
Donovan, Dick	MUDDOCK, JOYCE EMMERSON PRESTON
Dooley, Martin	DUNNE, PETER FINLEY
Dorman, Luke	BINGLEY, DAVID ERNEST
Dorset, Richard	SHAVER, RICHARD SHARPE
Dorsett, Danielle	DANIELS, DOROTHY
Douglas, Albert	ARMSTRONG, DOUGLAS ALBERT
Douglas, Arthur	MORETON, DOUGLAS ARTHUR
Douglas, Barbara	OVSTEDAL, BARBARA
Douglas, Michael	BRIGHT, ROBERT
Douglas, Michael	CRICHTON, DOUGLAS
Douglas, Michael	CRICHTON, JOHN MICHAEL
Douglas, R. M.	MASON, DOUGLAS RANKINE
Douglas, Thorne	HAAS, BENJAMIN LEOPOLD
Dowdy, Mrs. Regera	GOREY, EDWARD ST. JOHN
Dower, Penn	PENDOWER, JACQUES
Dowley, D. M.	MARRISON, LESLIE WILLIAM
Downes, Quentin	HARRISON, MICHAEL

PSEUDONYMS	**TRUE NAMES**
Doyle, Mike	DOYLE, CHARLES
Draco, F.	DAVIS, JULIA
Dragonet	SIMS, GEORGE R.
Drake, Joan	DAVIES, JOAN H.
Draper, Hastings	JEFFRIES, RODERIC
Drew, Nicholas	HARLING, ROBERT
Drinkrow, John	HARDWICK, MOLLIE
Droch	BRIDGES, ROBERT
Drummond, Charles	GILES, KENNETH
Drummond, Ivor	LONGRIGG, ROGER ERSKINE
Drummond, J.	CHANCE, JOHN NEWTON
Drummond, V. H.	SWETENHAM, MRS. ANTHONY
Drummond, Violet Hilda	SWETENHAM, MRS. ANTHONY
Dryden, John	ROWLAND, DONALD SYDNEY
Dryden, Lennox	STEEN, MARGUERITE
Dubois, Charles	COUNSELMAN, MARY ELIZABETH
Dubois, M.	KENT, ARTHUR
Dudley, Helen	HOPE-SIMPSON, JACYNTH
Dudley, Nancy	TAYLOR, LOIS DWIGHT
Dudley-Gordon, Tom	BARKER, DUDLEY
Dudley-Gordon, Tom	CAMPBELL, GORDON
Dudley-Gordon, Tom	GUTHRIE, TOM
Dudley-Smith, T.	TREVOR, ELLESTON
Duka, Ivo	DUCHACEK, IVO D.
Duke, Will	GAULT, WILLIAM CAMPBELL
Dumas, Claudine	MALZBERG, BARRY NORMAN
Duncan, Alex	DUKE, MADELAINE
Duncan, Duke	RATHBONE, ST. GEORGE HENRY
Duncan, W. R.	DUNCAN, MR. AND MRS. ROBERT L.
Dunsany, Lord	PLUNKETT, EDWARD JOHN MORETON DRAK
Duplex	BRADLEY, IAN
Duplex	HALLOWS, N. F.
Dupont, Paul	FREWIN, LESLIE
Durham, Anne	WALKER, EMILY KATHLEEN
Durham, David	VICKERS, ROY C.

PSEUDONYMS	TRUE NAMES
Durrant, Sheila	GROVES, SHEILA
Durrant, Theo	WHITE, WILLIAM ANTHONY PARKER
Dustin, Charles	GIESY, JOHN ULRICH
Duval, Jeanne	COFFMAN, VIRGINIA EDITH
Du Vaul, Virginia C.	COFFMAN, VIRGINIA EDITH
Dwight, Allan	TAYLOR, LOIS DWIGHT
Dwyer, K. R.	KOONTZ, DEAN RAY
Dykes, Jack	OWEN, JACK
Dymoke, Juliet	DE SCHANSCHIEFF, JULIET DYMOKE
E. V. L.	LUCAS, E. V.
E. W. H.	HORNUNG, ERNEST WILLIAM
Eaglesfield, Francis	GUIRDHAM, ARTHUR
Earle, William	JOHNS, WILLIAM EARLE
Earp, Virgil	KEEVIL, HENRY JOHN
East, Michael	WEST, MORRIS
Easton, Edward	MALERICH, EDWARD P.
Eastway, Edward	THOMAS, EDWARD
Edgar, Josephine	MUSSI, MARY
Edginton, May	EDGINTON, HELEN MARION
Edmonds, Charles	CARRINGTON, CHARLES EDMUND
Edmondson, G. C.	COTTON, JOSE MARIO GARRY ORDONEZ EDMONDSON
Edwards, Norman	CARR, TERRY GENE
Edwards, Norman	WHITE, THEODORE EDWIN
Edwards, Phoebe	BLOCH, BARBARA
Edwards, Samuel	GERSON, NOEL
Egan, Lesley	LININGTON, BARBARA ELIZABETH
Egbert, H. M.	EMANUEL, VICTOR ROUSSEAU
Eisner, Simon	KORNBLUTH, CYRIL M.
Elder, Art	MONTGOMERY, RUTHERFORD GEORGE
Elder, Evelyn	BURGE, MILWARD RODON KENNEDY
Eldershaw, M. Barnard	BARNARD, MARJORIE FAITH
Eldershaw, M. Barnard	ELDERSHAW, FLORA SYDNEY PATRICIA
El Dnomyar, Evreh Eniatnof	LE FONTAINE, JOSEPH RAYMOND HERVE

PSEUDONYMS	TRUE NAMES
Elgin, Mary	STEWART, DOROTHY MARY
Elia	LAMB, CHARLES
Eliot, Anne	TAYLOR, LOIS DWIGHT
Eliot, George	EVANS, MARIAN OR MARY ANN
Elizabeth	RUSSELL, COUNTESS MARY ANNETTTE VON ARNIM BEAUCHAMP
Ellanby, Boyd	BOYD, WILLIAM C.
Elliot, Asa	BLINDER, ELLIOT
Ellis, Louise	WALKER, EMILY KATHLEEN
Ellis, Olivia	FRANCIS, ANNE
Elphinstone, Francis	POWELL-SMITH, VINCENT
Elsna, Hebe	ANSLE, DOROTHY PHOEBE
Elson, R. N.	NELSON, RADELL FARADAY
Embey, Philip	PHILIPP, ELLIOT ELIAS
Emsley, Clare	PLUMMER, CLARE EMSLEY
English, Richard	SHAVER, RICHARD SHARPE
Engren, Edith	MC CAIG, ROBERT JESSE
Ericson, Walter	FAST, HOWARD MELVIN
Ermine, Will	DRAGO, HARRY SINCLAIR
Erskine, Margaret	WILLIAMS, MARGARET WETHERBY
Erskine, Rosalind	LONGRIGG, ROGER ERSKINE
Esmond, Harriet	BURGE, MILWARD RODON KENNEDY
Esohg, Lama	GHOSE, AMAL
Essex, Mary	BLOOM, URSULA HARVEY
Estevan, John	SHELLABARGER, SAMUEL
Estoril, Jean	ALLAN, MABEL ESTHER
Eton, Robert	MEYNELL, LAURENCE WALTER
Euphan	TODD, BARBARA EUPHAN
Eustace, Robert	BARTON, EUSTACE ROBERT
Evan, Paul	LEHMAN, PAUL EVAN
Evans, Evan	FAUST, FREDERICK SCHILLER
Evans, Evan	STOKER, ALAN
Evans, Frances	CARTER, FRANCES MONET
Evans, Tabor	KNOTT, WILLIAM S.
Evans, Tabor	WHITTINGTON, HARRY
Everett, Wade	COOK, WILLIAM EVERETT

PSEUDONYMS	TRUE NAMES
Everett, Wade	LUTZ, GILES ALFRED
Ewing, Frederick R.	WALDO, EDWARD HAMILTON
Excellent, Matilda	FARSON, DANIEL NEGLEY
Eyre, Annette	WORBOYS, ANNETTE ISOBEL
F. O. O.	STREET, CECIL JOHN CHARLES
Fabrizius, Peter	FABRY, JOSEPH B.
Fair, A. A.	GARDNER, ERLE STANLEY
Fairbairn, Roger	CARR, JOHN DICKSON
Faire, Zabrina	STEVENSON, FLORENCE
Fairfield, John	LIVINGSTONE, HARRISON EDWARD
Falk, Lee	COPPER, BASIL
Falkirk, Richard	LAMBERT, DEREK
Fallon, George	BINGLEY, DAVID ERNEST
Fallon, Martin	PATTERSON, HENRY
Falstaff, Jake	FETZER, HERMAN
Family Doctor, A	HUTCHIN, KENNETH CHARLES
Farely, Alison	POLAND, DOROTHY
Fargo, Doone	NORWOOD, VICTOR GEORGE CHARLES
Farley, Ralph Milne	HOAR, ROGER SHERMAN
Farndale, James	FARNDALE, W. A. J.
Farquharson, Martha	FINLEY, MARTHA F.
Farr, John	WEBB, JACK
Farrell, Ben	CEBULASH, MEL
Farrell, David	SMITH, FREDERICK E.
Farrell, John Wade	MACDONALD, JOHN DANN
Farrow, James S.	TUBB, EDWIN CHARLES
Farson, Negley	FARSON, DANIEL NEGLEY
Faulis, Hugh	MUNRO, NEIL
Fecamps, Elise	CREASEY, JOHN
Fecher, Constance	HEAVEN, CONSTANCE
Feikema, Feike	MANFRED, FREDERICK FEIKEMA
Fellowes, Anne	MANTLE, WINIFRED LANGFORD
Fenner, Carol	WILLIAMS, CAROL
Fenner, James R.	TUBB, EDWIN CHARLES

PSEUDONYMS	TRUE NAMES
Fenton, Freda	ROWLAND, DONALD SYDNEY
Fenton, Mark	NORWOOD, VICTOR GEORGE CHARLES
Fenwick, E. P.	WAY, ELIZABETH FENWICK
Fenwick, Elizabeth	WAY, ELIZABETH FENWICK
Ferguson, Evelyn	NEVIN, EVELYN C.
Ferguson, Helen	WOODS, HELEN
Fern, Fanny	WILLIS, SARA PAYSON
Fernandez, Happy Craven	FERNANDEZ, GLADYS CRAVEN
Ferrars, E. X.	BROWN, MORNA DORIS
Ferrars, Elizabeth	BROWN, MORNA DORIS
Ferrat, Jacques Jean	MERWIN, SAMUEL KIMBALL, JR.
Fiacc, Padraic	O'CONNOR, PATRICK JOSEPH
Field, Charles	ROWLAND, DONALD SYDNEY
Field, Frank Chester	ROBERTSON, FRANK CHESTER
Field, Gans T.	WELLMAN, MANLEY WADE
Field, Peter	MANN, EDWARD BEVERLY
Field, Peter	MINES, SAMUEL
Field, Peter	REPP, EDWARD EARL
Fielding, A.	FEILDING, DOROTHY
Fielding, A. E.	FEILDING, DOROTHY
Fielding, Gabriel	BARNSLEY, ALAN GABRIEL
Fielding, Hubert	SCHONFIELD, HUGH JOSEPH
Fielding, Xan	FIELDING, A. W.
Finch, Matthew	FINK, MERTON
Finch, Merton	FINK, MERTON
Finlay, William	MACKAY, JAMES ALEXANDER
Finn, Mickey	JARROLD, ERNEST
Finnegan, Robert	RYAN, PAUL WILLIAM
Finney, Jack	FINNEY, WALTER BRADEN
Fisher, A. E.	FISHER, EDWARD
Fisher, Clay	ALLEN, HENRY WILSON
Fisher, Steve	FISHER, STEPHEN GOULD
Fisher, Wade	NORWOOD, VICTOR GEORGE CHARLES
Fiske, Sharon	HILL, PAMELA
Fitt, Mary	FREEMAN, KATHLEEN
Fitzalan, Roger	TREVOR, ELLESTON

PSEUDONYMS	TRUE NAMES
Fitzgerald, Barbara	NEWMAN, MONA ALICE JEAN
Fitzgerald, Hugh	BAUM, LYMAN FRANK
Fitzgerald, Julia	WATSON, JULIA
Fitznoodle	VALLENTINE, B. B.
Flannery, Sean	HAGBERG, DAVID J.
Fleming, Caroline	MATHER, ANNE
Fleming, Oliver	MACDONALD, PHILIP
Fletcher, George U.	PRATT, MURRAY FLETCHER
Flying Officer X	BATES, H. E.
Flynn, Jackson	SHIRREFFS, GORDON DONALD
Foda, Ann	FOXE, ARTHUR NORMAN
Foley, Rae	DENNISTON, ELINORE
Forbes, Aleck	RATHBONE, ST. GEORGE HENRY
Forbes, D. E.	FORBES, DELORIS FLORINE STANTON
Forbes, Daniel	KENYON, MICHAEL
Ford, David	HARKNETT, TERRY WILLIAM
Ford, Elbur	HIBBERT, ELEANOR ALICE
Ford, Elizabeth	BIDWELL, MARJORY ELIZABETH SARAH
Ford, Ford Madox	HUEFFER, FORD MADOX
Ford, Hilary	YOUD, CHRISTOPHER SAMUEL
Ford, Kirk	SPENCE, WILLIAM JOHN DUNCAN
Ford, Leslie	BROWN, ZENITH
Ford, Lewis	PATTEN, LEWIS BYFORD
Ford, Norrey	DILCOCK, NOREEN
Forman, Ginny	ZACHARY, HUGH
Forrest, Allen	SNOW, CHARLES HORACE
Forrest, Felix C.	LINEBARGER, PAUL MYRON ANTHONY
Forrest, Norman	MORLAND, NIGEL
Forrester, Frank	HERBERT, HENRY WILLIAM
Forrester, Mary	HUMPHRIES, ELSIE MARY
Fosse, Alfred	JELLY, GEORGE OLIVER
Foster, George	HASWELL, CHETWYND JOHN DRAKE
Foster, Iris	POSNER, RICHARD
Foster, Jeanne	WILLIAMS, DOROTHY JEANNE
Foster, Richard	CROSSEN, KENDALL FOSTER
Foster, Simon	GLEN, DUNCAN

PSEUDONYMS	TRUE NAMES
Foulds, E. V.	FOULDS, ELFRIDA VIPONT
Fowler, Sydney	WRIGHT, SYDNEY FOWLER
Fox, Anthony	FULLERTON, ALEXANDER
Fox, Petronella	BALOGH, PENELOPE
Foxx, Jack	PRONZINI, BILL
Fra Elbertus	HUBBARD, ELBERT
Francis C. D. E.	HOWARTH, PATRICK
Franklin, Max	DEMING, RICHARD
Fraser, Jane	PILCHER, ROSAMUNDE
Frazer, Andrew	LESSER, MILTON
Frazer, Robert Caine	CREASEY, JOHN
Frazier, Arthur	BULMER, HENRY KENNETH
Frederic, Mike	COX, WILLIAM ROBERT
Frederick, John	BURGE, MILWARD RODON KENNEDY
Frederick, John	FAUST, FREDERICK SCHILLLER
Fredricks, Dr. Frank	FRANCK, FREDERICK
Freeman, Cynthia	FEINBERG, BEA
Freeman, Thomas	FEHRENBACH, T. R.
French, Ashley	ROBINS, DENISE NAOMI
French, Paul	ASIMOV, ISAAC
Freyer, Fredric	BALLINGER, WILLIAM SANBORN
Frick, C. H.	IRWIN, CONSTANCE
Friedman, Elias	FRIEDMAN, JACOB HORACE
Friedman, John	FRIEDMAN, JACOB HORACE
Friend, Ed	WORMSER, RICHARD EDWARD
Frome, David	BROWN, ZENITH
Frost, Frederick	FAUST, FREDERICK SCHILLER
Froy, Herald	DEGHY, GUY
Froy, Herald	WATERHOUSE, KEITH
Furey, Michael	WARD, ARTHUR HENRY SARSFIELD
G. K. C.	CHESTERTON, GILBERT KEITH
Gade, Henry	PALMER, RAYMOND A.
Gage, Wilson	STEELE, MARY QUINTARD
Gainham, Sarah	AMES, SARAH RACHEL

PSEUDONYMS	TRUE NAMES
Gaite, Francis	COLES, CYRIL HENRY
Gaite, Francis	MANNING, ADELAIDE FRANCIS OKE
Galaxan, Sol	COPPEL, ALFRED
Galway, Robert Conington	MC CUTCHAN, DONALD PHILIP
Gant, Richard	FREEMANTLE, BRIAN
Gard, Janice	REEVES, JOYCE
Gard, Joyce	REEVES, JOYCE
Garden, Bruce	MACKAY, JAMES ALEXANDER
Gardner, Jeffrey	FOX, GARDNER FRANCIS
Gardner, Miriam	BRADLEY, MARION ZIMMER
Garland, Bennett	GARFIELD, BRIAN FRANCIS WYNNE
Garland, George	ROARK, GARLAND
Garner, Graham	ROWLAND, DONALD SYDNEY
Garner, Rolf	BERRY, BRYAN
Garnett, Mary Clew	HAINS, T. JENKINS
Garnett, Roger	MORLAND, NIGEL
Garrett, Gordon	GARRETT, RANDALL PHILLIP
Garth, Will	KUTTNER, HENRY
Garve, Andrew	WINTERTON, PAUL
Gasciogne, Marguerite	LAZARUS, MARGUERITE
Gash, Jonathan	GRANT, JOHN
Gast, Kelly P.	COTTON, JOSE MARIO GARRY ORDONEZ EDMONDSON
Gaston, Bill	GASTON, WILLIAM JAMES
Gay, Amelia	HOGARTH, GRACE
Gayle, Emma	FAIRBURN, ELEANOR
Gearing-Thomas, G.	NORWOOD, VICTOR GEORGE CHARLES
George, Eliot	FREEMAN, GILLIAN
George, Eugene	CHEVALIER, PAUL EUGENE GEORGE
George, Jonathan	BURGE, MILWARD RODON KENNEDY
Gibb, Lee	DEGHY, GUY
Gibb, Lee	WATERHOUSE, KEITH
Gibbons, Margaret	MACGILL, MRS. PATRICK MARGARET
Gibbs, Henry	RUMBOLD-GIBBS, HENRY ST. JOHN CLAIR
Gibbs, Mary Ann	BIDWELL, MARJORY ELIZABETH SARAH

PSEUDONYMS	TRUE NAMES
Gibson, Charles	GARVICE, CHARLES
Gibson, Josephine	JOSLIN, SESLYE
Gilbert, Anna	LAZARUS, MARGUERITE
Gilbert, Anthony	MALLESON, LUCY BEATRICE
Gilbert, Manu	WEST, JOYCE
Gilbert, Sister Mary	DE FREES, MADELINE
Gilbert, Miriam	PRESBURG, MIRIAM
Gilbert, Nan	GILBERTSON, MILDRED
Gill, Patrick	CREASEY, JOHN
Gillen, Lucy	STRATTON, REBECCA
Gillette, Bob	SHAW, BYNUM G.
Gilman, George G.	HARKNETT, TERRY WILLIAMS
Gilman, Robert Cham	COPPEL, ALFRED
Gilmore, Anthony	BATES, HIRAM GILMORE, III
Giovanni, Nicki	GIOVANNI, YOLANDE C.
Gissing, George	GLOUSTON, J. STORER
Glamis, Walter	SCHACHNER, NATHAN
Glaser, Comstock	GLASER, KURT
Glen, Duncan	MUNRO, RONALD EADIE
Goaman, Muriel	COX, EDITH MURIEL
Godey, John	FREEDGOOD, MORTON
Godfrey, William	YOUD, CHRISTOPHER SAMUEL
Goforth, Ellen	FRANCIS, DOROTHY BRENNER
Goldstone, A.	GOLDSTONE, LAWRENCE ARTHUR
Goodwin, Suzanne	EBEL, SUZANNE
Gordon, Bill	ATHANAS, WILLIAM VERNE
Gordon, David	GARRETT, RANDALL PHILLIP
Gordon, Diana	ANDREWS, LUCILLA MATHEW
Gordon, Donald	PAYNE, DONALD GORDON
Gordon, Fritz	JARVIS, FREDERICK G. H.
Gordon, Jane	LEE, ELSIE
Gordon, Katharine	PEARSON, KATHARINE
Gordon, Lew	BALDWIN, GORDON CURTIS
Gordon, Ray	WAINWRIGHT, JOHN
Gordon, Rex	HOUGH, STANLEY BENNETT
Gordon, Stewart	SHIRREFFS, GORDON DONALD

PSEUDONYMS	TRUE NAMES
Gordon, Stuart	GORDON, RICHARD
Gordons, The	GORDON, GORDON
Gordons, The	GORDON, MILDRED
Gorham, Michael	FOLSOM, FRANKLIN BREWSTER
Gorky or Gorki, Maxim	PESHKOV, ALEXI MAXIMOVITCH
Gorman, Ginny	ZACHARY, HUGH
Gorsline, S. M.	GORSLINE, MARIE
Goryan, Sirak	SAROYAN, WILLIAM
Gottesman, S. D.	LOWNDES, ROBERT AUGUSTINE WARD
Gould, Alan	CANNING, VICTOR
Gould, Stephen	FISHER, STEPHEN GOULD
Graaf, Peter	YOUD, CHRISTOPHER SAMUEL
Graduate of Oxford, A	RUSKIN, JOHN
Grady, Tex	WEBB, JACK
Graeme, Bruce	JEFFRIES, GRAHAM MONTAGUE
Graeme, David	JEFFRIES, GRAHAM MONTAGUE
Graeme, Roderic	JEFFRIES, RODERIC
Graham, Charles S.	TUBB, EDWIN CHARLES
Graham, Ennis	MOLESWORTH, MARY LOUISA
Graham, James	PATTERSON, HENRY
Graham, Neill	DUNCAN, WILLIAM MURDOCH
Graham, Robert	HALDEMAN, JOE WILLIAM
Graham, Tom	LEWIS, HARRY SINCLAIR
Granados, Paul	KENT, ARTHUR
Grandower, Elissa	WAUGH, HILLARY BALDWIN
Grange, Peter	NICOLE, CHRISTOPHER ROBIN
Granite, Tony	POLITELLA, DARIO
Grant, Ambrose	RAYMOND, RENE BARBAZON
Grant, Anthony	PARES, MARION STAPYLTON
Grant, Jonathan	ADAMS, CLIFTON
Grant, Landon	GRIBBLE, LEONARD REGINALD
Grant, Margaret	FRANKEN, ROSE DOROTHY
Grant, Maxwell	GIBSON, WALTER B.
Grant, Maxwell	LYNDS, DENNIS
Grant, Richard	FREEMANTLE, BRIAN HARRY
Grantland, Keith	NUTT, CHARLES

PSEUDONYMS	TRUE NAMES
Graves, Valerie	BRADLEY, MARION ZIMMER
Gray, Angela	DANIELS, DOROTHY
Gray, Berkeley	BROOKS, EDWY SEARLES
Gray, Dorothy Kate	HAYNES, DOROTHY K.
Gray, Dulcie	DENISON, DULCIE WINIFRED CATHERINE
Gray, Elizabeth Janet	VINING, ELIZABETH GRAY
Gray, Ellington	JACOB, NAOMI ELLINGTON
Gray, Harriet	ROBINS, DENISE NAOMI
Gray, Jane	EVANS, CONSTANCE MAY
Gray, Russell	FISCHER, BRUNO
Gray, Zane	GRAY, PEARL ZANE
Grayson, David	BAKER, RAY STANNARD
Great Merlini, The	RAWSON, CLAYTON
Greaves, Richard	MC CUTCHEON, GEORGE BARR
Green, Charles M.	GARDNER, ERLE STANLEY
Greenwood, Grace	LIPPINCOTT, SARA JANE
Greenwood, Ted	GREENWOOD, EDWARD ALISTER
Greer, Francesca	JANAS, FRANKIE-LEE
Greer, Richard	GARRETT, RANDALL PHILLIP
Gregory, John	HOSKINS, ROBERT
Gregory, Sebastian Largo	LE FONTAINE, JOSEPH RAYMOND HERVE
Gregory, Stephen	PENDLETON, DONALD EUGENE
Greig, Charles	CRUICKSHANK, CHARLES GREIG
Greig, Maysie	GREIG-SMITH, JENNIFER
Grendon, Stephen	DERLETH, AUGUST WILLIAM
Grenville, Pelham	WODEHOUSE, PELHAM GRENVILLE
Grex, Leo	GRIBBLE, LEONARD REGINALD
Grey, Belinda	PETERS, MAUREEN
Grey, Brenda	MACKINLAY, LEILA ANTOINETTE STERLING
Grey, Carol	LOWNDES, ROBERT AUGUSTINE WARD
Grey, Charles	TUBB, EDWIN CHARLES
Grey, Georgina	ROBY, MARY LINN
Grey, Louis	GRIBBLE, LEONARD REGINALD
Grey, Zane	GRAY, PEARL ZANE

PSEUDONYMS	TRUE NAMES
Grey Owl (Washaquonasin)	BELANEY, ARCHIBALD STANSFIELD
Gridban, Volsted	FEARN, JOHN RUSSELL
Gridban, Volsted	TUBB, EDWIN CHARLES
Grieve, C. M.	MACDIARMID, HUGH
Griff, Alan	SUDDABY, DONALD
Griffin, Andrew	HECKELMANN, CHARLES NEWMAN
Griffin, David	MAUGHAM, ROBERT CECIL ROMER
Griffin, Jonathan	GRIFFIN, ROBERT JOHN THURLOW
Griffith, George	GRIFFITH-JONES, GEORGE CHETWYND
Grile, Dod	BIERCE, AMBROSE
Grinnell, David	WOLLHEIM, DONALD ALLEN
Grode, Redway	GOREY, EDWARD ST. JOHN
Groener, Carl	LOWNDES, ROBERT AUGUSTINE WARD
Grove, Frederick Philip	GREVE, FELIX PAUL BERTHOLD FRIEDRICH
Grover, Marshall	MEARS, LEONARD F.
Groves, Georgina	SYMONS, DOROTHY GERALDINE
Gulick, Bull	GULICK, GROVER C.
Gunn, Victor	BROOKS, EDWY SEARLES
Gwendolyn, Jacob Tonson	BENNETT, ARNOLD
H. B.	BELLOC, HILAIRE
H. D.	DOOLITTLE, HILDA
H. F. E.	EVERETT-GREEN, EVELYN
H. H.	JACKSON, HELEN HUNT
Haddon, Christopher	PALMER, JOHN LESLIE
Hagar, Judith	POLEY, JUDITH ANNE
Haggard, Paul	LONGSTREET, STEPHEN
Haggard, William	CLAYTON, RICHARD HENRY MICHAEL
Hagon, Priscilla	ALLAN, MABEL ESTHER
Hale, Michael	BULLOCK, MICHAEL
Haliburton, Hugh	ROBERTSON, JAMES LOGIE
Hall, Adam	TREVOR, ELLESTON
Hall, Aylmer	HALL, NORAH E. L.
Hall, Evan	HALLERAN, EUGENE EDWARDS

PSEUDONYMS	TRUE NAMES
Hall, Claudia	FLOREN, LEE
Hall, Holworthy	PORTER, HAROLD EVERETT
Hall, John Ryder	ROTSLER, WILLIAM
Hall, O. M.	HALL, OAKLEY MAXWELL
Hallard, Peter	CATHERALL, ARTHUR
Haller, Bill	BECHKO, PEGGY ANNE
Halliday, Brett	DRESSER, DAVIS
Halliday, Dorothy	DUNNETT, DOROTHY
Halliday, Michael	CREASEY, JOHN
Halls, Geraldine	JAY, GERALDINE MARY
Hamill, Ethel	WEBB, JEAN FRANCIS
Hamilton, Clive	LEWIS, CLIVE STAPLES
Hamilton, Gail	DODGE, MARY ABAGAIL
Hamilton, Hervey	ROBINS, DENISE NAOMI
Hamilton, Julia	WATSON, JULIA
Hamilton, Priscilla	GELLIS, ROBERTA LEAH
Hamilton, Wade	FLOREN, LEE
Hamilton, William	CANAWAY, W. H.
Hammond, Jane	POLAND, DOROTHY
Hammond, Ralph	INNES, RALPH HAMMOND
Hampton, Mark	NORWOOD, VICTOR GEORGE CHARLES
Hannon, Ezra	HUNTER, EVAN
Harbison, Robert	BRYANS, ROBERT HARBISON
Hard Pan	BONNER, GERALDINE
Hardin, Clement	NEWTON, DWIGHT BENNETT
Harding, George	RAUBENHEIMER, GEORGE HARDING
Harding, Matthew Whitman	FLOREN, LEE
Harding, Todd	REYNOLDS, DALLAS MC CORD
Harding, Wes	KEEVIL, HENRY JOHN
Hardy, Adam	BULMER, HENRY KENNETH
Hardy, Laura	HOLLAND, SHEILA
Hardy, Russ	SNOW, CHARLES HORACE
Hare, Cyril	CLARK, ALFRED ALEXANDER GORDON
Hargrave, Leonie	DISCH, THOMAS MICHAEL
Harlan, Glen	CEBULASH, MEL
Harland, Marion	TERHUNE, MARY VIRGINIA

PSEUDONYMS	TRUE NAMES
Harle, Elizabeth	ROBERTS, IRENE
Harley, John	MARSH, JOHN
Harlow, John	SNOW, CHARLES HORACE
Harman, Jane	HARKNETT, TERRY WILLIAMS
Harper, Daniel	BROSSARD, CHANDLER
Harriford, Daphne	HARRIS, MARION ROSE
Harris, Christopher	FRY, CHRISTOPHER
Harris, J. B.	HARRIS, JOHN WYNDHAM PARKES LUCAS BEYNON
Harris, Johnson	HARRIS, JOHN WYNDHAM PARKES LUCAS BEYNON
Harris, Larry Mark	GARRETT, RANDALL PHILLIP
Harrison, Bruce	PANGBORN, EDGAR
Harrison, Chip	BLOCK, LAWRENCE
Harrison, Whit	WHITTINGTON, HARRY
Harsch, Hilya	JELLY, GEORGE OLIVER
Hart, Caroline	GARVICE, CHARLES
Hart, Jon	HARVEY, JOHN B.
Harte, Marjorie	MC EVOY, MARJORIE
Harvester, Simon	RUMBOLD-GIBBS, HENRY ST. JOHN CLAIR
Harvey, Caroline	POTTER, JOANNA
Harvey, Rachel	BLOOM, URSULA HARVEY
Hastings, Graham	JEFFRIES, RODERIC
Haswell, Jock	HASWELL, CHETWYND JOHN DRAKE
Hatton, Julia	CURTIS, JULIA ANN KEMBLE
Havil, Anthony	PHILIPP, ELLIOT ELIAS
Hawk, Alex	GARFIELD, BRIAN FRANCIS WYNNE
Hawk, Alex	KELTON, ELMER
Hawk, Alex	LUTZ, GILES ALFRED
Hay, Timothy	BROWN, MARGARET WISE
Hayes, Timothy	FEARN, JOHN RUSSELL
Hayes, Timothy	RUBEL, JAMES LYON
Haygood, G. Arnold	SLAUGHTER, FRANK GILL
Hayward, Richard	KENDRICK, BAYNARD HARDWICK
Hazard, Jack	BOOTH, EDWIN

PSEUDONYMS	TRUE NAMES
Head, Matthew	CANADAY, JOHN EDWIN
Headley, Elizabeth	CAVANNA, BETTY
Healey, Ben	HEALEY, BENJAMIN JAMES
Heard, Gerald	HEARD, HENRY FITZGERALD
Heath, Sandra	WILSON, SANDRA
Heath, Sharon	RITCHIE, CLAIRE
Heath, Veronica	BLACKETT, VERONICA HEATH
Hebden, Mark	HARRIS, JOHN
Hedges, Joseph	HARKNETT, TERRY WILLIAMS
Hegan, Alice Caldwell	RICE, ALICE CALDWELL
Hegesippus	SCHONFIELD, HUGH JOSEPH
Held, Peter	VANCE, JOHN HOLBROOK
Henderson-Howat, Gerald	HOWAT, GERALD
Hennessey, Hugh	DONOVAN, JOHN
Hennessy, Max	HARRIS, JOHN
Henry, O.	PORTER, WILLIAM SIDNEY OR SYDNEY
Henry, Will	ALLEN, HENRY WILSON
Henson, Jim	HENSON, JAMES MAURY
Herald, Kathleen	PEYTON, KATHLEEN M.
Herbert, Henry K.	KNIBBS, HENRY HERBERT
Herbert, John	BRUNDAGE, JOHN HERBERT
Hermes	CANAWAY, W. H.
Hertzog, Peter	COOKE, PHILIP ST. GEORGE, III
Hervé, Joseph	LE FONTAINE, JOSEPH RAYMOND HERVE
Hervey, Raymond	LE FONTAINE, JOSEPH RAYMOND HERVE
Hext, Harrington	PHILLPOTTS, EDEN
Hicks, Eleanor	COERR, ELEANOR BEATRICE
Higgins, Jack	PATTERSON, HENRY
Highland, Dora	AVALLONE, MICHAEL ANGELO, JR.
Hildick, Wallace	HILDICK, E. W.
Hill, Alexis	CRAIG, MARY FRANCIS
Hill, Grace Livingston	HILL-LUTZ, GRACE LIVINGSTON
Hill, H. Haverstock	WALSH, JAMES MORGAN
Hill, James	JAMESON, MARGARET STROM
Hinde, Thomas	CHITTY, SIR THOMAS WILLES
Hippius, Zinaida	GIPIUS, ZINAIDA

PSEUDONYMS	TRUE NAMES
Hobart, Robert	LEE, NORMAN
Hobart, Robertson	LEE, NORMAN
Hobson, Polly	EVANS, JULIA
Hockaby, Stephen	MITCHELL, GLADYS MAUDE WINIFRED
Hodemart, Peter	AUDEMARS, PIERRE
Hodson, Arthur	NICKSON, ARTHUR THOMAS
Hofer, Peter	KORTNER, PETER
Hogarth, Charles	CREASEY, JOHN
Hogarth, John	FINNIN, MARY
Hogarth, Jr.	KENT, ROCKWELL
Holbrook, John	VANCE, JOHN HOLBROOK
Holden, Matthew	PARKINSON, ROGER
Holland, Katrin	FREYBE, HEIDI HUBERTA
Holland, Kel	WHITTINGTON, HARRY
Hollinshead, Judith	HAWTHORNE, JULIAN
Hollis, H. H.	RHAMEY, BEN
Holm, Saxe	JACKSON, HELEN HUNT
Holme, K. E.	HILL, CHRISTOPHER
Holmes, A. R.	BATES, HIRAM GILMORE, III
Holmes, Gordon	SHIEL, MATTHEW PHIPPS
Holmes, H. H.	WHITE, WILLIAM ANTHONY PARKER
Holmes, John	SOUSTER, RAYMOND
Holt, Conrad G.	FEARN, JOHN RUSSELL
Holt, Victoria	HIBBERT, ELEANOR ALICE
Holt, Tex	JOSCELYN, ARCHIE LYNN
Holton, Leonard	WIBBERLEY, LEONARD PATRICK O'CONNOR
Home, Michael	BUSH, CHARLIE CHRISTMAS
Homes, Geoffrey	MAINWARING, DANIEL
Honeyman, Brenda	CLARKE, BRENDA
Hope, Alice L.	LIGHTNER, ALICE MARTHA
Hope, Anthony	HAWKINS, SIR ANTHONY HOPE
Hope, Brian	CREASEY, JOHN
Hope, Laura Lee	ADAMS, HARRIET STRATEMEYER
Hope, Margaret	KNIGHT, ALANNA
Hope, Marion	PARKER, MARION DOMINICA HOPE

PSEUDONYMS	TRUE NAMES
Hopkins, Hiram	SELTZER, CHARLES ALDEN
Hopkins, Lightnin'	HOPKINS, SAM
Hopkins, Lyman	FOLSOM, FRANKLIN BREWSTER
Hopkinson, Tom	HOPKINSON, SIR HENRY THOMAS
Hopley, George	HOPLEY-WOOLRICH, CORNELL GEORGE
Hornung, E. W.	HORNUNG, ERNEST WILLIAM
Horsley, David	BINGLEY, DAVID ERNEST
Horton, Felix Lee	FLOREN, LEE
Houdini, Harry	WEISS, EHRICH
Houston, R. B.	RAE, HUGH CRAWFORD
Howard, Captain	SENARENS, LUIS PHILIP
Howard, Hartley	OGNALL, LEOPOLD HORACE
Howard, Jean	MACGIBBON, JEAN
Howard, Linden	MANLEY-TUCKER, AUDRIE
Howard, Mark	RIGSBY, VECHEL HOWARD
Howard, Mary	MUSSI, MARY
Howard, Vechel	RIGSBY, VECHEL HOWARD
Howard, Virginia Tier	ELLISON, VIRGINIA HOWELL
Howes, Jane	SHIRAS, WILMAR HOUSE
Hoy, Elizabeth	CONARAIN, ALICE NINA
Hubbard, Cal	HUBBARD, ELBERT
Hubbard, L. Ron	HUBBARD, LAFAYETTE RON
Huchet, Claire	BISHOP, CLAIRE HUCHET
Hudson, Jan	SMITH, GEORGE HENRY
Hudson, Jeffrey	CRICHTON, JOHN MICHAEL
Hughes, Brenda	COLLOMS, BRENDA
Hughes, Colin	CREASEY, JOHN
Hughes, Elizabeth	ZACHARY, HUGH
Hughes, Matilda	MAC LEOD, CHARLOTTE MATILDA
Hughes, Zach	ZACHARY, HUGH
Hull, Opal I.	LEHNUS, OPAL HULL
Hull, Richard	SAMPSON, RICHARD HENRY
Humphrys, Geoffrey	HUMPHRYS, LESLIE GEORGE
Hunt, Charlotte	HODGES, DORIS M.
Hunt, Clarence	HOLMAN, CLARENCE HUGH
Hunt, Francesca	HOLLAND, ISABELLE

PSEUDONYMS	TRUE NAMES
Hunt, Gill	BRUNNER, JOHN KILIAN HOUSTON
Hunt, Gill	TUBB, EDWIN CHARLES
Hunt, Harrison	BALLARD, WILLIS TODHUNTER
Hunt, Harrison	DAVIS, NORBERT
Hunt, Kyle	CREASEY, JOHN
Hunter	LUTZ, GILES ALFRED
Hunter, Elizabeth Mary Teresa	CHACE, ISOBEL
Hunter, Hall	MARSHALL, EDISON TESLA
Hunter, John	BALLARD, WILLIS TODHUNTER
Hunter, Leigh	ETCHISON, BIRDIE L.
Huston, Fran	MILLER, R. S.
Hyde, Eleanor	COWEN, FRANCES
Iams, Jack	IAMS, SAMUEL H., JR.
Iles, Bert	ROSS, ZOLA HELEN
Iles, Francis	COX, ANTHONY BERKELEY
Incogniteau, Jean-Louis	KEROUAC, JEAN-LOUIS LEBRID
Ines, Morgan	BRADLEY, MARION ZIMMER
Ingham, Daniel	LAMBOT, ISOBEL MARY
Inglis, Susan	MACKIE, DORIS
Innes, Jean	SAUNDERS, JEAN
Innes, Michael	STEWART, JOHN INNES MACKINTOSH
Inspector F	RUSSELL, WILLIAM
Irani, Merwan S.	BABA, MEHER
Ireland, Doreen	LORD, DOUGLAS
Irish, William	HOPLEY-WOOLRICH, CORNELL GEORGE
Ironquill	WARE, EUGENE FITCH
Irvin, Patrick	HOWARD, ROBERT E.
Irwin, G. H.	PALMER, RAYMOND A.
Irwin, G. H.	SHAVER, RICHARD SHARPE
Ives, John	GARFIELD, BRIAN FRANCIS WYNNE
Ives, Morgan	BRADLEY, MARION ZIMMER
Jacks, Oliver	GANDLEY, KENNETH ROYCE
Jackson, E. F.	TUBB, EDWIN CHARLES

PSEUDONYMS	TRUE NAMES
Jackson, Everatt	MUGGESON, MARGARET ELIZABETH
Jackson, Neville	GLASKIN, G. M.
Jackson, Sara	THOMAS, SARA
Jacobs, Leah	GELLIS, ROBERTA LEAH
Jacobs, T. C. H.	PENDOWER, JACQUES
Jaffa, George	WALLACE-CLARKE, GEORGE
James, Cy	WATTS, PETER CHRISTOPHER
James, Dan	SAYERS, JAMES DENISON
James, David	HAGBERG, DAVID J.
James, Dudley	CAESAR, R. D.
James, Dudley	MAYNE, WILLIAM
James, Dynely	MAYNE, WILLIAM
James, Margaret	BENNETTS, PAMELA
James, P. D.	WHITE, PHYLLIS DOROTHY
James, Phyllis Dorothy	WHITE, PHYLLIS DOROTHY
James, Will	DUFAULT, JOSEPH ERNEST NEPHTALI
James, William M.	HARKNETT, TERRY WILLIAMS
James, William M.	HARVEY, JOHN B.
Jameson, Eric	TRIMMER, ERIC J.
Janet, Lillian	O'DANIEL, JANET
Janet, Lillian	RESSLER, LILLIAN
Janifer, Laurence M.	GARRETT, RANDALL PHILLIP
Jansen, Hank	NORWOOD, VICTOR GEORGE CHARLES
Jansen, Jared	CEBULASH, MEL
Japrisot, Sebastian	ROSSI, JEAN BAPTISTE
Jason, Jerry	SMITH, GEORGE HENRY
Jason, Johnny	GLUT, DON F.
Jason, Stuart	FLOREN, LEE
Jason, Veronica	JOHNSTON, VELDA
Jay, Charlotte	JAY, GERALDINE MARY
Jay, Marion	SPALDING, RUTH
Jeake, Samuel	AIKEN, CONRAD
Jefford, Bat	BINGLEY, DAVID ERNEST
Jeffrey, William	PRONZINI, BILL
Jeffreys, J. O.	HEALEY, BENJAMIN JAMES
Jeffs, Rae	SEBLEY, FRANCES RAE

PSEUDONYMS	TRUE NAMES
Jennifer, Susan	HOSKINS, ROBERT
Jennings, Dean	FRAZEE, CHARLES STEVE
Jerome, Joseph	SEWELL, BROCARD
Jocelyn, Richard	CLUTTERBUCK, RICHARD
John, Nancy	SAWYER, JOHN
John, Nancy	SAWYER, NANCY
Johns, Avery	COUSINS, MARGARET
Johns, Foster	SELDES, GILBERT
Johns, Geoffrey	WARNER, GEOFFREY JOHN
Johns, Kenneth	BULMER, HENRY KENNETH
Johnson, A. E.	JOHNSON, ANNABELL JONES
Johnson, A. E.	JOHNSON, EDGAR RAYMOND
Johnson, Benjamin F.	RILEY, JAMES WHITCOMB
Johnson, Crockett	LEISK, DAVID JOHNSON
Johnson, Frosty	JOHNSON, FORREST B.
Johnson, Henry	HAMMOND, JOHN
Johnson, Jan	JOHNSON, PAULA JANICE
Johnson, Mel	MALZBERG, BARRY NORMAN
Johnson, Mike	SHARKEY, JOHN MICHAEL
Johnson, Sabina Thorne	THORNE, SABINA
Jones, Annabel	BRAND, MARY CHRISTIANNA MILNE
Jones, Frank	FEARN, JOHN RUSSELL
Jones, Helen	HINCKLEY, HELEN
Jones, J. Faragut	STREIB, DAN
Jones, Joanna	BURGE, MILWARD RODON KENNEDY
Jones, Luke	WATTS, PETER CHRISTOPHER
Jones, William Monarch	GUTHRIE, THOMAS ANSTEY
Jordan, Nell	BARKER, E. M.
Jorgensen, Ivar	FAIRMAN, PAUL W.
Jorgensen, Ivar	GARRETT, RANDALL PHILLIP
Jorgensen, Ivar	SILVERBERG, ROBERT
Josiah Allen's Wife	HOLLEY, MARIETTA
Judd, Cyril	MERRIL, JOSEPHINE JUDITH
Judd, Cyril M.	KORNBLUTH, CYRIL M.
Justicar	POWELL-SMITH, VINCENT
Justificus	PAPPAS, GEORGE S.

PSEUDONYMS	TRUE NAMES
Kains, Josephine	GOULART, RONALD JOSEPH
Kane, Jim	GERMANO, PETER B.
Kane, Julia	ROBINS, DENISE NAOMI
Kanto, Peter	ZACHARY, HUGH
Karol, Alexander	KENT, ARTHUR
Karta, Nat	NORWOOD, VICTOR GEORGE CHARLES
Kavan, Anna	WOODS, HELEN
Kavanagh, Paul	BLOCK, LAWRENCE
Kavanaugh, Cynthia	DANIELS, DOROTHY
Kaye, Tom	KAYE, BARRINGTON
Kearney, Julian	GOULART, RONALD JOSEPH
Keefe, Jack	LARDNER, RING
Keene, Carolyn	ADAMS, HARRIET STRATEMEYER
Keene, Faraday	JARRETT, CORA
Keene, James	COOK, WILLIAM EVERETT AND IDA
Keene, Lieutenant	RATHBONE, ST. GEORGE HENRY
Keith, Carlton	ROBERTSON, KEITH CARLTON
Keith, David	STEEGMULLER, FRANCIS
Keith, J. Kilmeny	MALLESON, LUCY BEATRICE
Kell, Joseph	WILSON, JOHN ANTHONY BURGESS
Kellow, Kathleen	HIBBERT, ELEANOR ALICE
Kelway, Christine	GWINN, CHRISTINE MARGARET
Kemp, Sarah	BUTTERWORTH, MICHAEL
Kendall, Lace	STOUTENBERG, ADRIEN
Kendrake, Carleton	GARDNER, ERLE STANLEY
Kendricks, James	FOX, GARDNER FRANCIS
Kennedy, Cody, Jr.	REESE, JOHN
Kennedy, Elliott	FOX, GARDNER FRANCIS
Kennedy, Elliott	GODFREY, LIONEL
Kennedy, Milward	BURGE, MILWARD RODON KENNEDY
Kennedy, Robert Milward	BURGE, MILWARD RODON KENNEDY
Kennedy, X. J.	KENNEDY, JOSEPH CHARLES
Kenneggy, Richard	NETTELL, RICHARD
Kenny, Charles J.	GARDNER, ERLE STANLEY
Kenny, Kathryn	KRULL, KATHLEEN
Kenny, Kevin	KRULL, KATHLEEN

PSEUDONYMS	TRUE NAMES
Kensinger, George	FICHTER, GEORGE S.
Kent, Alexander	REEMAN, DOUGLAS
Kent, David	BIRNEY, HERMAN HOFFMAN
Kent, Fortune	TOOMBS, JOHN
Kent, Helen	POLLEY, JUDITH ANNE
Kent, Kelvin	BARNES, ARTHUR KELVIN
Kent, Mallory	LOWNDES, ROBERT AUGUSTINE WARD
Kent, Pamela	BARRIE, SUSAN
Kent, Philip	BULMER, HENRY KENNETH
Kenton, Maxwell	SOUTHERN, TERRY
Kenton, Noel	CAPON, HARRY PAUL
Kenyon, Bernice	GILKYSON, BERNICE KENYON
Keppel, Charlotte	TORDAY, URSULA
Kerby, Susan	BURTON, ELIZABETH
Kern, Gregory	TUBB, EDWIN CHARLES
Kerouac, Jack	KEROUAC, JEAN-LOUIS LEBRID
Kerr, Ben	ARD, WILLIAM THOMAS
Kerr, Carole	CARR, MARGARET
Kerr, M. E.	MEAKER, MARIJANE
Kerr, Michael	HOSKINS, ROBERT
Kershaw, Peter	LUCIE-SMITH, EDWARD
Kevern, Barbara	SHEPHERD, DONALD LEE
Keverne, Richard	HOSKEN, CLIFFORD JAMES WHEELER
Kiefer, Middleton	KIEFER, WARREN
Kiefer, Middleton	MIDDLETON, HARRY
Kimbro, Jean	KIMBRO, JOHN M.
Kimbrough, Katheryn	KIMBRO, JOHN M.
Kineji, Maborushi	GIBSON, WALTER B.
King, Arthur	LAKE, KENNETH ROBERT
King, Norman A.	TRALINS, S. ROBERT
King, Paul	DRACKETT, PHIL
King, Vincent	VINSON, REX THOMAS
Kingsley, Charlotte Mary	HANSHEW, THOMAS W.
Kingston, Syd	BINGLEY, DAVID ERNEST
Kinkaid, Matt	ADAMS, CLIFTON
Kinsey, Elizabeth	CLYMER, ELEANOR

PSEUDONYMS	TRUE NAMES
Kirk, Michael	KNOX, WILLIAM
Kirke, Edmuns	GILMORE, JAMES R.
Kirtland, G. B.	SESYLE, JOSLIN
Kitt, Tamara	DE REGNIERS, BEATRICE S.
Knauff, Ellen Raphael	HARTLEY, ELLEN R.
Knickerbocker, Cholly	KELLAR, JOHN W.
Knickerbocker, Diedrich	IRVING, WASHINGTON
Knight, David	PRATHER, RICHARD SCOTT
Knight, Frank	KNIGHT, FRANCIS EDGAR
Knight, Gareth	WILBY, BASIL LEE
Knight-Patterson, W. M.	KULSKI, W. W.
Knott, Bill	KNOTT, WILLIAM S.
Knott, Will C.	KNOTT, WILLIAM S.
Knox, Bill	KNOX, WILLIAM
Knox, Calvin M.	SILVERBERG, ROBERT
Knye, Cassandra	DISCH, THOMAS MICHAEL
Knye, Cassandra	SLADEK, JOHN THOMAS
Koning, Hans	KONIGSBERG, HANS
Kosch, Erich	KOS, ERIC
Kramer, George	HEUMAN, WILLIAM
Krauss, Bruno	BULMER, HENRY KENNETH
Krin, Sylvie	FANTONI, BARRY
Kroll, Burt	ROWLAND, DONALD SYDNEY
Kruger, Paul	SEBENTHAL, ROBERTA ELIZABETH
Kyd, Thomas	HARBAGE, ALFRED BENNETT
Kyle, Duncan	BROXHOLME, JOHN
Kyle, Elisabeth	DUNLOP, AGNES M. R.
Kyle, Sefton	VICKERS, ROY C.
Lacey, Amy	AMY, WILLIAM LACEY
Lacy, Ed	ZINBERG, LEONARD S.
Ladd, Veronica	MINER, JANE CLAYPOOL
La Fayette, Rene	HUBBARD, LAFAYETTE RON
La Fontaine, Raymond	LE FONTAINE, JOSEPH RAYMOND HERVE
Laker, Rosalind	OVSTEDAL, BARBARA

PSEUDONYMS	TRUE NAMES
Lamb, Charlotte	HOLLAND, SHEILA
Lamb, William	JAMESON, MARGARET STROM
Lambert, Christinne	FREYBE, HEIDI HUBERTA
Lamont, Marianne	RUNDLE, ANNE
L'Amour, Louis	LA MOORE, LOUIS DEARBORN
Lancaster, Sheila	HOLLAND, SHEILA
Lancaster, Vicky	ANSLE, DOROTHY PHOEBE
Lance, Leslie	SWATRIDGE, IRENE MAUDE
Land, Jane	BORLAND, KATHRYN
Land, Jane	SPEICHER, HELEN ROSS
Land, Jane and Ross	BORLAND, KATHRYN
Land, Jane and Ross	SPEICHER, HELEN ROSS
Lane, Grant	FISHER, STEPHEN GOULD
Lane, Mary D.	DELANEY, MARY MURRAY
Lanf, Frances	MANTLE, WINIFRED LANGFORD
Lang, Grace	FLOREN, LEE
Lang, King	TUBB, EDWIN CHARLES
Langart, Darrel T.	GARRETT, RANDALL PHILLIP
Lange, John	CRICHTON, JOHN MICHAEL
Langford, Jane	MANTLE, WINIFRED LANGFORD
Langholm, Neil	BULMER, HENRY KENNETH
Langley, Helen	ROWLAND, DONALD SYDNEY
Langstaff, Launcelot	IRVING, WASHINGTON
Langstaff, Launcelot	PAULDING, JAMES KIRK
Lansing, Henry	ROWLAND, DONALD SYDNEY
Lant, Harvey	ROWLAND, DONALD SYDNEY
Lantern	MARQUIS, DON
Lantry, Mike	TUBB, EDWIN CHARLES
Lara	GRIFFITH-JONES, GEORGE CHETWYND
Latham, Mavis	CLARK, MAVIS THORPE
Latham, Philip	RICHARDSON, ROBERT SHIRLEY
Lathen, Emma	HENNISSART, MARTHA
Lathen, Emma	LATIS, MARY J.
Lattin, Anne	TAYLOR, LOIS DWIGHT
Lauder, George	DICK-LAUDER, SIR GEORGE
Launay, Droo	LAUNAY, ANDRE

PSEUDONYMS	TRUE NAMES
Laurie, Annie	BONFILS, MRS. CHARLES
Laurin, Anne	MC LAURIN, ANNE
Lavond, Paul Dennis	LOWNDES, ROBERT AUGUSTINE WARD
Lawless, Anthony	MACDONALD, PHILIP
Lawrence, Lesley	LEWIS, LESLEY
Lawrence, P.	TUBB, EDWIN CHARLES
Lawrence, Stephen P.	MURPHY, LAWRENCE AUGUSTUS
Lawson, Chet	TUBB, EDWIN CHARLES
Lawson, Michael	RYDER, M. L.
Lawson, Dr. Philip	TRIMMER, ERIC J.
Lawson, W. B.	JENKS, GEORGE C.
Lawton, Charles	HECKELMANN, CHARLES NEWMAN
Lea, Ed	RICHELSON, GERALDINE
Lear, Peter	LOVESEY, PETER
Leaver, Ruth	TOMALIN, RUTH
Le Cagat, Benat	WHITAKER, RODNEY
Le Carre, John	CORNWELL, DAVID JOHN MOORE
Lee, Andrew	AUCHINCLOSS, LOUIS
Lee, Edward Edson	EDWARDS, LEO
Lee, Howard	GOULART, RONALD JOSEPH
Lee, Julian	LATHAM, JEAN LEE
Lee, Matt	MERWIN, SAMUEL KIMBALL, JR.
Lee, Ranger	SNOW, CHARLES HORACE
Lee, William	BURROUGHS, WILLIAM SEWARD
Le Fontaine, J. R.	LE FONTAINE, JOSEPH RAYMOND HERVE
Le Fontaine, Ray	LE FONTAINE, JOSEPH RAYMOND HERVE
Leibenguth, Charla Ann	BANNER, CHARLA ANN LEIBENGUTH
Leigh, Roberta	LINDSAY, RACHEL
Leighton, Len	PATTEN, LEWIS BYFORD
Leinster, Murray	JENKINS, WILLIAM FITZGERALD
Lejeune, Anthony	THOMPSON, EDWARD ANTHONY
Le Mon, Lynn	WERT, LYNETTE L.
Leonard, Hugh	BYRNE, JOHN KEYES
Leppoc, Derfla	COPPEL, ALFRED
Le Sieg, Theo	GEISEL, THEODOR SEUSS
Leslie, Miriam	KETCHUM, PHILIP L.

PSEUDONYMS	TRUE NAMES
Leslie, O. H.	SLESAR, HENRY
Lester, Jane	WALKER, EMILY KATHLEEN
L'Estrange, Anna	ELLERBECK, ROSEMARY ANNE L'ESTRANGE
Lewes, Cady	DE VOTO, BERNARD AUGUSTINE
Lewesdon, John	DANIELL, ALBERT SCOTT
Lewis, C. D.	DAY-LEWIS, CECIL
Lewis, C. Day	DAY-LEWIS, CECIL
Lewis, C. S.	LEWIS, CLIVE STAPLES
Lewis, Charles	DIXON, ROGER
Lewis, Mervyn	FREWER, GLYN
Lewis, Roy	LEWIS, J. R.
Lewis, Voltaire	RITCHIE, EDWIN
Leyton, Sophie	WALSH, SHEILA
Lieksman, Anders	HAAVIKKO, PAAVO JUHANI
Lilly, Ray	CURTIS, RICHARD
Lin, Frank	ATHERTON, GERTRUDE FRANKLIN
Lincoln, Geoffrey	MORTIMER, JOHN
Lindars, Barnabas	LINDARS, FREDERICK C.
Linden, Oliver	ABRAHAMS, DORIS CAROLINE
Lippincott, Sara Jane	GREENWOOD, GRACE
Little, Conyth	LITTLE, CONSTANCE
Little, Conyth	LITTLE, GWENYTH
Little, Frances	MACAULEY, FRANCES C.
Livingston, Grace	HILL-LUTZ, GRACE LIVINGSTON
Lloyd, Levanah	PETERS, MAUREEN
Locke, Martin	DUNCAN, WILLIAM MURDOCH
Lockridges, The	LOCKRIDGE, FRANCES AND RICHARD
Logan, Ford	NEWTON, DWIGHT BENNETT
Logan, Jake	RIFKIN, SHEPPARD
Logan, Mark	NICOLE, CHRISTOPHER ROBIN
Lohrman, Paul	SHAVER, RICHARD SHARPE
Lomax, Bliss	DRAGO, HARRY SINCLAIR
London, Jack	LONDON, JOHN GRIFFITH
London, Laura	CURTIS, SHARON
London, Laura	CURTIS, THOMAS DALE

PSEUDONYMS	TRUE NAMES
Long, Lyda Belknap	LONG, FRANK BELKNAP
Long, William Stuart	STUART, VIVIAN
Longbaugh, Harry	GOLDMAN, WILLIAM
Longdon, George	RAYER, FRANCIS GEORGE
Longway, A. Huge	LANG, ANDREW
Lorac, E. C. R.	RIVETT, EDITH CAROLINE
Loraine, Philip	ESTRIDGE, ROBIN
Loran, Martin	BAXTER, JOHN
Lord, Jeffrey	NELSON, RADELL FARADAY
Lord, Nancy	TITUS, EVE
Loring, Peter	SHELLABARGER, SAMUEL
Loris	VON HOFMANNSTAHL, HUGO
Lorraine, Paul	FEARN, JOHN RUSSELL
Lorrimer, Claire	CLARK, PATRICIA DENISE
Lothrop, Amy	BARTLETT, ANNA
Loti, Pierre	VIAUD, L. M. JULIEN
Lourie, Helen	STORR, CATHERINE
Lovell, Marc	MC SHANE, MARK
Low, Dorothy Mackie	LOW, LOIS DOROTHEA
Lowing, Anne	GEACH, CHRISTINE
Loxmith, John	BRUNNER, JOHN KILIAN HOUSTON
Lucas, Victoria	PLATH, SYLVIA
Ludlow, Geoffrey	MEYNELL, LAURENCE WALTER
Luellen, Valentina	POLLEY, JUDITH ANNE
Lum, Peter	CROWE, LADY BETTINA
Lurgan, Lester	KNOWLES, MABEL WINIFRED
Luther, Martin	LEY, ROBERT ARTHUR
Lyall, David	SWAN, ANNIE S.
Lymington, John	CHANCE, JOHN NEWTON
Lynch, Eric	BINGLEY, DAVID ERNEST
Lynch, Frances	COMPTON, DAVID GUY
Lynn, Irene	ROWLAND, DONALD SYDNEY
Lynn, Margaret	BATTYE, GLADYS STARKEY
Lyons, Delphine C.	SMITH, EVELYN E.
Lyton, Ann	RAYNER, CLAIRE BERENICE

PSEUDONYMS	TRUE NAMES
Maborushi, Kineji	GIBSON, WALTER B.
McBain, Ed	HUNTER, EVAN
McCabe, Cameron	BORNEMAN, ERNEST
McCall, Anthony	KANE, HENRY
McCall, Vincent	MORLAND, NIGEL
McCann, Edson	ALVAREZ-DEL REY, RAMON FELIPE SAN JUAN MARIO SILVIO ENRICO
McCann, Edson	POHL, FREDERIK
MacCauley, Frances C.	LITTLE, FRANCIS
McCord, Whip	NORWOOD, VICTOR GEORGE CHARLES
McCorquodale, Barbara	CARTLAND, BARBARA HAMILTON
McCoy, Marshall	MEARS, LEONARD F.
MacCreigh, James	POHL, FREDERIK
McCrorey, Sanders	COUNSELMAN, MARY ELIZABETH
McCulloch, John Tyler	BURROUGHS, EDGAR RICE
MacDonald, Anson	HEINLEIN, ROBERT
MacDonald, Golden	BROWN, MARGARET WISE
Macdonald, John	MILLAR, KENNETH
Macdonald, John Ross	MILLAR, KENNETH
Macdonald, Marcia	HILL-LUTZ, GRACE LIVINGSTON
Macdonald, Ross	MILLAR, KENNETH
MacDonall, Robertson	MAIR, GEORGE BROWN
MacDougal, John	LOWNDES, ROBERT AUGUSTINE WARD
MacDuff, Andrew	FYFE, HORACE BROWNE
McElroy, Lee	KELTON, ELMER
MacFarlane, Stephen	CROSS, JOHN KEIR
McGirr, Edmund	GILES, KENNETH
McGowan, Inez	GRAHAM, ROGER PHILLIPS
McGrath, Morgan	RAE, HUGH CRAWFORD
McHugh, Stuart	ROWLAND, DONALD SYDNEY
McIntosh, J. T.	MACGREGOR, JAMES MURDOCH
MacIntyre, Elisabeth	ELDERSHAW, ELISABETH
McKenna, Evelyn	JOSCELYN, ARCHIE LYNN
McKenzie, Paige	BLOOD, MARIE
Mackinlock, Duncan	WATTS, PETER CHRISTOPHER
McLaglen, John J.	HARVEY, JOHN B.

PSEUDONYMS	TRUE NAMES
MacLaren, Ian	WATSON, JOHN MACLAREN
MacLean, Art	SHIRREFFS, GORDON DONALD
MacLean, Arthur	TUBB, EDWIN CHARLES
MacLeod, Robert	KNOX, WILLIAM
McLowery, Frank	KEEVIL, HENRY JOHN
McMahon, Pat	HOCH, EDWARD DENTINGER
MacNeil, Duncan	MC CUTCHAN, DONALD PHILIP
MacNeil, Neil	BALLARD, WILLIS TODHUNTER
McQuill, Thirsty	WALLACE, BRUCE
MacRae, Mason	RUBEL, JAMES LYON
McRoberts, Agnessan	MEEK, PAULINE PALMER
MacThomas, Ruaraidh	THOMSON, DERICK S.
Madison, Frank	ROWLAND, DONALD SYDNEY
Maddock, Stephen	WALSH, JAMES MORGAN
Maddox, Carl	TUBB, EDWIN CHARLES
Maine, Charles Eric	MC ILWAIN, DAVID
Maine, Trevor	CATHERALL, ARTHUR
Majors, Simon	FOX, GARDNER FRANCIS
Malloch, Peter	DUNCAN, WILLIAM MURDOCH
Mallory, Drew	GARFIELD, BRIAN FRANCIS WYNNE
Mallowan, Agatha Christie	MALLOWAN, DAME AGATHA MARY CLARISSA
Manly, Marline	RATHBONE, ST. GEORGE HENRY
Mann, Abel	CREASEY, JOHN
Mann, Charles	HECKELMANN, CHARLES NEWMAN
Mann, Chuck	HECKELMANN, CHARLES NEWMAN
Mann, Deborah	BLOOM, URSULA HARVEY
Mann, James	HARVEY, JOHN B.
Manners, Alexandra	RUNDLE, ANNE
Manning, David	FAUST, FREDERICK SCHILLER
Manning, Marsha	GRIMSTEAD, HETTIE
Manning, Roy	EAST, FRED
Manning-Sanders, Ruth	SANDERS, RUTH
Manor, Jason	HALL, OAKLEY MAXWELL
Manton, Peter	CREASEY, JOHN
Maras, Karl	BULMER, HENRY KENNETH

PSEUDONYMS	TRUE NAMES
March, Stanton	GRIFFITH-JONES, GEORGE CHETWYND
Marchant, Catherine	COOKSON, CATHERINE ANN
Marcus, Joanna	ANDREWS, LUCILLA MATHEW
Marin, A. C.	COPPEL, ALFRED
Markham, Robert	AMIS, KINGSLEY WILLIAM
Marlot, Raymond	ANGREMY, JEAN-PIERRE
Marlowe, Hugh	PATTERSON, HENRY
Marlowe, Stephen	LESSER, MILTON
Marlowe, Webb	MC COMAS, JESSE FRANCIS
Marreco, Anne	ACLAND, ALICE
Marric, J. J.	CREASEY, JOHN
Marsden, James	CREASEY, JOHN
Marsh, Jean	MARSHALL, EVELYN
Marshall, Gary	SNOW, CHARLES HORACE
Marshall, Joanne	RUNDLE, ANNE
Marshall, Lovat	DUNCAN, WILLIAM MURDOCH
Marshall, Raymond	RAYMOND, RENE BARBAZON
Marsten, Richard	HUNTER, EVAN
Martell, James	BINGLEY, DAVID ERNEST
Martin, Ellis	RYAN, MARAH ELLIS
Martin, Richard	CREASEY, JOHN
Martin, Ruth	RAYNER, CLAIRE BERENICE
Martin, Stella	HEYER, GEORGETTE
Marvel, Ik	MITCHELL, DONALD G.
Mason, Chuck	ROWLAND, DONALD SYDNEY
Mason, Frank	BUDRYS, ALGIRDAS JONAS
Mason, Frank W.	MASON, FRANCIS VAN WYCK
Mason, Lee W.	MALZBERG, BARRY NORMAN
Mason, Tally	DERLETH, AUGUST WILLIAM
Masterson, Whit	MC ILWAIN, DAVID
Masterson, Whit	MILLER, BILL
Masterson, Whit	WADE, ROBERT
Mather, Berkely	DAVIES, JOHN EVAN WESTON
Mattheson, Rodney	CREASEY, JOHN
Matthews, Anthony	BARKER, DUDLEY
Matthews, Kevin	FOX, GARDNER FRANCIS

PSEUDONYMS	TRUE NAMES
Maugham, Robin	MAUGHAM, ROBERT CECIL ROMER
Maxwell, John	FREEMANTLE, BRIAN HARRY
Maxwell, Vicky	WORBOYS, ANNETTE ISOBEL
May, Sophie	CLARKE, REBECCA SOPHIA
May, Wynne	MAY, WINIFRED JEAN
Maybury, Anne	BUXTON, ANNE
Mayfield, Julia	HASTINGS, PHYLISS DORA
Mayo, James	COULTER, STEPHEN
Mayo, Jim	LA MOORE, LOUIS DEARBORN
Meade, L. T.	MEADE, ELIZABETH THOMASINA
Meade, Richard	HAAS, BENJAMIN LEOPOLD
Meldrum, James	BROXHOLME, JOHN
Melikow, Loris	VON HOFMANNSTAHL, HUGO
Melmoth, Sebastian	WILDE, OSCAR FINGAL
Meloney, Franken	FRANKEN, ROSE DOROTHY
Melville, Anne	POTTER, MARGARET EDITH
Melville, Jennie	BUTLER, GWENDOLINE
Mentor	LAKE, KENNETH ROBERT
Meredith, Anne	MALLESON, LUCY BEATRICE
Meredith, Owen	BULWER-LYTTON, EDWARD ROBERT
Merezhkovski, Zinaida	GIPPIUS, ZINAIDA
Merlin, Christina	HEAVEN, CONSTANCE
Merlin, David	MOREAU, DAVID MERLIN
Merlini, The Great	RAWSON, CLAYTON
Merrick, Mark	RATHBONE, ST. GEORGE HENRY
Merrill, P. J.	ROTH, HOLLY
Merriman, Pat	ATKEY, PHILIP
Messer, Mona	HOCKING, MONA NAOMI ANNE MESSER
Metcalf, Suzanne	BAUM, LYMAN FRANK
Michaels, Barbara	MERTZ, BARBARA LOUISE GROSS
Michaels, Dale	RIFKIN, SHEPPARD
Michaels, Kristin	WILLIAMS, JEANNE
Michaels, Steve	AVALLONE, MICHAEL ANGELO, JR.
Miles, John	BICKHAM, JACK MILES
Miles, Keith	TRALINS, S. ROBERT

PSEUDONYMS	TRUE NAMES
Miles, Miska	MARTIN, PATRICIA MILES
Militant	SANDBURG, CARL A.
Millard, Joe	MILLARD, JOSEPH JOHN
Miller, Benjamin	LOOMIS, NOEL MILLER
Miller, Frank	LOOMIS, NOEL MILLER
Miller, Joaquin	MILLER, CINCINNATUS HEINE
Miller, Jon	MILLER, JOHN GORDON
Miller, Olive Thorne	MILLER, HARRIETT MANN
Miller, Wade	MC ILWAIN, DAVID
Miller, Wade	MILLER, BILL
Miller, Wade	WADE, ROBERT
Miller, Warne, M. D.	RATHBONE, ST. GEORGE HENRY
Milne, A. A.	MILNE, ALAN ALEXANDER
Mitchell, Clyde T.	GARRETT, RANDALL PHILLIP
Mitchell, Scott	GODFREY, LIONEL
Mitchum, Hank	NEWTON, DWIGHT BENNETT
Moamrath, M. M.	PUMILIA, JOSEPH F.
Molin, Charles	MAYNE, WILLIAM
Monahan, John	BURNETT, WILLIAM RILEY
Monig, Christopher	CROSSEN, KENDELL FOSTER
Monro, Gavin	MUNRO-HIGGS, GERTRUDE
Monroe, Lyle	HEINLEIN, ROBERT
Moor, Emily	DEMING, RICHARD
Moore, Amos	HUBBARD, GEORGE BARRON
Moore, Austin	MUIR, AUGUSTUS
Moore, Caroline	CONE, MOLLY
Moran, J-L.	WHITAKER, RODNEY
Moran, Mike	ARD, WILLIAM THOMAS
Morck, Paal	ROLVAAG, OLLE EDVART
Moresby, Louis	BECK, LILY ADAMS
Moreton, John	COHEN, MORTON
Morgan, Claire	HIGHSMITH, PATRICIA
Morgan, G. J.	ROWLAND, DONALD SYDNEY
Morgan, Glebe	ROWLAND, DONALD SYDNEY
Morgan, Marjorie	CHIBNALL, MARJORIE MC CALLUM
Morice, Anne	SHAW, FELICITY

PSEUDONYMS	TRUE NAMES
Morich, Stanton	GRIFFITH-JONES, GEORGE CHETWYND
Morino, Nick	DEMING, RICHARD
Morland, Dick	HILL, REGINALD
Morland, Peter Henry	FAUST, FREDERICK SCHILLER
Morley, Susan	CROSS, JOHN KEIR
Morley, Wilfred Owen	LOWNDES, ROBERT AUGUSTINE WARD
Morren, Theophil	VON HOFMANNSTAHL, HUGO
Morris, John	CARGILL, MORRIS
Morris, John	HEARNE, JOHN
Morris, Julian	WEST, MORRIS
Morris, Sara	BURGE, MILWARD RODON KENNEDY
Morrison, Richard	LOWNDES, ROBERT AUGUSTINE WARD
Morrison, Robert	LOWNDES, ROBERT AUGUSTINE WARD
Morrison, Roberta	WEBB, JEAN FRANCIS
Morse, Carol	HALL, MARJORY
Mortimer, Chapman	CHAPMAN-MORTIMER, WILLIAM CHARLES
Mortimer, Charles	CHAPMAN-MORTIMER, WILLIAM CHARLES
Morton, Anthony	CREASEY, JOHN
Morton, Stanley	FREEDGOOD, MORTON
Moss, Nancy	MOSS, ROBERT
Moss, Roberta	MOSS, ROBERT
Mossman, Burt	KEEVIL, HENRY JOHN
Mossop, Irene	SWATRIDGE, IRENE MAUDE
Motley, Mary	DE RENEVILLE, MARY MARGARET MOTLEY
Mountfield, David	GRANT, NEIL
Muddock, J. E.	MUDDOCK, JOYCE EMMERSON PRESTON
Mude, O.	GOREY, EDWARD ST. JOHN
Muir, Dexter	GRIBBLE, LEONARD REGINALD
Mun	MUNRO, LEAF
Mundy, Max	SCHOFIELD, SYLVIA ANNE
Munro, Mary	HOWE, DORIS
Munro, Ronald Eadie	GLEN, DUNCAN

PSEUDONYMS	TRUE NAMES
Murdoch, H. J.	MACGREGOR, JAMES MURDOCH
Murphy, C. L.	MURPHY, LAWRENCE AUGUSTUS
Murray, Beatrice	POSNER, RICHARD
Murray, Edna	ROWLAND, DONALD SYDNEY
Murray, Frances	BOOTH, ROSEMARY
Murray, Jill	WALKER, EMILY KATHLEEN
Mussey, Virginia T. H.	ELLISON, VIRGINIA HOWELL
Myers, Harriet Kathryn	WHITTINGTON, HARRY
Nabokoff, Vladimir	NABOKOV, VLADIMIR
Napier, Mark	LAFFIN, JOHN
Napier, Mary	WRIGHT, PATRICIA
Narmyx	DOUGLAS, NORMAN
Nasby, Petroleum V.	LOCKE, DAVID
Nash, Newlyn	HOWE, DORIS
Nash, Newlyn	HOWE, MURIEL
Nathan, Daniel	DANNAY, FREDERIC
Naylor, Eliot	FRANKAU, PAMELA
Neal, Hilary	NORTON, OLIVE MARION
Neighbour, Rhona M.	MARTIN, RHONA
Neilson, Marguerite	TOMPKINS, JULIA
Nelson, Johnny	MEARS, LEONARD F.
Nelson, Marguerite	FLOREN, LEE
Nelson, R. N.	NELSON, RADELL FARADAY
Nelson, Ray	NELSON, RADELL FARADAY
Nesbit, Troy	FOLSOM, FRANKLIN BREWSTER
Neville, Margot	GOYDER, MARGOT
Neville, Margot	JOSKE, ANNE NEVILLE GOYDER
Newell, Crosby	BONSALL, CROSBY NEWELL
Newman, Barbara	NEWMAN, MONA ALICE JEAN
Newman, Margaret	POTTER, MARGARET EDITH
Newton, David C.	CHANCE, JOHN NEWTON
Nicholas, F. R. E.	FREELING, NICHOLAS
Nichols, Peter	YOUD, CHRISTOPHER SAMUEL
Nicholson, C. R.	NICOLE, CHRISTOPHER ROBIN

PSEUDONYMS	TRUE NAMES
Nicholson, Christina	NICOLE, CHRISTOPHER ROBIN
Nicholson, Jane	STEEN, MARGUERITE
Nicholson, Robin	NICOLE, CHRISTOPHER ROBIN
Nile, Dorothea	AVALLONE, MICHAEL ANGELO, JR.
Noble, Charles	PAWLEY, MARTIN
Nodset, Joan L.	LEXAU, JOAN M.
Noel, John	BIRD, DENNIS LESLIE
Nolan, Chuck	EDSON, JOHN THOMAS
Noon, Ed	AVALLONE, MICHAEL ANGELO, JR.
Noone, Edwina	AVALLONE, MICHAEL ANGELO, JR.
Norden, Charles	DURRELL, LAWRENCE GEORGE
Norden, Helen Brown	LAWRENSON, HELEN
Norman, James	SCHMIDT, JAMES NORMAN
Norman, John	LANGE, JOHN FREDERICK, JR.
North, Andrew	NORTON, ALICE MARY
North, Colin	BINGLEY, DAVID ERNEST
North, Gil	HORNE, GEOFFREY
North, Howard	TREVOR, ELLESTON
North, Sara	BONHAM, BARBARA
Norton, Andre	NORTON, ALICE MARY
Norton, Bess	NORTON, OLIVE MARION
Norton, Bram	BRAMESCO, NORTON J.
Norvil, Manning	BULMER, HENRY KENNETH
Norway, Kate	NORTON, OLIVE MARION
Novak, Joseph	KOSINSKI, JERZY
Nye, Harold G.	HARDING, LEE JOHN
O'Brian, Frank	GARFIELD, BRIAN FRANCIS WYNNE
O'Brien, Clancy	SMITH, GEORGE HENRY
O'Brien, Robert C.	CONLY, ROBERT LESLIE
O'Brien, Sallee	JANAS, FRANKIE-LEE
O'Connor, Patrick	WIBBERLY, LEONARD PATRICK O'CONNOR
O'Donnell, K. M.	MALZBERG, BARRY NORMAN
O'Dowd, Cornelius	LEVER, CHARLES

PSEUDONYMS	TRUE NAMES
Ogilvy, Gavin	BARRIE, J. M.
O'Gorman, Ned	O'GORMAN, EDWARD CHARLES
O'Grady, Rohan	SKINNER, JUNE O'GRADY
O'Hara, Kevin	CUMBERLAND, MARTEN
O'Hara, Mary	ALSOP, MARY O'HARA
O'Hara, Scott	MAC DONALD, JOHN DANN
O'Laoghaire, Liam	O'LEARY, LIAM
Oldfield, Peter	BARTLETT, VERNON
Old Sleuth	HALSEY, HARLAN P.
Oldstyle, Jonathan	IRVING, WASHINGTON
Old Wilmer	LARDNER, RING
O'Leary	KUEHNELT-LEDDIHN, ERIK
Oliver, Mark	TYLER-WHITTLE, MICHAEL
Olsen, Bob	OLSEN, ALFRED JOHN, JR.
Olsen, D. B.	HITCHENS, JULIA CLARA CATHERINE DELORES BIRK OLSEN
Olsen, T. V.	OLSEN, THEODORE VICTOR
O'Malley, Frank	O'ROURKE, FRANK
O'Malley, Patrick	O'ROURKE, FRANK
O'Nair, Mairi	EVANS, CONSTANCE MAY
O'Neal, Zibby	O'NEAL, ELIZABETH
O'Neill, Egan	LININGTON, BARBARA ELIZABETH
O'Neill, Rose Cecil	WILSON, MRS. HARRY LEON
Optic, Oliver	ADAMS, WILLIAM T.
Orczy, Baroness	ORCZY, EMMA MAGDELENA ROSALIA MARIA JOSEFA BARBARA
Ormond, Frederic	DEY, FREDERIC MERRILL VAN RENSSELAER
Ormsbee, David	LONGSTREET, STEPHEN
Orwell, George	BLAIR, ERIC ARTHUR
Osborne, David	SILVERBERG, ROBERT
O'Shea, Sean	TRALINS, S. ROBERT
Oswalt, Sabine	MACCORMACK, SABINE G.
Otis, James	KALER, JAMES OTIS
O'Toole, Rex	TRALINS, S. ROBERT
Ouida	DE LA RAMEE, LOUISE

PSEUDONYMS	TRUE NAMES
Overy, Claire May	BASS, CLARA MAY
Owen, Caroline Dale	SNEDEKER, CAROLINE DALE
Owen, Edmund	TELLER, NEVILLE
Owen, Hugh	FAUST, FREDERICK SCHILLER
Owen, Tom	WATTS, PETER CHRISTOPHER
Oxenham, Elsie	DUNKERLEY, ELSIE JEANNETTE
Padgett, Lewis	KUTTNER, HENRY
Padgett, Lewis	MOORE, CATHERINE LUCILLE
Page, Emma	TIRBUTT, HONORIA
Page, Lorna	ROWLAND, DONALD SYDNEY
Page, Marco	KURNITZ, HARRY
Palinurus	CONNELLY, CYRIL
Pansy	ALDEN, ISABELLA MACDONALD
Paradise, Mary	EDEN, DOROTHY
Parish, Peggy	PARISH, MARGARET CECILE
Park, Jordan	KORNBLUTH, CYRIL M.
Park, Jordan	POHL, FREDERIK
Park, Robert	GARDNER, ERLE STANLEY
Parker, Leslie	THIRKELL, ANGELA
Parley, Peter	GOODRICH, SAMUEL GRISWOLD
Parson Lot	KINGSLEY, CHARLES
Partington, Mrs.	SHILLABER, BENJAMIN P.
Partridge, Anthony	OPPENHEIM, EDWARD PHILLIPS
Passante, Dom	FEARN, JOHN RUSSELL
Pater, Elias	FRIEDMAN, JACOB HORACE
Paterson, Judith	JONES, JUDITH PATERSON
Paterson-Jones, Judith	JONES, JUDITH PATERSON
Patrick, Maxine	MAXWELL, PATRICIA ANNE
Patrick, Q.	WEBB, RICHARD WILSON
Patrick, Q.	WHEELER, HUGH CALLINGHAM
Patterson, Harry	PATTERSON, HENRY
Patterson, Olive	ROWLAND, DONALD SYDNEY
Patton, Frank	PALMER, RAYMOND A.
Patton, Frank	SHAVER, RICHARD SHARPE

PSEUDONYMS	TRUE NAMES
Paul, Barbara	OVSTEDAL, BARBARA
Paul, John	WEBB, CHARLES HENRY
Paxton, Lois	LOW, LOIS DOROTHEA
Paye, Robert	CAMPBELL, GABRIELLE MARGARET VERE
Payne, Alan	JAKES, JOHN WILLIAM
Peace, Frank	COOK, WILLIAM EVERETT
Pearce, A. H.	QUIBELL, AGATHA HUNT
Pedler, Kit	PEDLER, CHRISTOPHER MAGNUS HOWARD
Peekner, Ray	PUECHNER, RAY
Pelkie, J. W.	PALMER, RAYMOND A.
Pell, Robert	HAGBERG, DAVID J.
Pemberton, Thomas	HOPKINSON, SIR HENRY THOMAS
Pembroke, Thomas	HOPKINSON, SIR HENRY THOMAS
Pembroke, Thomas	HORTON, MILES
Pender, Marilyn	PENDOWER, JACQUES
Pendleton, Don	CUNNINGHAM, CHET
Penmare, William	NISOT, ELIZABETH
Penn, Anne	PENDOWER, JACQUES
Penoyre, Mary	MORGAN, MARY PENOYRE
Pentecost, Hugh	PHILIPS, JUDSON PENTECOST
Peregoy, Calvin	MC CLARY, THOMAS CALVERT
Perkins, Virginia Chase	CHASE, VIRGINIA
Perley	POORE, BENJAMIN PERLEY
Perowne, Barry	ATKEY, PHILIP
Peters, Bill	MC GIVERN, WILLIAM PETER
Peters, Bryan	GEORGE, PETER BRYAN
Peters, Elizabeth	MERTZ, BARBARA LOUISE GROSS
Peters, Ellis	PARGETER, EDITH MARY
Peters, Geoffrey	PALMER, MADELYN
Peters, Linda	CATHERALL, ARTHUR
Peters, Ludovic	BRENT, PETER LUDWIG
Peters, Roy	NICKSON, ARTHUR THOMAS
Petrie, Rhona	BUCHANAN, EILEEN MARIE DUELL
Peyton, K.	PEYTON, KATHLEEN M.

PSEUDONYMS	TRUE NAMES
Peyton, K. M.	PEYTON, KATHLEEN M.
Pfaal, Hans	POE, EDGAR ALLAN
Pflaum, Susanna Whitney	PFLAUM-CONNOR, SUSANNA
Phillips, Frank	NOWLAN, PHILIP FRANCIS
Phillips, Mark	GARRETT, RANDALL PHILLIP
Phillips, Mark	HARRIS, LARRY MARK
Phillips, Richard	DICK, PHILIP K.
Phillips, Rog	GRAHAM, ROGER PHILLIPS
Phiz	BROWNE, HABLOT K.
Pickard, John Q.	BORG, PHILIP ANTHONY JOHN
Pierce, Matthew	LUCEY, JAMES D.
Pike, Charles R.	BULMER, HENRY KENNETH
Pike, Charles R.	HARKNETT, TERRY WILLIAMS
Pike, Robert L.	FISH, ROBERT L.
Pilgrim, Anne	ALLAN, MABEL ESTHER
Pilgrim, David	PALMER, JOHN LESLIE
Pilgrim, David	SAUNDERS, HILARY ADAM ST. GEORGE
Pilgrim, Derral	ZACHARY, HUGH
Pindar, Peter	WOLCOTT, JOHN
Pine, William	HARKNETT, TERRY WILLIAMS
Piper, Evelyn	MODELL, MERRIAM
Plaidy, Jean	HIBBERT, ELEANOR ALICE
Player, Robert	JORDAN, ROBERT FURNEAUX
Plum, Jennifer	KURLAND, MICHAEL JOSEPH
Plummer, Ben	BINGLEY, DAVID ERNEST
Pocock, Robert	POCOCK, HENRY ROGER ASHWELL
Pollock, Mary	BLYTON, ENID MARY
Ponder, Patricia	MAXWELL, PATRICIA ANNE
Pope John Paul II	WOJTYLA, KAROL
Porlock, Martin	MACDONALD, PHILIP
Portal, Ellis	POWE, BRUCE
Porte Crayon	STROTHER, DAVID H.
Porter, Alvin	ROWLAND, DONALD SYDNEY
Porter, Gene Stratton	PORTER, GENEVA GRACE STRATTON
Post, Mortimer	BLAIR, WALTER
Powell, Richard Stillman	BARBOUR, RALPH HENRY

PSEUDONYMS	TRUE NAMES
Power, Cecil	ALLEN, CHARLES GRANT BLAIRFINDIE
Powers, M. L.	TUBB, EDWIN CHARLES
Preedy, George	CAMPBELL, GABRIELLE MARGARET VERE
Prentis, Richard	AGATE, JAMES
Prescott, Caleb	BINGLEY, DAVID ERNEST
Preston, Richard	LINDSAY, JACK
Price, Evadne	SMITH, HELEN ZENNA
Price, Jennifer	HOOVER, HELEN
Proctor, Everitt	MONTGOMERY, RUTHERFORD GEORGE
Prole, Lozania	BLOOM, URSULA HARVEY
Pseudonym, A	BRENT, MADELINE
Pumilla, Joe	PUMILLA, JOSEPH F.
Pure, Simon	SWINNERTON, FRANK
Putnam, John	BECKWITH, BURNHAM PUTNAM
Putnam, J. Wesley	DRAGO, HARRY SINCLAIR
Putney, Gail J.	FULLERTON, GAIL
Q	QUILLER-COUCH, SIR ARTHUR
Quarles	POE, EDGAR ALLAN
Quarry, Nick	ALBERT, MARVIN H.
Quartermain, James	LYNNE, JAMES BROOM
Queen, Ellery	DANNAY, FREDERIC
Queen, Ellery	LEE, MANFRED BENNINGTON
Queen, Ellery	VANCE, JOHN HOLBROOK
Queen, Ellery	WALDO, EDWARD HAMILTON
Queen, Ellery, Jr.	DANNAY, FREDERIC
Queen, Ellery, Jr.	HOLDING, JAMES
Queen, Ellery, Jr.	LEE, MANFRED BENNINGTON
Quentin, Patrick	WEBB, RICHARD WILSON
Quentin, Patrick	WHEELER, HUGH CALLINGHAM
Quest, Erica	SAWYER, JOHN
Quest, Erica	SAWYER, NANCY
Quiller, Andrew	BULMER, HENRY KENNETH
Quin, Dan	LEWIS, ALFRED HENRY

PSEUDONYMS	TRUE NAMES
Quin, Mike	RYAN, PAUL WILLIAM
Quitman, Wallace	PALMER, RAYMOND A.
Rackham, John	PHILLIFENT, JOHN THOMAS
Radcliffe, Janette	ROBERTS, JANET LOUISE
Radford, E. and M. A.	RADFORD, EDWIN ISAAC
Radford, E. and M. A.	RADFORD, MONA AUGUSTA
Rafferty, S. S.	HURLEY, JOHN J.
Ralston, Jan	DUNLOP, AGNES M. R.
Ralston, Jan	KYLE, ELIZABETH
Ramal, Walter	DE LA MARE, WALTER
Ramsey, Eric	HAGBERG, DAVID J.
Rand, Brett	NORWOOD, VICTOR GEORGE CHARLES
Rand, Mat	HECKELMANN, CHARLES NEWMAN
Rand, William	ROSS, WILLIAM
Randall, Clay	ADAMS, CLIFTON
Randall, Janet	YOUNG, JANET RANDALL
Randall, Robert	GARRETT, RANDALL PHILLIP
Randall, Robert	SILVERBERG, ROBERT
Randell, Beverley	PRICE, BEVERLY JOAN
Randolph, Marion	RODELL, MARIE FREID
Random, Alex	ROWLAND, DONALD SYDNEY
Rangely, Olivia	ZACHARY, HUGH
Ranger, Ken	CREASEY, JOHN
Rankine, John	MASON, DOUGLAS RANKINE
Ransome, Stephen	DAVIS, FREDERICK CLYDE
Rattray, Simon	TREVOR, ELLESTON
Rawlins, Eustace Robert	BARTON, EUSTACE ROBERT
Raworth, Tom	RAWORTH, THOMAS MOORE
Ray, Wesley	GAULDEN, RAY
Raycraft, Stan	SHAVER, RICHARD SHARPE
Raymond, Charlotte	LE FONTAINE, JOSEPH RAYMOND HERVE
Raymond, Joseph	LE FONTAINE, JOSEPH RAYMOND HERVE
Raymond, Mary	HEATHCOTT, MARY
Rayner, Olive Pratt	ALLEN, CHARLES GRANT BLAIRFINDIE

PSEUDONYMS	TRUE NAMES
Rayner, Richard	MC ILWAIN, DAVID
Read, Jan	READ, JOHN HILTON
Read, Miss	SAINT, DORA JESSIE
Reade, Hamish	GRAY, SIMON
Rebel, Adam	ROAN, TOM
Redmayne, Barbara	HOWE, MURIEL
Reed, Eliot	AMBLER, ERIC
Reed, Eliot	RODDA, CHARLES
Reed, Kit	REED, LILLIAN
Reed, Peter	MACDONALD, JOHN DANN
Rees, Dilwyn	DANIEL, GLYN EDMUND
Reeve, Joel	COX, WILLIAM ROBERT
Regan, Brad	NORWOOD, VICTOR GEORGE CHARLES
Regester, Seeley	VICTOR, METTA FULLER
Reilly, William K.	CREASEY, JOHN
Reiner, Max	CALDWELL, JANET MIRIAM TAYLOR HOLLAND
Reitchi, Jack	REITCHI, JOHN GEORGE
Remington, Mark	BINGLEY, DAVID ERNEST
Remy, Pierre-Jean	ANGREMY, JEAN-PIERRE
Renault, Mary	CHALLANS, MARY
Renier, Elizabeth	BAKER, BETTY DOREEN
Reno, Clint	BALLARD, WILLIS TODHUNTER
Reno, Mark	KEEVIL, HENRY JOHN
Renton, Cam	ARMSTRONG, RICHARD
Revere, M. P.	WILLIAMSON, ALICE MURIEL
Revere, M. P.	WILLIAMSON, CHARLES NORRIS
Reynolds, Mack	REYNOLDS, DALLAS MC CORD
Reynolds, Maxine	REYNOLDS, DALLAS MC CORD
Rhamey, Ben	HOLETS, H. H.
Rhode, John	STREET, CECIL JOHN CHARLES
Rice, Craig	RANDOLPH, GEORGIANA ANN
Rich, Barbara	GRAVES, ROBERT RANKE
Rich, Barbara	JACKSON, MRS. SCHUYLER B.
Richard, Bob	RICKARD, ROBERT J. M.
Richards, Clay	CROSSEN, KENDELL FOSTER

PSEUDONYMS	TRUE NAMES
Richards, Frank	HAMILTON, CHARLES HAROLD ST. JOHN
Richards, Henry	MORRISSEY, JOSEPH LAWRENCE
Richards, Hilda	HAMILTON, CHARLES HAROLD ST. JOHN
Richmond, Grace	MARSH, JOHN
Richmond, Hugh	YOUNG, GORDAN RAY
Richmond, Roe	RICHMOND, ROALDUS FREDERICK
Rickard, Bob	RICKARD, ROBERT J. M.
Rider, Brett	GOODEN, ARTHUR HARRY
Ridgeway, Jason	LESSER, MILTON
Riding, Laura	GOTTSCHALK, LAURA RIDING
Riding, Laura	JACKSON, MRS. SCHUYLER B.
Riefe, Barbara	RIEFE, ALAN
Riley, Tex	CREASEY, JOHN
Rimmer, W. J.	ROWLAND, DONALD SYDNEY
Ring, Douglas	PRATHER, RICHARD SCOTT
Ringo, Johnny	KEEVIL, HENRY JOHN
Ringold, Clay	HOGAN, ROBERT RAY
Ripley, Jack	WAINWRIGHT, JOHN
Ritchie, Jack	REITCHI, JOHN GEORGE
Riverside, John	HEINLEIN, ROBERT
Rives, Amelie	TROUBETSKOI, PRINCESS
Rix, Donna	ROWLAND, DONALD SYDNEY
Roberts, I. M.	ROBERTS, IRENE
Roberts, Ivor	ROBERTS, IRENE
Roberts, James Hall	DUNCAN, ROBERT LIPSCOMB
Roberts, John	BINGLEY, DAVID ERNEST
Roberts, Ken	LAKE, KENNETH ROBERT
Roberts, Lawrence	FISH, ROBERT L.
Robertson, Elspeth	ELLISON, JOAN AUDREY
Robeson, Kenneth	DENT, LESTER
Robeson, Kenneth	ERNST, PAUL
Robeson, Kenneth	GOULART, RONALD JOSEPH
Robins, Patricia	CLARK, PATRICIA DENISE
Robson, Dirk	ROBINSON, DEREK
Rochard, Henry	CHARLIER, ROGER HENRI
Rocklynne, Ross	ROCKLIN, ROSS LOUIS

PSEUDONYMS	TRUE NAMES
Rockwell, Matt	ROWLAND, DONALD SYDNEY
Rodger, Alec	RODGER, THOMAS ALEXANDER
Roffman, Jan	SUMMERTON, MARGARET
Rogers, Floyd	SPENCE, WILLIAM JOHN DUNCAN
Rogers, Keith	HARRIS, MARION ROSE
Rogers, Melva	GRAHAM, ROGER PHILLIPS
Rogers, Mick	GLUT, DON F.
Rogers, Pat	PORGES, ARTHUR
Rohmer, Sax	WARD, ARTHUR HENRY SARSFIELD
Roland, Mary	BRAND, MARY CHRISTIANNA MILNE
Rollo Books	ABBOTT, JACOB
Rolls, Anthony	VULLIAMY, COLWYN EDWARD
Rome, Anthony	ALBERT, MARVIN H.
Romney, Steve	BINGLEY, DAVID ERNEST
Ronns, Edward	AARONS, EDWARD SIDNEY
Roos, Kelley	ROOS, AUDREY
Roos, Kelley	ROOS, WILLIAM
Roscoe, Charles	ROWLAND, DONALD SYDNEY
Rose, Laurence F.	FEARN, JOHN RUSSELL
Rosetti, Minerva	ROWLAND, DONALD SYDNEY
Ross, Albert	GOLDSTEIN, ARTHUR DAVID
Ross, Angus	GIGGAL, KENNETH
Ross, Barnaby	DANNAY, FREDERIC
Ross, Barnaby	LEE, MANFRED BENNINGTON
Ross, Carlton	BROOKS, EDWY SEARLES
Ross, Catherine	BEATY, BETTY
Ross, Clarissa	ROSS, WILLIAM
Ross, Dana	ROSS, WILLIAM
Ross, Eden	PHILPOTTS, ADELAIDE
Ross, Helaine	DANIELS, DOROTHY
Ross, Jonathan	ROSSITER, JOHN
Ross, Laurence	HYLAND, ANN
Ross, Leonard Q.	ROSTEN, LEO
Ross, Marilyn	ROSS, WILLIAM
Ross, Z. H.	ROSS, ZOLA HELEN
Rosse, Jan	STRAKER, J. F.

PSEUDONYMS	TRUE NAMES
Rostand, Robert	HOPKINS, ROBERT SYDNEY
Rothman, Judith	PETERS, MAUREEN
Rourke, James	HECKELMANN, CHARLES NEWMAN
Rousseau, Victor	EMANUEL, VICTOR ROUSSEAU
Rowen, Deirdre	WILLIAMS, DOROTHY JEANNE
Rowland, Iris	ROBERTS, IRENE
Rowlands, Effie	ALBANESI, MADAME EFFIE ADELAIDE MARIA
Roy, Brandon	BARCLAY, FLORENCE LOUISA
Roy, Rob	MACGREGOR, JOHN
Royce, Kenneth	GANDLEY, KENNETH ROYCE
Rudd, Margaret	NEWLIN, MARGARET RUDD
Rudomin, Esther	HAUTZIG, ESTHER
Ruell, Patrick	HILL, REGINALD
Ruppert, Chester	GRAHAM, ROGER PHILLIPS
Rusholm, Peter	POWELL, ERIC
Russell, James	HARKNETT, TERRY WILLIAMS
Russell, Shane	NORWOOD, VICTOR GEORGE CHARLES
Rusticus	FOWLER, J. K.
Rutherford, Douglas	MC CONNELL, JAMES DOUGLAS RUTHERFORD
Ruthin, Margaret	CATHERALL, ARTHUR
Rutledge, Brett	PAUL, ELLIOT HAROLD
Ryan, Tim	DENT, LESTER
Rybot, Doris	PONSONBY, DORIS ALMON
Rydell, Forbes	FORBES, DELORIS FLORINE STANTON
Rydell, Forbes	RYDELL, HELEN
Rydell, Wendell	RYDELL, WENDY
Ryder, Jonathan	LUDLUM, ROBERT
Ryder, Thom	HARVEY, JOHN B.
Rye, Anthony	YOUD, CHRISTOPHER SAMUEL
Sabin, Mark	FOX, NORMAN ARNOLD
Sabre, Dirk	LAFFIN, JOHN
Sadler, Mark	LYNDS, DENNIS
Sage, Juniper	BROWN, MARGARET WISE

PSEUDONYMS	TRUE NAMES
St. John, Leonie	BAYER, WILLIAM
St. John, Mabel	COOPER, HENRY ST. JOHN
St. John, Nicole	JOHNSTON, NORMA
St. John, Philip	ALVAREZ-DEL RAY, RAMON FELIPE SAN JUAN MARIO SILVIO ENRICO
St. George, Harry	RATHBONE, ST. GEORGE HENRY
St. Paul, Sterner	MEEK, STERNER ST. PAUL
Saki	MUNRO, H. H.
Salisbury, Carola	BUTTERWORTH, MICHAEL
Salisbury, John	CAUTE, DAVID
Salop, Lynne	HAWES, LYNNE SALOP
Salter, Cedric	KNIGHT, FRANCIS EDGAR
Salter, Mary D.	AINSWORTH, MARY D. SALTER
Sanborn, B. X.	BALLINGER, WILLIAM SANBORN
Sand, George	DUPIN, AMANDINE AURORE LUCIE
Sanders, Daphne	RANDOLPH, GEORGIANA ANN
Sanders, Jeanne	RUNDLE, ANNE
Sanders, Martin	BURGE, MILWARD RODON KENNEDY
Sandon, J. D.	HARVEY, JOHN B.
Sands, Martin	BURGE, MILWARD RODON KENNEDY
Sandys, Oliver	JERVIS, MARGUERITE FLORENCE
Sapper	MC NEILE, HERMAN CYRIL
Sarban	WALL, JOHN W.
Saunders, Caleb	HEINLEIN, ROBERT
Saunders, John	NICKSON, ARTHUR THOMAS
Saunders, Mack	KETCHUM, PHILIP L.
Saunders, Richard	FRANKLIN, BENJAMIN
Saunders, Wes	BOUNDS, SYDNEY JAMES
Savage, David	HOSSENT, HARRY
Savage, Richard	ROE, IVAN
Sawtelle, William Carter	GRAHAM, ROGER PHILLIPS
Saxon, Alex	PRONZINI, BILL
Saxon, John A.	BELLEM, ROBERT LESLIE
Saxon, Richard	MORRISSEY, JOSEPH LAWRENCE
Saxton, Judith	TURNER, JUDITH
Scarrott, Michael	FISHER, A. STANLEY

PSEUDONYMS	TRUE NAMES
Schofield, Jonathan	STREIB, DAN
Schofield, Paul	TUBB, EDWIN CHARLES
Sclanders, Dorn	FEARN, JOHN RUSSELL
Scofield, Jonathan	TOOMBS, JOHN
Scotland, Jay	JAKES, JOHN WILLIAM
Scott, Alastair	ALLEN, KENNETH S.
Scott, Anthony	DRESSER, DAVIS
Scott, Dan	BARKER, SQUIRE OMAR
Scott, Dana	ROBERTSON, CONSTANCE NOYES
Scott, Jane	MC ELFRESH, ELIZABETH ADELINE
Scott, Janey	LINDSAY, RACHEL
Scott, Milward	RAYER, FRANCIS GEORGE
Scott, Valerie	ROWLAND, DONALD SYDNEY
Scott, Warwick	TREVOR, ELLESTON
Scrum, R.	CRUMB, R.
Seager, Joan	FEARN, JOHN RUSSELL
Seale, Sara	MAC PHERSON, A. D. L.
Sea-Lion	BENNETT, GEOFFREY MARTIN
Sealsfield, Charles	POSTL, KARL
Seare, Nicholas	WHITAKER, RODNEY
Searls, Hank	SEARLS, HENRY HUNT, JR.
Sebastian, Lee	SILVERBERG, ROBERT
Sedges, John	BUCK, PEARL S.
Seed, Jenny	SEED, CECILE EUGENIE
Segundo, Bart	ROWLAND, DONALD SYDNEY
Selden, George	THOMPSON, GEORGE SELDEN
Sellings, Arthur	LEY, ROBERT ARTHUR
Seuss	GEISEL, THEODOR SEUSS
Seuss, Dr.	GEISEL, THEODOR SEUSS
Severn, David	UNWIN, DAVID STORR
Seymour, Alan	WRIGHT, SYDNEY FOWLER
Shane, Bart	ROWLAND, DONALD SYDNEY
Shane, John	DURST, PAUL
Shane, Rhondo	NORWOOD, VICTOR GEORGE CHARLES
Shane, Victor	NORWOOD, VICTOR GEORGE CHARLES
Shannon, Dell	LININGTON, BARBARA ELIZABETH

PSEUDONYMS	TRUE NAMES
Shannon, Steve	BOUMA, JOHANAS L.
Sharkey, Jack	SHARKEY, JOHN MICHAEL
Sharp, Luke	BARR, ROBERT
Shaul, Frank	ROWLAND, DONALD SYDNEY
Shaw, Brian	TUBB, EDWIN CHARLES
Shaw, Bryan	FEARN, JOHN RUSSELL
Shaw, Irene	ROBERTS, IRENE
Shawn, Frank S.	GOULART, RONALD JOSEPH
Shearing, Joseph	CAMPBELL, GABRIELLE MARGARET VERE
Shelbourne, Cecily	EBEL, SUZANNE
Sheldon, Lee	LEE, WAYNE CYRIL
Sheldon, Racoona	SHELDON, ALICE HASTINGS
Sheldon, Roy	TUBB, EDWIN CHARLES
Shepherd, John	BALLARD, WILLIS TODHUNTER
Shepherd, Michael	LUDLUM, ROBERT
Shepherd, Neal	MORLAND, NIGEL
Sheraton, Neil	SMITH, NORMAN EDWARD MACE
Sheridan, Lee	LEE, ELSIE
Sherman, Michael	LOWNDES, ROBERT AUGUSTINE WARD
Sherman, Peter Michael	LOWNDES, ROBERT AUGUSTINE WARD
Shone, Patric	HANLEY, JAMES
Shore, Norman	SMITH, NORMAN EDWARD MACE
Short, Luke	GLIDDEN, FREDERICK DILLEY
Shumsky, Zena	COLLIER, ZENA
Shura, Mary Francis	CRAIG, MARY FRANCIS
Shute, Nevil	NORWAY, NEVIL SHUTE
Shy, Timothy	LEWIS, D. B. WYNDHAM
Siady, Fred M.	SAIDY, FAREED MILHEM
Sibert, Willa	CATHER, WILLA
Sidney, Margaret	LOTHROP, HARRIET MULFORD
Sihanouk, Nordom	SIAHNOUK, SAMDECH NORDOM
Siller, Van	VAN SILLER, HILDA
Siluriensis, Leolinus	MACHEN, ARTHUR
Silver, Nicholas	FAUST, FREDERICK SCHILLER
Silver, Richard	BULMER, HENRY KENNETH

PSEUDONYMS	TRUE NAMES
Silvester, Frank	BINGLEY, DAVID ERNEST
Simon, Robert	MUSTO, BARRY
Simons, Jim	SIMONS, JAMES MARCUS
Sims, John	HOPSON, WILLIAM L.
Sims, Lieutenant A. K.	WHITSON, JOHN HARVEY
Sinclair, Alisdair	CLYNE, DOUGLAS
Sinclair, Grant	DRAGO, HARRY SINCLAIR
Sinclair, James	STAPLES, REGINALD
Singer, Adam	KARP, DAVID
Sinjohn, John	GALSWORTHY, JOHN
Slate, John	FEARN, JOHN RUSSELL
Slater, Cedric	KNIGHT, FRANCIS EDGAR
Slaughter, Anson	ATHANAS, WILLIAM VERNE
Slick, Sam	HALIBURTON, T. C.
Sloane, Sara	BLOOM, URSULA HARVEY
Small, Ernest	LENT, BLAIR
Smith, Bryan	KNOWLES, MABEL WINIFRED
Smith, Caesar	TREVOR, ELLESTON
Smith, Carmichael	LINEBARGER, PAUL MYRON ANTHONY
Smith, Charles	HECKELMANN, CHARLES NEWMAN
Smith, Cordwainer	LINEBARGER, PAUL MYRON ANTHONY
Smith, Johnston	CRANE, STEPHEN
Smith, Lew	FLOREN, LEE
Smith, Shelley	BODINGTON, NANCY HERMIONE
Smith, T. Carlyle	BANGS, JOHN KENDRICK
Smith, Wade	SNOW, CHARLES HORACE
Snow, Lyndon	ANSLE, DOROTHY PHOEBE
Sohl, Jerry	SOHL, GERALD ALLAN
Somers, Bart	FOX, GARDNER FRANCIS
Somers, Paul	GARVE, ANDREW
Somers, Paul	WINTERTON, PAUL
Somers, Suzanne	DANIELS, DOROTHY
Soskin, V. H.	ELLISON, VIRGINIA HOWELL
Sosthenes	COAD, FREDERICK ROY
Soutter, Fred	LAKE, KENNETH ROBERT
Spade, Rupert	PAWLEY, MARTIN

PSEUDONYMS	TRUE NAMES
Spain, John	ADAMS, CLEVE FRANKLIN
Spanner, Valerie	GRAYLAND, VALERIE MERLE
Spaulding, Leonard	BRADBURY, RAY
Spellman, Roger G.	COX, WILLIAM ROBERT
Spence, Bill	SPENCE, WILLIAM JOHN DUNCAN
Spence, Duncan	SPENCE, WILLIAM JOHN DUNCAN
Spencer, John	VICKERS, ROY C.
Spencer, Leonard G.	GARRETT, RANDALL PHILLIP
Spillane, Mickey	SPILLANE, FRANK MORRISON
Sprague, Carter	MERWIN, SAMUEL KIMBALL, JR.
Spurr, Clinton	ROWLAND, DONALD SYDNEY
Spy	WARD, LESLIE
Squires, Phil	BARKER, SQUIRE OMAR
Stagge, Jonathan	WEBB, RICHARD WILSON
Stagge, Jonathan	WHEELER, HUGH CALLINGHAM
Stairs, Gordon	AUSTIN, MARY
Stambler, Helen	LATNER, HELEN
Stamper, Alex	KENT, ARTHUR
Stanfield, Anne	COFFMAN, VIRGINIA EDITH
Stanhope, Lavinia	SCHLEIN, MIRIAM
Stanley, Bennett	HOUGH, STANLEY BENNETT
Stanton, John	WALLIS, G. C.
Stanton, Paul	BEATY, DAVID
Stanton, Schuyler	BAUM, LYMAN FRANK
Stanton, Vance	AVALLONE, MICHAEL ANGELO, JR.
Stark, Joshua	OLSEN, THEODORE VICTOR
Stark, Richard	WESTLAKE, DONALD EDWIN
Starr, Henry	BINGLEY, DAVID ERNEST
Starr, John	COUNSELMAN, MARY ELIZABETH
Starr, Roland	ROWLAND, DONALD SYDNEY
Statten, Vargo	FEARN, JOHN RUSSELL
Steber, A. R.	GRAHAM, ROGER PHILLIPS
Steber, A. R.	PALMER, RAYMOND A.
Steel, Byron	STEEGMULLER, FRANCIS
Steel, Morris J.	PALMER, RAYMOND A.
Steele, Curtis	DAVIS, FREDERICK CLYDE

PSEUDONYMS	TRUE NAMES
Steele, Howard	STEELE, HARWOOD ELMES ROBERT
Steele, Morris J.	PALMER, RAYMOND A.
Steffanson, Con	GOULART, RONALD JOSEPH
Stein, Ben	STEIN, BENJAMIN
Steptoe, Lydia	BARNES, DJUNA
Sterling, Brett	HAMILTON, EDMOND
Sterling, Maria Sandra	FLOREN, LEE
Stern, Paul Frederick	ERNST, PAUL FREDERICK
Stern, Stuart	RAE, HUGH CRAWFORD
Stevens, Blaine	WHITTINGTON, HARRY
Stevens, Francis	BENNETT, GERTRUDE BARROWS
Stevens, J. D.	ROWLAND, DONALD SYDNEY
Stevens, John	TUBB, EDWIN CHARLES
Stevens, R. L.	HOCH, EDWARD DENTINGER
Stevens, Robert Tyler	STAPLES, REGINALD
Stevenson, John P.	GRIERSON, EDWARD DOBBYN
Stewart, David	POLITELLA, DARIO
Stewart, Jay	PALMER, CHARLES STUART
Stewart, Jean	NEWMAN, MONA ALICE JEAN
Stewart, John Innes Mackintosh	INNES, MICHAEL
Stewart, Will	WILLIAMSON, JOHN STEWART
Stine, Hank	STINE, HENRY EUGENE
Stirling, Jessica	COGHLAN, MARGARET M.
Stirling, Jessica	RAE, HUGH CRAWFORD
Stockbridge, Dorothy	TILLET, DOROTHY STOCKBRIDGE
Stockton, Frank R.	STOCKTON, FRANCIS RICHARD
Stone, Hampton	STEIN, AARON MARC
Stone, Thomas H.	HARKNETT, TERRY WILLIAMS
Stoner, Oliver	BISHOP, MORCHARD
Stong, Pat	HOUGH, RICHARD ALEXANDER
Storm, Christopher	OLSEN, THEODORE VICTOR
Storm, Virginia	SWATRIDGE, IRENE MAUD
Story, Josephine	LORING, EMILIE
Strachey, Barbara	HALPERN, BARBARA STRACHEY
Strange, John Stephen	TILLET, DOROTHY STOCKBRIDGE
Strange, Lord	DRUMMOND, JOHN

PSEUDONYMS	TRUE NAMES
Stranger, Joyce	WILSON, JOYCE MURIEL
Stratton, Thomas	COULSON, ROBERT STRATTON
Stratton, Thomas	DE WEESE, THOMAS EUGENE
Stravolgi, Bartolomeo	TUCCI, NICCOLO
Street, C. J. C.	STREET, CECIL JOHN CHARLES
Stretton, Hesba	SMITH, SARAH
Strong, Pat	HOUGH, RICHARD ALEXANDER
Strong, Susan	REES, JOAN
Strong, Zachary	MANN, EDWARD BEVERLY
Strover, Dorothea	TINNE, DOROTHEA
Stuart, Alex	GORDON, RICHARD
Stuart, Alex R.	GORDON, RICHARD
Stuart, Clay	WHITTINGTON, HARRY
Stuart, Eleanor	PORTER, ELEANOR HODGMAN
Stuart, Ian	MACLEAN, ALISTAIR STUART
Stuart, Jason	FLOREN, LEE
Stuart, Logan	WILDING, PHILIP
Stuart, Sidney	AVALLONE, MICHAEL ANGELO, JR.
Stultifer, Morton	CURTIS, RICHARD
Sture-Vasa, Mary	ALSOP, MARY O'HARA
Sturgeon, Theodore	WALDO, EDWARD HAMILTON
Sturrock, Jeremy	HEALEY, BENJAMIN JAMES
Stuyvesant, Alice	WILLIAMSON, ALICE MURIEL
Stuyvesant, Alice	WILLIAMSON, CHARLES NORRIS
Subond, Valerie	GRAYLAND, VALERIE MERLE
Suffling, Mark	ROWLAND, DONALD SYDNEY
Sullivan, Sean Mei	SOHL, GERALD ALLAN
Sullivan, Vernon	VIAN, BORIS
Summers, Diana	SMITH, GEORGE HENRY
Summers, Essie	SUMMERS, ETHEL SNELSON
Summers, Jeanne	RUNDLE, ANNE
Summers, Rowena	SAUNDERS, JEAN
Sundarananda	NAKASHIMA, GEORGE KATSUTOSHI
Sundial	MARQUIS, DON
Super Santa	BERMAN, ED
Sutherland, Elizabeth	MARSHALL, ELIZABETH SOUTHERLAND

PSEUDONYMS	TRUE NAMES
Sutton, Henry	SLAVITT, DAVID
Sutton, I. M.	COAD, FREDERICK ROY
Sutton, John	TULLETT, DENIS
Sydney, Cynthia	TRALINS, S. ROBERT
Syntax, Dr.	COOMBE, WILLIAM
Taine, John	BELL, ERIC TEMPLE
Talbot, Kay	ROWLAND, DONALD SYDNEY
Talbot, Lawrence	BRYANT, EDWARD WINSLOW
Tall, Stephen	CROOK, COMPTON NEWBY
Tarrant, John	EGLETON, CLIVE
Tate, Allen	ORLEY, JOHN
Tate, Ellalice	HIBBERT, ELEANOR ALICE
Taylor, H. Baldwin	WAUGH, HILLARY BALDWIN
Temple, Dan	NEWTON, DWIGHT BENNETT
Tempest, Jan	SWATRIDGE, IRENE MAUD
Tempest, Sarah	PONSONBY, DORIS ALMON
Tempest, Victor	PHILIPP, ELLIOT ELIAS
Tenn, William	KLASS, PHILIP
Tenneshaw, S. M.	GARRETT, RANDALL PHILLIP
Tenneshaw, S. M.	SILVERBERG, ROBERT
Terry, C. V.	SLAUGHTER, FRANK GILL
Terry, William	HARKNETT, TERRY WILLIAMS
Terson, Peter	PATTERSON, PETER
Tertz, Abram	SINTAVSKY, ANDREY
Tey, Josephine	MACKINTOSH, ELIZABETH
Thames, C. H.	LESSER, MILTON
Thayer, Geraldine	DANIELS, DOROTHY
Thayer, Lee	THAYER, EMMA REDINGTON
Thomas, Joan Gale	ROBINSON, JOAN MARY GALE
Thomas, Ivor	BULMER-THOMAS, IVOR
Thomas, K.	FEARN, JOHN RUSSELL
Thomas, Lee	FLOREN, LEE
Thomas, Paul	MANN, THOMAS
Thompson, China	BRAND, MARY CHRISTIANNA MILNE

PSEUDONYMS	TRUE NAMES
Thompson, Eileen	PANOWSKI, EILEEN JANET THOMPSON
Thompson, Wolf	SETON, ERNEST THOMPSON
Thomson, Edward	TUBB, EDWIN CHARLES
Thomson, Joan	CHARNOCK, JOAN PAGET
Thomson, Jonathan H.	THOMSON, DAISY HICKS
Thorne, Nicola	ELLERBECK, ROSEMARY ANNE L'ESTRANGE
Thorpe, Sylvia	THIMBLETHORPE, JUNE SYLVIA
Thribb, E. J.	FANTONI, BARRY
Tibber, Robert	FRIEDMAN, ROSEMARY
Tibber, Rosemary	FRIEDMAN, ROSEMARY
Tilbury, Quenna	WALKER, EMILY KATHLEEN
Tillray, Les	GARDNER, ERLE STANLEY
Tilton, Alice	TAYLOR, PHOEBE ATWOOD
Tinker, Beamish	JESSE, F. TENNYSON
Tinne, E. D.	TINNE, DOROTHEA
Tiptree, James, Jr.	SHELDON, ALICE HASTINGS
Titan, Earl	FEARN, JOHN RUSSELL
Titcomb, Timothy	HOLLAND, J. G.
Titmarsh, Michael Angelo	THACKERY, WILLIAM MAKEPEACE
Todd, Paul	POSNER, RICHARD
Tomkinson, Constance	WEEKS, LADY CONSTANCE AVARD
Torrie, Malcolm	MITCHELL, GLADYS MAUDE WINIFRED
Towne, Stuart	RAWSON, CLAYTON
Tracy, Leland	TRALINS, S. ROBERT
Trailrider	HYLAND, ANN
Trainor, Richard	TRALINS, S. ROBERT
Traube, Ruy	TRALINS, S. ROBERT
Traver, Robert	VOELKER, JOHN DONALDSON
Travers, Colonel J. M.	RATHBONE, ST. GEORGE HENRY
Travers, Kenneth	HUTCHIN, KENNETH CHARLES
Travers, Will	ROWLAND, DONALD SYDNEY
Travis, Gerry	TRIMBLE, LOUIS PRESTON
Travis, Will	KEEVIL, HENRY JOHN
Treat, Lawrence	GOLDSTONE, LAWRENCE ARTHUR
Tredgold, Nye	TRANTER, NIGEL GODWIN

PSEUDONYMS	TRUE NAMES
Tree, Gregory	BARDIN, JOHN FRANKLIN
Trehearne, Elizabeth	ALBRITTON, CAROL
Trehearne, Elizabeth	MAXWELL, PATRICIA ANNE
Tresilian, Liz	GREEN, ELISABETH SARA
Tressidy, Jim	NORWOOD, VICTOR GEORGE CHARLES
Trevanian	WHITAKER, RODNEY
Treves, Kathleen	WALKER, EMILY KATHLEEN
Trevor, Glen	HILTON, JAMES
Trevor, William	COX, WILLIAM TREVOR
Tring, A. Stephen	MEYNELL, LAURENCE WALTER
Trollope, Joanna	POTTER, JOANNA
Trout, Kilgore	FARMER, PHILIP JOSE
Troy, Katherine	BUXTON, ANNE
Troy, Simon	WARRINER, THURMAN
Tubb, E. C.	TUBB, EDWIN CHARLES
Tucker, Link	BINGLEY, DAVID ERNEST
Turner, Bill	TURNER, W. PRICE
Turner, Clay	BALLARD, WILLIS TODHUNTER
Turner, Len	FLOREN, LEE
Turner, Mary	LAMBOT, ISOBEL MARY
Twain, Mark	CLEMENS, SAMUEL LANGHORNE
Twist, Ananias	NUNN, WILLIAM CURTIS
Unada	GLIEWE, UNADA G.
Uncle Gordon	ROE, F. GORDON
Uncle Remus	HARRIS, JOEL CHANDLER
Underhill, Charles	HILL, REGINALD
Underwood, Michael	EVELYN, JOHN MICHAEL
Underwood, Miles	GLASSCO, JOHN
Ungerer, Tomi	UNGERER, JEAN THOMAS
Updyke, James	BURNETT, WILLIAM RILEY
Usco	GERD, JACOB STERN
Uttley, Alison	UTTLEY, ALICE JANE
V. V. V.	LUCAS, E. V.

PSEUDONYMS	TRUE NAMES
Valentine, Alec	ISAACS, ALAN
Valentine, Douglas	WILLIAMS, GEORGE VALENTINE
Valentine, Jo	ARMSTRONG, CHARLOTTE
Vanardy, Varick	DEY, FREDERIC MERRILL VAN RENSSELAER
Vance, Gerald	GARRETT, RANDALL PHILLIP
Vance, Gerald	GRAHAM, ROGER PHILLIPS
Vance, Jack	VANCE, JOHN HOLBROOK
Van Dine, S. S.	WRIGHT, WILLARD HUNTINGTON
Van Dyne, Edith	BAUM, LYMAN FRANK
Vane, Bret	KENT, ARTHUR
Vane, Michael	HUMPHRIES, SYDNEY VERNON
Van Heller, Marcus	ZACHARY, HUGH
Van Lhin, Erik	ALVAREZ-DEL REY, RAMON FELIPE SAN JUAN MARIO SILVIO ENRICO
Van See, John	VANCE, JOHN HOLBROOK
Van Someren, Liesje	PUTLAND-VAN SOMEREN, ELIZABETH
Vardre, Leslie	DAVIES, LESLIE PURNELL
Varley, John Philip	MITCHELL, LANGDON E.
Vedder, John K.	GRUBER, FRANK
Venables, Terry	WILLIAMS, GORDON
Venison, Alfred	POUND, EZRA
Venning, Michael	RANDOLPH, GEORIGANA ANN
Vercors	BRULLER, JEAN
Verdon, Dorothy	TRALINS, S. ROBERT
Verne, Jules	OLCHEWITZ, M.
Verval, Alain	GREENWOOD, THOMAS
Verval, Alain	LANDE, LAWRENCE MONTAGNE
Veryan, Patricia	BANNISTER, PATRICIA V.
Vestal, Stanley	CAMPBELL, WALTER STANLEY
Vicarion, Count Palmiro	LOGUE, CHRISTOPHER
Victor, Charles B.	PUECHNER, RAY
Vigil	KOESTLER, ARTHUR
Vigil, Lawrence	FINNIN, MARY
Viliers, Guy	GOULDING, PETER GEOFFREY
Vincent, Harl	SCHOEPFLIN, HAROLD VINCENT

PSEUDONYMS	TRUE NAMES
Vindicator	HOPKINSON, SIR HENRY THOMAS
Vine, Sarah	ROWLAND, DONALD SYDNEY
Vinson, Elaine	ROWLAND, DONALD SYDNEY
Vipont, Charles	FOULDS, ELFRIDA VIPONT
Vipont, Elfrida	FOULDS, ELFRIDA VIPONT
Vitezovic, T.	KUEHNELT-LEDDIHN, ERIK
Voltaire	AROUET, FRANÇOIS-MARIE
Von Hutten, Baroness Betsy Riddle	RIDDLE, BETSY
Von Rachen, Kurt	HUBBARD, LAFAYETTE RON
Von Tempski, Armine	BALL, ARMINE
Voyle, Mary	MANNING, ROSEMARY
Wade, Alan	VANCE, JOHN HOLBROOK
Wade, Bob	MC ILWAIN, DAVID
Wade, Everett	COOK, WILLIAM EVERETT
Wade, Henry	AUBREY-FLETCHER, HENRY LANCELOT
Wade, Jennifer	DE WEESE-WEHEN, JOY
Wade, Robert	MC ILWAIN, DAVID
Wagstaff, Theophile	THACKERY, WILLIAM MAKEPEACE
Wainer, Cord	DEWEY, THOMAS BLANCHARD
Waldo, Dave	CLARKE, DAVID WALDO
Walford, Christian	DILCOCK, NOREEN
Walker, Harry	WAUGH, HILLARY BALDWIN
Walker, J.	CRAWFORD, JOHN RICHARD
Walker, Lucy	SANDERS, DOROTHY LUCIE
Walker, Max	AVALLONE, MICHAEL ANGELO, JR.
Walker, Reeve	HECKELMANN, CHARLES NEWMAN
Wallace, Ian	PRITCHARD, JOHN WALLACE
Wallis, B.	WALLIS, GEORGE C.
Wallis, B. and G. C.	WALLIS, GEORGE C.
Walsh, Jill Paton	PATON WALSH, GILLIAN
Walters, Hugh	HUGHES, WALTER LLEWELLYN
Walters, Rick	ROWLAND, DONALD SYDNEY
Warborough, Martin Leach	ALLEN, CHARLES GRANT BLAIRFINDIE
Ward, Artemus	BROWNE, CHARLES FARRAR

PSEUDONYMS	TRUE NAMES
Ward, Jonas	ARD, WILLIAM THOMAS
Ward, Jonas	COX, WILLIAM ROBERT
Ward, Jonas	GARFIELD, BRIAN FRANCIS WYNNE
Ward, Malanie	CURTIS, RICHARD
Wardell, Nora Helen	HERON-ALLEN, EDWARD
Wardle, Don	SNOW, CHARLES HORACE
Ware, Wallace	KARP, DAVID
Warneford, Inspector Robert, RN	RUSSELL, WILLIAM
Warner, Matt	FICHTER, GEORGE S.
Warre, Mary Douglas	GREIG-SMITH, JENNIFER
Warren, Andrew	TUTE, WARREN
Warren, Mary Douglas	GREIG-SMITH, JENNIFER
Water, Silas	LOOMIS, NOEL MILLER
Waterhouse, Arthur	FEARN, JOHN RUSSELL
Waters	RUSSELL, WILLIAM
Watkins, Gerrold	MALZBERG, BARRY NORMAN
Watson, Will	FLOREN, LEE
Wayland, Patrick	O'CONNOR, RICHARD
Wayne, Anderson	DRESSER, DAVIS
Wayne, Donald	DODD, WAYNE D.
Wayne, Joseph	PATTEN, LEWIS BYFORD
Weary, Ogred	GOREY, EDWARD ST. JOHN
Weaver, Ward	MASON, FRANCIS VAN WYCK
Webb, Christopher	WIBBERLEY, LEONARD PATRICK O'CONNOR
Webb, Neil	ROWLAND, DONALD SYDNEY
Webster, Jean	WEBSTER, ALICE JANE CHANDLER
Webster, Noah	KNOX, WILLIAM
Weegee	FELLIG, ARTHUR
Weiner, Henri	LONGSTREET, STEPHEN
Welch, Ronald	FELTON, RONALD OLIVER
Welcome, John	BRENNAN, JOHN NEEDHAM HUGGARD
Welles, Elizabeth	ROBY, MARY LINN
Wellington, Anne	HEWETT, ANITA
Wellington, John	FARNILL, BARRIE
Wells, H. G.	WELLS, HERBERT GEORGE

PSEUDONYMS	TRUE NAMES
Wells, Hondo	WHITTINGTON, HARRY
Wells, John J.	COULSON, JUANITA
Wells, Tobias	FORBES, DELORIS FLORINE STANTON
Welsh, Ronald	FELTON, RONALD OLIVER
Wentworth, Patricia	ELLES, DORA AMY
Wernheim, John	FEARN, JOHN RUSSELLL
Wesley, Elizabeth	MC ELFRESH, ELIZABETH ADELINE
Wesley, James	RIGONI, ORLANDO
West, C. P.	WODEHOUSE, PELHAM GRENVILLE
West, Nathanael	WEINSTEIN, NATHAN WELLENSTEIN
West, Tom	EAST, FRED
West, Ward	BORLAND, HAROLD GLEN
Western, Mark	CRISP, ANTHONY THOMAS
Westgate, John	BLOOMFIELD, ANTHONY JOHN WESTGATE
Westmacott, Mary	MALLOWAN, DAME AGATHA MARY CLARISSA
Weston, Allen	HOGARTH, GRACE
Weston, Allen	NORTON, ALICE MARY
Weston, Helen Gray	DANIELS, DOROTHY
Weston, William	MILSOM, CHARLES HENRY
Wetherell, Elizabeth	WARNER, SUSAN BOGERT
Wharton, Anthony	MC ALLISTER, ALISTER
Whitaker, Rod	WHITAKER, RODNEY
Whitbread, Jane	LEVIN, JANE WHITBREAD
Whitby, Sharon	PETERS, MAUREEN
White, George M.	WALSH, JAMES MORGAN
White, Harry	WHITTINGTON, HARRY
White, Jonathan	HARVEY, JOHN B.
White, Ted	WHITE, THEODORE EDWIN
Whitney, Hallam	WHITTINGTON, HARRY
Whittington, Peter	MACKAY, JAMES ALEXANDER
Whittle, Tyler	TYLER-WHITTLE, MICHAEL
Wick, Carter	WHITTINGTON, HARRY
Wick, Carter	WILCOX, COLIN
Wick, Stuart	FREEMAN, KATHLEEN

PSEUDONYMS	TRUE NAMES
Wiest, Grace L.	DELOUGHERY, GRACE L.
Wigan, Christopher	BINGLEY, DAVID ERNEST
Wigg, T. I. G.	MC CUTCHAN, DONALD PHILIP
Wilde, Jimmy	CREASEY, JOHN
Wilde, Jocelyn	TOOMBS, JOHN
Wilder, Cherry	GRIMM, CHERRY BARBARA
Wiley, John	GRAHAM, ROGER PHILLIPS
Wiley, Margaret L.	MARSHALL, MARGARET LENORE
Wilkins, Mary	FREEMAN, MARY ELEANOR WILKINS
Will	LIPKIND, WILLIAM
Williams, Arnold	MEADOWCROFT, ERNEST
Williams, J. R.	WILLIAMS, DOROTHY JEANNE
Williams, J. Walker	WODEHOUSE, PELHAM GRENVILLE
Williamson, Mrs. Harcourt	WILLIAMSON, ALICE MURIEL AND CHARLES NORRIS
Williamson, Jack	WILLIAMSON, JOHN STEWART
Willis, Ted	WILLIS, EDWARD HENRY
Willoughby, Cass	OLSEN, THEODORE VICTOR
Willoughby, Hugh	HARVEY, NIGEL
Willoughby, Lee Davis	WEBB, JEAN FRANCIS
Wills, Chester	SNOW, CHARLES HORACE
Wills, Thomas	ARD, WILLIAM THOMAS
Wilmer, Dale	MC ILWAIN, DAVID
Wilmer, Dale	MILLER, BILL
Wilmer, Dale	WADE, ROBERT
Wilson, Barbara	GARRETT, RANDALL PHILLIP
Wilson, Barbara	HARRIS, LARRY MARK
Wilson, Christine	GEACH, CHRISTINE
Wilson, Dave	FLOREN, LEE
Wilson, David	MACARTHUR, DAVID WILSON
Wilson, Dick	WILSON, RICHARD GARRATT
Wilson, Gwendoline	EWENS, GWENDOLINE WILSON
Wilson, Mary	ROBY, MARY LINN
Winch, John	CAMPBELL, GABRIELLE MARGARET VERE
Winchester, Kay	WALKER, EMILY KATHLEEN

PSEUDONYMS	TRUE NAMES
Windham, Basil	WODEHOUSE, PELHAM GRENVILLE
Wine, Dick	POSNER, RICHARD
Winfield, Arthur M.	STRATEMEYER, EDWARD
Winiki, Ephriam	FEARN, JOHN RUSSELL
Winslow, Kent	WOODWORTH, FRED
Winstan, Matt	NICKSON, ARTHUR THOMAS
Winter, H. G.	BATES, HIRAM GILMORE, III
Wodehouse, P. G.	WODEHOUSE, PELHAM GRENVILLE
Wodge, Dreary	GOREY, EDWARD ST. JOHN
Wood, Catherine	ETCHISON, BIRDIE L.
Wood, Kerry	WOOD, EDGAR ALLARDYCE
Woodcott, Keith	BRUNNER, JOHN KILIAN HOUSTON
Woodruff, Philip	MASON, PHILIP
Woods, Lawrence	LOWNDES, ROBERT AUGUSTINE WARD
Woods, P. F.	BAYLEY, BARRINGTON JOHN
Woods, Sara	BOWEN-JUDD, SARA
Woodward, Lilian	MARSH, JOHN
Woolrich, Cornell	HOPLEY-WOOLRICH, CORNELL GEORGE
Worboys, Anne Eyre	WORBOYS, ANNETTE ISOBEL
Worchester, Roland	RAYER, FRANCIS GEORGE
Worth, Peter	GRAHAM, ROGER PHILLIPS
Wright, Francesca	ROBINS, DENISE NAOMI
Wright, Kenneth	ALVAREZ-DEL REY, RAMON FELIPE SAN JUAN MARIO SILVIO ENRICO
Wright, Rowland	WELLS, CAROLYN
Wright, S. Fowler	WRIGHT, SYDNEY FOWLER
Wylie, Laura	MATTHEWS, PATRICIA ANNE
Wyndham, Esther	LUTYENS, MARY
Wyndham, John	HARRIS, JOHN WYNDHAM PARKES LUCAS BEYNON
Wyndham, Lee	HYNDMAN, JANE LEE
Wynne, Brian	GARFIELD, BRIAN FRANCIS WYNNE
Wynne, Frank	GARFIELD, BRIAN FRANCIS WYNNE
Wynne, May	KNOWLES, MABEL WINIFRED
X, Mr.	HOCH, EDWARD DENTINGER

PSEUDONYMS	TRUE NAMES
Xeno	LAKE, KENNETH ROBERT
Yaffe, Alan	YORINKS, ARTHUR
Yarnall, Sophia	JACOBS, SOPHIA YARNALL
Yates, Dornford	MERCER, CECIL WILLIAM
Ybarra, I. R.	WOODWORTH, FRED
York, Alison	NICOLE, CHRISTOPHER ROBIN
York, Andrew	NICOLE, CHRISTOPHER ROBIN
York, Georgia	HOFFMAN, LEE
York, Jeremy	CREASEY, JOHN
York, Margaret	NICHOLSON, MARGARET BETA
Yorke, Katherine	ELLERBECK, ROSEMARY ANNE L'ESTRANGE
Yorke, Margaret	NICHOLSON, MARGARET BEDA
Yorke, Roger	BINGLEY, DAVID ERNEST
Youd, C. S.	YOUD, CHRISTOPHER SAMUEL
Young, Angela	YARDLEY, ALICE
Young, Carter Travis	CHARBONNEAU, LOUIS HENRY
Young, Collier	BLOCH, ROBERT
Young, Jan	YOUNG, JANET RANDALL
Young, Rose	HARRIS, MARION ROSE
Young, Wilson	TIPPETTE, GILES
Yuill, P. B.	WILLIAMS, GORDON
Yuill, P. B.	VENABLES, TERRY
Yun, Leong Gor	ELLISON, VIRGINIA HOWELL
Zachary, Elizabeth	ZACHARY, HUGH
Zetford, Tully	BULMER, HENRY KENNETH
Ziliox, Marc	FICHTER, GEORGE S.
Ziller, Robert	ZIEGLER, RICHARD
Zinberg, Len	ZINBERG, LEONARD S.
Zonik, Eleanor Dorothy	GLASER, ELEANOR DOROTHY

– 7 –

First Books by Collectible Authors

This list will provide the correct title of an author's first book(s), and is important for anyone hoping to assemble complete author collections. Many authors published their first book using a pseudonym, or anonymously, and I have also provided that information. It makes no difference if you collect only first editions, since any edition will do when trying to assemble a complete author collection. I have included hundreds of authors whose names do not appear on any other list in this book, particularly if the author did not use any pseudonym(s).

Usually an author's first book is the most difficult to find, but not necessarily the most expensive. There are several reasons for this. First, publishers are often reluctant to take a chance on a large printing for the first book of a new author; thus first books are often small printings—sometimes as few as six copies for copyright purposes.

You will also discover that first books are likely to be books of verse or nonfiction. Many authors who have achieved prominence in a certain genre, such as mysteries or mainstream fiction, may have had their first book published in a different genre, such as a juvenile, a school text, some form of nonfiction, or perhaps, a scientific tome—sometimes even as a doctoral dissertation.

Often they are privately printed editions—a euphemism for self-published, in some instances. A very high percentage of them, particularly in the science fiction/adventure and mystery fields, were originally published as paperbacks.

Because of these factors, the first book often becomes the key book in assembling an author collection. When a first edition is required, it often becomes nearly impossible to locate one, and the price can become truly astronomical.

If I were a beginning collector interested in assembling a collection likely to increase in value—to use that word that most antiquarian booksellers hate, INVESTMENT—I would go for a collection of first books by authors either in a particular genre, such as mystery or children's books, or for a general collection of either fiction or nonfiction.

Please note: All books are listed in alphabetical order by the author's name unless no author is shown on the title page; then they are listed by the first word in the title. If you want to know whether an author's name is the true name or a pseudonym, or if that author may have used or still uses one or more pseudonyms, first look up the name in Chapter 5. If it does not appear there, check Chapter 6 to find the true name, then refer back to Chapter 5 to see if there are any other pseudonyms listed. If you do not find the name in either of these chapters, it probably means that the name is the true name and that there are no known pseudonyms. In some cases it may be the pseudonym or true name of a new author who will perhaps be included in another edition of this book.

Also, when an author published more than one book in his first year of publication, I have noted them all without trying to indicate precedence.

AUTHOR	TITLE/FIRST EDITION INFORMATION
Aarons, Edward Sidney	DEATH IN A LIGHTHOUSE, as Edward Ronns. New York: Phoenix, 1938.
Abbey, Edward	JONATHAN TROY. New York: Dodd Mead, 1954.
Abrahams, Doris Caroline	THE MOON ON MY LEFT, as Caryl Brahms. London, 1930.
Acland, Alice	CAROLINE NORTON. 1948.
Adams, Andy	THE LOG OF A COWBOY. Boston: Houghton Mifflin; London: Constable, 1903.
Adams, Cleve Franklin	AND SUDDEN DEATH. New York: Dutton, 1940.
Adams, Clifton	THE DESPERADO. New York: Fawcett, 1950; London: Fawcett, 1953.
Adams, Leonie	THOSE NOT ELECT. New York, 1925.
Adams, Peter Robert Charles	THE LAND AT MY DOOR. N.p., 1965.

AUTHOR	TITLE/FIRST EDITION INFORMATION
Adams, Richard	WATERSHIP DOWN. London; New York, 1972.
Ade, George	ARTIE. N.p., 1896.
Adlard, Mark	INTERFACE. London: Sidgwick & Jackson, 1971; New York: Ace, 1977.
Agee, James	PERMIT ME VOYAGE. New Haven, Conn., 1934.
Ahlswede, Ann	DAY OF THE HUNTER. New York: Ballantine, 1960. HUNTING WOLF. New York: Ballantine, 1960.
Aiken, Conrad	EARTH TRIUMPHANT AND OTHER TALES IN VERSE. New York, 1914.
Aiken, Joan Delano	ALL YOU'VE EVER WANTED AND OTHER STORIES. London: Cape, 1953.
Ainsworth, Ruth Gallard	TALES ABOUT TONY. London, 1936.
Albanesi, Madame Effie Adelaide Maria	MARGERY DAW, anonymously. London; New York, 1886.
Albee, Edward	THE ZOO STORY AND THE SANDBOX. New York, 1960. THE ZOO STORY, THE DEATH OF BESSIE SMITH, THE SANDBOX. New York, 1960; London, 1962.
Albert, Marvin H.	LIE DOWN WITH LIONS. New York: Fawcett, 1955; London: Red Seal, 1957.
Alcott, Louisa May	FLOWER FABLES. Boston: Briggs, 1855.
Aldington, Richard	IMAGES 1910-1915. London, 1915.
Aldiss, Brian Wilson	THE BRIGHTFOUNT DIARIES. London: Faber, 1955.
Aldrich, Thomas Bailey	THE BELLS: A COLLECTION OF CHIMES. New York: Derby, 1855.
Alger, Horatio, Jr.	BERTHA'S CHRISTMAS VISION: AN AUTUMN SHEAF. Boston, 1856.
Algren, Nelson	SOMEBODY IN BOOTS. New York, 1935.
Allbeury, Theodore Edward Le Bouthillier	A CHOICE OF ENEMIES, as Ted Allbeury. New York: St. Martin's, 1972; London: Davies, 1973.

AUTHOR	TITLE/FIRST EDITION INFORMATION
Allen, Charles Grant Blairfindie	PHYSIOLOGICAL AESTHETICS, as Grant Allen. London: King, 1877; New York: Appleton, 1878.
Allen, Henry Wilson	NO SURVIVORS, as Will Henry. New York: Random House, 1950; London: Corgi, 1952.
Allen, Terry D. and Don B.	DOCTOR IN BUCKSKIN, as T. D. Allen. New York: Harper, 1951.
Allen, William Hervey, Jr.	BALLADS OF THE BORDER. Privately printed, 1916.
Allen, Woody	DON'T DRINK THE WATER. New York, 1967.
Allingham, Margery Louise	BLACKKERCHIEF DICK: A TALE OF MERSEA ISLAND. London: Hodder & Stoughton; New York: Doubleday, 1923.
Alsop, Mary O'Hara	LET US SAY GRACE, as Mary Sture-Vasa. Boston: Christopher, 1930.
Ambler, Eric	THE DARK FRONTIER. London: Hodder & Stoughton, 1936.
Arlen, Michael	THE LONDON VENTURE. London: Heinemann; New York: Dodd Mead, 1920.
Armstrong, Charlotte	LAY ON, MACDUFF. New York: Coward McCann, 1942; London: Gifford, 1943.
Ashton, Elizabeth	THE PIED TULIP. London: Mills & Boon, 1969; Toronto: Harlequin, 1970.
Asimov, Isaac	PEBBLE IN THE SKY. New York: Doubleday, 1950; London: Corgi, 1958. I, ROBOT. New York: Gnome, 1950; London: Grayson, 1952.
Asprin, Robert Lynn	THE COLD CASH WAR. New York: St. Martin's; London: New English Library, 1977.
Athanas, William Verne	THE PROUD ONES, as Verne Athanas. New York: Simon & Schuster, 1952; London: Rich & Cowan, 1953.
Atherton, Gertrude Franklin	WHAT DREAMS MAY COME, as Frank Lin. Chicago: Belford Clarke, 1888; as Gertrude Atherton. London: Routledge, 1889.

AUTHOR	TITLE/FIRST EDITION INFORMATION
Atkey, Philip	ARREST THESE MEN! as Barry Perowne. London: Cassell, 1932.
Atkins, Frank	THE DEVIL-TREE OF EL DORADO, as Fenton Ash. London: Hutchinson, 1896; New York: New Amsterdam, 1897.
Atkins, John Alfred	THE DISTRIBUTION OF FISH. London: Fabian Society, 1941.
Aubrey-Fletcher, Henry Lancelot	THE VERDICT OF YOU ALL, as Henry Wade. London: Constable, 1926; New York: Payson & Clarke, 1927.
Austin, Mary	THE LAND OF LITTLE RAIN. Boston: Houghton Mifflin, 1903.
Ayres, Ruby Mildred	CASTLES IN SPAIN: THE CHRONICLES OF AN APRIL MONTH. London: Cassell, 1912.
Baker, Betty Doreen	THE GENEROUS VINE, as Elizabeth Renier. London: Hurst & Blackett, 1962; New York: Ace, 1972.
Baldwin, Faith	MAVIS OF GREEN HILL. Boston; London, 1921.
Baldwin, Gordon Cortis	TROUBLE RANGE. London: Hale, 1956; New York: Arcadia, 1959. TRAIL NORTH. London: Hale, 1956; New York: Arcadia, 1957.
Baldwin, James	GO TELL IT ON THE MOUNTAIN. New York, 1953.
Baldwin, Joseph G.	THE FLUSH TIMES OF ALABAMA AND MISSISSIPPI. New York, 1853.
Ballantyne, Robert Michael	HUDSON'S BAY; OR, EVERY-DAY LIFE IN THE WILDS OF NORTH AMERICA, as R. M. Ballantyne. Edinburgh: Blackwood, 1848.
Ballard, James Graham	THE WIND FROM NOWHERE, as J. G. Ballard. New York: Berkley, 1962; London: Penguin, 1967. THE VOICES OF TIME AND OTHER STORIES, as J. G. Ballard. New York: Berkley, 1962. BILLENIUM AND

AUTHOR	TITLE/FIRST EDITION INFORMATION
	OTHER STORIES, as J. G. Ballard. New York: Berkley, 1962.
Ballard, Willis Todhunter	SAY YES TO MURDER. New York: Putnam, 1942.
Bangs, John Kendrick	THE LORGNETTE, as J. K. B. New York, 1886.
Bannister, Patricia V.	THE LORD AND THE GYPSY, as Patricia Veryan. New York: Walker, 1978; as DEBT OF HONOUR. London: Souvenir Press, 1980.
Barclay, Florence Louisa	GUY MERVYN, as Brandon Roy. 3 vols. London, 1891.
Barker, Squire Omar	VIENTOS DE LAS SIERRAS, WINDS OF THE MOUNTAINS, as S. Omar Barker. Privately printed, 1922.
Barnes, Arthur Kelvin	INTERPLANETARY HUNTER. New York: Gnome, 1956.
Barrett, Neal, Jr.	KELWIN. New York: Lancer, 1970.
Barrie, Sir James Matthew	BETTER DEAD. London, 1888.
Barrie, Susan	MISTRESS OF BROWN FURROWS. London, 1952.
Barry, Jane	THE LONG MARCH. New York: Appleton Century Crofts, 1955.
Barth, John Simmons	THE FLOATING OPERA. New York: Appleton Century Crofts, 1956.
Barthelme, Donald	COME BACK, DR. CALIGARI. Boston, 1964.
Bassler, Thomas J.	HALF PAST HUMAN, as T. J. Bass. New York: Ballantine, 1971.
Bates, Hiram Gilmore, III	SPACE HAWK: THE GREATEST OF INTERPLANETARY ADVENTURES, as Anthony Gilmore, with D. W. Hall. New York: Greenberg, 1952.
Battye, Gladys Starkey	TO SEE A STRANGER, as Margaret Lynn. London: Hodder & Stoughton, 1961; New York: Doubleday, 1962.

AUTHOR	TITLE/FIRST EDITION INFORMATION
Baum, Lyman Frank	THE BOOK OF HAMBURGS: A BRIEF TREATISE UPON THE MATING, REARING, AND MANAGEMENT OF THE DIFFERENT VARIETIES OF HAMBURGS (chickens), by L. Frank Baum. Hartford, Conn.: Stoddard, 1886.
Baxter, John	THE OFF-WORLDERS. New York: Ace, 1966; as THE GOD KILLERS. Sydney, Australia: Horwitz, 1968.
Bayley, Barrington John	STAR VIRUS. New York: Ace, 1970.
Beach, Rex Ellingwood	THE SPOILERS. New York: Harper, 1906; London: Hodder & Stoughton, 1912.
Beagle, Peter S.	A FINE AND PRIVATE PLACE. New York, 1960.
Bean, Myrtle Amelia	THE FANCHER TRAIN. New York: Doubleday, 1958; as THE VENGEANCE TRAIL. London: Hamish Hamilton, 1958.
Bear, Gregory Dale	HEGIRA, as Greg Bear. New York: Dell, 1979. PSYCHLONE, as Greg Bear. New York: Ace, 1979.
Beaty, Betty	SOUTH TO THE SUN. London, 1956.
Bechdolt, Frederick Ritchie	9009, with James Hopper. New York: McClure, 1908.
Bechko, Peggy Anne	NIGHT OF THE FLAMING GUNS. New York: Doubleday, 1974. GUNMAN'S JUSTICE. New York: Doubleday, 1974.
Beck, Lily Adams	THE KEY OF DREAMS. New York, 1922. THE NINTH VIBRATION AND OTHER STORIES. New York, 1922.
Beecher, Harriet Elizabeth	PRIZE-TALE: A NEW ENGLAND SKETCH. Lowell, Mass., 1834.
Beecher, John	"AND I WILL BE HEARD." New York, 1940.
Bell, Eric Temple	THE CYCLOTOMIC QUINARY QUINTIC. New York: Columbia University, 1912.
Bellah, James Warner	SKETCH BOOK OF A CADET FROM GASCONY. New York: Knopf, 1923.

AUTHOR	TITLE/FIRST EDITION INFORMATION
Bellamy, Edward	SIX TO ONE: A NANTUCKET IDYL. New York: Putnam; London: Sampson Low, 1878.
Bellingham, Helen Mary Dorothea	THE GREEN LACQUER PAVILION. London; New York, 1926.
Belloc, Joseph Hilaire Pierre	VERSES AND SONNETS. London, 1896.
Bellow, Saul	DANGLING MAN. New York, 1944.
Benet, Stephen Vincent	THE DRUG-SHOP; OR, ENDYMION IN EDMONSTOUN. Privately printed, 1917.
Benet, William Rose	MERCHANTS FROM CATHAY AND OTHER POEMS. New York, 1913.
Benford, Gregory Albert	DEEPER THAN THE DARKNESS. New York: Ace, 1970; London: Gollancz, 1979.
Bennett, Enoch Arnold	A MAN FROM THE NORTH, as Arnold Bennett. London, 1898.
Bennett, Gertrude Barrows	THE HEADS OF CERBERUS, as Francis Stevens. Reading: Polaris Press, 1952.
Bennetts, Pamela	THE BORGIA PRINCE. London, 1968.
Berckman, Evelyn Domenica	THE EVIL OF TIME. New York: Dodd Mead, 1954; London: Eyre & Spottiswoode, 1955.
Beresford, Elisabeth	THE TELEVISION MYSTERY. London, 1957.
Beresford, John Davys	THE EARLY HISTORY OF JACOB STAHL. London: Sidgwick & Jackson; Boston: Little, Brown, 1911.
Berger, Thomas Louis	CRAZY IN BERLIN. New York: Scribner, 1958.
Bernstein, Aline	THREE BLUE SUITS. New York, 1933.
Berrigan, Daniel	TIME WITHOUT NUMBER. New York, 1957.
Berry, Bryan	AND THE STARS REMAIN. London: Panther, 1952. BORN IN CAPTIVITY. London: Panther, 1952. DREAD VISITOR. London: Panther, 1952.
Berry, Don	TRASK. New York: Viking; London: Hutchinson, 1960.

AUTHOR	**TITLE/FIRST EDITION INFORMATION**
Berryman, John	POEMS. Norfolk, Va., 1942.
Bessie, Alvah C.	DWELL IN THE WILDERNESS. New York, 1935.
Best, Oswald Herbert	GARRAM THE HUNTER, as Herbert Best. New York: Doubleday, 1930; London: Lane, 1935.
Bester, Alfred	THE DEMOLISHED MAN. Chicago: Shasta; London: Sidgwick & Jackson, 1953. WHO HE? New York: Dial, 1953.
Betjeman, John	MOUNT ZION, OR IN TOUCH WITH THE INFINITE. London, 1931.
Bevan, Gloria	THE DISTANT TRAP. London, 1969.
Bickham, Jack Miles	GUNMAN'S GAMBLE. New York: Ace, 1958; London: Hale, 1959.
Bidwell, Marjory Elizabeth Sarah	FOG, as Elizabeth Ford. London, 1933.
Bigg, Patricia Nina	THE FLICKERING CANDLE, as Patricia Ainsworth. London, 1968.
Biggers, Earl Derr	SEVEN KEYS TO BALDPATE. Indianapolis: Bobbs Merrill, 1913; London: Mills & Boon, 1914.
Biggle, Lloyd, Jr.	THE ANGRY ESPERS. New York: Ace, 1961; London: Hale, 1968.
Binder, Otto Oscar	THE NEW LIFE, as John Coleridge. New York: Columbia, 1940. MARTIAN MARTYRS, as John Coleridge. New York: Columbia, 1940.
Bindloss, Harold Edward	IN THE NIGER COUNTRY. Edinburgh: Blackwood, 1898.
Bingham, John Michael Ward, Lord Clanmoris	MY NAME IS MICHAEL SIBLEY. London: Gollancz; New York: Dodd Mead, 1952.
Bingley, David Ernest	MOSSYHORN TRAIL, as Christopher Wigan. London: Mills & Boon, 1957. OPERATION PEDESTAL, as David Horsley. London: Brown Watson, 1957.
Birney, Herman Hoffman	KING OF THE MESA, as Hoffman Birney. Philadelphia, 1927; London: Long, 1928.

AUTHOR	TITLE/FIRST EDITION INFORMATION
Bischoff, David Frederick	THE SEEKER, with Christopher Lampton. Toronto: Laser, 1976.
Bishop, Michael	A FUNERAL FOR THE EYES OF FIRE. New York: Ballantine, 1975; London: Sphere, 1978.
Bixby, Jerome Lewis	THE DEVIL'S SCRAPBOOK. New York: Brandon, 1964. SPACE BY THE TALE. New York: Ballantine, 1964.
Black, Laura	GLENDRACO. New York; London, 1977.
Blackburn, Paul	THE DISSOLVING FABRIC. Mallorca, 1955.
Blackmore, Jane	TOWARDS TOMORROW. London, 1941.
Blackmur, R. P.	T. S. ELIOT. Cambridge, England, 1928.
Blackwood, Algernon Henry	THE EMPTY HOUSE AND OTHER GHOST STORIES. London: Nash, 1906; New York: Vaughan, 1915.
Blair, Eric Arthur	DOWN AND OUT IN PARIS AND LONDON, as George Orwell. London: Gollancz; New York: Harper, 1933.
Blair, Kathryn	GREEN LEAVES, as Rosalind Brett. Hanley, England, 1947. PAGAN INTERLUDE, as Rosalind Brett. Hanley, England, 1947. SECRET MARRIAGE, as Rosalind Brett. London, 1947.
Blake, Forrester Avery	RIDING THE MUSTANG TRAIL. New York: Scribner, 1935.
Blake, Stephanie	FLOWERS OF FIRE. Chicago, 1977.
Blish, James Benjamin	JACK OF EAGLES. New York: Greenberg, 1952; London: Nova, 1955.
Bloch, Robert	SEA-KISSED. London: Utopian, 1945. THE OPENER OF THE WAY. Sauk City, Wis.: Arkham, 1945.
Bloom, Ursula Harvey	TIGER. Privately printed, 1903. WINIFRED. Privately printed, 1903.
Blunden, Edmund Charles	PASTORALS: A BOOK OF VERSES. London, 1916.

AUTHOR	TITLE/FIRST EDITION INFORMATION
Bly, Robert	THE SILENCE IN THE SNOWY FIELDS. Middletown, Conn., 1962.
Bodenheim, Maxwell	MINNA AND MYSELF. New York, 1918.
Bodington, Nancy Hermione	BACKGROUND FOR MURDER, as Shelley Smith. London: Swan, 1942.
Bogan, Louise	BODY OF THIS DEATH: POEMS. New York, 1923.
Boland, Bertram John	WHITE AUGUST, as John Boland. London: Joseph; New York: Arcadia, 1955.
Bone, Jesse F.	OBSERVATIONS ON THE OVARIES OF INFERTILE AND REPORTEDLY INFERTILE DAIRY CATTLE. Corvallis: Oregon State College, 1954.
Bonham, Frank	LOST STAGE VALLEY. New York: Simon & Schuster, 1948; Kingswood, England: World's Work, 1950.
Booth, Edwin	SHOWDOWN AT WARBIRD. New York, Ace: 1957. JINX RIDER. New York: Ace, 1957.
Booth, Rosemary	PONIES ON THE HEATHER, as Frances Murray. London: Collins, 1966.
Borg, Philip Anthony John	SHERIFF OF CLINTON, as Jack Borg. London: Jenkins, 1954. HELLBENT TRAIL, as Jack Borg. London: Jenkins, 1954.
Borland, Harold Glen	HEAPS OF GOLD, as Hal Borland. Privately printed, 1922.
Borland, Kathryn	SOUTHERN YANKEES, as Alice Abbott. Indianapolis, 1960.
Bosworth, Allan Rucker	WHEREVER THE GRASS GROWS. New York: Doubleday, 1941; London: Cassell, 1942. STEEL TO THE SUNSET, as Alamo Boyd. New York: Arcadia, 1941.
Bouma, Johanas L.	DANGER TRAIL. New York: Popular Library, 1954.
Bounds, Sydney James	DIMENSION OF HORROR. London: Panther, 1953. VENGEANCE VALLEY, as Wes Saunders. Leicester, England: Fiction House, 1953.

AUTHOR	TITLE/FIRST EDITION INFORMATION
Bourdillon, Francis	AMONG THE FLOWERS, AND OTHER POEMS. London, 1878.
Bova, Benjamin William	THE STAR CONQUERORS, as Ben Bova. Philadelphia: Winston, 1959.
Bowen-Judd, Sara	BLOODY INSTRUCTIONS, as Sara Woods. London: Collins; New York: Harper, 1962.
Bower, Bertha Muzzy	CHIP, OF THE FLYING U, as B. M. Bower. New York: Dillingham, 1906; London: Nelson, 1920.
Bowles, Jane	TWO SERIOUS LADIES. New York, 1943.
Bowles, Paul	TWO POEMS. New York, 1934.
Boyle, Kay	SHORT STORIES. Paris, 1929.
Brackett, Leigh Douglass	NO GOOD FROM A CORPSE. New York: Coward McCann, 1944.
Bradbury, Raymond Douglas	DARK CARNIVAL, as Ray Bradbury. Sauk City, Wis.: Arkham, 1947; London: Hamish Hamilton, 1948.
Bradford, Richard Roark	RED SKY AT MORNING. Philadelphia: Lippincott, 1968; London: Hodder & Stoughton, 1969.
Bradley, Marion Zimmer	SONGS FROM RIVENDELL. Privately printed, 1959.
Bragg, William Frederick	STARR OF WYOMING, as W. F. Bragg. London: Wright & Brown, 1936.
Braine, John	ROOM AT THE TOP. London, 1957.
Braithwaite, William S.	LYRICS OF LIFE AND LOVE. Boston, 1904.
Braun, Matthew	MATTIE SILKS, as Matt Braun. New York: Popular Library, 1972; London: Coronet, 1974. BLACK FOX, as Matt Braun. New York: Fawcett, 1972; London: Coronet, 1973.
Brennan, John Needham Huggard	RED COATS GALLOPING, as John Welcome. London: Constable, 1949.
Brent, Madeleine	TREGARON'S DAUGHTER. London; New York, 1971.
Brent, Peter Ludwig	CRY VENGEANCE, as Ludovic Peters. London; New York: Abelard Schuman, 1961.

AUTHOR	TITLE/FIRST EDITION INFORMATION
Bretnor, Reginald	THROUGH SPACE AND TIME WITH FERDINAND FEGHOOT, as Grendel Briarton. Berkeley, Calif.: Paradox, 1962.
Breuer, Miles John	THE GIRL FROM MARS, with Jack Williamson. New York: Stellar, 1929.
Brinnin, John Malcolm	THE GARDEN IS POLITICAL. New York, 1942.
Britt, Katrina	A KISS IN A GONDOLA. London, 1968.
Broderick, Damien	A MAN RETURNED. Sydney, Australia: Horwitz, 1965.
Bromfield, Louis	THE GREEN BAY TREE. New York, 1924.
Bromige, Iris Amy Edna	THE TRACEYS. London, 1946.
Brooks, Gwendolyn	A STREET IN BRONZEVILLE. New York, 1945.
Broster, Dorothy Kathleen	CHANTEMERLE with Gertrude Winifred Taylor. London; New York, 1911.
Brown, Dee Alexander	WAVE HIGH THE BANNER. Philadelphia: Macrae Smith, 1942.
Brown, Fredric	THE FABULOUS CLIPJOINT. New York: Dutton, 1947; London: Boardman, 1949.
Brown, James Cooke	LOGLAN, with L. F. Brown. 5 vols. Gainesville, Fla.: Loglan Institute, 1963-1975.
Brown, Joseph Paul Summers	JIM KANE, as J. P. S. Brown. New York: Dial, 1970; as POCKET MONEY, as J. P. S. Brown. London: Sphere, 1972.
Brunner, John Kilian Houston	HORSES AT HOME. London: Spring, 1958.
Bryher, Winifred	THE LAMENT FOR ADONIS. London, 1918.
Bryant, Edward Winslow, Jr.	AMONG THE DEAD AND OTHER EVENTS LEADING UP TO THE APOCALYPSE. New York: Macmillan, 1973.
Buchan, John	SIR QUIXOTE OF THE MOORS. London; New York, 1895.
Buchanan, Eileen Marie Duell	DEATH IN DEAKINS WOOD, as Rhona Petrie. London: Gollancz, 1963; New York: Dodd Mead, 1964.

AUTHOR	TITLE/FIRST EDITION INFORMATION
Budrys, Algirdas Jonas	FALSE NIGHT, as Algis Budrys. New York: Lion, 1954; London: Mayflower, 1963.
Buechner, Frederick	A LONG DAY'S DYING. New York, 1950.
Bullen, Frank T.	THE CRUISE OF THE "CACHALOT." London, 1898.
Bulmer, Henry Kenneth	SPACE TREASON, as Kenneth Bulmer, with A. V. Clarke. London: Panther, 1952. CYBERNETIC CONTROLLER, as Kenneth Bulmer, with A. V. Clarke. London: Panther, 1952. ENCOUNTER IN SPACE, as Kenneth Bulmer. London: Panther, 1952.
Bunner, H. C.	A WOMAN OF HONOR. Boston, 1883.
Bunting, Basil	REDIMICULUM MATELLARUM. Milan, 1930.
Burchardt, William Robert	THE WILDCATTERS, as Bill Burchardt. New York: Ace, 1963.
Burdette, Robert J.	THE RISE AND FALL OF THE MUSTACHE. Burlington, 1877.
Burdick, Eugene Leonard	THE NINTH WAVE. Boston: Houghton Mifflin; London: Gollancz, 1956.
Burford, Lolah	VICE AVENGED: A MORAL TALE. New York; London, 1971.
Burge, Milward Rodon Kennedy	THE BLESTON MYSTERY, as Robert Milward Kennedy, with A. Gordon MacDonnell. London: Gollancz, 1928; New York: Doubleday, 1929.
Burgess, Frank Gelett	THE PURPLE COW! San Francisco, 1895. 8 leaves.
Burghley, Rose	AND BE THY LOVE. London, 1958.
Burgin, George Brown	HIS LORDSHIP, AND OTHERS. London, 1893.
Burke, Kenneth	THE WHITE OXEN AND OTHER STORIES. New York, 1924.
Burnett, Frances Hodgson	THAT LASS O LOWRIE'S. New York, 1877.

AUTHOR	TITLE/FIRST EDITION INFORMATION
Burnett, William Riley	LITTLE CAESAR, as W. R. Burnett. New York: Dial; London: Cape, 1929.
Burns, John Horne	THE GALLERY. New York, 1947.
Burns, Walter Noble	A YEAR WITH A WHALER. New York: Outing, 1913.
Burroughs, Edgar Rice	TARZAN OF THE APES. Chicago: McClurg, 1914; London: Methuen, 1917.
Burroughs, William Seward	JUNKIE: CONFESSIONS OF AN UNREDEEMED DRUG ADDICT, as William Lee. New York: Ace, 1953; London: Digit, 1957.
Burt, Katharine	THE BRANDING IRON. Boston: Houghton Mifflin; London: Constable, 1919.
Busch, Niven	TWENTY-ONE AMERICANS, BEING PROFILES OF SOME PEOPLE IN OUR TIME, TOGETHER WITH SILLY PICTURES OF THEM DRAWN BY DE MISKEY. New York: Doubleday, 1930.
Butler, Gwendoline	RECEIPT FOR MURDER. London, 1956.
Butler, Samuel	A FIRST YEAR IN CANTERBURY SETTLEMENT. London, 1863.
Butterworth, Michael	THE SOUNDLESS SCREAM. London: Long; New York: Doubleday, 1967.
Butts, Mary	SPEED THE PLOW AND OTHER STORIES. London, 1923.
Buxton, Anne	THE BEST LOVE OF ALL, as Anne Maybury. London: Mills & Boon, 1932. THE ENCHANTED KINGDOM, as Anne Maybury. London: Mills & Boon, 1932. THE LOVE THAT IS STRONGER THAN LIFE, as Anne Maybury. London: Mills & Boon, 1932. LOVE TRIUMPHANT, as Anne Maybury. London: Mills & Boon, 1932.
Bynner, Witter	AN ODE TO HARVARD AND OTHER POEMS. Boston, 1907.
Cabell, James Branch	THE EAGLE'S SHADOW. New York, 1904.

AUTHOR	TITLE/FIRST EDITION INFORMATION
Cadell, Violet Elizabeth	MY DEAR AUNT FLORA. London, 1946.
Cain, James Mallahan	OUR GOVERNMENT. New York, 1930.
Caine, Thomas Henry Hall	RICHARD III AND MACBETH: A DRAMATIC STUDY, as Hall Caine. London, 1877.
Caird, Janet Hinshaw	ANGUS THE TARTAN PARTAN. London, 1961.
Caldwell, Erskine	THE BASTARD. New York, 1929.
Caldwell, Janet Miriam Taylor Holland	DYNASTY OF DEATH, as Taylor Caldwell. New York, 1938.
Calisher, Hortense	IN THE ABSENCE OF ANGELS. Boston, 1951.
Callaghan, Morley	STRANGE FUGITIVE. New York, 1928.
Cameron, Lou	ANGEL'S FLIGHT. New York: Fawcett, 1960; London: Muller, 1962.
Campbell, Gabrielle Margaret Vere	THE VIPER OF MILAN, as Marjorie Bowen. London: Alston Rivers; New York: McClure Phillips, 1906.
Campbell, Roy	THE FLAMING TERRAPIN. London, 1924.
Capote, Truman	OTHER VOICES, OTHER ROOMS. New York, 1948.
Capps, Benjamin Franklin	HANGING AT COMANCHE WELLS. New York: Ballantine, 1962.
Carleton, William M.	FAX: A CAMPAIGN POEM. Chicago, 1868.
Carr, Robyn	CHELYNNE. Boston, 1980
Carter, Forrest	THE REBEL OUTLAW, JOSEY WALES. Gantt, Ala.: Whipporwill, 1973; as GONE TO TEXAS. London: Weidenfeld & Nicolson, 1975.
Carter, Linwood Vrooman	THE WIZARD OF LEMURIA, as Lin Carter. New York: Ace, 1965.
Cartland, Barbara Hamilton	JIG-SAW. London, 1925.
Case, David	THE CELL: THREE TALES OF HORROR. New York, 1969.

AUTHOR	TITLE/FIRST EDITION INFORMATION
Case, Robert Ormond	JUST BUCKAROOS. New York: Chelsea House, 1927.
Castaneda, Carlos	THE TEACHINGS OF DON JUAN/A YAQUI WAY OF KNOWLEDGE. Berkeley, Calif., 1968.
Cather, Willa Sibert	APRIL TWILIGHTS. Boston: Badger, 1903.
Cawein, Madison J.	BLOOMS OF THE BERRY. Louisville, Ky., 1887.
Chance, John Newton	MURDER IN OILS. London: Gollancz, 1935. WHEELS IN THE FOREST. London: Gollancz, 1935.
Chandler, Raymond Thornton	THE BIG SLEEP. New York, 1939.
Channing, William Ellery	THE DUTIES OF CHILDREN. Boston, 1807.
Chapman, Hester Wolferstan	SHE SAW THEM GO BY. London; Boston, 1933.
Chappell, Mollie	LITTLE TOM SPARROW. Leeds, England, 1950.
Charbonneau, Louis Henry	NO PLACE ON EARTH. New York: Doubleday, 1958; London: Jenkins, 1966.
Chase, Borden	EAST RIVER. New York: Crowell, 1935.
Cheever, John	THE WAY SOME PEOPLE LIVE. New York, 1943.
Chesnutt, Charles W.	THE CONJURE WOMAN. Boston, 1899.
Chesterton, Gilbert Keith	GREYBEARDS AT PLAY: LITERATURE AND ART FOR OLD GENTLEMEN: RHYMES AND SKETCHES, as G. K. Chesterton. London: Brimley Johnson, 1900. THE WILD KNIGHT AND OTHER POEMS, as G. K. Chesterton. London: Richards, 1900.
Chisholm, Arthur Murray	THE BOSS OF WIND RIVER, as A. M. Chisholm. New York: Doubleday, 1911.
Chivers, Thomas Holley	THE PATH OF SORROW. Franklin, 1832.
Clark, Charles Heber	OUT OF THE HURLY-BURLY, as Max Adeler. Philadelphia, 1874. Also the first book illustrated by A. B. Frost.

AUTHOR	**TITLE/FIRST EDITION INFORMATION**
Clark, Patricia Denise	THE ADVENTURES OF THE THREE BABY BUNNIES, as Patricia Robins. London: Nicholson & Watson, 1934.
Clark, Walter van Tilburg	CHRISTMAS COMES TO HJALSEN, RENO. Reno, Nev.: Reno Publishing House, 1930.
Clarke, Arthur Charles	INTERPLANETARY FLIGHT: AN INTRODUCTION TO ASTRONAUTICS. London: Temple Press, 1950; New York: Harper, 1951.
Clarke, David Waldo	MODERN ENGLISH WRITERS, as Dave Waldo. London: Longman, 1947.
Clavell, James	KING RAT. Boston, 1962.
Cleeve, Brian Talbot	THE FAR HILLS. London, 1952.
Clemens, Samuel Langhorne	THE CELEBRATED JUMPING FROG OF CALAVERAS COUNTY AND OTHER SKETCHES, as Mark Twain. New York: Webb, 1867.
Cleugh, Sophia	MATILDA, GOVERNESS OF THE ENGLISH. New York, 1924.
Cobb, Irvin S.	BACK HOME. New York, 1912.
Coburn, Walter J.	THE RINGTAILED RANNYHANS, as Walt Coburn. New York: Century, 1927.
Cockrell, Marian	YESTERDAY'S MADNESS. New York, 1943.
Cody, Stetson	CACTUS CLANCY RIDES. London: Allen, 1949.
Coffman, Virginia Edith	MOURA. New York, 1959.
Coghlan, Peggie	THE SPOILED EARTH, as Jessica Stirling, with Hugh C. Rae. London: Hodder & Stoughton, 1974; as STRATHMORE. New York: Delacorte, 1975.
Coldsmith, Donald C.	HORSIN' AROUND, as Don Coldsmith. San Antonio, Tex.: Naylor, 1975.
Collin, Marion	ROMANTIC FICTION, with Anne Britton. London, 1960.

AUTHOR	TITLE/FIRST EDITION INFORMATION
Collins, Wilkie	MEMOIRS OF THE LIFE OF WILLIAM COLLINS, R. A. 2 vols. London, 1848.
Comfort, Will Levington	TROOPER TALES: A SERIES OF SKETCHES OF THE REAL AMERICAN PRIVATE SOLDIER. New York: Street & Smith, 1899.
Compton-Burnett, Ivy	DOLORES. Edinburgh, 1911.
Conarain, Alice Nina	LOVE IN APRON STRINGS, as Elizabeth Hoy. London, 1933.
Condon, Richard Thomas	THE OLDEST CONFESSION. New York: Appleton Century Crofts, 1958; as THE HAPPY THIEVES. New York: Bantam, 1962.
Conly, Robert Leslie	THE SILVER CROWN, as Robert C. O'Brien. New York: Atheneum, 1968; London: Gollancz, 1973.
Connolly, Cyril	THE ROCK POOL. Paris, 1936.
Conroy, Jack	THE DISINHERITED. New York, 1933.
Constiner, Merle	HEARSE OF A DIFFERENT COLOR. New York: Phoenix, 1952.
Cook, Ida	WIFE TO CHRISTOPHER, as Mary Burchell. London, 1936.
Cook, William Everett	FRONTIER FEUD, as Will Cook. New York: Popular Library, 1954. PRAIRIE GUNS, as Will Cook. New York: Popular Library, 1954.
Cook, William Wallace	HIS FRIEND THE ENEMY. New York: Dillingham, 1903.
Cookson, Catherine Ann	KATE HANNIGAN. London, 1950.
Coolidge, Dane	HIDDEN WATER. Chicago: McClurg, 1910.
Coolidge, Susan	THE NEW YEAR'S BARGAIN. Boston: Roberts; London: Warne, 1872.
Cooper, Courtney Ryley	US KIDS: VERSES. Kansas City, Mo.: Kellog Baxter, 1910.
Cooper, Henry St. John	BULL-DOGS AND BULL-DOG BREEDING. London: Jarrolds, 1905.

AUTHOR	TITLE/FIRST EDITION INFORMATION
Cooper, Jilly	HOW TO STAY MARRIED. London, 1969.
Coover, Robert	THE ORIGIN OF THE BRUNISTS. New York, 1966.
Corle, Edwin	MOJAVE: A BOOK OF STORIES. New York: Liveright, 1934.
Cornwell, David John Moore	CALL FOR THE DEAD, as John LeCarre. London: Gollancz, 1961; New York: Walker, 1962.
Cort, Van	THE RANGERS OF BLOODY SILVER. New York: Phoenix, 1941; as BLOOD ON THE MOON. London: Hodder & Stoughton, 1941.
Costain, Thomas Bertram	FOR MY GREAT FOLLY. New York, 1942.
Coulson, Juanita	CRISIS ON CHEIRON. New York: Ace, 1967.
Courtney, Caroline	DUCHESS IN DISGUISE. New York; London, 1979. A WAGER FOR LOVE. New York; London, 1979. LOVE UNMASKED. New York; London, 1979.
Coward, Noel	"I'LL LEAVE IT TO YOU." London, 1920.
Cowen, Frances	IN THE CLUTCH OF THE GREEN HAND. London, 1929.
Cox, William Robert	MAKE MY COFFIN STRONG. New York: Fawcett, 1954; London: Fawcett, 1955.
Coxe, Louis	THE SEA FARING AND OTHER POEMS. New York, 1947
Cozzens, James Gould	CONFUSION. Boston, 1924.
Craig, Mary Francis	SIMPLE SPIGOTT. New York, 1960.
Crews, Harry	THE GOSPEL SINGER. New York, 1968.
Cronin, A. J.	HATTER'S CASTLE. London, 1931.
Crook, Compton Newby	THE STARDUST VOYAGES, as Stephen Tall. New York: Berkley, 1975.
Crosby, Caresse	CROSSES OF GOLD: A BOOK OF VERSE. Paris, 1925.
Crosby, Harry C.	THE DAY THE MACHINES STOPPED, as Christopher Anvil. Derby, Conn.: Monarch, 1964.

AUTHOR	TITLE/FIRST EDITION INFORMATION
Crothers, Samuel McCord	MISS MUFFET'S CHRISTMAS PARTY. St. Paul, Minn., 1892.
Crowe, Cecily	MISS SPRING. New York, 1953.
Cullen, Countee	COLOR. New York, 1925.
Cullum, Ridgewell	THE DEVIL'S KEG. London: Chapman & Hall, 1903; as THE STORY OF THE FOSS RIVER RANCH. Boston: Page, 1903.
Culp, John Hewett, Jr.	BORN OF THE SUN. New York: Sloane, 1959; London: Deutsch, 1963.
Cunningham, Chet	BUSHWHACKERS AT CIRCLE K. New York: Avalon, 1969.
Cunningham, Eugene	THE REGULATION GUY. New York: Cornhill, 1922. GYPSYING THROUGH CENTRAL AMERICA. New York: Dutton; London: Unwin, 1922.
Curry, Peggy Simson	FIRE IN THE WATER. New York: McGraw Hill, 1951; London: Muller, 1952.
Curtis, Thomas Dale and Sharon	A HEART TOO PROUD, as Laura London. New York: Dell, 1978.
Curwood, James Oliver	THE COURAGE OF CAPTAIN PLUM. Indianapolis: Bobbs Merrill, 1908; London: Hodder & Stoughton, 1925. THE WOLF HUNTERS: A TALE OF ADVENTURE IN THE WILDERNESS. Indianapolis: Bobbs Merrill, 1908; London: Cassell, 1917.
Cushman, Dan	MONTANA, HERE I BE! New York: Macmillan, 1950; London: Laurie, 1953.
Dahlberg, Edward	BOTTOM DOGS. London, 1929.
Dailey, Janet	NO QUARTER ASKED. London: Mills & Boon, 1974; Toronto: Harlequin, 1976. SAVAGE LAND. London: Mills & Boon, 1974; Toronto: Harlequin, 1976.
Danbury, Iris	THE GENTLE INVADER. London, 1957.

AUTHOR	TITLE/FIRST EDITION INFORMATION
Daniels, Dorothy	THE DARK RIDER, as Geraldine Thayer. New York, 1961. THE CADUCEUS TREE, as Suzanne Somers. New York, 1961.
Dannay, Frederic	THE ROMAN HAT MYSTERY, as Ellery Queen, with Manfred B. Lee. New York: Stokes; London: Gollancz, 1929.
Darcy, Clare	GEORGINA. New York, 1971.
Davenport, Marcia	MOZART. New York, 1932.
Davidson, Donald	AN OUTLAND PIPER. Boston, 1924.
Davies, John Evan Weston	THE ACHILLES AFFAIR, as Berkely Mather. London: Collins; New York: Scribner, 1959.
Davies, W. H.	THE SOUL'S DESTROYER, AND OTHER POEMS. London, 1905.
Davis, Dorothy Salisbury	THE JUDAS CAT. New York, 1949.
Davis, Harold Lenoir	HONEY IN THE HORN, as H. L. Davis. New York: Harper; London: Lovat Dickson & Thompson, 1935.
Davis, Rebecca	MARGARET HOWTH: A STORY OF TO-DAY. Boston, 1862.
Day, Robert S.	THE LAST CATTLE DRIVE. New York: Putnam; London: Secker & Warburg, 1977.
Day-Lewis, Cecil	BEECHEN VIGIL & OTHER POEMS. London, 1925.
Decker, William	TO BE A MAN. Boston: Little, Brown, 1967.
Deeping, George Warwick	UTHER AND IGRAINE. London; New York, 1903.
Deland, Margaret	THE OLD GARDEN AND OTHER VERSES. Boston, 1886.
De la Pasture, Edmee Elizabeth Monica	ZELLA SEES HERSELF, as E. M. Delafield. London; New York, 1917.
De la Roche, Mazo Louise	EXPLORERS OF THE DAWN. New York; London, 1922.
Delderfield, Ronald Frederick	THESE CLICKS MADE HISTORY: THE STORIES OF STANLEY "GLORIOUS" DEVON, FLEET STREET PHOTOGRAPHER. Exmouth, England, 1946.

AUTHOR	TITLE/FIRST EDITION INFORMATION
Dell, Ethel Mary	THE WAY OF AN EAGLE. New York, 1911.
Dell, Floyd	WOMEN AS WORLD BUILDERS. Chicago, 1913.
Delmar, Vina	BAD GIRL. New York, 1928.
De Morgan, William	JOSEPH VANCE. London, 1906.
Denver, Lee	GUN FEUD AT SUNROCK. London: Skeffington, 1951.
De Rosso, Henry Andrew	.44, as H. A. De Rosso. New York: Lion, 1953; London: Mills & Boon, 1957.
De Schanschieff, Juliet Dymoke	THE SONS OF THE TRIBUNE: AN ADVENTURE ON THE ROMAN WALL. London, 1956.
Deutsch, Babette	BANNERS. New York, 1919.
De Voto, Bernard Augustine	THE CROOKED MILE. New York: Minton Balch, 1924.
De Vries, Peter	BUT WHO WAKES THE BUGLER? Boston, 1940.
De Weese-Wehen, Joy	STAIRWAY TO A SECRET. New York: Dutton, 1953.
Dewlen, Al	THE NIGHT OF THE TIGER. New York, 1956.
Dick, Philip Kindred	SOLAR LOTTERY. New York: Ace, 1955; as WORLD OF CHANCE. London: Rich & Cowan, 1956. A HANDFUL OF DARKNESS. London: Rich & Cowan, 1955; Boston: Gregg Press, 1978.
Didion, Joan	RUN RIVER. New York, 1963.
Di Donato, Pietro	CHRIST IN CONCRETE. Chicago, 1939.
Dingwell, Joyce	AUSTRALIAN HOSPITAL. London, 1955.
Diver, Katherine Helen Maud	THE ENGLISHWOMAN IN INDIA, as Maud Diver. Edinburgh, 1909.
Dobson, Austin	VIGNETTES IN RHYME. London, 1873.
Doctorow, Edgar Laurence	WELCOME TO HARD TIMES, as E. L. Doctorow. New York, 1960.

AUTHOR	TITLE/FIRST EDITION INFORMATION
Dodge, Mary Mapes	THE IRVINGTON STORIES, as M. E. Dodge. New York: O'Kane, 1865. HANS BRINKER; OR, THE SILVER SKATES: A STORY OF LIFE IN HOLLAND. New York: O'Kane, 1865; as THE SILVER SKATES. London: Sampson Low, 1867.
Dodgson, Charles Lutwidge	THE FIFTH BOOK OF EUCLID TREATED ALGEBRAICALLY, as C. L. Dodgson. Oxford: Parker, 1858.
Donleavy, J. P.	THE GINGER MAN. Paris, 1955.
Doolittle, Hilda	SEA GARDEN: IMAGIST POEMS, as H. D. London, 1916.
Dorn, Edward	WHAT I SEE IN THE MAXIMUS POEMS. Ventura, Calif., 1960.
Douglas, Lord Alfred	POEMES. Paris, 1896.
Dowler, James Ross	PARTNER'S CHOICE. New York, 1958.
Doyle, Arthur Conan	A STUDY IN SCARLET. London: Ward Lock, 1888; Philadelphia: Lippincott, 1890.
Drago, Harry Sinclair	WHOSO FINDETH A WIFE, as J. Wesley Putnam. New York, 1914.
Dresser, Davis	MARDI GRAS MADNESS, as Anthony Scott. New York, 1934.
Drinkwater, John	POEMS. Birmingham, 1903.
Dufault, Joseph Ernest Nephtali	COWBOYS NORTH AND SOUTH, as Will James. New York; London: Scribner, 1924.
Duffield, Anne	MISS MAYHEW AND MING YUN: A STORY OF EAST AND WEST. New York, 1928.
Du Maurier, Daphne	THE LOVING SPIRIT. London; New York, 1931.
Dunbar, Paul Laurence	OAK AND IVY. Dayton, Ohio, 1893.
Duncan, Robert Lipscomb	THE Q DOCUMENT, as James Hall Roberts. New York: Morrow, 1964; London: Cape, 1965.
Dunkerley, Elsie Jeanette	GOBLIN ISLAND, as Elsie Oxenham. London: Collins, 1907.

AUTHOR	TITLE/FIRST EDITION INFORMATION
Dunlop, Agnes M. R.	THE BEGONIA BED, as Elisabeth Kyle. London: Constable; Indianapolis: Bobbs Merrill, 1934.
Dunne, John Gregory	DELANO: THE STORY OF THE CALIFORNIA GRAPE STRIKE. New York, 1967.
Dunnett, Dorothy	THE GAME OF KINGS. New York, 1961.
Durham, Marilyn	THE MAN WHO LOVED CAT DANCING. New York; London, 1972.
Durrell, Lawrence George	QUAINT FRAGMENT: POEMS WRITTEN BETWEEN THE AGES OF SIXTEEN AND NINETEEN. London: Cecil Press, 1931.
Durst, Paul	DIE, DAMN YOU! New York, 1952.
East, Fred	MEDDLING MAVERICK, as Tom West. New York: Dutton, 1944; London: Ward Lock, 1946.
Eastlake, William Derry	GO IN BEAUTY. New York, 1956.
Easton, Robert Olney	THE HAPPY MAN. New York, 1943.
Ebel, Suzanne	LOVE, THE MAGICIAN. London, 1956.
Eberhart, Mignon Good	THE PATIENT IN ROOM 18. New York; London, 1929.
Eberhart, Richard	A BRAVERY OF EARTH. London, 1930.
Eddison, E. R.	THE WORM OUROBOROS. London, 1922.
Eden, Dorothy	SINGING SHADOWS. London, 1940.
Edginton, Helen Marion	THE WEIGHT CARRIERS, as May Edginton. London, 1909.
Edmonds, Walter Dumaux	ROME HAUL. Boston, 1929.
Edson, John Thomas	TRAIL BOSS. London, 1961.
Edwards, Anne	A CHILD'S BIBLE. London, 1967.
Ehrlich, John Gunther	REVENGE, as Jack Ehrlich. New York, 1958.
Eliot, Thomas Stearns	PRUFROCK AND OTHER OBSERVATIONS. London, 1917.

AUTHOR	TITLE/FIRST EDITION INFORMATION
Elkin, Stanley	BOSWELL. New York, 1964.
Ellerbeck, Rosemary Anne L'Estrange	INCLINATION TO MURDER. London, 1965.
Elles, Dora Amy	A CHILD'S RHYME BOOK, as Patricia Wentworth. London: Melrose, 1910. A MARRIAGE UNDER THE TERROR. London: Melrose; New York: Putnam, 1910.
Ellison, Harlan Jay	RUMBLE. New York: Pyramid, 1958. THE DEADLY STREETS. New York: Ace, 1958; London: Digit, 1959.
Ellison, Ralph	INVISIBLE MAN. New York, 1952.
Elston, Allan Vaughan	COME OUT AND FIGHT! New York, 1941.
Emanuel, Victor Rousseau	DERWENT'S HORSE, as Victor Rousseau. London: Methuen, 1901.
Erdman, Loula Grace	SEPARATE STAR. New York, 1944.
Ernenwein, Leslie	GUNSMOKE GALOOT. New York, 1941.
Erskine-Lindop, Audry Beatrice Noel	FORTUNE MY FOE. New York, 1947.
Ertz, Susan	MADAME CLAIRE. London; New York, 1923.
Estleman, Loren D.	THE OKLAHOMA PUNK. Canoga Park, Calif., 1976.
Estridge, Robin	THE FUTURE IS TOMORROW. London: Davies, 1947.
Evans, Max	SOUTHWEST WIND. San Antonio, Tex., 1958.
Evarts, Hal George, Sr.	THE CROSS-PULL. New York; London, 1920.
Evarts, Hal George, Jr.	ROLLING AHEAD. Paris, 1945 .
Evelyn, John Michael	MURDER ON TRIAL, as Michael Underwood. London: Hammond, 1954; New York: Washburn, 1958.
Everett, Edward	A DEFENSE OF CHRISTIANITY. Boston, 1814.

AUTHOR	TITLE/FIRST EDITION INFORMATION
Everson, Bill William	THESE ARE THE RAVENS. San Leandro, Calif., 1935.
Ewing, Juliana Horatia	MELCHIOR'S DREAM AND OTHER TALES. London: Bell & Daldy, 1862; Boston: Roberts, 1886.
Exley, Frederick	A FAN'S NOTES. New York, 1968.
Fante, John	WAIT UNTIL SPRING, BANDINI. New York, 1938.
Farnes, Eleanor	MERRY GOES THE TIME. London, 1935.
Farnol, John Jeffrey	MY LADY CAPRICE. London; New York, 1907.
Farrell, Cliff	FOLLOW THE NEW GRASS. New York, 1945.
Farrell, James Thomas	YOUNG LONIGAN: A BOYHOOD IN CHICAGO. New York, 1932.
Fast, Howard Melvin	TWO VALLEYS. New York: Dial; London: Dickson, 1934.
Faulkner, William	THE MARBLE FAUN. Boston, 1924.
Faust, Frederick Schiller	THE UNTAMED, as Max Brand. New York: Putnam, 1919; London: Hodder & Stoughton, 1952.
Fearing, Kenneth Flexner	ANGEL ARMS. New York, 1929.
Feibleman, James K.	DEATH OF THE GOD IN MEXICO. New York, 1931.
Feinberg, Bea	A WORLD FULL OF STRANGERS, as Cynthia Freeman. New York, 1975.
Fellows, Catherine	LEONORA. London, 1972.
Felton, Ronald Oliver	THE BLACK CAR MYSTERY, as Ronald Welch. London: Pitman, 1950.
Ferber, Edna	DAWN O'HARA: THE GIRL WHO LAUGHED. New York, 1911.
Fergusson, Harvey	CAPITOL HILL. New York, 1923.
Ferlinghetti, Lawrence	PICTURE OF THE GONE WORLD. San Francisco, 1955.

AUTHOR	**TITLE/FIRST EDITION INFORMATION**
Ferrini, Vincent	NO SMOKE. Portland, 1941.
Field, Eugene	TRIBUNE PRIMER. Denver, 1881.
Field, Rachel Lyman	THE POINTED PEOPLE: VERSES AND SILHOUETTES. New Haven, Conn.; London, 1924.
Finley, Glenna	DEATH STRIKES OUT. New York, 1957.
Finney, Charles G.	THE CIRCUS OF DOCTOR LAO. New York, 1935.
Firbank, Arthur Ronald	ODETTE D'ANTREVERNES. London, 1905.
Fisher, Vardis Alvero	SONNETS: TO AN IMAGINARY MADONNA. New York, 1927.
Fitzgerald, F. Scott	THIS SIDE OF PARADISE. New York, 1920.
Fitzgerald, Robert	POEMS. New York, 1935.
Fitzgerald, Valerie	ZEMINDAR. London, 1981.
Flanner, Janet	THE CUBICAL CITY. New York, 1926.
Fleming, Ian Lancaster	CASINO ROYALE. London, 1953.
Fletcher, John Gould	FIRE AND WINE. London: May, 1913.
Flynn, Robert Lopez	NORTH TO YESTERDAY. New York; London, 1967.
Flynn, Thomas Theodore	IT'S MURDER! as T. T. Flynn. London, 1950.
Foreman, Leonard London	DON DESPERADO, as L. L. Foreman. New York, 1941.
Forester, C. S.	A PAWN AMONG KINGS. London, 1924.
Forster, Edward Morgan	WHERE ANGELS FEAR TO TREAD, as E. M. Forster. Edinburgh: Blackwood, 1905; New York: Knopf, 1920.
Foster, Walter Bertram	THE LOST GALLEON OF DOUBLOON ISLAND, as W. Bert Foster. Philadelphia, 1901.
Fowler, Kenneth Abrams	OUTCAST OF MURDER MESA. New York, 1954.
Fowles, John	THE COLLECTOR. London, 1963.

AUTHOR	TITLE/FIRST EDITION INFORMATION
Fox, John, Jr.	A CUMBERLAND VENDETTA AND OTHER STORIES. New York, 1896.
Fox, Norman Arnold	GUN-HANDY. New York, 1941.
Frankau, Gilbert	ETON ECHOES: A VOLUME OF HUMOROUS VERSE. Eton, England, 1901.
Franken, Rose Dorothy	PATTERN. New York, 1925.
Frazee, Charles Steve	RANGE TROUBLE, as Dean Jennings. New York: Phoenix, 1951. SHINING MOUNTAINS. New York: Rinehart, 1951; London: Muller, 1953.
Frederic, Harold	SETH'S BROTHER'S WIFE. New York, 1887.
Friedman, Bruce Jay	STERN. New York, 1962.
Friedman, I. K.	THE LUCKY NUMBER. Chicago, 1896.
Fry, Christopher	THE BOY WITH A CART. London, 1939.
Fry, Roger	GIOVANNI BELLINI. London, 1899.
Gaddis, William	THE RECOGNITIONS. New York, 1955.
Gaines, Ernest	CATHERINE CARMIER. New York, 1964.
Gallagher, Patricia	THE SONS AND THE DAUGHTERS. New York; London, 1961.
Gandley, Kenneth Royce	MY TURN TO DIE, as Kenneth Royce. London: Barker, 1958.
Gann, Walter	THE TRAIL BOSS. Boston, 1937.
Gardiner, Dorothy	THE TRANSATLANTIC GHOST. New York; London, 1933.
Gardner, John	RESURRECTION. New York, 1966.
Garfield, Brian Francis Wynne	RANGE JUSTICE. New York, 1960.
Garland, Hannibal Hamlin	MAIN-TRAVELLED ROADS: SIX MISSISSIPPI VALLEY STORIES. Boston, 1891.
Garvice, Charles	EVE AND OTHER VERSES. Privately printed, 1873.
Gaskin, Catherine	THIS OTHER EDEN. London, 1947.
Gass, William H.	OMENSETTER'S LUCK. New York, 1966.

AUTHOR	TITLE/FIRST EDITION INFORMATION
Gaulden, Ray	THE ROUGH AND LONELY LAND. London, 1957.
Gavin, Catherine Irvine	LOUIS PHILIPPE, KING OF THE FRENCH. London, 1933.
Geisel, Theodor Seuss	AND TO THINK THAT I SAW IT ON MULBERRY STREET, as Dr. Seuss. New York: Vanguard, 1937; London: Country Life, 1939.
Gellis, Roberta Leah	KNIGHT'S HONOR. New York, 1964.
George, Henry	OUR LAND AND LAND POLICY, NATIONAL AND STATE. San Francisco, 1871.
Germano, Peter B.	TRAIL BOSS FROM TEXAS, as Barry Cord. New York: Phoenix; London: Foulsham, 1948.
Giggal, Kenneth	THE MANCHESTER THING, as Angus Ross. London: Long, 1970.
Gilbert, William Schwenk	A NEW AND ORIGINAL EXTRAVAGANZA ENTITLED DULCAMARA; OR, THE LITTLE DUCK AND THE GREAT QUACK. London, 1866.
Gilder, Richard Watson	THE NEW DAY. New York, 1876.
Giles, Janice Holt	THE ENDURING HILLS. Philadelphia, 1950.
Giles, Kenneth	SOME BEASTS NO MORE. London: Gollancz, 1965; New York: Walker, 1968.
Gill, Brendan	DEATH IN APRIL AND OTHER POEMS. Windham, Conn., 1935.
Gipson, Frederick Benjamin	FABULOUS EMPIRE: COLONEL ZACK MILLER'S STORY, as Fred Gipson. Boston, 1946.
Gissing, George	WORKERS IN THE DAWN. London, 1880.
Glasscock, Anne	KENNEDY'S GOLD, as Michael Bonner. New York: Doubleday, 1960; London: Collins, 1961.

AUTHOR	TITLE/FIRST EDITION INFORMATION
Glidden, Frederick Dilley	THE FEUD AT SINGLE SHOT, as Luke Short. New York: Farrar & Rinehart; London: Collins, 1936.
Glidden, Jonathan H.	THE CRIMSON HORSESHOE, as Peter Dawson. New York: Dodd Mead; London: Collins, 1941. THE STAGLINE FEUD, as Peter Dawson. New York: Dodd Mead, 1941; London: Collins, 1942.
Gluyas, Constance	THE KING'S BRAT. Englewood Cliffs, N.J., 1972.
Glyn, Elinor	THE VISITS OF ELIZABETH. London, 1900.
Godden, Margaret Rumer	CHINESE PUZZLE. London, 1936.
Godwin, Gail	THE PERFECTIONISTS. New York, 1970.
Golding, William Gerald	POEMS. London: Macmillan, 1934; New York: Macmillan, 1935.
Goldstone, Lawrence Arthur	BRINGING SHERLOCK HOME, as Lawrence Treat. New York: Doubleday, 1930.
Gooden, Arthur Henry	CROSS KNIFE RANCH. London, 1933.
Goodman, Paul	TEN LYRIC POEMS. New York, 1934.
Gordon, Charles William	GWEN'S CANYON, as Ralph Connor. Toronto: Westminster, 1898. BEYOND THE MARSHES, as Ralph Connor. Toronto: Westminster, 1898. BLACK ROCK: A TALE OF THE SELKIRKS, as Ralph Connor. Toronto: Westminster; Chicago: Revell; and London: Hodder & Stoughton, 1898.
Gordon, Ethel Edison	WHERE DOES THE SUMMER GO? New York, 1967.
Goudge, Elizabeth de Beauchamp	THE FAIRIES' BABY AND OTHER STORIES. London, 1919.
Goyder, Margot, and Anne Neville	MARIETTA IS STOLEN, as Margot Neville. London: Parsons, 1922.
Goyen, William	THE HOUSE OF BREATH. New York, 1950.
Graham, Roger Phillips	TIME TRAP, as Rog Phillips. Chicago: Century, 1949.

AUTHOR	TITLE/FIRST EDITION INFORMATION
Grahame, Kenneth	PAGAN PAPERS. London, 1894.
Grau, Shirley Ann	THE BLACK PRINCE AND OTHER STORIES. New York, 1955.
Graves, John	GOODBYE TO A RIVER. New York, 1960.
Graves, Robert Ranke	OVER THE BRAZIER. London: Poetry Bookshop, 1916; New York: St. Martin's, 1975. GOLIATH AND DAVID. London: Chiswick, 1916.
Gray, Pearl Zane	BETTY ZANE, as Zane Grey. New York, 1903.
Green, Henry	BLINDNESS. New York, 1926.
Greene, Graham	BABBLING APRIL: COLLECTED POEMS. Oxford, 1925.
Gregory, Horace	CHELSEA ROOMING HOUSE. New York, 1930.
Gregory, Jackson	UNDER HANDICAP. New York, 1914.
Greig-Smith, Jennifer	PEGGY OF BEACON HILL, as Maysie Greig. Boston, 1924.
Greve, Felix Paul Berthold Friedrich	WANDERUNGEN, as Frederick Philip Grove. Privately printed, 1902. HELENA UND DAMON, as Frederick Philip Grove. Privately printed, 1902.
Grimm, Cherry Barbara	THE LUCK OF BRIN'S FIVE, as Cherry Wilder. New York: Atheneum, 1977; London: Angus & Robertson, 1979.
Grimstead, Hettie	PAINTED VIRGIN. London, 1931.
Grove, Frederick Herridge	FLAME OF THE OSAGE, as Fred Grove. New York, 1958.
Gruber, Frank	PEACE MARSHALL. New York, 1939.
Grundy, Mabel Sarah Barnes	A THAMES CAMP. Bristol, England, 1902.
Guiney, Louise Imogen	SONGS AT THE START. Boston, 1884.
Gulick, Grover C.	COWBOY, FISHERMAN, HUNTER, as Bill Gulick, with Larry Mersfelder. Kansas City, Mo., 1942.

AUTHOR	TITLE/FIRST EDITION INFORMATION
Guthrie, Alfred Bertram, Jr.	MURDERS AT MOON DANCE, as A. B. Guthrie. New York, 1943.
Guthrie, Ramon	TROBAR CLUS. Northampton, 1923.
Guthrie, Thomas Anstey	VICE VERSA; OR, A LESSON TO FATHERS, as F. Anstey. London: Smith Elder; New York: Appleton, 1882.
Haas, Benjamin Leopold	THE FORAGERS, as Ben Haas. New York: Simon & Schuster, 1962; London: Davies, 1963.
Haggard, Henry Rider	CETYWAYO AND HIS WHITE NEIGHBOURS; OR, REMARKS ON RECENT EVENTS IN ZULULAND, NATAL, AND THE TRANSVAAL. London: Trubner, 1882.
Haines, Pamela	TEA AT GUNTER'S. London, 1974.
Hale, Lucretia Peabody	THE STRUGGLE FOR LIFE. Boston: Walker Wise, 1861.
Haley, J. Evetts	THE XIT RANCH OF TEXAS. Chicago, 1929.
Hall, James Norman	KITCHENER'S MOB. Boston, 1916.
Hall, Oakley Maxwell	MURDER CITY, as O. M. Hall. New York, 1949.
Halleran, Eugene Edward	NO RANGE IS FREE, as E. E. Halleran. Philadelphia, 1944.
Hamilton, Charles Harold St. John	SCHOOLBOY SERIES: THE SECRET OF THE SCHOOL, THE BLACK SHEEP OF SPARSHOTT, FIRST MAN IN, LOOKING AFTER LAMB, as Frank Richards. 4 vols. London: Merrett, 1946.
Hamilton, Donald Bengtsson	DATE WITH DARKNESS. New York, 1947.
Hammett, Samuel Dashiell	RED HARVEST. New York, 1929.
Hampson, Anne	ETERNAL SUMMER. London, 1969.
Harbage, Alfred Bennett	THOMAS KILLIGREW: CAVALIER DRAMATIST. Philadelphia: University of Pennsylvania; London: Oxford University, 1930.

AUTHOR	TITLE/FIRST EDITION INFORMATION
Hardwick, Mollie	THE JOLLY TOPER, with Michael Hardwick. London, 1961.
Hardy, William George	ABRAHAM, PRINCE OF UR. New York, 1935.
Harknett, Terry Williams	THE BENEVOLENT BLACKMAILER. London: Hale, 1962. THE SCRATCH ON THE SURFACE. London: Hale, 1962.
Harris, Joel Chandler	UNCLE REMUS: HIS SONGS AND HIS SAYINGS: THE FOLKLORE OF THE OLD PLANTATION. New York: Appleton, 1881; as UNCLE REMUS AND HIS LEGENDS OF THE OLD PLANTATION. London: Bogue, 1881; as UNCLE REMUS; OR, MR. FOX, MR. RABBIT, AND MR. TERRAPIN. London: Routledge, 1881.
Harris, John Wyndham Parkes Lucas Beynon	THE SECRET PEOPLE, as John Beynon. London: Newnes, 1935; as J. B. Harris. New York: Lancer, 1964. FOUL PLAY, as John Beynon. London: Newnes, 1935.
Harris, Larry Mark	PAGAN PASSIONS, with Randall Garrett. New York: Galaxy, 1959.
Harris, Marilyn	KING'S EX. New York; London, 1967.
Harris, Mark	TRUMPET TO THE WORLD. New York, 1946.
Harris, Rosemary Jeanne	THE SUMMER-HOUSE. London, 1956.
Harrison, Edith Elizabeth Tatchell	COFFEE AT DOBREE'S. London, 1965.
Harte, Bret	CONDENSED NOVELS AND OTHER PAPERS. New York, 1867.
Harvey, John B.	AVENGING ANGEL, as Thom Ryder. London, 1975.
Hastings, Phyllis Dora	AS LONG AS YOU LIVE. London, 1951.
Hawkes, John	FIASCO HALL, as J. C. B. Hawkes, Jr. Cambridge, Mass., 1943.
Hawkins, Sir Anthony Hope	A MAN OF MARK, as Anthony Hope. London, 1890.

AUTHOR	TITLE/FIRST EDITION INFORMATION
Hay, John	JIM BLUDSO OF THE PRAIRIE BELL, AND LITTLE BREECHES. Boston, 1871.
Haycox, Ernest	FREE GRASS. New York, 1929.
Healey, Benjamin James	WAITING FOR A TIGER, as Ben Healey. London: Hale; New York, 1965.
Heaven, Constance	QUEEN'S DELIGHT, as Constance Fecher. London, 1966.
Hecht, Anthony	A SUMMONING OF STONES. New York, 1954.
Heckelmann, Charles Newman	JUNGLE MENACE. New York, 1937. CLARKVILLE'S BATTERY; OR, BASE-BALL VERSUS GANGSTERS, as Charles Lawton. New York, 1937.
Heinlein, Robert Anson	ROCKET SHIP GALILEO. New York: Scribner, 1947; London: New English Library, 1971.
Heller, Joseph	CATCH-22. New York, 1961.
Hemingway, Ernest	THREE STORIES AND TEN POEMS. Paris, 1923.
Hendryx, James Beardsley	THE PROMISE: A TALE OF THE GREAT NORTHWEST. New York, 1915.
Hennissart, Martha	BANKING ON DEATH, as Emma Lathen, with Mary J. Latis New York: Macmillan, 1961; London: Gollancz, 1962.
Henty, George Alfred	A SEARCH FOR A SECRET, as G. A. Henty. 3 vols. London: Tinsley, 1867.
Herbst, Josephine	NOTHING IS SACRED. New York, 1928.
Hergesheimer, Joseph	THE LAY ANTHONY. New York, 1914.
Heron-Allen, Edward	DE FIDICULIS OPUSCULUM, as Christopher Blayre. 9 vols. Privately printed, 1882-1941.
Heuman, William	GUNS AT BROKEN BOW. New York, 1950. FIGHTING FIVE. New York, 1950.
Heyer, Georgette	THE BLACK MOTH. London; Boston, 1921.
Heyward, Du Bose	SKYLINES AND HORIZONS. New York, 1924.

AUTHOR	TITLE/FIRST EDITION INFORMATION
Hibbert, Eleanor Alice	DAUGHTER OF ANNA, as Victoria Holt. London, 1941.
Hichens, Robert Smythe	THE COASTGUARD'S SECRET. London, 1886.
Hill, Grace Livingston	A CHAUTAUQUA IDYL. Boston, 1887.
Hill, Pamela	FLAMING JANET: A LADY OF GALLOWAY. London, 1954.
Hillyer, Robert	SONNETS AND OTHER LYRICS. Cambridge, 1917.
Hilton, James	CATHERINE HERSELF. London: Unwin, 1920.
Himes, Chester Bomar	IF HE HOLLERS LET HIM GO. New York, 1947.
Hintze, Naomi Agans	BURIED TREASURE WAITS FOR YOU. Indianapolis, 1962.
Hitchens, Julia Clara Catherine Dolores Birk Olsen	THE CLUE IN THE CLAY, as D. B. Olsen. New York: Phoenix, 1938.
Hobart, Donald Bayne	THE WHISTLING WADDY: A WESTERN STORY. New York, 1928. DOUBLE SHUFFLE. New York, 1928.
Hodge, Jane Aiken	MAULEVER HALL. London; New York, 1964.
Hoffman, Lee	GUNFIGHT AT LARAMIE. New York: Ace, 1966; London: Gold Lion, 1975. THE LEGEND OF BLACKJACK SAM. New York: Ace, 1966.
Hogan, Robert Ray	EX-MARSHALL. New York, 1956.
Holland, Isabelle	CECILY. Philadelphia, 1967.
Holland, Sheila	LOVE IN A MIST. London: Hale, 1971.
Holmes, John Clellon	GO. New York, 1952.
Holmes, Oliver Wendell	POEMS. Boston, 1836.
Hopley-Woolrich, Cornell George	COVER CHARGE, as Cornell Woolrich. New York: Boni & Liveright, 1926.
Hopson, William L.	GUN-THROWER. New York; London, 1940.
Horgan, Paul	LAMB OF GOD. Privately printed, 1927.

AUTHOR	TITLE/FIRST EDITION INFORMATION
Horne, Geoffrey	WINTER. London: Hutchinson, 1957.
Horner, Lance	MANDINGO, with Kyle Onstott. Richmond, Va., 1957.
Hosken, Clifford James Wheeler	CARTERET'S CURE, as Richard Keverne. London: Constable; Boston: Houghton Mifflin, 1926.
Hough, Emerson	THE SINGING MOUSE STORIES. New York, 1895.
Housman, Laurence	A FARM IN FAIRYLAND. London, 1894.
Houston, Tex	THE SHERIFF OF HAMMER COUNTY. London, 1956.
Hovey, Richard	POEMS. Washington, 1880.
Howard, Robert Ervin	A GENT FROM BEAR CREEK. London, 1937.
Howatch, Susan Elizabeth	THE DARK SHORE. New York, 1965.
Howe, Mark A. De Wolfe	RARI NANTES: BEING VERSES AND A SONG. Boston, 1893.
Hubbard, George Barron	WITHOUT COMPROMISE, as George Hubbard, with Lilian Bennet-Thompson. New York: Century, 1922.
Hueffer, Ford H. Madox	THE BROWN OWL. London, 1892.
Huffaker, Clair	BADGE FOR A GUNFIGHTER. New York; London, 1957.
Hufford, Susan	MIDNIGHT SAILING. New York, 1975.
Hughes, Langston	THE WEARY BLUES. New York, 1926.
Hughes, Richard Arthur Warren	THE SISTERS' TRAGEDY. Oxford, 1922.
Hughes, Ted	THE HAWK IN THE RAIN. London, 1957.
Hughes, Walter Llewellyn	BLAST OFF AT WOOMERA, as Hugh Walters. London: Faber, 1957; as BLAST-OFF AT 0300. New York: Criterion, 1958.
Hull, Edith Maude	THE SHEIK, as E. M. Hull. London, 1919.
Humphrey, William	THE LAST HUSBAND AND OTHER STORIES. New York; London, 1953.
Huneker, James	MEZZOTINTS IN MODERN MUSIC. New York, 1899.

AUTHOR	TITLE/FIRST EDITION INFORMATION
Hunt, Leigh	JUVENILIA; OR, A COLLECTION OF POEMS, as J. H. L. Hunt. London, 1801.
Hunter, Elizabeth Mary Teresa	THE AFRICAN MOUNTAIN, as Isobel Chace. London, 1960.
Hunter, Evan	THE BIG FIX. N.p.: Falcon, 1952. FIND THE FEATHERED SERPENT. Philadelphia: Winston, 1952.
Hurley, John J.	FATAL FLOURISHES, as S. S. Rafferty. New York: Avon, 1979.
Hurst, Fannie	JUST AROUND THE CORNER: ROMANCE EN CASSEROLE. New York, 1914.
Huxley, Aldous Leonard	THE BURNING WHEEL. Oxford: Blackwell, 1916.
Hyndman, Jane Lee	SIZZLING PAN RANCH, as Lee Wyndham. New York: Crowell, 1951.
Iams, Samuel H., Jr.	NOWHERE WITH MUSIC. New York: Longman, 1938.
Iannuzzi, John Nicholas	WHAT'S HAPPENING? New York: Barnes; London: Yoseloff, 1963.
(If)	IF ALL ELSE FAILS, WE CAN WHIP THE HORSE'S EYES AND MAKE HIM SLEEP, as Craig Strete [A Cherokee Indian writer].Amsterdam, 1976.
Ingelow, Jean	A RHYMING CHRONICLE OF INCIDENTS AND FEELINGS, anonymously. London: Longman, 1850.
Innes, Ralph Hammond	THE DOPPELGANGER. London: Jenkins, 1937.
Irwin, Margaret Emma Faith	HOW MANY MILES TO BABYLON? London: Constable, 1913.
Ish-Kishor, Sulamith	THE BIBLE STORY. New York: United Synagogue, 1921.

AUTHOR	TITLE/FIRST EDITION INFORMATION
Jackman, Stuart Brooke	PORTRAIT IN TWO COLOURS. London: Faber, 1948; New York: Scribner, 1949.
Jackson, Jesse	CALL ME CHARLEY. New York: Harper, 1945.
Jackson, Shirley Hardie	THE ROAD THROUGH THE WALL. New York: Farrar Straus, 1948.
Jacob, Naomi Ellington	JACOB USSHER. London: Butterworth, 1925.
Jacob, Piers Anthony Dillingham	CHTHON, as Piers Anthony. New York: Ballantine, 1967; London: Macdonald, 1970.
Jakes, John William	THE TEXANS RIDE NORTH. Philadelphia: Winston, 1952.
James, Phyllis Dorothy	COVER HER FACE. London: Faber, 1962; New York: Scribner, 1966.
Jarrell, Randall	FIVE YOUNG AMERICAN POETS, with others. New York: New Directions, 1940.
Jarrett, Cora	PECCADILLOES, as Faraday Keene. New York: Day, 1929; London: Noel Douglas, 1930.
Jay, Geraldine Mary	THE KNIFE IS FEMININE, as Charlotte Jay. London: Collins, 1951.
Jeffries, Roderic	BRANDY AHOY! as Roderic Graeme. London: Hutchinson, 1951.
Jellicoe, Ann	SOME UNCONSCIOUS INFLUENCES IN THE THEATRE. London; New York: Cambridge University, 1967.
Jenkins, William Fitzgerald	SCALPS, as Murray Leinster. New York: Brewer & Warren, 1930; as WINGS OF CHANCE. London: Hamilton, 1935.
Jenks, George Charles	DOUBLE CURVE DAN, THE PITCHER DETECTIVE. New York: Beadle & Adams, 1883.
Jepson, Selwyn	THE QUALIFIED ADVENTURER. London: Hutchinson; New York: Harcourt Brace, 1922.

AUTHOR	TITLE/FIRST EDITION INFORMATION
Jervis, Marguerite Florence	THE ACTIVITIES OF LAVIE JUTT, as Marguerite Barclay, with Armiger Barclay. London, 1911.
Jesse, Fryniwyd Tennyson	THE MILKY WAY. London: Heinemann, 1913; New York: Doran, 1914.
Jessup, Richard	THE CUNNING AND THE HAUNTED. New York: Fawcett, 1957; London: Fawcett, 1958.
Jobson, Hamilton	THEREFORE I KILLED HIM. London: Long, 1968.
Johns, William Earl	THE CAMELS ARE COMING. London: Hamilton, 1932. MOSSYFACE, as William Earl. London: Mellifont, 1932. THE PICTORIAL FLYING COURSE, with Harry M. Schofield. London: Hamilton, 1932. FIGHT PLANES AND ACES. London: Hamilton, 1932.
Johnson, Annabell Jones	AS A SPECKLED BIRD. New York: Crowell, 1956; London: Hodder & Stoughton, 1958.
Johnson, Barbara Ferry	LIONORS. New York: Avon, 1975; London: Sphere, 1977.
Johnson, Dorothy Marie	BEULAH BUNNY TELLS ALL. New York: Morrow, 1942; as MISS BUNNY INTERVENES. London: Chapman & Hall, 1948.
Johnson, Edgar Raymond	THE BIG ROCK CANDY, with Annabell Jones Johnson. New York: Crowell, 1957.
Johnson, Emil Richard	SILVER STREET. New York: Harper, 1968; as THE SILVER STREET KILLER. London: Hale, 1969.
Johnston, Mary	THE PRISONERS OF HOPE: A TALE OF COLONIAL VIRGINIA. Boston: Houghton Mifflin, 1898; as THE OLD DOMINION. London: Constable, 1899.
Johnston, Norma	THE WISHING STAR. New York: Funk & Wagnalls, 1963.

AUTHOR	TITLE/FIRST EDITION INFORMATION
Johnston, Velda	ALONG A DARK PATH. New York: Dodd Mead, 1967; Aylesbury, England: Milton House, 1974.
Jones, Dennis Feltham	COLOSSUS. London: Hart Davis, 1966; New York: Putnam, 1967.
Jones, Diana Wynne	CHANGEOVER. London: Macmillan, 1970.
Jones, Douglas C.	THE TREATY OF MEDICINE LODGE: THE STORY OF THE GREAT TREATY COUNCIL AS TOLD BY EYEWITNESSES. Norman: University of Oklahoma, 1966.
Jones, Langdon	THE EYE OF THE LENS. New York: Macmillan, 1972.
Jones, Nard	OREGON DETOUR. New York: Payson & Clarke, 1930.
Jones, Neil Ronald	THE PLANET OF THE DOUBLE SUN. New York: Ace, 1967. THE SUNLESS WORLD. New York: Ace, 1967. SPACE WAR. New York: Ace, 1967. TWIN WORLDS. New York: Ace, 1967.
Jones, Raymond F.	RENAISSANCE. New York: Gnome, 1951. THE ALIEN. New York: Galaxy, 1951. THE TOYMAKER. Los Angeles: Fantasy, 1951.
Jordan, June	WHO LOOK AT ME! New York: Crowell, 1969.
Jordan, Robert Furneaux	THE CHARM OF THE TIMBER HOUSE. London: Nicholson & Watson, 1936.
Joscelyn, Archie Lynn	THE GOLDEN BOWL. Cleveland: World, 1931.
Joslin, Sesyle	WHAT DO YOU SAY, DEAR? New York: Scott, 1958; London: Faber, 1960.
Jowett, Margaret	CANDIDATE FOR FAME. London: Oxford University, 1955.
Judah, Aaron	TOMMY WITH THE HOLE IN HIS SHOE. London: Faber, 1957.
Juster, Norton	THE PHANTOM TOLLBOOTH. New York: Epstein & Carroll, 1961; London: Collins, 1962.

AUTHOR	TITLE/FIRST EDITION INFORMATION
Kahl, Virginia C.	AWAY WENT WOLFGANG! New York: Scribner, 1954.
Kamm, Josephine Mary	ALL QUIET AT HOME. London: Longman, 1936.
Kane, Frank	ABOUT FACE. New York: Curl, 1947.
Kane, Henry	A HALO FOR NOBODY. New York: Simon & Schuster, 1947; London: Boardman, 1950.
Kantor, MacKinlay	DIVERSEY. New York: Coward McCann, 1928.
Kapp, Colin	TRANSFINITE MAN. New York: Berkely, 1964; as THE DARK MIND. London: Corgi, 1965.
Karp, David	THE VOICE OF THE FOUR FREEDOMS. Privately printed, 1942.
Kaye, Geraldine	TALES FOR MALAYAN CHILDREN. Singapore: Moore, 1956.
Keating, Henry Raymond Fitzgerald	DEATH AND THE VISITING FIREMEN. London: Gollancz, 1959; New York: Doubleday, 1973.
Keats, Ezra Jack	MY DOG IS LOST, with Pat Cherr. New York: Crowell, 1960.
Keeler, Harry Stephen	THE VOICE OF THE SEVEN SPARROWS. London: Hutchinson, 1924; New York: Dutton, 1928.
Keene, Day	THIS IS MURDER, MR. HERBERT, AND OTHER STORIES. New York: Avon, 1948.
Keeping, Charles William James	BLACK DOLLY. Leicester, England: Brockhampton, 1966; as MOLLY O' THE MOORS. Cleveland: World, 1966.
Keith, Harold Verne	BOYS' LIFE OF WILL ROGERS. New York: Crowell, 1937.
Kelland, Clarence Budington	QUIZZER NO. 20, BEING QUESTIONS AND ANSWERS ON INSURANCE. Detroit: Sprague, 1911.

AUTHOR	**TITLE/FIRST EDITION INFORMATION**
Keller, David Henry	THE KELLERS OF HAMILTON TOWNSHIP: A STUDY IN DEMOCRACY. Privately printed, 1922.
Kelley, Leo Patrick	THE COUNTERFEITS. New York: Belmont, 1967.
Kelley, William Melvin	A DIFFERENT DRUMMER. New York: Doubleday, 1962; London: Hutchinson, 1963.
Kelly, Eric Philbrook	THE TRUMPETER OF KRAKOW. New York: Macmillan, 1928; London: Chatto & Windus, 1968.
Kelly, Mary Theresa	A COLD COMING. London: Secker & Warburg, 1956; New York: Walker, 1968.
Kelton, Elmer	HOT IRON. New York: Ballantine, 1956.
Kemelman, Harry	FRIDAY THE RABBI SLEPT LATE. New York: Crown, 1964; London: Hutchinson, 1965.
Kendall, Carol	THE BLACK SEVEN. New York: Harper, 1946; London: Lane, 1950.
Kendrick, Baynard Hardwick	BLOOD ON LAKE LOUISA. New York: Greenberg, 1934; London: Methuen, 1937.
Kennedy, Margaret	A CENTURY OF REVOLUTION 1789-1920. London: Methuen, 1922.
Kenrick, Tony	THE ONLY GOOD BODY'S A DEAD ONE. London: Cape, 1970; New York: Simon & Schuster, 1971.
Kenyon, Michael	MAY YOU DIE IN IRELAND. London: Collins; New York: Morrow, 1965.
Keppel-Jones, Arthur Mervyn	DO WE GOVERN OURSELVES? Johannesburg, South Africa: Society of Friends of Africa, 1945.
Kerr, Anne Judith	THE TIGER WHO CAME TO TEA. London: Collins; New York: Coward McCann, 1968.
Kersh, Gerald	JEWS WITHOUT JEHOVAH. London: Wishart, 1934.

AUTHOR	TITLE/FIRST EDITION INFORMATION
Kesey, Ken Elton	ONE FLEW OVER THE CUCKOO'S NEST. New York: Viking, 1962; London: Methuen, 1963.
Ketchum, Philip L.	DEATH IN THE LIBRARY. New York: Crowell, 1937.
Key, Alexander Hill	THE RED EAGLE. New York: Volland, 1930.
Keyes, Daniel	FLOWERS FOR ALGERNON. New York: Harcourt Brace; London: Cassell, 1966.
Keyes, Frances Parkinson	THE OLD GRAY HOMESTEAD. Boston: Houghton Mifflin; London: Hodder & Stoughton, 1919.
Kidd, Flora	VISIT TO ROWANBANK. London: Mills & Boon, 1966. WHISTLE AND I'LL COME. London: Mills & Boon, 1966. Toronto: Harlequin, 1967. NURSE AT ROWANBANK. Toronto: Harlequin, 1966. London: Mills & Boon, 1967.
Killough, Karen Lee	A VOICE OUT OF RAMAH. New York: Ballantine, 1979. THE DOPPELGANGER GAMBIT. New York: Ballantine, 1979.
Kimbro, John M.	THE HOUSE ON WINDSWEPT RIDGE, as Katheryn Kimbrough. New York: Popular Library, 1971; London: Sphere, 1973. THE TWISTED CAMEO, as Katheryn Kimbrough. New York: Popular Library, 1971; London: Sphere, 1973.
Kimenye, Barbara	KALASANDA. Nairobi; London: Oxford University, 1965.
King, General Charles	CAMPAIGNING WITH CROOK. Milwaukee, Wis.: Sentinel, 1880.
King, Charles Daly	BEYOND BEHAVIORISM: THE FUTURE OF PSYCHOLOGY, as Robert Courtney. New York: Grant, 1927.
King, David Clive	HAMID OF ALEPPO. New York: Macmillan, 1958.

AUTHOR	**TITLE/FIRST EDITION INFORMATION**
King, Rufus Frederick	NORTH STAR: A DOG STORY FOR THE CANADIAN NORTHWEST. New York: Watt, 1925.
King, Stephen	THINNER, as Richard Bachman.
Kingman, Mary Lee	PIERRE PIDGEON. Boston: Houghton Mifflin, 1943.
Kipling, Joseph Rudyard	SCHOOLBOY LYRICS. Lahore: privately printed, 1881.
Kirk, Russell Amos	RANDOLPH OF ROANOKE: A STUDY IN CONSERVATIVE THOUGHT. Chicago: University of Chicago, 1951.
Kirst, Hans Hellmut	THE NIGHT OF THE GENERALS. 1963.
Kitchin, Clifford Henry Benn	CURTAINS. Oxford: Blackwell, 1919.
Kjelgaard, James Arthur	FOREST PATROL. New York: Holiday House, 1941; London: Sampson Low, 1948.
Klass, Philip	OF ALL POSSIBLE WORLDS, as William Tenn. New York: Ballantine, 1955; London: Joseph, 1956.
Klein, Norma	MOM, THE WOLF MAN, AND ME. New York: Pantheon, 1972.
Kline, Otis Adelbert	THE PLANET OF PERIL. Chicago: McClurg, 1929.
Klinger, Henry	WANTON FOR MURDER. New York: Doubleday, 1961.
Kneale, Thomas Nigel	TOMATO CAIN AND OTHER STORIES. London: Collins, 1949; New York: Knopf, 1950.
Knebel, Fletcher	NO HIGH GROUND, with Charles W. Bailey II. New York: Harper; London: Weidenfeld & Nicolson, 1960.
Knibbs, Henry Herbert	FIRST POEMS, as Henry K. Herbert. Rochester, N.Y.: Genesee Press, 1908.
Knight, Alanna	LEGEND OF THE LOCH. London: Hurst & Blackett, 1969; New York: Lancer, 1970.
Knight, Damon Francis	HELL'S PAVEMENT. New York: Lion, 1955; London: Banner, 1958.

AUTHOR	**TITLE/FIRST EDITION INFORMATION**
Knight, Francis Edgar	THE ALBATROSS COMES HOME, as Frank Knight. London: Hollis & Carter, 1949.
Knight, Norman Louis	A TORRENT OF FACES, with James Blish. New York: Doubleday, 1967; London: Faber, 1968.
Knowles, Mabel Winifred	LOVE'S OBJECT; OR, SOME THOUGHTS FOR YOUNG GIRLS, as May Wynne. London: Nisbet, 1899.
Knox, Ronald Arbuthnott	SIGNA SEVERA. Privately printed, 1906.
Knox, William	DEADLINE FOR A DREAM. London: Long, 1957; as IN AT THE KILL. New York: Doubleday, 1961.
Koestler, Arthur	VON WEISSEN NACHTEN UND ROTEN TAGEN. Kharkov: Ukrainian State, 1933.
Konigsburg, Elaine Lobl	FROM THE MIXED-UP FILES OF MRS. BASIL E. FRANKWEILER. New York: Atheneum, 1967; London: Macmillan, 1969.
Koontz, Dean Ray	STAR QUEST. New York: Ace, 1968.
Kornbluth, Cyril M.	GUNNER CADE, as Cyril M. Judd, with Judith Merril. New York: Simon & Schuster, 1952; London: Gollancz, 1964. OUTPOST MARS, as Cyril M. Judd, with Judith Merril. New York: Abelard, 1952; London: New English Library, 1966. TAKEOFF, as C. M. Kornbluth. New York: Doubleday, 1952. THE NAKED STORM, as Simon Eisner. New York: Lion, 1952.
Krasilovsky, Phyllis	THE MAN WHO DIDN'T WASH HIS DISHES. New York: Doubelday, 1950; Kingswood, England: World's Work, 1962.
Kraus, Joanna Halpert	SEVEN SOUND AND MOTION STORIES. Rowayton, Conn.: New Plays, 1971.
Kraus, Robert	JUNIOR, THE SPOILED CAT. New York; London: Oxford University, 1955.
Krause, Herbert	WIND WITHOUT RAIN. Indianapolis: Bobbs Merrill, 1939. NEIGHBOR BOY. Iowa City: Midland House, 1939.

AUTHOR	TITLE/FIRST EDITION INFORMATION
Krauss, Ruth	A GOOD MAN AND HIS WIFE. New York: Harper, 1944.
Krumgold, Joseph Quincy	THANKS TO MURDER. New York: Vanguard; London: Gollancz, 1935.
Kurland, Michael Joseph	TEN YEARS TO DOOMSDAY, with Chester Anderson. New York: Pyramid, 1964.
Kurnitz, Harry	FAST COMPANY, as Marco Page. New York: Dodd Mead; London: Heinemann, 1938.
Kuskin, Karla	ROAR AND MORE. New York: Harper, 1956.
Kuttner, Henry	LAWLESS GUNS, as Will Garth. New York: Dodge, 1937.
Kyne, Peter Bernard	THE THREE GODFATHERS. New York: Doran, 1913; London: Hodder & Stoughton, 1914.
La Bern, Arthur Joseph	IT ALWAYS RAINS ON SUNDAY. London: Nicholson & Watson, 1945.
La Farge, Oliver Hazard Perry	TRIBES AND TEMPLES: A RECORD OF THE EXPEDITION TO MIDDLE AMERICA CONDUCTED BY THE TULANE UNIVERSITY OF LOUISIANA IN 1925. 2 vols. New Orleans: Tulane University, 1926-1927.
Lafferty, Raphael Aloysius	PAST MASTER. New York: Ace; London: Rapp & Whiting, 1968.
Lake, David John	JOHN MILTON: PARADISE LOST. Calcutta: Mukhopadhyay, 1967.
La Moore, Louis Dearborn	SMOKE FROM THIS ALTAR, as Louis L'Amour. Oklahoma City: Lusk, 1939.
Lampman, Evelyn Sibley	CRAZY CREEK. New York: Doubleday, 1948.
Lane, Roumelia	ROSE OF THE DESERT. London: Mills & Boon, 1967; Toronto: Harlequin, 1968. HIDEAWAY HEART. London: Mills & Boon, 1967; Toronto: Harlequin, 1968.

AUTHOR	TITLE/FIRST EDITION INFORMATION
Lang, Andrew	BALLADS AND LYRICS OF OLD FRANCE, WITH OTHER POEMS. London: Longman, 1872.
Lange, John Frederick, Jr.	TARNSMAN OF GOR, as John Norman. New York: Ballantine, 1966; London: Sidgwick & Jackson, 1969.
Langley, John	RUSTLER'S BRAND. London: Lane, 1954.
Langton, Jane Gillson	THE MAJESTY OF GRACE. New York: Harper, 1961.
Lanier, Sterling Edmund	THE WAR FOR THE LOT. Chicago: Follett, 1969.
Latham, Jean Lee	555 POINTERS FOR BEGINNING ACTORS AND DIRECTORS. Chicago: Dramatic Publishing, 1935.
Latimer, Jonathan Wyatt	MURDER IN THE MADHOUSE. New York: Doubleday; London: Hurst & Blackett, 1935.
Latis, Mary J.	BANKING ON DEATH, as Emma Lathen, with Martha Hennissart. New York: Macmillan, 1961; London: Gollancz, 1962.
La Tourrette, Jacqueline	THE JOSEPH STONE. New York: Norton, 1971.
Lattimore, Eleanor Frances	LITTLE PEAR. New York: Harcourt Brace, 1931; London: Museum Press, 1947.
Laumer, John Keith	HOW TO DESIGN AND BUILD FLYING MODELS. New York: Harper, 1960; London: Hale, 1975.
Lawrence, Ann Margaret	TOM ASS; OR, THE SECOND GIFT. London: Macmillan, 1972; New York: Walck, 1973.
Lawrence, Hildegarde	BLOOD UPON THE SNOW. New York: Simon & Schuster, 1944; London: Chapman & Hall, 1946.
Lawrence, Mildred	SUSAN'S BEARS. New York: Grosset & Dunlap, 1945.
Lawson, Robert	COUNTRY COLIC. Boston: Little, Brown, 1944.

AUTHOR	TITLE/FIRST EDITION INFORMATION
Lazarus, Marguerite	IMAGES OF ROSE, as Anna Gilbert. London; New York, 1974.
Lea, Alec Richard	THE OUTWARD URGE. London: Rich & Cowan, 1944.
Lea, Tom	JOHN W. NORTON, AMERICAN PAINTER 1876-1934, with Thomas E. Tallmadge. Chicago: Lakeside Press, 1935.
Leaf, Wilbur Munro	LO, THE POOR INDIAN, as Mun. New York: Leaf, Mahony, Seidel & Stokes, 1934. GRAMMAR CAN BE FUN. New York: Stokes, 1934; London: Ward Lock, 1951.
Lear, Edward	ILLUSTRATIONS OF THE FAMILY OF PSITTACIDAE, OR PARROTS. Privately printed, 1832.
Leasor, Thomas James	NOT SUCH A BAD DAY. Leicester, England: Blackfriars Press, 1946.
Leblanc, Maurice Marie Emile	ARSENE LUPIN, with Edgar Jepson. 1909.
Lee, Benjamin	PAGANINI STRIKES AGAIN. London: Hutchinson, 1970.
Lee, Dennis Beynon	KINGDOM OF ABSENCE. Toronto: House of Anansi, 1967.
Lee, Elsie	HOW TO GET THE MOST OUT OF YOUR TAPE RECORDING, as Lee Sheridan, with Michael Sheridan. Flushing, N.Y.: Robins, 1958. MORE FUN WITH YOUR TAPE RECORDERS AND STEREO, as Lee Sheridan, with Michael Sheridan. Los Angeles: Trend, 1958.
Lee, Manfred B.	THE ROMAN HAT MYSTERY, as Ellery Queen, with Frederic Dannay. New York: Stokes; London: Gollancz, 1929.
Lee, Mildred	THE INVISIBLE SUN. Philadelphia: Westminster, 1946.
Lee, Tanith	THE BETROTHED. Sideup, England: Slughorn Press, 1968.
Lee, Wayne Cyril	PRAIRIE VENGEANCE. New York: Arcadia, 1954; London: Barker, 1955.

AUTHOR	TITLE/FIRST EDITION INFORMATION
Leeson, Robert Arthur	UNITED WE STAND: AN ILLUSTRATED ACCOUNT OF TRADE UNION EMBLEMS. Bath, England: Adams & Dart, 1971.
Le Fanu, Joseph Sheridan	THE COCK AND THE ANCHOR. 1845.
Le Feuvre, Amy	ERIC'S GOOD NEWS. London: Religious Tract Society, 1894; Chicago: Revell, 1896.
LeFontaine, Joseph Raymond Herve	A MANUAL FOR CRYOGENIC FLUID CONTROLS. Dayton, Ohio: Koehler, 1958.
LeGuin, Ursula Kroeber	ROCANNON'S WORLD. New York: Ace, 1966; London: Tandem, 1972.
Lehman, Paul Evan	IDAHO. New York: Macauley, 1933; as COWBOY IDAHO. London: Ward Lock, 1933.
Leiber, Fritz Reuter, Jr.	NIGHT'S BLACK AGENTS. Sauk City, Wis.: Arkham House, 1947; London: Spearman, 1975.
Leisk, David Johnson	BARNABY, as Crockett Johnson. New York: Holt, 1943.
Leitch, Adelaide	FLIGHTLINE NORTH. St. John's, Newfoundland: Guardian, 1952.
Lemarchand, Elizabeth Wharton	DEATH OF AN OLD GIRL. London: Hart Davis, 1967; New York: Award, 1970.
Le May, Alan	PAINTED PONIES. New York: Doran; London: Cassell, 1927.
L'Engle, Madeleine	18 WASHINGTON SQUARE, SOUTH. Boston: Baker, 1944.
Lenski, Lois Lenore	SKIPPING VILLAGE. New York: Stokes, 1927.
Leonard, Elmore	THE BOUNTY HUNTERS. Boston: Houghton Mifflin, 1953; London: Hale, 1956.
Le Queux, William Tufnell	GUILTY BONDS. London: Routledge, 1891; New York: Fenno, 1895.
Leroux, Gaston	THE MYSTERY OF THE YELLOW ROOM. 1908.
Leslie, Doris	THE STARLING. London: Hurst & Blackett; New York: Century, 1927.

AUTHOR	TITLE/FIRST EDITION INFORMATION
Lesser, Milton	EARTHBOUND. Philadelphia: Winston, 1952; London: Hutchinson, 1955.
Lessing, Doris May	THE GRASS IS SINGING. London: Joseph; New York: Crowell, 1950.
Levin, Ira	A KISS BEFORE DYING. New York: Simon & Schuster, 1953; London: Joseph, 1954.
Lewin, Michael Z.	HOW TO BEAT COLLEGE TESTS: A PRACTICAL GUIDE TO EASE THE BURDEN OF USELESS COURSES. New York: Dial, 1970.
Lewis, Alfred Henry	WOLFVILLE. New York: Stokes; London: Lawrence & Bullen, 1897.
Lewis, Clive Staples	SPIRITS IN BONDAGE: A CYCLE OF LYRICS, as Clive Hamilton. London: Heinemann, 1919.
Lewis, Ernest Michael Roy	THE FUTURE OF AUSTRALIA, as Roy Lewis. New Delhi: Hindustan Times Press, 1944.
Lewis, Harry Sinclair	HIKE AND THE AEROPLANE, as Tom Graham. New York: Stokes, 1912.
Lewis, Hilda Winifred	PEGASUS YOKED. London: Hurst & Blackett, 1933.
Lewis, John Royston	CASES FOR DISCUSSION. Oxford: Pergamon Press, 1965.
Lewis, Maynah	NO PLACE FOR LOVE. London: Hurst & Blackett, 1963.
Lewty, Marjorie	NEVER IT CALL IT LOVING. London: Mills & Boon, 1958; Toronto: Harlequin, 1968.
Lexau, Joan M.	OLAF READS. New York: Dial, 1961.
Ley, Alice Chetwynd	THE JEWELLED SNUFF BOX. London: Hale, 1959; New York: Beagle, 1974.
Ley, Robert Arthur	TIME TRANSFER AND OTHER STORIES, as Arthur Sellings. London: Joseph, 1956.

AUTHOR	TITLE/FIRST EDITION INFORMATION
Lichtenberg, Jacqueline	HOUSE OF ZEOR. New York: Doubleday, 1974.
Lifton, Betty Jean	JOJI AND THE DRAGON. New York: Morrow, 1957.
Lightner, Alice Martha	THE PILLAR AND THE FLAME, as Alice L. Hopf. New York: Vinal, 1928.
Lindsay, David	A VOYAGE TO ARCTURUS. London: Methuen, 1920; New York: Macmillan, 1963.
Lindsay, Norman Alfred William	A CURATE IN BOHEMIA. Sydney, Australia: Bookstall, 1913; London: Laurie, 1937.
Lindsay, Rachel	IN NAME ONLY, as Roberta Leigh. London: Falcon, 1951; Toronto: Harlequin, 1973.
Linebarger, Paul Myron Anthony	THE POLITICAL DOCTRINES OF SUN YAT-SEN, as P. M. A. Linebarger. Baltimore: Johns Hopkins University, 1937.
Lingard, Joan Amelia	LIAM'S DAUGHTER. London: Hodder & Stoughton, 1963.
Linington, Barbara Elizabeth	THE PROUD MAN. New York: Viking, 1955.
Linklater, Eric Robert Russell	POOBIE. Edinburgh: Porpoise Press, 1925.
Lionni, Leo	LITTLE BLUE AND LITTLE YELLOW. New York: McDowell Obolensky, 1959; Leicester, England: Brockhampton, 1962.
Lipkind, William	WINNEBAGO GRAMMAR. New York: Columbia University, 1945.
Lippincott, Joseph Wharton	BUN, A WILD RABBIT. Philadelphia, 1918.
Little, Constance and Gwyneth	THE GREY MIST MURDERS. New York: Doubleday, 1938.
Little, Flora Jean	IT'S A WONDERFUL WORLD. Guelph, Ontario. Privately printed, 1947.
Litvonov, Ivy	GROWING PAINS. London: Heinemann; New York: Doran, 1913.
Lively, Penelope	ASTERCOTE. London: Heinemann, 1970; New York: Dutton, 1971.
Livingston, Myra Cohn	WHISPERS AND OTHER POEMS. New York: Harcourt Brace, 1958.

AUTHOR	**TITLE/FIRST EDITION INFORMATION**
Llewellyn, David William Alun	BALLADS AND SONGS. London: Stockwell, 1921.
Lobel, Anita	SVEN'S BRIDGE. New York: Harper, 1965.
Lobel, Arnold	A ZOO FOR MISTER MUSTER. New York: Harper, 1962.
Locke, Elsie Violet	THE SHEPHERD AND THE SCULLERY-MAID. Christchurch, New Zealand: New Zealand Communist Party, 1950.
Lockridge, Frances	HOW TO ADOPT A CHILD. New York: Children, 1928.
Lockridge, Richard Orson	MR. AND MRS. NORTH. New York: Stokes, 1936; London: Joseph, 1937.
Lockridge, Richard Orson and Frances Louise	THE NORTHS MEET MURDER. New York: Stokes; London: Joseph, 1940.
Lofting, Hugh John	THE STORY OF DR. DOLITTLE, BEING THE HISTORY OF HIS PECULIAR LIFE AND ASTONISHING ADVENTURES IN FOREIGN PARTS. New York: Stokes; London: Cape, 1920.
Lofts, Norah	I MET A GYPSY. London: Methuen; New York: Knopf, 1935.
London, John Griffith	THE SON OF THE WOLF: TALES OF THE FAR NORTH, as Jack London. Boston: Houghton Mifflin, 1900; London: Isbister, 1902.
Long, Charles Russell	THE INFINITE BRAIN. New York: Avalon, 1957.
Long, Frank Belknap	A MAN FROM GENOA AND OTHER POEMS. Athol, Mass.: Cook, 1926.
Loomis, Noel Miller	MURDER GOES TO PRESS. New York: Phoenix, 1937.
Loring, Emilie	FOR THE COMFORT OF THE FAMILY: A VACATION EXPERIMENT, as Josephine Story. New York: Doran, 1914.
Lott, Milton	THE LAST HUNT. Boston: Houghton Mifflin, 1954; London: Collins, 1955.

AUTHOR	TITLE/FIRST EDITION INFORMATION
Lovecraft, Howard Phillips	THE MATERIALIST TODAY, as H. P. Lovecraft. Privately printed, 1926.
Lovesey, Peter	THE KINGS OF DISTANCE: A STUDY OF FIVE GREAT RUNNERS. London: Eyre & Spottiswoode, 1968.
Low, Lois Dorothea	ISLE FOR A STRANGER, as Dorothy Mackie Low. London: Hurst & Blackett, 1962; New York: Ace, 1968.
Lowndes, Marie Adelaide Belloc	H.R.H. THE PRINCE OF WALES; AN ACCOUNT OF HIS CAREER, anonymously. London: Richards; New York: Appleton, 1898.
Lowndes, Robert Augustine Ward	MYSTERY OF THE THIRD MINE. Philadelphia: Winston, 1953.
Ludlum, Robert	THE SCARLATTI INHERITANCE. Cleveland: World; London: Hart Davis, 1971.
Lupoff, Richard Allen	EDGAR RICE BURROUGHS: MASTER OF ADVENTURE. New York: Canaveral Press, 1965.
Lustgarten, Edgar Marcus	A CASE TO ANSWER. London: Eyre & Spottiswoode, 1947; as ONE MORE UNFORTUNATE. New York: Scribner, 1947.
Lutyens, Mary	FORTHCOMING MARRIAGES. London: Murray; New York: Dutton, 1933.
Lutz, Giles Alfred	FIGHT OR RUN. New York: Popular, 1954.
Lutz, John Thomas	THE TRUTH OF THE MATTER. New York: Pocket Books, 1971.
Lyall, Gavin Tudor	THE WRONG SIDE OF THE SKY. London: Hodder & Stoughton; New York: Scribner, 1961.
Lynch, Patricia Nora	THE GREEN DRAGON. London: Harrap, 1925.
Lynn, Elizabeth A.	A DIFFERENT LIGHT. New York: Berkley, 1978; London: Gollancz, 1979.

AUTHOR	**TITLE/FIRST EDITION INFORMATION**
Macardle, Dorothy Margaret Callan	EARTH-BOUND: NINE STORIES OF IRELAND. Worcester, Mass.: Harrigan Press, 1924. TRAGEDIES OF KERRY 1922-1923. Dublin: Emton Press, 1924.
McBain, Laurie Lee	DEVIL'S DESIRE. New York: Avon, 1975.
McCaffrey, Anne Inez	RESTOREE. New York: Ballantine; London: Rapp & Whiting, 1967.
McCaig, Robert Jesse	TOLL MOUNTAIN. New York: Dodd Mead, 1953; London: Collins, 1954.
McCarry, Charles	CITIZEN NADER. New York: Saturday Review Press, 1972.
McCarthy, Gary	THE DERBY MAN. New York: Doubleday, 1976; London: Hale, 1978.
McClary, Thomas Calvert	REBIRTH, WHEN EVERYONE FORGOT. New York: Bartholomew House, 1944.
McCloskey, John Robert	LENTIL. New York: Viking, 1940.
McCloy, Helen Worrell Clarkson	DANCE OF DEATH. New York: Morrow, 1938; as DESIGN FOR DYING. London: Heinemann, 1938.
McClure, James Howe	THE STEAM PIG. London: Gollancz, 1971; New York: Harper, 1972.
McConnell, James Douglas Rutherford	COMES THE BLIND FURY, as Douglas Rutherford. London: Faber, 1950.
McCord, David Thompson Watson	ODDLY ENOUGH. Cambridge, Mass.: Washburn & Thomas, 1926.
McCoy, Horace	THEY SHOOT HORSES, DON'T THEY? New York: Simon & Schuster; London: Barker, 1935.
McCulley, Johnston	BROADWAY BAB. New York: Watt, 1919; London: Hutchinson, 1926.
McCurtin, Peter	HANGTOWN. New York: Belmont, 1970; as ARIZONA HANGTOWN. London: Hale, 1972. MAFIOSA. New York: Belmont, 1970; London: New English Library, 1971.
McCutchan, Donald Philip	WHISTLE AND I'LL COME. London: Harrap, 1957.

AUTHOR	TITLE/FIRST EDITION INFORMATION
McCutcheon, George Barr	GRAUSTARK: THE STORY OF A LOVE BEHIND THE THRONE. Chicago: Stone, 1901; London: Richards, 1902.
MacDonald, Allan William Colt	RESTLESS GUNS. New York: Chelsea, 1929; London: Collins, 1934.
MacDonald, George	PHANTASTES: A FAERIE ROMANCE FOR MEN AND WOMEN. London: Smith Elder, 1858; Boston: Loring, 1870.
McDonald, Gregory	RUNNING SCARED. New York: Obolensky, 1964; London: Gollancz, 1977.
MacDonald, John Dann	THE BRASS CUPCAKE. New York: Fawcett, 1950; London: Muller, 1955.
MacDonald, Philip	AMBROTOX AND LIMPING DICK, as Oliver Fleming, with Ronald MacDonald. London: Ward Lock, 1920.
McElfresh, Elizabeth Adeline	MY HEART WENT DEAD. New York: Phoenix, 1949.
McEvoy, Marjorie	NO CASTLE OF DREAMS. London: Jenkins, 1960; New York: Lenox Hill, 1971. A RED, RED ROSE. London: Jenkins, 1960.
McGaughy, Dudley Dean	GUNS TO THE SUNSET, as Dean Owen. New York: Phoenix, 1948; London: Wright & Brown, 1950.
McGerr, Patricia	PICK YOUR VICTIM. New York: Doubleday, 1946; London: Collins, 1947.
MacGibbon, Jean	WHEN THE WEATHER'S CHANGING, as Jean Howard. London: Putnam, 1945.
MacGill, Mrs. Patrick Margaret	THE "GOOD-NIGHT" STORIES, as Margaret Gibbon. London: Year Book Press, 1912.
McGinley, Phyliss	ON THE CONTRARY. New York: Doubleday, 1934.
McGivern, William Peter	BUT DEATH RUNS FASTER. New York: Dodd Mead, 1948; London: Boardman, 1949.
McGraw, Eloise Jarvis	SAWDUST IN HIS SHOES. New York: Coward McCann, 1950.

AUTHOR	TITLE/FIRST EDITION INFORMATION
MacGregor, Ellen	TOMMY AND THE TELEPHONE. Chicago: Whitman, 1947.
McGregor, Iona	AN EDINBURGH REEL. London: Faber, 1968.
MacGregor, James Murdoch	WORLD OUT OF MIND, as J. T. McIntosh. New York: Doubleday, 1953; London: Museum Press, 1955.
McGuane, Thomas Francis, III	THE SPORTING CLUB. New York: Simon & Schuster, 1968; London: Deutsch, 1969.
McGuire, Dominic Paul	MURDER IN BOSTALL. London: Skeffinton, 1931; as THE BLACK ROSE MURDER. New York: Brentano's, 1932.
McHugh, Vincent	TOUCH ME NOT. New York: Cape & Smith, 1930.
McIlwain, David	SPACEWAYS, as Charles Eric Maine. London: Hodder & Stoughton, 1953; as SPACEWAYS SATELLITE. New York: Avalon, 1958.
MacInnes, Helen Clark	ABOVE SUSPICION. Boston: Little, Brown; London: Harrap, 1941.
MacIntyre, Elisabeth	AMBROSE KANGAROO: A STORY THAT NEVER ENDS. Sydney, Australia: Consolidated, 1941; New York: Scribner, 1942.
McIntyre, Vonda Neel	THE EXILE WAITING. New York: Doubleday, 1975; London: Gollancz, 1976.
Mackay, Constance D'Arcy	COSTUMES AND SCENERY FOR AMATEURS. New York: Holt, 1915.
Mackay, Mary	A ROMANCE OF TWO WORLDS, as Marie Corelli. 2 vols. London, 1886. VENDETTA; OR, THE STORY OF OUR FORGOTTEN, as Marie Corelli. 3 vols. London, 1886.
McKee, David John	BRONTO'S WINGS. London: Dobson, 1964.
Mackelworth, Ronald Walter	FIREMANTLE, as R. W. Mackelworth. London: Hale, 1968; as THE DIABOLS. New York: Paperback Library, 1969.

AUTHOR	**TITLE/FIRST EDITION INFORMATION**
Macken, Walter	QUENCH THE MOON. London: Macmillan; New York: Viking, 1948.
McKenna, Richard Milton	THE SAND PEBBLES. New York: Harper, 1962; London: Gollancz, 1963.
MacKenzie, Donald	OCCUPATION: THIEF. Indianapolis: Bobbs Merrill, 1955; as FUGITIVES. London: Elek, 1955.
MacKenzie, Jean	STORM ISLAND. Toronto: Macmillan, 1968.
Mackie, Doris	MARRIED MAN'S GIRL, as Susan Inglis. London: Mills & Boon, 1934.
Mackinlay, Leila Antoinette Sterling	LITTLE MOUNTEBANK. London: Mills & Boon, 1930.
Mackintosh, Elizabeth	THE MAN IN THE QUEUE, as Gordon Daviot. London: Methuen; New York: Dutton, 1929. KIF: AN UNVARNISHED HISTORY. London: Benn; New York: Appleton, 1929.
McLaughlin, Dean Benjamin, Jr.	DOME WORLD. New York: Pyramid, 1962.
McLaughlin, Lorrie Bell	WEST TO THE CARIBOO. Toronto: Macmillan, 1962; New York: St. Martin's; London: Macmillan, 1963.
MacLean, Alistair Stuart	H.M.S. ULYSSES. London: Collins, 1955; New York: Doubleday, 1956.
McLean, Allan Campbell	THE HILL OF THE RED FOX. London: Collins, 1955; New York: Dutton, 1956.
MacLean, Katherine Anne	COSMIC CHECKMATE, with Charles V. De Vet. New York: Ace, 1962. THE DIPLOIDS AND OTHER FLIGHTS OF FANCY. New York: Avon, 1962.
MacLeod, Charlotte Matilda	MYSTERY OF THE WHITE KNIGHT. New York: Avalon, 1965. THE FOOD OF LOVE, as Matilda Hughes. New York: Avalon, 1965. NEXT DOOR TO DANGER. New York: Avalon, 1965.
MacLeod, Jean S.	LIFE FOR TWO. London: Mills & Boon, 1936.

AUTHOR	TITLE/FIRST EDITION INFORMATION
MacLeod, Robert	THE APPALOOSA. New York: Fawcett, 1966.
McMullen, Mary	STRANGLEHOLD. New York: Harper, 1951; as DEATH OF MISS X. London: Collins, 1952.
McMurty, Larry	HORSEMAN, PASS BY. New York: Harper, 1961; as HUD. New York: Popular, 1963; London: Sphere, 1971.
McNeile, Herman Cyril	THE LIEUTENANT AND OTHERS, as Sapper. London: Hodder & Stoughton, 1915.
McNeill, Janet	MY FRIEND SPECS MC CANN. London: Faber, 1955. A CHILD IN THE HOUSE. London: Hodder & Stoughton, 1955.
McNichols, Charles Longstreth	CRAZY WEATHER. New York: Macmillan, 1944; London: Gollancz, 1945. JAPAN: ITS RESOURCES AND INDUSTRIES, with Clayton D. Carus. New York: Harper, 1944.
McNickle, William D'Arcy	THE SURROUNDED. New York: Dodd Mead, 1936.
MacPherson, A. D. L.	BEGGARS MAY SING, as Sara Seale. London, 1932; Toronto: Harlequin, 1968.
MacPherson, Margaret	THEM SHINTY BOYS. London: Collins; New York: Harcourt Brace, 1963.
McShane, Mark	THE STRAIGHT AND THE CROOKED. London: Long, 1960.
MacVicar, Angus	THE PURPLE ROCK. London: Paul, 1933.
Maddock, Reginald Bertram	CORRIGAN AND THE WHITE COBRA [TOMB OF OPI, YELLOW PERIL, BLACK RIDERS, GOLDEN PAGODA, DREAM-MAKERS, BLUE CRATER, GREEN TIGER, RED LIONS, LITTLE PEOPLE], as R. B. Maddock. 10 vols. London: Nelson, 1956-1963.
Maddocks, Margaret Kathleen Avern	COME LASSES AND LADS. London: Hurst & Blackett, 1944.

AUTHOR	TITLE/FIRST EDITION INFORMATION
Mahy, Margaret	THE DRAGON OF AN ORDINARY FAMILY. New York: Watts; London: Heinemann, 1969.
Maling, Arthur Gordon	DECOY. New York: Harper, 1969; London: Joseph, 1971.
Mallowan, Dame Agatha Mary Clarissa	THE MYSTERIOUS AFFAIR AT STYLES, as Agatha Christie. London: Lane, 1920; New York: Dodd Mead, 1927.
Malzberg, Barry Norman	ORACLE OF THE THOUSAND HANDS. New York: Olympia, 1968.
Manfred, Frederick Feikema	THE GOLDEN BOWL. St. Paul, Minn.: Webb, 1944; London: Dobson, 1947.
Manley-Tucker, Audrie	LEONIE. London: Mills & Boon, 1958.
Mann, Edward Beverly	THE MAN FROM TEXAS. New York: Morrow, 1931; London: Hurst & Blackett, 1934.
Mann, Jessica	A CHARITABLE END. London: Collins; New York: McKay, 1971.
Manning, Laurence Edward	THE HOW AND WHY OF BETTER GARDENING. New York: Van Nostrand, 1951.
Manning, Rosemary	FROM HOLST TO BRITTEN: A STUDY OF MODERN CHORAL MUSIC. London: Workers' Music, 1949.
Manning-Sanders, Ruth	THE PEDLAR AND OTHER POEMS. London: Selwyn & Blount, 1919.
Markoosie	HARPOON OF THE HUNTER. Montreal; London: McGill-Queen's University Press, 1970.
Marlowe, Dan James	DOORWAY TO DEATH. New York: Avon; London: Digit, 1959.
Marlowe, Derek	A DANDY IN ASPIC. London: Gollancz; New York: Putnam, 1966.
Marquand, John Phillips	PRINCE AND BOATSWAIN: SEA TALES FROM THE RECOLLECTIONS OF REAR-ADMIRAL CHARLES E. CLARK, with James Morgan. Greenfield, Mass.: Hall, 1915.

AUTHOR	TITLE/FIRST EDITION INFORMATION
Marsh, Edith Ngaio	A MAN LAY DEAD. London: Bles, 1934; New York: Sheridan, 1942.
Marshall, Edison Tesla	THE VOICE OF THE PACK. Boston: Little, Brown; London: Hodder & Stoughton, 1920.
Marshall, Evelyn	THE SHORE HOUSE MYSTERY, as Jean Marsh. London: Hamilton, 1931.
Marshall, Rosamond van der Zee	L'ENFANT DU CIRQUE. 1930.
Martin, David	BATTLEFIELDS AND GIRLS: POEMS. Glasgow, Scotland: Maclellan, 1942.
Martin, George Raymond Richard	A SONG FOR LYA AND OTHER STORIES. New York: Avon, 1976; London: Coronet, 1978.
Martin, Patricia Miles	SYLVESTER JONES AND THE VOICE OF THE FOREST. New York: Lothrop, 1958.
Martin, Rhona	GALLOWS WEDDING. London: Bodley Head, 1978; New York: Coward McCann, 1979.
Masefield, John	SALT-WATER BALLADS. London: Grant Richards, 1902; New York: Macmillan, 1913.
Mason, Alfred Edward Woodley	A ROMANCE OF WASTDALE. London: Mathews; New York: Stokes, 1895.
Mason, Douglas Rankine	THE BLOCKADE OF SINITRON, as John Rankine. London: Nelson, 1966. INTERSTELLAR TWO-FIVE, as John Rankine. London: Dobson, 1966. FROM CARTHAGE THEN I CAME, as Douglas R. Mason. New York: Doubleday, 1966; London: Hale, 1968.
Mason, Francis van Wyck	SEEDS OF MURDER. New York: Doubleday, 1930; London: Eldon, 1937.
Masson, David Irvine	HAND-LIST OF INCUNABULA IN THE UNIVERSITY LIBRARY, LIVERPOOL. Privately printed, 1948; supplement, 1955.
Masur, Harold Q.	BURY ME DEEP. New York: Simon & Schuster, 1947; London: Boardman, 1948.
Mather, Anne	CAROLINE. London: Hale, 1965.

AUTHOR	TITLE/FIRST EDITION INFORMATION
Matheson, Richard Burton	SOMEONE IS BLEEDING. New York: Lion, 1953.
Mathews, John Joseph	WAH 'KON-TAH: THE OSAGE AND THE WHITE MAN'S ROAD. Norman: University of Oklahoma, 1932.
Matthews, Patricia Anne	HORROR AT GULL HOUSE, as Patty Brisco, with Clayton Matthews. New York: Belmont, 1970. MERRY'S TREASURE, as Patty Brisco. New York: Avalon, 1970.
Mathis, Sharon Bell	BROOKLYN STORY. New York: Hill & Wang, 1970.
Mattingley, Christobel	THE PICNIC DOG. London: Hamish Hamilton, 1970.
Maugham, Robert Cecil Romer	THE 1946 MS, as Robin Maugham. London: War Facts Press, 1943.
Maugham, William Somerset	LIZA OF LAMBETH. London: Unwin, 1897; New York: Doran, 1921.
May, Winifred Jean	A CLUSTER OF PALMS, as Wynne May. London: Mills & Boon, 1967.
Mayne, William	FOLLOW THE FOOTPRINTS. London: Oxford University, 1953.
Mead, Edward Shepherd	THE MAGNIFICENT MAC INNES, as Shepherd Mead. New York: Farrar Straus, 1949.
Meade, Elizabeth Thomasina	LOTY'S LAST HOME, as L. T. Meade. London: Shaw, 1875.
Meader, Stephen Warren	THE BLACK BUCCANEER. New York: Harcourt Brace, 1920.
Meaker, Marijane	DINKY HOCKER SHOOTS SMACK! as M. E. Kerr. New York: Harper, 1972; London: Gollancz, 1973.
Means, Florence Crannell	RAFAEL AND CONSUELO, with Harriet Louise Fullen. New York: Friendship Press, 1929.
Mears, Leonard F.	TROUBLE TOWN, as Johnny Nelson. Sydney, Australia: Cleveland, 1955. DRIFT, as Marshall Grover. Sydney, Australia: Scripts,

AUTHOR	TITLE/FIRST EDITION INFORMATION
	n.d. COLORADO PURSUIT, as Marshall Grover. Sydney, Australia: Scripts, n.d. BORN TO DRIFT, as Marshall Grover. Sydney, Australia: Scripts, n.d. COLD TRAIL TO KIRBY, as Marshall Grover. Sydney, Australia: Scripts, n.d.
Meek, Sterner St. Paul	JERRY: THE ADVENTURES OF AN ARMY DOG, as S. P. Meek. New York: Morrow, 1932.
Meggs, Brown Moore	SATURDAY GAMES. New York: Random House, 1974; London: Collins, 1975.
Meigs, Cornelia Lynde	THE KINGDOM OF THE WINDING ROAD. New York; London: Macmillan, 1915.
Meltzer, David	POEMS, with Donald Schenker. Privately printed, 1957.
Melwood, Eileen Mary	NETTLEWOOD. London: Deutsch, 1974; New York: Seabury, 1975.
Mercer, Cecil William	THE BROTHER OF DAPHNE, as Dornford Yates. London: Ward Lock, 1914.
Meredith, Richard Carlton	THE SKY IS FILLED WITH SHIPS. New York: Ballantine, 1969. WE ALL DIED AT BREAKAWAY STATION. New York: Ballantine, 1969.
Merriam, Eve	FAMILY CIRCLE. New Haven, Conn.: Yale, 1946.
Merril, Josephine Judith	SHADOW ON THE HEARTH, as Judith Merril. New York: Doubleday, 1950; London: Sidgwick & Jackson, 1953.
Merrill, Jean	HENRY, THE HAND-PAINTED MOUSE. New York: Coward McCann, 1951.
Merritt, Abraham	THE MOON POOL, as A. Merritt. New York; London: Putnam, 1919.
Mertz, Barbara Louise Gross	TEMPLES, TOMBS, AND HIEROGLYPHS: THE STORY OF EGYPTOLOGY, as Barbara G. Mertz. New York: Coward McCann; London: Gollancz, 1964.

AUTHOR	TITLE/FIRST EDITION INFORMATION
Merwin, Samuel Kimball, Jr.	MURDER IN MINIATURES, as Sam Merwin, Jr. New York: Doubleday, 1940.
Meyer, Nicholas	TARGET PRACTICE. New York: Harcourt Brace, 1974; London: Hodder & Stoughton, 1975.
Meyers, Roy Lethbridge	DOLPHIN BOY. New York: Ballantine, 1967; as THE DOLPHIN RIDER. London: Rapp & Whiting, 1968.
Meynell, Laurence Walter	MOCKBEGGAR. London: Harrap, 1924; New York: Appleton, 1925.
Michener, James A.	THE UNIT IN THE SOCIAL STUDIES, with Harold M. Long. Cambridge, Mass.: Harvard, 1940.
Milburn, George	A HANDBOOK FOR AMATEUR MAGICIANS. Girard, Kans.: Haldeman-Julius, 1926.
Miles, Favell Mary	THE RED FLAME, as Lady Miles. London: Hutchinson: 1921. RED, WHITE, AND GREY, as Lady Miles. London: Hutchinson, 1921.
Milhous, Katherine	LOVINA. New York; London: Scribner, 1940.
Millar, Kenneth	THE DARK TUNNEL. New York: Dodd Mead, 1944; as I DIE SLOWLY. London: Lion, 1955.
Millar, Margaret Ellis	THE INVISIBLE WORM. New York: Doubleday, 1941; London: Long, 1943.
Millard, Joseph John	MANSION OF EVIL. New York: Fawcett, 1950.
Miller, Bill	DEADLY WEAPON, as Wade Miller, with Robert Wade. New York: Farrar & Straus, 1946; London: Sampson Low, 1947.
Miller, Peter Schuyler	GENUS HOMO, as P. Schuyler Miller, with L. Sprague de Camp. Reading, Pa.: Fantasy Press, 1950.
Miller, Walter Michael, Jr.	A CANTICLE FOR LEIBOWITZ. Philadelphia: Lippincott; London: Weidenfeld & Nicolson, 1960.

AUTHOR	**TITLE/FIRST EDITION INFORMATION**
Millhiser, Marlys Joy	MICHAEL'S WIFE. New York: Putnam, 1972.
Milne, Alan Alexander	LOVERS IN LONDON, as A. A. Milne. London: Alston Rivers, 1905.
Minarik, Else Holmelund	LITTLE BEAR. New York: Harper, 1957; Kingswood, England: World's Work, 1965.
Mitchell, Gladys Maude Winifred	SPEEDY DEATH. London: Gollancz; New York: Dial, 1929.
Mitchell, Margaret Munnerlyn	GONE WITH THE WIND. New York; London: Macmillan, 1936.
Mitchell, Sibyl Elyne Keith	AUSTRALIA'S ALPS, as Elyne Mitchell. Sydney, Australia; London: Angus & Robertson, 1942.
Mitchison, Naomi Margaret	THE CONQUERED. London: Cape; New York: Harcourt Brace, 1923.
Modell, Merriam	THE SOUND OF YEARS, as Evelyn Piper. New York: Simon & Schuster, 1946; London: Cassell, 1947.
Moffat, Gwen	SPACE BELOW MY FEET. London: Hodder & Stoughton; New York: Houghton Mifflin, 1961.
Molesworth, Mary Louisa	LOVER AND HUSBAND, as Ennis Graham. 3 vols. London: Skeet, 1869.
Momaday, Navarre Scott	HOUSE MADE OF DAWN. New York: Harper, 1968; London: Gollancz, 1969.
Monjo, Ferdinand Nicolas, III	INDIAN SUMMER. New York: Harper, 1968; Kingswood, England: World's Work, 1969.
Monteilhet, Hubert	THE PRAYING MANTISES. 1962.
Monteleone, Thomas F.	SEEDS OF CHANGE. Toronto: Laser, 1975.
Montgomery, Lucy Maud	ANNE OF GREEN GABLES. Boston: Page; London: Pitman, 1908.
Montgomery, Rutherford George	TROOPERS THREE. New York: Doubleday, 1932.
Moorcock, Michael	THE STEALER OF SOULS AND OTHER STORIES. London: Spearman, 1963; New York: Lancer, 1967.

AUTHOR	TITLE/FIRST EDITION INFORMATION
Moore, Brian	THE EXECUTIONERS, as Michael Bryan. Toronto: Harlequin, 1951. WREATH FOR A REDHEAD, as Michael Bryan. Toronto: Harlequin, 1951.
Moore, Catherine Lucille	THE BRASS RING, as Lewis Padgett, with Henry Kuttner. New York: Duell, 1946; London: Sampson Low, 1947.
Moore, Doris Elizabeth Langley	THE TECHNIQUE OF THE LOVE AFFAIR, as A Gentlewoman. London: Howe; New York: Simon & Schuster, 1928.
Moore, Patrick Alfred	THE MASTER OF THE MOON. London: Museum Press, 1952.
Moore, Ward	BREATHE IN THE AIR AGAIN. New York: Harper, 1942.
Moorhead, Diana	IN SEARCH OF MAGIC. Auckland, New Zealand; Leicester, England: Brockhampton, 1971.
Morey, Walter Nelson	NORTH TO DANGER, with Virgil Burford. New York: Day, 1954.
Morgan, Alison Mary	FISH. London: Chatto & Windus, 1971; as A BOY CALLED FISH. New York: Harper, 1973.
Morgan, Dan	CEE TEE MAN. London: Panther, 1955.
Morland, Nigel	CACHEXIA: A COLLECTION OF PROSE POEMS, with Peggy Barwell. Paris: Barbier, 1930. PEOPLE WE HAVE NEVER MET: A BOOK OF SUPERFICIAL CAMEOS, with Peggy Barwell. Paris: Barbier, 1931.
Morressy, John	THE BLACKBOARD CAVALIER. New York: Doubleday, 1966; London: Gollancz, 1967.
Morris, Janet Ellen	HIGH COUCH ON SILISTRA. New York; London: Bantam, 1977. THE GOLDEN SWORD. New York; London: Bantam, 1977.
Morris, William	THE EARTHLY PARADISE. 3 vols. 1868-1870.
Morris, Wright Marion	MY UNCLE DUDLEY. New York: Harcourt Brace, 1942.

AUTHOR	TITLE/FIRST EDITION INFORMATION
Morrison, Arthur	THE SHADOWS AROUND US: AUTHENTIC TALES OF THE SUPERNATURAL. London: Simpkin Marshall, 1891.
Morrissey, Joseph Lawrence	CITY OF THE HIDDEN EYES, as J. L. Morrissey. London: Consul, 1964.
Motley, Annette	MY LADY'S CRUSADE. London: Futura, 1977.
Mowat, Farley McGill	PEOPLE OF THE DEER. Boston: Little, Brown; London: Joseph, 1952.
Mowery, William Byron	THE SILVER HAWK. New York: Doubleday, 1929.
Moyes, Patricia	DEAD MEN DON'T SKI. London: Collins, 1959; New York: Rinehart, 1960.
Mukerji, Dhan Gopal	RAJANI: SONGS OF THE NIGHT. San Francisco: Elder, 1916.
Mulford, Clarence Edward	BAR-20. New York: Outing, 1907; London: Hodder & Stoughton, 1914.
Murphy, Lawrence Augustus	THE NAKED RANGE, as Steven C. Lawrence. New York: Ace, 1956.
Murray, Max	THE WORLD'S BACK DOORS. London: Cape, 1927; New York: Cape & Smith, 1929.
Muskett, Netta Rachel	THE JADE SPIDER. London: Hutchinson, 1927.
Mussi, Mary	WINDIER SKIES, as Mary Howard. London, 1930.
Myers, John	THE HARP AND THE BLADE. New York: Dutton, 1941.
Nebel, Louis Frederick	SLEEPERS EAST. Boston: Little, Brown, 1933; London: Gollancz, 1934.
Neels, Betty	AMAZON IN AN APRON. London: Mills & Boon, 1969. BLOW HOT, BLOW COLD. London: Mills & Boon, 1969; as SURGEON FROM HOLLAND. Toronto: Harlequin, 1970. SISTER PETERS IN AMSTERDAM. London: Mills & Boon, 1969; Toronto: Harlequin, 1970.

AUTHOR	TITLE/FIRST EDITION INFORMATION
Neihardt, John Gneisenau	THE DIVINE ENCHANTMENT: A MYSTICAL POEM. New York: White, 1900.
Neilan, Sarah	THE BRAGANZA PURSUIT. London: Hodder & Stoughton; New York: Dutton, 1976.
Nelson, Radell Faraday	THE GANYMEDE TAKEOVER, as Ray Nelson, with Philip K. Dick. New York: Ace, 1967; London: Arrow, 1971.
Nesbit, Edith	THE PROPHET'S MANTLE, as Fabian Bland, with Hubert Bland. London: Drane, 1885; Chicago: Belford Clarke, 1889.
Ness, Evaline	A GIFT FOR SULA SULA. New York: Scribner, 1963.
Neville, Emily Cheney	IT'S LIKE THIS, CAT. New York: Harper, 1963; London: Angus & Robertson, 1969.
Neville, Kris Ottman	EPOXY RESINS, with Henry Lee. New York: McGraw Hill, 1957.
Nevins, Francis Michael, Jr.	PUBLISH AND PERISH. New York: Putnam, 1975; London: Hale, 1977.
Newberry, Clare Turlay	HERBERT THE LION. New York: Brewer Warren and Putnam, 1931.
Newcomb, Simon	A CRITICAL EXAMINATION OF OUR FINANCIAL POLICY DURING THE SOUTHERN REBELLION. New York: Appleton, 1865.
Newman, Bernard	HOW TO RUN AN AMATEUR CONCERT PARTY. London: Reynolds, 1925.
Newton, Dwight Bennett	GUNS OF THE RIMROCK. New York: Phoenix, 1946; London: Sampson Low, 1947.
Nichols, John	THE STERILE CUCKOO. New York: McKay, 1965.
Nichols, John Beverly	PRELUDE. London: Chatto & Windus, 1920.
Nichols, Ruth	A WALK OUT OF THE WORLD. Toronto: Longman; New York: Harcourt Brace, 1969. CEREMONY OF INNOCENCE. London: Faber, 1969.

AUTHOR	TITLE/FIRST EDITION INFORMATION
Nicholson, Margaret Beda	SUMMER FLIGHT, as Margaret Yorke. London: Hale, 1957.
Nickson, Arthur Thomas	TIN STAR SHERIFF, as Matt Winstan. London: Jenkins, 1956.
Nicole, Christopher Robin	WEST INDIAN CRICKET. London: Phoenix, 1957.
Nielsen, Helen Berniece	THE KIND MAN. New York: Washburn; London: Gollancz, 1951.
Niven, Frederick John	THE LOST CABIN MINE. London: Lane, 1908; New York: Lane, 1909.
Niven, Laurence van Cott	WORLD OF PTAVVS, as Larry Niven. New York: Ballantine, 1966; London: Macdonald, 1968.
Nolan, Frederick	THE LIFE AND DEATH OF JOHN HENRY TUNSTALL. Albuquerque: University of New Mexico, 1965.
Nolan, William Francis	ADVENTURE ON WHEELS: THE AUTOBIOGRAPHY OF A ROAD RACING CHAMPION, with John Fitch. New York: Putnam, 1959.
Norman, Lilith	THE CITY OF SYDNEY: OFFICIAL GUIDE. Sydney, Australia: City Council, 1959.
Norris, Benjamin Franklin	YVERNELLE: A LEGEND OF FUEDAL FRANCE. Philadelphia: Lippincott, 1891.
Norris, Kathleen Thompson	MOTHER. New York: Macmillan, 1911.
North, Sterling	(POEMS). Chicago: University of Chicago, 1925.
Norton, Alice Mary	THE PRINCE COMMANDS, as Andre Norton. New York; London: Appleton Century, 1934.
Norton, Mary	THE MAGIC BED-KNOB; OR, HOW TO BECOME A WITCH IN TEN EASY LESSONS. New York: Hyperion, 1943.
Norway, Kate	SISTER BROOKES OF BYND'S. London: Mills & Boon, 1957; as NURSE BROOKES. Toronto: Harlequin, 1958.

AUTHOR	TITLE/FIRST EDITION INFORMATION
Norway, Nevil Shute	MARAZAN, as Nevil Shute. London: Cassell, 1926.
Nourse, Alan Edward	TROUBLE ON TITAN, as Alan E. Nourse. Philadelphia: Winston, 1954; London: Hutchinson, 1956.
Nowlan, Philip Francis	BUCK ROGERS ON THE MOON OF SATURN. Racine, Wis.: Whitman, 1934. BUCK ROGERS IN THE DANGEROUS MISSION. New York: Blue Ribbon Press, 1934.
Nutt, Charles	THE HUNGER AND OTHER STORIES, as Charles Beaumont. New York: Putnam, 1957; as SHADOW PLAY, as Charles Beaumont. London: Panther, 1964. RUN FROM THE HUNTER, as Keith Grantland, with John E. Tomerlin. New York: Fawcett, 1957; London: Boardman, 1959.
Nye, Nelson Coral	TWO-FISTED COWPOKE. New York: Greenberg, 1936; London: Nicholson & Watson, 1937.
Nye, Robert	JUVENILIA 1. Lowestoft, England: Scorpion Press, 1961.
Obets, Bob	BLOOD-MOON RANGE. New York: Pyramid, 1957.
O'Connor, John Woolf	CONQUEST: A NOVEL OF THE OLD SOUTHWEST. New York: Harper, 1930.
O'Connor, Richard	THOMAS: ROCK OF CHICKAMAUGA. New York: Prentice Hall, 1948.
O'Dell, Scott	REPRESENTATIVE PHOTOPLAYS ANALYZED. Hollywood, Calif.: Palmer, 1924.
Odle, E. V.	THE HISTORY OF ALFRED RUDD. London: Collins, 1922.
O'Donnell, Lillian	DEATH ON THE GRASS. New York: Arcadia, 1960.
O'Donnell, Peter	MODESTY BLAISE. London: Souvenir Press; New York: Doubleday, 1965.

AUTHOR	TITLE/FIRST EDITION INFORMATION
Offord, Lenore Glen	MURDER ON RUSSIAN HILL. Philadelphia: Macrae Smith, 1938; as MURDER BEFORE BREAKFAST. London: Jarrolds, 1938.
Offutt, Andrew Jefferson	EVIL IS LIVE SPELLED BACKWARDS. New York: Paperback Library, 1970.
Ogilvie, Elisabeth May	HIGH TIDE AT NOON. New York: Crowell, 1944; London: Harrap, 1945.
Oliver, Symmes Chadwick	MISTS OF DAWN, as Chad Oliver. Philadelphia: Winston, 1952; London: Hutchinson, 1954.
Olsen, Alfred John, Jr.	RHYTHM RIDES THE ROCKET, as Bob Olsen. New York: Columbia, 1940.
Olsen, Theodore Victor	HAVEN OF THE HUNTED. New York: Ace, 1956.
O'Malley, Lady Mary Dolling	PEKING CIRCUS, as Ann Bridge. London; Boston: 1932.
Oman, Carola Mary Anima	THE MENIN ROAD AND OTHER POEMS. London: Hodder & Stoughton, 1919.
Onadipe, Nathaniel Kolawole	THE ADVENTURES OF SOUZA, THE VILLAGE LAD, as Kola Onadipe. Lagos: African University, 1963.
Onstott, Kyle	YOUR DOG AS A HOBBY, with Irving C. Ackerman. New York, 1940.
Oppenheim, Edward Phillips	THE PEER AND THE WOMAN. New York: Taylor, 1892; London: Ward Lock, 1895.
Orczy, Emma Magdalena Rosalia Maria Josefa Barbara	THE EMPEROR'S CANDLESTICKS, as Baroness Orczy. London: Pearson, 1899; New York: Doscher, 1908.
Orgel, Doris	THE TALE OF GOCKEL, HINKEL, AND GACKELIAH. New York: Random House, 1961.
Ormerod, Roger	TIME TO KILL. London: Hale, 1974.
Ormondroyd, Edward	DAVID AND THE PHOENIX. Chicago: Follett, 1957.

AUTHOR	TITLE/FIRST EDITION INFORMATION
O'Rourke, Frank	"E" COMPANY. New York: Simon & Schuster, 1945.
Ostenso, Martha	A FAR LAND. New York: Seltzer, 1924.
Ottley, Reginald Leslie	STAMPEDE. London: Laurie, 1961.
Overholser, Wayne D.	BUCKAROO'S CODE. New York: Macmillan, 1947; Redhill, England: Wells Gardner, 1948.
Overton, Jenny Margaret Mary	CREED COUNTRY. London: Faber, 1969; New York: Macmillan, 1970.
Ovstedal, Barbara	SOVEREIGN'S KEY, as Rosalind Laker. London: Hale, 1969.
Packard, Frank Lucius	ON THE IRON AT BIG CLOUD. New York: Crowell, 1911.
Paine, Albert Bigelow	RHYMES BY TWO FRIENDS, with William Allen White. Privately printed, 1873.
Palmer, Charles Stuart	ACE OF JADES. New York: Mohawk, 1931.
Palmer, Cyril Everard	A BROKEN VESSEL. Kingston, Jamaica: Pioneer Press, 1960.
Pangborn, Edgar	A-100, as Bruce Harrison. New York: Dutton, 1930.
Panshin, Alexei	RITE OF PASSAGE. New York: Ace, 1968; London: Sidgwick & Jackson, 1969. STAR WELL. New York: Ace, 1968. THE THURB REVOLUTION. New York: Ace, 1968. HEINLEIN IN DIMENSION: A CRITICAL ANALYSIS. Chicago: Advent, 1968.
Pargeter, Edith Mary	HORTENSIUS, FRIEND OF NERO. London: Lovat Dickson, 1936; New York: Greystone, 1937. IRON-BOUND. London: Lovat Dickson, 1936.
Pargeter, Margaret	WINDS FROM THE SEA. London: Mills & Boon; Toronto: Harlequin, 1975.
Parish, Margaret Cecile	GOOD HUNTING, LITTLE INDIAN, as Peggy Parish. New York: Scott, 1962. MY BOOK OF MANNERS, as Peggy Parish.

AUTHOR	TITLE/FIRST EDITION INFORMATION
	New York: Golden, 1962; London: Golden Pleasure, 1963.
Park, Rosina Ruth Lucia	THE HARP IN THE SOUTH. Sydney, Australia: Angus & Robertson; London: Joseph; Boston: Houghton Mifflin, 1948.
Parker, Richard	ESCAPE FROM THE ZOO. London: Sylvan Press, 1945.
Parker, Robert Brown	THE GODWULF MANUSCRIPT. Boston: Houghton Mifflin, 1973; London: Deutsch, 1974.
Patchett, Mary Elwyn Osborne	AJAX, THE WARRIOR. London: Lutterworth, 1953; as AJAX, GOLDEN DOG OF THE AUSTRALIAN BUSH. Indianapolis: Bobbs Merrill, 1953.
Paton Walsh, Gillian	HENGEST'S TALE. London: Macmillan; New York: St. Martin's, 1966.
Patten, Brian	PORTRAITS. Liverpool, England: Privately printed, 1962.
Patten, Lewis Byford	MASSACRE AT WHITE RIVER. New York: Ace, 1952; London: Ward Lock, 1961.
Patterson, Henry	SEVEN PILLARS TO HELL, as Hugh Marlowe. London; New York: Abelard Schuman, 1963.
Pattinson, Nancy Evelyn	MY DREAM IS YOURS, as Nan Asquith. London, 1954.
Pattullo, George	THE UNTAMED: RANGE LIFE IN THE SOUTHWEST. New York: Fitzgerald, 1911.
Paul, Elliot Harold	INDELIBLE. Boston: Houghton Mifflin, 1922; London: Jarrolds, 1924.
Pauley, Barbara Anne	BLOOD KIN. New York: Doubleday, 1972.
Peake, Lilian	MAN OF GRANITE: London: Mills & Boon, 1971; Toronto: Harlequin, 1975. THIS MOMENT IN TIME. London: Mills & Boon, 1971; Toronto: Harlequin, 1972.
Pearce, Ann Philippa	MINNOW ON THE SAY. London: Oxford University, 1955; as THE MINNOW LEADS TO TREASURE. Cleveland: World, 1958.

AUTHOR	TITLE/FIRST EDITION INFORMATION
Pease, Howard	THE TATTOOED MAN. New York: Doubleday; London: Heinemann, 1926.
Peck, Richard	OLD TOWN: A COMPLEAT GUIDE, with Norman Strasma. Chicago, 1965.
Peck, Robert Newton	THE HAPPY SADIST. New York: Doubleday, 1962.
Pedler, Christopher Magnus Howard	MUTANT 59, THE PLASTIC EATER, as Kit Pedler, with Gerry Davis. London: Souvenir Press, 1971; New York: Viking, 1972.
Pedler, Margaret Bass	THIS SPLENDID FOLLY. London: Mills & Boon, 1918; New York: Doran, 1921.
Peet, William Bartlett	HUBERT'S HAIR-RAISING ADVENTURE, as Bill Peet. Boston: Houghton Mifflin, 1959; London: Deutsch, 1960.
Pemberton, Max	THE DIARY OF A SCOUNDREL. London: Ward & Downey, 1891.
Pendelton, Donald Eugene	FRAME UP, as Stephen Gregory. Fresno, Calif.: Vega, 1960.
Pendower, Jacques	THE TERROR OF TORLANDS, as T. C. H. Jacobs. London: Stanley Paul, 1930.
Percy, Walker	ALPHA YES, TERRA NO! New York: Ace, 1965. THE CAVES OF MARS. New York: Ace, 1965. SAGA OF LOST EARTHS. New York: Ace, 1965. THE STAR MILL. New York: Ace, 1965.
Perkins, Lucy Fitch	THE GOOSE GIRL: A MOTHER'S LAP-BOOK OF RHYMES AND PICTURES. Chicago: McClurg, 1906.
Perry, George Sessions	WALLS RISE UP. New York: Doubleday, 1939.
Perry, Ritchie John Allen	THE FALL GUY. London: Collins; Boston: Houghton Mifflin, 1972.
Peter, Elizabeth O.	CONFIDENT TOMORROWS. London: Hurst & Blackett, 1931.
Peters, Maureen	ELIZABETH THE BELOVED. London: Hale, 1965; New York: Beagle, 1972.

AUTHOR	TITLE/FIRST EDITION INFORMATION
Peters, Natasha	SAVAGE SURRENDER. New York: Ace, 1977; London: Arrow, 1978.
Petersham, Maud Sylvia Fuller and Miska	MIKI. New York: Doubleday, 1929.
Petry, Ann Lane	THE STREET. Boston: Houghton Mifflin, 1946; London: Joseph, 1947.
Peyton, Kathleen W.	SABRE, THE HORSE FROM THE SEA, as Kathleen Herald. London: Black, 1948; New York: Macmillan, 1963.
Philips, Judson Pentecost	RED WAR, as Judson Philips, with Thomas A. Johnson. New York: Doubleday, 1936. HOLD 'EM GIRLS: THE INTELLIGENT WOMAN'S GUIDE TO MEN AND FOOT-BALL, with Robert W. Wood, Jr. New York: Putnam, 1936.
Philliphent, John Thomas	SPACE PUPPET, as John Rackham. London: Pearson, 1954. JUPITER EQUILATERAL, as John Rackham. London: Pearson, 1954. THE MASTER WEED, as John Rackham. London: Pearson, 1954.
Phillpotts, Eden	MY ADVENTURE IN THE FLYING SCOTSMAN: A ROMANCE OF LONDON AND NORTH-WESTERN RAILWAY SHARES. London: Hogg, 1888.
Phipson, Joan Margaret	CHRISTMAS IN THE SUN. Sydney, Australia; London: Angus & Robertson, 1951.
Picard, Barbara Leonie	THE MERMAID AND THE SIMPLETON. London: Oxford University, 1949; New York: Criterion, 1970.
Piercy, Marge	BREAKING CAMP. Middletown, Conn.: Wesleyan University, 1968.
Pilcher, Rosamunde	HALF-WAY TO THE MOON. London: Mills & Boon, 1949.
Piper, Henry Beam	MURDER IN THE GUNROOM, as H. Beam Piper. New York: Knopf, 1953.
Piserchia, Doris Elaine	MISTER JUSTICE. New York: Ace, 1973; London: Dobson, 1977.

AUTHOR	TITLE/FIRST EDITION INFORMATION
Plagemann, Bentz	WILLIAM WALTER. New York: Greystone, 1941.
Platt, Charles	THE GARBAGE WORLD. New York: Berkley, 1967; London: Panther, 1968.
Plowman, Stephanie	NELSON. London: Methuen, 1955.
Plummer, Clare Emsley	PAINTED CLAY, as Clare Emsley. London: 1947.
Pocock, Henry Roger Ashwell	TALES OF WESTERN LIFE, LAKE SUPERIOR, AND THE CANADIAN PRAIRIE, as H. R. A. Pocock. Ottawa, Canada: Mitchell, 1888.
Pohl, Frederik	THE SPACE MERCHANTS, with C. M. Kornbluth. New York: Ballantine, 1953; London: Heinemann, 1955. DANGER MOON, as James MacCreigh. Sydney, Australia: American Science Fiction, 1953.
Politi, Leo	LITTLE PANCHO. New York: Viking, 1938.
Polland, Madeleine Angela	CHILDREN OF THE RED KING. London: Constable, 1960; New York: Holt Rinehart, 1961.
Ponsonby, Doris Almon	THE GAZEBO, as D. A. Ponsonby. London: Hutchinson, 1945; as IF MY ARMS COULD HOLD, as Doris Ponsonby. New York: Liveright, 1947.
Poole, Jane Penelope Josephine	A DREAM IN THE HOUSE. London: Hutchinson, 1961.
Popkin, Zelda	DEATH WEARS A WHITE GARDENIA. Philadelphia: Lippincott, 1938; London: Hutchinson, 1939.
Porter, Eleanor Hodgman	CROSS CURRENT: THE STORY OF MARGARET. Boston: Wilde, 1907; London: Harrap, 1928.
Porter, Geneva Grace Stratton	THE SONG OF THE CARDINAL: A LOVE STORY, as Gene Stratton Porter. Indianapolis: Bobbs Merrill, 1903; London: Hodder & Stoughton, 1913.
Porter, Joyce	DOVER ONE. London: Cape; New York: Scribner, 1964.

AUTHOR	TITLE/FIRST EDITION INFORMATION
Porter, Sheena	THE BRONZE CHRYSANTHEMUM. London: Oxford University, 1961; Princeton, N.J.: Van Nostrand, 1965.
Porter, William Sydney	CABBAGES AND KINGS, as O. Henry. New York: McClure, 1904; London: Nash, 1912.
Portis, Charles McColl	NORWOOD. New York: Simon & Schuster, 1966; London: Cape, 1967.
Post, Melville Davisson	THE STRANGE SCHEMES OF RANDOLPH MASON. New York: Putnam, 1896.
Postgate, Raymond William	THE INTERNATIONAL (SOCIALIST BUREAU) DURING THE WAR. London: The Herald, 1918.
Potter, Helen Beatrix	THE TALE OF PETER RABBIT. Privately printed, 1900.
Potter, Joanna	ELIZA STANHOPE, as Joanna Trollope. London: Hutchinson, 1978; New York: Dutton, 1979.
Potter, Margaret Edith	MURDER TO MUSIC, as Margaret Newman. London, 1959.
Potts, Jean	SOMEONE TO REMEMBER. Philadelphia: Westminster, 1943.
Pournelle, Jerry Eugene	RED HEROIN, as Wade Curtis. New York: Berkley, 1969.
Powell, James	A MAN MADE FOR TROUBLE. Canoga Park, Calif.: Major, 1976; London: Hale, 1981.
Power, Rhoda Dolores	UNDER COSSACK AND BOLSHEVIK. London: Methuen, 1919; as UNDER THE BOLSHEVIK REIGN OF TERROR, New York: McBride & Nast, 1919.
Powys, John Cowper	ODES AND OTHER POEMS. London: Rider, 1896.
Pragnell, Festus	THE GREEN MAN OF KILSONA. London: Allan, 1936; as THE GREEN MAN OF GRAYPEC. New York: Greenberg, 1950.
Prather, Richard Scott	CASE OF THE VANISHING BEAUTY. New York: Fawcett, 1950; London: Fawcett, 1957.

AUTHOR	TITLE/FIRST EDITION INFORMATION
Pratt, Murray Fletcher	THE HEROIC YEARS: FOURTEEN YEARS OF THE REPUBLIC 1801-1815. New York: Smith & Haas, 1934.
Prebble, John Edward Curtis	WHERE THE SEA BREAKS. London: Secker & Warburg, 1944.
Prescott, John Brewster	THE BEAUTIFUL SHIP: A STORY OF THE GREAT LAKES. New York: Longman, 1952.
Preston, Ivy Alice	THE SILVER STREAM. Christchurch, New Zealand: Pegasus Press, 1959.
Price, Anthony	THE LABYRINTH MAKERS. London: Gollancz, 1970; New York: Doubleday, 1971.
Price, Susan	THE DEVIL'S PIPER. London: Faber, 1973; New York: Morrow, 1976.
Priest, Christopher	INDOCTRINAIRE. London: Faber; New York: Harper, 1970.
Priestley, John Boynton	THE CHAPMAN OF RHYMES. London: Alexander Moring, 1918.
Prior, Allan	A FLAME IN THE AIR. London: Joseph, 1951.
Procter, Maurice	NO PROUD CHIVALRY. London: Longman, 1947.
Pronzini, Bill	THE STALKER. New York: Random House, 1971; London: Hale, 1974.
Propper, Milton Morris	THE STRANGE DISAPPEARANCE OF MARY YOUNG. New York: Harper, 1929; London: Harrap, 1932.
Pudney, John Sleigh	SPRING ENCOUNTER. London: Methuen, 1933.
Purdom, Thomas Edward	I WANT THE STARS, as Tom Purdom. New York: Ace, 1964.
Purdum, Herbert R.	MY BROTHER JOHN. New York: Doubleday, 1966.
Pye, Virginia Frances Kennedy	ST. MARTIN'S HOLIDAY. London: Heinemann, 1930.

AUTHOR	TITLE/FIRST EDITION INFORMATION
Pyle, Howard	THE MERRY ADVENTURES OF ROBIN HOOD OF GREAT RENOWN IN NOTTINGHAMSHIRE. New York: Scribner; London: Sampson Low, 1883.
Pynchon, Thomas	V. Philadelphia: Lippincott; London: Cape, 1963.
Radford, Edwin Isaac and Mona Augusta	MURDER JIGSAW, as E. and M. A. Radford. London: Melrose, 1944.
Rae, Gwynedd	MOSTLY MARY. London: Mathews & Marrot, 1930; New York: Morrow, 1931.
Rae, Hugh Crawford	SKINNER. London: Blond; New York: Viking, 1965.
Raine, William McLeod	A DAUGHTER OF THE RAASAY: A TALE OF THE '45. New York: Stokes, 1902; as FOR LOVE AND HONOUR. London: Isbister, 1904.
Rand, Ayn	WE THE LIVING. New York: Macmillan; London: Cassell, 1936.
Randall, Florence Engel	HEDGEROW. New York: Harcourt Brace; London: Heinemann, 1967.
Randall, Marta	A CITY IN THE NORTH. New York: Warner, 1976.
Randall, Rona	THE MOON RETURNS. London: Collins, 1942.
Randolph, Georgiana Ann	8 FACES AT 3, as Craig Rice. New York: Simon & Schuster; London: Eyre & Spottiswoode, 1939.
Ransome, Arthur Michell	THE SOULS OF THE STREETS AND OTHER LITTLE PAPERS. London: Langham, 1904.
Raphael, Rick	CODE THREE. New York: Simon & Schuster, 1965; London: Gollancz, 1966. THE THIRST QUENCHERS. London: Gollancz, 1965.
Raskin, Ellen	NOTHING EVER HAPPENS ON MY BLOCK. New York: Atheneum, 1966.

AUTHOR	TITLE/FIRST EDITION INFORMATION
Rathbone, Julian	DIAMONDS BID. London: Joseph, 1966; New York: Walker, 1967.
Rathbone, St. George Henry	OLD SHADOW, as Marline Manly. Chicago: Pictorial, 1871.
Rawlings, Marjorie Kinnan	SOUTH MOON UNDER. New York: Scribner; London: Faber, 1933.
Rawson, Clayton	DEATH FROM A TOP HAT. New York: Putnam; London: Collins, 1938.
Ray, Mary Eva Pedder	THE VOICE OF APOLLO. London: Cape, 1964; New York: Farrar Straus, 1965.
Rayer, Francis George	LADY IN DANGER. Dublin: Grafton, 1948.
Rayner, Claire Berenice	THE FINAL YEAR. London: Corgi, 1962. MOTHERS AND MIDWIVES. London: Allen & Unwin, 1962.
Rayner, William	THE REAPERS. London: Faber, 1961.
Read, Herbert Edward	SONGS OF CHAOS. London: Elkin Mathews, 1915; New York: St. Martin's, 1975.
Reamy, Tom	BLIND VOICES. New York: Berkley, 1978; London: Sidgwick & Jackson, 1979.
Reaney, James Crerar	THE RED HEART. Toronto: McClelland & Stewart, 1949.
Reed, Ishmael	THE FREE-LANCE PALLBEARERS. New York: Doubleday, 1967; London: MacGibbon & Kee, 1968.
Reed, Lillian	ARMED CAMPS, as Kit Reed. London: Faber, 1959; New York: Dutton, 1970.
Reed, Talbot Baines	THE ADVENTURES OF A THREE-GUINEA WATCH. London: Religious Tract Society, 1883.
Rees, George Leslie Clarke	DIGIT DICK ON THE GREAT BARRIER REEF [AND THE TASMANIAN DEVIL, IN BLACK SWAN LAND, AND THE LOST OPALS]. 4 vols. Sydney, Australia: Sands, 1942-1957.
Reese, John	SHEEHAN'S MILL. New York: Doubleday, 1943.

AUTHOR	TITLE/FIRST EDITION INFORMATION
Reeve, Arthur Benjamin	THE SILENT BULLET: ADVENTURES OF CRAIG KENNEDY, SCIENTIFIC DETECTIVE. New York: Dodd Mead, 1912; as THE BLACK HAND. London: Nash, 1912.
Reeves, James	THE NATURAL NEED. Deya, Mallorca: Seizin Press; London: Constable, 1936.
Reid, Henrietta	ISLAND OF SECRETS. London: Mills & Boon, 1965.
Reid, Meta Mayne	THE LAND IS DEAR. London: Melrose, 1936.
Reilly, Helen	THE THIRTY-FIRST BULLFINCH. New York: Doubleday, 1930.
Reitci, John George	A NEW LEAF AND OTHER STORIES, as Jack Ritchie. New York: Dell, 1971.
Rendell, Ruth	FROM DOON WITH DEATH. London: Hutchinson, 1964; New York: Doubleday, 1965.
Repp, Edward Earl	CYCLONE JIM, as E. Earl Repp. New York: Godwin, 1935; London: Wright & Brown, 1936. HELL ON THE PECOS, as E. Earl Repp. New York: Godwin, 1935; London: Wright & Brown, 1936.
Rey, Hans Augusto	ZEBROLOGY. London: Chatto & Windus, 1937.
Rey, Margret	HOW THE FLYING FISHES CAME INTO BEING, with H. A. Rey. London: Chatto & Windus, 1938.
Reynolds, Dallas McCord	THE CASE OF THE LITTLE GREEN MEN, as Mack Reynolds. New York: Phoenix, 1951.
Rhodes, Eugene Manlove	GOOD MEN AND TRUE. New York: Holt, 1910.
Richards, Laura Elizabeth	FIVE MICE IN A MOUSE-TRAP, BY THE MAN IN THE MOON, DONE IN VERNACULAR, FROM THE LUNACULAR. Boston: Estes, 1880.

AUTHOR	TITLE/FIRST EDITION INFORMATION
Richardson, Robert Shirley	PRELIMINARY ELEMENTS OF OBJECT COMAS SOLA (1927), with others. Berkeley: University of California, 1927.
Richmond, Roaldus Frederick	CONESTOGA WAGON, as Roe Richmond. New York: Phoenix, 1949; London: Clerke & Cockeran, 1951.
Richmond, Walter and Leigh	SHOCK WAVES, as Walt and Leigh Richmond. New York: Ace, 1967. THE LOST MILLENNIUM, as Walt and Leigh Richmond. New York: Ace, 1967.
Richter, Conrad Michael	BROTHERS OF NO KIN AND OTHER STORIES. New York: Hinds, 1924.
Riddle, Betsy	MISS CARMICHAEL'S CONSCIENCE: A STUDY IN FLUCTUATIONS, as Baroness von Hutten. Philadelphia, 1900.
Ridge, Antonia	THE HANDY ELEPHANT AND OTHER STORIES. London: Faber, 1946.
Riefe, Alan	TALES OF HORROR. New York: Pocket Books, 1965.
Rigsby, Vechel Howard	VOYAGE TO LEANDRO. New York: Harper, 1939.
Riley, Louise	THE MYSTERY HORSE. Toronto: Copp Clark; New York: Messner, 1950; Oxford: Blackwell, 1957.
Rinehart, Mary Roberts	THE CIRCULAR STAIRCASE. Indianapolis: Bobbs Merrill, 1908; London: Cassell, 1909.
Ritchie, Claire	THE SHELTERED FLAME. London: Hodder & Stoughton, 1949.
Roan, Tom	WHISPERING RANGE. New York: King, 1934; London: Nicholson & Watson, 1935.
Roark, Garland	WAKE OF THE RED WITCH. Boston: Little, Brown, 1946.
Roberts, Charles George Douglas	ORION AND OTHER POEMS, as Charles G. D. Roberts. Philadelphia: Lippincott, 1880.
Roberts, Elizabeth Madox	IN THE GREAT STEEP'S GARDEN: POEMS. Colorado Springs: Gowdy Simmons, 1915.

AUTHOR	TITLE/FIRST EDITION INFORMATION
Roberts, Irene	LOVE SONG OF THE SEA. London: Fleetway, 1960. JUMP INTO HELL! London: Brown Watson, 1960.
Roberts, Janet Louise	JEWELS OF TERROR. New York: Lancer, 1970. LOVE SONG. New York: Pinnacle, 1970.
Roberts, Keith John Kingston	THE FURIES. London: Hart Davis; New York: Berkley, 1966.
Roberts, Willo Davis	MURDER AT GRAND BAY. New York: Arcadia, 1955.
Robertson, Frank Chester	THE FOREMAN OF THE FORTY-BAR. New York: Barse & Hopkins, 1925; London: Collins, 1927.
Robertson, Keith Carlton	TICKTOCK AND JIM. Philadelphia: Winston, 1948; as WATCH FOR A PONY. London: Heinemann, 1949.
Robinett, Stephen	STARGATE. New York: St. Martin's, 1976; London: Hale, 1978.
Robins, Denise Naomi	THE MARRIAGE BOND. London: Hodder & Stoughton, 1924. SEALED LIPS. London: Hodder & Stoughton, 1924.
Robinson, Frank Malcolm	THE POWER. Philadelphia: Lippincott, 1956; London: Eyre & Spottiswoode, 1957.
Robinson, Joan Mary Gale	A STANDS FOR ANGEL. London: Mowbray, 1939; as A IS FOR ANGEL. New York: Lothrop, 1953.
Robinson, Spider	TELEMPATH. New York: Berkley, 1976; London: Macdonald & Jane's, 1978.
Roby, Mary Linn	STILL AS THE GRAVE. New York: Dodd Mead, 1964; London: Collins, 1965.
Rocklin, Ross Louis	THE MEN AND THE MIRROR, as Ross Rocklynne. New York: Ace, 1973. THE SUN DESTROYERS, as Ross Rocklynne. New York: Ace, 1973.
Rodell, Marie Freid	BREATHE NO MORE, as Marion Randolph. New York: Holt; London: Heinemann, 1940.

AUTHOR	TITLE/FIRST EDITION INFORMATION
Roderdus, Frank	JOURNEY TO UTAH. New York: Doubleday, 1977; London: Hale, 1978. DUSTER. Independence, Mo.: Independence Press, 1977.
Rodgers, Mary	THE ROTTEN BOOK. New York: Harper, 1969.
Rogers, Joel Townsley	ONCE IN A RED MOON. New York: Brentano's, 1923.
Rogers, Rosemary	SWEET SAVAGE LOVE. New York: Avon, 1974; London: Futura, 1977. THE WILDEST HEART. New York: Avon, 1974; London: Futura, 1978.
Rohmer, Richard	THE GREEN NORTH. Toronto: Maclean Hunter, 1970.
Rolvaag, Olle Edvart	ORDFORKLARING TIL NORDAHL ROLFSENS LAESEBOK FOR FOLKESKOLEN II. Minneapolis: Augsburg, 1909.
Rome, Margaret	THE LOTTERY OF MATTHEW DEVLIN. London: Mills & Boon, 1968. THE MARRIAGE OF CAROLINE LINDSAY. London: Mills & Boon, 1968; Toronto: Harlequin, 1974.
Roos, Audrey and William	MADE UP TO KILL, as Kelley Roos. New York: Dodd Mead, 1940; as MADE UP FOR MURDER. London: Jarrolds, 1941.
Roose-Evans, James	DIRECTING A PLAY: JAMES ROOSE-EVANS ON THE ART OF DIRECTING AND ACTING. London: Studio Vista; New York: Theatre Arts, 1968.
Roshwald, Mordecai Marceli	ADAM VE'HINUKNO [MAN AND EDUCATION]. Tel-Aviv: Dvir, 1954.
Ross, Diana	THE WORLD AT WORK [GETTING YOU THINGS, MAKING YOU THINGS]. 2 vols. London: Country Life, 1939.
Ross, Sinclair	AS FOR ME AND MY HOUSE. New York: Reynal, 1941.
Ross, Zola Helen	THREE DOWN VULNERABLE, as Z. H. Ross. Indianapolis: Bobbs Merrill, 1946.

AUTHOR	TITLE/FIRST EDITION INFORMATION
Rossi, Jean Baptiste	THE 10:30 FROM MARSEILLES, as Sebastien Japrisot. 1963.
Rossiter, John	THE BLOOD RUNNING COLD, as Jonathan Ross. London: Cassell, 1968.
Roth, Holly	THE CONTENT ASSIGNMENT. New York: Simon & Schuster; London: Hamish Hamilton, 1954.
Rotsler, William	CONTEMPORARY EROTIC CINEMA. New York: Ballantine, 1973.
Rounds, Glen Harold	OL' PAUL, THE MIGHTY LOGGER. New York: Holiday House, 1936.
Rowland, Donald Sydney	THE BATTLE DONE, as Donald S. Rowland. London: Brown Watson, 1958.
Rubel, James Lyon	THE MEDICO OF PAINTED SPRINGS, as Mason Macrae. New York: Phoenix, 1934; London: Mills & Boon, 1935.
Ruck, Amy Roberta	HIS OFFICIAL FIANCEE, as Berta Ruck. London: Hutchinson; New York: Dodd Mead, 1914.
Rundle, Anne	THE MOON MARRIAGE. London: Hurst & Blackett, 1967.
Rush, Philip	ROGUE'S LUTE. London: Dakars, 1944.
Rushing, Jane Gilmore	WALNUT GROVE. New York: Doubleday, 1964.
Russ, Joanna	PICNIC ON PARADISE. New York: Ace, 1968; London: Macdonald, 1969.
Russell, Bertrand Arthur William	GERMAN SOCIAL DEMOCRACY. London: Longman, 1896; New York: Simon & Schuster, 1965.
Russell, Charles Marion	RAWHIDE RAWLINS STORIES. Great Falls: Montana Newspaper Association, 1921.
Russell, Eric Frank	SINISTER BARRIER. Kingswood, England: World's Work, 1943; Reading: Fantasy Press, 1948.
Russell, Martin James	NO THROUGH ROAD. London: Collins, 1965; New York: Coward McCann, 1966.

AUTHOR	TITLE/FIRST EDITION INFORMATION
Russell, Ray	THE CASE AGAINST SATAN. New York: Obolensky, 1962; London: Souvenir, 1963. SARDONICUS AND OTHER STORIES. New York: Ballantine, 1962.
Ryan, Marah Ellis	MERZE: THE STORY OF AN ACTRESS. Chicago: Rand McNally, 1889.
Sabatini, Rafael	THE LOVERS OF YVONNE. London: Pearson, 1902; as THE SUITORS OF YVONNE. New York: Putnam, 1902.
Saberhagen, Frederick Thomas	THE GOLDEN PEOPLE, as Fred Saberhagen. New York: Ace, 1964.
Sachs, Marilyn	AMY MOVES IN. New York: Doubleday, 1964.
St. Clair, Margaret	AGENT OF THE UNKNOWN. New York: Ace, 1956. THE GREEN QUEEN. New York: Ace, 1956.
Sale, Richard Bernard	NOT TOO NARROW, NOT TOO DEEP. New York: Simon & Schuster; London: Cassell, 1936.
Salkey, Felix Andrew Alexander	A QUALITY OF VIOLENCE, as Andrew Salkey. London: Hutchinson, 1959.
Sallis, James	A FEW LAST WORDS. London: Hart Davis, 1969; New York: Macmillan, 1970.
Sanders, Dorothy Lucy	FAIRIES ON THE DOORSTEP, as Dorothy Lucie Sanders. Sydney, Australia: Australasian, 1948; as POOL OF DREAMS, as Lucy Walker. New York: Ballantine, 1973. THE RANDY, as Dorothy Lucie Sanders. Sydney, Australia: Australasian, 1948.
Sanders, Lawrence	HANDBOOK OF CREATIVE CRAFTS, with Richard Carol. New York: Pyramid, 1968.
Sandoz, Mari Susette	OLD JULES. Boston: Little, Brown, 1935; London: Chapman & Hall, 1937.
Santee, Ross	MEN AND HORSES. New York: Century, 1926.

AUTHOR	TITLE/FIRST EDITION INFORMATION
Sargent, Pamela	CLONED LIVES. New York: Fawcett, 1976.
Saville, Leonard Malcolm	MYSTERY AT WITCHEND. London: Newnes, 1943; as SPY IN THE HILLS. New York: Farrar & Rinehart, 1945.
Sawley, Petra	NO TIME FOR LOVE. London: Gresham, 1967. NO PLACE FOR LOVE. London: Gresham, 1967. LOVE ON ICE. London: Gresham, 1967.
Sawyer, John and Nancy	VICTIM OF LOVE, as Nancy Buckingham. London: 1967.
Sawyer, Ruth	THE PRIMROSE RING. New York; London: Harper, 1915.
Sayers, Dorothy Leigh	OP.1. Oxford: Blackwell, 1918.
Sayers, James Denson	CAN THE WHITE RACE SURVIVE? Washington, D.C.: Independent, 1929.
Scarborough, Dorothy	FUGITIVE VERSES. Waco, Tex.: Baylor University, 1912.
Scarry, Richard McClure	THE GREAT BIG CAR AND TRUCK BOOK. New York: Simon & Schuster, 1951.
Schachner, Nathan	AARON BURR, as Nat Schachner. New York: Stokes, 1937.
Schaefer, Jack Warner	SHANE. Boston: Houghton Mifflin, 1949; London: Deutsch, 1954.
Scherf, Margaret Louise	THE CORPSE GROWS A BEARD. New York: Putnam, 1940; London: Patridge, 1946.
Schlee, Ann	THE STRANGERS. London: Macmillan, 1971; New York: Atheneum, 1972.
Schlein, Miriam	A DAY AT THE PLAYGROUND. New York: Simon & Schuster, 1951.
Schmidt, James Norman	MURDER, CHOP CHOP, as James Norman. New York: Morrow, 1942; London: Joseph, 1943.
Schmidt, Stanley Albert	NEWTON AND THE QUASI-APPLE. New York: Doubleday, 1975.
Schmitz, James Henry	AGENT OF VEGA. New York: Gnome, 1960.

AUTHOR	TITLE/FIRST EDITION INFORMATION
Schoepflin, Harold Vincent	THE DOOMSDAY PLANET, as Vincent Harl. New York: Belmont, 1966.
Scortia, Thomas Nicholas	WHAT MAD ORACLE? Evanston, Ill.: Regency, 1961.
Scott, Reginald Thomas Maitland	SECRET SERVICE SMITH. New York: Dutton, 1923; London: Hodder & Stoughton, 1924.
Searls, Henry Hunt, Jr.	THE BIG X, as Hank Searls. New York: Harper; London: Heinemann, 1959.
Seed, Cecile Eugenie	THE DANCING MULE, as Jenny Seed. London: Nelson, 1964.
Seeley, Mabel	THE LISTENING HOUSE. New York: Doubleday, 1938; London: Collins, 1939.
Seelye, John Douglas	THE TRUE ADVENTURES OF HUCKLEBERRY FINN, AS TOLD TO JOHN SEELYE. Evanston, Ill.: Northwestern University, 1970.
Seifert, Elizabeth	YOUNG DOCTOR GALAHAD. New York: Dodd Mead, 1938; as YOUNG DOCTOR. London: Collins, 1939.
Seltzer, Charles Alden	THE COUNCIL OF THREE. New York: Abbey, 1900.
Selwyn, Francis	CRACKSMAN ON VELVET. London: Deutsch; New York: Stein & Day, 1974.
Senarens, Luis Philip	A.D.T.; OR, THE MESSENGER BOY DETECTIVE, as Police Captain Howard. New York: Champion, 1882. THE GIRL DETECTIVE, as Police Captain Howard. New York: Champion, 1882. THE MYSTERY OF ONE NIGHT, as Police Captain Howard. New York: Champion, 1882. YOUNG VIDOCQ, as Police Captain Howard. New York: Champion, 1882.
Sendak, Maurice Bernard	KENNY'S WINDOW. New York: Harper, 1956.
Seredy, Kate	THE GOOD MASTER. New York: Viking, 1935; London: Harrap, 1937.

AUTHOR	TITLE/FIRST EDITION INFORMATION
Serling, Edward Rodman	STORIES FROM THE TWILIGHT ZONE, as Rod Serling. New York: Bantam, 1960.
Serraillier, Ian Lucien	THREE NEW POETS, with others. Billericay, England: Grey Walls Press, 1942.
Serviss, Garrett Putnam	ASTRONOMY WITH AN OPERA-GLASS. New York: Appleton, 1888.
Seton, Anya	MY THEODOSIA. Boston: Houghton Mifflin, 1941; London: Hodder & Stoughton, 1945.
Seton, Ernest Evan Thompson	A LIST OF ANIMALS IN MANITOBA. Toronto: Oxford University, 1886.
Sewell, Anna	BLACK BEAUTY, HIS GROOMS AND COMPANIONS: THE AUTOBIOGRAPHY OF A HORSE, TRANSLATED FROM THE ORIGINAL EQUINE. London: Jarrolds, 1877; New York: Angell, 1878.
Sewell, Helen Moore	A HEAD FOR HAPPY. New York: Macmillan, 1931.
Seymour, Alan	THE ONE DAY OF THE YEAR. London: Souvenir, 1967.
Shannon, Monica	CALIFORNIA FAIRY TALES. New York: Doubleday; London: Heinemann, 1926.
Shappiro, Herbert Arthur	THE BLACK RIDER. New York: Arcadia, 1941.
Sharkey, John Michael	THE SECRET MARTIANS, as Jack Sharkey. New York: Ace, 1960. MURDER, MAESTRO, PLEASE, as Jack Sharkey. New York; London: Abelard Schuman, 1960.
Sharmat, Marjorie Weinman	REX. New York: Harper, 1967.
Sharp, Edith Lambert	NKWALA. Boston: Little, Brown, 1958; London: Dent, 1959.
Sharp, Margery	RHODODENDRON PIE. London: Chatto & Windus; New York: Appleton, 1930.
Shaver, Richard Sharpe	I REMEMBER LEMURIA, AND THE RETURN OF SATHANAS. Evanston, Ill.: Venture, 1948.

AUTHOR	TITLE/FIRST EDITION INFORMATION
Shaw, Felicity	THE HAPPY EXILES. London: Hamish Hamilton; New York: Harper, 1956.
Shaw, Robert	NIGHT WALK, as Bob Shaw. New York: Banner, 1967; London: New English Library, 1970.
Shea, Cornelius	LOVE AND LURE; OR, THE HEART OF A "BAD" MAN: A ROMANCE OF ARIZONA. New York: Broadway, 1912. LOOK OUT FOR PAINT. Boston: Baker, 1912.
Sheckley, Robert	UNTOUCHED BY HUMAN HANDS. New York: Ballantine, 1954; London: Joseph, 1955.
Sheldon, Alice Hastings	TEN THOUSAND LIGHT-YEARS FROM HOME, as James Tiptree, Jr. London: Eyre Methuen, 1975.
Shellabarger, Samuel	THE DOOR OF DEATH. New York: Century, 1928; London: Methuen, 1929. THE CHEVALIER BAYARD: A STUDY IN FADING CHIVALRY. New York: Century, 1928.
Shelley, John Lascola	GUNPOINT! New York: Graphic, 1956; London: Hale, 1959.
Shelley, Noreen	PIGGY GRUNTER'S RED UMBRELLA [NURSEY RHYMES, AT THE FIRE, AT THE CIRCUS]. 4 vols. Sydney, Australia: Johnson, 1944.
Shepherd, Donald Lee	DARK EDEN, as Barbara Kevern. New York: Pocket Books, 1973.
Sherriff, Robert Charles	JOURNEY'S END, as R. C. Sherriff, with Vernon Bartlett. London: Gollancz; New York: Stokes, 1930. Play version. London: Gollancz; New York: Brentano's, 1929.
Sherry, Sylvia	STREET OF THE SMALL NIGHT MARKET. London: Cape, 1966; as SECRET OF THE JADE PAVILION. Philadelphia: Lippincott, 1967.
Shiel, Matthew Phipps	PRINCE ZALESKI, as M. P. Shiel. London: Lane; Boston: Roberts, 1895.
Shiras, Wilmar House	SLOW DAWNING, as Jane Howes. St. Louis: Herder, 1946.

AUTHOR	TITLE/FIRST EDITION INFORMATION
Shotwell, Louisa Rossiter	THIS IS THE INDIAN AMERICAN [YOUR NEIGHBOR, THE MIGRANT]. 3 vols. New York: Friendship Press, 1955-1958.
Shrake, Edwin	BLOOD RECKONING. New York: Bantam, 1962.
Silko, Leslie	LAGUNA WOMAN: POEMS. Greenfield Center, N.Y.: Greenfield Review Press, 1974.
Sillitoe, Alan	WITHOUT BEER OR BREAD. London: Outposts, 1957.
Silverberg, Robert	REVOLT ON ALPHA C. New York: Crowell, 1955.
Simak, Clifford Donald	THE CREATOR. Los Angeles: Crawford, 1946.
Simenon, Georges	THE STRANGE CASE OF PETER THE LETT. 1933.
Simon, Roger Lichtenberg	HEIR. New York: Macmillan, 1968.
Simpson, Helen de Guerry	PHILOSOPHIES IN LITTLE. Sydney, Australia: Angus & Robertson, 1921.
Sims, George Frederick Robert	THE SWALLOW LOVERS. London: Privately printed, 1942.
Sinclair, Olga Ellen	THE MAN AT THE MANOR. London: Gresham, 1967; New York: Dell, 1972. GYPSIES. Oxford: Blackwell, 1967.
Sinclair, Upton	SPRINGTIME AND HARVEST: A ROMANCE. New York: Sinclair Press, 1901; as KING MIDAS. New York; London: Funk & Wagnalls, 1901.
Singer, Isaac Bashevis	THE FAMILY MOSKAT. New York: Knopf, 1950; London: Secker & Warburg, 1966.
Siodmak, Kurt	SCHLUSS IN TONFILMATELIER. Berlin: Scherl, 1930.
Skinner, Burrhus Frederic	THE BEHAVIOR OF ORGANISMS: AN EXPERIMENTAL ANALYSIS, as B. F. Skinner. New York: Appleton, 1938.

AUTHOR	**TITLE/FIRST EDITION INFORMATION**
Skinner, June O'Grady	O'HOULIHAN'S JEST: A LAMENT FOR THE IRISH, as Rohan O'Grady. New York: Macmillan; London: Gollancz, 1961.
Sky, Kathleen	BIRTHRIGHT. Toronto: Laser, 1975.
Sladek John Thomas	THE HOUSE THAT FEAR BUILT, as Cassandra Knye, with Thomas M. Disch. New York: Paperback Library, 1966.
Slaughter, Frank Gill	THAT NONE SHOULD DIE. New York: Doubleday, 1941; London: Jarrolds, 1942.
Sleigh, Barbara	CARBONEL. London: Parrish, 1955; Indianapolis: Bobbs Merrill, 1957.
Slesar, Henry	THE GRAY FLANNEL SHROUD. New York: Random House, 1959; London: Deutsch, 1960.
Sloane, William Milligan, III	BACK HOME: A GHOST PLAY. New York: Longman, 1931.
Slobodkin, Louis	THE FRIENDLY ANIMALS. New York: Vanguard, 1944. MAGIC MICHAEL. New York: Macmillan, 1944.
Slobodkina, Esphyr	CAPS FOR SALE. New York: Scott, 1940; Kingswood, England: World's Work, 1959.
Smith, Cicely Fox	SONGS OF GREATER BRITAIN AND OTHER POEMS. London: Simpkin, 1899. THE FOREMOST TRAIL. London: Sampson Low, 1899.
Smith, Clark Ashton	THE STAR-TREADER AND OTHER POEMS. San Francisco: Robertson, 1912.
Smith, Doris Edna Elliott	STAR TO MY BARQUE. London: Ward Lock, 1964.
Smith, Edward Elmer	THE SKYLARK OF SPACE, as E. E. Smith, with Mrs. Lee Hawkins Garby. Providence, R.I.: Buffalo, 1946; London: Digit, 1959.
Smith, Lady Eleanor Furneaux	RED WAGON: A STUDY OF THE TOBER. London: Gollancz; Indianapolis: Bobbs Merrill, 1930.
Smith, Emma	MAIDENS' TRIP. London: Putnam, 1948.

AUTHOR	TITLE/FIRST EDITION INFORMATION
Smith, Ernest Bramah	ENGLISH FARMING AND WHY I TURNED IT UP. London, 1894.
Smith, Evelyn E.	THE BUILDING BOOK. New York: Howell Soskin, 1947.
Smith, George Henry	1976: YEAR OF TERROR. New York: Epic, 1961. SCOURGE OF THE BLOOD CULT. New York: Epic, 1976. THE COMING OF THE RATS. New York: Pike, 1961; London: Digit, 1964.
Smith, George Oliver	VENUS EQUILALATERAL. Philadelphia: Prime Press, 1947; London: Futura, 1975.
Smith, Helen Zenna	JUST JANE, as Evadne Price. London: Hamilton, 1928.
Smith, Joan	AN AFFAIR OF THE HEART. New York: Fawcett, 1977. ESCAPADE. New York: Fawcett, 1977.
Smith, Sarah	THE STORY OF OLD LONDON, as Hesba Stretton. London: Religious Tract Society, 1869; New York: Whittaker, 1886.
Smith, William Jay	POEMS. Pawlet, Vt.: Banyan Press, 1947.
Snedeker, Caroline Dale	THE COWARD OF THERMOPYLAE. New York: Doubleday, 1911; as THE SPARTAN. London: Hodder & Stoughton, 1913.
Snow, Charles Horace	DUST OF GOLD. London: Methuen, 1928.
Snyder, Zilpha Keatley	SEASON OF PONIES. New York: Atheneum, 1964.
Sobol, Donald J.	THE DOUBLE QUEST. New York: Watts, 1957.
Softly, Barbara	PLAIN JANE. London: Macmillan, 1961; New York: St. Martin's, 1962.
Sohl, Gerald Allan	THE HAPLOIDS, as Jerry Sohl. New York: Rinehart, 1952.
Sorensen, Virginia	A LITTLE LOWER THAN THE ANGELS. New York: Knopf, 1942.
Southall, Ivan Francis	OUT OF THE DAWN: THREE SHORT STORIES. Privately printed, 1942.

AUTHOR	TITLE/FIRST EDITION INFORMATION
Speare, Elizabeth George	THE WITCH OF BLACKBIRD POND. Boston: Houghton Mifflin, 1958; London: Gollancz, 1960.
Spearman, Frank Hamilton	THE NERVE OF FOLEY AND OTHER RAILROAD STORIES. New York: Harper, 1900.
Speicher, Helen Ross	SOUTHERN YANKEES, as Alice Abbott. Indianapolis: Bobbs Merrill, 1960.
Spence, Eleanor	PATTERSON'S TRACK. Melbourne, Australia: Oxford University, 1958; London: Angus & Robertson, 1959.
Spence, William John Duncan	DARK HELL, as Duncan Spence. London: Brown Watson, 1959.
Sperry, Armstrong	ONE DAY WITH MANU. Philadelphia: Winston, 1933.
Spicer, Bart	THE DARK LIGHT. New York: Dodd Mead, 1949; London: Collins, 1950.
Spicer, Betty Coe	FINAL COPY, as Jay Barbette, with Bart Spicer. New York: Dodd Mead, 1950; London: Barker, 1952.
Spillane, Frank Morrison	I, THE JURY, as Mickey Spillane. New York: Dutton, 1947; London: Barker, 1952.
Spinrad, Norman	THE SOLARIANS. New York: Paperback Library, 1966; London: Sphere, 1979.
Sprigg, Christopher St. John	THE AIRSHIP: ITS DESIGN, HISTORY, OPERATION, AND FUTURE. London: Sampson Low, 1931.
Spykman, Elizabeth Choate	A LEMON AND A STAR. New York: Harcourt Brace, 1955; London: Macmillan, 1956.
Stableford, Brian Michael	CRADLE OF THE SUN. New York: Ace; London: Sidgwick & Jackson, 1969.
Stafford, Jean	BOSTON ADVENTURE. New York: Harcourt Brace, 1944; London: Faber, 1948.
Stapledon, William Olaf	LATTER-DAY PSALMS. Liverpool, England: Young, 1914.

AUTHOR	TITLE/FIRST EDITION INFORMATION
Starrett, Charles Vincent Emerson	ARTHUR MACHEN: A NOVELIST OF ECSTASY AND SIN, as Vincent Starrett. Chicago: Hill, 1918.
Stasheff, Christopher	THE WARLOCK IN SPITE OF HIMSELF. New York: Ace, 1969.
Stead, Robert James Campbell	THE EMPIRE BUILDERS AND OTHER POEMS. Toronto: Briggs, 1908.
Steel, Danielle	GOING HOME. New York: Pocket Books, 1973; London: Sphere, 1980.
Steele, Harwood Elmes Robert	CLEARED FOR ACTION, as Howard Steele. London: Unwin, 1914.
Steele, Mary Quintard	JOURNEY OUTSIDE. New York: Viking, 1969; London: Macmillan, 1970.
Steele, William Owen	THE GOLDEN ROOT. New York: Aladdin, 1951.
Steelman, Robert James	STAGES SOUTH. New York: Ace, 1956.
Steen, Marguerite	THE GILT CAGE. London: Bles, 1926; New York: Doran, 1927.
Stegner, Wallace Earle	REMEMBERING LAUGHTER. Boston: Little, Brown; London: Heinemann, 1937.
Steig, William	MAN ABOUT TOWN. New York: Long & Smith, 1932.
Stein, Aaron Marc	SPIRALS. New York: Covici Friede, 1930.
Steinbeck, John Ernst	CUP OF GOLD: A LIFE OF HENRY MORGAN, BUCCANEER, WITH OCCASIONAL REFERENCE TO HISTORY. New York: McBride, 1929; London: Heinemann, 1937.
Stephenson, Andrew Michael	NIGHTWATCH. London: Futura, 1977; New York: Dell, 1979.
Steptoe, John Lewis	STEVIE. New York: Harper, 1969; London: Longman, 1970.
Stern, Richard Martin	THE BRIGHT ROAD TO FEAR. New York: Ballantine, 1958; London: Secker & Warburg, 1959.
Stevens, James Floyd	PAUL BUNYAN. New York: Knopf, 1925.

AUTHOR	TITLE/FIRST EDITION INFORMATION
Stevenson, Anne	RALPH DACRE. New York: Walker; London: Collins, 1967.
Stevenson, Dorothy Emily	MEADOW-FLOWERS. London: Macdonald, 1915.
Stevenson, Florence	THE STORY OF AIDA, BASED ON THE OPERA BY GUISEPPE VERDI. New York: Putnam, 1965.
Stevenson, Robert Louis Balfour	THE PENTLAND RISING: A PAGE OF HISTORY, 1666. Privately printed, 1866.
Stevenson, William Henri	THE YELLOW WIND: AN EXCURSION IN AND AROUND RED CHINA. Boston: Houghton Mifflin; London: Cassell, 1959.
Stewart, Agnes Charlotte	THE BOAT IN THE REEDS. London: Blackie, 1960.
Stewart, Dorothy Mary	VISIBILITY NIL, as Mary Elgin. London, 1963.
Stewart, George Rippey	THE TECHNIQUE OF ENGLISH VERSE. New York: Holt, 1930.
Stewart, John Innes Mackintosh	DEATH AT THE PRESIDENT'S LODGING, as Michael Innes. London: Gollancz, 1936; as SEVEN SUSPECTS. New York: Dodd Mead, 1937.
Stewart, Mary Florence Elinor	MADAM, WILL YOU TALK? London: Hodder & Stoughton, 1955; New York: Mill, 1956.
Stilwell, Hart	BORDER CITY. New York: Doubleday, 1945; London: Hurst & Blackett, 1948.
Stine, Henry Eugene	SEASON OF THE WITCH, as Hank Stine. New York: Essex House, 1968.
Stockton, Francis Richard	TING-A-LING, as Frank R. Stockton. Boston: Hurd & Stoughton, 1870; London: Ward & Downey, 1889.
Stoker, Abraham	THE DUTIES OF CLERKS OF PETTY SESSIONS IN IRELAND, as Bram Stoker. Privately printed, 1879.
Stolz, Mary Slattery	TO TELL YOUR LOVE. New York: Harper, 1950.

AUTHOR	TITLE/FIRST EDITION INFORMATION
Stong, Philip Duffield	STATE FAIR. New York: Century; London: Barker, 1932.
Storey, Margaret	KATE AND THE FAMILY TREE. London: Bodley Head, 1965; as THE FAMILY TREE. Nashville, Tenn.: Nelson, 1973.
Storr, Catherine	INGEBORG AND RUTHY. London: Harrap, 1940.
Stout, Rex Todhunter	FER-DE-LANCE. New York: Farrar & Rinehart, 1934; London: Cassell, 1935.
Stover, Leon Eugene	STONEHENGE, with Harry Harrison. New York: Scribner; London: Davies, 1972. LA SCIENCE-FICTION AMERICAINE: ESSAI D'ANTHROPOLOGIE CULTURELLE. Paris: Aubier Montaigne, 1972.
Straight, Michael Whitney	MAKE THIS THE LAST WAR: THE FUTURE OF THE UNITED NATIONS. New York: Harcourt Brace; London: Allen & Unwin, 1943.
Straker, John Foster	POSTMAN'S KNOCK. London: Harrap, 1954.
Stratton, Rebecca	THE ROSS INHERITANCE. London: Mills & Boon, 1969. GOOD MORNING, DOCTOR HOUSTON. London: Mills & Boon, 1969; Toronto: Harlequin, 1970. THE SILVER FISHES. London: Mills & Boon, 1969; Toronto: Harlequin, 1970. A WIFE FOR ANDREW. London: Mills & Boon, 1969; Toronto: Harlequin, 1970. All as Lucy Gillen.
Streatfield, Noel	THE WHICHARTS. London: Heinemann, 1931; New York: Coward McCann, 1932.
Street, Cecil John Charles	WITH THE GUNS, as F. O. O. London: Nash, 1916.
Stribling, Theodore Sigismund	THE CRUISE OF THE DRY DOCK. Chicago: Reilly & Britton, 1917.
Strong, Leonard Alfred George	DALLINGTON RHYMES, as L. A. G. Strong. Oxford: Holywell, 1919.

AUTHOR	TITLE/FIRST EDITION INFORMATION
Stubbs, Jean	THE ROSE-GROWER. London: Macmillan, 1962; New York: St. Martin's, 1963.
Stucley, Elizabeth Florence	POLLYCON: A BOOK FOR THE YOUNG ECONOMIST. Oxford: Blackwell, 1933.
Sublette, Clifford MacClellan	THE SCARLET COCKEREL. Boston: Atlantic Monthly Press, 1925; London: Hodder & Stoughton, 1926.
Sudbery, Rodie	THE HOUSE IN THE WOOD. London: Deutsch, 1968; as A SOUND OF CRYING. New York: McCall, 1970.
Suddaby, Donald	SCARLET-DRAGON: A LITTLE CHINESE PHANTASY. Blackburn, England: Privately printed, 1923.
Summers, Ethel Snelson	NEW ZEALAND INHERITANCE, as Essie Summers. London: Mills & Boon, 1957; as HEATHERLEIGH. Toronto: Harlequin, 1963.
Summerton, Margaret	THE SUNSET HOUR. London: Hodder & Stoughton, 1957.
Sutcliffe, Rosemary	THE ARMOURER'S HOUSE. London; New York: Oxford University, 1951.
Sutherland, Efua Theodora	PLAYTIME IN AFRICA. London: Brown Knight & Truscott, 1960; New York: Atheneum, 1962.
Sutton, Evelyn Mary	MY CAT LIKES TO HIDE IN BOXES. London: Hamish Hamilton, 1973; New York: Parents Magazine, 1974.
Sutton, Jefferson H.	FIRST ON THE MOON, as Jeff Sutton. New York: Ace, 1958.
Sutton, Jefferson H. and Eugenia Geneva	THE RIVER, as Jeff and Jean Sutton. New York: Belmont, 1966.
Swan, Annie S.	UPS AND DOWNS: A FAMILY CHRONICLE. London: Charing Cross, 1878.
Swarthout, Glendon Fred	WILLOW RUN. New York: Crowell, 1943.
Swatridge, Irene Maude	WELL PLAYED, JULIANA! as Irene Mossop. London, 1928.

AUTHOR	TITLE/FIRST EDITION INFORMATION
Syme, Neville Ronald	FULL FATHOM FIVE. London: Lunn, 1946.
Symonds, John	WILLIAM WASTE. London: Low & Marston, 1947.
Symons, Dorothy Geraldine	ALL SOULS. London; New York: Longman, 1950.
Symons, Julian Gustave	CONFUSIONS ABOUT X. London: Fortune Press, 1939.
Szilard, Leo	THE VOICE OF THE DOLPHINS AND OTHER STORIES. New York: Simon & Schuster; London: Gollancz, 1961.
Tate, Joan	JENNY. London: Heinemann, 1964.
Tate, Peter	THE THINKING SEAT. New York: Doubleday, 1969; London: Faber, 1970.
Tattersall, Honor Jill	A SUMMER'S CLOUD. London: Collins, 1965.
Taylor, Lois Dwight	SPANIARD'S MARK, as Anne Eliot. New York: 1933.
Taylor, Phoebe Atwood	THE CAPE COD MYSTERY. Indianapolis: Bobbs Merrill, 1931.
Taylor, Robert Lewis	ADRIFT IN A BONEYARD. New York: Doubleday, 1947.
Taylor, Sydney Brenner	ALL-OF-A-KIND FAMILY. Chicago: Wilcox & Follett, 1951; London: Blackie, 1961.
Taylor, Theodore	THE MAGNIFICENT MITSCHER. New York: Norton, 1954.
Telfair, Richard	WYOMING JONES. New York: Fawcett, 1958; London: Fawcett, 1959.
Temple, William Frederick	FOUR-SIDED TRIANGLE. London: Long, 1949; New York: Fell, 1951.
Tennant, Emma Christina	THE COLOUR OF RAIN, as Catherine Aydy. London: Weidenfeld & Nicholson, 1964.
Tevis, Walter Stone	THE HUSTLER. New York: Harper, 1959; London: Joseph, 1960.

AUTHOR	TITLE/FIRST EDITION INFORMATION
Thane, Elswyth	RIDERS OF THE WIND. New York: Stokes, 1926; London: Murray, 1928.
Thayer, Emma Redington	ALICE AND THE WONDERLAND PEOPLE, as Lee Thayer. New York: Bungalow Book and Toy, 1914.
Thiele, Colin Milton	PROGRESS TO DENIAL. Adelaide, Australia: Jindyworobak, 1945. SPLINTERS AND SHARDS. Adelaide, Australia: Jindyworobak, 1945.
Thimblethorpe, June Sylvia	THE SCANDALOUS LADY ROBIN, as Sylvia Thorpe. London: Hutchinson, 1950; New York: Fawcett, 1975.
Thomas, Donald Michael	PERSONAL AND POSSESSIVE, as D. M. Thomas. London: Outposts, 1964.
Thomas, Ross	THE COLD WAR SWAP. New York: Morrow, 1966; as SPY IN THE VODKA. London: Hodder & Stoughton, 1967.
Thomason, John William, Jr.	FIX BAYONETS! New York: Scribner, 1926.
Thompson, Edward Anthony	CROWDED AND DANGEROUS, as Anthony Lejeune. London: Macdonald, 1959.
Thompson, George Selden	THE DOG THAT COULD SWIM UNDER WATER, as George Selden. New York: Viking, 1956.
Thompson, Thomas	RANGE DRIFTER. New York: Doubleday, 1949; London: Hodder & Stoughton, 1950.
Thomson, Basil Home	THE DIVERSIONS OF A PRIME MINISTER. Edinburgh: Blackwood, 1894.
Thomson, June	NOT ONE OF US. New York: Harper, 1971; London: Constable, 1972.
Thorpe, Kay	DEVON INTERLUDE. London: Mills & Boon, 1968; Toronto: Harlequin, 1969. THE LAST OF THE MALLORYS. London: Mills & Boon; Toronto: Harlequin, 1968. OPPORTUNE MARRIAGE. London: Mills & Boon, 1968; Toronto: Harlequin, 1975.
Thurber, James Grover	IS SEX NECESSARY? OR, WHY YOU FEEL THE WAY YOU DO, with E. B.

AUTHOR	TITLE/FIRST EDITION INFORMATION
	White. New York: Harper, 1929; London: Heinemann, 1930.
Thurston, Robert Donald	ALICIA II. New York: Putnam, 1978. BATTLESTAR, with Glen A. Larson. New York: Berkley; London: Futura, 1978.
Thwaite, Ann	THE YOUNG TRAVELLERS IN JAPAN. London: Phoenix, 1958.
Tidyman, Ernest	FLOWER POWER. New York: Paperback Library, 1968. THE ANZIO DEATH TRAP. New York: Belmont, 1968.
Tillett, Dorothy Stockbridge	PATHS OF JUNE, as Dorothy Stockbridge. New York: Dutton, 1920.
Tippette, Giles	THE BANK ROBBER. New York: Macmillan, 1970.
Tirbutt, Honoria	IN LOVING MEMORY, as Emma Page. London: Collins, 1970.
Titus, Eve	ANATOLE. New York: McGraw Hill, 1956; London: Lane, 1957.
Todd, Barbara Euphan	THE 'NORMOUS SATURDAY FAIRY BOOK, with Marjory Royce and Moira Meighn. London: Paul, 1924.
Todd, Herbert Eatton	BOBBY BREWSTER AND THE WINKERS' CLUB. Leicester, England: Ward, 1949.
Tolbert, Frank Xavier, Sr.	NIEMAN-MARCUS: THE STORY OF THE PROUD DALLAS STORE. New York: Holt, 1953.
Tolkien, John Ronald Reuel	A MIDDLE ENGLISH VOCABULARY, as J. R. R. Tolkien. London; New York: Oxford University, 1922.
Tomalin, Ruth	THRENODY FOR DORMICE. London: Fortune Press, 1947.
Tompkins, Walker Allison	OZAR, THE AZTEC. London: Gramol, 1935.
Torday, Ursula	THE BALLAD-MAKER OF PARIS. London, 1935.

AUTHOR	TITLE/FIRST EDITION INFORMATION
Townsend, John Rowe	GUMBLE'S YARD. London: Hutchinson, 1961; as TROUBLE IN THE JUNGLE. Philadelphia: Lippincott, 1969.
Train, Arthur Cheney	MCALLISTER AND HIS DOUBLE. New York: Scribner; London: Newnes, 1905.
Tranter, Nigel Godwin	THE FORTALICES AND EARLY MANSIONS OF SOUTHERN SCOTLAND 1400-1650. Edinburgh: Moray Press, 1935.
Travers, Pamela Lyndon	MARY POPPINS. London: Howe; New York: Reynal & Hitchcock, 1934.
Treadgold, Mary	WE COULDN'T LEAVE DINAH. London: Cape, 1941; as LEFT TILL CALLED FOR. New York: Doubleday, 1941.
Trease, Robert Geoffrey	THE SUPREME PRIZE AND OTHER POEMS. London: Stockwell, 1926.
Treece, Henry	38 POEMS. London: Fortune Press, 1940.
Trench, John Chenevix	DOCKEN DEAD. London: Macdonald, 1953; New York: Macmillan, 1954.
Tresselt, Alvin	RAIN DROP SPLASH. New York: Lothrop, 1946.
Trevor, Elleston	INTO THE HAPPY GLADE, as T. Dudley-Smith. London: Swan, 1943. OVER THE WALL, as T. Dudley-Smith, London: Swan, 1943. ANIMAL LIFE STORIES: RIPPLESWIM THE OTTER, SCAMPER-FOOT THE PINE MARTEN, SHADOW THE FOX. 3 vols. London: Swan, 1943-1945.
Trevor, Lucy Meriol	THE FOREST AND THE KINGDOM. London: Faber, 1949.
Trimble, Louis Preston	SPORTS OF THE WORLD. Los Angeles: Golden West, 1939.
Tripp, Miles Barton	FAITH IS A WINDSOCK. London: Davies, 1952.
Tubb, Edwin Charles	SATURN PATROL, as King Lang. London: Warren, 1951. PLANETFALL, as Gill Hunt. London: Warren, 1951.

AUTHOR	TITLE/FIRST EDITION INFORMATION
Tucker, Arthur Wilson "Bob"	THE CHINESE DOLL, as Wilson Tucker. New York: Rinehart, 1946; London: Cassell, 1948.
Tudor, Tasha	PUMPKIN MOONSHINE. New York; London: Oxford University, 1938.
Tunis, John Roberts	SPORTS, HEROES, AND HYSTERICS. New York: Day, 1928.
Turkle, Brinton	OBADIAH THE BOLD. New York: Viking, 1965.
Turner, Ethel Sybil	SEVEN LITTLE AUSTRALIANS. London: Ward Lock, 1894; Philadelphia: McKay, 1904.
Turner, George Reginald	YOUNG MAN OF TALENT. London: Cassell, 1959; as SCOBIE. New York: Simon & Schuster, 1959.
Turner, Philip William	THE CHRISTMAS STORY: A CAROL SERVICE FOR CHILDREN. London: Church Information Office, 1964.
Tuttle, Lisa	WINDHAVEN, with George R. R. Martin. New York: Simon & Schuster, 1980.
Tuttle, Wilber Coleman	REDDY BRANT, HIS ADVENTURES. New York: Century, 1920.
Tyre, Nedra	RED WINE FIRST. New York: Simon & Schuster, 1947.
Uchida, Yoshiko	THE DANCING KETTLE AND OTHER JAPANESE FOLK TALES. New York: Harcourt Brace, 1949.
Ude, Wayne	BUFFALO AND OTHER STORIES. Amherst, Mass.: Lynx House, 1979.
Udry, Janice May	LITTLE BEAR AND THE BEAUTIFUL KITE. Racine, Wis.: Whitman, 1955.
Uhnak, Dorothy	POLICEWOMAN: A YOUNG WOMAN'S INITIATION INTO THE REALITIES OF JUSTICE. New York: Simon & Schuster, 1964.

AUTHOR	TITLE/FIRST EDITION INFORMATION
Ungerer, Jean Thomas	THE MELLOPS GO FLYING, as Tomi Ungerer. New York: Harper, 1957; London: Methuen, 1957. THE MELLOPS GO DIVING FOR TREASURE. New York: Harper, 1957.
Unwin, David Storr	RICK AFIRE! as David Severn. London: Lane, 1942.
Unwin, Nora Spicer	ROUND THE YEAR: VERSES AND PICTURES. London: Chatto & Windus, 1939; New York: Holiday House, 1940.
Upchurch, Boyd Bradfield	THE LAST STARSHIP FROM EARTH, as John Boyd. New York: Weybright & Talley, 1965; London: Gollancz, 1969. THE SLAVE STEALER, as John Boyd. New York: Weybright & Talley, 1968; London: Jenkins, 1969.
Upfield, Arthur William	THE HOUSE OF CAIN. London: Hutchinson, 1928; New York: Dorrance, 1929.
Upton, Bertha Hudson	THE ADVENTURES OF TWO DUTCH DOLLS—AND A GOLLIWOGG. London; New York: Longman, 1895.
Uttley, Alice Jane	THE SQUIRREL, THE HARE, AND THE LITTLE GREY RABBIT, as Alison Uttley. London: Heinemann, 1929.
Vaizey, Jessie Bell	A ROSE-COLOURED THREAD, as Mrs. George de Horne Vaizey. London: Bowden, 1898.
Vance, John Holbrook	THE DYING EARTH, as Jack Vance. New York: Curl, 1950; London: Mayflower, 1972.
Vance, Louis Joseph	TERENCE O'ROURKE, GENTLEMAN ADVENTURER. New York: Wessels, 1905; London: Richards, 1906.
Vance, William E.	THE BRANDED LAWMAN. New York: Ace, 1952.
Van de Wetering, Janwillem	OUTSIDER IN AMSTERDAM. 1974.
Van Gulik, Robert H.	DEE GOONG AN. 1949.

AUTHOR	TITLE/FIRST EDITION INFORMATION
Van Scyoc, Sydney Joyce	SALTFLOWER. New York: Avon, 1971.
Van Siller, Hilda	ECHO OF A BOMB, as Van Siller. New York: Doubleday, 1943; London: Jarrolds, 1944.
Van Slyke, Helen Lenore	THE RICH AND THE RIGHTEOUS. New York: Doubleday, 1971; London: Cassell, 1972.
Van Stockum, Hilda	A DAY ON SKATES. New York; London: Harper, 1934.
Van Vogt, Alfred Elton	SLAN, as A. E. van Vogt. Sauk City, Wis.: Arkham House, 1946; London: Weidenfeld & Nicolson, 1953.
Varley, John	THE OPHIUCHI HOTLINE. New York: Dial, 1977; London: Sidgwick & Jackson, 1978.
Venables, Terry	HAZELL PLAYS SOLOMON, as P. B. Yuill, with Gordon Williams. London: Macmillan, 1975; New York: Walker, 1975.
Verney, John	VERNEY ABROAD. London: Collins, 1954.
Vernon, Roger Lee	THE SPACE FRONTIER. New York: New American Library, 1955.
Verrill, Alpheus Hyatt	GASOLENE ENGINES: THEIR OPERATION, USE , AND CARE, as A. Hyatt Verrill. New York: Henley, 1912. KNOTS, SPLICES, AND ROPE WORK, as A. Hyatt Verrill. New York: Henley, 1912.
Vickers, Roy C.	LORD ROBERTS: THE STORY OF HIS LIFE. London: Pearson, 1914.
Vidal, Eugene Luther Gore	WILLIWAW. New York: Dutton, 1946; London: Panther, 1965.
Vinge, Joan Carol Dennison	THE OUTCASTS OF HEAVEN BELT. New York: New American Library, 1978. FIRESHIP. New York: Dell, 1978; London: Sidgwick & Jackson, 1981.
Vinge, Vernor Steffen	GRIMM'S WORLD. New York: Berkley, 1976; London: Hamlyn, 1978. THE WITLING. New York: DAW; London: Dobson, 1976.

AUTHOR	TITLE/FIRST EDITION INFORMATION
Vining, Elizabeth Gray	MEREDITHS' ANN. New York: Doubleday; London: Heinemann, 1927.
Vinson, Rex Thomas	LIGHT A LAST CANDLE, as Vincent King. New York: Ballantine, 1969; London: Rapp & Whiting, 1970.
Viorst, Judith Stahl	PROJECTS: SPACE. New York: Washington Square Press, 1962.
Vipont, Elfrida	QUAKERISM: AN INTERNATIONAL WAY OF LIFE, as E. V. Foulds. Manchester, England: 1930 Committee, 1930.
Von Arnim, Countess Mary Annette	ELIZABETH AND HER GERMAN GARDEN, as Elizabeth. London; New York, 1898.
Vonnegut, Kurt, Jr.	PLAYER PIANO. New York: Scribner, 1952; London: Macmillan, 1953.
Vulliamy, Colwyn Edward	CHARLES KINGSLEY AND CHRISTIAN SOCIALISM. London: Fabian Society, 1914.
Waber, Bernard	LORENZO. Boston: Houghton Mifflin, 1961.
Wade, Robert	DEADLY WEAPON, as Wade Miller, with Bill Miller. New York: Farrar & Straus, 1946; London: Sampson Low, 1947.
Wagoner, David Russell	DRY SUN, DRY WIND. Bloomington, Ind.: Indiana University, 1953.
Wahl, Jan	PLEASANT FIELDMOUSE. New York: Harper, 1964; Kingswood, England: World's Work, 1969. THE BEAST BOOK. New York: Harper, 1964.
Wahloo, Per, and Maj Sjowall	ROSEANNA. 1967.
Wainwright, John	DEATH IN A SLEEPING CITY. London: Collins, 1965.
Waldo, Edward Hamilton	"IT," as Theodore Sturgeon. Philadelphia: Prime Press, 1948. WITHOUT SORCERY, as Theodore Sturgeon. Philadelphia: Prime Press, 1948.

AUTHOR	TITLE/FIRST EDITION INFORMATION
Walker, David Harry	THE STORM AND THE SILENCE. Boston: Houghton Mifflin, 1949; London: Cape, 1950.
Wall, John W.	RINGSTONES AND OTHER CURIOUS TALES, as Sarban. London: Davies; New York: Coward McCann, 1951.
Wallace, Floyd	ADDRESS: CENTAURI. New York: Gnome, 1955.
Wallace, Richard Horatio Edgar	THE MISSION THAT FAILED! A TALE OF THE RAID AND OTHER POEMS, as Edgar Wallace. Cape Town, South Africa: Maskew Miller, 1898.
Walling, Robert Alfred John	FLAUNTING MOLL AND OTHER STORIES. London: Harper, 1898.
Wallis, George C.	THE CHILDREN OF THE SPHINX, as G. C. Wallis. London: Simpkin Marshall, 1924.
Walsh, James Morgan	THE BRETHREN OF THE COMPASS, as J. M. Walsh, with E. J. Blythe. London: Jarrolds, 1925. THE WHITE MASK, as J. M. Walsh. London: Hamilton, 1925; New York: Doran, 1927.
Walsh, Sheila	THE GOLDEN SONGBIRD. London: Hurst & Blackett; New York: New American Library, 1975.
Walsh, Thomas Francis Morgan	NIGHTMARE IN MANHATTAN. Boston: Little, Brown, 1950; London: Hamish Hamilton, 1951.
Wambaugh, Joseph Aloysius, Jr.	THE NEW CENTURIONS. Boston: Little, Brown, 1970; London: Joseph, 1971.
Wandrei, Donald	ECSTASY AND OTHER POEMS. Athol, Mass.: Cook, 1928.
Ward, Arthur Sarsfield	PAUSE! anonymously. London: Greening, 1910.
Ward-Thomas, Evelyn Bridget Patricia	IMPERIAL HIGHNESS, as Evelyn Anthony. London, 1953.
Warren, Charles Marquis	ONLY THE VALIANT. New York: Macmillan, 1943; London: Corgi, 1953.

AUTHOR	TITLE/FIRST EDITION INFORMATION
Warriner, Thurman	METHOD IN HIS MURDER. London: Hodder & Stoughton; New York: Macmillan, 1950.
Waterloo, Stanley	HOW IT LOOKS. New York: Brentano's, 1888.
Waters, Frank Joseph	FEVER PITCH. New York: Liveright, 1930.
Watkins, William John	FIVE POEMS. Chula Vista, Calif.: Word Press, 1968.
Watkins-Pitchford, Denys James	WILD LONE. London: Eyre & Spottiswoode; New York: Scribner, 1938.
Watson, Clyde	FATHER FOX'S PENNYRHYMES. New York: Crowell, 1971.
Watson, Colin	COFFIN, SCARCELY USED. London: Eyre & Spottiswoode, 1958; New York: Putnam, 1967.
Watson, Ian	JAPAN: A CAT'S EYE VIEW. Osaka: Bunken, 1969.
Watson, Julia	THE LOVECHILD, as Julia Fitzgerald. London, 1967.
Watts, Peter Christopher	OUT OF YESTERDAY. London: Hodder & Stoughton, 1950.
Waugh, Hillary Baldwin	MADAM WILL NOT DINE TONIGHT. New York: Coward McCann, 1947; London: Boardman, 1949; as IF I LIVE TO DINE. Hasbrouck Heights, N.J.: Graphic, 1949.
Way, Margaret	BLAZE OF SILK. London: Mills & Boon, 1970; Toronto: Harlequin, 1971. KING COUNTRY. London: Mills & Boon, 1970; Toronto: Harlequin, 1971. THE TIME OF THE JACARANDA. London: Mills & Boon; Toronto: Harlequin, 1970.
Wayne, Anne Jenifer	THIS IS THE LAW: STORIES OF WRONGDOERS BY FAULT OR FOLLY. London: Sylvan Press, 1948.
Webb, Jack	THE BIG SIN. New York: Rinehart, 1952; London: Boardman, 1953. HIGH MESA, as Tex Grady. New York: Dutton, 1952; London: Foulsham, 1954.

AUTHOR	TITLE/FIRST EDITION INFORMATION
Webb, Jean Francis	LOVE THEY MUST. New York: Washburn, 1933.
Webster, Alice Jane Chandler	WHEN PATTY WENT TO COLLEGE, as Jean Webster. New York: Century, 1903; as PATTY AND PRISCILLA. London: Hodder & Stoughton, 1915.
Weinbaum, Stanley Grauman	DAWN OF FLAME. New York: Ruppert, 1936.
Weir, Rosemary	THE SECRET JOURNEY. London: Parrish, 1957.
Welch, James	RIDING THE EARTHBOY 40. Cleveland: World, 1971.
Wellman, Manly Wade	THE INVADING ASTEROID. New York: Stellar, 1932.
Wellman, Paul Iselin	BRONCHO APACHE. New York; London: Macmillan, 1936.
Wells, Carolyn	THE STORY OF BETTY. New York: Century, 1899.
Wells, Herbert George	TEXT-BOOK OF BIOLOGY, as H. G. Wells, 2 vols. London: Clive, 1893. HONOURS PHYSIOGRAPHY, as H. G. Wells, with R. A. Gregory. London: Hughes, 1893.
Wersba, Barbara	THE BOY WHO LOVED THE SEA. New York: Coward McCann, 1961.
West, Joyce Tarlton	SHEEP KINGS. Wellington, New Zealand: Tombs, 1936.
West, Kingsley	A TIME FOR VENGEANCE. New York: Doubleday, 1961.
West, Wallace George	BETTY BOOP IN SNOW-WHITE. Racine, Wis.: Whitman, 1934. ALICE IN WONDERLAND. Racine, Wis.: Whitman, 1934. PARAMOUNT NEWSREEL MEN WITH ADMIRAL BYRD IN LITTLE AMERICA. Racine, Wis.: Whitman, 1934.
Westall, Robert	THE MACHINE-GUNNERS. London: Macmillan, 1975; New York: Morrow, 1976.

AUTHOR	TITLE/FIRST EDITION INFORMATION
Westerman, Percy Francis	A LAD OF GRIT. London: Blackie, 1908.
Westlake, Donald Edwin	THE MERCENARIES. New York: Random House, 1960; London: Boardman, 1961.
Weston, Carolyn	TORMENTED. New York: Surrey House, 1956.
Westwood, Gwen	MONKEY BUSINESS. London: Hamish Hamilton, 1965.
White, Ethel Lina	THE WISH-BONE. London: Ward Lock, 1927.
White, James	THE SECRET VISITOR. New York: Ace, 1957; London: Digit, 1961.
White, Jon Ewbank Manchip	DRAGON AND OTHER POEMS. London: Fortune Press, 1943.
White, Lionel	THE SNATCHERS. New York: Fawcett, 1953; London: Miller, 1958.
White, Stewart Edward	THE CLAIM JUMPERS: A ROMANCE. New York: Appleton, 1901; London: Hodder & Stoughton, 1905.
White, Terence Hanbury	LOVED HELEN AND OTHER POEMS, as T. H. White. London: Chatto & Windus; New York: Viking, 1929. THE GREEN BAY TREE; OR, THE WICKED MAN TOUCHES WOOD, as T. H. White. Cambridge, England: Heffer, 1929.
White, Theodore Edwin	INVASION FROM 2500, as Norman Edwards, with Terry Carr. Derby, Conn.: Monarch, 1964.
White, William Anthony Parker	THE CASE OF THE SEVEN OF CALVARY, as Anthony Boucher. New York: Simon & Schuster; London: Hamish Hamilton, 1937.
Whitechurch, Victor Lorenzo	THE COURSE OF JUSTICE. London: Isbister, 1903.
Whitfield, Raoul	GREEN ICE. New York: Knopf, 1930; as THE GREEN ICE MURDERS. New York: Avon, 1947. WINGS OF GOLD. New York: Knopf, 1930.

AUTHOR	TITLE/FIRST EDITION INFORMATION
Whitney, Phyllis Ayame	A PLACE FOR ANN. Boston: Houghton Mifflin, 1941.
Whitson, John Harvey	CAPTAIN CACTUS. New York: Beadle & Adams, 1888.
Whittington, Harry	VENGEANCE VALLEY. New York: Phoenix, 1945; London: Ward Lock, 1947.
Wibberley, Leonard Patrick O'Connor	THE LOST HARPOONER, as Patrick O'Connor. New York: Washburn, 1947; London: Harrap, 1959.
Wiegand, William George	AT LAST, MR. TOLLIVER. New York: Rinehart, 1950; London: Hodder & Stoughton, 1951.
Wier, Ester Alberti	THE ANSWER BOOK ON NAVAL SOCIAL CUSTOMS [AND AIR FORCE SOCIAL CUSTOMS], with Dorothy Hickey. 2 vols. Harrisburg, Pa.: Military Services Publishing, 1956-1957.
Wiese, Kurt	KAROO THE KANGAROO. New York: Coward McCann, 1929. THE CHINESE INK STICK. New York: Doubleday, 1929.
Wiggin, Kate Douglas	THE STORY OF PATSY: A REMINISCENCE. San Francisco: Murdock, 1883; London: Gay & Bird, 1889.
Wilcox, Collin	THE BLACK DOOR. New York: Dodd Mead, 1967; London: Cassell, 1968.
Wilder, Laura Ingalls	LITTLE HOUSE IN THE BIG WOODS. New York: Harper, 1932; London: Methuen, 1956.
Wilhelm, Kate	THE MILE-LONG SPACESHIP. New York: Berkley, 1963; as ANDOVER AND THE ANDROID. London: Dobson, 1966. MORE BITTER THAN DEATH. New York: Simon & Schuster, 1963; London: Hale, 1965.
Wilkinson, Anne Cochran Boyd	COUNTERPOINT TO SLEEP. Montreal: First Statement Press, 1951.
Willard, Barbara	LOVE IN AMBUSH, with Elizabeth Helen Devas. London: Howe, 1930.

AUTHOR	TITLE/FIRST EDITION INFORMATION
Williams, Charles	HILL GIRL. New York: Fawcett, 1951; London: Red Seal, 1958.
Williams, Claudette	SPRING GAMBIT. New York: Fawcett, 1976.
Williams, Dorothy Jeanne	TAME THE WILD STALLION, as J. R. Williams. Englewood Cliffs, N.J.: Prentice Hall, 1957; Kingswood, England: World's Work, 1958.
Williams, George Valentine	WITH OUR ARMY IN FLANDERS. London: Arnold, 1915.
Williams, Gordon	THE LAST DAY OF LINCOLN CHARLES. London: Secker & Warburg, 1965; New York: Stein & Day, 1966.
Williams, Jay	THE STOLEN ORACLE. New York: Oxford University, 1943.
Williams, John Alfred	THE ANGRY ONES. New York: Ace, 1960.
Williams, John Edward	NOTHING BUT THE NIGHT. Denver: Swallow, 1948.
Williams, Robert Moore	THE CHAOS FIGHTERS. New York: Ace, 1955. CONQUEST OF THE SPACE SEA. New York: Ace, 1955.
Williams, Ursula Moray	JEAN-PIERRE. London: Black, 1931.
Williamson, Alice Muriel	THE BARN STORMERS, BEING THE TRAGICAL SIDE OF A COMEDY, as Mrs. Harcourt Williamson. New York: Stokes, 1897.
Williamson, C. N. and A. M.	THE LIGHTNING CONDUCTOR: THE STRANGE ADVENTURES OF A MOTOR-CAR. London: Methuen, 1902; New York: Holt, 1903.
Williamson, Charles Norris	MEMOIRS OF THE LIFE AND WRITINGS OF THOMAS CARLYLE, as C. N. Williamson, with Richard Herne Shepherd. London: Allen, 1881.
Williamson, John Stewart	THE GIRL FROM MARS, as Jack Williamson, with Miles J. Breuer. New York: Stellar, 1929.

AUTHOR	TITLE/FIRST EDITION INFORMATION
Willis, Edward Henry	FIGHTING YOUTH OF RUSSIA, as Ted Willis. London: Russia Today Society, 1942.
Wills, Maitland Cecil Melville	AUTHOR IN DISTRESS. London: Heritage, 1934; as NUMBER 18. London: Lane, 1934.
Wilson, Barbara Ker	SCOTTISH FOLK TALES AND LEGENDS. London: Oxford University; New York: Walck, 1954.
Wilson, Colin Henry	THE OUTSIDER. London: Gollancz; Boston: Houghton Mifflin, 1956.
Wilson, Harry Leon	ZIGZAG TALES FROM THE EAST TO THE WEST. New York: Keppler & Schwarzmann, 1894.
Wilson, John Anthony Burgess	TIME FOR A TIGER, as Anthony Burgess. London: Heinemann, 1956.
Wilson, Joyce Muriel	WILD CAT ISLAND, as Joyce Stranger. London: Methuen, 1961.
Wilson, Richard	THE GIRLS FROM PLANET 5. New York: Ballantine, 1955; London: Hale, 1968.
Wilson, Robert Anton	PLAYBOY'S BOOK OF FORBIDDEN WORDS. Chicago: Playboy Press, 1972.
Winsor, Kathleen	FOREVER AMBER. New York: Macmillan, 1944; London: Macdonald, 1945.
Winsper, Violet	LUCIFER'S ANGEL. London: Mills & Boon; Toronto: Harlequin, 1961. WIFE WITHOUT KISSES. London: Mills & Boon, 1961; Toronto: Harlequin, 1973.
Winston, Daoma	TORMENTED LOVERS. Derby, Conn.: Monarch, 1962.
Winther, Sophus Keith	THE REALISTIC WAR NOVEL. Seattle: University of Washington, 1930.
Wister, Owen	THE NEW SWISS FAMILY ROBINSON. Cambridge, Mass.: Sever, 1882.
Witting, Clifford	MURDER IN BLUE. London: Hodder & Stoughton; New York: Scribner, 1937.
Wodhams, Jack	THE AUTHENTIC TOUCH. New York: Curtis, 1971.

AUTHOR	TITLE/FIRST EDITION INFORMATION
Wojciechowska, Maia Teresa	MARKET DAY FOR TI ANDRE. New York: Viking, 1952.
Wolf, Gary K.	KILLERBOWL. New York: Doubleday, 1975; London: Sphere, 1976.
Wolfe, Bernard	HOW TO GET A JOB IN THE AIRCRAFT INDUSTRY. Mount Vernon, N.Y.: Wallach, 1943.
Wolfe, Gene Rodman	OPERATION ARES. New York: Berkley, 1970; London: Dobson, 1977.
Wollheim, Donald Allen	THE SECRET OF SATURN'S RINGS [THE MARTIAN MOONS, THE NINTH PLANET]. 3 vols. Philadelphia: Winston, 1954-59.
Wood, Edgar Allardyce	THE MAGPIE MENACE, as Kerry Wood. Red Deer, Canada: Kerry Wood, 1936.
Wood, Mrs. Henry	EAST LYNNE. 1861.
Wood, Lorna	THE CRUMB-SNATCHERS. London: Cape, 1933.
Woodiwiss, Kathleen E.	THE FLAME AND THE FLOWER. New York: Avon, 1972; London: Futura, 1975.
Woods, Helen	A CHARMED CIRCLE, as Helen Ferguson. London: Cape, 1929.
Woolf, Douglas	THE HYPOCRITIC DAYS. Majorca: Divers Press, 1955.
Worboys, Annette Isobel	DREAM OF PETALS WHIM, as Anne Eyre Worboys. London: Ward Lock, 1961. PALM ROCK AND PARADISE, as Anne Eyre Worboys. London: Ward Lock, 1961.
Wormser, Richard Edward	THE MAN WITH THE WAX FACE. New York: Smith & Haas, 1934.
Wren, Percival Christopher	THE INDIAN TEACHER'S GUIDE TO THE THEORY AND PRACTICE OF MENTAL, MORAL, AND PHYSICAL EDUCATION, as P. C. Wren. Bombay, India: Longman, 1910.
Wright, Austin Tappan	ISLANDIA. New York: Rinehart, 1942.

AUTHOR	TITLE/FIRST EDITION INFORMATION
Wright, Harold Bell	THAT PRINTER OF UDELL'S: A STORY OF THE MIDDLE WEST. Chicago: Book Supply, 1903; London: Hodder & Stoughton, 1910.
Wright, Sydney Fowler	SCENES FROM THE MORTE D'ARTHUR, as Alan Seymour. London: Erskine MacDonald, 1919.
Wright, Willard Huntington	EUROPE AFTER 8:15, with H. L. Mencken and George Jean Nathan. New York: Lane, 1914.
Wrightson, Alice Patricia	THE CROOKED SNAKE. Sydney, Australia; London: Angus & Robertson, 1955.
Wylie, Philip Gordon	HEAVY LADEN. New York: Knopf, 1928.
Yarbro, Chelsea Quinn	OGILVIE, TALLANT, AND MOON. New York: Putnam, 1976. TIME OF THE FOURTH HORSEMAN. New York: Doubleday, 1976; London: Sidgwick & Jackson, 1980.
Yates, Elizabeth	HIGH HOLIDAY. London: Black, 1938.
Yep, Laurence Michael	SWEETWATER. New York: Harper, 1973; London: Faber, 1976.
Yerby, Frank Garvin	THE FOXES OF HARROW. New York: Dial, 1946; London: Heinemann, 1947.
Yolen, Jane	SEE THIS LITTLE LINE? New York: McKay, 1963. PIRATES IN PETTICOATS. New York: McKay, 1963.
Yonge, Charlotte Mary	LE CHATEAU DE MELVILLE; OU, RECREATIONS DU CABINET D'ETUDE. London: Simkin, 1838.
Young, Delbert Alton	MUTINY ON HUDSON BAY. Toronto: Gage, 1964.
Young, Gordon Ray	SAVAGES. New York: Doubleday, 1921; London: Cape, 1922.
Young, Michael Dunlop	WILL THE WAR MAKE US POORER? with Henry Bunbury. London: Oxford University, 1943.

AUTHOR	TITLE/FIRST EDITION INFORMATION
Young, Robert Franklin	THE WORLDS OF ROBERT F. YOUNG. New York: Simon & Schuster, 1965; London: Gollancz, 1966.
Young, Scott Alexander	RED SHIELD IN ACTION: A RECORD OF CANADIAN SALVATION ARMY WAR SERVICES IN THE SECOND GREAT WAR. Toronto: Clarke, 1949.
Zagat, Arthur Leo	SEVEN OUT OF TIME. Reading, Pa.: Fantasy, 1949.
Zangwill, Israel	MOTZA KLEIS, anonymously, with Louis Cowen. London: Privately printed, 1882.
Zebrowski, George	THE OMEGA POINT. New York: Ace, 1972; London: New English Library, 1974.
Zelazny, Roger Joseph	THIS IMMORTAL. New York: Ace, 1966; London: Hart Davis, 1967. THE DREAM MASTER. New York: Ace, 1966; London: Hart Davis, 1968.
Zinberg, Leonard S.	WALK HARD—TALK LOUD, as Len Zinberg. Indianapolis: Bobbs Merrill, 1940.
Zindel, Paul	THE PIGMAN. New York: Harper, 1968; London: Bodley Head, 1969.
Zion, Eugene	ALL FALLING DOWN, as Gene Zion. New York: Harper, 1951; Kingswood, England: World's Work, 1969.
Zolotow, Charlotte	THE PARK BOOK. New York: Harper, 1944.

8

Collectible Book Illustrators

Books, posters, and magazines illustrated by, and books by or about, any of these illustrators are collectible and often bring substantial premiums over unillustrated editions of otherwise collectible books. Many of the books illustrated by these artists are reprint editions of classics, often done in elaborate bindings. Sometimes they are also limited editions signed by the artist.

Such books are the exception to the usual collector's requirement that a book be a first edition. This is because the book is in itself a form of first edition due to the presence of the artist's illustrations for the first time.

Please note: Names that are pseudonyms are followed by the illustrator's true name(s) in parentheses.

Abbey, Edwin Austin
Ambrus, Victor
Anglund, Joan Walsh
Ardizzone, Edward
Armstrong, Rolf
Artzybasheff, Boris
Averill, Esther Holden

Babbitt, Natalie
Bacon, John R.
Bacon, Peggy
Banner, Angela
Baum, L. Frank
Beardsley, Aubrey
Beggarstaffs, The (James Pryde and William Nicholson)
Behn, Harry
Bemelmans, Ludwig
Beneker, Gerrit A.
Berry, Erick
Bewick, Thomas
Bianco, Pamela
Bice, Clare
Bird, Elisha Brown
Biro, Val
Bisset, Donald
Blaine, Mahlon
Blake, William

Bodecker, Niels Mogens
Bonnard, Paul
Bonnard, Pierre
Bonsall, Crosby Newell
Bonte, B. Willard
Boston, Peter
Bradley, Will
Bragdon, Claude Fayette
Brangwyn, Frank
Bright, Robert
Brisley, Joyce Lankester
Britton, L. N.
Brooke, Leonard Leslie
Bull, Charles Livingston
Burton, Virginia Lee
Byrd, David

Calaora, Lorraine
Carleton, B.
Carlu, Jean
Carqueville, Will
Carre, Jean
Chagall, Marc
Chambers, C. E.
Chambers, Robert William
Cheret, Jules
Christy, Howard Chandler
Clarke, Harry
Cox, Charles H.
Cox, Palmer
Coughlin, John C.
Crane, Walter
Cruikshank, George

Dali, Salvador
Darling, Louis
Darly, F. O. A. C.
D'Aulaire, Edgar Parin
Davis, Paul
Day, Francis
De Angeli, Marguerite Lofft
De Lans, Eugenie
Denslow, W. W. (William Wallace Denslow)
Dimitri, Ivan
Dixon, Maynard (Lafayette Maynard Dixon)
Dore, Gustav
Dougherty, James
Dow, Arthur Wesley
Downe, Albro
Drummond, Violet Hilda
DuBois, William Pene
Dulac, Edmund
Dunn, Harvey
Dürer, Albrecht
Duvoisin, Roger Antoine

Eddy, Henry B.
Edwards, George Wharton
Ellis, Harvey
Emerson, R. L.
Enright, Elizabeth
Enright, Maginal
Erte (Romain DeTirtoff)

Falls, C. B.
Falter, John
Field, Rachel Lyman
Fischer, Anton Otto
Fisher, Harrison
Flack, Marjorie
Flag, James Montgomery

Flora, James Royer
Floyd, Gareth
Foreman, Michael
Forsythe, Clyde
Fortnum, Peggy
Freeman, Barbara Constance
Freeman, Don
Frost, A. B.
Fry, Rosalie Kingsmill

Gag, Wanda
Galdone, Paul
Gibbs, Cecelia May
Gibson, Charles Dana
Gilbert, F. Allan
Gill, Eric
Gill, Margery
Goff, Seymour
Gordon, Margaret
Gorey, Edward
Gramatky, Hardie
Greenaway, Kate
Greenough, W. C.
Greulle, Johnny
Grohe, Glenn
Gurvin, Abe

Hader, Berta Hoerner
Haeberle, R. L.
Hale, Kathleen
Haley, Gail Einhart
Haywood, Carolyn
Held, John, Jr.
Hendee, A.
Hirsch, Joseph
Hoff, Sydney
Hogarth, William
Holling, Holling Clancy
Homer, Winslow
Hough, Charlotte
Houston, James Archibald
Hughes, Shirley
Hunt, James

Icart, Louis

Jansen, R. H.
James, Will
Johnson, Crockett

Keats, Ezra Jack
Keeping, Charles William James
Kenney, Clayton
Kent, Rockwell
King, Alexander
Kuskin, Karla

Lattimore, Eleanor Frances
Lawson, Robert
Leaf, Munro
Lenski, Lois
Leyendecker, J. C.
Lindsay, Norman
Lobel, Anita
Lobel, Arnold

McCloskey, John Robert
McCreary, Harrison
McKee, David John
McVicker, Harry W.
Maitland, Antony

Martin, David Stone
Mayer, Hy
Michaelson, J.
Milhous, Katherine
Mora, F. Luis
Morgan, Wallace
Morse, Alice C.
Mucha, Alphonse

Nankivell, Frank Arthur
Neill, John R.
Newell, Peter (Sheaf Hersey)
Nielsen, Kay
Norton, M. E.

O'Neill, Rose
Orr, A. E.
Orr, Forrest
Ottman, Chci
Outcault, Richard Felton

Parrish, Maxfield
Paus, Herbert
Peixotto, Ernest
Pendergast, Maurice
Penfield, Edward
Pennell, Joseph
Perkins, Lucy Fitch
Perlin, Bernard
Petersham, Maud Sylvia Fuller
Phillips, S. Coles
Podwal, Marc
Pogany, Willie
Politi, Leo
Porter, Bruce
Potter, Helen Beatrix
Potthast, Edward Henry
Pyle, Howard

Rackham, Arthur
Raemakers, Louis
Raleigh, Henry
Raskin, Ellen
Reed, Ethel
Remington, Frederic
Reuterdahl, H.
Rey, Hans Augusto
Rhead, Louis J.
Richardson, Frederick
Riesenberg, Sidney
Riguer, Aljandro de
Robinson, Charles
Robinson, Joan Mary Gale
Robinson, W. Heath
Rockwell, Norman
Rogers, A. P.
Rogers, Bruce
Rosenberg, Henry M.
Rounds, Glen Harold
Russell, Charles M.

St. John, J. Allen
Sarg, Tony
Sattler, Joseph
Scarry, Richard
Scotson-Clark, George Frederick
Schoonover, Frank
Schweinfurth, J. A.
Sendak, Maurice
Seredy, Kate
Seton, Ernest Evan Thompson
Seuss, Dr. (Theodor Seuss Geisel)

Sewell, Helen Moore
Shahn, Ben
Shepard, Ernest
Sheridan, J. E.
Sloan, John
Slobodkin, Louis
Slobodkina, Esphyr
Smith, Dan V.
Smith, F. Berkeley
Smith, Jessie Wilcox
Smith, Lawrence D.
Soper, Eileen
Sperry, Armstrong
Steig, William
Steinlen, Theophile-Alexandre
Sterner, Albert
Stewardson, John
Strathman, F.
Szyk, Arthur

Tenniel, John
Toulouse-Lautrec, Henri de
Treidler, Adolph
Twachtman, John

Underwood, C. F.

Valenti, Angelo
Valentine, D. G.
Verney, John
Verrees, J. Paul

Wagner, Robert Leicester
Walton, Tony
Ward, Byron
Warren, Ferdinand
Watson, Henry Sumner
Weisgard, Leonard
Wells, E. B.
Whitehead, Walter
Wiese, Kurt
Williams, Garth
Williams, John Scott
Wood, Page
Woodbury, Charles Herbert
Wyeth, N. C.

Yeats, Jack B.
Young, Ellsworth

Zagat, A. L.

– 9 –

Anonymously Written Books: Their Authors and Values

Most of these titles were published in later editions with the author identified, and of course many of them are still in print, since they are classics. Remember, even though the author's name will be missing, the book should still show the other information I have supplied. This list will prove useful at garage sales or flea markets, or when browsing in old book stores or antique shops.

AB-SA-RA-KA, HOME OF THE CROWS [Mrs. Henry B. Carrington]. Philadelphia, 1868. With folding map. Cloth. $200-300.

ACELDAMA, A PLACE TO BURY STRANGERS IN. BY A GENTLEMAN OF THE UNIVERSITY OF CAMBRIDGE [Aleister Crowley]. London, 1898. Wrappers. $400-700.

THE ADVENTURES OF A BROWNIE, AS TOLD TO MY CHILD . . . BY THE AUTHOR OF "JOHN HALIFAX, GENTLEMAN" [Dinah M. Craik]. London, 1872. Cloth. $250-400.

THE ADVENTURES OF A POST CAPTAIN. BY A NAVAL OFFICER [Alfred Thornton]. London, (1817). 25 colored plates. Boards. $350-600.

THE ADVENTURES OF ROBIN DAY [Robert Montgomery Bird]. 2 vols. Philadelphia, 1839. Purple cloth. Paper label on spines. $250-400.

THE ADVENTURES OF TIMOTHY PEACOCK, ESQUIRE. BY A MEMBER OF THE VERMONT BAR [Daniel Pierce Thompson]. Middlebury, Vt., 1835. Cloth. $300-600.

THE ADVENTURES OF ULYSSES [Charles Lamb]. London, 1808. Boards. Paper label. Frontispiece. Engraved title page. $700-1,100.

THE ADVENTURES OF A YANKEE, OR THE SINGULAR LIFE OF JOHN LEDYARD. BY A YANKEE [John Ledyard]. Boston, 1831. Woodcuts. Boards and leather. $300-500.

THE ADVENTURES OF A YOUNGER SON [Edward John Trelawny]. 3 vols. London, 1831. Boards. Author's first book. $400-600.

THE AGE OF BRONZE [George Gordon Noel, Lord Byron]. London, 1823. Wrappers. $400-700.

ALARIC AT ROME: A PRIZE POEM. RECITED IN RUGBY SCHOOL. JUNE XII, MDCCCXL [Matthew Arnold]. Rugby, England, 1840. Pink pictorial wrappers. 12 pp. Author's first book of verse. At least $7,500.

ALNWICK CASTLE, WITH OTHER POEMS [Fitz-Greene Halleck]. New York, 1827. Wrappers. $250-350.

ALTOWAN; OR INCIDENTS OF LIFE AND ADVENTURE IN THE ROCKY MOUNTAINS. BY AN AMATEUR TRAVELLER [Sir William Drummond Stewart]. 2 vols. New York, 1846. Cloth. $350-500.

AMERICAN ARGUMENTS FOR BRITISH RIGHTS [William Loughton Smith]. London, 1806. Wrappers. $150-250.

THE AMERICAN CRUISER [Captain George Little]. Boston, 1846. Cloth. $100-150.

THE AMERICAN SHOOTER'S MANUAL. BY A GENTLEMAN OF PHILADELPHIA COUNTY [Attributed to Dr. Jesse Y. Kester]. Philadelphia, 1827. Leather. Frontispiece. 2 plates. Errata. $2,000 or more.

THE ANALYSIS OF THE HUNTING FIELD [Robert Smith Surtees]. London, 1846. 7 colored plates by Henry Alken. 43 woodcuts. Green cloth. $800-1,100.

THE ANGEL IN THE HOUSE [Coventry Patmore]. London, 1854. Cloth. $100-150.

ANNE OF GEIERSTEIN; OR, THE MAIDEN OF THE MIST [Sir Walter Scott]. 3 vols. Edinburgh, 1829. Boards. $300-500.

THE ANTIQUARY [Sir Walter Scott]. 3 vols. Edinburgh, 1816. $350-500.

AN APPEAL TO THE CLERGY OF THE CHURCH OF SCOTLAND [Robert Louis Stevenson]. Edinburgh, 1875. 12 pp. No covers. At least $5,000.

ARTHUR MERVYN; OR MEMOIRS OF THE YEAR 1793. BY THE AUTHOR OF WIELAND [Charles Brockden Brown]. 2 vols. Philadelphia, 1799-1800. Leather. At least $500.

"ASK MAMA"; OR, THE RICHEST COMMONER IN ENGLAND [Robert Smith Surtees]. London, (1857 and) 1858. 13 parts in red wrappers. 13 color plates and 69 woodcuts by John Leech. At least $750.

ATLANTIS. [William Gilmore Simms]. New York, 1832. Wrappers. $300-400.

THE ATTACHE; OR, SAM SLICK IN ENGLAND [Thomas Chandler Haliburton]. Second series, 2 vols. London, 1844. Plum cloth. 48 pages of ads at end of vol. 2. At least $150.

AUTHORSHIP: A TALE [John Neal]. Boston, 1930. Boards and cloth. $100-150.

THE AUTOCRAT OF THE BREAKFAST TABLE [Oliver Wendell Holmes]. Boston, 1858. Cloth. Illustrated. Several "points" are involved in identifying a true first issue of the first edition. $500 and up.

AYESHA, THE MAID OF KARS. BY THE AUTHOR OF "ZOHRA," ETC. [James Morier]. 3 vols. London, 1834. Boards. $300 and up.

BEAUTY AND THE BEAST [Attributed to Charles Lamb]. London, (ca.1810-1813). Boards. Printed paper case. $1,000 and up.

THE BEE-HUNTER; OR, THE OAK OPENINGS [James Fenimore Cooper]. 3 vols. London, 1848. Boards. $200-300.

BEPPO, A VENETIAN STORY [George Gordon Noel, Lord Byron]. London, 1818. Wrappers. At least $750.

A BIOGRAPHICAL NOTE OF COMMODORE JESSE D. ELLIOTT. BY A CITIZEN OF NEW YORK [Russell Jarvis]. Philadelphia, 1835. Boards. $100 and up.

BIOGRAPHY OF JAMES LAWRENCE, ESQ. [Washington Irving]. New Brunswick, N.J., 1813. Portrait. Boards. $150-250.

THE BLOSSOMS OF MORALITY [Richard Johnson]. Philadelphia, 1810. 51 wood engravings. Leather and boards. At least $50.

A BOOK OF COMMANDMENTS, FOR THE GOVERNMENT OF THE CHURCH OF CHRIST [Joseph Smith, Jr.]. Zion (Independence), Mo., 1833. Boards. At least $10,000.

BORDER BEAGLES: A TALE OF MISSISSIPPI [William Gilmore Simms]. 2 vols. Philadelphia, 1840. Boards and cloth. $300-400.

THE BORDERERS: A TALE. BY THE AUTHOR OF "THE SPY" [James Fenimore Cooper]. 3 vols. London, 1829. Boards. At least $750.

THE BRAVO: A VENETIAN STORY [James Fenimore Cooper]. 3 vols. London, 1831. Boards. At least $750.

A BRIEF DESCRIPTION OF WESTERN TEXAS [W. G. Kingsbury]. San Antonio, Tex., 1873. Pictorial wrappers. $600 and up.

A BRIEF HISTORY OF CHRIST'S HOSPITAL [Charles Lamb]. London, 1820. Boards. $450 and up.

THE BROTHERS: A TALE OF THE FRONDE [Henry William Herbert]. 2 vols. New York, 1835. Brown cloth. Author's first book. At least $250.

CALAVAR: OR, THE KNIGHT OF THE CONQUEST [Robert Montgomery Bird]. 2 vols. Philadelphia, 1834. Purple cloth. Author's first book. $250 and up.

CALIFORNIA ILLUSTRATED. BY A RETURNED CALIFORNIAN [J. M. Letts]. New York, 1852. 48 plates. Cloth. $350-500.

CALIFORNIA SKETCHES, WITH RECOLLECTIONS OF THE GOLD MINES [Leonard Kip]. Albany, N.Y., 1850. Half leather. At least $750.

CAPT. SMITH AND PRINCESS POCAHONTAS: AN INDIAN TALE [John Smith]. Philadelphia, 1805. Boards. With undated copyright notice. At least $2,000.

CARELESS JOHN, THE ENGLISH "SQUIRE:" A POEM IN TEN CANTOS [William A. Chatto]. London, 1821. Cloth. 24 colored plates. $400-600.

CARL WERNER, AN IMAGINATIVE STORY [William Gilmore Simms]. 2 vols. New York, 1838. Cloth. At least $350.

CASTLE DISMAL; OR, THE BACHELOR'S CHRISTMAS [William Gilmore Simms]. New York, 1844. Boards. $250-350.

CASTLE RACKRENT; AN HIBERNIAN TALE [Maria Edgeworth]. London, 1800. Boards. At least $500.

THE CHAINBEARER, OR, THE LITTLEPAGE MANUSCRIPTS [James Fenimore Cooper]. 3 vols. London, 1845. Tan boards. At least $350.

THE CHILD'S BOTANY [Samuel Griswold Goodrich]. Boston, 1828. Boards. $100-150.

A CHRISTMAS GIFT FROM FAIRY-LAND [James Kirk Paulding]. New York, (1838). Cloth. $150-250.

CLASS POEM [James Russell Lowell]. Cambridge, Mass., 1838. Wrappers. Author's first published work. $250-350.

CLASS POEM, 1915 [Archibald MacLeish]. (New Haven, Conn.), 1915. Author's first separately published work. 4 pp. At least $2,500.

THE CLOCKMAKER; OR THE SAYINGS AND DOINGS OF SAMUEL SLICK OF SLICKVILLE [Thomas Chandler Haliburton]. Halifax, 1836. Cloth. $250-300.

COLLEGE MUSINGS, OR TWIGS FROM PARNASSUS [William Russell Smith]. Tuscaloosa, Ala., 1833. Boards. First Alabama book of poetry. At least $750.

THE COMING RACE [Edward Bulwer-Lytton]. Edinburgh, 1871. Cloth. At least $450.

CONFESSIONS OF AN ENGLISH OPIUM-EATER [Thomas de Quincey]. London, 1822. Boards. At least $1,200.

THE CONFESSIONS OF HARRY LORREQUER [Charles Lever]. Dublin, 1839. Illustrated by Phiz. 11 parts in pink wrappers. Author's first book. $450-600.

COUNT JULIAN; OR, THE LAST DAYS OF THE GOTH [William Gilmore Simms]. Baltimore, Md., 1845. $250 and up.

COUNT JULIAN: A TRAGEDY [Walter Savage Landor]. London, 1812. Boards. $350-450.

CROMWELL: AN HISTORICAL NOVEL [Henry William Herbert]. 2 vols. New York, 1838. Brown cloth. 12 pages of ads. $175-250.

THE CURSE OF MINERVA [George Gordon Noel, Lord Byron]. London, 1812. Dark brown wrappers. 25 pp. At least $2,500.

THE DAMSEL OF DARIEN [William Gilmore Simms]. 2 vols. Philadelphia, 1839. Boards or wrappers. $350-500.

DATE 1601. CONVERSATION AS IT WAS BY THE SOCIAL FIRESIDE, IN THE TIMES OF THE TUDORS [Samuel Langhorne Clemens]. (West Point, N.Y., 1882). 7 single unbound leaves. At least $500.

THE DEERSLAYER; OR, THE FIRST WAR-PATH. BY THE AUTHOR OF "THE LAST OF THE MOHICANS" [James Fenimore Cooper]. 2 vols. Philadelphia, 1841. $2,250 or more.

DEMOS: A STORY OF ENGLISH SOCIALISM [George Gissing]. 3 vols. London, 1886. $700-800.

DERRY DOWN DERRY: A BOOK OF NONSENSE [Edward Lear]. London, (1846). Oblong. Printed wrappers. Limited edition of 175. Author's first children's book. $2,250 or more.

THE DESCENDANT [Ellen Glasgow]. New York, 1897. Author's first book. $100-125.

A DESCRIPTION OF TREMONT HOUSE [William G. Eliot]. Boston, 1830. Boards. $60-75.

DESPERATE REMEDIES: A NOVEL [Thomas Hardy]. 3 vols. London, 1871. $2,750-3,250.

DESTINY; OR, THE CHIEF'S DAUGHTER [Susan Edmonstone Ferrier]. 3 vols. Edinburgh, 1831. $350-450.

THE DISCARDS. BY OLD WOLF [Lucullus V. McWhorter]. 3 vols. (Yakima, Wash.), 1920. Wrappers. $125-175.

A DISCOURSE ON THE ABORIGINES OF THE VALLEY OF THE OHIO [William Henry Harrison]. Cincinnati, 1838. Folding map. Sewed. 22 pp. $175-225.

DISIECTA MEMBRA [Norman Douglas]. London, 1915. 54 pp. Wrappers. Limited edition. $175-225.

DOMESTIC MANNERS OF THE AMERICANS [Frances Trollope]. 2 vols. London, 1832. $450-550.

THE DOOMED CITY [Charles H. Mackintosh]. Detroit, 1871. Folding map. 54 pp. Wrappers. $45-60.

THE DUN COW: AN HYPER-SATYRICAL DIALOGUE IN VERSE [Walter Savage Landor]. London, 1808. 12 leaves. Wrappers. $1,200 or more.

THE DUTCHMAN'S FIRESIDE [James Kirk Paulding]. 2 vols. New York, 1831. $175-225.

DYLLIA NOVA QUINQUE HEROUM ATQUE HEROIDUM [Walter Savage Landor]. Oxford, 1815. 2 parts in one. Boards $350-450.

THE ECHO [Richard Alsop, Lemuel Hopkins, Theodore Dwight, et al.]. (New York, 1807). $100-125.

AN 1862 TRIP TO THE WEST [Lyman B. Goff]. Pawtucket, R.I., (1926). $750 or more.

ELIA: ESSAYS WHICH HAVE APPEARED UNDER THAT SIGNATURE IN THE LONDON MAGAZINE [Charles Lamb]. London, 1823. First issue. $800 or more.

ELIZABETH BENNET; OR, PRIDE AND PREJUDICE: A NOVEL [Jane Austen]. 2 vols. Philadelphia, 1832. First American edition of *Pride and Prejudice*. $450-550.

THE EMBARGO, OR SKETCHES OF THE TIMES; A SATIRE BY A YOUTH OF THIRTEEN [William Cullen Bryant]. Boston, 1808. 12 pp. Wrappers. $1,100 or more.

EMILY PARKER, OR IMPULSE, NOT PRINCIPLE [Lydia Maria Child]. Boston, 1827. Boards. $175-225.

EMMA. BY THE AUTHOR OF PRIDE AND PREJUDICE [Jane Austen]. 3 vols. London, 1816. $4,500 or more.

ENGLISH BARDS AND SCOTCH REVIEWERS [George Gordon Noel, Lord Byron]. London, (1809). 54 pp. Boards. $2,250 or more.

THE ENGLISH DANCE OF DEATH [William Combe]. London, 1814-1816. 74 color plates by Thomas Rowlandson. 24 parts in wrappers. $1,100 or more.

EPILOGOS [Robert Duncan]. Los Angeles, 1967. Wrappers. Limited edition. Signed. With original drawing by Duncan. $175-225.

EPIPSYCHIDION: VERSES, ETC. [Percy Bysshe Shelley]. London, 1821. Wrappers. $3,000 or more.

AN EPITOME OF ELECTRICITY AND GALVANISM. BY TWO GENTLEMEN OF PHILADELPHIA [Jacob Green and Ebenezer Hazard]. Philadelphia, 1809. Boards. $175-225.

EREWHON, OR OVER THE RANGE [Samuel Butler]. London, 1872. $225-275.

AN ESSAY ON MIND, WITH OTHER POEMS [Elizabeth Barrett Browning]. London, 1826. Boards. $900 or more.

ESSAYS FROM POOR ROBERT THE SCRIBE [Charles Miner]. Doylestown, Pa., 1815. $175-225.

ESSAYS OF HOWARD ON DOMESTIC ECONOMY [Mordecai Manuel Noah]. New York, 1820. $100-125.

EUGENE ARAM: A TALE [Edward Bulwer-Lytton]. 3 vols. London, 1832. $175-225.

AN EULOGY ON THE LIFE OF GEN. GEORGE WASHINGTON [Robert Treat Paine, Jr.]. Newburyport, Mass., 1800. Wrappers. $125-150.

EUPHRANOR: A DIALOGUE ON YOUTH [Edward Fitzgerald]. London, 1851. $225-275.

EVENINGS IN NEW ENGLAND. BY AN AMERICAN LADY [Lydia Maria Child]. Boston, 1824. $175-225.

EVENTS IN INDIAN HISTORY, BEGINNING WITH AN ACCOUNT OF THE ORIGIN OF THE AMERICAN INDIANS [James Wimer]. Lancaster, Pa., 1841. Leather. $175-225.

AN EXAMINATION OF THE PRESIDENT'S REPLY TO THE NEW HAVEN REMONSTRANCE [William Coleman]. New York, 1801. Wrappers. $85-100.

AN EYEWITNESS. SATAN IN SEARCH OF A WIFE [Charles Lamb]. London, 1831. Wrappers. Illustrated by George Cruikshank. $600-750.

EZRA POUND: HIS METRIC AND POETRY [T. S. Eliot]. New York, 1917. Rose boards. $450-525.

A FABLE FOR CRITICS [James Russell Lowell]. New York, 1848. $225-250.

THE FAIRY BOOK [Dinah M. Craik]. New York, 1837. $150-200.

FAITH GARTNEY'S GIRLHOOD [Mrs. A. D. T. Whitney]. Boston, 1863. $85-100.

A FAITHFUL PICTURE OF THE POLITICAL SITUATION IN NEW ORLEANS [Edward James Workman]. New Orleans, 1807. $450-525.

FALKLAND [Edward Bulwer-Lytton]. London, 1827. Boards. $850-1,000.

FALKNER: A NOVEL [Mary Wollstonecraft Shelley]. 3 vols. London, 1837. $450-600.

THE FAMILY ROBINSON CRUSOE [Johann David Wyss]. 2 vols. London, 1814. First English edition. $4,500 or more.

FANNY [Fitz-Greene Halleck]. New York, 1819. $350-425.

FANSHAWE: A TALE [Nathaniel Hawthorne]. Boston, 1828. Boards. $12,500 or more.

THE FEAST OF THE POETS. BY THE EDITOR OF THE EXAMINER [Leigh Hunt]. London, 1814. Boards. $275-350.

THE FIRST SETTLERS OF NEW ENGLAND; OR, CONQUEST OF THE PEQUODS, NARRAGANSETS AND POKANOKETS. BY A LADY OF MASSACHUSETTS [Lydia Maria Child]. Boston, (1829). Boards. $85-100.

A FOOL'S ERRAND. BY ONE OF THE FOOLS [Albion W. Tourgee]. New York, 1879. $85-100.

FOREST AND STREAM FABLES [Rowland Evans Robinson]. New York, (1866). $160-200.

THE FORTUNES OF COLONEL TORLOGH O'BRIEN [Joseph Sheridan Le Fanu]. Dublin, 1847. 10 parts. $450-525.

THE FORTUNES OF NIGEL [Sir Walter Scott]. 3 vols. Edinburgh, 1822. Boards. $450-525.

THE FORTUNES OF PERKIN WARBECK [Mary Wollstonecraft Shelley]. 3 vols. London, 1830. Boards. $550-650.

FRANK FAIRLEIGH; OR SCENES FROM THE LIFE OF A PRIVATE PUPIL [Frank E. Smedley]. London, 1850. 15 parts. Wrappers. Illustrated by George Cruikshank. $800 or more.

FRANKENSTEIN; OR THE MODERN PROMETHEUS [Mary Wollstonecraft Shelley]. 3 vols. London, 1818. Boards. $8,500 or more.

THE FRUGAL HOUSEWIFE. BY THE AUTHOR OF HOBOMOK [Lydia Maria Child]. Boston, 1829. Boards. $175-225.

FUGITIVE PIECES [George Gordon Noel, Lord Byron]. N.p., (1806). Wrappers. $10,000 or more.

THE GAMEKEEPER AT HOME [Richard Jeffries]. London, 1878. $275-350.

GANCONAGH. JOHN SHERMAN AND DHOYA [William Butler Yeats]. London, (1891). Cloth or wrappers. $650-800.

THE GENIUS OF OBLIVION AND OTHER POEMS. BY A LADY OF NEW-HAMPSHIRE [Sarah Josepha Hale]. Concord, Mass., 1823. Boards. $250-325.

GEORGIA SCENES, CHARACTERS, INCIDENTS, ETC., IN THE FIRST HALF CENTURY OF THE REPUBLIC. BY A NATIVE GEORGIAN [Augustus Baldwin Longstreet]. Augusta, Ga., 1835. Boards. $1,100 or more.

GETTING A WRONG START: A TRUTHFUL AUTOBIOGRAPHY [Emerson Hough]. New York, 1915. $40-50.

A GIFT FROM FAIRY-LAND [James Kirk Paulding]. New York, (1838). $350-425.

GINX'S BABY: HIS BIRTH AND OTHER MISFORTUNES [John Edward Jenkins]. London, 1870. $60-75.

THE GREEN MOUNTAIN BOYS [Daniel Pierce Thompson]. 2 vols. Montpelier, Vt., 1839. Boards. $575-750.

GREYSLAYER: A ROMANCE OF THE MOHAWK [Charles Fenno Hoffman]. 2 vols. New York, 1840. $375-450.

GROUPED THOUGHTS AND SCATTERED FANCIES [William Gilmore Simms]. Richmond, Va., 1845. Wrappers. $225-275.

GRYLL GRANGE. BY THE AUTHOR OF HEADLONG HALL [Thomas Love Peacock]. London, 1861. $450-575.

GUIDE, GAZETTEER AND DIRECTORY OF NEBRASKA RAILROADS [J. M. Wolfe]. Omaha, Nebr., 1872. Wrappers. $275-350.

GUY MANNERING; OR, THE ASTROLOGER [Sir Walter Scott]. 3 vols. Edinburgh, 1815. Boards. $350-425.

GUY RIVERS: A TALE OF GEORGIA [William Gilmore Simms]. 2 vols. New York, 1834. $450-525.

HANDLEY CROSS: OR, MR. JORROCK'S HUNT [Robert Smith Surtees]. London, 1853-1854. 17 parts in wrappers. Illustrated by John Leech. $1,650 or more.

HAROLD THE DAUNTLESS [Sir Walter Scott]. Edinburgh, 1817. Boards. $275-350.

THE HASHEESH EATER [Fitz-Hugh Ludlow]. New York, 1857. $225-275.

HAWBUCK GRANGE; OR, THE SPORTING ADVENTURES OF THOMAS SCOTT ESQ. [Robert Smith Surtees]. London, 1847. Illustrated by Phiz. $275-350.

HEADLONG HALL [Thomas Love Peacock]. London, 1816. Boards. $550-650.

THE HEADSMAN [James Fenimore Cooper]. 3 vols. London, 1833. Boards. $650-800.

THE HEIDENMAUER; OR, THE BENEDICTINES [James Fenimore Cooper]. 3 vols. London, 1832. Boards. $450-525.

HENRIETTA TEMPLE: A LOVE STORY [Benjamin Disraeli]. 3 vols. London, 1837. $450-600.

HINTS TOWARD FORMING THE CHARACTER OF A YOUNG PRINCESS [Hannah Moore]. 2 vols. London, 1805. Boards. $175-225.

HISTORICAL SKETCH BOOK AND GUIDE TO NEW ORLEANS AND ENVIRONS [Lafcadio Hearn, et al.]. New York, 1885. Wrappers. $450-525.

HISTORY OF ALAMEDA COUNTY, CALIFORNIA [J. P. Munro-Fraser]. Oakland, Calif., 1883. $275-350.

HISTORY OF CRAWFORD AND RICHLAND COUNTIES, WISCONSIN [C. W. Butterfield and George A. Ogle]. Springfield, Ill., 1884. $125-150.

HISTORY OF THE DETECTION AND TRIAL OF JOHN A. MUREL, THE GREAT WESTERN LAND PIRATE [Augustus Q. J. Walton]. Lexington, Ky., 1835. Wrappers. $1,150 or more.

THE HISTORY OF HENRY ESMOND [William Makepeace Thackery]. 3 vols. London, 1852. $375-450.

A HISTORY OF THE INDIAN WARS WITH THE FIRST WHITE SETTLERS OF THE UNITED STATES [Daniel C. Sanders]. Montpelier, Vt., 1812. $550-650.

THE HISTORY OF JOHNNY QUAE GENUS [William Combe]. London, 1822. Wrappers. Illustrated by Thomas Rowlandson. $1,200 or more.

HISTORY OF THE LATE WAR IN THE EASTERN COUNTRY [Robert B. McAfee]. Lexington, Ky., 1816. Boards or leather. $450-600.

A HISTORY OF MADEIRA [William Combe]. London, 1821. $900-1,100.

HISTORY OF MARIN COUNTY, CALIFORNIA [J. P. Munro-Fraser]. San Francisco, 1880. $400-500.

HISTORY OF NEVADA COUNTY, CALIFORNIA [Frank L. Wells]. Oakland, Calif., 1880. $500-650.

HISTORY OF SAN JOAQUIN COUNTY, CALIFORNIA [Frank T. Gilbert]. Oakland, Calif., 1879. $450-600.

HISTORY OF SAN LUIS OBISPO COUNTY, CALIFORNIA [Myron Angel]. Oakland, Calif., 1883. $375-450.

HISTORY OF SANTA BARBARA AND VENTURA COUNTIES, CALIFORNIA [Jesse D. Mason]. Oakland, Calif., 1883. $175-225.

HISTORY OF A SIX WEEKS' TOUR THROUGH A PART OF FRANCE, SWITZERLAND, GERMANY, AND HOLLAND [Percy Bysshe Shelley]. London, 1817. Boards. $1,200 or more.

HOBOMOK, A TALE OF EARLY TIMES [Lydia Maria Child]. Boston, 1824. Boards. $300-400.

HOME AS FOUND. BY THE AUTHOR OF HOMEWARD BOUND [James Fenimore Cooper]. 2 vols. Philadelphia, 1838. $650-800.

HORSE-SHOE ROBINSON [John Pendleton Kennedy]. 2 vols. Philadelphia, 1835. $450-550.

HOW TO WIN IN WALL STREET [Joaquin Miller]. New York, 1881. $60-80.

THE HUMOURIST [George Cruikshank]. 4 vols. London, 1819-1820. Illustrated by Cruikshank. $850 or more.

THE HUNTERS OF KENTUCKY [Benjamin Bilson]. New York, 1847. Wrappers. $175-225.

HYMNS FOR INFANT MINDS [Ann and Jane Taylor]. Boston, 1814. Wrappers. $50-65.

HYPERION: A ROMANCE. BY THE AUTHOR OF "OUTRE-MER" [Henry Wadsworth Longfellow]. 2 vols. New York, 1839. Boards. $600-800.

AN IDEAL HUSBAND. BY THE AUTHOR OF LADY WINDERMERE'S FAN [Oscar Wilde]. London, 1899. Trade edition. $250-325.

IDLENESS AND INDUSTRY EXEMPLIFIED, IN THE HISTORY OF JAMES PRESTON AND IVY LAWRENCE [Maria Edgeworth]. Philadelphia, 1803. $175-225.

THE ILLINOIS CENTRAL RAILROAD COMPANY, OFFERS OVER 2,000,000 ACRES, ETC. [John Wilson]. New York, 1856. $150-200.

ILLINOIS IN 1837; A SKETCH [S. Augustus Mitchell]. Philadelphia, 1837. $150-175.

IMAGINARY CONVERSATIONS OF LITERARY MEN AND STATESMEN [Walter Savage Landor]. 2 vols. London, 1824. $175-225.

AN IMPARTIAL APPEAL TO THE REASON, INTEREST, AND PATRIOTISM OF THE PEOPLE OF ILLINOIS, ON THE INJURIOUS EFFECTS OF SLAVE LABOUR [Morris Birkbeck]. (Philadelphia), 1824. $2000 or more.

THE IMPARTIAL INQUIRER [John Lowell]. Boston, 1811. $60-80.

THE IMPORTANCE OF BEING EARNEST. BY THE AUTHOR OF LADY WINDERMERE'S FAN [Oscar Wilde]. London, 1899. $175-225.

INCIDENTAL NUMBERS [Elinor Wylie]. London, 1912. $4,000 or more.

INCIDENTS OF BORDER LIFE [Joseph Pritts]. Chambersburg, Pa., 1839. $100-125.

INDEX [Norman Douglas]. London, 1915. Wrappers. $85-100.

AN INDEX TO "IN MEMORIAM" [Charles L. Dodgson]. London, 1862. $350-425.

INDIAN COUNCIL IN THE VALLEY OF THE WALLA-WALLA [Lawrence Kip]. San Francisco, 1855. Wrappers. $850 or more.

INDIAN SUMMER [William Ellery Leonard]. (Madison, Wis., 1912), Wrappers. $45-60.

THE INDIANS: OR, NARRATIVES OF MASSACRES AND DEPREDATIONS, ETC. BY A DESCENDANT OF THE HUGUENOTS [Johannes H. Bevier]. Rondout, N.Y., 1846. $110-135.

THE INFIDEL; OR, THE FALL OF MEXICO [Robert Montgomery Bird]. 2 vols. Philadelphia, 1835. $650-800.

THE INHERITANCE [Susan Edmonstone Ferrier]. 3 vols. Edinburgh, 1824. $300-400.

IN MEMORIAM [Alfred, Lord Tennyson]. London, 1850. $350-425.

IRENE THE MISSIONARY [John W. DeForest]. Boston, 1879. $60-75.

IVANHOE: A ROMANCE [Sir Walter Scott]. 3 vols. Edinburgh, 1820. $1,700 or more.

JOAQUIN (THE CLAUDE DUVAL OF CALIFORNIA); OR, THE MARAUDER OF THE MINES [Henry L. Williams]. New York, (1865). Wrappers. $200-275.

JOHN BULL IN AMERICA; OR, THE NEW MUNCHAUSEN [James Kirk Paulding]. New York, 1825. $200-225.

JOHN HALIFAX, GENTLEMAN [Dinah M. Craik]. 3 vols. London, 1856. $700-850.

JOHN MARR AND OTHER SAILORS [Herman Melville]. New York, 1888. Wrappers. Limited edition of 25. $850.

JOHN WOODVIL: A TRAGEDY [Charles Lamb]. London, 1802. $625.

JONAH: CHRISTMAS, 1917 [Aldous Huxley]. Oxford, 1917. Limited edition of 50. $1,200.

JOURNAL HISTORIQUE DE L'ESTABLISSEMENT DES FRANCAIS A LA LOUISIANE [Bernard de la Harpe]. Nouvelle-Orleans, 1831. $400.

JOURNAL OF THE EXPEDITION OF DRAGOONS UNDER THE COMMAND OF COL. HENRY DODGE TO THE ROCKY MOUNTAINS DURING THE SUMMER OF 1835 [Lieutenant G. P. Kingsbury]. Washington, D.C., 1836. Maps. Wrappers, $325; Cloth, $225.

JOURNAL OF A TOUR AROUND HAWAII, THE LARGEST OF THE SANDWICH ISLANDS [William Ellis]. Boston, 1825. $750.

JUSTICE AND EXPEDIENCY; OR SLAVERY CONSIDERED WITH A VIEW TO ITS RIGHTFUL AND EFFECTUAL REMEDY, ABOLITION [John Greenleaf Whittier]. Haverhill, Mass., 1833. $525.

KEEP COOL [John Neal]. 2 vols. Baltimore, Md., 1817. $275.

THE KEMPTON-WACE LETTERS [Jack London and Anna Strunsky]. New York, 1903. $125.

KENILWORTH [Sir Walter Scott]. 3 vols. Edinburgh, 1821. $850.

THE KENTUCKIAN IN NEW YORK. BY A VIRGINIAN [W. A. Caruthers]. 2 vols. New York, 1834. $300.

KLOSTERHEIM: OR THE MASQUE. BY AN ENGLISH OPIUM EATER [Thomas de Quincey]. Edinburgh, 1832. $625.

KONINGSMARKE, THE LONG FINNE: A STORY OF THE NEW WORLD [James Kirk Paulding]. 2 vols. New York, 1823. $250.

LADIES ALMANACK. WRITTEN AND ILLUSTRATED BY A LADY OF FASHION [Djuna Barnes]. Paris, 1928. Wrappers. Limited edition of 1,000. $1,200.

LARA, A TALE. JACQUELINE, A TALE [George Gordon Noel, Lord Byron and Samuel Rogers]. London, 1814. $725.

THE LAST DAYS OF POMPEII [Edward Bulwer-Lytton]. 2 vols. New York, 1834. $250.

THE LAST MAN [Mary Wollstonecraft Shelley]. 3 vols. London, 1826. $1,200.

THE LAST OF THE MOHICANS. BY THE AUTHOR OF "THE PIONEERS" [James Fenimore Cooper]. 2 vols. Philadelphia, 1826. $6,500 or more.

LAWYERS AND LEGISLATORS, OR NOTES ON THE AMERICAN MINING COMPANIES [Benjamin Disraeli]. London, 1825. $175.

LEATHER STOCKING AND SILK [John E. Cooke]. New York, 1854. $325.

LEAVES FROM MARGARET SMITH'S JOURNAL [John Greenleaf Whittier]. Boston, 1849. Wrappers. $150.

LEGENDS OF THE CONQUEST OF SPAIN. BY THE AUTHOR OF "THE SKETCH BOOK" [Washington Irving]. Philadelphia, 1835. $450 or more.

LETTERS FROM THE SOUTH [James Kirk Paulding]. 2 vols. New York, 1817. $150.

LIFE AND ADVENTURES OF BRONCHO JOHN: HIS SECOND TRIP UP THE TRAIL, BY HIMSELF [John H. Sullivan]. Valparaiso, Ind., 1908. Wrappers. $165.

THE LIFE AND MOST SURPRISING ADVENTURES OF ROBINSON CRUSOE OF YORK, MARINER [Daniel Defoe]. Philadelphia, 1803. $225.

MACARIA; OR, ALTARS OF SACRIFICE [Augusta Jane Evans Wilson]. Richmond, Va., 1864. Wrappers. $450.

MAID MARIAN [Thomas Love Peacock]. London, 1822. $650.

MAJOR JONES'S COURTSHIP; OR ADVENTURES OF A CHRISTMAS EVE [William Tappan Thompson]. Savannah, Ga., 1850. Wrappers. $125.

MARTIN FABER, THE STORY OF A CRIMINAL [William Gilmore Simms]. 2 vols. New York, 1838. $375.

MELLICHAMPE: A LEGEND OF THE SANTEE [William Gilmore Simms]. 2 vols. New York, 1836. $475.

MEMORANDA: DEMOCRATIC VISTAS [Walt Whitman]. Washington, D.C., 1871. Wrappers. $650.

MERRY-MOUNT; A ROMANCE OF THE MASSACHUSETTS COLONY [John Lothrop Motley]. 2 vols. Boston, 1849. $125.

THE MERRY TALES OF THE THREE WISE MEN OF GOTHAM [James Kirk Paulding]. New York, 1826. $125.

THE NARRATIVE OF ARTHUR GORDON PYM [Edgar Allan Poe]. New York, 1838. $1,500 or more.

NARRATIVE OF THE CAPTURE AND BURNING OF FORT MASSACHUSETTS [Reverend John Norton]. Albany, N.Y., 1870. Limited edition of 100. $125.

NARRATIVE OF THE MASSACRE AT CHICAGO, AUGUST 15, 1812, AND SOME PRECEDING EVENTS [Mrs. Juliette A. Kinzie]. Chicago, 1844. Wrappers. $3,000 or more.

A NARRATIVE OF OCCURRENCES IN INDIAN COUNTRIES OF NORTH AMERICA [Samuel Hull Wilcocke]. London, 1807. Wrappers. $950.

NATURE [Ralph Waldo Emerson]. Boston, 1836. $950.

NAUTICAL REMINISCENCES. BY THE AUTHOR OF "A MARINER'S SKETCHES" [Nathaniel Ames]. Providence, R.I., 1832. $125.

THE NAVAL MONUMENT [Abel Bowen]. Boston, 1816. $325.

THE OAK OPENINGS; OR, THE BEE-HUNTER. BY THE AUTHOR OF "THE PIONEERS" [James Fenimore Cooper]. 2 vols. New York, 1848. Wrappers. $525.

OBSERVATIONS ON THE WISCONSIN TERRITORY [William Rudolph Smith]. Philadelphia, 1835. $525.

ODE TO NAPOLEON BUONOPARTE [George Gordon Noel, Lord Byron]. London, 1814. Wrappers. $1,500 or more.

THE OGILVIES [Dinah Maria Mulock]. 3 vols. London, 1849. $475.

ON THE PLAINS; OR, THE RACE FOR LIFE [Edward S. Ellis]. New York, 1863. Wrappers. $375.

ONTWA, THE SON OF THE FOREST: A POEM [Henry Whiting]. New York, 1832. $1,200 or more.

ORIGIN AND TRADITIONAL HISTORY OF THE WYANDOTTS [Peter D. Clarke]. Toronto, 1870. $125.

OSCEOLA; OR, FACT AND FICTION: A TALE OF THE SEMINOLE WAR. BY A SOUTHERNER [James Birchett Ransom]. New York, 1838. $325.

THE PARTISAN: A TALE OF THE REVOLUTION [William Gilmore Simms]. 2 vols. New York, 1835. $475.

PASSION-FLOWERS [Julia Ward Howe]. Boston, 1854. $275.

THE PATHFINDER: OR, THE INLAND SEA. BY THE AUTHOR OF "THE PIONEERS" [James Fenimore Cooper]. 2 vols. Philadelphia, 1840. $650.

PAULINE: A FRAGMENT OF A CONFESSION [Robert Browning]. London, 1833. $18,000 or more.

PELAYO: A STORY OF THE GOTH [William Gilmore Simms]. 2 vols. New York, 1838. $425.

PEN KNIFE SKETCHES; OR, CHIPS OFF THE OLD BLOCK [Alonzo Delano]. Sacramento, Calif., 1853. Wrappers. $650.

PERSONAL REMINESCENCES OF A MARYLAND SOLDIER [G. W. Booth]. Baltimore, Md., 1898. $175.

PHOTOGRAPHIC SKETCH BOOK OF THE WAR [Alexander Gardner]. 2 vols. Washington, D.C., 1865-1866. 100 gold-tone albumen prints. $17,000 or more.

PHYLOS THE TIBETIAN. AN EARTH DWELLER'S RETURN [Frederick S. Oliver]. Milwaukee, Wis., 1940. $85.

THE QUAKER PARTISANS [William Gilmore Simms]. Philadelphia, 1869. $275.

QUENTIN DURWARD [Sir Walter Scott]. 3 vols. Edinburgh, 1823. $1,000.

THE REDSKINS [James Fenimore Cooper]. 2 vols. New York, 1846. Wrappers. $1,250 or more.

THE REIGN OF TERROR IN KANZAS [Charles W. Briggs]. Boston, 1856. Wrappers. $675.

REMINISCENCES OF A CAMPAIGN IN MEXICO [John B. Robertson]. Nashville, Tenn., 1849. $300.

THE RESOURCES OF ARIZONA [Patrick Hamilton]. Florence, Ariz., 1881. Wrappers. $400.

RICHARD HURDIS; OR, THE AVENGER OF BLOOD [William Gilmore Simms]. 2 vols. Philadelphia, 1838. $425.

RICHMOND DURING THE WAR; FOUR YEARS OF PERSONAL OBSERVATION [Sally A. Brock]. New York, 1867. $150.

ROB OF THE BOWL [John Pendleton Kennedy]. 2 vols. Philadelphia, 1838. $375.

ROLLO LEARNING TO TALK [Jacob Abbott]. Philadelphia, 1841. $90.

SAN FRANCISCO BAY AND CALIFORNIA IN 1776 [Pedro Font]. Providence, R.I., 1911. $275.

SATANSTOE; OR, THE LITTLEPAGE MANUSCRIPTS [James Fenimore Cooper]. 2 vols. New York, 1845. Wrappers. $1,250 or more.

SCENES IN THE ROCKY MOUNTAINS, OREGON, CALIFORNIA, NEW MEXICO, TEXAS AND GRAND PRAIRIES. BY A NEW ENGLANDER [Rufus B. Sage]. Philadelphia, 1846. Cloth or wrappers. $900 or more.

SEVEN AND NINE YEARS AMONG THE CAMANCHES AND APACHES [Edwin Eastman]. Jersey City, N.J., 1873. $110.

SIMPLE TRUTHS IN VERSE, FOR THE AMUSEMENT AND INSTRUCTION OF CHILDREN, AT AN EARLY AGE [Mary Belson Elliot]. Baltimore, Md., ca. 1820. $75.

SIX TO ONE; A NANTUCKET IDYL [Edward Bellamy]. New York, 1878. $275.

TALES OF THE NORTHWEST; OR, SKETCHES OF INDIAN LIFE AND CHARACTER [William J. Snelling]. Boston, 1830. $425.

TALES OF TERROR; WITH AN INTRODUCTORY DIALOGUE [Matthew G. Lewis]. London, 1801. Wraps. $75.

TEN THOUSAND A YEAR [Samuel Warren]. 6 vols. Philadelphia, 1840-1841. $950.

THOUGHTS ON THE PROPOSED ANNEXATION OF TEXAS TO THE UNITED STATES [Theodore Sedgewick]. New York, 1844. Wrappers. $175.

A THOUSAND MILES IN A CANOE FROM DENVER TO LEAVENWORTH [W. A. Spencer]. Bushnell, Nebr., 1880. Wrappers. $425.

THE VAGABOND: A NEW STORY FOR CHILDREN [Samuel Griswold Goodrich]. Hartford, Conn., 1819. Wrappers. $165.

VIRGINIA ILLUSTRATED [David Hunter Strother]. New York, 1857. $165.

VIVIAN GREY [Benjamin Disraeli]. 5 vols. London, 1826. $650.

THE WAR IN FLORIDA [Woodburn Potter]. Baltimore, 1836. $325.

THE WAR IN TEXAS [Benjamin Lundy]. Philadelphia, 1836. Wrappers. $400.

WESTWARD HO! [James Kirk Paulding]. 2 vols. New York, 1832. $275.

-10-

Western Americana Books, and Their Values

This is one of the most popular collecting categories. From an investment standpoint, it is perhaps the most important. It sub-divides into numerous, smaller categories such as ranching, gun-fighting, Indian wars, exploration, railroads, stage coaching, or what have you.

Remember: condition is important. The values given here are for first-edition books in very good to fine condition, and with a dust jacket if the book was originally issued with one. "Points" often need to be verified to properly identify many of these books. A librarian or rare bookseller should be consulted for verification of edition and value.

AUTHOR	TITLE/EDITION INFORMATION/VALUE
Abbey, James	CALIFORNIA. A TRIP ACROSS THE PLAINS IN THE SPRING OF 1850. New Albany, (1850). 64 pp. Wrappers. $3,000-4,000.
Abbott, E. C., and Helena Huntington Smith	WE POINTED THEM NORTH. New York, (1939). $85-100.
Adams, Ramon	THE RAMPAGING HERD. Norman, Okla., 1959. $225-275.
Aken, David	PIONEERS OF THE BLACK HILLS. (Milwaukee, Wis., ca.1920). $100-125.
Aldridge, Reginald	LIFE ON A RANCH. New York, 1884. Wrappers. $250-500.
Allan, J. T.	CENTRAL AND WESTERN NEBRASKA, AND THE EXPERIENCES OF ITS STOCK

AUTHOR	**TITLE/EDITION INFORMATION/VALUE**
	GROWERS. Omaha, Nebr., 1883. Wrappers. $225-275.
Alter, J.	JAMES BRIDGER: TRAPPER, FRONTIERSMAN, SCOUT, AND GUIDE. Salt Lake City, Utah, (1925). $150-200.
Applegate, Jesse	A DAY WITH THE COW COLUMN IN 1843. Chicago, 1934. $85-110.
Armour, Samuel	HISTORY OF ORANGE COUNTY, CALIFORNIA. Los Angeles, 1921. $125-145.
Bailey, Washington	A TRIP TO CALIFORNIA IN 1853. LeRoy, Ill., 1915. Wrappers. $350-450.
Bandini, Joseph	A DESCRIPTION OF CALIFORNIA IN 1828. Berkeley, Calif., 1951. $85-100.
Banta, William, and J. W. Caldwell, Jr.	TWENTY-SEVEN YEARS ON THE FRONTIER, OR FIFTY YEARS IN TEXAS. Austin, Tex., 1893. $1,800 or more.
Barreiro, Antonio	OJEADA SOBRE NUEVO-MEXICO. Puebla, Mexico, 1832. $850-1,100.
Bartlett, John Russell	PERSONAL NARRATIVE OF EXPLORATIONS AND INCIDENTS IN TEXAS, NEW MEXICO, CALIFORNIA, ETC. New York, 1854. Folding map. 44 plates. $550-750.
Bass, W. W., editor	ADVENTURES IN THE CANYONS OF THE COLORADO BY TWO OF ITS EARLIEST EXPLORERS, JAMES WHITE AND H. W. HAWKINS. Grand Canyon, 1920. Wrappers. $175-225.
Baylies, Francis	A NARRATIVE OF GENERAL WOOL'S CAMPAIGN IN MEXICO. Albany, N.Y., 1851. $350-500.
Becker, Robert H.	DESIGNS ON THE LAND: DISENOS OF CALIFORNIA RANCHOS. San Francisco, 1964. $175-450.
Beechey, F. W.	AN ACCOUNT OF A VISIT TO CALIFORNIA. (San Francisco, 1941). $175-225.

AUTHOR	TITLE/EDITION INFORMATION/VALUE
Benedict, Carl Peters	A TENDERFOOT KID ON GYP WATER. Austin, Tex., 1943. $175-225.
Benson, Henry C.	LIFE AMONG THE CHOCTAW INDIANS. Cincinnati, 1860. $225-300.
Benton, Frank	COWBOY LIFE ON THE SIDETRACK. Denver, (1903). $125-175.
Biggers, Don H.	FROM CATTLE RANGE TO COTTON PATCH. Abilene, Kans., (ca. 1908). Wrappers. $450-600.
(Biographical)	BIOGRAPHICAL SOUVENIR OF THE STATE OF TEXAS. Chicago, 1889. At least $1,200.
Bonnell, George W.	TOPOGRAPHICAL DESCRIPTION OF TEXAS. Austin, Tex., 1840. $2,200-3,500.
Bonner, T. D.	THE LIFE AND ADVENTURES OF JAMES P. BECKWOURTH, MOUNTAINEER, SCOUT AND PIONEER, ETC. New York, 1856. $225-275.
Brady, William	GLIMPSES OF TEXAS. Houston, 1871. Wrappers or cloth. $1,200-1,500.
Braman, D. E. E.	INFORMATION ABOUT TEXAS. Philadelphia, 1857. $450-600.
(Brand)	BRAND BOOK OF THE WESTERN SOUTH DAKOTA STOCK GROWERS' ASSOCIATION. Omaha, Nebr., (1901). $275-325.
(Brief)	A BRIEF DESCRIPTION OF WESTERN TEXAS [W. G. Kingsbury]. San Antonio, Tex., 1873. $650-800.
Brown, Samuel R.	THE WESTERN GAZETTEER, OR EMIGRANT'S DIRECTORY. Auburn, 1817. $500-750.
Brown, William C.	THE SHEEPEATER CAMPAIGN IN IDAHO. Boise, 1926. Map. Wrappers. $250-325.
Browne, J. Ross	ADVENTURES IN THE APACHE COUNTRY. New York, 1869. $175-250.

AUTHOR	TITLE/EDITION INFORMATION/VALUE
Bruffey, George A.	EIGHTY-ONE YEARS IN THE WEST. Butte, Mont., 1925. Wrappers. $85-100.
Bryant, Edwin	WHAT I SAW IN CALIFORNIA. New York, 1848. $300-400.
Buffum, E. Gould	SIX MONTHS IN THE GOLD MINES. Philadelphia, 1850. Wrappers or cloth. $500-650.
Burns, John H.	MEMOIRS OF A COW PONY. Boston, (1906). $275-350.
Burton, Harley	A HISTORY OF THE JA RANCH. Austin, Tex., 1928. $450-600.
Calhoun, James S.	OFFICIAL CORRESPONDENCE OF JAMES S. CALHOUN WHILE INDIAN AGENT AT SANTA FE. Washington, 1815. $125-150.
Campbell, J. L.	IDAHO AND MONTANA GOLD REGIONS. Chicago, 1965. $1,700 and up.
Campbell, J. L.	THE GREAT AGRICULTURAL and MINERAL WEST. Chicago, 1866. Wrappers. $1,700 or more.
Canfield, Chauncey L., editor	THE DIARY OF A FORTY-NINER. San Francisco, 1906. $125-175.
Cannon, George Q.	WRITINGS FROM THE "WESTERN STANDARD." PUBLISHED IN SAN FRANCISCO. Liverpool, England, 1864. $125-175.
Capron, Elisha S.	HISTORY OF CALIFORNIA. Boston, 1854. $85-125.
Carey, C. H.	HISTORY OF OREGON. Chicago, 1922. $60-85.
Carr, John	PIONEER DAYS IN CALIFORNIA. Eureka, Calif., 1891. $125-150.
Carroll, H. Bailey	THE TEXAN SANTA FE TRAIL. Canyon, Tex., 1951. Boxed. $85-100.
Carson, James H.	LIFE IN CALIFORNIA. Tarrytown, N.Y., 1931. $50-65.

AUTHOR	TITLE/EDITION INFORMATION/VALUE
Carstarphen, J. E.	MY TRIP TO CALIFORNIA. Louisiana, Mo., 1914. $100-125.
Carter, Robert G.	MASSACRE OF SALT CREEK PRAIRIE AND THE COW-BOY'S VERDICT. Washington, 1919. Wrappers. At least $350.
Carter, Robert G.	PURSUIT OF KICKING BIRD: A CAMPAIGN IN THE TEXAS "BAD LANDS." Washington, 1920. Wrappers. $300 or more.
Carter, W. A.	HISTORY OF FANNIN COUNTY, TEXAS. Bonham, Tex., 1885. $900 or more.
Castenada, Carlos E.	OUR CATHOLIC HERITAGE IN TEXAS, 1519-1810. 5 vols. Austin, Tex., 1936-42. $750 or more.
Cates, Cliff D.	PIONEER HISTORY OF WISE COUNTY, TEXAS. Decatur, Tex., 1907. Wrappers. $225-300.
Celiz, Fray Francisco	DIARY OF THE ALARCON EXPEDITION INTO TEXAS, 1718-1719. Los Angeles, 1935. $150-200.
Chamisso, Adelbert von	A SOJOURN AT SAN FRANCISCO BAY 1816. San Francisco, 1936. $150-175.
Chase, Charles M.	THE EDITOR'S RUN IN NEW MEXICO AND COLORADO. Lyndon, Vt., 1882. Wrappers. $225-300.
Child, Andrew	OVERLAND ROUTE TO CALIFORNIA. Milwaukee, Wis., 1852. At least $5,000.
Chittenden, Hiram	THE AMERICAN FUR TRADE OF THE FAR WEST. 3 vols. New York, 1902. $375-450.
Clappe, Louise A. K. S.	CALIFORNIA IN 1851; 1852: THE DAME SHIRLEY LETTERS. 2 vols. San Francisco, 1933. $100-150.
Clark, Charles M.	A TRIP TO PIKE'S PEAK AND NOTES BY THE WAY. Chicago, 1861. $650 or more.
Clark, Stanley	THE LIFE AND ADVENTURES OF THE AMERICAN COWBOY. (Providence, R.I.), 1897. $150-175.

AUTHOR	TITLE/EDITION INFORMATION/VALUE
Clarke, A. B.	TRAVELS IN MEXICO AND CALIFORNIA. Boston, 1852. Wrappers. $800 or more.
Clay, John	MY LIFE ON THE RANGE. Chicago, (1924). $200-250.
Clum, Woodworth	APACHE AGENT: THE STORY OF JOHN P. CLUM. Boston, 1936. $60-85.
Cobbett, Thomas B.	COLORADO MINING DIRECTORY. Denver, 1879. $450 and up.
Coke, Henry J.	A RIDE OVER THE ROCKY MOUNTAINS TO OREGON AND CALIFORNIA. London, 1852. $175-225.
Collins, Mrs. Nat	THE CATTLE QUEEN OF MONTANA. St. James, Minn., 1893. Wrappers. $1,100 or more.
Colton, Walter	THREE YEARS IN CALIFORNIA. New York, 1850. $175-225.
Conklin, E.	PICTURESQUE ARIZONA. New York, 1878. $200-250.
Connelley, William E.	WILD BILL AND HIS ERA. New York, 1933. $85-100.
(Constitution)	THE CONSTITUTION OF THE REPUBLIC OF MEXICO AND THE STATE OF COAHUILA AND TEXAS. New York, 1832. $1,100 or more.
(Constitution)	CONSTITUTION OF THE STATE OF WEST TEXAS. Austin, Tex., (1868). Wrappers. $650 or more.
Cook, D. J.	HANDS UP, OR 20 YEARS OF DETECTIVE LIFE IN THE MOUNTAINS AND ON THE PLAINS. Denver, 1882. $275-325.
Cook, James H.	FIFTY YEARS ON THE OLD FRONTIER. New Haven, Conn., 1923. $60-75.
Cooke, Philip St. George	THE CONQUEST OF NEW MEXICO AND CALIFORNIA. New York, 1878. $175-250.
Costanso, Miguel	THE SPANISH OCCUPATION OF CALIFORNIA. San Francisco, 1934. $175-225.

AUTHOR	TITLE/EDITION INFORMATION/VALUE
Couts, Cave J.	FROM SAN DIEGO TO THE COLORADO IN 1849. Los Angeles, 1932. $125-175.
Cowan, Robert E.	A BIBLIOGRAPHY OF THE HISTORY OF CALIFORNIA AND THE PACIFIC WEST, 1510-1906. San Francisco, 1914. At least $350.
Cox, Isaac	THE ANNALS OF TRINITY COUNTY. San Francisco, 1940. $65-85.
Cox, James	HISTORICAL AND BIOGRAPHICAL RECORD OF THE CATTLE INDUSTRY AND THE CATTLEMAN OF TEXAS AND ADJACENT TERRITORY. St. Louis, 1895. $3,200 and up.
Cox, Ross	ADVENTURES ON THE COLUMBIA RIVER. 2 vols. London, 1831. $800 or more.
Coy, Owen C.	PICTORIAL HISTORY OF CALIFORNIA. Berkeley, Calif., 1925. $110-125.
Cremony, John C.	LIFE AMONG THE APACHES. San Francisco, 1868. $225-250.
Creuzbaur, Robert, compiler	ROUTE FROM THE GULF OF MEXICO AND THE LOWER MISSISSIPPI VALLEY TO CALIFORNIA AND THE PACIFIC OCEAN. New York, 1849. $4,500 or more.
Crocket, George L.	TWO CENTURIES IN EAST TEXAS. Dallas, (ca.1932). $175-225.
Cuming, F.	SKETCHES OF A TOUR TO THE WESTERN COUNTRY. Pittsburgh, Pa., 1810. $350-450.
Cunningham, Eugene	FAMOUS IN THE WEST. El Paso, Tex., 1926. Wrappers. $175-225.
Cunningham, Eugene	TRIGGERNOMETRY: A GALLERY OF GUNFIGHTERS. New York, 1934. $100-150.
Curtiss, Daniel S.	WESTERN PORTRAITURE, AND EMIGRANTS' GUIDE. New York, 1852. $225-275.
Cutts, James M.	THE CONQUEST OF CALIFORNIA AND NEW MEXICO. Philadelphia, 1847. $175-225.

AUTHOR	TITLE/EDITION INFORMATION/VALUE
Dale, Edward Everett	THE RANGE CATTLE INDUSTRY. Norman, Okla., 1930. $175-225.
Damon, Samuel C.	A JOURNEY TO LOWER OREGON AND UPPER CALIFORNIA, 1848-49. San Francisco, 1927. $150-200.
Dana, Edmund	GEOGRAPHICAL SKETCHES ON THE WESTERN COUNTRY; DESIGNED FOR EMIGRANTS AND SETTLERS. Cincinnati, 1819. $450-600.
Darby, William	THE EMIGRANT'S GUIDE TO THE WESTERN AND SOUTHWESTERN STATES AND TERRITORIES. New York, 1818. $350-450.
David, Ellis	A COMMERCIAL ENCYCLOPEDIA OF THE PACIFIC SOUTHWEST. Oakland, Calif., 1915. $125-150.
Davidson, Gordon Charles	THE NORTH WEST COMPANY. Berkeley, Calif., 1918. $125-150.
Davis, William Heath	SIXTY YEARS IN CALIFORNIA. San Francisco, 1889. $250-300.
Davis, William W. H.	EL GRINGO; OR NEW MEXICO AND HER PEOPLE. New York, 1857. $150-225.
Davis, William W. H.	THE SPANISH CONQUEST OF NEW MEXICO: 1527-1703. Doylestown, 1869. $175-225.
Dawson, Nicholas	CALIFORNIA IN '41. TEXAS IN '51. MEMOIRS. (Austin, Tex., ca. 1910). $600-750.
Dawson, Thomas F., and F. J. V. Skiff	THE UTE WAR: A HISTORY OF THE WHITE RIVER MASSACRE, ETC. Denver, 1879. Wrappers. At least $2,000.
De Barthe, Joe	THE LIFE AND ADVENTURES OF FRANK GROUARD, CHIEF OF SCOUTS. St. Joseph, Mo., (1894). $275-325.
De Cordova, J.	TEXAS: HER RESOURCES AND HER PUBLIC MEN. Philadelphia, 1858. $400-500.

AUTHOR	TITLE/EDITION INFORMATION/VALUE
De Cordova, J.	THE TEXAS IMMIGRANT AND TRAVELLER'S GUIDE BOOK. Austin, Tex., 1856. $400 or more.
Delay, Peter J.	HISTORY OF YUBA AND SUTTER COUNTIES, CALIFORNIA. Los Angeles, 1924. $125-175.
Denny, Arthur	PIONEER DAYS ON PUGET SOUND. Seattle, Wash., 1888. $100 or more.
(Depredations)	DEPREDATIONS AND MASSACRE BY THE SNAKE RIVER INDIANS. (Washington, D.C.), 1861. $125-150.
De Quille, Dan (William Wright)	HISTORY OF THE BIG BONANZA. Hartford, Conn., 1876. $125-150.
De Quille, Dan (William Wright)	A HISTORY OF THE COMSTOCK SILVER LODE AND MINES. Virginia City, Nev., (1889). $175-225.
De Wolff, J. H.	PAWNEE BILL (MAJ. GORDON W. LILLIE): HIS EXPERIENCE AND ADVENTURES ON THE WESTERN PLAINS. N.p., 1902. $150-175.
Dexter, A. Hersey	EARLY DAYS IN CALIFORNIA. (Denver), 1886. $225-275.
Dimsdale, Thomas J.	THE VIGILANTES OF MONTANA. Virginia City, Mont., 1866. $1,700 or more.
Disturnell, John, publisher	THE EMIGRANT'S GUIDE TO NEW MEXICO, CALIFORNIA, AND OREGON. New York, 1849. $800 or more.
Dobie, J. Frank	THE FIRST CATTLE IN TEXAS AND THE SOUTHWEST. Austin, Tex., 1939. $100-125.
Dobie, J. Frank	GUIDE TO LIFE AND LITERATURE OF THE SOUTHWEST. Austin, Tex., 1943. Wrappers. $45-75.
Dodge, Grenville M.	UNION PACIFIC RAILROAD, REPORT OF G. M. DODGE, CHIEF ENGINEER, TO THE BOARD OF DIRECTORS. TO IDAHO, MONTANA, OREGON, AND

AUTHOR	TITLE/EDITION INFORMATION/VALUE
	PUGET'S SOUND. Washington, 1869. Wrappers. $350 or more.
Dodge, Richard Irving	THE PLAINS OF THE GREAT WEST AND THEIR INHABITANTS. New York, 1877. $100-125.
Donoho, M. H.	CIRCLE-DOT, A TRUE STORY OF COW-BOY LIFE 40 YEARS AGO. Topeka, Kans., 1907. $85-100.
Douglas, C. L.	CATTLE KINGS OF TEXAS. Dallas, (1939). $100 or more; also a limited edition: $350 or more.
Douglas, C. L.	FAMOUS TEXAS FEUDS. Dallas, (1936). $125-150.
Downie, William	HUNTING FOR GOLD: PERSONAL EXPERIENCES IN THE EARLY DAYS ON THE PACIFIC COAST. San Francisco, 1893. $175-225.
(Draft)	DRAFT OF A CONSTITUTION PUB-LISHED UNDER THE DIRECTION OF A COMMITTEE OF CITIZENS OF COLO-RADO. Denver, 1875. At least $175.
(Dragoon)	DRAGOON CAMPAIGNS TO THE ROCKY MOUNTAINS. BY A DRAGOON [James Hildreth]. New York, 1836. $350-450.
Drake, Benjamin	THE LIFE AND ADVENTURES OF BLACK HAWK. Cincinnati, 1838. $175-225.
Drannan, Captain William F.	THIRTY-ONE YEARS ON THE PLAINS AND IN THE MOUNTAINS. Chicago, 1899. $175-225.
Driggs, George W.	OPENING OF THE MISSISSIPPI; OR TWO YEARS' CAMPAIGNING IN THE SOUTH-WEST. Madison, Wis., 1864. $175-225.
Duflot de Mofras, Eugene	EXPLORATION DU TERRITOIRE DE L'OREGON. 2 vols. Paris, 1844. $3,750 or more.
Duflot de Mofras, Eugene	TRAVELS ON THE PACIFIC COAST. 2 vols. Santa Ana, Calif., 1937. $175-225.

AUTHOR	TITLE/EDITION INFORMATION/VALUE
Dunn, John	HISTORY OF THE OREGON TERRITORY AND BRITISH NORTH-AMERICAN FUR TRADE. London, 1844. $500 or more.
Dunn, John	THE OREGON TERRITORY AND THE BRITISH NORTH-AMERICAN FUR TRADE. Philadelphia, 1845. Wrappers. $350.
Duval, John C.	EARLY TIMES IN TEXAS. Austin, Tex., 1892. $175-225.
Dwinelle, John W.	THE COLONIAL HISTORY OF THE CITY OF SAN FRANCISCO. San Francisco, 1863. $675 or more.
Dyer, Mrs. D. B.	"FORT RENO," OR PICTURUSQUE "CHEYENNE AND ARRAPAHOE ARMY LIFE," BEFORE THE OPENING OF OKLAHOMA. New York, 1896. $175-225.
Edelman, George W.	A GUIDE TO THE VALUE OF CALIFORNIA GOLD. Philadelphia, 1850. $1,500 or more.
Edward, David B.	THE HISTORY OF TEXAS. Cincinnati, 1836. $450 and up.
Edwards, Frank S.	A CAMPAIGN IN NEW MEXICO WITH COL. DONIPHAN. Philadelphia, 1847. Wrappers. $350-450.
Edwards, Philip Leget	CALIFORNIA IN 1837. Sacramento, Calif., 1890. Wrappers. $175-225.
Edwards, Philip Leget	SKETCH OF THE OREGON TERRITORY; OR, THE EMIGRANT'S GUIDE. Liberty, Mo., 1842. Wrappers. $5,500—perhaps much more.
Edwards, W. F., publisher	W. F. EDWARDS' TOURISTS' GUIDE AND DIRECTORY OF THE TRUCKEE BASIN. Truckee, Calif., 1883. $500 or more.
Elliott, W. W.	HISTORY OF THE ARIZONA TERRITORY. San Francisco, 1884. $850-1,000.

AUTHOR	TITLE/EDITION INFORMATION/VALUE
Ellis, Edward S.	THE LIFE AND TIMES OF CHRISTOPHER CARSON. New York, (1861). $100-125.
Emmons, Samuel Franklin	GEOLOGY AND MINING INDUSTRY OF LEADVILLE, COLORADO. 2 vols. Washington, 1883. $350-425.
Englehardt, Zephyrin	THE FRANCISCANS OF ARIZONA. Harbor Springs, Mich., 1899. Wrappers. $225-275.
Englehardt, Zephyrin	THE FRANCISCANS IN CALIFORNIA. Harbor Springs, Mich., 1897. Wrappers. $225-275.
Esshom, Frank	PIONEERS AND PROMINENT MEN OF UTAH. Salt Lake City, Utah, 1913. $110-135.
(Ethnologic)	AN ETHNOLOGIC DICTIONARY OF THE NAVAJO LANGUAGE, BY THE FRANCISCAN FATHERS. St. Michaels, Ariz., 1910. Wrappers. $600-750.
Evans, Elwood	PUGET SOUND: ITS PAST, PRESENT AND FUTURE. Olympia, Wash., 1869. Wrappers. $225-275.
Evans, Elwood	WASHINGTON TERRITORY. Olympia, Wash., 1877. Wrappers. $275-325.
Evans, Estwick	A PEDESTRIOUS TOUR, OF 4,000 MILES, THROUGH THE WESTERN STATES AND TERRITORIES. Concord, N.H., 1819. $650 or more.
(Evidence)	EVIDENCE CONCERNING PROJECTED RAILWAYS ACROSS THE SIERRA NEVADA MOUNTAINS. Carson City, Nev., 1865. $800 or more.
Ewell, Thomas T.	A HISTORY OF HOOD COUNTY, TEXAS. Granbury, Tex., 1895. $600-800.
(Facts)	FACTS CONCERNING THE CITY OF SAN DIEGO, THE GREAT SOUTHWESTERN SEA-PORT OF THE UNITED STATES, WITH A MAP SHOWING THE

AUTHOR	TITLE/EDITION INFORMATION/VALUE
	CITY AND ITS SURROUNDINGS. San Diego, Calif., (1888). Wrappers. $225-300.
Fairfield, Asa Merrill	FAIRFIELD'S PIONEER HISTORY OF LASSEN COUNTY, CALIFORNIA. San Francisco, (1916). $175-225.
Falconer, Thomas	LETTERS AND NOTES ON THE TEXAN SANTA FE EXPEDITION, 1841-1842. New York, 1930. $175-225.
Falconer, Thomas	ON THE DISCOVERY OF THE MISSISSIPPI, AND ON, OREGON, AND NORTHWESTERN BOUNDARY OF THE UNITED STATES. London, 1844. $575-750.
Farnham, S. B.	THE NEW YORK AND IDAHO GOLD MINING CO. New York, 1864. $225-300.
Farnham, Thomas J.	HISTORY OF OREGON TERRITORY. New York, 1844. Wrappers. $225-300.
Farnham, Thomas J.	TRAVELS IN THE CALIFORNIAS. New York, 1844. $1,750 or more.
Farnham, Thomas J.	TRAVELS IN THE GREAT WESTERN PRAIRIES. Poughkeepsie, N.Y., 1841. $550-650.
Finley, Ernest L.	HISTORY OF SONOMA COUNTY. Santa Rosa, Calif., 1937. $85-100.
Fleming, E. B.	EARLY HISTORY OF HOPKINS COUNTY, TEXAS. N.p., 1902. $400-500.
Flint, Timothy	INDIAN WARS OF THE WEST. Cincinnati, 1833. $225-300.
Foote, Henry Stuart	TEXAS AND THE TEXANS. 2 vols. Philadelphia, 1841. $500-650.
Forbes, Alexander	CALIFORNIA: A HISTORY. London, 1839. $550-650.
Foreman, Grant	PIONEER DAYS IN THE EARLY SOUTHWEST. Cleveland, 1926. $125-175.
Forney, Colonel John W.	WHAT I SAW IN TEXAS. Philadelphia, (1872). Wrappers. $275-350.

AUTHOR	TITLE/EDITION INFORMATION/VALUE
Forrest, Earle R.	MISSIONS AND PUEBLOS OF THE OLD SOUTHWEST. Cleveland, 1929. $175-225.
Foster, Charles	THE GOLD PLACERS OF CALIFORNIA. Akron, Ohio, 1849. Wrappers. $3,000-3,750.
Foster, George G., editor	THE GOLD REGIONS OF CALIFORNIA. New York, 1848. Wrappers. $350-500.
Foster, Isaac	THE FOSTER FAMILY, CALIFORNIA PIONEERS. (Santa Barbara, Calif., 1925). $125-150.
Fountain, Albert J.	BUREAU OF IMMIGRATION OF THE TERRITORY OF NEW MEXICO: REPORT OF DONA ANA COUNTY. Santa Fe, N. Mex., 1882. Wrappers. $175-225.
Fremont, John Charles	OREGON AND CALIFORNIA: THE EXPLORING EXPEDITION TO THE ROCKY MOUNTAINS, OREGON, AND CALIFORNIA. Buffalo, N.Y., 1849. $85.
French, Captain W. J.	WILD JIM, THE TEXAS COWBOY AND SADDLE KING. Antioch, Ill., 1890. Wrappers. $450-600.
French, William	SOME RECOLLECTIONS OF A WESTERN RANCHMAN. London, (1927). $400-450.
Fridge, Ike	HISTORY OF THE CHISUM WAR. COWBOY LIFE ON THE FRONTIER. Electra, Tex., (1927). Wrappers. $450 or more.
Frink, Margaret A.	JOURNAL OF THE ADVENTURES OF A PARTY OF CALIFORNIA GOLD-SEEKERS. (Oakland, Calif., 1897). $450-600.
Frost, John	HISTORY OF THE STATE OF CALIFORNIA. Auburn, Calif., 1850. $175-225.
Frost, John	THE MEXICAN WAR AND ITS WARRIORS. New Haven, Conn., 1849. $250-300.
Fry, Frederick	FRY'S TRAVELER'S GUIDE, AND DESCRIPTIVE JOURNAL OF THE GREAT NORTHWESTERN TERRITORIES. Cincinnati, 1865. $550-650.

AUTHOR	**TITLE/EDITION INFORMATION/VALUE**
Fulmore, Z. T.	THE HISTORY AND GEOGRAPHY OF TEXAS AS TOLD IN COUNTY NAMES. (Austin, Tex., 1915). $125-175.
Gallagher James	THE WESTERN SKETCH-BOOK. Boston, 1850. $175-225.
Gallatin, Albert	LETTERS OF ALBERT GALLATIN ON THE OREGON QUESTION. Washington, 1846. $100-125.
Gard, Wayne	ALONG THE EARLY TRAILS OF THE SOUTHWEST. Austin, Tex., 1969. Limited and signed edition. $175-225.
Garland, Hamlin	THE BOOK OF THE AMERICAN INDIAN. New York, 1923. 34 plates by Frederic Remington. $175-250.
Garrard, Lewis H.	WAH-TO-YAH, AND THE TAOS TRAIL. Cincinnati, 1850. $650-800.
Garrett, Pat F.	THE AUTHENTIC LIFE OF BILLY, THE KID. Santa Fe, N. Mex., 1882. Wrappers. $4,250 or more.
(Gem)	A GEM: "THE CITY OF THE PLAINS." ABILENE: THE CENTRE OF THE "GOLDEN BELT." Burlington, Iowa, 1887. Wrappers. $100-125.
(Geological)	GEOLOGICAL SURVEY OF TEXAS: FIRST ANNUAL REPORT. Austin, Tex., 1890. $350 or more.
Gerstaecker, Friedrich	CALIFORNIA GOLD MINES. Oakland, Calif., 1946. Signed. $100-125.
Gerstaecker, Friedrich	SCENES OF LIFE IN CALIFORNIA. San Francisco, 1942. Limited edition. $85-110.
Giddings, Marsh	FIRST ANNUAL MESSAGE TO THE LEGISLATIVE ASSEMBLY OF THE TERRITORY OF NEW MEXICO. Santa Fe, N. Mex., 1871. Wrappers. $150-200.
Gillett, James B.	SIX YEARS WITH THE TEXAS RANGERS. Austin, Tex., (1921). $125-150.

AUTHOR	TITLE/EDITION INFORMATION/VALUE
Gilmor, Harry	FOUR YEARS IN THE SADDLE. New York, 1866. $85-100.
(Gold)	GOLD, SILVER, LEAD, AND COPPER MINES OF ARIZONA. (Philadelphia, 1867). Wrappers. $550 or more.
Goldsmith, Oliver	OVERLAND IN FORTY-NINE. Detroit, 1896. $950 or more.
Goodnight, Charles, III	THE LOVING BRAND BOOK. Austin, Tex., 1965. Limited edition. $275.
Goodyear, W. A.	THE COAL MINES OF THE WESTERN COAST OF THE UNITED STATES. San Francisco, 1877. $125-150.
Gordon, Samuel	RECOLLECTIONS OF OLD MILESTOWN, MONTANA. Miles City, Mont., 1918. $175-200.
Gouge, William M.	THE FISCAL HISTORY OF TEXAS. Philadelphia, 1852. $175-225.
Gould, Stephen	THE ALAMO CITY GUIDE. (San Antonio, Tex.), 1882. Wrappers. At least $1,000.
Gove, Captain Jesse A.	THE UTAH EXPEDITION, 1857-58. Concord, 1928. $65-80.
Graham, W. A.	MAJOR RENO VINDICATED. Hollywood, Calif., 1935. Wrappers. $85-100.
Grant, Blanche C., editor	KIT CARSON'S OWN STORY. Taos, N. Mex., 1926. Wrappers. $85-100.
Graves, Richard S.	OKLAHOMA OUTLAWS. (Oklahoma City, 1915). Wrappers. $65-80.
Greeley, Horace	AN OVERLAND JOURNEY FROM NEW YORK TO SAN FRANCISCO. New York, 1860. $85-100.
Green, Ben K.	THE COLOR OF HORSES. Flagstaff, Ariz., (1974). Trade edition. $40-50.
Green, Ben K.	THE LAST TRAIL DRIVE THROUGH DOWNTOWN DALLAS. Flagstaff, Ariz., (1971). Trade edition. $30-35.

AUTHOR	TITLE/EDITION INFORMATION/VALUE
Green, Jonathan S.	JOURNAL OF A TOUR ON THE NORTHWEST COAST OF AMERICA IN THE YEAR 1829. New York, 1915. Limited edition. $325-375.
Green, Thomas J.	JOURNAL OF THE TEXIAN EXPEDITION AGAINST MIER. New York, 1845. $400-500.
Greenhow, Robert	THE GEOGRAPHY OF OREGONGE AND CALIFORNIA. Boston, 1845. Wrappers. $350-400.
Greenhow, Robert	THE HISTORY OF OREGON AND CALIFORNIA. Boston, 1844. $200-250.
Greer, James K.	BOIS D'ARC TO BARB'D WIRE. Dallas, 1936. $175-225.
Greer, James K.	COLONEL JACK HAYES: TEXAS FRONTIER LEADER AND CALIFORNIA BUILDER. New York, 1952. $125-150.
Greer, James K., editor	A TEXAS RANGER AND FRONTIERSMAN. Dallas, 1932. $110-135.
Gregory, Joseph W.	GREGORY'S GUIDE FOR CALIFORNIA TRAVELLERS VIA THE ISTHMUS OF PANAMA. New York, 1850. Wrappers. $1,750 or more.
Gregory, Samuel	HISTORY OF MEXICO; WITH AN ACCOUNT OF THE TEXAN REVOLUTION. Boston, 1847. Wrappers. $175-225.
Grinnell, George Bird	TWO GREAT SCOUTS AND THEIR PAWNEE BATTALION. Cleveland, 1928. $75-100.
Griswold, N. W.	BEAUTIES OF CALIFORNIA. San Francisco, 1883. Wrappers. $175-225.
Grover, La Fayette, editor	THE OREGON ARCHIVES. Salem, Oreg., 1853. $850-1,000.
Gunn, Douglas	SAN DIEGO: CLIMATE, RESOURCES, TOPOGRAPHY, PRODUCTION, ETC. San Diego, Calif., 1886. Wrappers. $450 or more.

AUTHOR	TITLE/EDITION INFORMATION/VALUE
Hafen, Le Roy R., editor	THE MOUNTAIN MEN AND THE FUR TRADE OF THE FAR WEST. 10 vols. Glendale, Calif., 1965-1972. $400-500.
Hafen, Le Roy R.	THE OVERLAND MAIL, 1849-1869. Cleveland, 1926. $75-100.
Hafen, Le Roy R.	OVERLAND ROUTES TO THE GOLD FIELDS. Glendale, Calif., 1942. $60-75.
Hafen, Le Roy R.	THE OLD SPANISH TRAIL. Glendale, Calif., 1954. $30-40.
Hafen, Le Roy R. and Ann W., editors	THE FAR WEST AND THE ROCKIES, 1820-75. 15 vols. Glendale, Calif., 1954-1961. $400-500.
Hafen, Le Roy R., and W. J. Ghent	BROKEN HAND: THE LIFE STORY OF THOMAS FITZPATRICK, CHIEF OF THE MOUNTAIN MEN. Denver, 1931. Limited and signed edition. $275-325.
Hafen, Le Roy R., and Francis Marion Young	FORT LARAMIE AND THE PAGEANT OF THE WEST, 1834-1890. Glendale, Calif., 1938. $60-75.
Hale, Edward Everett	A TRACT FOR THE DAY: HOW TO CONQUER TEXAS BEFORE TEXAS CONQUERS US. Boston, 1845. Wrappers. $175 or more.
Hale, John	CALIFORNIA AS IT IS. San Francisco, 1954. Limited edition. $200-225.
Hale, Will (William Hale Stone)	TWENTY-FOUR YEARS A COWBOY AND RANCHMAN IN SOUTHERN TEXAS AND OLD MEXICO. Hedrick, Oklahoma Territory, (1905). Wrappers. $4,500 or more.
Haley, J. Evetts	FORT CONCHO ON THE TEXAS FRONTIER. San Angelo, (Tex., 1952). Trade edition. $85-100.
Haley, J. Evetts	THE HERALDRY OF THE RANGE. Canyon, Tex., 1949. $425-500.
Haley, J. Evetts	JEFF MILTON: A GOOD MAN WITH A GUN. Norman, Okla., 1948. $85-100.

AUTHOR	**TITLE/EDITION INFORMATION/VALUE**
Haley, J. Evetts	LIFE ON THE TEXAS RANGE. Austin, Tex., 1952. $85-100.
Haley, J. Evetts	THE XIT RANCH OF TEXAS. Chicago, 1929. $225 or more.
Hall, Edward H.	THE GREAT WEST. New York, 1864. Wrappers. $225-300.
Hall, Fredrick	THE HISTORY OF SAN JOSE AND SURROUNDINGS. San Francisco, 1871. $150-175.
Hall, J.	SONORA: TRAVELS AND ADVENTURES IN SONORA. Chicago, 1881. $1,500 or more.
Hall, James	THE ROMANCE OF WESTERN HISTORY. Cincinnati, 1857. $60-75.
Hall, James	SKETCHES OF HISTORY, LIFE, AND MANNERS IN THE WEST. Cincinnati, 1834. $175-225.
Hall, James	STATISTICS OF THE WEST. Cincinnati, 1836. $125-165.
Halley, William	CENTENNIAL YEAR BOOK OF DESCRIPTION OF THE CONTRA COSTA UNDER SPANISH, MEXICAN, AND AMERICAN RULE. Oakland, Calif., 1876. $100-150.
Hamilton, Patrick	THE RESOURCES OF ARIZONA. Prescott, Ariz., 1881. Wrappers. $225 or more.
Hamilton, W. T.	MY SIXTY YEARS ON THE PLAINS. New York, 1905. $125-150.
(Hand-Book)	HAND-BOOK OF NESS COUNTY, THE BANNER COUNTY OF WESTERN KANSAS. Chicago, 1887. Wrappers. $200-250.
Hardin, John Wesley	THE LIFE OF JOHN WESLEY HARDIN. Seguin, Tex., 1896. Wrappers. $125-150.
Hare, George H.	GUIDE TO SAN JOSE AND VICINITY. San Jose, Calif., 1872. Wrappers. $175-225.
Harlan, Jacob Wright	CALIFORNIA, '46 TO '88. San Francisco, 1888. $125-150.

AUTHOR	TITLE/EDITION INFORMATION/VALUE
Harlow, Neal	THE MAPS OF SAN FRANCISCO BAY. San Francisco, 1950. Limited edition. $550 or more.
Harman, S. W.	HELL ON THE BORDER. Fort Smith, Ark., (1898). Wrappers. $550-625.
Harris, Sarah Hollister	AN UNWRITTEN CHAPTER OF SALT LAKE, 1851-1901. New York, 1901. $225-275.
Harris, W. B.	PIONEER LIFE IN CALIFORNIA. Stockton, Calif., 1884. Wrappers. $275 or more.
Hart, John A., et al	HISTORY OF PIONEER DAYS IN TEXAS AND OKLAHOMA. (Guthrie, Okla., 1906). $175-225.
Hartley, Oliver C.	DIGEST OF THE LAWS OF TEXAS. Philadelphia, 1850. $175-225.
Harvey, Henry	HISTORY OF THE SHAWNEE INDIANS. Cincinnati, 1855. $150 or more.
Haskins, C. W.	THE ARGONAUTS OF CALIFORNIA. New York, 1890. $250 or more.
Hastain, E.	TOWNSHIP PLATS OF THE CREEK NATION. Muskogee, Okla., 1910. $300 or more.
Hastings, Frank S.	A RANCHMAN'S RECOLLECTIONS. Chicago, 1921. $125 or more.
Hastings, Lansford W.	THE EMIGRANT'S GUIDE TO OREGON AND CALIFORNIA. Cincinnati, 1845. Wrappers or boards. At least $11,000.
Hastings, Lansford W.	A NEW HISTORY OF OREGON AND CALIFORNIA. Cincinnati, 1849. $450 or more.
Hawley, A. T.	THE CLIMATE, RESOURCES, AND ADVANTAGES OF HUMBOLDT COUNTY. Eureka, Calif., 1879. Wrappers. $500 or more.
Hawley, A. T.	THE PRESENT CONDITION, GROWTH, PROGRESS AND ADVANTAGES OF LOS ANGELES CITY AND COUNTY, SOUTHERN CALIFORNIA. Los Angeles, 1876. Map. Wrappers. At least $500.

AUTHOR	TITLE/EDITION INFORMATION/VALUE
Hawley, W. A.	THE EARLY DAYS OF SANTA BARBARA. New York, 1910. Wrappers. At least $125.
Hayden, Ferdinand V.	GEOLOGICAL AND GEOGRAPHICAL ATLAS OF COLORADO. (Washington), 1877. 20 2-page maps. $225 or more.
Hayden, Ferdinand V.	SUN PICTURES OF ROCKY MOUNTAIN SCENERY. New York, 1870. 30 mounted photos. $2,500 or more.
Hayden, Ferdinand V.	THE YELLOWSTONE NATIONAL PARK. Boston, 1876. Illustrated by Thomas Moran. 2 maps. $3,500 or more.
Heckendorn and Wilson	MINERS AND BUSINESS MEN'S DIRECTORY (for Toulumne, California). Columbia, Calif., 1856. Wrappers. $1,700 or more.
Helm, Mary S.	SCRAPS OF EARLY TEXAS HISTORY. Austin, Tex., 1884. $375 or more.
Herndon, William H., and Jesse W. Weik	HERNDON'S LINCOLN: THE TRUE STORY OF A GREAT LIFE. 3 vols. Chicago, (1889). 63 plates. $250 or more.
Hewitt, Randall H.	ACROSS THE PLAINS AND OVER THE DIVIDE. New York, (1906). 58 plates. Folding map. $125-150.
Hewitt, Randall H.	NOTES BY THE WAY: MEMORANDA OF A JOURNEY ACROSS THE PLAINS, FROM DUNDEE, ILL., TO OLYMPIA, W.T. MAY 7 TO NOVEMBER 3, 1862. Olympia, Wash., 1863. Wrappers. $3,500 or more.
Hilton, A.	OKLAHOMA AND INDIAN TERRITORY ALONG THE FRISCO. St. Louis, 1905. Wrappers. 2 maps. $125-175.
Hind, Henry Youle.	NORTH-WEST TERRITORY. Toronto, 1859. Folding maps. Plans. $350-425.
Hinkle, James F.	EARLY DAYS OF A COWBOY ON THE PECOS. Roswell, N. Mex., 1937. Wrappers. $450-525.

AUTHOR	TITLE/EDITION INFORMATION/VALUE
Hinton, Richard J.	THE HAND-BOOK OF ARIZONA. San Francisco, 1878. Maps. $125-150.
(Historical)	HISTORICAL AND DESCRIPTIVE REVIEW OF THE INDUSTRIES OF TACOMA, 1887. Los Angeles, 1887. Unbound. $125-150.
(Historical)	HISTORICAL AND DESCRIPTIVE REVIEW OF THE INDUSTRIES OF WALLA WALLA. N.p., 1891. Wrappers. $175-225.
(History)	HISTORY OF ALAMEDA COUNTY, CALIFORNIA [J. P. Munro-Fraser]. Oakland, Calif., 1883. $275-350.
(History)	HISTORY OF AMADOR COUNTY, CALIFORNIA. Oakland, Calif., 1881. $200-250.
(History)	HISTORY OF THE ARKANSAS VALLEY, COLORADO. Chicago, 1881. $140.
(History)	HISTORY OF THE CITY OF DENVER, ARAPAHOE COUNTY, AND COLORADO. Chicago, 1880. $275.
(History)	HISTORY OF IDAHO TERRITORY. San Francisco, 1884. Maps. $300.
(History)	HISTORY OF LOS ANGELES COUNTY, CALIFORNIA. Oakland, Calif., 1880. Folding map. $500.
(History)	HISTORY OF MARIN COUNTY, CALIFORNIA [J. P. Munro-Fraser]. San Francisco, 1880. $400.
(History)	HISTORY OF MENDOCINO COUNTY, CALIFORNIA. San Francisco, 1880. $350.
(History)	HISTORY OF MILAM, WILLIAMSON, BASTROP, TRAVIS, LEE AND BURLESON COUNTIES, TEXAS. Chicago, 1893. $400.
(History)	HISTORY OF MONTANA, 1739-1885. Chicago, 1885. Folding map. $325.

AUTHOR	TITLE/EDITION INFORMATION/VALUE
(History)	HISTORY OF NAPA AND LAKE COUNTIES, CALIFORNIA. San Francisco, 1881. $350.
(History)	HISTORY OF NEVEDA. Oakland, Calif., 1881. 116 plates. $575.
(History)	HISTORY OF NEVEDA COUNTY, CALIFORNIA [Frank L. Wells]. Oakland, Calif., 1880. Folio. $500.
(History)	HISTORY OF SAN JOAQUIN COUNTY, CALIFORNIA [Frank T. Gilbert]. Oakland, Calif., 1879. $475.
(History)	HISTORY OF SAN LUIS OBISPO COUNTY, CALIFORNIA [Myron Angel]. Oakland, Calif., 1883. $400.
(History)	HISTORY OF SANTA BARBARA AND VENTURA COUNTIES, CALIFORNIA [by Jesse D. Mason]. Oakland, Calif., 1883. $175.
(History)	HISTORY OF SONOMA COUNTY, CALIFORNIA. San Francisco, 1880. $175.
(History)	A HISTORY OF TEXAS, OR THE EMIGRANT'S GUIDE TO THE NEW REPUBLIC. BY A RESIDENT EMIGRANT. New York, 1844. Color plate. $450.
Hittell, John S.	THE COMMERCE AND INDUSTRIES OF THE PACIFIC COAST OF NORTH AMERICA. San Francisco, 1882. Folding map in color. $145.
Hittell, John S.	A HISTORY OF THE CITY OF SAN FRANCISCO. San Francisco, 1878. $140.
Hittell, John S.	THE RESOURCES OF VALLEJO. (Vallejo, Calif., 1869). Folding map. Wrappers. $350.
Hittell, John S.	YOSEMITE: ITS WONDERS AND ITS BEAUTIES. San Francisco, 1868. 20 mounted photo views by "Helios" (Eadweard Muybridge). At least $1,500.
Hittell, Theodore H., editor	ADVENTURES OF JAMES CAPEN ADAMS, MOUNTAINEER AND

AUTHOR	TITLE/EDITION INFORMATION/VALUE
	GRIZZLY BEAR HUNTER, OF CALIFORNIA. San Francisco, 1869. $225.
Hodge, Hiram C.	ARIZONA AS IT IS. New York, 1877. Map. $175.
Holden, W. C.	ALKALI TRAILS. Dallas, (1930). Maps. $135.
Holden, W. C.	ROLLIE BURNS; OR, AN ACCOUNT OF THE RANCHING INDUSTRY ON THE SOUTH PLAINS. Dallas, (1932). Maps. $140.
Holden, W. C.	THE SPUR RANCH. Boston, (1934). $175.
Holder, Charles F.	ALL ABOUT PASADENA AND ITS VICINITY. Boston, 1889. Wrappers. $125.
Holder, Charles F.	THE CHANNEL ISLANDS OF CALIFORNIA. Chicago, 1910. $90.
Holley, Mary Austin	TEXAS: OBSERVATIONS, HISTORICAL, GEOGRAPHICAL AND DESCRIPTIVE. Baltimore, 1833. Folding map. At least $1,500.
Hollister, Ovando J.	THE SILVER MINES OF COLORADO. Central City, Colo., 1867. Wrappers. $550.
Hollister, Urioah S.	THE NAVAJO AND HIS BLANKET. Denver, 1903. Color plates. $175.
Honig, Louis O.	THE PATHFINDER OF THE WEST: JAMES BRIDGER. Kansas City, 1951. $65.
Hopkins, Harry C.	HISTORY OF SAN DIEGO: ITS PUEBLO LANDS AND WATER. San Diego, (1929). $75.
Horgan, Paul	GREAT RIVER: THE RIO GRANDE IN AMERICAN HISTORY. 2 vols. New York, 1954. $45.
Houstoun, Mrs. Matilda C.	TEXAS AND THE GULF OF MEXICO. 2 vols. London, 1844. $450.
Howard, Olover Otis	NEZ PERCE JOSEPH. Boston, 1881. Maps. $175.
Hughes, John T.	CALIFORNIA: ITS HISTORY, POPULATION, CLIMATE, SOIL, PRODUCTIONS, AND HARBORS. Cincinnati, 1848. Wrappers. $225.

AUTHOR	TITLE/EDITION INFORMATION/VALUE
Hulaniski, F. J., editor	HISTORY OF CONTRA COSTA COUNTY, CALIFORNIA. Berkeley, Calif., 1917. $175.
Hunt, George M.	EARLY DAYS UPON THE PLAINS OF TEXAS. Lubbock, Tex., (1919). $250.
Hunt, Richard S., and Jesse F. Randel	GUIDE TO THE REPUBLIC OF TEXAS. New York, 1839. Folding map. $875.
Hunt, Richard S., and Jesse F. Randel	A NEW GUIDE TO TEXAS. New York, 1845. Folding map. $675.
Hunter, J. Marvin	THE TRAIL DRIVERS OF TEXAS. 2 vols. (San Antonio, Tex., 1920-1923). $200.
Hunter, J. Marvin, and Noah H. Rose	THE ALBUM OF GUN-FIGHTERS. (Bandera, Tex., 1951). $85.
Hunter, John D.	MANNERS AND CUSTOMS OF SEVERAL INDIAN TRIBES LOCATED WEST OF THE MISSISSIPPI. Philadelphia, 1823. $225.
Huntington, D. B.	VOCABULARY OF THE UTAH AND SHO-SHO-NE, OR SNAKE DIALECT, WITH INDIAN LEGENDS AND TRADITIONS. Salt Lake City, 1872. Sewed. $140.
Hutchings, James M.	SCENES OF WONDER AND CURIOSITY IN CALIFORNIA. San Francisco, (1860). $125.
Hyde, George E.	THE EARLY BLACKFEET AND THEIR NEIGHBORS. Denver, 1933. Wrappers. $125.
Hyde, George E.	THE PAWNEE INDIANS. 2 vols. Denver, 1934. Wrappers. $125.
Hyde, George E.	RED CLOUD'S FOLK. Norman, Okla., 1937. $65.
Hyde, George E.	RANGERS AND REGULARS. Denver, 1933. Wrappers. $100.
(Idaho)	IDAHO: A GUIDE IN WORD AND PICTURE. Caldwell, 1937. $200.
Ide, Simeon	THE CONQUEST OF CALIFORNIA: A BIOGRAPHY OF WILLIAM B. IDE. Oakland, Calif., 1944. $70.

AUTHOR	TITLE/EDITION INFORMATION/VALUE
Ide, William Brown	WHO CONQUERED CALIFORNIA? [Simeon Ide]. Claremont, N.H., ca. 1880s. $325.
(Illustrated)	THE ILLUSTRATED ATLAS AND HISTORY OF YOLO COUNTY, CALIFORNIA. San Francisco, 1879. Map. 50 plates. Large folio. $400.
(Illustrated)	AN ILLUSTRATED HISTORY OF LOS ANGELES COUNTY. Chicago, 1889. $300.
(Illustrated)	AN ILLUSTRATED HISTORY OF SAN JOAQUIN COUNTY. Chicago, 1890. $300.
(Indian)	THE INDIAN COUNCIL IN THE VALLEY OF THE WALLA-WALLA, 1855 [Lawrence Kip]. San Francisco, 1855. Wrappers. $850.
(Industrial)	THE INDUSTRIAL PRODIGY OF THE NEW SOUTHWEST. Muskogee, Indian Territory, (ca. 1902). Wrappers. $100.
Ingersoll, Luther A.	CENTURY ANNALS OF SAN BERNARDINO COUNTY. Los Angeles, 1904. $125.
Inman, Colonel Henry	THE OLD SANTA FE TRAIL. New York, 1897. Map. 8 plates by Frederic Remington. $175.
Inman, Colonel Henry	STORIES OF THE OLD SANTA FE TRAIL. Kansas City, 1881. $135.
Inman, Colonel Henry, editor	BUFFALO JONES' 40 YEARS OF ADVENTURE. Topeka, Kans., 1899. 43 plates. $185.
Inman, Colonel Henry, and William F. Cocy	THE GREAT SALT LAKE TRAIL. New York, 1898. Map. 8 plates. $185.
Irving, John Treat, Jr.	INDIAN SKETCHES, TAKEN DURING AN EXPEDITION TO THE PAWNEE TRIBES. 2 vols. Philadelphia, 1835. $300.
Ives, Joseph C.	REPORT UPON THE COLORADO RIVER OF THE WEST. Washington, 1861. 4 folding maps. Plates. $225.
Ivins, Virginia W.	PEN PICTURES OF EARLY WESTERN DAYS. (Keokuk, Iowa), 1905. $115.

AUTHOR	TITLE/EDITION INFORMATION/VALUE
Jackson, A. P., and E. C. Cole	OKLAHOMA! POLITICALLY AND TOPOGRAPHICALLY DESCRIBED. Kansas City, (1885). Wrappers. $550.
Jackson, A. W.	BARBARIANA; OR SCENERY, CLIMATE, SOILS AND SOCIAL CONDITIONS OF SANTA BARBARA CITY AND COUNTY. San Francisco, 1888. Wrappers. $115.
James, W. S.	COW-BOY LIFE IN TEXAS. Chicago, (1893). 34 plates. Wrappers. $275.
James, William F., and George H. McMurry	HISTORY OF SAN JOSE, CALIFORNIA. San Jose, 1933. $70.
Jefferson, H. E.	OKLAHOMA: THE BEAUTIFUL LAND. Chicago, 1889. Wrappers. $550.
Jennings, N. A.	A TEXAS RANGER. New York, 1899. $300.
Jocknick, Sidney	EARLY DAYS ON THE WESTERN SLOPE OF COLORADO. Denver, 1913. $175.
Johnson, Don Carlos	A BRIEF HISTORY OF SPRINGVILLE, UTAH. Springville, 1900, Wrappers. $225.
Johnson, Overton, and William H. Winter	ROUTE ACROSS THE ROCKY MAOUNTAINS, ETC. Lafayette, Ind., 1846. $1,700 or more.
Johnson, Sidney S.	TEXANS WHO WORE THE GRAY. Tyler, Tex., (ca. 1907). $375.
Jones, Anson B.	MEMORANDA AND OFFICIAL CORRESPONDENCE RELATING TO THE REPUBLIC OF TEXAS, ITS HISTORY AND ANNEXATION. New York, 1859. $175.
Jones, Jonathan H.	A CONDENSED HISTORY OF THE APACHE AND COMANCHE INDIAN TRIBES. San Antonio, Tex., 1899. $500.
Jones, William Carey	LAND TITLES IN CALIFORNIA. San Francisco, 1852. Wrappers. $725.
Judd, A. N.	AMPAIGNING AGAINST THE SIOUX. (Watsonville, Calif., 1906). Wrappers. At least $825.

AUTHOR	TITLE/EDITION INFORMATION/VALUE
Keleher, William A.	THE FABULOUS FRONTIER. Santa Fe, N. Mex., (1945). $115.
Keleher, William A.	THE MAXWELL LAND GRANT. Santa Fe, N. Mex., (1942). $185.
Kelley, Hall J.	GENERAL CIRCULAR TO ALL PERSONS OF GOOD CHARACTER WHO WISH TO EMIGRATE TO THE OREGON TERRITORY. Charlestown, Mass., 1831. Wrappers. $675.
Kelley, Hall J.	A GEOGRAPHICAL SKETCH OF THAT PART OF NORTH AMERICA CALLED OREGON. Boston, 1830. Folding map. Wrappers. $1,500 or more.
Kelley, Hall J.	HISTORY OF THE COLONIZATION OF THE OREGON TERRITORY. Worcester, Mass., 1850. Sewed. $1,200 or more.
Kelley, Hall J.	A HISTORY OF THE SETTLEMENT OF OREGON AND THE INTERIOR OF UPPER CALIFORNIA. Springfield, Mass., 1868. Wrappers. At least $5,500.
Kelly, Charles	OLD GREENWOOD: THE STORY OF CALEB GREENWOOD, TRAPPER, PATHFINDER AND EARLY PIONEER OF THE WEST. Salt Lake City, 1936. $160.
Kelly, Charles	THE OUTLAW TRAIL: A HISTORY OF BUTCH CASSIDY AND HIS WILD BUNCH. Salt Lake City, 1938. $140.
Kelly, Charles, and Maurice L. Howe	MILES L. GOODYEAR, FIRST CITIZEN OF UTAH. Salt Lake City, 1937. $80.
Kelly, George Fox	LAND FRAUDS OF CALIFORNIA. N.p., 1864. Wrappers. $550.
Kelly, William	AN EXCURSION TO CALIFORNIA OVER THE PRAIRIE, ROCKY MOUNTAINS, AND GREAT SIERRA NEVEDA. 2 vols., London, 1851. $450.
Kendall, George Wilkins	NARRATIVE OF THE TEXAN SANTA FE EXPEDITION. 2 vols. New York, 1844. Folding map. Plates. $500.

AUTHOR	TITLE/EDITION INFORMATION/VALUE
Kendall, George Wilkins	THE WAR BETWEEN THE UNITED STATES AND MEXICO. New York, 1841. Map. Colored plates. At least $2,000.
Kennedy, William	TEXAS: ITS GEOGRAPHY, NATURAL HISTORY, AND TOPOGRAPHY. New York, 1844. Wrappers. $225.
Kennedy, William	TEXAS: THE RISE, PROGRESS AND PROSPECTS OF THE REPUBLIC OF TEXAS. 2 vols. London, 1841. Charts. Maps. $550.
King, Frank M.	LONGHORN TRAIL DRIVERS. (Los Angeles, 1940). $115.
King, Frank M.	WRANGLIN' IN THE PAST. (Los Angeles, 1935). $115.
Kinzie, Mrs. Juliette A.	WAU-BUN, THE "EARLY DAY" IN THE NORTH-WEST. New York, 1856. $125.
Kip, Lawrence	ARMY LIFE IN THE PACIFIC. New York, 1859. $400.
Kneedler, H. S.	THE COAST COUNTRY OF TEXAS. Cincinnati, 1896. Wrappers. $175.
Knox, Dudley W.	NAVAL SKETCHES OF THE WAR IN CALIFORNIA. New York, 1939. $200.
Kroeber, Alfred L.	HANDBOOK OF THE INDIANS OF CALIFORNIA. Washington, 1925. Maps. Plates. $175.
Kuykendall, Ivan Lee	GHOST RIDERS OF THE MOGOLLON. San Antonio, Tex., (1954). $375.
Kuykendall, Judge W. L.	FRONTIER DAYS. N.p., 1917. $85.
La Frentz, F. W.	COWBOY STUFF. New York, 1927. 49 plates. $550.
Lane, Walter P.	ADVENTURES AND RECOLLECTIONS OF GEN. WALTER WALTER P. LANE. Marshall, Tex., 1887. Wrappers. $1,000.
Lang, H. O., editor	HISTORY OF THE WILLIAMETTE VALLEY. Portland, Oreg., 1885. $90.

AUTHOR	TITLE/EDITION INFORMATION/VALUE
Lang, William W.	A PAPER ON THE RESOURCES AND CAPABILITIES OF TEXAS. (New York), 1881. Wrappers. $125.
Langley, Henry G.	THE SAN FRANCISCO DIRECTORY FOR THE YEAR 1858. San Francisco, 1858. $400.
Langston, Mrs. George	HISTORY OF EASTLAND COUNTY, TEXAS. Dallas, 1904. $250.
(Laramie)	LARAMIE, HAHN'S PEAK AND PACIFIC RAILWAY SYSTEM: THE DIRECT GATEWAY TO SOUTHERN WYOMING, NORTHERN COLORADO, AND EASTERN UTAH. N.p. (1910). Wrappers. Folio. $250.
La Salle, Charles E.	COLONEL CROCKET, THE TEXAS TRAILER. New York, (1871). Wrappers. $125.
Latrobe, Charles Joseph	THE RAMBLER IN MEXICO. London, 1836. $275.
(Laws)	LAWS AND DECREES OF THE STATE OF COAHUILA AND TEXAS, IN SPANISH AND ENGLISH. Houston, 1839. $625.
(Laws)	LAWS AND REGULATIONS OF UNION DISTRICT, CLEAR CREEK COUNTY, C.T. Central City, (Colorado Territory), 1864. Wrappers. $675.
(Laws)	LAWS FOR THE BETTER GOVERNMENT OF CALIFORNIA. San Francisco, 1848. First English book printed in California. At least $5,500.
(Laws)	LAWS OF THE CHEROKEE NATION. Tahlequah, Indian Territory, 1852. $1,500.
(Laws)	LAWS OF THE CHOCTAW NATION, MADE AND ENACTED BY THE GENERAL COUNCIL FROM 1886 TO 1890. Atoka, Indian Territory. In Choctaw and English. $300.

AUTHOR	TITLE/EDITION INFORMATION/VALUE
(Laws)	LAWS OF THE GREGORY DISTRICT, FEBRUARY 18 and 20, 1860. Denver, 1860. Wrappers. $1,200.
(Laws)	LAWS OF THE TERRITORY OF NEW MEXICO. Santa Fe, N. Mex., 1862. Wrappers. $300.
(Laws)	LAWS OF THE TOWN OF SAN FRANCISCO. San Francisco, 1847. Wrappers. $1,250.
Layne, J. Gregg	ANNALS OF LOS ANGELES. San Francisco, 1935. $65.
Lea, Pryor	AN OUTLINE OF THE CENTRAL TRANSIT, IN A SERIES OF SIX LETTERS TO HON. JOHN HEMPHILL. Galveston, Tex., 1859. Wrappers. $125.
Lea, Tom	THE KING RANCH. 2 vols. Boston, (1957). $150.
(Leadville)	LEADVILLE CHRONICLE ANNUAL. Leadville, Colo., 1881. Wrappers. $175.
(Leadville)	LEADVILLE, COLORADO: THE MOST WONDERFUL MINING CAMP IN THE WORLD [John L. Loomis]. Colorado Springs, 1879. Wrappers. $325.
Le Conte, Joseph	A JOURNAL OF RAMBLINGS THROUGH THE HIGH SIERRAS OF CALIFORNIA. San Francisco, 1875. Photos. At least $1,800.
(Lee)	THE LEE TRIAL! AN EXPOSÉ OF THE MOUNTAIN MEADOWS MASSACRE. Salt Lake City, 1875. Wrappers. $950.
Leeper, David Rohrer	THE ARGONAUTS OF FORTY-NINE. South Bend, Ind., 1894. $85.
Leese, Jacob P.	HISTORICAL OUTLINE OF LOWER CALIFORNIA. New York, 1865. Wrappers. $175.
Leigh, William R.	THE WESTERN PONY. New York, (1933). Color plates. $500.

AUTHOR	TITLE/EDITION INFORMATION/VALUE
Leonard, H. L. W.	OREGON TERRITORY. Cleveland, 1846. Wrappers. At least $3,000.
Lester, C. Edwards	SAM HOUSTON AND HIS REPUBLIC. New York, 1846. Maps. $350.
(Letter)	LETTER FROM THE SECRETARY OF STATE, ACCOMPANYING CERTAIN LAWS OF THE NORTHWESTERN AND INDIAN TERRITORIES OF THE UNITED STATES. (Washington), 1902. Sewed. $150.
Levy, Daniel	LES FRANCAIS EN CALIFORNIE. San Francisco, 1884. Wrappers. $175.
Lewis, Meriwether, and William Clark	HISTORY OF THE EXPEDITION UNDER THE COMMAND OF CAPTAINS LEWIS AND CLARK. 2 vols. Philadelphia, 1814. Folding map. Charts. Possibly as much as $50,000—see a specialist.
Lewis, Meriwether, and William Clark	ORIGINAL JOURNALS OF THE LEWIS AND CLARK EXPEDITION, 1804-1806. 8 vols. New York, 1904-1905. Atlas. $1,500.
Lewis, Meriwether, and William Clark	TRAVELS TO THE SOURCE OF THE MISSOURI RIVER AND ACROSS THE AMERICAN CONTINENT TO THE PACIFIC OCEAN. London, 1814. Map. Charts. $3,000.
Lockwood, Frank C.	THE APACHE INDIANS. New York, 1938. $85.
Lockwood, Frank C.	ARIZONA CHARACTERS. Los Angeles, 1928. $125.
Lockwood, Frank C.	PIONEER DAYS IN ARIZONA. New York, 1932. $90.
(Lone)	THE LONE STAR GUIDE DESCRIPTIVE OF COUNTRIES ON THE LINE OF THE INTERNATIONAL AND GREAT NORTHERN RAILROAD OF TEXAS [H. M. Hoxie]. St. Louis, (ca. 1877). Folding map. Table. Wrappers. $225.
Loughborough, John	THE PACIFIC TELEGRAPH AND RAILWAY. St. Louis, 1849. Folding maps. Unbound. $750.

AUTHOR	TITLE/EDITION INFORMATION/VALUE
Lowman, Al	THIS BITTERLY BEAUTIFUL LAND: A TEXAS COMMONPLACE BOOK. (Austin, Tex., 1972). Folio. $500.
Luhan, Mabel Dodge	TAOS AND ITS ARTISTS. New York, 1947. $175.
Luke, L. D.	ADVENTURES AND TRAVELS IN THE NEW WONDER LAND OF YELLOWSTONE PARK. Utica, N.Y., 1886. $85.
Lyman, Albert	JOURNAL OF A VOYAGE TO CALIFORNIA, AND LIFE IN THE GOLD DIGGINGS. Hartford, Conn., 1852. Wrappers. $1,500.
McCall, Ansel J.	PICK AND PAN: A TRIP TO THE DIGGINGS IN 1849. Bath, N.Y., 1889. Wrappers. $725.
McCalla, William L.	ADVENTURES IN TEXAS. Philadelphia, 1841. $625.
McCollum, William	CALIFORNIA AS I SAW IT. Buffalo, N.Y., 1850. Wrappers. At least $8,000.
McConnell, Joseph Carroll	THE WEST TEXAS FRONTIER. Jacksboro, Tex., 1933. $125.
McConnell, W. J.	EARLY HISTORY OF IDAHO. Caldwell, 1913. $85.
McCormick, Richard C.	ARIZONA: ITS RESOURCES AND PROSPECTS. New York, 1865. Folding map. Wrappers. $125.
McCormick, S. J.	ALMANAC FOR THE YEAR 1864; CONTAINING USEFUL INFORMATION RELATIVE TO THE POPULATION, PROGRESS AND RESOURCES OF OREGON, WASHINGTON AND IDAHO. Portland, (1863). Wrappers. $225 or more.
McCoy, Joseph G.	HISTORIC SKETCHES OF THE CATTLE TRADE OF THE WEST AND SOUTHWEST. Kansas City, 1874. $1,000.

AUTHOR	TITLE/EDITION INFORMATION/VALUE
McDanield, H. F., and N. A. Taylor	THE COMING EMPIRE; OR, 2,000 MILES IN TEXAS ON HORSEBACK. New York, (1877). $125.
McEachran, D.	NOTES OF A TRIP TO BOW RIVER, NORTH-WEST TERRITORIES. Montreal, 1881. $225.
McGlashan, C. F.	HISTORY OF THE DONNER PARTY: A TRAGEDY OF THE SIERRAS. Truckee, Calif., (1879). $700.
McIlvaine, William, Jr.	SKETCHES OF SCENERY AND NOTES OF PERSONAL ADVENTURE, IN CALIFORNIA AND MEXICO. Philadelphia, 1850. Plates. $1800.
McIntire, Jim	EARLY DAYS IN TEXAS: A TRIP TO HELL AND HEAVEN. Kansas City, Mo., (1902). Plates. $300.
Mack, Effie	NEVADA: A HISTORY OF THE STATE. Glendale, 1936. Map. $85.
Mackay, Malcolm S.	COW-RANGE AND HUNTING TRAIL. New York, 1925. $225.
McKee, James Cooper	NARRATIVE OF THE SURRENDER OF A COMMAND OF U.S. FORCES AT FORT FILLMORE, N.M., IN JULY A.D. 1861. New York, 1881. Wrappers. Second edition. $225.
McKee, Dr. W. H.	THE TERRITORY OF NEW MEXICO AND ITS RESOURCES. New York, 1866. Wrappers. At least $2,500.
McKnight, George S.	CALIFORNIA 49ER: TRAVELS FROM PERRYSBURG TO CALIFORNIA. Perrysburg, Ohio, 1903. Wrappers. $175.
McMurtrie, Douglas C.	THE BEGINNINGS OF PRINTING IN UTAH. Chicago, 1931. $100.
McMurtrie, Douglas C.	PIONEER PRINTING IN TEXAS. Austin, Tex., 1932. Wrappers. $100.
McMurtrie, Douglas C., and Albert H. Allem	EARLY PRINTING IN COLORADO. Denver, 1935. $100.

AUTHOR	TITLE/EDITION INFORMATION/VALUE
McNeil, Samuel	MC NEIL'S TRAVELS IN 1849, TO, THROUGH AND FROM THE GOLD REGIONS. Columbus, Ohio, 1850. Wrappers. At least $6,000.
Magoffin, Susan Shelby	DOWN THE SANTA FE TRAIL AND INTO MEXICO. New Haven, Conn., 1926. Maps. $150.
Maillard, N. Doran	THE HISTORY OF THE REPUBLIC OF TEXAS, FROM THE DISCOVERY OF THE COUNTRY TO THE PRESENT TIME. London, 1842. Folding map. $475.
Mangam, William D.	THE CLARKS OF MONTANA. (New York, 1939). Wrappers. $350.
Manly, William Lewis	DEATH VALLEY IN '49. San Jose, Calif., 1894. $125.
(March)	THE MARCH OF THE FIRST. Denver, 1863. Sewed. At least $3,500.
Marcy, Randolph B.	THE PRAIRIE TRAVELER: A HAND-BOOK FOR OVERLAND EXPEDITIONS. New York, 1859. Map. $375.
Marks, B.	SMALL SCALE FARMING IN CENTRAL CALIFORNIA. San Francisco, 1888. Wrappers. $125.
Marsh, James B.	FOUR YEARS IN THE ROCKIES. Newcastle, Penn., 1884. $400.
Marshall, William I.	ACQUISITION OF OREGON, AND THE LONG SUPPRESSED EVIDENCE ABOUT MARCUS WHITMAN. 2 vols. (Seattle, Wash.), 1905. $200.
Mathews, A. E.	CANYON CITY, COLORADO, AND ITS SURROUNDINGS. New York, 1870. Map. At least $3,500.
Mathews, A. E.	PENCIL SKETCHES OF COLORADO. (New York), 1866. At least $4,500.
Mathews, A. E.	PENCIL SKETCHES OF MONTANA. New York, 1868. At least $3,500.

AUTHOR	TITLE/EDITION INFORMATION/VALUE
Mathews, Alfred E.	GEMS OF ROCKY MOUNTAIN SCENERY. New York, 1869. $1,750.
Mathews, Alfred E.	INTERESTING NARRATIVE; BEING A JOURNAL OF THE FLIGHT OF ALFRED E. MATHEWS, OF STARK CO., OHIO, FROM THE STATE OF TEXAS. (New Philadelphia, Ohio), 1861. Sewed. $1,250.
Mathews, Mrs. M. M.	TEN YEARS IN NEVADA. Buffalo, N.Y., 1880. $225.
Maynard, G. W.	REPORT ON THE PROPERTY OF THE ALICE GOLD AND SILVER MINING CO., BUTTE. New York, 1882. Maps. Wrappers. $125.
Meeker, Ezra	WASHINGTON TERRITORY WEST OF THE CASCADE MOUNTAINS. Olympia Wash., 1870. Wrappers. $825.
(Memorial)	MEMORIAL AND BIOGRAPHICAL HISTORY OF JOHNSON AND HILL COUNTIES, TEXAS. Chicago, 1892. $350.
(Memorial)	MEMORIAL AND BIOGRAPHICAL HISTORY OF MC LENNAN, FALLS, BELL AND CORYELL COUNTIES, TEXAS. Chicago, 1893. $425.
(Memorial)	MEMORIAL TO THE PRESIDENT AND CONGRESS FOR THE ADMISSION OF WYOMING TERRITORY TO THE UNION. Cheyenne, Wyo., 1889. Wrappers. $135.
Mercer, A. S.	THE BANDITTI OF THE PLAINS. (Cheyenne, Wyo., 1894). Map. At least $3,500.
Mercer, A. S.	WASHINGTON TERRITORY: THE GREAT NORTH-WEST. Utica, N.Y., 1865. Wrappers. $950.
(Mexican)	MEXICAN TREACHERIES AND CRUELTIES [Lieutenant G. N. Allen]. Boston, 1847. Wrappers. $100.
(Mexico)	MEXICO AND THE UNITED STATES: AN AMERICAN VIEW OF THE MEXICAN QUESTION. BY A CITIZEN OF

AUTHOR	TITLE/EDITION INFORMATION/VALUE
	CALIFORNIA. San Francisco, 1866. Wrappers. $125.
(Mexico)	MEXICO IN 1842 TO WHICH IS ADDED, AN ACCOUNT OF TEXAS AND YUCATAN, AND OF THE SANTA FE EXPEDITION [George F. Folsom]. New York, 1842. Folding map. $400.
Miles, William	JOURNAL OF THE SUFFERINGS AND HARDSHIPS OF CAPT. PARKER H. FRENCH'S OVERLAND EXPEDITION TO CALIFORNIA. Chambersburg, Penn., 1851. Wrappers. At least $4,000.
Miller, Joaquin	AN ILLUSTRATED HISTORY OF MONTANA. 2 vols. Chicago, 1984. $200.
Mills, William W.	FORTY YEARS AT EL PASO, 1858-1898. (Chicago, 1901). $225.
Mitchell, G. R.	THE PACIFIC GOLD COMPANY OF GILPIN COUNTY, COLORADO. Boston, 1866. Wrappers. $150.
Mitchell, John D.	LOST MINES OF THE GREAT SOUTHWEST. (Phoenix, Ariz., 1933). $100.
Mitchell, S. Augustus, publisher	ACCOMPANIMENT TO MITCHELL'S NEW MAP OF TEXAS, OREGON AND CALIFORNIA, WITH THE REGIONS ADJOINING. Philadelphia, 1846. Folding map. $650.
Mitchell, S. Augustus, publisher	DESCRIPTION OF OREGON AND CALIFORNIA, EMBRACING AN ACCOUNT OF THE GOLD REGIONS. Philadelphia, 1849. Folding map. $725.
Moellhausen, Baldwin	DIARY OF A JOURNEY FROM THE MISSISSIPPI TO THE COASTS OF THE PACIFIC WITH A UNITED STATES GOVERNMENT EXPEDITION. 2 vols. London, 1858. Folding map. $1,250.
Molker, A. J.	A HISTORY OF NATRONA COUNTY, WYOMING. Chicago, 1923. $175.

AUTHOR	TITLE/EDITION INFORMATION/VALUE
(Montana)	MONTANA, ITS CLIMATE, INDUSTRIES AND RESOURCES. Helena, Mont., 1884. Wrappers. $175.
(Montana)	MONTANA TERRITORY, HISTORY AND BUSINESS DIRECTORY 1879 [F. W. Warner]. Helena, Mont., (1879). Map. $450.
Morfi, Juan Agustin	HISTORY OF TEXAS, 1673-1779. Albuquerque, N. Mex., 1935. Map. $225.
Morgan, Dale L.	JEDEDIAH SMITH AND THE OPENING OF THE WEST. Indianapolis, (1953). $65.
Morgan, Dale L., and Carl I. Wheat	JEDEDIAH SMITH AND HIS MAPS OF THE AMERICAN WEST. San Francisco, 1954. 7 folding maps. $650.
Morgan, Dick T.	MORGAN'S MANUAL OF THE U.S. HOMESTEAD AND TOWNSITE LAWS. Guthrie, Okla., 1893. Wrappers. $250.
Morgan, Martha M., editor	A TRIP ACROSS THE PLAINS IN THE YEAR 1849. San Francisco, 1864. Wrappers. At least $6,500.
Morgan, Thomas J.	A GLANCE AT TEXAS. Columbus, Ohio, 1844. $1,750.
Morphis, J. M.	HISTORY OF TEXAS. New York, 1874. Folding map. $175.
Morrell, Z. N.	FLOWERS AND FRUITS FROM THE WILDERNESS; OR 36 YEARS IN TEXAS. Boston, 1872. $150.
Morse, John F., and Samuel Colville	ILLUSTRATED HISTORICAL SKETCHES OF CALIFORNIA. Sacramento, Calif., 1854. Wrappers. $750.
Mowry, Sylvester	MEMOIR OF THE PROPOSED TERRITORY OF ARIZONA. Washington, 1857. Map. Wrappers. At least $2,500.
Muir, John	THE MOUNTAINS OF CALIFORNIA. New York, 1894. $300.
Muir, John, editor	PICTURESQUE CALIFORNIA. 2 vols. San Francisco, (1888). 130 plates. Folio. $850.

AUTHOR	TITLE/EDITION INFORMATION/VALUE
Mullan, John	MINERS' AND TRAVELERS' GUIDE TO OREGON. New York, 1865. Folding map. $425.
Mullan, John	REPORT ON THE CONSTRUCTION OF A MILITARY ROAD FROM FORT WALLA-WALLA TO FORT BENTON. Washington, 1863. 4 folding maps. 11 plates. $300.
Mumey, Nolie	BLOODY TRAILS ALONG THE RIO GRANDE. Denver, 1938. Map. $50.
Mumey, Nolie	CALAMITY JANE. Denver, 1950. Folding map. 2 pamphlets. Signed. $200.
Mumey, Nolie	CREEDE: HISTORY OF A COLORADO MINING TOWN. Denver, 1949. $75.
Mumey, Nolie	HISTORY OF THE EARLY SETTLEMENTS OF DENVER. Glendale, Calif., 1942. Map. $75.
Mumey, Nolie	MARCH OF THE FIRST DRAGOONS TO THE ROCKY MOUNTAINS IN 1835. Denver, 1957. Folding map. $75.
Mumey, Nolie	OLD FORTS AND TRADING POSTS OF THE WEST. Denver, 1956. $75.
Mumey, Nolie	PIONEER DENVER, INCLUDING SCENES OF CENTRAL CITY, COLORADO CITY, AND NEVEDA CITY. Denver, 1948. Folding plate. $90.
Mumey, Nolie	POKER ALICE. Denver, 1951. Folding map. Wrappers. $75.
Mumey, Nolie	THE TETON MOUNTAINS. Denver, 1947. $75.
(Murder)	MURDER BY DEPUTY U.S. MARSHALL E. M. THORNTON OF E. M. DALTON WAYLAID AND ASSASSINATED IN COLD BLOOD. Salt Lake City, 1886. Wrappers. $150.
Napton, William B.	OVER THE SANTA FE TRAIL. Kansas City, 1905. Wrappers. $175.

AUTHOR	TITLE/EDITION INFORMATION/VALUE
Neil, John B.	BIENNIAL MESSAGE OF THE GOVERNOR OF IDAHO TO THE 11TH SESSION OF THE LEGISLATURE OF IDAHO TERRITORY. Boise City, Idaho, 1880. Wrappers. $140.
(New)	THE NEW EMPIRE: OREGON, WASHINGTON, IDAHO. Portland, Oreg., 1888. Folding map. Wrappers. $85.
(New)	THE NEW TEXAS SPELLING BOOK [E. H. Cushing]. Houston, 1863. $1,200.
(New)	NEW YORK AND ORO-FINO GOLD AND SILVER MINING CO. OF IDAHO. New York, 1865. Wrappers. $140.
Newberry, J. S.	REPORT ON THE PROPERTIES OF THE RAMSHORN CONSOLIDATED SILVER MINING COMPANY AT BAY HORSE, IDAHO. New York, (1881). Wrappers. $140.
Newell, Rev. Chester	HISTORY OF THE REVOLUTION IN TEXAS. New York, 1838. Folding map. $500.
Newmark, Harris	SIXTY YEARS IN SOUTHERN CALIFORNIA, 1853-1913. New York, 1916. $60.
Nimmo, Joseph, Jr.	RANGE AND RANCH CATTLE TRAFFIC. (Washington, 1884). 4 folding maps. Wrappers. $1,800.
Nordhoff, Charles	CALIFORNIA FOR HEALTH, PLEASURE AND RESIDENCE. New York, 1872. Map. $125.
North, Thomas	FIVE YEARS IN TEXAS; OR, WHAT YOU DID NOT HEAR DURING THE WAR. Cincinnati, 1879. $125.
(Northern)	THE NORTHERN ROUTE TO IDAHO [D. D. Merrill]. St. Paul, (N. Mex., 1864). Folding map. At least $1,500.
(Notes)	NOTES ON CALIFORNIA AND THE PLACERS [James Delavan]. New York, 1850. Wrappers. At least $2,000.

AUTHOR	TITLE/EDITION INFORMATION/VALUE
(Official)	OFFICIAL HISTORICAL ATLAS OF ALAMEDA COUNTY. Oakland, Calif., 1878. Folding maps, folio. $375.
Ogden, George	LETTERS FROM THE WEST. New Bedford, Mass., 1823. $675.
Older, Mr. and Mrs. Fremont	THE LIFE OF GEORGE HEARST, CALIFORNIA PIONEER. San Francisco, 1933. $450.
Oldham, Williamson S., and George W. White	DIGEST OF THE GENERAL STATUTE LAWS OF THE STATE OF TEXAS. Austin, Tex., 1859. $200.
Olmsted, Frederick Law	A JOURNEY THROUGH TEXAS. New York, 1857. Folding map. $175.
Onderdonk, James L.	IDAHO: FACTS AND STATISTICS. San Francisco, 1885. Wrappers. $225.
(Oregon)	OREGON: AGRICULTURAL, STOCK RAISING, MINERAL RESOURCES, CLIMATE, ETC. [Union Pacific Rail Road]. Council Bluffs, Iowa, 1888. Wrappers. $200.
Orr, N. M.	THE CITY OF STOCKTON. Stockton, Calif., 1874. Wrappers. $160.
Orr and Ruggles	SAN JOAQUIN COUNTY. Stockton, Calif., 1887. Map. Wrappers. $175.
Otero, Miguel Antonio	THE REAL BILLY THE KID. New York, 1936. $60.
Packard, Wellman, and G. Larison	EARLY EMIGRATION TO CALIFORNIA. Bloomington, Ill., 1928. Wrappers. $450.
Palladino, Lawrence B.	INDIAN AND WHITE IN THE NORTHWEST. Baltimore, 1894. $200.
Palmer, Joel	JOURNAL OF TRAVELS OVER THE ROCKY MOUNTAINS, TO THE MOUTH OF THE COLUMBIA RIVER. Cincinnati, 1847. Wrappers. $2,300 or more.
Parker, A. A.	A TRIP TO THE WEST AND TEXAS. Concord, (N.H.), 1835. $450.

AUTHOR	TITLE/EDITION INFORMATION/VALUE
Parker, Aaron	FORGOTTEN TRAGEDIES OF INDIAN WARFARE IN IDAHO. Grangeville, Idaho, 1925. Wrappers. $125.
Parker, Frank, editor	WASHINGTON TERRITORY! THE PRESENT AND PROSPECTIVE FUTURE OF THE UPPER COLUMBIA COUNTRY. Walla Walla, Wash., 1881. Wrappers. $450.
Parker, Henry W.	HOW OREGON WAS SAVED TO THE U.S. New York, 1901. Wrappers. $45.
Parker, Samuel	JOURNAL OF AN EXPLORING TOUR BEYOND THE ROCKY MOUNTAINS. Ithaca, N.Y., 1838. $550.
Parker, (Nathan H.), and (D. H.) Huyett	THE ILLUSTRATED MINERS' HANDBOOK AND GUIDE TO PIKE'S PEAK. St. Louis, 1859. 2 folding maps. At least $6,500.
Parkman, Francis	THE CALIFORNIA AND OREGON TRAIL. 2 vols. New York, 1849. Wrappers; or 1 vol. Cloth. At least $10,000.
Parsons, George Frederic	THE LIFE AND ADVENTURES OF JAMES W. MARSHALL. Sacramento, 1870. $175.
(Pasadena)	PASADENA AS IT IS TODAY FROM A BUSINESS STANDPOINT. (Pasadena, Calif., 1886). Wrappers. $175.
(Pasadena)	PASADENA, LOS ANGELES COUNTY, SOUTHERN CALIFORNIA. Los Angeles, 1898. Wrappers. $125.
Patterson, Lawson B.	TWELVE YEARS IN THE MINES OF CALIFORNIA. Cambridge, Mass., 1862. $175.
Paulison, C. M. K.	ARIZONA: THE WONDERFUL COUNTRY. Tucson, Ariz., 1881. Wrappers. $3,000.
Payne, John Howard	INDIAN JUSTICE: A CHEROKEE MURDER TRAIL AT TAHLEQUAH IN 1840. Oklahoma City, 1934. $175.
Peters, De Witt C.	KIT CARSON'S LIFE. Hartford, Conn., 1874. $135.

AUTHOR	**TITLE/EDITION INFORMATION/VALUE**
Peters, De Witt C.	THE LIFE AND ADVENTURES OF KIT CARSON, THE NESTOR OF THE ROCKY MOUNTAINS. New York, 1858. $175.
Petter, Rodolphe	ENGLISH-CHEYENNE DICTIONARY. Kettle Falls, Wash., 1913-1915. Folio. $250.
Phillips, D. L.	LETTERS FROM CALIFORNIA. Springfield, Ill., 1877. $165.
(Pioneering)	PIONEERING ON THE PLAINS. JOURNEYS TO MEXICO IN 1848. THE OVERLAND TRIP TO CALIFORNIA [Alexander W. McCoy, et al]. (Kaukauna, Wis., 1924). Wrappers. $200.
Platt, P. L., and N. Slater	THE TRAVELERS' GUIDE ACROSS THE PLAINS, UPON THE OVERLAND ROUTE TO CALIFORNIA. Chicago, 1852. Folding map. Wrappers. At least $9,500.
Pleasants, W. J.	TWICE ACROSS THE PLAINS, 1849-1856. San Francisco, 1906. $500.
Polley, J. B.	HOOD'S TEXAS BRIGADE. New York, 1910. $400.
Pollock, J. M.	THE UNVARNISHED WEST: RANCHING AS I FOUND IT. London, (1911). $350.
Poor, M. C.	DENVER, SOUTH PARK AND PACIFIC. Denver, 1949. Map. $375.
Porter, Lavinia Honeyman	BY OX TEAM TO CALIFORNIA. Oakland, Calif., 1910. $525.
(Portrait)	PORTRAIT AND BIOGRAPHICAL RECORD OF DENVER AND VICINITY. Chicago, 1898. $400.
Poston, Charles D.	APACHE LAND. San Francisco, 1878. $150.
Poston, Charles D.	SPEECH OF THE HON. CHARLES D. POSTON, OF ARIZONA, ON INDIAN AFFAIRS. New York, 1865. Wrappers. $800.
Powell, H. M. T.	THE SANTA FE TRAIL TO CALIFORNIA, 1849-1852. San Francisco, (1931). Maps. At least $1,500.

AUTHOR	TITLE/EDITION INFORMATION/VALUE
Powell, J. W.	CANYONS OF THE COLORADO. Meadville, Penn., 1895. 10 folding plates. $1,500.
Prescott, William H.	THE HISTORY OF THE CONQUEST OF MEXICO. 3 vols. New York, 1843. Maps. $250.
(Proceedings)	PROCEEDINGS OF THE FIRST ANNUAL SESSION OF THE TERRITORIAL GRANGE OF MONTANA. Diamond City, Mont., 1875. $350.
(Progressive)	PROGRESSIVE MEN OF SOUTHERN IDAHO. Chicago, 1904. $375.
Prosch, J. W.	MCCARVER AND TACOMA. Seattle, Wash., (1906). $100.
(Prospectus)	PROSPECTUS OF HOPE GOLD COMPANY. New York, 1864. Wrappers. $150.
(Prospectus)	PROSPECTUS OF THE LEADVILLE AND TEN MILE NARROW GAUGE RAILWAY COMPANY OF LEADVILLE, COL. Leadville, Colo., 1880. Wrappers. $275.
(Puget)	PUGET SOUND BUSINESS DIRECTORY AND GUIDE TO WASHINGTON TERRITORY, 1872. Olympia, Wash., (1872). $650.
(Puget)	PUGET SOUND DIRECTORY, 1887 [R. L. Polk]. N.p., 1887. $650.
Quickfall	WESTERN LIFE, AND HOW I BECAME A BRONCO BUSTER [Bob Grantham]. London, (1890). Wrappers. $550.
Raht, Carlysle Graham	THE ROMANCE OF DAVIS MOUNTAINS AND BIG BEND COUNTRY. El Paso, Tex., (1919). $90.
Raine, William MacLeod	CATTLE BRANDS: A SKETCH OF BYGONE DAYS IN THE COW-COUNTRY. Boston, (1920). Wrappers. $125.
Raines, C. W.	A BIBLIOGRAPHY OF TEXAS. Austin, Tex., 1896. $150.

AUTHOR	TITLE/EDITION INFORMATION/VALUE
Ramsdell, Charles W.	RECONSTRUCTION IN TEXAS. New York, 1910. Wrappers. $125.
Rankin, M. Wilson	REMINISCENCES OF FRONTIER DAYS. Denver, (1938). $125.
Rankin, Melinda	TEXAS IN 1850. Boston, 1850. $325.
Raymond, Dora Neill	CAPTAIN LEE HALL OF TEXAS. Norman, Okla., 1940. $45.
Recio, Jesus T.	TOMOCHIE! EPISODIOS DE LA COMPANIA DE CHIHUAHUA, 1893. Rio Grande City, Tex., 1894. $400.
Reed, Nathaniel	THE LIFE OF TEXAS JACK. (Tulsa, Okla., 1936.) Wrappers. $825.
Reed, S. G.	A HISTORY OF THE TEXAS RAILROADS. Houston, (1941). $225.
Reid, John C.	REID'S TRAMP, OR A JOURNAL OF THE INCIDENTS OF TEN MONTHS TRAVEL THROUGH TEXAS, NEW MEXICO, ARIZONA, SONORA, AND CALIFORNIA. Selma, Ala., 1858. At least $9,000.
Reid, Samuel C., Jr.	THE SCOUTING EXPEDITIONS OF MC CULLOCH'S TEXAS RANGERS. Philadelphia, 1847. $325.
(Relief)	RELIEF BUSINESS DIRECTORY, NAMES AND NEW LOCATIONS IN SAN FRANCISCO, OAKLAND, BERKELEY AND ALAMEDA OF 4,000 SAN FRANCISCO FIRMS AND BUSINESS MEN. Berkeley, Calif., 1906. Wrappers. $250.
(Reminiscences)	REMINISCENCES OF A CAMPAIGN IN MEXICO [John B. Robertson]. Nashville, Tenn., 1849. $275.
Remy, Jules, and Julius L. Brenchley	A JOURNEY TO GREAT SALT LAKE CITY. 2 vols. London, 1861. Maps. $600.
Renfrow, W. C.	OKLAHOMA AND THE CHEROKEE STRIP. Chicago, 1893. Folding map. Wrappers. $100.

AUTHOR	TITLE/EDITION INFORMATION/VALUE
(Report)	REPORT FROM A SELECT COMMITTEE OF THE HOUSE OF REPRESENTATIVES, ON THE OVERLAND EMIGRATION ROUTE FROM MINNESOTA TO BRITISH OREGON. St. Paul, Minn., 1858. Wrappers. $750.
(Report)	REPORT OF THE SECRETARY OF THE INTERIOR, COMMUNICATING THE REPORT OF J. ROSS BROWNE, ON THE LATE INDIAN WAR IN OREGON AND WASHINGTON TERRITORIES. Washington, 1858. Sewed. $150.
(Report)	REPORT ON THE GOVERNOR'S MESSAGE, RELATING TO THE "POLITICAL SITUATION," "POLYGAMY," AND "GOVERNMANTAL ACTION." Salt Lake City, 1882. Wrappers. $150.
(Reports)	REPORTS OF THE COMMITTEE SENT IN 1873, BY THE MEXICAN GOVERNMENT, TO THE FRONTIER OF TEXAS. New York, 1875. 3 folding maps. $250.
(Reports)	REPORTS OF TERRITORIAL OFFICERS OF THE TERRITORY OF COLORADO. Central City, Colo., 1871. Wrappers. $125.
(Resources)	RESOURCES AND DEVELOPMENT OF THE TERRITORY OF WASHINGTON. Seattle, Wash., 1886. Sewed. $125.
Revere, Joseph W.	A TOUR OF DUTY IN CALIFORNIA. New York, 1849. Folding map. $450.
Richardson, Rupert N., and C. C. Rister	THE GREATER SOUTHWEST. Glendale, Calif., 1934. $65.
Ridge, John R.	JOAQUIN MURIETA, THE BRIGAND CHIEF OF CALIFORNIA. San Francisco, 1932. Folding poster. $95.
Ridings, Sam P.	THE CHISHOLM TRAIL. Guthrie, Okla., (1936). Folding map. $100.
Ripley, R. S.	THE WAR WITH MEXICO. New York, 1849. $250.

AUTHOR	TITLE/EDITION INFORMATION/VALUE
Rister, Carl Coke	THE SOUTHWESTERN FRONTIER, 1865-1881. Cleveland, 1928. Maps. $185.
Roberts, Mrs. D. W.	A WOMAN'S REMINISCENCES OF SIX YEARS IN CAMP WITH THE TEXAS RANGERS. Austin, (1928). Wrappers. $85.
Roberts, Oran M.	DESCRIPTION OF TEXAS. St. Louis, 1881. 5 2-page maps. $225.
Roberts, W. H.	NORTHWESTERN WASHINGTON. Port Townsend, Wash., 1880. Folding map. Wrappers. $450.
Robertson, John W.	FRANCIS DRAKE AND OTHER EARLY EXPLORERS ALONG THE PACIFIC COAST. San Francisco, 1927. 28 maps. $225.
Robertson, Wyndham, Jr.	OREGON, OUT RIGHT AND TITLE. Washington, 1846. Folding map. Wrappers or boards. $1,300.
Robinson, Jacob	SKETCHES OF THE GREAT WEST. Portsmouth, N.H., 1848. Wrappers. At least $5,000.
Robinson, William Davis	MEMOIRS OF THE MEXICAN REVOLUTION. Philadelphia, 1820. $350.
Rock, Marion Tuttle	ILLUSTRATED HISTORY OF OKLAHOMA. Topeka, Kans., 1890. 90 plates. $525.
(Rocky)	ROCKY MOUNTAIN DIRECTORY AND COLORADO GAZATTIER FOR 1871. Denver, (1870). $275.
Rogers, A. N.	COMMUNICATION RELATIVE TO THE LOCATION OF THE U.P.R.R. ACROSS THE ROCKY MOUNTAINS THROUGH COLORADO TERRITORY. Central City, Colo., 1867. Wrappers. $550.
Rollinson, John K.	HISTORY OF THE MIGRATION OF OREGON-RAISED HERDS TO MID-WESTERN MARKETS: WYOMING CATTLE TRAILS. Caldwell, Idaho, 1948. $150.
Rollinson, John K.	HOOFPRINTS OF A COWBOY AND A U.S. RANGER. Caldwell, Idaho, 1941. $85.

AUTHOR	TITLE/EDITION INFORMATION/VALUE
Roosevelt, Theodore	THE WINNING OF THE WEST. 4 vols. New York, 1889-1896. $450.
Root, Frank A., and William E. Connelley	THE OVERLAND STAGE TO CALIFORNIA. Topeka, Kans., 1901. Map. $175.
Rose, Victor M.	ROSS' TEXAS BRIGADE. Louisville, Ky., 1881. $1,000.
Ross, Alexander	ADVENTURES OF THE FIRST SETTLERS ON THE OREGON OR COLUMBIA RIVER. London, 1949. Folding map. $1,300.
Ross, Alexander	THE FUR HUNTERS OF THE FAR WEST. 2 vols. London, 1855. Map. $650.
(Rules)	RULES AND ORDERS OF THE HOUSE OF REPRESENTATIVES OF THE TERRITORY OF WASHINGTON, 1864-5. Olympia, Washington Territory, 1864. Wrappers. $225.
(Rules)	RULES AND REGULATIONS OF THE UTAH AND NORTHERN RAILWAY, FOR THE GOVERNMENT PF EMPLOYEES. Salt Lake City, 1879. $150.
(Rules)	RULES, REGULATIONS, AND BY-LAWS OF THE BOARD OF COMMISSIONERS TO MANAGE THE YOSEMITE VALLEY AND MARIPOSA BIG TREE GROVE. Sacramento, 1885. Wrappers. $175.
Russell, Alex J.	THE RED RIVER COUNTRY, HUDSON'S BAY AND NORTH-WEST TERRITORIES. Ottawa, Canada, 1869. Folding map. Wrappers. $175.
Russell, Osborne	JOURNAL OF A TRAPPER, OR NINE YEARS IN THE ROCKY MOUNTAINS. (Boise, Idaho, 1914). $450.
Ruxton, George E.	LIFE IN THE FAR WEST. Edinburgh, 1849. $250.
Ryan, William R.	PERSONAL ADVENTURES IN UPPER AND LOWER CALIFORNIA IN 1848-49. London, 1850. 23 plates. $350.

AUTHOR	TITLE/EDITION INFORMATION/VALUE
Sabin, Edwin L.	BUILDING THE PACIFIC RAILWAY. Philadelphia, 1919. $65.
Sabin, Edwin L.	KIT CARSON DAYS (1809-1868). Chicago, 1914. $100.
Salpointe, John B.	A BRIEF SKETCH OF THE MISSION OF SAN XAVIER DEL BAC WITH A DESCRIPTION OF ITS CHURCH. San Francisco, 1880. Wrappers. $200.
(Salt)	THE SALT LAKE CITY DIRECTORY AND BUSINESS GUIDE [Edward L. Sloan]. Salt Lake City, 1869. $200.
(San Bernardino)	SAN BERNARDINO COUNTY, CALIFORNIA, ILLUSTRATED DESCRIPTION OF. San Bernardino, 1881. Wrappers. $200.
(San Bernardino)	SAN BERNARDINO COUNTY, CALIFORNIA. INGERSOLL'S CENTURY ANNALS OF SAN BERNARDINO COUNTY, 1769-1904. Los Angeles, 1904. $125.
(San Francisco)	SAN FRANCISCO BAY AND CALIFORNIA IN 1776 [Pedro Font]. Providence, R.I., 1911. $250.
(San Francisco)	SAN FRANCISCO BOARD OF ENGINEERS: REPORT UPON CITY GRADES. San Francisco, 1854. Wrappers. $185.
(San Francisco)	SAN FRANCISCO DIRECTORY FOR THE YEAR 1852-53. San Francisco, 1852. $875.
Santee, Ross	MEN AND HORSES. New York, (1926). $125.
Santleben, August	A TEXAS PIONEER. New York, 1910. $300.
Sawyer, Eugene T.	THE LIFE AND CAREER OF TIBURCIO VASQUEZ. (San Jose, Calif., 1875). Wrappers. $350.
Saxton, Charles	THE OREGONIAN; OR HISTORY OF THE OREGON TERRITORY. Oregon City, Oreg., 1846. Wrappers. At least $1,800.

AUTHOR	TITLE/EDITION INFORMATION/VALUE
(Scenes)	SCENES IN THE ROCKY MOUNTAINS, OREGON, CALIFORNIA, NEW MEXICO AND GRAND PRIARIES. BY A NEW ENGLANDER [Rufus B. Sage]. Philadelphia, 1846. Wrappers. $850.
Scharmann, H. B.	OVERLAND JOURNEY TO CALIFORNIA. (New York, 1918). $175.
Schmitz, Joseph M.	TEXAN STATECRAFT, 1836-1845. San Antonio, Tex., 1941. $65.
Schoolcraft, Henry R.	NARRATIVE JOURNAL OF TRAVELS THROUGH THE NORTHWESTERN REGIONS OF THE U.S. Albany, N.Y., 1821. Folding map. 7 plates. $250.
Schoolcraft, Henry R., and James Allen	EXPEDITION TO NORTH-WEST INDIANS. (Washington, 1834). Wrappers. $225.
Schwettman, Martin W.	SANTA RITA, THE UNIVERSITY OF TEXAS OIL DISCOVERY. N.p., 1943. Wrappers. $75.
Sealsfield, Charles	THE CABIN BOOK; OR, SKETCHES OF LIFE IN TEXAS. New York, 1844. 3 parts. Wrappers. $750.
Seyd, Ernest	CALIFORNIA AND ITS RESOURCES. London, 1858. 2 folding maps. $575.
Seymour, E. S.	EMIGRANT'S GUIDE TO THE GOLD MINES OF UPPER CALIFORNIA. Chicago, 1849. Wrappers. At least $2,500.
Sherwood, J. Ely	CALIFORNIA: HER WEALTH AND RESOURCES. New York, 1848. Wrappers. $1,350.
Shields, G. O.	CRUISING IN THE CASCADES. Chicago, 1889. $125.
Shinn, Charles Howard	GRAPHIC DESCRIPTION OF PACIFIC COAST OUTLAWS. (San Francisco, 1890-1895). Wrappers. $425.
Shinn, Charles Howard	MINING CAMPS. New York, 1885. $175.
Shinn, Charles Howard	PACIFIC RURAL HANDBOOK. San Francisco, 1879. $135.

AUTHOR	TITLE/EDITION INFORMATION/VALUE
Shipley, Conway	SKETCHES IN THE PACIFIC. London, 1851. Plates. Folio. At least $5,500.
Shipman, Mrs. O. L.	TAMING THE BIG BEND. Marfa, Tex., 1926. Folding map. $275.
Silliman, Benjamin	A DESCRIPTION OF THE RECENTLY DISCOVERED PETROLEUM REGION IN CALIFORNIA. New York, 1864. Wrappers. $850.
(Silver)	SILVER MINES OF VIRGINIA AND AUSTIN, NEVADA. Boston, 1865. Wrappers. $375.
Simpson, James H.	REPORT OF THE SECRETARY OF WAR AND MAP OF WAGON ROADS IN UTAH. (Washington, 1859). Folding map. $175.
Simpson, Thomas	NARRATIVE OF THE DISCOVERIES ON THE NORTHWEST COAST OF AMERICA. London, 1843. Maps. $450.
Siringo, Charles	A HISTORY OF "BILLY THE KID." (Santa Fe, N. Mex., 1920). Wrappers. $850.
Siringo, Charles A.	RIATA AND SPURS. Boston, 1927. Plates. $375.
Siringo, Charles A.	TEXAS COWBOY, OR FIFTEEN YEARS ON THE HURRICANE DECK OF A SPANISH PONY. Chicago, 1885. Wrappers or cloth. At least $5,500.
Sitgreaves, Lorenzo	REPORT OF AN EXPEDITION DOWN THE ZUNI AND COLORADO RIVERS. Washington, 1853. Folding map. 79 plates. $400.
(Sketches)	SKETCHES OF MISSION LIFE AMONG THE INDIANS OF OREGON. New York, 1854. $275.
Sloan, Edward L., editor	SALT LAKE CITY: GAZETTEER AND DIRECTORY. Salt Lake City, 1874. $250.
Sloan, Robert W.	UTAH GAZETTEER AND DIRECTORY OF LOGAN, OGDEN, PROVO AND SALT LAKE CITIES. Salt Lake City, 1884. $250.

AUTHOR	TITLE/EDITION INFORMATION/VALUE
Smart, Stephen F.	LEADVILLE, TEN MILE AND ALL OTHER NOTED COLORADO MINING CAMPS. Kansas City, 1879. 2 folding maps. Wrappers. $500.
Smith, Ashbel	REMINISCENCES OF THE TEXAS REPUBLIC. Galveston, Tex., 1876. $275.
Smith, Frank Meriweather, editor	SAN FRANCISCO VIGILANCE COMMITTEE OF '56. San Francisco, 1883. Wrappers. $200.
Smith, James F.	THE CHEROKEE LAND LOTTERY, ETC. New York, 1838. $275.
Smith, Jodie, editor	HISTORY OF THE CHISUM WAR [Ike Fridge]. (Electra, Tex., 1927). Wrappers. $125.
Taft, Robert	ARTISTS AND ILLUSTRATORS OF THE OLD WEST. New York, 1953. $65.
Tarascon, Louis A., et al.	PETITION PRAYING THE OPENING OF A WAGON ROAD FROM THE RIVER MISSOURI, NORTH OF THE RIVER KANSAS, TO THE RIVER COLUMBIA. Washington, 1824. Sewed. $275.
Taylor, Bayard	ELDORADO, OR, ADVENTURES IN THE PATH OF EMPIRE. 2 vols. New York, 1850. $700.
Taylor, Thomas U.	JESSE CHISHOLM. Bandera, Tex., (1939). $125.
(Territory)	THE TERRITORY OF WYOMING: ITS HISTORY, SOIL, CLIMATE, RESOURCES, ETC. [J. K. Jeffrey]. Laramie City, Wyoming Territory, 1874. Wrappers. $625.
(Texas)	TEXAS IN 1840, OR THE EMIGRANT'S GUIDE TO THE NEW REPUBLIC [A. B. Lawrence and C. J. Stille]. New York, 1840. $550.
(Texas)	TEXAS, THE HOME FOR THE EMIGRANT FROM EVERYWHERE [J. B. Robertson]. Houston, 1875. Wrappers. $250.

AUTHOR	TITLE/EDITION INFORMATION/VALUE
Thom, Adam	THE CLAIMS TO THE OREGON TERRITORY CONSIDERED. London, 1844. Wrappers. $225.
Thompson, R. A.	CENTRAL SONOMA: A BRIEF DESCRIPTION OF THE TOWNSHIP AND TOWN OF SANTA ROSA, SONOMA COUNTY, CALIFORNIA. Santa Rosa, Calif., 1884. Wrappers. $250.
Thompson, R. A.	CONQUEST OF CALIFORNIA. Santa Rosa, Calif., 1896. Wrappers. $110.
Udell, John	INCIDENTS OF TRAVEL TO CALIFORNIA, ACROSS THE GREAT PLAINS. Jefferson, Ohio, 1856. $450.
Van Tramp, John C.	PRAIRIE AND ROCKY MOUNTAIN ADVENTURES. Columbus, Ohio, 1858. $140.
Vaughn, Robert	THEN AND NOW, OR 36 YEARS IN THE ROCKIES. Minneapolis, 1900. $165.
Velasco, Jose Francisco	SONORA: ITS EXTENT, POPULATION, NATURAL PRODUCTIONS, INDIAN TRIBES, MINES, MINERAL LANDS, San Francisco, 1861. $225.
Vischer, Edward	SKETCHES OF THE WASHOE MINING REGION. San Francisco, 1862. Portfolio with 29 plates. Wrappers. $1,800.
(Visit)	A VISIT TO TEXAS. New York, 1834. Folding color map. $700.
Voorhees, Luke	PERSONAL RECOLLECTIONS OF PIONEER LIFE ON THE MOUNTAINS AND PLAINS OF THE GREAT WEST. Cheyenne, Wyo., (1920). $140.
Wagner, Henry R.	THE CARTOGRAPHY OF THE NORTHWEST COAST OF AMERICA TO THE YEAR 1800. 2 vols. Berkeley, Calif., 1937. Folio. Boxed. $575.

AUTHOR	TITLE/EDITION INFORMATION/VALUE
Wagner, Henry R.	THE PLAINS AND THE ROCKIES. San Francisco, 1920. $350; San Francisco, 1921. $125.
Wagner, Henry R.	SPANISH EXPLORATIONS IN THE STRAIT OF JUAN DE FUCA. Santa Ana, Calif., 1933. Maps. $250.
Wagner, Henry R.	THE SPANISH SOUTHWEST, 1542-1794. Berkeley, Calif., 1924. $400.
Wagner, Henry R.	THE SPANISH VOYAGES TO THE NORTHWEST COAST OF AMERICA. San Francisco, 1929. Maps. $225.
Walker, Tacetta	STORIES OF EARLY DAYS IN WYOMING: BIG HORN BASIN. Casper, Wyo., (1936). $40.
Wallace, Ed. R.	PARSON HANKS: 14 YEARS IN THE WEST. Arlington, Tex., (1906). $175.
Walters, Lorenzo D.	TOMBSTONE'S YESTERDAY. Tucson, Ariz., 1928. $125.
Walton, W. M.	LIFE AND ADVENTURES OF BEN THOMPSON, THE FAMOUS TEXAN. Austin, Tex., 1884. Wrappers. $1,800.
Ware, Joseph E.	THE EMIGRANT'S GUIDE TO CALIFORNIA. St. Louis, (1849). Folding map. $2,800.
Warre, Henry J.	SKETCHES IN NORTH AMERICA AND THE OREGON TERRITORY. (London, 1848). Maps. Plates. Folio. At least $12,000.
Waters, Frank	MASKED GODS: NAVAHO AND PUEBLO CEREMONIALISM. Albuquerque, N. Mex., 1950. $85.
Watkins, C. L.	PHOTOGRAPHIC VIEWS OF THE FALLS AND VALLEY OF YO-SEMITE. San Francisco, 1863. Map and mounted photographs. Folio. At least $12,000.
Watkins. C. L.	PHOTOGRAPHS OF THE COLUMBIA RIVER AND OREGON. San Francisco, (1873). 51 mounted albumen prints. Large folio. At least $125,000.

AUTHOR	TITLE/EDITION INFORMATION/VALUE
Watkins, C. L.	PHOTOGRAPHS OF THE PACIFIC COAST. San Francisco, (1873). 49 mounted albumen prints. Large folio. At least $125,000.
Watkins, C. L.	WATKINS NEW SERIES COLUMBIA RIVER SCENERY, OREGON. N.p., (1880). 40 plates. At least $10,000.
Watson, Douglas S.	CALIFORNIA IN THE FIFTIES. San Francisco, 1936, 50 views. Folio. $450.
Watson, Douglas S.	THE SPANISH OCCUPATION OF CALIFORNIA. San Francisco, 1934. $125.
Watts, J. L.	CHEROKEE CITIZENSHIP AND A BRIEF HISTORY OF INTERNAL AFFAIRS IN THE CHEROKEE NATION. Muldrow, Indian Territory, Okla., 1895. Wrappers. $175.
Webb, Walter Prescott	THE TEXAS RANGERS. Boston, 1935. $100.
Werth, John J.	A DISSERTATION ON THE RESOURCES AND POLICY OF CALIFORNIA. Benicia, Calif., 1851. $1,300.
Weston, Edward	CALIFORNIA AND THE WEST. New York, 1940. $250.
Weston, Edward	MY CAMERA ON POINT LOBOS. Yosemite National Park and Boston, 1950. Folio. Spiral bound. $450.
Weston, Silas	FOUR MONTHS IN THE MINES OF CALIFORNIA; OR, LIFE IN THE MOUNTAINS. Providence, R.I., 1854, 24 pp. Wrappers. $375. Second edition of next entry.
Weston, Silas	LIFE IN THE MOUNTAINS; OR, FOUR MONTHS IN THE MINES OF CALIFORNIA. Providence, R.I., 1854, 36 pp. Wrappers. $425. First edition of previous item.
Wetherbee, J., Jr.	A BRIEF SKETCH OF COLORADO TERRITORY AND THE GOLD MINES OF THAT REGION. Boston, 1863. Wrappers. At least $2,000.
Wheat, Carl I.	BOOKS OF THE GOLD RUSH. San Francisco, 1949. $275.

AUTHOR	TITLE/EDITION INFORMATION/VALUE
Wheat, Carl I.	THE MAPS OF THE CALIFORNIA GOLD REGION, 1848. San Francisco, 1942. 26 maps. Folio. $1,200.
Wheat, Carl I.	THE PIONEER PRESS OF CALIFORNIA. Oakland, Calif., 1948. $200.
Whilldin, M. A.	DESCRIPTION OF WESTERN TEXAS. Galveston, Tex., 1876. Folding map. Plates. Wrappers. $600.
Whitely, Ike	RURAL LIFE IN TEXAS. Atlanta, Ga., 1891. Wrappers. $325.
Whitney, J. D.	THE AURIFEROUS GRAVELS OF THE SIERRA NEVEDA OF CALIFORNIA. Cambridge, Mass., 1880. Folding map and plates. $150.
Whitney, J. D.	THE YOSEMITE BOOK. New York, 1868. 28 photo plates. 2 maps. $3,500.
Wilbarger, J. W.	INDIAN DEPREDATIONS IN TEXAS. Austin, Tex., 1889. Plates. $725.
Wilkes, Charles	WESTERN AMERICA, INCLUDING CALIFORNIA AND OREGON. Philadelphia, 1949. 3 folding maps. Wrappers. $875.
Wilkes, George	THE HISTORY OF OREGON, GEOGRAPHICAL AND POLITICAL. New York, 1845. Folding map. Wrappers. $1,750.
Wilkeson, Samuel	WILKESON'S NOTES ON PUGET SOUND. (New York, 1870). Wrappers. $350.
Willcox, R. N.	REMINISCENCES OF CALIFORNIA LIFE. (Avery, Ohio), 1897. $225.
Willey, S. H.	AN HISTORICAL PAPER RELATING TO SANTA CRUZ, CALIFORNIA. San Francisco, 1876. Wrappers. $165.
Williams, Joseph	NARRATIVE OF A TOUR FROM THE STATE OF INDIANA TO THE OREGON TERRITORY. Cincinnati, 1843. Wrappers. $6,500.

AUTHOR	TITLE/EDITION INFORMATION/VALUE
Williams, O. W.	IN OLD NEW MEXICO, 1879-1880: REMINISCENCES OF JUDGE O. W. WILLIAMS. N.p., n.d.. Wrappers. $125.
Wilson, John Albert	HISTORY OF LOS ANGELES COUNTY, CALIFORNIA. Oakland, Calif., 1880. $500.
Wilson, Obed G.	MY ADVENTURES IN THE SIERRAS. Franklin, Ohio, 1902. $85.
Wiltsee, Ernest A.	GOLD RUSH STEAMERS. San Francisco, 1938. $125.
Winkler, A. V.	THE CONFEDERATE CAPITAL AND HOOD'S TEXAS BRIGADE. Austin, Tex., 1894. $225.
Wislizenus, Frederick A.	MEMOIR OF A TOUR TO NORTHERN MEXICO. Washington, 1848. 3 folding maps. $250.
Wood, W. D.	REMINISCENCES OF RECONSTRUCTION IN TEXAS. (San Marcos, Tex.), 1902. Wrappers. $150.
Woodman, David, Jr.	GUIDE TO TEXAS EMIGRANTS. Boston, 1835. Map. At least $2,500.
Wooten, Dudley G.	A COMPREHENSIVE HISTORY OF TEXAS, 1865 TO 1897. 2 vols. Dallas, 1898. 23 plates. $350.
Wright, E. W.,	LEWIS AND DRYDEN'S MARINE HISTORY OF THE PACIFIC NORTHWEST. Portland, Oreg., 1895. $550.
Wyeth, John B.	OREGON; OR A SHORT HISTORY OF A LONG JOURNEY. Cambridge, Mass., 1833. Wrappers. $1,800.

11

General Americana Books, and Their Values

This is a very important collecting category. The authors and titles presented here are those that are best known to the general public. Only titles having a current market value of at least $100 are listed. It is reasonable to assume that all first-edition books by any of the authors listed will have value, but do *not* assume that all books by the same author will have comparable values.

The values given here are for first-edition books in very good to fine condition, and with a dust jacket if the book was originally issued with one. "Points" often need to be verified to properly identify many of these books. A librarian or rare bookseller should be consulted for verification of edition and value.

AUTHOR	TITLE/EDITION INFORMATION/VALUE
Alexander, E. P.	MILITARY MEMOIRS OF A CONFEDERATE. New York, 1907. $135-160.
Allen, J. A.	NOTES ON THE NATURAL HISTORY OF PORTIONS OF MONTANA AND DAKOTA. Boston, 1874. Wrappers. $110-135.
Allen, William A.	ADVENTURES WITH INDIANS AND GAME. Chicago, 1903. $175-225.
Andreas, A. T.	ATLAS MAP OF PEORIA COUNTY, ILLINOIS. Chicago, 1873. $350-425.
Andreas, A. T.	HISTORY OF CHICAGO. 3 vols. Chicago, 1884-1886. $375-425.

AUTHOR	TITLE/EDITION INFORMATION/VALUE
Andreas, A. T.	HISTORY OF THE STATE OF KANSAS. Chicago, 1883. $450-550.
Andreas, A. T.	ILLUSTRATED HISTORICAL ATLAS OF THE STATE OF IOWA. Chicago, 1875. $450 or more.
Armstrong, Moses K.	HISTORY AND RESOURCES OF DAKOTA, MONTANA AND IDAHO. Yanktown, Dakota Territory, 1866. Wrappers. $3,750-4,250.
Ashley, Clifford W.	THE YANKEE WHALER. Boston, 1926. Trade edition. $225-300.
Atwater, Caleb	A HISTORY OF THE STATE OF OHIO. Cincinnati, (1838). $175-200.
Atwater, Caleb	MYSTERIES OF WASHINGTON CITY. Washington City (Washington, D.C.), 1844. $135-160.
Babbitt, E. L.	THE ALLEGHENY PILOT. Freeport, Pa., 1855. Wrappers. $175-225.
Baily, Francis	JOURNAL OF A TOUR IN UNSETTLED PARTS OF NORTH AMERICA IN 1796 & 1797. London, 1856. $600-750.
Balme, J. R.	AMERICAN STATES, CHURCHES AND SLAVERY. London, 1863. $45-65.
Barbe-Marbois, François	THE HISTORY OF LOUISIANA, PARTICULARLY THE CESSION OF THAT COLONY TO THE U.S.A. Philadelphia, 1830. $375-425.
Barnard, George N.	PHOTOGRAPHIC VIEW OF SHERMAN'S CAMPAIGN. New York, (1866). 61 gold-tone albumen prints. $10,000 or more.
Barnes, David M.	THE DRAFT RIOTS IN NEW YORK, JULY, 1863. New York, 1863. Wrappers. $175-225.
Barrows, R. M.	THE KITBOOK FOR SOLDIERS, SAILORS, AND MARINES. Chicago, (1943). $75-125.

AUTHOR	TITLE/EDITION INFORMATION/VALUE
Barrows, Willard	NOTES ON IOWA TERRITORY. Cincinnati, 1845. $1,500 or more.
Barton, James L.	COMMERCE OF THE LAKES. Buffalo, N.Y., 1847. Wrappers. $125-150.
Bates, Finis L.	ESCAPE AND SUICIDE OF JOHN WILKES BOOTH. Memphis, Tenn., 1907. $85-100.
Beard, Charles A.	AN ECONOMIC INTERPRETATION OF THE CONSTITUTION OF THE UNITED STATES. New York, 1913. $225-275.
Beck, Lewis C.	A GAZETEER OF THE STATES OF ILLINOIS AND MISSOURI. Albany, N.Y., 1823. $850 or more.
Benson, Henry C.	LIFE AMONG THE CHOCTAW INDIANS. Cincinnati, 1860. $225-275.
Bevier, Robert S.	HISTORY OF THE FIRST AND SECOND MISSOURI CONFEDERATE BRIGADES, 1861-65. St. Louis, 1879. $175-225.
Bickerstaff, Isaac	THE RHODE-ISLAND ALMANAC FOR 1842. Providence, R.I., (1841). Wrappers. $175-225.
Bingham, Helen M.	HISTORY OF GREEN COUNTY, WISCONSIN. Milwaukee, Wis., 1877. $85-100.
Birkbeck, Morris	AN APPEAL TO THE PEOPLE OF ILLINOIS, ON THE QUESTION OF A CONVENTION. Shawneetown, Ill., 1823. Wrappers. $550-750.
Birkbeck, Morris	NOTES ON A JOURNEY IN AMERICA FROM THE COAST OF VIRGINIA TO THE TERRITORY OF ILLINOIS. Philadelphia, 1817. $300-375.
Blackbird, Andrew J.	HISTORY OF THE OTTAWA AND CHIPPEWA INDIANS OF MICHIGAN. Ypsilanti, Mich., 1887. $175-225.
Blanchard, Rufus, publisher	CITIZEN'S GUIDE FOR THE CITY OF CHICAGO: COMPANION TO BLANCHARD'S MAP OF CHICAGO. Chicago,

AUTHOR	TITLE/EDITION INFORMATION/VALUE
	(1868). Wrappers. Map bound in. $750 or more.
Blowe, Daniel	A GEOGRAPHICAL, COMMERCIAL, AND AGRICULTURAL VIEW OF THE UNITED STATES OF AMERICA. Liverpool, England, (1820). $250-325.
Bond, J. Wesley	MINNESOTA AND ITS RESOURCES. Chicago, 1856. $125-175.
Bonney, Edward	BANDITTI OF THE PRAIRIES; OR, THE MURDERER'S DOOM! Chicago, 1850. Wrappers. $4,200 or more.
Bosworth, Newton	HOCHELAGA DEPICTA: THE EARLY HISTORY AND PRESENT STATE OF THE CITY AND ISLAND OF MONTREAL. Montreal, 1839. $225-275.
Bouchette, Joseph	A TOPOGRAPHICAL DESCRIPTION OF THE PROVINCE OF LOWER CANADA, WITH REMARKS UPON UPPER CANADA. London, 1815. $325-375.
Bourke, John G.	ON THE BORDER WITH CROOK. New York, 1891. $175-225.
Bowditch, Nathaniel	THE NEW AMERICAN PRACTICAL NAVIGATOR. Newburyport, Mass., 1802. $1,500 or more.
Brackenridge, H. M.	JOURNAL OF A VOYAGE UP THE MISSOURI. Baltimore, Md., 1815. $350 or more.
Bradbury, John	TRAVELS IN THE INTERIOR OF AMERICA. Liverpool, England, 1817. $1,100-1,500.
Bradley, Joshua	ACCOUNTS OF RELIGIOUS REVIVALS IN MANY PARTS OF THE UNITED STATES FROM 1815 TO 1818. Albany, N.Y., 1819. $60-75.
Brice, Wallace	A HISTORY OF FORT WAYNE. Fort Wayne, Ind., 1868. $110-135.
Briggs, L. Vernon	HISTORY OF SHIPBUILDING ON NORTH RIVER, PLYMOUTH COUNTY, MASSACHUSETTS. Boston, 1889. $175-225.

AUTHOR	TITLE/EDITION INFORMATION/VALUE
Britton, Wiley	MEMOIRS OF THE REBELLION ON THE BORDER. Chicago, 1882. $85-100.
Brower, Jacob V.	MEMOIRS OF EXPLORATIONS IN THE BASIN OF THE MISSISSIPPI. 8 vols. St. Paul, Minn., 1898-1904. $450 or more.
Brown, Henry	HISTORY OF ILLINOIS. New York, 1844. $175-225.
Brown, Jesse, and A. M. Willard	THE BLACK HILLS TRAILS. Rapid City, S. Dak., 1924. $125-150.
Brown, Samuel R.	THE WESTERN GAZETTEER, OR EMIGRANT'S DIRECTORY. Auburn, N.Y., 1817. $450-550.
Brown, William H.	THE EARLY HISTORY OF THE STATE OF ILLINOIS. Chicago, 1840. Wrappers. $1,100-1,400.
Browne, J. Ross	ETCHINGS OF A WHALING CRUISE. New York, 1846. $350-425.
Brunson, Edward	PROFITS IN SHEEP AND CATTLE IN CENTRAL AND WESTERN KANSAS. Kansas City, Mo., 1883. Wrappers. $225-275.
Buffum, E. Gould	SIX MONTHS IN THE GOLD MINES. Philadelphia, 1850. Cloth or wrappers. $350-500.
Burney, James	HISTORY OF THE BUCCANEERS OF AMERICA. London, 1816. $375-450.
Burnham, Daniel H., and Edward H. Bennett	PLAN OF CHICAGO. Chicago, 1909. $325-375.
Butcher, S. D.	S. D. BUTCHER'S PIONEER HISTORY OF CUSTER COUNTRY. Broken Bow, Nebr., 1901. $125-150.
Butler, Mann	A HISTORY OF THE COMMONWEALTH OF KENTUCKY. Louisville, Ky., 1834. $325-375.
Butterfield, C. W.	AN HISTORICAL ACCOUNT OF THE EXPEDITION AGAINST SANDUSKY. Cincinnati, 1873. $125-150.
Butterfield, C. W.	HISTORY OF SENECA COUNTY, OHIO. Sandusky, Ohio, 1848. $125-150.

AUTHOR	TITLE/EDITION INFORMATION/VALUE
Byers, William N., and John H. Kellom	A HAND BOOK TO THE GOLD FIELDS OF NEBRASKA AND KANSAS. Chicago, 1859. Wrappers. $5,250 or more.
Byrd, William (of Westover)	THE WRITINGS OF "COLONEL WILLIAM BYRD OF WESTOVER IN VIRGINIA, ESQ." New York, 1901. $125-150.
Byrne, B. M.	LETTERS ON THE CLIMATE, SOILS, AND PRODUCTIONS OF FLORIDA. Jacksonville, Fla., 1851. Wrappers. $325-375.
(Cabinet)	THE CABINET OF NATURAL HISTORY AND AMERICAN RURAL SPORT. 3 vols. Philadelphia, 1830-32-33. $17,000 or more.
Cable, George W.	THE CREOLES OF LOUISIANA. New York, 1884. $85-100.
Caldwell, J. A.	HISTORY OF BELMONT AND JEFFERSON COUNTIES, OHIO. Wheeling, Ohio, 1880. $125-175.
Caldwell, J. F. J.	HISTORY OF A BRIGADE OF SOUTH CAROLINIANS. Philadelphia, 1866. $225-275.
Campbell, Patrick	TRAVELS IN THE INTERIOR INHABITED PARTS OF NORTH AMERICA. Toronto, 1937. $135-160.
Cannon, J. P.	INSIDE OF REBELDOM: THE DAILY LIFE OF A PRIVATE IN THE CONFEDERATE ARMY. Washington, D.C., 1900. $100-150.
Canova, Andrew P.	LIFE AND ADVENTURES IN SOUTH FLORIDA. Palatka, Fla., 1885. Wrappers. $225-275.
Carlyle, Thomas	OCCASIONAL DISCOURSE ON THE NIGGER QUESTION. London, 1853. Wrappers. $350-425.
Carr, John	EARLY TIMES IN MIDDLE TENNESSEE. Nashville, Tenn., 1857. $175-225.

AUTHOR	TITLE/EDITION INFORMATION/VALUE
Carr, Spencer	A BRIEF SKETCH OF LA CROSSE, WISCONSIN. La Crosse, Wis., 1854. Wrappers. $275-325.
Casler, John	FOUR YEARS IN THE STONEWALL BRIGADE. Guthrie, Okla., 1893. $125-150.
Castleman, Alfred L.	ARMY OF THE POTOMAC: BEHIND THE SCENES. Milwaukee, Wis., 1863. $85-100.
Catlin, George	LETTERS AND NOTES ON THE MANNERS, CUSTOMS, AND CONDITIONS OF THE NORTH AMERICAN INDIANS. 2 vols. London, 1841. $1,000 or more.
Catlin, George	NORTH AMERICAN INDIAN PORTFOLIO. London, 1844. Large folio. $15,000 or more.
Catlin, George	O-KEE-PA, A RELIGIOUS CEREMONY. London, 1867. $1,500 or more.
(Cattle)	CATTLE RAISING IN SOUTH DAKOTA. (Forest City, S. Dak., 1904). Wrappers. $125-135.
(Celebration)	CELEBRATION OF THE 73RD ANNIVERSARY OF THE DECLARATION OF INDEPENDENCE . . . ON BOARD THE BARQUE "HANNAH SPRAGUE," ETC. New York, 1849. Wrappers. $100-125.
Chadwick, Henry	THE GAME OF BASE BALL: HOW TO LEARN IT, HOW TO PLAY IT, AND HOW TO TEACH IT. New York, (1868). $85-100.
Charlevoix, Pierre F. X.	JOURNAL OF A VOYAGE TO NORTH AMERICA. 2 vols. Chicago, 1923. $175-225.
Childs, C. G., engraver	VIEWS IN PHILADELPHIA AND ITS VICINITY. Philadelphia, 1827(-1830). $2,000 and up.
Chittenden, Hiram M.	HISTORY OF EARLY STEAMBOAT NAVIGATION ON THE MISSOURI RIVER. 2 vols. New York, 1903. $175-225.

AUTHOR	TITLE/EDITION INFORMATION/VALUE
Claiborne, John Herbert	SEVENTY-FIVE YEARS IN OLD VIRGINIA. New York, 1905. $60-75.
Clark, Walter, editor	HISTORIES OF THE SEVERAL REGIMENTS AND BATTALIONS FROM NORTH CAROLINA IN THE GREAT WAR, 1861-1865. 5 vols. Raleigh, N.C., 1901. $200-250.
Clarke, Lewis	NARRATIVE OF THE SUFFERINGS OF LEWIS CLARKE DURING A CAPTIVITY OF MORE THAN TWENTY-FIVE YEARS. Boston, 1845. Wrappers. $125-150.
Clayton, William	THE LATTER-DAY SAINTS' EMIGRANTS' GUIDE. St. Louis, 1848. Wrappers. $3,500 or more.
Coffin, Joshua	A SKETCH OF THE HISTORY OF NEWBURY, NEWBURYPORT, AND WEST NEWBURYPORT. Boston, 1845. $125-175.
Cohn, David L.	NEW ORLEANS AND ITS LIVING PAST. Boston, 1941. Limited and signed edition. $85-100.
Colbert, E.	CHICAGO: HISTORICAL AND STATISTICAL SKETCH OF THE GARDEN CITY. Chicago, 1868. Wrappers. $125-150.
Collins, Charles	COLLINS' HISTORY AND DIRECTORY OF THE BLACK HILLS. Central City, Dakota Territory, 1878. Wrappers. $2,000 and up.
Collins, Charles, compiler	COLLINS' OMAHA DIRECTORY. (Omaha, Nebr., 1866). $800 or more.
Collins, Lieutenant R. M.	CHAPTERS FROM THE UNWRITTEN HISTORY OF THE WAR BETWEEN THE STATES. St. Louis, 1893. $225-275.
Colt, Mirian Davis	WENT TO KANSAS. Watertown, N.Y., 1862. $375-450.
Colton, Calvin	TOUR OF THE AMERICAN LAKES. 2 vols. London, 1853. $175-225.
Conclin, George	CONCLIN'S NEW RIVER GUIDE, OR A GAZETEER OF ALL THE TOWNS ON

AUTHOR	TITLE/EDITION INFORMATION/VALUE
	THE WESTERN WATERS. Cincinnati, 1850. Wrappers. 44 full-page maps. $125-175.
(Confederate)	CONFEDERATE RECEIPT BOOK. Richmond, Va., 1863. Wrappers. $350-450.
Connelley, William E.	QUANTRILL AND THE BORDER WARS. Cedar Rapids, Iowa, 1910. $100-125.
Connolly, A. P.	THRILLING NARRATIVE OF THE MINNESOTA MASSACRE AND THE SIOUX WAR OF 1862-1863. Chicago, (1896). $175-225.
(Constitution)	CONSTITUTION AND LAWS OF THE CHEROKEE NATION. St. Louis, 1875. $375-425.
(Constitution)	CONSTITUTION AND LAWS OF THE MUSKOGEE NATION. St. Louis, 1880. $225-275.
(Constitution)	CONSTITUTION AND PLAYING RULES OF THE INTERNATIONAL BASEBALL ASSOCIATION . . . AND THE CHAMPIONSHIP RECORD FOR 1877. Jamaica Plains, Mass., 1878. Wrappers. $125-175.
(Constitution)	CONSTITUTION OF THE STATE OF SEQUOYAH. (Muscogee, Indian Territory, 1905). Wrappers, $3,500 or more. Second edition, $3,000 or more.
Cook, John R.	THE BORDER AND THE BUFFALO. Topeka, Kans., 1907. $50-65.
Coon, James Churchill	LOG OF THE CRUISE OF 1889 D.T.S.C., NEW SMYRNA TO LAKE WORTH, EAST COAST OF FLORIDA. Lake Helen, Fla., 1889. Wrappers. $125-175.
Coulter, E. Merton	TRAVELS IN THE CONFEDERATE STATES: A BIBLIOGRAPHY. Norman, Okla., 1948. $65-90.
Courtauld, George	ADDRESS TO THOSE WHO MAY BE DISPOSED TO REMOVE TO THE UNITED STATES OF AMERICA. Sudbury, Canada, 1820. Wrappers $1,350 and up.

AUTHOR	TITLE/EDITION INFORMATION/VALUE
Cox, Sandford C.	RECOLLECTIONS OF THE EARLY SETTLEMENT OF THE WABASH VALLEY. Lafayette, Ind., 1860. $115-135.
Crakes, Sylvester	FIVE YEARS A CAPTIVE AMONG THE BLACK-FEET INDIANS. Columbus, Ohio, 1858. $325-375.
Crawford, Lucy	THE HISTORY OF THE WHITE MOUNTAINS. Portland, Maine, 1846. $110-135.
Crotty, D. G.	FOUR YEARS CAMPAIGNING IN THE ARMY OF THE POTOMAC. Grand Rapids, Mich., 1894. $85-100.
Cuffe, Paul	NARRATIVE OF THE LIFE AND ADVENTURES OF PAUL CUFFE, A PEQUOT INDIAN. New York, 1838. Wrappers. $200-250.
Cumings, Samuel	THE WESTERN PILOT. Cincinnati, 1825. $750 or more.
Curley, Edwin A.	NEBRASKA: ITS ADVANTAGES AND DRAWBACKS. London, 1875. $100-150.
Curtis, Edward S.	THE NORTH AMERICAN INDIAN. 20 vols. Cambridge, Mass., 1907-1930. 20 portfolios. Limited and signed edition. $60,000—perhaps much more.
Cushman, H. B.	A HISTORY OF THE CHOCTAW, CHICKSAW AND NATCHEZ INDIANS. Greenville, Tex., 1899. $275-325.
Custer, Elizabeth B.	"BOOTS AND SADDLES" OR LIFE IN DAKOTA WITH GENERAL CUSTER. New York, 1885. $50-65.
Custer, Elizabeth B.	TENTING ON THE PLAINS. New York, 1887. $45-60.
Custer, George A.	MY LIFE ON THE PLAINS. New York, 1874. $175-200.
Dacus, J. A.	LIFE AND ADVENTURES OF FRANK AND JESSE JAMES. St. Louis, 1880. $325-375.

AUTHOR	TITLE/EDITION INFORMATION/VALUE
Dalton, Emmett	WHEN THE DALTONS RODE. Garden City, N.Y., 1931. $60-75.
Daniels, William M.	A CORRECT ACCOUNT OF THE MURDER OF GENERALS JOSEPH AND HYRUM SMITH, AT CARTHAGE, ON THE 27TH DAY OF JUNE, 1944. Nauvoo, Ill., 1845. Wrappers. $2,750-3,250.
Darby, William	A GEOGRAPHICAL DESCRIPTION OF THE STATE OF LOUISIANA. Philadelphia, 1816. $325-375.
Darby, William	A TOUR FROM THE CITY OF NEW YORK, TO DETROIT, IN THE MICHIGAN TERRITORY. New York, 1819. $225-275.
Darlington, Mary Carson, editor	FORT PITT AND LETTERS FROM THE FRONTIER. Pittsburgh, Pa., 1892. Limited large paper edition. $175-225.
Daubeny, Charles	JOURNAL OF A TOUR THROUGH THE UNITED STATES AND CANADA. 1837-1838. Oxford, 1843. $175-250.
Davis, Paris M.	AN AUTHENTICK HISTORY OF THE LATE WAR BETWEEN THE UNITED STATES AND GREAT BRITAIN. Ithaca, N.Y., 1829. $125-150.
Davis, William J., editor, (by Adam R. Johnson)	THE PARTISAN RANGERS OF THE CONFEDERATE STATES ARMY. Louisville, Ky., 1904. $125-175.
Dawson, Simon J.	REPORT ON THE EXPLORATION OF THE COUNTRY BETWEEN LAKE SUPERIOR AND THE RED RIVER SETTLEMENT AND THE ASSINIBOINE AND SASKATCHEWAN. Toronto, 1859. $225-275.
Day, Sherman	REPORT OF THE COMMITTEE ON INTERNAL IMPROVEMENTS, ON THE USE OF THE CAMELS ON THE PLAINS, MAY 30, 1885. (Sacramento, Calif.), 1885. Unbound. $60-75.

AUTHOR	TITLE/EDITION INFORMATION/VALUE
Debar, J. H.	THE WEST VIRGINIA HANDBOOK AND IMMIGRANT'S GUIDE. Parkersburg, W. Va., 1870. $125-175.
(Declaration)	DECLARATION OF THE IMMEDIATE CAUSE WHICH INDUCE AND JUSTIFY THE SECESSION OF SOUTH CAROLINA FROM THE FEDERAL UNION, AND THE ORDINANCE OF SECESSION. Charleston, S.C., 1869. Wrappers. $450-550.
De Hass, Wills	HISTORY OF THE EARLY SETTLEMENT AND INDIAN WARS OF WESTERN VIRGINIA. Wheeling, W. Va., 1851. $225-275.
Delafield, John, Jr.	AN INQUIRY INTO THE ORIGIN OF THE ANTIQUITIES OF AMERICA. New York, 1839. 18-foot-long folding plate. $175-225.
Delano, Alonzo	LIFE ON THE PLAINS AND AMONG THE DIGGINGS. Auburn, N.Y., 1854. $450 or more.
Delano, Amasa	A NARRATIVE OF VOYAGES AND TRAVELS, IN THE NORTHERN AND SOUTHERN HEMISPHERES. Boston, 1817. $500 or more.
Delano, Judah	WASHINGTON (D.C.) DIRECTORY. Washington, D.C., 1822. $550 or more.
De Roos, Fred F.	PERSONAL NARRATIVE OF TRAVELS IN THE UNITED STATES AND CANADA IN 1826. London, 1827. $350-425.
(Description)	A DESCRIPTION OF CENTRAL IOWA, WITH SPECIAL REFERENCE TO POLK COUNTY AND DES MOINES, THE STATE CAPITAL. Des Moines, Iowa, 1858. Wrappers. $450-525.
(Descriptive)	A DESCRIPTIVE ACCOUNT OF THE CITY OF PEORIA,. Peoria, Ill., 1859. Wrappers. $150-175.

AUTHOR	TITLE/EDITION INFORMATION/VALUE
De Tonty, Henri	RELATION OF HENRI DE TONTY CONCERNING THE EXPLORATIONS OF LA SALLE. Chicago, 1898. Limited edition. Text in French and English. $225-275.
De Voto, Bernard	ACROSS THE WIDE MISSOURI. Boston, 1947. Limited edition. Boxed. $125-150.
Dickins, James	1861 TO 1865, BY AN OLD JOHNNIE: PERSONAL RECOLLECTIONS AND EXPERIENCES OF THE CONFEDERATE ARMY. Cincinnati, 1897. $125-175.
Dietz, August	THE POSTAL SERVICE OF THE CONFEDERATE STATES OF AMERICA. Richmond, Va., 1929. $125-175.
Diomedi, Alexander	SKETCHES OF MODERN INDIAN LIFE. (Woodstock, Md., 1894). Wrappers. $140-170.
(Directory)	DIRECTORY OF THE CITY OF MINERAL POINT FOR THE YEAR 1859. Mineral Point, Wis., 1859. $225-275.
Disturnell, John	THE INFLUENCE OF CLIMATE IN NORTH AND SOUTH AMERICA. New York, 1867. $125-150.
Disturnell, John, publisher	DISTURNELL'S GUIDE THROUGH THE MIDDLE, NORTHERN, AND EASTERN STATES. New York, 1847. Maps. $75-100.
Disturnell, John, publisher	THE GREAT LAKES OR INLAND SEAS OF AMERICA. New York, 1868. $175-225.
Disturnell, John, publisher	THE UPPER LAKES OF NORTH AMERICA: A GUIDE. New York, 1857. $125-150.
Doddridge, Joseph	NOTES, ON THE SETTLEMENT AND INDIAN WARS, OF THE WESTERN PARTS OF VIRGINIA AND PENNSYLVANIA, ETC. Wellsburgh, Va., 1924. $500 or more.
Dodge, Grenville M.	HOW WE BUILT THE UNION PACIFIC RAILWAY. Council Bluffs, Iowa, (1908). Wrappers. $125-175.
Dodge, Richard Irving	THE BLACK HILLS. New York, 1876. $125-150.

AUTHOR	TITLE/EDITION INFORMATION/VALUE
Dodge, Richard Irving	OUR WILD INDIANS. Hartford, Conn., 1882. $100-125.
Dodge, William Sumner	A WAIF OF THE WAR; OR, THE HISTORY OF THE 75TH ILLINOIS INFANTRY. Chicago, 1866. $165-200.
(Domestic)	DOMESTIC COOKERY: THE EXPERIENCED AMERICAN HOUSEKEEPER. New York, 1823. $150-175.
Douglas, James	THE GOLD FIELDS OF CANADA. Quebec, 1863. Wrappers. $150-175.
Dow, George Francis	THE ARTS AND CRAFTS IN NEW ENGLAND. Topsfield, Mass., 1927. $175-225.
Dow, George Francis	WHALE SHIPS AND WHALING. Salem, Mass., 1925. Limited edition. $150-175.
Dow, George Francis, and John H. Edmonds	THE PIRATES OF THE NEW ENGLAND COAST. Salem, Mass., 1923. $90-125.
Drake, Benjamin	TALES AND SKETCHES OF THE QUEEN CITY. Cincinnati, 1838. $90-125.
Drake, Benjamin, and E. D. Mansfield	CINCINATTI IN 1826. Cincinnati, 1827. $125-175.
Drake, Daniel	AN ACCOUNT OF EPIDEMIC CHOLERA, AS IT APPEARED IN CINCINNATI. Cincinnati, 1832. Wrappers. $250-300.
Drake, Daniel	NATURAL AND STATISTICAL VIEW, OR PICTURE OF CINCINNATI AND THE MIAMI COUNTRY. Cincinnati, 1815. $400 or more.
Drake, Morgan	LAKE SUPERIOR RAILROAD: LETTER TO THE HON. LEWIS CASS. Pontiac, Mich., 1853. Wrappers. $275-325.
Drayton, John	MEMOIRS OF THE AMERICAN REVOLUTION. 2 vols. Charleston, S.C., 1821. $650-725.
Drayton, John	A VIEW OF SOUTH-CAROLINA. Charleston, S.C., 1802. $850 or more.
Drips, Joseph H.	THREE YEARS AMONG THE INDIANS IN DAKOTA. Kimball, S. Dak., 1894. Wrappers $800 and up.

AUTHOR	TITLE/EDITION INFORMATION/VALUE
Drysdale, Isabel	SCENES IN GEORGIA. Philadelphia, (1827). $100-125.
Duncan, John M.	TRAVELS THROUGH PART OF THE UNITED STATES AND CANADA IN 1818 AND 1819. 2 vols. Glasgow, Scotland, 1823. $400 or more; 2 vols. New York, 1823. $125-175.
Duncan, L. Wallace	HISTORY OF MONTGOMERY COUNTY, KANSAS. Iola, Kans., 1903. $125-175.
Duncan, L. Wallace	HISTORY OF WILSON AND NEOSHO COUNTIES, KANSAS. Fort Scott, Kans., 1902. $125-175.
Dunlap, William	A HISTORY OF THE AMERICAN THEATRE. New York, 1832. $125-175.
Dunlap, William	A HISTORY OF THE NEW NETHERLANDS. 2 vols. New York, 1839-1840. $225-275.
Dunlap, William	HISTORY OF THE RISE AND PROGRESS OF THE ARTS OF DESIGN IN THE UNITED STATES. 2 vols. New York, 1834. $225-275.
Dustin, Fred	THE CUSTER TRAGEDY. Ann Arbor, Mich., 1939. 3 folding maps. Limited edition. $350-425.
Dwight, Timothy	TRAVELS IN NEW-ENGLAND AND NEW YORK. 4 vols. New Haven, Conn., 1821-1822. 3 maps. $225-275.
Dyer, Frederick H.	A COMPENDIUM OF THE WAR OF THE REBELLION. Des Moines, Iowa, 1908. $90-120.
Early, Lieutenant General Jubal A.	A MEMOIR OF THE LAST YEAR OF THE WAR FOR INDEPENDENCE IN THE CONFEDERATE STATES OF AMERICA. Toronto, 1866. $175-225.

AUTHOR	**TITLE/EDITION INFORMATION/VALUE**
Eastman, Mary H.	THE AMERICAN ABORIGINAL PORTFOLIO. Philadelphia, (1853). 26 plates. $550-650.
Easton, John	A NARRATIVE OF THE CAUSES WHICH LED TO PHILLIP'S INDIAN WAR. Albany, N.Y., 1858. Map. $75-100.
Eaton, Rachel Caroline	JOHN ROSS AND THE CHEROKEE INDIANS. Menasha, Wis., 1914. $175-225.
Eckenrode, Hamilton J.	THE REVOLUTION IN VIRGINIA. Boston, 1916. $60-75.
Edwards, Billy	GLADIATORS OF THE PRIZE RING, OR PUGILISTS OF AMERICA. Chicago, (1895). Folio. $125-175.
Edwards, J. C.	SPEECH IN RELATION TO THE TERRITORY IN DISPUTE BETWEEN THE STATE OF MISSOURI AND THE UNITED STATES. Washington, D.C., 1843. 20 pp. Sewed. $125-175.
Edwards, John N.	NOTED GUERRILLAS. St. Louis, 1877. $125-150.
Edwards, John N.	SHELBY AND HIS MEN, OR THE WAR IN THE WEST. Cincinnati, 1867. $60-75.
Edwards, John N.	SHELBY'S EXPEDITION TO MEXICO. Kansas City, Mo., 1872. $100-125.
Edwards, Samuel E.	THE OHIO HUNTER. Battle Creek, Mich., 1866. $600-700.
Egle, William H.	HISTORY OF DAUPHINE AND LEBANON COUNTIES (PENNSYLVANIA). Philadelphia, 1883. $100-125.
Egle, William H.	AN ILLUSTRATED HISTORY OF THE COMMONWEALTH OF PENNSYLVANIA. Harrisburg, Pa., 1876. $60-75.
Elliott, David Stewart	LAST RAID OF THE DALTONS. Coffeyville, Kans., 1892. Wrappers. $375-450.
Ellis, Edward S.	THE LIFE AND ADVENTURES OF COL. DAVID CROCKETT. New York, 1861. $100-125.

AUTHOR	TITLE/EDITION INFORMATION/VALUE
Ellis, William	THE AMERICAN MISSION IN THE SANDWICH ISLANDS. Honolulu, 1866. $225-275.
Ellsworth, Henry W.	VALLEY OF THE UPPER WABASH, INDIANA. New York, 1838. 3 folding lithographs. Map. $225-275.
Ellsworth, Lincoln	THE LAST WILD BUFFALO HUNT. New York, 1916. $60-75.
Emerson, Charles L.	RISE AND PROGRESS OF MINNESOTA TERRITORY. St. Paul, Minn., 1855. Wrappers. $375-425.
Emory, William H.	NOTES OF A MILITARY RECONNAISSANCE. Washington, D.C., 1848. 68 plates. Maps. Plans. $175-225.
Erwin, Milo	THE HISTORY OF WILLIAMSON COUNTY, ILLINOIS. Marion, Ill., 1876. $125-175.
Ethell, Henry C.	THE RISE AND PROGRESS OF CIVILIZATION IN THE HAIRY NATION AND THE HISTORY OF DAVIS COUNTY. Bloomfield, Iowa, 1883. $125-175.
Etzenhouser, R.	FROM PALMYRA, NEW YORK, 1839, TO INDEPENDENCE, MISSOURI, 1894. Independence, Mo., 1894. Wrappers. $125-150.
Everett, Horace	REGULATING THE INDIAN DEPARTMENT. (Washington, D.C., 1834). $225-275.
Everts and Kirk	THE OFFICIAL STATE ATLAS OF NEBRASKA. Philadelphia, 1885. 207 colored maps. Plates. $450 or more.
Evjen, John O.	SCANDINAVIAN IMMIGRANTS IN NEW YORK, 1639-1674. Minneapolis, Minn., 1916. $100-125.
Fairbanks, George R.	EARLY HISTORY OF FLORIDA. St. Augustine, Fla., 1857. 82 pp. Sewed. $250-325.
Fairbanks, George R.	THE SPANIARDS IN FLORIDA. Jacksonville, Fla., 1868. Wrappers. $175-250.

AUTHOR	TITLE/EDITION INFORMATION/VALUE
Fairchild, T. B.	A HISTORY OF THE TOWN OF CUYAHOGA FALLS, SUMMIT COUNTY. Cleveland, 1876. $125-175.
Finney & Davis, publishers	BIOGRAPHICAL AND STATISTICAL HISTORY OF THE CITY OF OSHKOSH. Oshkosh, Wis., 1867. $100-125.
(First)	FIRST ANNUAL REPORT OF THE DIRECTORS OF THE CENTRAL MINING CO. Detroit, 1855. Wrappers. $100-125.
(First)	FIRST ANNUAL REVIEW OF PIERCE COUNTY. Prescott, Wis., 1855. Wrappers. $125-150.
(First)	THE FIRST SETTLEMENT AND EARLY HISTORY OF PALMYRA, WAYNE COUNTY, NEW YORK. Palmyra, N.Y., 1858. Wrappers. 10 pp. $125-175.
Fisher, Richard S.	INDIANA: ITS GEOGRAPHY, STATISTICS, COUNTY TOPOGRAPHY. New York, 1852. Folding map. $175-225.
Fletcher, Charles H.	JEFFERSON COUNTY, IOWA, CENTENNIAL HISTORY. Fairfield, Iowa, 1876. Wrappers. $100-125.
Flickinger, Robert E.	PIONEER HISTORY OF POCAHONTAS COUNTY, IOWA. Fonda, Iowa, 1904. $85-100.
Flower, Richard	LETTERS FROM ILLINOIS, 1820-1821. London, 1822. Wrappers. $750-850.
Forbes, James Grant	SKETCHES, HISTORICAL AND TOPOGRAPHICAL, OF THE FLORIDAS. New York, 1821. Map. $550 or more.
Foster, James S.	ADVANTAGES OF DAKOTA TERRITORY. Yankton, Dakota Territory, 1873. Wrappers. $1,200 or more.
Foster, James S.	OUTLINES OF HISTORY OF THE TERRITORY OF DAKOTA AND EMIGRANT'S GUIDE TO THE FREE LANDS OF THE NORTHWEST. Yankton, Dakota Territory, 1870. Map. Wrappers. $2,750 or more.

AUTHOR	TITLE/EDITION INFORMATION/VALUE
Fox, Lady Mary	ACCOUNT OF AN EXPEDITION TO THE INTERIOR OF NEW HOLLAND. London, 1837. $325 or more.
Franks, David	THE NEW-YORK DIRECTORY. New York, 1786. 82 pp. $3,500 or more.
Frink, F. W.	A RECORD OF RICE COUNTY, MINNESOTA, IN 1868. Faribault, Minn., 1868. Wrappers. $125-175.
Fulkerson, H. S.	RANDOM RECOLLECTIONS OF EARLY DAYS IN MISSISSIPPI. Vicksburg, Miss., 1885. Wrappers. $450-525.
Fuller, C. L.	POCKET MAP AND DESCRIPTIVE OUTLINE HISTORY OF THE BLACK HILLS OF DAKOTA AND WYOMING. Rapid City, S. Dak., 1887. Wrappers. Folding map. $700-850.
Fuller, Emeline	LEFT BY THE INDIANS, OR RAPINE, MASSACRE AND CANNIBALISM ON THE OVERLAND TRAIL IN 1860. Mt. Vernon, Iowa, 1892. Wrappers. $250-325.
Fullmer, John S.	ASSASSINATION OF JOSEPH AND HYRUM SMITH, THE PROPHET AND THE PATRIARCH OF THE CHURCH OF JESUS CHRIST OF LATTER-DAY SAINTS. Liverpool, England, 1855. $600-750.
Gale, George	UPPER MISSISSIPPI. Chicago, 1867. $125-150.
Garden, Alexander	ANECDOTES OF THE REVOLUTIONARY WAR IN AMERICA. 2 vols. Charleston, S.C., 1822. First and second series. $325-400.
Garneau, Joseph, Jr.	NEBRASKA: HER RESOURCES, ADVANTAGES AND DEVELOPMENT. Omaha, Nebr., 1893. Wrappers. $225-275.
Garner, James W.	RECONSTRUCTION IN MISSISSIPPI. New York, 1901. $175-225.

AUTHOR	TITLE/EDITION INFORMATION/VALUE
Gass, Patrick	A JOURNAL OF THE VOYAGES AND TRAVELS OF A CORPS OF DISCOVERY, UNDER THE COMMAND OF CAPT. LEWIS AND CAPT. CLARK, ETC. Pittsburgh, Pa., 1807. $850-1,000.
(General)	GENERAL AND STATISTICAL DESCRIPTION OF PIERCE COUNTY (WISCONSIN). (Prescott, Wis., 1854). 9 pp. Sewed. $125-150.
(General)	GENERAL ORDERS AFFECTING THE VOLUNTEER FORCE: ADJUTANT GENERAL'S OFFICE, 1863. Washington, D.C., 1864. $175-225.
Gerhard, Fred	ILLINOIS AS IT IS. Chicago, 1857. 3 folding maps. $175-225.
Gilbert, Paul T., and Charles L. Bryson	CHICAGO AND ITS MAKERS. Chicago, 1929. $125-175.
Gilham, William B.	MANUAL OF INSTRUCTION FOR THE VOLUNTEERS AND MILITIA OF THE CONFEDERATE STATES. Richmond, Va., 1861. $450 or more.
Gilleland, J. C.	THE OHIO AND MISSISSIPPI PILOT. Pittsburgh, Pa., 1820. 16 maps. $1,700 or more.
Glass, E. L. N.	HISTORY OF THE TENTH CAVALRY, 1866-1921. Tucson, Ariz., 1921. $85-100.
Glenn, Allen	HISTORY OF CASS COUNTY (MISSOURI). Topeka, Kans,, 1917. $125-175.
Goldsborough, Charles W.	THE UNITED STATES' NAVAL CHRONICLE. VOL 1. Washington City (Washington, D.C.), 1824. $175-225.
Goodwin, H. C.	PIONEER HISTORY; OR CORTLAND COUNTY AND THE BORDER WARS OF NEW YORK. New York, 1859. $100-125.
Gould, E. W.	FIFTY YEARS ON THE MISSISSIPPI. St. Louis, 1889. $200-250.

AUTHOR	TITLE/EDITION INFORMATION/VALUE
Graham, W. A., editor	THE OFFICIAL RECORD OF A COURT OF INQUIRY CONVENED . . . REQUEST OF MAJOR MARCUS A. RENO TO INVESTIGATE HIS CONDUCT AT THE BATTLE OF THE LITTLE BIG HORN, ETC. 2 vols. Pacific Palisades, Calif., 1951. Folio. Limited edition. $400 or more.
Grant, U. S.	GENERAL ORDERS, NO. 67. Washington, D.C., 1868. Sewed. $100-125.
Graydon, Alexander	MEMOIRS OF A LIFE, CHIEFLY PASSED IN PENNSYLVANIA, WITHIN THE LAST 60 YEARS. Harrisburg, Pa., 1811. $175-200.
(Great)	THE GREAT EASTERN GOLD MINING CO. New York, 1880. Wrappers. $175-225.
(Great)	GREAT TRANS-CONTINENTAL RAIL-ROAD GUIDE. Chicago, 1869. Wrappers. $225-275.
Grece, Charles F.	FACTS AND OBSERVATIONS RESPECTING CANADA, AND THE UNITED STATES OF AMERICA. London, 1819. $250-325.
Green, Max	THE KANZAS REGION. New York, 1856. Wrappers. 2 maps. $175-225.
Haines, Elijah M.	THE AMERICAN INDIAN. Chicago, 1888. $100.
Haines, Elijah M.	HISTORICAL AND STATISTICAL SKETCHES OF LAKE COUNTY, STATE OF ILLINOIS. Waukegan, Ill., 1852. Wrappers. $275.
Hair, James T., publisher	GAZETTEER OF MADISON COUNTY, ILLINOIS. Alton, Ill., 1866. $125.
Hakes, Harlo	LANDMARKS OF STEUBEN COUNTY, NEW YORK. Syracuse, N.Y., 1896. $85.
Halbert, Henry S., and Timothy H. Ball	THE CREEK WAR OF 1813 AND 1814. Chicago, 1895. Folding map. $125.

AUTHOR	TITLE/EDITION INFORMATION/VALUE
Hale, Edward Everett	KANZAS AND NEBRASKA. Boston, 1854. Folding map. $165.
Hall, Captain Basil	TRAVELS IN NORTH AMERICA. 3 vols. Edinburgh, 1829. Folding map. Table. $250.
Hall, Francis	TRAVELS IN CANADA AND THE UNITED STATES IN 1816 AND 1817. London, 1818. Folding map. $275.
Hancock, R. R.	HANCOCK'S DIARY; OR, A HISTORY OF THE 2ND TENNESSEE CONFEDERATE CAVALRY. Nashville, Tenn., 1887. $150.
Hanson, George A.	OLD KENT: THE EASTERN SHORE OF MARYLAND. Baltimore, Md,, 1876. $65.
Harlow, Alvin F.	OLD TOWPATHS. New York, 1926. $100.
Harlow, Alvin F.	OLD WAYBILLS. New York, 1934. $100.
Harmon, Daniel Williams	A JOURNAL OF VOYAGES AND TRAVELS IN THE INTERIOUR OF NORTH AMERICA. Andover, Mass., 1820. Folding map. $675.
Harris, Thaddeus Mason	THE JOURNAL OF A TOUR INTO THE TERRITORY NORTHWEST OF THE ALLEGHANY MOUNTAINS. Boston, 1805. Folding maps. Plate. $375.
Harris, Thomas M.	ASSASSINATION OF LINCOLN. Boston, (1892). $45.
Harrison, William Henry	A DISCOURSE ON THE ABORIGINES OF THE VALLEY OF THE OHIO. Cincinnati, 1838. Folding map. Wrappers. $250.
Hatfield, Edwin F.	HISTORY OF ELIZABETH, NEW JERSEY. New York, 1865. $145.
Hawkins, Alfred	HAWKIN'S PICTURE OF QUEBEC; WITH HISTORICAL RECOLLECTIONS. Quebec, 1834. $300.
Hawley, Zerah	A JOURNAL OF A TOUR THROUGH CONNECTICUT, MASSACHUSETTS, NEW YORK. New Haven, Conn., 1822. $450.

AUTHOR	**TITLE/EDITION INFORMATION/VALUE**
Haymond, Creed	THE CENTRAL PACIFIC RAILROAD. Washington, D.C., (1888). Wrappers. $145.
Haymond, Henry	HISTORY OF HARRISON COUNTY, WEST VIRGINIA. Morgantown, W. Va., (1910). $135.
Haywood, John	THE CIVIL AND POLITICAL HISTORY OF THE STATE OF TENNESSEE. Knoxville, Tenn., 1823. $575.
Haywood, John	THE NATURAL AND ABORIGINAL HISTORY OF TENNESSEE. Nashville, Tenn., 1823. $675.
Headley, John W.	CONFEDERATE OPERATIONS IN CANADA AND NEW YORK. New York, 1906. $115.
Heckewelder, John	AN ACCOUNT OF THE HISTORY, MANNERS, AND CUSTOMS OF THE INDIAN NATIONS. Philadelphia, 1818. $125.
Heckewelder, John	A NARRATIVE OF THE MISSION OF THE UNITED BRETHEREN AMONG THE DELAWARE AND MOHEGAN INDIANS. Philadelphia, 1820. $175.
Hennepin, Father Louis	A DESCRIPTION OF LOUISIANA. New York, 1880. $175.
Henry, Alexander	TRAVELS AND ADVENTURES IN CANADA AND THE INDIAN TERRITORIES. New York, 1809. $575.
Henry, John Joseph	AN ACCURATE AND INTERESTING ACCOUNT OF THE HARDSHIPS AND SUFFERINGS OF THAT BAND OF HEROES, WHO TRAVERSED THE WILDERNESS IN THE CAMPAIGN AGAINST QUEBEC IN 1775. Lancaster, Pa., 1812. $350.
Henry, John Joseph	CAMPAIGN AGAINST QUEBEC. Watertown, N.Y., 1844. $125.
(Illustrated)	ILLUSTRATED ALBUM OF BIOGRAPHY OF POPE AND STEVENS COUNTIES, MINNESOTA. Chicago, 1888. $175.

AUTHOR	TITLE/EDITION INFORMATION/VALUE
(Illustrated)	ILLUSTRATED HISTORICAL ATLAS OF THE STATE OF INDIANA. Chicago, 1876. $275.
(Indian)	THE INDIAN MISSION, IN THE UNITED STATES. Philadelphia, 1841. Wrappers. At least $1,750.
Jackson, Andrew	MESSAGE FROM THE PRESIDENT OF THE UNITED STATES, IN COMPLIANCE WITH A RESOLUTION OF THE SENATE CONCERNING THE FUR TRADE AND INLAND TRADE TO MEXICO. (Washington, D.C., 1832). Unbound. $300.
James, Edwin, editor	ACCOUNT OF AN EXPEDITION FROM PITTSBURG TO THE ROCKY MOUNTAINS. 3 vols. Philadelphia, 1822-1823. Maps. Atlas. $1,400.
James, Edwin, editor	A NARRATIVE OF THE CAPTIVITY AND ADVENTURES OF JOHN TANNER. New York, 1830. $675.
James, Fred	THE KLONDIKE GOLDFIELDS AND HOW TO GET THERE. London, 1897. Wrappers. $450.
Jerome, Chauncey	HISTORY OF THE AMERICAN CLOCK BUSINESS FOR THE PAST 60 YEARS. New Haven, Conn., 1860. Wrappers. $175.
Johnson, Crisfield	THE HISTORY OF CUYAHOGA COUNTY, OHIO. Cleveland, 1879. $100.
Johnson, Edwin F.	RAILROAD TO THE PACIFIC, NORTHERN ROUTE. New York, 1854. 3 maps. $350.
Johnson, Harrison	JOHNSON'S HISTORY OF NEBRASKA. Omaha, Nebr., 1880. Folding map. $150.
Johnston, Carrier Polk, and W. H. S. McGlumphy	HISTORY OF CLINTON AND CALDWELL COUNTIES, MISSOURI. Topeka, Kans., 1923. $100.
Johnston, Charles	A NARRATIVE OF THE INCIDENTS ATTENDING THE CAPTURE, DETEN-

AUTHOR	TITLE/EDITION INFORMATION/VALUE
	TION, AND RANSOM OF. New York, 1827. $235.
Jones, A. D.	ILLINOIS AND THE WEST. Boston, 1838. Folding map. $125.
Jones, Charles C., Jr.	THE DEAD TOWNS OF GEORGIA. Savannah, Ga., 1878. Maps. $125.
Jones, Charles C., Jr.	THE HISTORY OF GEORGIA. 2 vols. Boston, 1883 Maps. Plates. $200.
Jones, Charles C., Jr.	THE HISTORY OF SAVANNAH. Syracuse, N.Y., 1890. $200.
Jones, David	A JOURNAL OF TWO VISITS MADE TO SOME NATIONS OF INDIANS ON THE WEST SIDE OF THE RIVER OHIO, IN THE YEARS 1772 AND 1773. Burlington, N.J., 1774. At least $7,500.
Jones, Herschel	ADVENTURES IN AMERICANA. 2 vols. New York, 1928. 300 plates. $350.
Jones, Samuel	PITTSBURGH IN THE YEAR EIGHTEEN-HUNDRED AND TWENTY-SIX. Pittsburgh, Pa., 1826. At least $1,200.
(Journal)	JOURNAL OF THE CONVENTION TO FORM A CONSTITUTION FOR THE STATE OF WISCONSIN: BEGUN AND HELD AT MADISON ON THE 5TH DAY OF OCTOBER, 1846. Madison, Wis., 1847. $175.
(Journal)	JOURNAL OF AN EXCURSION MADE BY THE CORPS OF CADETS, UNDER CAPT. PATRIDGE. Concord, N.H., 1822. Wrappers. $100.
Kane, Paul	WANDERINGS OF AN ARTIST AMONG THE INDIANS OF NORTH AMERICA. London, 1859. Folding map. Color plates. At least $1,500.
Kane, Thomas Leiper	THE MORMONS. Philadelphia, 1850. Wrappers. $275.

AUTHOR	TITLE/EDITION INFORMATION/VALUE
Keating, William H.	NARRATIVE OF AN EXPEDITION TO THE SOURCE OF ST. PETER'S RIVER, LAKE WINNEPEEK. 2 vols. Philadelphia, 1824. Folding map. $375.
Keller, George	A TRIP ACROSS THE PLAINS. (Masillon, Ohio, 1851). Wrappers. At least $5,000.
Kelly, L. V.	THE RANGE MEN: THE STORY OF THE RANCHERS AND INDIANS OF ALBERTA. Toronto, 1913. $325.
Kercheval, Samuel	A HISTORY OF THE VALLEY OF VIRGINIA. Winchester, Va., 1833. $675.
King, Charles	THE FIFTH CAVALRY IN THE SIOUX WAR TO 1876: CAMPAIGNING WITH CROOK. Milwaukee, Wis., 1880. Wrappers. $275.
King, Richard	NARRATIVE OF A JOURNEY TO THE SHORES OF THE ARCTIC OCEAN, IN 1833, 1834, AND 1835. 2 vols. London, 1836. Maps. $500.
(Klondyke)	THE KLONDYKE MINES AND THE GOLDEN VALLEY OF THE YUKON. N.p, 1897. Wrappers. $125.
Knight, Dr., and John Slover	INDIAN ATROCITIES. Nashville, Tenn., 1843. At least $1,750.
Knoblock, Byron W.	BANNERSTONES OF THE NORTH AMERICAN INDIAN. La Grange, Ill., 1939. 270 plates. $225.
Kohl, L. G.	KITCHI-GAMI: WANDERINGS ROUND LAKE SUPERIOR. London, 1860. $325.
La Bree, Ben, editor	THE CONFEDERATE SOLDIER IN THE CIVIL WAR, 1861-1865. Louisville, Ky., 1895. Folio. $250.
Lamson, David R.	TWO YEARS' EXPERIENCE AMONG THE SHAKERS. West Boylston, Mass., 1848. $125.
Lancaster, Robert A., Jr.	HISTORIC VIRGINIA HOMES AND CHURCHES. Philadelphia, 1915. $110.

AUTHOR	TITLE/EDITION INFORMATION/VALUE
Langworthy, Lucius H.	DUBUQUE: ITS HISTORY, MINES, INDIAN LEGENDS. Dubuque, Iowa, (1855). Wrappers. $250.
Lanier, Sidney	FLORIDA: ITS SCENERY, CLIMATE, AND HISTORY. Philadelphia, 1876. $250.
Lanman, Charles	ADVENTURES IN THE WILDS OF THE UNITED STATES AND BRITISH AMERICAN PROVINCES. 2 vols. Philadelphia, 1856. $675.
Lanman, Charles	HAW-HO-NOO, OR RECORDS OF A TOURIST. Philadelphia, 1850. $350.
Lanman, Charles	A SUMMER IN THE WILDERNESS. New York, 1847. $350.
Lanman, Charles	A TOUR TO THE RIVER SAGUENAY. Philadelphia, 1848. Wrappers. $300.
Lapham, I. A.	A GEOGRAPHICAL AND TOPOGRAPHICAL DESCRIPTION OF WISCONSIN. Milwaukee, Wis., 1844. Folding map. $450.
Larimer, Mrs. Sarah L.	THE CAPTURE AND ESCAPE; OR, LIFE AMONG THE SIOUX. Philadelphia, 1870. $125.
Larimer, William	REMINISCENCES OF GEN. WILLIAM LARIMER AND OF HIS SON WILLIAM H. H. LARIMER. Lancaster, Pa., 1918. Folding chart. $450.
Laroque, François	A JOURNAL OF FRANCOIS A. LAROQUE FROM THE ASSINIBOINE TO THE YELLOWSTONE, 1805. Ottawa, Canada, 1910. Wrappers. $275.
Larpenteur, Charles	FORTY YEARS A FUR TRADER OF THE UPPER MISSISSIPPI. 2 vols. New York, 1898. 6 maps. $135.
La Salle, Nicolas de	RELATIONS OF THE DISCOVERY OF THE MISSISSIPPI RIVER. Chicago, 1898. French and English text. $350.
La Salle, René Robert Cavelier de	RELATION OF THE DISCOVERIES AND VOYAGES OF CAVELIER DE LA SALLE. Chicago, 1901. French and English text. $350.

AUTHOR	TITLE/EDITION INFORMATION/VALUE
Latham, H.	TRANS-MISSOURI STOCK RAISING. Omaha, Nebr., 1871. Map. Wrappers. At least $550.
Latour, A. Lacarriere	HISTORICAL MEMOIR OF THE WAR IN WEST FLORIDA AND LOUISIANA IN 1814-1815. 2 vols. Philadelphia, 1816. Atlas. $1,800.
(Law)	LAW OF DESCENT AND DISTRIBUTION GOVERNING LANDS OF THE CREEK NATION, AS HELD BY C. W. RAYMOND, JUDGE OF THE U. S. COURT FOR THE INDIAN TERRITORY. N.p, 1903. Wrappers. $250.
(Laws)	LAWS OF THE CHOCTAW NATION, MADE AND ENACTED BY THE GENERAL COUNCIL FROM 1886 TO 1890. Atoka, Indian Terrritory, 1890. Choctaw and English text. $300.
McAdam, R. W.	CHICKASAWS AND CHOCTAWS. COMPRISING THE TREATIES OF 1855 AND 1866. Ardmore, Okla., 1891. Wrappers. $350.
MacCabe, Julius P. Bolivar	DIRECTORY OF THE CITY OF DETROIT. Detroit, 1837. $850.
MacCabe, Julius P. Bolivar	DIRECTORY OF THE CITY OF MILWAUKEE. Milwaukee, Wis., 1847. $450.
MacCabe, Julius P. Bolivar	A DIRECTORY OF CLEVELAND AND THE CITIES OF OHIO FOR THE YEARS 1837-1838. Cleveland, 1837. $875.
McCall, George A.	LETTERS FROM THE FRONTIERS. Philadelphia, 1868. $300.
McCall, Hugh	THE HISTORY OF GEORGIA. 2 vols. Savannah, Ga., 1811-1816. $450.
McClintock, John S.	PIONEER DAYS IN THE BLACK HILLS. Deadwood, S. Dak., (1939). $125.
McClintock, Walter	OLD INDIAN TRAILS. Boston, 1923. $60.
McClintock, Walter	THE OLD NORTH TRAIL. London, 1910. Folding map. $100.

AUTHOR	TITLE/EDITION INFORMATION/VALUE
M'Clung, John A.	SKETCHES OF WESTERN ADVENTURE. Maysville, Ky., 1832. $875.
McConkey, Mrs. Harriet E.	DAKOTA WAR; OR, INDIAN MASSACRE AND WAR IN MINNESOTA. St. Paul, Minn., 1863. $350.
McCorkle, John, and O. S. Barton	THREE YEARS WITH QUANTRELL. Armstrong. Mo., (1914). Wrappers. $250.
McCoy, Isaac	HISTORY OF BAPTIST INDIAN MISSIONS. Washington, D.C., 1840. $300.
McCoy, Isaac	REMARKS ON THE PRACTICABILITY OF INDIAN REFORM. Boston, 1827. Wrappers. $350.
McCoy, Isaac	REMOVE INDIANS WESTWARD. (Washington, D.C.), 1829. Sewed. $125.
M'Donell, Alexander	A NARRATIVE OF TRANSACTIONS IN THE RED RIVER COUNTRY. London, 1819. Folding map. At least $1,500.
McGee, Joseph H.	STORY OF THE GRAND RIVER COUNTRY, 1821-1905. (Gallatin, Mo., 1909). Wrappers. $125.
McKay, Richard C.	SOUTH STREET: A MARITIME HISTORY OF NEW YORK. New York, (1934). 48 illustrations. $175.
McKim, Randolph H.	A SOLDIER'S RECOLLECTIONS: LEAVES FROM THE DIARY OF A YOUNG CONFEDERATE. New York, 1911. $75.
McLeod, Donald	HISTORY OF WISKONSAN, FROM ITS FIRST DISCOVERY TO THE PRESENT PERIOD. Buffalo, N.Y., 1846. Folding map. Plates. $325.
Martin, Aaron	AN ATTEMPT TO SHOW THE INCONSISTENCY OF SLAVE-HOLDING, WITH THE RELIGION OF THE GOSPEL. Lexington, Ky., 1807. Sewed. At least $2,000.
Martineau, Harriet	SOCIETY IN AMERICA. 3 vols. London, 1837. $625.

AUTHOR	TITLE/EDITION INFORMATION/VALUE
Mason, Emily V., editor	THE SOUTHERN POEMS OF THE WAR. Baltimore, Md., 1867. $125.
Mason, Z. H.	A GENERAL DESCRIPTION OF ORANGE COUNTY, FLORIDA. Orlando, Fla., (1881). Map. Wrappers. $325.
Matson, N.	REMINISCENCES OF BUREAU COUNTY. Princeton, Ill., 1872. $90.
(Narrative)	NARRATIVE AND REPORT OF THE CAUSES AND CIRCUMSTANCES OF THE DEPLORABLE CONFLAGARATION AT RICHMOND. N.p., 1812. $150.
(Narrative)	A NARRATIVE OF THE ADVENTURES AND SUFFERINGS OF CAPT. DANIEL D. HEUSTIS. Boston, 1847. Wrappers. $1,200.
(Narrative)	NARRATIVE OF THE CAPTIVITY AND PROVIDENTIAL ESCAPE OF MRS. JANE LEWIS [William P. Edwards]. (New York), 1833. Wrappers. $325.
(Narrative)	NARRATIVE OF THE CAPTURE AND BURNING OF FORT MASSACHUSETTS [Reverend John Norton]. Albany, N.Y., 1870. $110.
(Narrative)	A NARRATIVE OF THE FACTS AND CIRCUMSTANCES RELATING TO THE KIDNAPPING AND PRESUMED MURDER OF WILLIAM MORGAN. Batavia, N.Y., 1827. Sewed. $275.
(Narrative)	NARRATIVE OF THE MASSACRE AT CHICAGO, AUGUST 15, 1812, AND SOME PRECEDING EVENTS [Mrs. Juliette A. Kinzie]. Chicago, 1844. Map. Wrappers. At least $3,000.
(Narrative)	A NARRATIVE OF OCCURRENCES IN THE INDIAN COUNTRY OF NORTH AMERICA [Samuel Hull Wilcocke]. London, 1807. Wrappers. $850.

AUTHOR	**TITLE/EDITION INFORMATION/VALUE**
(Narrative)	A NARRATIVE OF THE SUPPRESSION BY COL. BURR OF THE "HISTORY OF THE ADMINISTRATION OF JOHN ADAMS" [James Cheetham]. New York, 1802. Sewed. $250.
(Necessity)	THE NECESSITY OF A SHIP-CANAL BETWEEN THE EAST AND WEST [J. W. Foster]. Chicago, 1863. Wrappers. $145.
Neese, George M.	THREE YEARS IN THE CONFEDERATE HORSE ARTILLERY. New York, 1911. $90.
O'Bryan, William	A NARRATIVE OF TRAVELS IN THE UNITED STATES AND ADVICE TO EMIGRANTS AND TRAVELLERS GOING TO THAT INTERESTING COUNTRY. London, 1836. $350.
(Observations)	OBSERVATIONS ON THE WISCONSIN TERRITORY [William Rudolph Smith]. Philadelphia, 1835. Folding map. $525.
Oliphant, Laurence	MINNESOTA AND THE FAR WEST. Edinburgh, 1855. Folding map. Plates. $175.
Oliver, John W., publisher	GUIDE TO THE NEW GOLD REGION OF WESTERN KANSAS AND NEBRASKA. New York, 1859. Folding map. Wrappers. At least $5,000.
(Only)	ONLY AUTHENTIC LIFE OF ABRAHAM LINCOLN, ALIAS "OLD ABE," A SON OF THE WEST. (New York, 1864). Wrappers. $450.
(Ordnance)	ORDNANCE MANUAL FOR THE USE OF THE OFFICERS OF THE CONFEDERATE STATES OF AMERICA. Charleston, S.C., 1863. $650.
(Origin)	ORIGIN AND TRADITIONAL HISTORY OF THE WYANDOTTS [Peter D. Clarke]. Toronto, 1870. $90.
Orr, George	THE POSSESSION OF LOUISIANA BY THE FRENCH. London, 1803. $175.

AUTHOR	TITLE/EDITION INFORMATION/VALUE
Osgood, Ernest Staples	THE DAY OF THE CATTLEMAN. Minneapolis, 1929. Maps. $175.
Palmer, H. E.	THE POWDER RIVER INDIAN EXPEDITION, 1865. Omaha, Nebr., 1887. Wrappers. $325.
Palmer, William J.	REPORT OF SURVEYS ACROSS THE CONTINENT. Philadelphia, 1869. 3 maps. Photo plates. Wrappers. $850.
Parker, Solomon	PARKER'S AMERICAN CITIZEN'S SURE GUIDE. Sag Harbor, N.Y., 1808. $185.
Parkman, Francis	HISTORY OF THE CONSPIRACY OF PONTIAC AND THE WAR OF THE NORTH AMERICAN TRIBES. Boston, 1851. 4 maps. $165.
Parkman, Francis	THE OLD REGIME IN CANADA. Boston, 1874. Large paper edition. $165.
Patterson, A. W.	HISTORY OF THE BACKWOODS; OR, THE REGION OF THE OHIO. Pittsburgh, Pa., 1843. Folding map. $450.
Pattie, James O.	THE PERSONAL NARRATIVE OF JAMES O. PATTIE, OF KENTUCKY. Cincinnati, 1831. Plates. At least $10,000.
Patton, Reverend W. W., and R. N. Isham	U. S. SANITARY COMMISSION, NO. 38: REPORT ON THE CONDITION OF CAMPS AND HOSPITALS AT CAIRO PADAUCAH AND ST. LOUIS. Chicago, 1861. Sewed. $125.
Paulding, James Kirk	SLAVERY IN THE UNITED STATES. New York, 1836. $85.
Ramsay, David	THE HISTORY OF SOUTH CAROLINA. 2 vols. Charleston, S.C., 1809. 2 folding maps. $575.
Ramsey, J. G. M.	THE ANNALS OF TENNESSEE. Charleston, S.C., 1853. Folding map. $300.

AUTHOR	TITLE/EDITION INFORMATION/VALUE
Ranck, George W.	HISTORY OF LEXINGTON, KENTUCKY. Cincinnati, 1872. $85.
Randall, Thomas E.	HISTORY OF THE CHIPPEWA VALLEY. Eau Claire, Wis., 1875. $85.
Reagan, John H.	MEMOIRS, WITH SPECIAL REFERENCE TO SECESSION AND THE CIVIL WAR. New York, 1906. $225.
Redmond, Pat. H.	HISTORY OF QUINCY (ILL.) AND ITS MEN OF MARK. Quincy, Ill., 1869. $125.
Reed, J. W.	MAP OF AND GUIDE TO THE KANSAS GOLD REGIONS. New York, 1859. Wrappers. At least $3,500.
Reed, Wallace P.	HISTORY OF ATLANTA, GEORGIA. Syracuse, N.Y., 1889. Portraits. $85.
Reed, William	LIFE ON THE BORDER, SIXTY YEARS AGO. Fall River, Mass., 1882. Wrappers. $65.
Rees, William	DESCRIPTION OF THE CITY OF KEOKUK. Keokuk, Iowa, 1854. Wrappers. $275.
Rees, William	THE MISSISSIPPI BRIDGE CITIES: DAVENPORT, ROCK ISLAND AND MOLINE. (Rock Island, Ill.), 1854. Sewed. $175.
(Regulations)	REGULATIONS FOR THE UNIFORM AND DRESS OF THE ARMY OF THE UNITED STATES. Philadelphia, 1851. 25 chromolithos. $575.
Reid, A. J.	THE RESOURCES AND MANUFACTURING CAPACITY OF THE LOWER FOX RIVER VALLEY. Appleton, Wis., 1874. Folding map. Panorama. Wrappers. $85.
(Reign)	THE REIGN OF TERROR IN KANZAS [Charles W. Briggs]. Boston, 1856. Wrappers. $675.
(Remarks)	REMARKS ADDRESSED TO THE CITIZENS OF ILLINOIS, ON THE PROPOSED INTRODUCTION OF SLAVERY [Morris Birkbeck]. N.p., (1824). At least $3,500.

AUTHOR	TITLE/EDITION INFORMATION/VALUE
(Report)	REPORT OF A COMMITTEE APPOINTED BY THE TRUSTEES OF THE TOWN OF MILWAUKEE, RELATIVE TO THE COMMERCE OF THAT TOWN AND THE NAVIGATION OF LAKE MICHIGAN [I. A. Lapham and F. Randall]. Milwaukee, Wis., 1842. Sewed. $375.
(Report)	REPORT OF THE BOARD OF CANAL COMMISSIONERS, TO THE GENERAL ASSEMBLY OF OHIO. Columbus, Ohio, 1824. Sewed. $175.
(Report)	REPORT OF THE BOARD OF INTERNAL IMPROVEMENTS FOR THE STATE OF KENTUCKY, AND REPORTS OF THE ENGINEERS. (Frankfort, Ky., 1836). Sewed. $125.
Reynolds, John	THE PIONEER HISTORY OF ILLINOIS. Belleville, Ill., 1852. $350.
Reynolds, John	SKETCHES OF THE COUNTRY ON THE NORTHERN ROUTE FROM BELLEVILLE, ILL., TO THE CITY OF NEW YORK, AND BACK BY THE OHIO VALLEY. Belleville, Ill., 1854. $675.
St. Clair, Major General	A NARRATIVE OF THE MANNER IN WHICH THE CAMPAIGN AGAINST THE INDIANS, IN THE YEAR 1791, WAS CONDUCTED. Philadelphia, 1812. $400.
St. John, John R.	A TRUE DESCRIPTION OF THE LAKE SUPERIOR COUNTRY. New York, 1846. 2 folding maps. $325.
Sale, Edith Tunis	MANORS OF VIRGINIA IN COLONIAL TIMES. Philadelphia, 1909. 49 plates. $135.
Sandburg, Carl	ABRAHAM LINCOLN: THE PRAIRIE YEARS. 2 vols. New York, (1926). Boxed. Signed. Large paper edition. $475.
Sandburg, Carl	ABRAHAM LINCOLN: THE WAR YEARS. 4 vols. New York, (1939-1941). Boxed. Signed. Large paper edition. $475.

AUTHOR	TITLE/EDITION INFORMATION/VALUE
Sanders, Daniel C.	A HISTORY OF THE INDIAN WARS WITH THE FIRST SETTLERS OF THE UNITED STATES. Montpelier, Vt., 1812. $650.
Sanders, Captain John	MEMOIR ON THE MILITARY RESOURCES OF THE VALLEY OF THE OHIO. Pittsburgh, Pa., 1845. Unbound. $185.
Sanford, Nettle	HISTORY OF MARSHALL COUNTY, IOWA. Clinton, Iowa, 1867. $165.
Sansom, Joseph	SKETCHES OF LOWER CANADA, HISTORICAL AND DESCRIPTIVE. New York, 1817. $225.
Sargent, George B.	NOTES ON IOWA. New York, 1848. Map. $900.
Satterlee, M. P.	A DETAILED ACCOUNT OF THE MASSACRE BY THE DAKOTA INDIANS OF MINNESOTA IN 1862. Minneapolis, 1923. Wrappers. $175.
Saunders, James E.	EARLY SETTLERS OF ALABAMA. New Orleans, 1899. $200.
Scharf, John Thomas	HISTORY OF THE CONFEDERATE STATES NAVY. New York, 1887. 42 plates. $165.
Scharf, John Thomas	HISTORY OF DELAWARE. 2 vols. Philadelphia, 1888. $175.
Scharf, John Thomas	HISTORY OF MARYLAND. 3 vols. Baltimore, Md., 1879. Folding maps. Charts. $225.
Scharf, John Thomas	HISTORY OF WESTCHESTER COUNTY, NEW YORK. 2 vols. Philadelphia, 1886. $325.
Scharf, John Thomas	HISTORY OF WESTERN MARYLAND. 2 vols. Philadelphia, 1882. Map. 109 plates. $175.
Schoolcraft, Henry R.	HISTORICAL AND STATISTICAL INFORMATION RESPECTING THE INDIAN TRIBES. 6 vols. Philadelphia, 1851-1857. Maps. Table. At least $2,250.
Schoolcraft, Henry R.	THE INDIAN TRIBES OF THE UNITED STATES. 2 vols. Philadelphia, 1884. 100 plates. $225.

AUTHOR	TITLE/EDITION INFORMATION/VALUE
Schoolcraft, Henry R.	INFORMATION RESPECTING THE HISTORY, CONDITIONS, AND PROSPECTS OF THE INDIAN TRIBES OF THE UNITED STATES. 6 vols. Philadelphia, 1853-1857. At least $1,750.
Schoolcraft, Henry R.	INQUIRIES RESPECTING THE HISTORY OF THE INDIAN TRIBES OF THE UNITED STATES. (Washington, D.C., 1847-1850). Wrappers. $575.
Schoolcraft, Henry R.	JOURNAL OF A TOUR INTO THE INTERIOR OF THE MISSOURI AND ARKANSAW. London, 1821. Folding map. $275.
(Tallapoosa)	TALLAPOOSA LAND, MINING AND MANUFACTURING CO., HARALSON COUNTY. Tallapoosa, Ga., 1887. Map. Wrappers. $125.
Tallent, Annie D.	THE BLACK HILLS; OR THE LAST HUNTING GROUNDS OF THE DAKOTAHS. St. Louis, 1899. 50 plates. $150.
Tanner, Henry S.	A BRIEF DESCRIPTION OF THE CANALS AND RAILROADS OF THE UNITED STATES. Philadelphia, 1834. Maps. $225.
Tanner, Henry S.	A NEW AMERICAN ATLAS. Philadelphia, 1823. 2 folding and 16 2-page maps. At least $3,500.
Tarascon, Louis A.	AN ADDRESS TO THE CITIZENS OF PHILADELPHIA, ON THE GREAT ADVANTAGES WHICH ARISE FROM THE TRADE OF THE WESTERN COUNTRY. Philadelphia, 1806. Wrappers. $875.
Taylor, F.	A SKETCH OF THE MILITARY BOUNTY TRACT OF ILLINOIS. Philadelphia, 1839. $225.
Taylor, James W.	NORTHWEST BRITISH AMERICA AND ITS RELATIONS TO THE STATE OF MINNESOTA. St. Paul, Minn., 1860. Map. At least $2,500.

AUTHOR	TITLE/EDITION INFORMATION/VALUE
Taylor, James W.	THE SIOUX WAR. St. Paul, Minn., 1862. $1,200.
Taylor, John W.	IOWA, THE "GREAT HUNTING GROUND" OF THE INDIANS; AND THE "BEAUTIFUL LAND" OF THE WHITE MAN. Dubuque, Iowa, 1860. Wrappers. $275.
Taylor, Joseph Henry	TWENTY YEARS ON THE TRAP LINE. Bismarck, N. Dak., 1891. Plates. $250.
Taylor, Oliver I.	DIRECTORY OF WHEELING AND OHIO COUNTY. Wheeling, W. Va., 1851. $175.
Thomas, David	TRAVELS THROUGH THE WESTERN COUNTRY IN THE SUMMER OF 1816. Auburn, N.Y., 1819. Folding map. $350.
Thomas, Henry W.	HISTORY OF THE DOLES-COOK BRIGADE, ARMY OF NORTHERN VIRGINIA. Atlanta, Ga., 1903. $125.
Thompson, Captain B. F.	HISTORY OF THE 112TH REGMENT OF ILLINOIS VOLUNTEER INFANTRY, 1862-1865. Toulon, Ill., 1885. $125.
Thompson, Daniel Pierce, editor	THE LAWS OF VERMONT, 1824-1834, INCLUSIVE. Montpelier, Vt., 1835. $350.
Thompson, David	HISTORY OF THE LATE WAR, BETWEEN GREAT BRITAIN AND THE U.S.A. Niagara, Canada, 1832. $275.
Thompson, Maurice	THE STORY OF LOUISIANA. Boston, (1888). $65.
Thwaites, Reuben Gold	HISTORIC WATERWAYS: SIX HUNDRED MILES OF CANOEING DOWN THE ROCK, FOX, AND WISCONSIN RIVERS. Chicago, 1888. $175.
Tierney, Luke	HISTORY OF THE GOLD DISCOVERIES ON THE SOUTH PLATTE RIVER. Pacific City, Iowa, 1859. Wrappers. At least $17,500.
Todd, Frederick P.	SOLDIERS OF THE AMERICAN ARMY, 1775-1941. New York, 1941. 24 hand-colored plates. Signed. $575.

AUTHOR	TITLE/EDITION INFORMATION/VALUE
Tower, Colonel Reuben	AN APPEAL TO THE PEOPLE OF NEW YORK IN FAVOR OF THE CONSTRUCTION OF THE CHENANGO CANAL. Utica, N.Y., 1830. Sewed. $125.
(Uniform)	UNIFORM AND DRESS OF THE ARMY OF THE CONFEDERATE STATES. Richmond, Va., 1861. 15 plates. $500.
(United States)	THE UNITED STATES ENROLLMENT LAWS FOR CALLING OUT THE NATIONAL FORCES. New York, 1864. Wrappers. $85.
(United States)	UNITED STATES "HISTORY" AS THE YANKEE MAKES IT AND TAKES IT. BY A CONFEDERATE SOLDIER [John Cussons]. Glen Allen, Va., 1900. Wrappers. $125.
Upham, Samuel C.	NOTES FROM SUNLAND, ON THE MANATEE RIVER, GULF COAST OF SOUTH FLORIDA. Braidentown, Fla., 1881. Wrappers. $175.
Van Buren, A. D.	JOTTINGS OF A YEAR'S SOJOURN IN THE SOUTH. Battle Creek, Mich., 1859. $125.
Van Cleve, Mrs. Charlotte O. C.	"THREE SCORE YEARS AND TEN"; LIFE-LONG MEMORIES OF FORT SNELLING, MINN., AND OTHER PARTS OF THE WEST. (Minneapolis), 1888. $85.
Van Zandt, Nicholas Biddle	A FULL DESCRIPTION OF THE SOIL, WATER, TIMBER, AND PRAIRIES OF EACH LOT, OR QUARTER SECTION OF THE MILITARY LANDS BETWEEN THE MISSISSIPPI AND ILLINOIS RIVERS. Washington, D.C., 1818. Folding map. At least $4,250.
(Vindication)	VINDICATION OF THE RECENT AND PREVAILING POLICY OF GEORGIA IN

AUTHOR	TITLE/EDITION INFORMATION/VALUE
	ITS INTERNAL AFFAIRS [Augustin S. Clayton]. Athens, Ga., 1827. Wrappers. $275.
Volney, C. F.	A VIEW OF THE SOIL AND CLIMATE OF THE UNITED STATES. Philadelphia, 1804. 2 folding maps. 2 folding plates. $225.
Wagner, Lieutenant Colonel A. L., and Commander J. D. Kelley	THE UNITED STATES ARMY AND NAVY: THEIR HISTORIES. Akron, Ohio, 1899. 43 plates. Folio. $225.
Wakefield, John A.	HISTORY OF THE WAR BETWEEN THE UNITED STATES AND THE SAC AND FOX NATIONS OF INDIANS. Jacksonville, Ill., 1834. $725.
Walker, Judson E.	CAMPAIGNS OF GENERAL CUSTER IN THE NORTH-WEST, AND THE FINAL SURRENDER OF SITTING BULL. New York, 1881. Wrappers. $275.
Wall, W. G.	WALL'S HUDSON RIVER PORTFOLIO. New York, (1826). 21 color plates. Folio. At least $5,000.
Walther, C. F., and I. N. Taylor	THE RESOURCES AND ADVANTAGES OF THE STATE OF NEBRASKA. (Omaha, Nebr., 1871). Folding map. Wrappers. $225.
(War)	THE WAR IN FLORIDA. BY A LATE STAFF OFFICER [Woodburn Potter]. Baltimore, Md., 1836. Folding map. $375.
Warder, T. B., and J. M. Catlett	BATTLE OF YOUNG'S BRANCH, OR, MANASSAS PLAIN. Richmond, Va., 1862. 2 folding maps. Wrappers or leather. $675.
Ware, Eugene	THE INDIAN WAR OF 1864. Topeka, Kans., 1911. $175.
Ware, Eugene	THE LYON CAMPAIGN IN MISSOURI. Topeka, Kans., 1907. $135.
Wayland, John W.	HISTORIC HOMES OF NORTHERN VIRGINIA AND THE EASTERN PANHANDLE OF WESTERN VIRGINIA. Staunton, Va., 1937. $95.

AUTHOR	TITLE/EDITION INFORMATION/VALUE
Wayland, John W.	HISTORY OF ROCKINGHAM COUNTY. Dayton, Va., 1912. $140.
Webb, Walter Prescott	THE GREAT PLAINS. Boston, (1931). $125.
Wells, William, and Otto Onken	WESTERN SCENERY; OR, LAND AND RIVER, HILL AND DALE, IN THE MISSISSIPPI VALLEY. Cincinnati, 1851. 19 views. At least $3,500.
Wetmore, Alphonso	GAZETTEER OF THE STATE OF MISSOURI. St. Louis, 1837. Folding map. $50.
Wetmore, Helen Cody	LAST OF THE GREAT SCOUTS: THE LIFE STORY OF COL. WILLIAM F. CODY, "BUFFALO BILL." (Duluth, Minn., 1899). 276 pp. $225.
Whitaker, Arthur Preston, editor	DOCUMENTS RELATING TO THE COMMERCIAL POLICY OF SPAIN IN THE FLORIDAS. DeLand, Fla., 1931. Maps. $85.
White, Philo	AGRICULTURAL STATISTICS OF RACINE COUNTY. Racine, Wis., 1852. Wrappers. $125.
Williams, G. T.	RECEIPTS AND SHIPMENTS OF LIVESTOCK AT UNION STOCK YARDS FOR 1890. Chicago, 1891. Wrappers. $350.
Williams, Jesse	A DESCRIPTION OF THE UNITED STATES LANDS OF IOWA. New York, 1840. Folding map. $750.
Williams, John Lee	THE TERRITORY OF FLORIDA. New York, 1837. Folding map. $300.
Williams, John Lee	A VIEW OF WEST FLORIDA. Philadelphia, 1827. Folding map. $175.
Williams, Thomas J. C.	A HISTORY OF WASHINGTON COUNTY. 2 vols. Hagerstown, Md., 1906. $95.
Williamson, Hugh	THE HISTORY OF NORTH CAROLINA. 2 vols. Philadelphia, 1812. Folding map. $425.
Williamson, James J.	MOSBY'S RANGERS. New York, 1896. $125.

AUTHOR	TITLE/EDITION INFORMATION/VALUE
Willis, Nathaniel Parker	AMERICAN SCENERY. 2 vols. London, 1840. 117 views by W. H. Bartlett. $1,000 or more.
Wilson, Woodrow	GEORGE WASHINGTON. New York, 1897. $125.
Wise, George	CAMPAIGNS AND BATTLES OF THE ARMY OF NORTHERN VIRGINIA. New York, 1916. $125.
Wood, James H.	THE WAR, STONEWALL JACKSON, HIS CAMPAIGNS AND BATTLES, THE REGIMENT, AS I SAW THEM. Cumberland, Md., (1910). $125.
Wood, Silas	A SKETCH OF THE FIRST SETTLEMENT OF THE SEVERAL TOWNS ON LONG ISLAND. Brooklyn, 1824. $275.
Woodruff, W. E.	WITH THE LIGHT GUNS IN '61-'65. Little Rock, Ark., 1903. $200.
Woods, Daniel B.	SIXTEEN MONTHS AT THE GOLD DIGGINGS. New York, 1851. $300.
Woods, John	TWO YEARS' RESIDENCE ON THE ENGLISH PRAIRIE, IN THE ILLINOIS COUNTRY. London, 1822. 2 maps. At least $1,250.
Woodson, W. H.	HISTORY OF CLAY COUNTY, MISSOURI. Topeka, Kans., 1920. $75.
Woolworth, James M.	NEBRASKA IN 1857. Omaha, Nebr., 1857. Color folding map. $650.
Wright, William	THE OIL REGIONS OF PENNSYLVANIA. New York, 1865. $225.
Yeary, Mamie	REMINISCENCES OF THE BOYS IN GRAY, 1861-1965. Dallas, 1912. $175.
Young, Andrew W.	HISTORY OF CHAUTAUQUA COUNTY, NEW YORK. Buffalo, N.Y., 1875. $135.
Young, Ansel	THE WESTERN RESERVE ALMANAC FOR THE YEAR 1844. Cleveland, (1843). Wrappers. $150.

– 12 –

Crime/Mystery/Adventure/Espionage Books, And Their Values

This genre is now enjoying a surge in popularity. It is one of the most popular genres for collectors of fiction, perhaps because it encompasses so many readily identifiable sub-genres, such as traditional British whodunits, locked-room puzzles, and series featuring dectective-hero sleuths like Sherlock Holmes and Hercule Poirot.

The authors and titles presented here are those that are best known to the general public. It is reasonable to assume that all first edition books by any of the authors listed will have value, but do *not* assume that all books by the same author will have comparable values.

The values given here are for first-edition books in very good to fine condition, and with a dust jacket if the book was originally issued with one. "Points" often need to be verified to properly identify many of these books. A librarian or rare bookseller should be consulted for verification of edition and value.

AUTHOR	TITLE/EDITION INFORMATION/VALUE
Aarons, Edward Sidney	DEATH IN A LIGHTHOUSE, as Edward Ronns. New York: Phoenix Press, 1938. $50.
Aarons, Edward Sidney	MURDER MONEY, as Edward Ronns. New York: Phoenix Press, 1938. $50.
Aarons, Edward Sidney	THE CORPSE HANGS HIGH, as Edward Ronns. New York: Phoenix Press, 1939. $50.
Aarons, Edward Sidney	NO PLACE TO LIVE, as Edward Ronns. Philadelphia: McKay, 1947. $40.

AUTHOR	TITLE/EDITION INFORMATION/VALUE
Aarons, Edward Sidney	TERROR IN THE TOWN, as Edward Ronns. Philadelphia: McKay, 1947. $40.
Aarons, Edward Sidney	GIFT OF DEATH, as Edward Ronns. Philadelphia: McKay, 1948. $40.
Aarons, Edward Sidney	NIGHTMARE. Philadelphia: McKay, 1948. $40.
Aarons, Edward Sidney	DEAD HEAT, as Paul Ayres. Drexel Hill, Pa.: Bell, 1950. $40.
Aarons, Edward Sidney	THE ART STUDIO MURDERS, as Edward Ronns. Kingston, N.Y.: Quin, 1950. $40.
Aarons, Edward Sidney	CATSPAW ORDEAL, as Edward Ronns. New York: Fawcett, 1950. $30.
Aarons, Edward Sidney	DARK MEMORY, as Edward Ronns. Kingston, N.Y.: Quin, 1950. $30.
Aarons, Edward Sidney	MILLION DOLLAR MURDER, as Edward Ronns. New York: Fawcett, 1950. $30.
Aarons, Edward Sidney	STATE DEPARTMENT MURDERS, as Edward Ronns. New York: Fawcett, 1950. $30.
Aarons, Edward Sidney	THE DECOY, as Edward Ronns. New York: Fawcett, 1951. $10.
Aarons, Edward Sidney	I CAN'T STOP RUNNING, as Edward Ronns. New York: Fawcett, 1951. $10.
Aarons, Edward Sidney	DON'T CRY, BELOVED, as Edward Ronns. New York: Fawcett, 1952. $10.
Aarons, Edward Sidney	PASSAGE TO TERROR, as Edward Ronns. New York: Fawcett, 1952. $10.
Aarons, Edward Sidney	ESCAPE TO LOVE. New York: Fawcett, 1952. $10.
Aarons, Edward Sidney	COME BACK, MY LOVE. New York: Fawcett, 1953. $10.
Aarons, Edward Sidney	DARK DESTINY, as Edward Ronns. Hasbrouck Heights, N.J.: Graphic, 1953. $10.
Aarons, Edward Sidney	THE SINNERS. New York: Fawcett, 1953. $10.
Aarons, Edward Sidney	THE NET, as Edward Ronns. Hasbrouck Heights, N.J.: Graphic, 1953. $10.

AUTHOR	TITLE/EDITION INFORMATION/VALUE
Aarons, Edward Sidney	SAY IT WITH MURDER, as Edward Ronns. Hasbrouck Heights, N.J.: Graphic, 1954. $10.
Aarons, Edward Sidney	GIRL ON THE RUN. New York: Fawcett, 1954. $10.
Aarons, Edward Sidney	ASSIGNMENT TO DISASTER. New York: Fawcett, 1955. $10.
Aarons, Edward Sidney	THEY ALL RAN AWAY, as Edward Ronns. Hasbrouck Heights, N.J.: Graphic, 1955. $10.
Aarons, Edward Sidney	POINT OF PERIL, as Edward Ronns. New York: Curl, 1956. $10.
Aarons, Edward Sidney	ASSIGNMENT—SUICIDE. New York: Fawcett, 1956. $10.
Aarons, Edward Sidney	ASSIGNMENT—TREASON. New York: Fawcett, 1956. $10.
Aarons, Edward Sidney	ASSIGNMENT—BUDAPEST. New York: Fawcett, 1957. $10.
Aarons, Edward Sidney	ASSIGNMENT—STELLA MARNI. New York: Fawcett, 1957. $10.
Aarons, Edward Sidney	DEATH IS MY SHADOW, as Edward Ronns. New York: Curl, 1957. $10.
Aarons, Edward Sidney	ASSIGNMENT—ANGELINA. New York: Fawcett, 1958. $10.
Aarons, Edward Sidney	ASSIGNMENT—MADELEINE. New York: Fawcett, 1958. $10.
Aarons, Edward Sidney	GANG RUMBLE, as Edward Ronns. New York: Avon, 1958. $10.
Aarons, Edward Sidney	ASSIGNMENT—CARLOTTA CORTEZ. New York: Fawcett, 1959. $10.
Aarons, Edward Sidney	ASSIGNMENT—HELENE. New York: Fawcett, 1959. $10.
Aarons, Edward Sidney	ASSIGNMENT—LILI LAMARIS. New York: Fawcett, 1959. $10.
Aarons, Edward Sidney	THE BIG BEDROOM, as Edward Ronns. New York: Pyramid, 1959. $10.
Aarons, Edward Sidney	ASSIGNMENT—MARA TIRANA. New York: Fawcett, 1960. $10.

AUTHOR	TITLE/EDITION INFORMATION/VALUE
Aarons, Edward Sidney	HELL TO ETERNITY. New York: Fawcett, 1960. $10.
Aarons, Edward Sidney	ASSIGNMENT—ZORAYA. New York: Fawcett, 1960. $10.
Aarons, Edward Sidney	ASSIGNMENT—ANKARA. New York: Fawcett, 1961. $10.
Aarons, Edward Sidney	ASSIGNMENT—LOWLANDS. New York: Fawcett, 1961. $10.
Aarons, Edward Sidney	THE DEFENDERS. New York: Fawcett, 1961. $10.
Aarons, Edward Sidney	ASSIGNMENT—BURMA GIRL. New York: Fawcett, 1962. $10.
Aarons, Edward Sidney	ASSIGNMENT—KARACHI. New York: Fawcett, 1962. $10.
Aarons, Edward Sidney	THE GLASS CAGE, as Edward Ronns. New York: Pyramid, 1962. $10.
Aarons, Edward Sidney	ASSIGNMENT—SORRENTO SIREN. New York: Fawcett, 1963. $10.
Aarons, Edward Sidney	ASSIGNMENT—MANCHURIAN DOLL. New York: Fawcett, 1963. $10.
Aarons, Edward Sidney	ASSIGNMENT—SULU SEA. New York: Fawcett, 1964. $10.
Aarons, Edward Sidney	ASSIGNMENT—THE GIRL IN THE GONDOLA. New York: Fawcett, 1964. $10.
Aarons, Edward Sidney	ASSIGNMENT—THE CAIRO DANCERS. New York: Fawcett, 1965. $10.
Aarons, Edward Sidney	ASSIGNMENT—PALERMO. New York: Fawcett, 1966. $10.
Aarons, Edward Sidney	ASSIGNMENT—CONG HAI KILL. New York: Fawcett, 1966. $10.
Aarons, Edward Sidney	ASSIGNMENT—SCHOOL FOR SPIES. New York: Fawcett, 1966. $10.
Aarons, Edward Sidney	ASSIGNMENT—BLACK VIKING. New York: Fawcett, 1967. $10.
Aarons, Edward Sidney	ASSIGNMENT—MOON GIRL. New York: Fawcett, 1967. $10.

AUTHOR	TITLE/EDITION INFORMATION/VALUE
Aarons, Edward Sidney	ASSIGNMENT—NUCLEAR NUDE. New York: Fawcett, 1968. $10.
Aarons, Edward Sidney	ASSIGNMENT—PEKING. New York: Fawcett, 1969. $10.
Aarons, Edward Sidney	ASSIGNMENT—STAR STEALERS. New York: Fawcett, 1970. $10.
Aarons, Edward Sidney	ASSIGNMENT—WHITE RAJAH. New York: Fawcett, 1970. $10.
Aarons, Edward Sidney	ASSIGNMENT—TOKYO. New York: Fawcett, 1971. $10.
Aarons, Edward Sidney	ASSIGNMENT—BANGKOK. New York: Fawcett, 1972. $10.
Aarons, Edward Sidney	ASSIGNMENT—GOLDEN GIRL. New York: Fawcett, 1972. $10.
Aarons, Edward Sidney	ASSIGNMENT—MALTESE MAIDEN. New York: Fawcett, 1972. $10.
Aarons, Edward Sidney	ASSIGNMENT—CEYLON. New York: Fawcett, 1973. $10.
Aarons, Edward Sidney	ASSIGNMENT—SILVER SCORPION. New York: Fawcett, 1973. $10.
Aarons, Edward Sidney	ASSIGNMENT—AMAZON QUEEN. New York: Fawcett, 1974. $10.
Aarons, Edward Sidney	ASSIGNMENT—SUMATRA. New York: Fawcett, 1974. $10.
Aarons, Edward Sidney	ASSIGNMENT—BLACK GOLD. New York: Fawcett, 1975. $10.
Aarons, Edward Sidney	ASSIGNMENT—QUAYLE QUESTION. New York: Fawcett, 1975. $10.
Aiken, Joan Delano	THE SILENCE OF HERONDALE. New York: Doubleday, 1964. $50.
Aiken, Joan Delano	THE FORTUNE HUNTERS. New York: Doubleday, 1965. $50.
Aiken, Joan Delano	TROUBLE WITH PRODUCT X. London: Gollancz, 1966; as BEWARE OF THE BANQUET. New York: Doubleday, 1966. $50.

AUTHOR	TITLE/EDITION INFORMATION/VALUE
Aiken, Joan Delano	HATE BEGINS AT HOME. London: Gollancz, 1967; as DARK INTERVAL. New York: Doubleday, 1967. $50.
Aiken, Joan Delano	THE RIBS OF DEATH. London: Gollancz, 1967; as THE CRYSTAL CROW. New York: Doubleday, 1968. $50.
Aiken, Joan Delano	THE WINDSCREEN WEEPERS AND OTHER TALES OF HORROR AND SUSPENSE. London: Gollancz, 1969. $40.
Aiken, Joan Delano	THE EMBROIDERED SUNSET. New York: Doubleday, 1970. $40.
Aiken, Joan Delano	THE GREEN FLASH AND OTHER TALES OF HORROR, SUSPENSE AND FANTASY. New York: Holt Rinehart, 1971. $40.
Aiken, Joan Delano	DIED ON A RAINY SUNDAY. New York: Holt Rinehart, 1972. $40.
Aiken, Joan Delano	THE BUTTERFLY PICNIC. London: Gollancz, 1972; as A CLUSTER OF SEPERATE SPARKS, New York: Doubleday, 1972. $40.
Aiken, Joan Delano	VOICES IN AN EMPTY HOUSE. New York: Doubleday, 1975. $30.
Aiken, Joan Delano	THE FAR FORESTS: TALES OF ROMANCE, FANTASY, AND SUSPENSE. New York: Viking, 1977. $30.
Aiken, Joan Delano	LAST MOVEMENT. New York: Doubleday, 1977. $30.
Aiken, Joan Delano	A TOUCH OF CHILL. London: Gollancz, 1979. $20.
Aiken, Joan Delano	A WHISPER IN THE NIGHT. London: Gollancz, 1982. $30.
Aird, Catherine	THE RELIGIOUS BODY. New York: Doubleday, 1966. $75.
Aird, Catherine	A MOST CONTAGIOUS GAME. New York: Doubleday, 1967. $50.
Aird, Catherine	HENRIETTA WHO? New York: Doubleday, 1968. $50.

AUTHOR	TITLE/EDITION INFORMATION/VALUE
Aird, Catherine	THE COMPLETE STEEL. London: Macdonald, 1969; as THE STATELY HOME MURDER. New York: Doubleday, 1970. $50.
Aird, Catherine	A LATE PHOENIX. New York: Doubleday, 1971. $40.
Aird, Catherine	HIS BURIAL TOO. New York: Doubleday, 1973. $40.
Aird, Catherine	SLIGHT MOURNING. New York: Doubleday, 1976. $30.
Aird, Catherine	PARTING BREATH. New York: Doubleday, 1978. $30.
Aird, Catherine	SOME DIE ELOQUENT. London: Collins, 1979. $30.
Albert, Marvin H.	THE HOODS COME CALLING, as Nick Quarry. New York: Fawcett, 1958. $40.
Albert, Marvin H.	THE GIRL WITH NO PLACE TO HIDE, as Nick Quarry. New York: Fawcett, 1959. $40.
Albert, Marvin H.	NO CHANCE IN HELL, as Nick Quarry. New York: Fawcett, 1960. $40.
Albert, Marvin H.	TILL IT HURTS, as Nick Quarry. New York: Fawcett, 1960. $40.
Albert, Marvin H.	SOME DIE HARD, as Nick Quarry. New York: Fawcett, 1961. $40.
Albert, Marvin H.	MIAMI MAYHEM, as Anthony Rome. London: Hale, 1961; as TONY ROME. New York: Dell, 1967. $30.
Albert, Marvin H.	THE LADY IN CEMENT, as Anthony Rome. London: Hale, 1962. $30.
Albert, Marvin H.	MY KIND OF GAME, as Anthony Rome. New York: Dell, 1962. $30.
Albert, Marvin H.	THE PINK PANTHER. New York: Bantam, 1964. $30.
Albert, Marvin H.	THE DON IS DEAD, as Nick Quarry. New York: Fawcett, 1972. $20.
Albert, Marvin H.	THE VENDETTA, as Nick Quarry. New York: Fawcett, 1973. $20.

AUTHOR	TITLE/EDITION INFORMATION/VALUE
Albert, Marvin H.	THE GARGOYLE CONSPIRACY. New York: Doubleday, 1975. $20.
Albert, Marvin H.	THE MEDUSA COMPLEX. New York: Arbor House, 1982. $20.
Albrand, Martha	NO SURRENDER. Boston: Little, Brown, 1942. $65.
Albrand, Martha	WITHOUT ORDERS. Boston: Little, Brown, 1943. $60.
Albrand, Martha	NONE SHALL KNOW. Boston: Little, Brown, 1945. $60.
Albrand, Martha	REMEMBERED ANGER. Boston: Little, Brown, 1946. $60.
Albrand, Martha	AFTER MIDNIGHT. New York: Random House, 1948. $50.
Albrand, Martha	DESPERATE MOMENT. New York: Random House, 1951. $30.
Albrand, Martha	THE HUNTED WOMAN. New York: Random House, 1952. $30.
Albrand, Martha	NIGHTMARE IN COPENHAGEN. New York: Random House, 1954. $30.
Albrand, Martha	THE MASK OF ALEXANDER. New York: Random House, 1955. $30.
Albrand, Martha	THE LINDEN AFFAIR. New York: Random House, 1956. $30.
Albrand, Martha	A DAY IN MONTE CARLO. New York: Random House, 1959. $30.
Albrand, Martha	MEET ME TONIGHT. New York: Random House, 1960. $30.
Albrand, Martha	A CALL FROM AUSTRIA. New York: Random House, 1963. $30.
Albrand, Martha	A DOOR FELL SHUT. New York: New American Library, 1966. $30.
Albrand, Martha	RHINE REPLICA. New York: Random House, 1969. $20.
Albrand, Martha	MANHATTAN NORTH. New York: Coward McCann, 1971. $20.

AUTHOR	TITLE/EDITION INFORMATION/VALUE
Albrand, Martha	ZURICH AZ/900. New York: Holt Rinehart, 1974. $20.
Albrand, Martha	A TASTE OF TERROR. New York: Putnam, 1977. $20.
Albrand, Martha	INTERMISSION. London: Hodder & Stoughton, 1978; as FINAL SCORE. New York: St. Martin's, 1978. $20.
Ambler, Eric	THE DARK FRONTIER. London: Hodder & Stoughton, 1936. $150.
Ambler, Eric	UNCOMMON DANGER. London: Hodder & Stoughton, 1937; as BACKGROUND TO DANGER. New York: Knopf, 1937. $135.
Ambler, Eric	EPITAPH FOR A SPY. London: Hodder & Stoughton, 1938. $135.
Ambler, Eric	CAUSE FOR ALARM. New York: Knopf, 1939. $125.
Ambler, Eric	A COFFIN FOR DIMITRIOS. New York, 1939. $175-225.
Ambler, Eric	JOURNEY INTO FEAR. New York: Knopf, 1940. $75.
Ambler, Eric	SKYTIP, as Eliot Reed. New York: Doubleday, 1950. $50.
Ambler, Eric	JUDGMENT ON DELTCHEV. New York: Knopf, 1951. $50.
Ambler, Eric	TENDER TO DANGER, as Eliot Reed. New York: Doubleday, 1951. $50.
Ambler, Eric	THE SCHIRMER INHERITANCE. New York: Knopf, 1953. $50.
Ambler, Eric	THE MARAS AFFAIR, as Eliot Reed. New York: Doubleday, 1953. $50.
Ambler, Eric	CHARTER TO DANGER, as Eliot Reed. London: Collins, 1954. $50.
Ambler, Eric	THE NIGHT-COMERS. London: Heinemann, 1956; as STATE OF SIEGE. New York: Knopf, 1956. $40.

AUTHOR	TITLE/EDITION INFORMATION/VALUE
Ambler, Eric	PASSPORT TO PANIC, as Eliot Reed. London: Collins, 1958. $40.
Ambler, Eric	PASSAGE OF ARMS. New York: Knopf, 1960. $40.
Ambler, Eric	THE LIGHT OF DAY. New York: Knopf, 1963. $40.
Ambler, Eric	THE ABILITY TO KILL AND OTHER PIECES. London: Bodley Head, 1963. $40.
Ambler, Eric	A KIND OF ANGER. New York: Atheneum, 1964. $40.
Ambler, Eric	DIRTY STORY. New York: Atheneum, 1967. $30.
Ambler, Eric	THE INTERCOM CONSPIRACY. New York: Atheneum, 1969. $30.
Ambler, Eric	THE LEVANTER. New York: Atheneum, 1972. $30.
Ambler, Eric	DOCTOR FRIGO. New York: Atheneum, 1974. $30.
Ambler, Eric	SEND NO MORE ROSES. London: Weidenfeld & Nicolson, 1977; as THE SIEGE OF THE VILLA LIPP. New York: Random House, 1977. $30.
Anthony, Evelyn	IMPERIAL HIGHNESS. London: Museum Press, 1953; as REBEL PRINCESS. New York: Crowell, 1953. $75.
Anthony, Evelyn	THE RENDEZVOUS. New York: Coward McCann, 1968. $50.
Anthony, Evelyn	THE LEGEND. New York: Coward McCann, 1969. $50.
Anthony, Evelyn	THE ASSASSIN. New York: Coward McCann, 1970. $50.
Anthony, Evelyn	THE TAMARIND SEED. New York: Coward McCann, 1971. $50.
Anthony, Evelyn	THE POELLENBERG INHERITANCE. New York: Coward McCann, 1972. $40.

AUTHOR	**TITLE/EDITION INFORMATION/VALUE**
Anthony, Evelyn	THE OCCUPYING POWER. London: Hutchinson, 1973; as STRANGER AT THE GATES. New York: Coward McCann, 1973. $40.
Anthony, Evelyn	THE MALASPIGA EXIT. London: Hutchinson, 1974; as MISSION TO MALASPIGA. New York: Coward McCann, 1974. $40.
Anthony, Evelyn	THE PERSIAN RANSOM. London: Hutchinson, 1975; as THE PERSIAN PRICE, New York: Coward McCann, 1975. $40.
Anthony, Evelyn	THE SILVER FALCON. New York: Coward McCann, 1977. $40.
Anthony, Evelyn	THE RETURN. New York: Coward McCann, 1978. $30.
Anthony, Evelyn	THE GRAVE OF TRUTH. London: Hutchinson, 1979. $30.
Anthony, Evelyn	THE JANUS IMPERATIVE. New York: Coward McCann, 1980. $30.
Anthony, Evelyn	THE DEFECTOR. New York: Coward McCann, 1981. $30.
Anthony, Evelyn	THE AVENUE OF THE DEAD. London: Hutchinson, 1981. $30.
Atlee, Philip	THE CASE OF THE SHIVERING CHORUS GIRLS, as James Atlee Phillips. New York: Coward McCann, 1942. $75.
Atlee, Philip	SUITABLE FOR FRAMING, as James Atlee Phillips. New York: Macmillan, 1949. $50.
Atlee, Philip	PAGODA, as James Atlee Phillips. New York: Macmillan, 1951. $50.
Atlee, Philip	THE DEADLY MERMAIDS, as James Atlee Phillips. New York: Dell, 1954. $40.
Atlee, Philip	THE GREEN WOUND. New York: Fawcett, 1963. $40.
Atlee, Philip	THE SILKEN BARONESS. New York: Fawcett, 1964; as THE SILK BARONESS CONTRACT, London, 1967. $40.

AUTHOR	**TITLE/EDITION INFORMATION/VALUE**
Atlee, Philip	THE DEATH BIRD CONTRACT. New York: Fawcett, 1966. $40.
Atlee, Philip	THE IRISH BEAUTY CONTRACT. New York: Fawcett, 1966. $40.
Atlee, Philip	THE PAPER PISTOL CONTRACT. New York: Fawcett, 1966. $40.
Atlee, Philip	THE STAR RUBY CONTRACT. New York: Fawcett, 1967. $30.
Atlee, Philip	THE SKELETON COAST CONTRACT. New York: Fawcett, 1968. $30.
Atlee, Philip	THE ROCKABYE CONTRACT. New York: Fawcett, 1968. $30.
Atlee, Philip	THE ILL WIND CONTRACT. New York: Fawcett, 1969. $30.
Atlee, Philip	THE TREMBLING EARTH CONTRACT. New York: Fawcett, 1969. $10.
Atlee, Philip	THE FER-DE-LANCE CONTRACT. New York: Fawcett, 1970. $10.
Atlee, Philip	THE CANADIAN BOMBER CONTRACT. New York: Fawcett, 1971. $10.
Atlee, Philip	THE WHITE WOLVERINE CONTRACT. New York: Fawcett, 1971. $10.
Atlee, Philip	THE JUDAH LION CONTRACT. New York: Fawcett, 1972. $10.
Atlee, Philip	THE KIWI CONTRACT. New York: Fawcett, 1972. $10.
Atlee, Philip	THE SHANKILL ROAD CONTRACT. New York: Fawcett, 1973. $10.
Atlee, Philip	THE SPICE ROUTE CONTRACT. New York: Fawcett, 1973. $10.
Atlee, Philip	THE KOWLOON CONTRACT. New York: Fawcett, 1974. $10.
Atlee, Philip	THE UNDERGROUND CITIES CONTRACT. New York: Fawcett, 1974. $10.
Atlee, Philip	THE BLACK VENUS CONTRACT. New York: Fawcett, 1975. $10.

AUTHOR	TITLE/EDITION INFORMATION/VALUE
Atlee, Philip	THE LOST DOMINO CONTRACT. New York: Fawcett, 1976. $10.
Avallone, Michael Angelo, Jr.	THE SPITTING IMAGE. New York: Holt Rinehart, 1953. $50.
Avallone, Michael Angelo, Jr.	THE TALL DOLORES. New York: Holt Rinehart, 1953. $45.
Avallone, Michael Angelo, Jr.	DEAD GAME. New York: Holt Rinehart, 1954. $45.
Avallone, Michael Angelo, Jr.	VIOLENCE IN VELVET. New York: New American Library, 1956. $40.
Avallone, Michael Angelo, Jr.	THE CASE OF THE BOUNCING BETTY. New York: Ace, 1957. $40.
Avallone, Michael Angelo, Jr.	THE CASE OF THE VIOLENT VIRGIN. New York: Ace, 1957. $40.
Avallone, Michael Angelo, Jr.	THE CRAZY MIXED-UP CORPSE. New York: Fawcett, 1957. $35.
Avallone, Michael Angelo, Jr.	THE VOODOO MURDERS. New York: Fawcett, 1957. $30.
Avallone, Michael Angelo, Jr.	MEANWHILE BACK AT THE MORGUE. New York: Fawcett, 1960. $30.
Avallone, Michael Angelo, Jr.	ALL THE WAY HOME. New York: Midwood, 1960. $30.
Avallone, Michael Angelo, Jr.	THE LITTLE BLACK BOOK. New York: Midwood, 1961. $30.
Avallone, Michael Angelo, Jr.	STAG STRIPPER. New York: Midwood, 1961. $30.
Avallone, Michael Angelo, Jr.	WOMEN IN PRISON. New York: Midwood, 1961. $30.
Avallone, Michael Angelo, Jr.	THE ALARMING CLOCK. London: Allen, 1961. $30.
Avallone, Michael Angelo, Jr.	FLIGHT HOSTESS ROGERS. New York: Midwood, 1962. $30.
Avallone, Michael Angelo, Jr.	NEVER LOVE A CALL GIRL. New York: Midwood, 1962. $30.
Avallone, Michael Angelo, Jr.	THE PLATINUM TRAP. New York: Midwood, 1962. $30.

AUTHOR	TITLE/EDITION INFORMATION/VALUE
Avallone, Michael Angelo, Jr.	SEX KITTEN. New York: Midwood, 1962. $30.
Avallone, Michael Angelo, Jr.	SINNERS IN WHITE. New York: Midwood, 1962. $30.
Avallone, Michael Angelo, Jr.	LUST AT LEISURE. Beacon, N.Y.: Beacon Signal, 1963. $30.
Avallone, Michael Angelo, Jr.	THE BEDROOM BOLERO. New York: Belmont, 1963; as THE BOLERO MURDERS. London: Hale, 1972. $30.
Avallone, Michael Angelo, Jr.	THE MAIN ATTRACTION, as Steve Michaels. New York: Belmont, 1963. $30.
Avallone, Michael Angelo, Jr.	THE LIVING BOMB. London: Allen, 1963. $350.
Avallone, Michael Angelo, Jr.	THERE IS SOMETHING ABOUT A DAME. New York: Belmont, 1963. $30.
Avallone, Michael Angelo, Jr.	SHOCK CORRIDOR. New York: Belmont, 1963. $30.
Avallone, Michael Angelo, Jr.	THE DOCTOR'S WIFE. New York: Beacon, 1963. $30.
Avallone, Michael Angelo, Jr.	TALES OF THE FRIGHTENED. New York: Belmont, 1963. $30.
Avallone, Michael Angelo, Jr.	AND SEX WALKED IN. Beacon, N.Y.: Beacon Signal, 1963. $30.
Avallone, Michael Angelo, Jr.	LUST IS NO LADY. New York: Belmont, 1964; as THE BRUTAL KOOK, London: Allen, 1965. $30.
Avallone, Michael Angelo, Jr.	FELICIA, as Mark Dane. New York: Belmont, 1964. $30.
Avallone, Michael Angelo, Jr.	THE CHINA DOLL, as Nick Carter. New York: Award, 1964. $30.
Avallone, Michael Angelo, Jr.	RUN SPY RUN, as Nick Carter. New York: Award, 1964. $30.
Avallone, Michael Angelo, Jr.	SAIGON, as Nick Carter. New York: Award, 1964. $30.
Avallone, Michael Angelo, Jr.	THE NIGHT WALKER, as Sidney Stuart. New York: Award, 1964. $30.

AUTHOR	TITLE/EDITION INFORMATION/VALUE
Avallone, Michael Angelo, Jr.	STATION SIX—SAHARA. New York: Popular Library, 1964. $30.
Avallone, Michael Angelo, Jr.	THE THOUSAND COFFINS AFFAIR. New York: Ace, New English Library, 1965. $30.
Avallone, Michael Angelo, Jr.	YOUNG DILLINGER, as Sidney Stuart. New York: Belmont, 1965. $30.
Avallone, Michael Angelo, Jr.	THE BIRDS OF A FEATHER AFFAIR. New York: New American Library, 1966. $30.
Avallone, Michael Angelo, Jr.	THE BLAZING AFFAIR. New York: New American Library, 1966. $30.
Avallone, Michael Angelo, Jr.	THE FAT DEATH. London: Allen, 1966. $30.
Avallone, Michael Angelo, Jr.	KALEIDOSCOPE. New York: Popular Library, 1966. $30.
Avallone, Michael Angelo, Jr.	THE FEBRUARY DOLL MURDERS. New York: New American Library, 1967. $30.
Avallone, Michael Angelo, Jr.	MADAME X. New York: Popular Library, 1966. $30.
Avallone, Michael Angelo, Jr.	THE FELONY SQUAD. New York: Popular Library, 1967. $30.
Avallone, Michael Angelo, Jr.	THE MAN FROM AVON. New York: Avon, 1967. $30.
Avallone, Michael Angelo, Jr.	ASSASSINS DON'T LIE IN BED. New York: New American Library, 1968. $30.
Avallone, Michael Angelo, Jr.	THE COFFIN THINGS. New York: Lancer, 1968. $30.
Avallone, Michael Angelo, Jr.	HAWAII FIVE-O. New York: New American Library, 1968. $30.
Avallone, Michael Angelo, Jr.	THE INCIDENT. New York: New American Library, 1968. $30.
Avallone, Michael Angelo, Jr.	THE HORRIBLE MAN. London: Hale, 1968; New York: Curtis, 1972. $30.
Avallone, Michael Angelo, Jr.	MANNIX. New York: Popular Library, 1968. $30.
Avallone, Michael Angelo, Jr.	THE FLOWER-COVERED CORPSE. London: Hale, 1969. $30.

AUTHOR	TITLE/EDITION INFORMATION/VALUE
Avallone, Michael Angelo, Jr.	THE DOOMSDAY BAG. New York: New American Library, 1969; as KILLER'S HIGHWAY. London: Hale, 1970. $30.
Avallone, Michael Angelo, Jr.	HAWAII FIVE-O: TERROR IN THE SUN. New York: New American Library, 1969. $30.
Avallone, Michael Angelo, Jr.	THE KILLING STAR. London: Hale, 1969. $30.
Avallone, Michael Angelo, Jr.	MISSING! New York: New American Library, 1969. $30.
Avallone, Michael Angelo, Jr.	A BULLET FOR PRETTY BOY. New York: Curtis, 1970. $20.
Avallone, Michael Angelo, Jr.	ONE MORE TIME. New York: Popular Library, 1970. $20.
Avallone, Michael Angelo, Jr.	DEATH DIVES DEEP. New York: New American Library, 1971. $20.
Avallone, Michael Angelo, Jr.	LITTLE MISS MURDER. New York: New American Library, 1971; as THE ULTIMATE CLIENT. London: Hale, 1971. $20.
Avallone, Michael Angelo, Jr.	WHEN WERE YOU BORN? Paris: Gallimard, 1971. $20.
Avallone, Michael Angelo, Jr.	THE NIGHT BEFORE CHAOS. Paris: Gallimard, 1971. $20.
Avallone, Michael Angelo, Jr.	THE CRAGHOLD LEGACY, as Edwina Noone. New York: Beagle, 1971. $20.
Avallone, Michael Angelo, Jr.	KEITH PARTRIDGE, MASTER-SPY, as Vance Stanton. New York: Curtis, 1971. $10.
Avallone, Michael Angelo, Jr.	SHOOT IT AGAIN, SAM. New York: Curtis, 1972; as THE MOVING GRAVEYARD, London: Hale, 1973. $10.
Avallone, Michael Angelo, Jr.	THE GIRL IN THE COCKPIT. New York: Curtis, 1972. $10.
Avallone, Michael Angelo, Jr.	LONDON BLOODY LONDON. New York: Curtis, 1972. $10.
Avallone, Michael Angelo, Jr.	THE FAT AND SKINNY MURDER MYSTERY, as Vance Stanton. New York: Curtis, 1972. $10.

AUTHOR	TITLE/EDITION INFORMATION/VALUE
Avallone, Michael Angelo, Jr.	THE WALKING FINGERS, as Vance Stanton. New York: Curtis, 1972. $10.
Avallone, Michael Angelo, Jr.	WHO'S THAT LAUGHING IN THE GRAVE? as Vance Stanton. New York: Curtis, 1972. $10.
Avallone, Michael Angelo, Jr.	KILL HER—YOU'LL LIKE IT. New York: Curtis, 1973. $10.
Avallone, Michael Angelo, Jr.	THE HOT BODY. New York: Curtis, 1973. $10.
Avallone, Michael Angelo, Jr.	KILLER ON THE KEYS. New York: Curtis, 1973. $10.
Avallone, Michael Angelo, Jr.	THE X-RATED CORPSE. New York: Curtis, 1973. $10.
Avallone, Michael Angelo, Jr.	153 OAKLAND STREET, as Dora Highland. New York: Popular Library, 1973. $10.
Avallone, Michael Angelo, Jr.	THE BEAST WITH RED HANDS, as Sidney Stuart. New York: Popular Library, 1973. $10.
Avallone, Michael Angelo, Jr.	DEATH IS A DARK MAN, as Dora Highland. New York: Popular Library, 1974. $10.
Avallone, Michael Angelo, Jr.	FALLEN ANGEL. New York: Warner, 1974. $10.
Avallone, Michael Angelo, Jr.	THE WEREWOLF WALKS TONIGHT. New York: Warner, 1974. $10.
Avallone, Michael Angelo, Jr.	DEVIL, DEVIL. New York: Warner, 1975. $10.
Avallone, Michael Angelo, Jr.	ONLY ONE MORE MIRACLE. New York: Scholastic, 1975. $10.
Avallone, Michael Angelo, Jr.	THE BIG STIFFS. London: Hale, 1977. $10.
Avallone, Michael Angelo, Jr.	DARK ON MONDAY. London: Hale, 1978. $10.
Avallone, Michael Angelo, Jr.	WHERE MONSTERS WALK. New York: Scholastic, 1978. $10.
Avallone, Michael Angelo, Jr.	FIVE MINUTE MYSTERIES. New York: Scholastic, 1978. $10.

AUTHOR	TITLE/EDITION INFORMATION/VALUE
Ballard, Willis Todhunter	SAY YES TO MURDER. New York: Putnam, 1942. $85.
Ballard, Willis Todhunter	MURDER CAN'T STOP. Philadelphia: McKay, 1946. $85.
Ballard, Willis Todhunter	MURDER PICKS THE JURY, as Harrison Hunt, with Norbert Davis. New York: Curl, 1947. $85.
Ballard, Willis Todhunter	DEALING OUT DEATH. Philadelphia: McKay, 1948. $85.
Ballard, Willis Todhunter	WALK IN FEAR. New York: Fawcett, 1952. $85.
Ballard, Willis Todhunter	DEATH TAKES AN OPTION, as Neil MacNeil. New York: Fawcett, 1958. $85.
Ballard, Willis Todhunter	THIRD ON A SEESAW, as Neil MacNeil. New York: Fawcett, 1959. $85.
Ballard, Willis Todhunter	TWO GUNS FOR HIRE, as Neil MacNeil. New York: Fawcett, 1959. $85.
Ballard, Willis Todhunter	LIGHTS, CAMERA, MURDER, as John Shepherd. New York: Belmont, 1960. $85.
Ballard, Willis Todhunter	HOT DAM, as Neil MacNeil. New York: Fawcett, 1960. $85.
Ballard, Willis Todhunter	THE DEATH RIDE, as Neil MacNeil. New York: Fawcett, 1960. $85.
Ballard, Willis Todhunter	PRETTY MISS MURDER. New York: Permabooks, 1961. $65.
Ballard, Willis Todhunter	THE SEVEN SISTERS. New York: Permabooks, 1962. $65.
Ballard, Willis Todhunter	MEXICAN SLAY RIDE, as Neil MacNeil. New York: Fawcett, 1962. $65.
Ballard, Willis Todhunter	THREE FOR THE MONEY. New York: Permabooks, 1963. $65.
Ballard, Willis Todhunter	END OF A MILLIONAIRE, as P. D. Ballard. New York: Fawcett, 1964. $65.
Ballard, Willis Todhunter	THE SPY CATCHERS, as Neil MacNeil. New York: Fawcett, 1966. $65.

AUTHOR	TITLE/EDITION INFORMATION/VALUE
Ballard, Willis Todhunter	MURDER LAS VEGAS STYLE. New York: Tower, 1967. $65.
Ballard, Willis Todhunter	BROTHERS IN BLOOD, as P. D. Ballard. New York: Fawcett, 1972. $45.
Ballard, Willis Todhunter	ANGEL OF DEATH, as P. D. Ballard. New York: Fawcett, 1973. $45.
Ballard, Willis Todhunter	THE DEATH BROKERS, as P. D. Ballard. New York: Fawcett, 1973. $45.
Ballard, Willis Todhunter	THE KREMLIN FILE, as Nick Carter. New York: Award, 1973. $45.
Bentley, E. C.	TRENT'S LAST CASE. London: Nelson, 1913; as THE WOMAN IN BLACK. New York: Century, 1913. $275.
Bentley, E. C.	TRENT'S OWN CASE, with H. Warner Allen. New York: Knopf, 1936. $175.
Bentley, E. C.	TRENT INTERVENES. New York: Knopf, 1938. $145.
Bentley, E. C.	ELEPHANT'S WORK: AN ENIGMA. New York: Knopf, 1950. $125.
Bentley, Nicolas Clerihew	GAMMON AND ESPIONAGE. London: Cresset, 1938. $165.
Bentley, Nicolas Clerihew	THE TONGUE-TIED CANARY. New York: Duell, 1949. $125.
Bentley, Nicolas Clerihew	THE FLOATING DUTCHMAN. New York: Duell, 1951. $85.
Bentley, Nicolas Clerihew	THIRD PARTY RISK. London: Joseph, 1953. $75.
Bentley, Nicolas Clerihew	THE EVENTS OF THAT WEEK. New York: St. Martin's, 1972. $50.
Bentley, Nicolas Clerihew	INSIDE INFORMATION. London: Deutsch, 1974. $50.
Biggers, Earl Derr	SEVEN KEYS TO BALDPATE. Indianapolis: Bobbs Merrill, 1913. $65.
Biggers, Earl Derr	LOVE INSURANCE. Indianapolis: Bobbs Merrill, 1914. $65.

AUTHOR	TITLE/EDITION INFORMATION/VALUE
Biggers, Earl Derr	INSIDE THE LINES, with Robert Welles Ritchie. Indianapolis: Bobbs Merrill, 1915. $65.
Biggers, Earl Derr	THE AGONY COLUMN. Indianapolis: Bobbs Merrill, 1916. $65.
Biggers, Earl Derr	THE HOUSE WITHOUT A KEY. Indianapolis: Bobbs Merrill, 1916. $65.
Biggers, Earl Derr	THE CHINESE PARROT. Indianapolis: Bobbs Merrill, 1926. $65.
Biggers, Earl Derr	FIFTY CANDLES. Indianapolis: Bobbs Merrill, 1926. $65.
Biggers, Earl Derr	BEHIND THAT CURTAIN. Indianapolis: Bobbs Merrill, 1928. $65.
Biggers, Earl Derr	THE BLACK CAMEL. Indianapolis: Bobbs Merrill, 1929. $65.
Biggers, Earl Derr	CHARLIE CHAN CARRIES ON. Indianapolis: Bobbs Merrill, 1930. $65.
Biggers, Earl Derr	KEEPER OF THE KEYS. Indianapolis: Bobbs Merrill, 1932. $65.
Biggers, Earl Derr	EARL DERR BIGGERS TELLS TEN STORIES. Indianapolis: Bobbs Merrill, 1933. $65.
Box, Edgar	DEATH IN THE FIFTH POSITION. New York: Dutton, 1952. $75-90.
Box, Edgar	DEATH BEFORE BEDTIME. New York: Dutton, 1953. $60-75.
Box, Edgar	DEATH LIKES IT HOT. New York: Dutton, 1954. $60-75.
Bramah, Ernest	MAX CARRADOS. London: Methuen, 1914. $450-550.
Bramah, Ernest	THE EYES OF MAX CARRADOS. New York: Doran, 1924. $450-550.
Bramah, Ernest	THE SPECIMEN CASE, New York: Doran, 1925. $400.
Bramah, Ernest	MAX CARRADOS MYSTERIES. London: Hodder & Stoughton, 1927. $350.
Bramah, Ernest	THE BRAVO OF LONDON. London: Cassell, 1934. $350.

AUTHOR	TITLE/EDITION INFORMATION/VALUE
Bramah, Ernest	BEST MAX CARRADOS DETECTIVE STORIES. New York: Dover, 1972. $350.
Buchan, John	THE WATCHER BY THE THRESHOLD AND OTHER TALES. Edinburgh: Blackwood, 1902. $450.
Buchan, John	THE MOON ENDURETH: TALES AND FANCIES. New York: Sturgis, 1912. $325.
Buchan, John	THE THIRTY-NINE STEPS. New York: Doran, 1915. $225-275.
Buchan, John	THE POWER-HOUSE. New York: Doran, 1916. $125.
Buchan, John	GREENMANTLE. New York: Doran, 1916. $125.
Buchan, John	MR. STANDFAST. New York: Doran, 1919. $110.
Buchan, John	HUNTINGTOWER. New York: Doran, 1922. $100.
Buchan, John	THE THREE HOSTAGES. Boston: Houghton Mifflin, 1924. $65.
Buchan, John	JOHN MACNAB. Boston: Houghton Mifflin, 1925. $65.
Buchan, John	THE DANCING FLOOR. Boston: Houghton Mifflin, 1926. $65.
Buchan, John	THE RUNAGATES CLUB. Boston: Houghton Mifflin, 1928. $65.
Buchan, John	THE COURTS OF THE MORNING. Boston: Houghton Mifflin, 1929. $65.
Buchan, John	CASTLE GAY. Boston: Houghton Mifflin, 1929. $65.
Buchan, John	THE GAP IN THE CURTAIN. Boston: Houghton Mifflin, 1932. $65.
Buchan, John	A PRINCE OF THE CAPTIVITY. Boston: Houghton Mifflin, 1933. $65.
Buchan, John	THE HOUSE OF THE FOUR WINDS. Boston: Houghton Mifflin, 1935. $65.

AUTHOR	TITLE/EDITION INFORMATION/VALUE
Buchan, John	THE ISLAND OF SHEEP, as THE MAN FROM THE NORLANDS. Boston: Houghton Mifflin, 1936. $65.
Buchan, John	SICK HEART RIVER, as MOUNTAIN MEADOW. Boston: Houghton Mifflin, 1941. $65.
Buechner, Frederick	A LONG DAY'S DYING. New York, 1950. $60-75.
Burnett, W. R.	LITTLE CAESAR. New York: Dial, 1929. $125-150.
Burnett, W. R.	THE SILVER EAGLE. New York: Dial, 1931. $65.
Burnett, W. R.	DARK HAZARD. New York: Harper, 1933. $65.
Burnett, W. R.	KING COLE. New York: Harper, 1936. $65.
Burnett, W. R.	HIGH SIERRA. New York: Knopf, 1940. $65.
Burnett, W. R.	THE QUICK BROWN FOX. New York: Knopf, 1942. $65.
Burnett, W. R.	NOBODY LIVES FOREVER. New York: Knopf, 1943. $65.
Burnett, W. R.	TOMORROW'S ANOTHER DAY. New York: Knopf, 1945. $65.
Burnett, W. R.	ROMELLE. New York: Knopf, 1946. $65.
Burnett, W. R.	THE ASPHALT JUNGLE. New York: Knopf, 1949. $65.
Burnett, W. R.	LITTLE MEN, BIG WORLD. New York: Knopf, 1951. $65.
Burnett, W. R.	VANITY ROW. New York: Knopf, 1952. $65.
Burnett, W. R.	BIG STAN, as John Monahan. New York: Fawcett, 1953. $65.
Burnett, W. R.	UNDERDOG. New York: Knopf, 1957. $65.
Burnett, W. R.	CONANT. New York: Popular Library, 1961. $65.
Burnett, W. R.	ROUND THE CLOCK AT VOLARI'S. New York: Fawcett, 1961. $65.

AUTHOR	TITLE/EDITION INFORMATION/VALUE
Burnett, W. R.	THE WIDOW BARONY. London: Macdonald, 1962. $65.
Burnett, W. R.	THE COOL MAN. New York: Fawcett, 1968. $65.
Cain, James Mallahan	THE POSTMAN ALWAYS RINGS TWICE. New York: Knopf, 1934. $550 or more.
Cain, James Mallahan	SERENADE. New York: Knopf, 1937. $65.
Cain, James Mallahan	MILDRED PIERCE. New York: Knopf, 1941. $65.
Cain, James Mallahan	LOVE'S LOVELY COUNTERFEIT. New York: Knopf, 1942. $65.
Cain, James Mallahan	THREE OF A KIND: CAREER IN C MAJOR, THE EMBEZZLER, DOUBLE INDEMNITY. New York: Knopf, 1943. $65.
Cain, James Mallahan	CAREER IN C MAJOR AND OTHER STORIES. New York: Avon, 1943. $65.
Cain, James Mallahan	PAST ALL DISHONOR. New York: Knopf, 1946. $65.
Cain, James Mallahan	SINFUL WOMAN. New York: Avon, 1947. $65.
Cain, James Mallahan	THE BUTTERFLY. New York: Knopf, 1947. $65.
Cain, James Mallahan	THE MOTH. New York: Knopf, 1948. $30-45.
Cain, James Mallahan	THREE OF HEARTS. London: Hale, 1949.
Cain, James Mallahan	JEALOUS WOMAN. New York: Avon, 1948.
Cain, James Mallahan	THE ROOT OF HIS EVIL. New York: Avon, 1951. $65.
Cain, James Mallahan	GALATEA. New York: Knopf, 1953. $65.
Cain, James Mallahan	MIGNON. New York: Dial, 1962. $65.
Cain, James Mallahan	THE MAGICIAN'S WIFE. New York: Dial, 1965. $65.
Cain, James Mallahan	RAINBOW'S END. New York: Mason Charter, 1975. $65.

AUTHOR	TITLE/EDITION INFORMATION/VALUE
Cain, James Mallahan	THE INSTITUTE. New York: Mason Charter, 1976. $65.
Carr, John Dickson	IT WALKS BY NIGHT. New York: Harper, 1930. $65.
Carr, John Dickson	CASTLE SKULL. New York: Harper, 1931. $65.
Carr, John Dickson	THE LOST GALLOWS. New York: Harper, 1931. $65.
Carr, John Dickson	POISON IN JEST. New York: Harper, 1932. $65.
Carr, John Dickson	THE CORPSE IN THE WAXWORKS. New York: Harper, 1932. $65.
Carr, John Dickson	HAG'S NOOK. New York: Harper, 1933. $65.
Carr, John Dickson	THE MAD HATTER MYSTERY. New York: Harper, 1933. $65.
Carr, John Dickson	THE BOWSTRING MURDERS, as Carr Dickson. New York: Morrow, 1933. $65.
Carr, John Dickson	THE PLAGUE COURT MURDERS, as Carter Dickson. New York: Morrow, 1934. $65.
Carr, John Dickson	THE BLIND BARBER. New York: Harper, 1934. $65.
Carr, John Dickson	THE EIGHT OF SWORDS. New York: Harper, 1934. $65.
Carr, John Dickson	DEVIL KINSMERE, as Roger Fairbairn. New York: Harper, 1934. $65.
Carr, John Dickson	THE WHITE PRIORY MURDERS, as Carter Dickson. New York: Morrow, 1934. $65.
Carr, John Dickson	THE RED WIDOW MURDERS, as Carter Dickson. New York: Morrow, 1935. $65.
Carr, John Dickson	DEATH-WATCH. New York: Harper, 1935. $65.
Carr, John Dickson	THE THREE COFFINS. New York: Harper, 1935. $65.
Carr, John Dickson	THE UNICORN MURDERS, as Carter Dickson. New York: Morrow, 1935. $65.

AUTHOR	TITLE/EDITION INFORMATION/VALUE
Carr, John Dickson	THE ARABIAN NIGHTS MURDER. New York: Harper, 1936. 65.
Carr, John Dickson	THE BURNING COURT. New York: Harper, 1937. $65.
Carr, John Dickson	THE FOUR FALSE WEAPONS, BEING THE RETURN OF BENCOLIN. New York: Harper, 1937. $65.
Carr, John Dickson	TO WAKE THE DEAD. New York: Harper, 1938. $65.
Carr, John Dickson	THE CROOKED HINGE. New York: Harper, 1938. $65.
Carr, John Dickson	THE PROBLEM OF THE GREEN CAPSULE. New York: Harper, 1939. $65.
Carr, John Dickson	THE PROBLEM OF THE WIRE CAGE. New York: Harper, 1939. $65.
Carr, John Dickson	THE MAN WHO COULD NOT SHUDDER. New York: Harper, 1940. $65.
Carr, John Dickson	THE CASE OF THE CONSTANT SUICIDES. New York: Harper, 1941. $65.
Carr, John Dickson	DEATH TURNS THE TABLES. New York: Harper, 1941. $60-80.
Chandler, Raymond	THE BIG SLEEP. New York: Knopf, 1939. $850 or more.
Chandler, Raymond	FAREWELL, MY LOVELY. New York: Knopf, 1940. $2,250 or more.
Chandler, Raymond	THE HIGH WINDOW. New York: Knopf, 1942. $850.
Chandler, Raymond	THE LADY IN THE LAKE. New York: Knopf, 1943. $550 or more.
Chandler, Raymond	FIVE MURDERERS. New York: Avon, 1944. $65.
Chandler, Raymond	FIVE SINISTER CHARACTERS. New York: Avon, 1945. $65.
Chandler, Raymond	FINGER MAN AND OTHER STORIES. New York: Avon, 1946. $65.

AUTHOR	TITLE/EDITION INFORMATION/VALUE
Chandler, Raymond	SPANISH BLOOD. Cleveland: World, 1946. $35-50.
Chandler, Raymond	THE LITTLE SISTER. Boston: Houghton Mifflin, 1949. $175-225.
Chandler, Raymond	THE SIMPLE ART OF MURDER. Boston: Houghton Mifflin, 1950. $350.
Chandler, Raymond	SMART ALECK KILL. London: Hamish Hamilton, 1953. $65.
Chandler, Raymond	THE LONG GOOD-BYE. Boston: Houghton Mifflin, 1954. $275-325.
Chandler, Raymond	PLAYBACK. Boston: Houghton Mifflin, 1958. $125-175.
Chandler, Raymond	KILLER IN THE RAIN. Boston, 1964. $135-175.
Chesterton, Gilbert Keith	THE TREMENDOUS ADVENTURES OF MAJOR BROWN. London: Shurmer Sibthorp, 1903. $500.
Chesterton, Gilbert Keith	THE CLUB OF QUEER TRADES. New York: Harper, 1905. $465.
Chesterton, Gilbert Keith	THE MAN WHO WAS THURSDAY: A NIGHTMARE. New York: Dodd Mead, 1908. $365.
Chesterton, Gilbert Keith	THE INNOCENCE OF FATHER BROWN. New York: Lane, 1911. $350 or more.
Chesterton, Gilbert Keith	THE WISDOM OF FATHER BROWN. New York: Lane, 1914. $325-375.
Chesterton, Gilbert Keith	THE MAN WHO KNEW TOO MUCH AND OTHER STORIES. New York: Harper, 1922. $265.
Chesterton, Gilbert Keith	THE INCREDULITY OF FATHER BROWN. New York: Dodd Mead, 1926. $365.
Chesterton, Gilbert Keith	THE SECRET OF FATHER BROWN. New York: Harper, 1927. $325-375.
Chesterton, Gilbert Keith	FOUR FAULTLESS FELONS. London, (1930). $135-160.

AUTHOR	TITLE/EDITION INFORMATION/VALUE
Chesterton, Gilbert Keith	THE SCANDAL OF FATHER BROWN. New York, 1935. $60-75.
Christie, Agatha	THE MYSTERIOUS AFFAIR AT STYLES. London, 1920. $2,250 or more.
Christie, Agatha	THE MAN IN THE BROWN SUIT. London, 1924. $275-325.
Christie, Agatha	THE HOUND OF DEATH AND OTHER STORIES. London, 1933. $225-275.
Christie, Agatha	MR. PARKER PYNE, DETECTIVE. New York, 1934. $650-750.
Christie, Agatha	MURDER IN MESOPOTOMIA. London, (1936). $325-375.
Christie, Agatha	POIROT LOSES A CLIENT. New York, 1937. $625-675.
Christie, Agatha	MURDER FOR CHRISTMAS. New York, 1939. $650-750.
Christie, Agatha	HERCULE POIROT'S CHRISTMAS. London, (1939). $175-225.
Christie, Agatha	SAD CYPRESS. London, (1940). $275-325.
Christie, Agatha	THE PATRIOTIC MURDERS. New York, 1941. $650-750.
Christie, Agatha	DEATH COMES AS THE END. London, 1945. $135-175.
Christie, Agatha	CROOKED HOUSE. New York, (1949). $175-225.
Christie, Agatha	DEAD MAN'S FOLLY. New York, (1956). $85-100.
Collins, Wilkie	THE WOMAN IN WHITE. New York, 1860. $350 or more.
Crofts, Freeman Wills	THE CASK. New York: Seltzer, 1924. $365.
Crofts, Freeman Wills	THE PIT-PROP SYNDICATE. New York: Seltzer, 1925. $225-275.
Crofts, Freeman Wills	THE PONSON CASE. New York: Boni, 1927. $225.
Crofts, Freeman Wills	THE GROOTE PARK MURDER. New York: Seltzer, 1925. $200-250.

AUTHOR	TITLE/EDITION INFORMATION/VALUE
Derleth, August	MURDER STALKS THE WAKELY FAMILY. New York: Loring & Mussey, 1934. $65.
Derleth, August	THE MAN ON ALL FOURS. New York: Loring & Mussey, 1934. $65.
Derleth, August	THREE WHO DIED. New York: Loring & Mussey, 1935. $65.
Derleth, August	SIGN OF FEAR. New York: Loring & Mussey, 1935. $65.
Derleth, August	SENTENCE DEFERRED. New York: Scribner, 1939. $65.
Derleth, August	THE NARRACONG RIDDLE. New York: Scribner, 1940. $65.
Derleth, August	THE SEVEN WHO WAITED. New York: Scribner, 1943. $65.
Derleth, August	MISCHIEF IN THE LANE. New York: Scribner, 1944. $65.
Derleth, August	NO FUTURE FOR LUANA. New York: Scribner, 1945. $65.
Derleth, August	THE LURKER AT THE THRESHOLD, with H. P. Lovecraft. Sauk City, Wis.: Arkham, 1945. $165.
Derleth, August	THE MEMOIRS OF SOLAR PONS. Sauk City, Wis., 1951. $85-100.
Derleth, August	DEATH BY DESIGN. New York: Arcadia, 1953. $65.
Derleth, August	FELL PURPOSE. New York: Arcadia, 1953. $65.
Derleth, August	THE RETURN OF SOLAR PONS. Sauk City, Wis., 1958. $85-100.
Derleth, August	THE REMINISCENCES OF SOLAR PONS. Sauk City, Wis., 1961. $85-100.
Derleth, August	THE TRAIL OF CTHULHU. Sauk City, Wis.: Arkham, 1962. $65.
Derleth, August	THE ADVENTURE OF THE ORIENT EXPRESS. Sauk City, Wis.: Mycroft & Moran, 1965. $65.

AUTHOR	TITLE/EDITION INFORMATION/VALUE
Derleth, August	MR. FAIRLIE'S FINAL JOURNEY. Sauk City, Wis.: Mycroft & Moran, 1968. $65.
Derleth, August	THE ADVENTURE OF THE UNIQUE DICKENSIANS. Sauk City, Wis.: Mycroft & Moran, 1968. $65.
Doyle, Arthur Conan	A STUDY IN SCARLET. London, 1888. Wrappers. $15,000 or more.
Doyle, Arthur Conan	THE ADVENTURES OF SHERLOCK HOLMES. New York: Harper, 1892. $550 or more.
Doyle, Arthur Conan	THE MYSTERY OF CLOOMBER. New York: Fenno, 1895. $465.
Doyle, Arthur Conan	THE SIGN OF FOUR. London, 1890. $1,750 or more.
Doyle, Arthur Conan	THE DOINGS OF RAFFLES HAW. New York: Lovell, 1892. $225-275.
Doyle, Arthur Conan	MY FRIEND THE MURDERER. New York: Lovell, 1893. $225-275.
Doyle, Arthur Conan	THE MEMOIRS OF SHERLOCK HOLMES. New York: Harper, 1894. $550 or more.
Doyle, Arthur Conan	THE HOUND OF THE BASKERVILLES. New York: McClure, 1902. $450 or more.
Doyle, Arthur Conan	THE RETURN OF SHERLOCK HOLMES. New York: McClure, 1905. $350 or more.
Doyle, Arthur Conan	THE VALLEY OF FEAR. New York: Doran, 1914. $65.
Doyle, Arthur Conan	HIS LAST BOW. New York: Doran, 1917. $175-225.
Doyle, Arthur Conan	THE CASE-BOOK OF SHERLOCK HOLMES. New York: Doran, (1927). $550 or more.
Doyle, Arthur Conan	THE SPECKLED BAND. London: French, 1912. $350 or more.
Ellin, Stanley Bernard	DREADFUL SUMMIT. New York: Simon & Schuster, 1948. $165.

AUTHOR	TITLE/EDITION INFORMATION/VALUE
Ellin, Stanley Bernard	THE KEY TO NICHOLAS STREET. New York: Simon & Schuster, 1952. $95.
Ellin, Stanley Bernard	MYSTERY STORIES. New York: Simon & Schuster, 1956. $85-100.
Ellin, Stanley Bernard	THE EIGHTH CIRCLE. New York: Random House, 1958. $65.
Ellin, Stanley Bernard	HOUSE OF CARDS. New York: Random House, 1967. $65.
Ellison, Harlan	RUMBLE. New York, (1958). Wrappers. $60-75.
Faulkner, William	SANCTUARY. New York, (1931). $950 or more.
Faulkner, William	LIGHT IN AUGUST. (New York, 1932). $600 or more.
Faulkner, William	ABSALOM, ABSALOM! New York, 1936. Trade edition. $275-325.
Faulkner, William	INTRUDER IN THE DUST. New York, (1948). $175 or more.
Faulkner, William	KNIGHT'S GAMBIT. New York, (1949). $175-225.
Fearing, Kenneth	THE HOSPITAL. New York: Random House, 1939. $65.
Fearing, Kenneth	DAGGER OF THE MIND. New York: Random House, 1941. $65.
Fearing, Kenneth	CLARK GIFFORD'S BODY. New York: Random House, 1942. $65.
Fearing, Kenneth	THE BIG CLOCK. New York: Harcourt Brace, (1946). $60-75.
Fleming, Ian Lancaster	CASINO ROYALE. New York: Macmillan, 1954. $1,500 or more.
Fleming, Ian Lancaster	LIVE AND LET DIE. London: Cape, 1954. $600 or more.
Fleming, Ian Lancaster	MOONRAKER. New York: Macmillan, 1955. $550.

AUTHOR	TITLE/EDITION INFORMATION/VALUE
Fleming, Ian Lancaster	DIAMONDS ARE FOREVER. New York: Macmillan, 1956. $500.
Fleming, Ian Lancaster	FROM RUSSIA, WITH LOVE. New York: Macmillan, 1957. $350.
Fleming, Ian Lancaster	DR. NO. New York: Macmillan, 1958. $125-150.
Fleming, Ian Lancaster	GOLDFINGER. New York: Macmillan, 1959. $100.
Fleming, Ian Lancaster	FOR YOUR EYES ONLY: FIVE SECRET OCCASIONS IN THE LIFE OF JAMES BOND. New York: Viking, 1960. $65.
Fleming, Ian Lancaster	THUNDERBALL. New York: Viking, 1961. $65.
Fleming, Ian Lancaster	THE SPY WHO LOVED ME. New York: Viking, 1962. $65.
Fleming, Ian Lancaster	ON HER MAJESTY'S SECRET SERVICE. New York: New American Library, 1963. Trade edition. $60-75.
Fleming, Ian Lancaster	YOU ONLY LIVE TWICE. New York: New American Library, 1964. $65.
Fleming, Ian Lancaster	THE MAN WITH THE GOLDEN GUN. New York: New American Library, 1965. $65.
Fleming, Ian Lancaster	OCTOPUSSY, AND THE LIVING DAY-LIGHTS. New York: New American Library, 1966. $65.
Fowles, John	THE COLLECTOR. London, (1963). $700 or more.
Fowles, John	THE FRENCH LIEUTENANT'S WOMAN. London, (1969). $175-225.
Francis, Dick	DEAD CERT. New York: Holt Rinehart, 1962. $65.
Francis, Dick	NERVE. New York: Harper, 1964. $50.
Francis, Dick	FOR KICKS. New York: Harper, 1965. $50.
Francis, Dick	ODDS AGAINST. New York: Harper, 1966. $50.
Francis, Dick	FLYING FINISH. New York: Harper, 1967. $500.

AUTHOR	TITLE/EDITION INFORMATION/VALUE
Francis, Dick	BLOOD SPORT. New York: Harper, 1968. $50.
Francis, Dick	FORFEIT. New York: Harper, 1969. $50.
Francis, Dick	ENQUIRY. New York: Harper, 1969. $50.
Francis, Dick	RAT RACE. New York: Harper, 1971. $50.
Francis, Dick	BONECRACK. New York: Harper, 1972. $50.
Francis, Dick	SMOKESCREEN. New York: Harper, 1972. $50.
Francis, Dick	SLAY-RIDE. New York: Harper, 1974. $50.
Francis, Dick	KNOCK-DOWN. New York: Harper, 1975. $50.
Francis, Dick	HIGH STAKES. New York: Harper, 1976. $50.
Francis, Dick	IN THE FRAME. New York: Harper, 1977. $50.
Francis, Dick	RISK. New York: Harper, 1978. $50.
Francis, Dick	TRIAL RUN. New York: Harper, 1979. $50.
Frank, Arthur	WHO KILLED NETTA MAUL? London: Gollancz, 1940. $50.
Frank, Arthur	TIME'S A THIEF. London: French, 1952. $50.
Frank, Arthur	TWENTY MINUTES WITH MRS. OAKENTUBB. London: Miller, 1955. $50.
Frank, Arthur	SHE WOULD NOT DANCE. London: Quekett, 1956. $50.
Frank, Arthur	ANOTHER MYSTERY IN SUVA. London: Heinemann, 1956. $50.
Frank, Arthur	MURDER IN THE TROPIC NIGHT. London: Jenkins, 1961. $35.
Frank, Arthur	THE THROBBING DARK. London: Jenkins, 1963. $35.
Frank, Arthur	THE ABANDONED WOMAN: THE STORY OF LUCY WALTER (1630-1658). London: Heinemann, 1964. $35.
Frank, Arthur	CONFESSION TO MURDER. London: United Writers, 1974. $35.

AUTHOR	TITLE/EDITION INFORMATION/VALUE
Frank, Arthur	THE PROFIT FROM MURDER. London: Hub, 1974. $35.
Frank, Arthur	CAPTAIN ROCCO RIDES TO SHEFFIELD. London: Chatto & Windus, 1975. $35.
Freeman, Richard Austin	THE ADVENTURES OF ROMNEY PRINGLE, as Clifford Ashdown, with J. J. Pitcairn. London, 1902. $1,200 or more.
Freeman, Richard Austin	THE RED THUMB MARK. London, 1907. $550 or more.
Freeman, Richard Austin	JOHN THORNDYKE'S CASES. London: Chatto & Windus, 1909. $450.
Freeman, Richard Austin	THE EYE OF OSIRIS: A DETECTIVE ROMANCE. London: Hodder & Stoughton, 1911. $450.
Freeman, Richard Austin	THE SINGING BONE. London: Hodder & Stoughton, 1912. $450 or more.
Freeman, Richard Austin	THE MYSTERY OF 31, NEW INN. Philadelphia: Winston, 1913. $450.
Freeman, Richard Austin	THE UTTERMOST FARTHING: A SAVANT'S VENDETTA. Philadelphia: Winston, 1914. $450.
Freeman, Richard Austin	A SILENT WITNESS. Philadelphia: Winston, 1915. $450.
Freeman, Richard Austin	THE EXPLOITS OF DANBY CROKER, BEING EXTRACTS FROM A SOMEWHAT DISREPUTABLE AUTOBIOGRAPHY. London: Duckworth, 1916. $450.
Freeman, Richard Austin	THE GREAT PORTRAIT MYSTERY. London: Hodder & Stoughton, 1918. $450.
Freeman, Richard Austin	HELEN VARDON'S CONFESSION. London: Hodder & Stoughton, 1922. $450.
Freeman, Richard Austin	THE CAT'S EYE. London, (1923). $225-275.
Freeman, Richard Austin	DR. THORNDYKE'S CASE BOOK. London: Hodder & Stoughton, 1923. $225.
Freeman, Richard Austin	THE MYSTERY OF ANGELINA FROOD. New York: Dodd Mead, 1925. $225.

AUTHOR	TITLE/EDITION INFORMATION/VALUE
Freeman, Richard Austin	THE SHADOW OF THE WOLF. New York: Dodd Mead, 1925. $225.
Freeman, Richard Austin	THE D'ARBLAY MYSTERY. New York: Dodd Mead, 1926. $225.
Freeman, Richard Austin	THE PUZZLE LOCK. New York: Dodd Mead, 1926. $225.
Freeman, Richard Austin	THE MAGIC CASKET. New York: Dodd Mead, 1927. $225.
Freeman, Richard Austin	A CERTAIN DR. THORNDYKE. New York: Dodd Mead, 1928. $225.
Freeman, Richard Austin	AS A THIEF IN THE NIGHT. New York: Dodd Mead, 1928. $225.
Freeman, Richard Austin	THE FAMOUS CASES OF DR. THORNDYKE. London: Hodder & Stoughton, 1929. $225.
Freeman, Richard Austin	MR. POTTERMACK'S OVERSIGHT. New York: Dodd Mead, 1930. $225.
Freeman, Richard Austin	DR. THORNDYKE INVESTIGATES. London: University of London Press, 1930. $225.
Freeman, Richard Austin	PONTIFEX, SON AND THORNDYKE. New York: Dodd Mead, 1931. $225.
Freeman, Richard Austin	WHEN ROGUES FALL OUT. London: Hodder & Stoughton, 1932. $225.
Freeman, Richard Austin	DR. THORNDYKE INTERVENES. New York: Dodd Mead, 1933. $225.
Freeman, Richard Austin	FOR THE DEFENCE: DR. THORNDYKE. London, 1934. $225.
Freeman, Richard Austin	THE PENROSE MYSTERY. New York: Dodd Mead, 1936. $225.
Freeman, Richard Austin	FELO DE SE? London: Hodder & Stoughton, 1937. $225-275.
Freeman, Richard Austin	THE STONEWARE MONKEY. New York: Dodd Mead, 1939. $225.
Freeman, Richard Austin	MR. POLTON EXPLAINS. New York: Dodd Mead, 1940. $225-275.

AUTHOR	TITLE/EDITION INFORMATION/VALUE
Greene, Graham	THE MAN WITHIN. New York: Doubleday, 1929. $1,100 or more.
Greene, Graham	THE NAME OF ACTION. New York: Doubleday, 1931. $175-225.
Greene, Graham	RUMOUR AT NIGHTFALL. New York: Doubleday, 1932. $150-200.
Greene, Graham	ORIENT EXPRESS: AN ENTERTAINMENT. New York: Doubleday, 1933. $675-800.
Greene, Graham	IT'S A BATTLEFIELD. New York: Doubleday, 1934. $275-325.
Greene, Graham	A GUN FOR SALE. London: Heinemann, 1936. $225-275.
Greene, Graham	BRIGHTON ROCK. New York: Viking, 1938. $150-200.
Greene, Graham	THE CONFIDENTIAL AGENT. New York: Viking, 1939. $175-225.
Greene, Graham	THE POWER AND THE GLORY. London: Heinemann, 1940. $175-225.
Greene, Graham	THE HEART OF THE MATTER. New York: Viking, 1948. $100-125.
Greene, Graham	THE THIRD MAN. New York: Viking, 1950. $175-225.
Greene, Graham	THE QUIET AMERICAN. London, (1955). $85-125.
Greene, Graham	OUR MAN IN HAVANA. New York: Viking, 1958. $150-175.
Hammett, Samuel Dashiell	RED HARVEST. New York: Knopf, 1929. $2,200 or more.
Hammett, Samuel Dashiell	THE DAIN CURSE. New York: Knopf, 1929. $1,200 or more.
Hammett, Samuel Dashiell	THE MALTESE FALCON. New York: Knopf, 1930. $2,200 or more.
Hammett, Samuel Dashiell	THE GLASS KEY. New York: Knopf, 1931. $1,200 or more.

AUTHOR	TITLE/EDITION INFORMATION/VALUE
Hammett, Samuel Dashiell	SECRET AGENT X-9. 2 vols. Philadelphia: McKay, 1934. $400-500.
Hammett, Samuel Dashiell	THE THIN MAN. New York: Knopf, 1934. $800-1,000.
Hornung, E. W.	MR. JUSTICE RAFFLES. London, 1909. $85-100.
Household, Geoffrey	ROGUE MALE. London, 1939. $135-175.
Lathen, Emma	BANKING ON DEATH. New York: Macmillan, 1961. $65.
Lathen, Emma	A PLACE FOR MURDER. New York: Macmillan, 1963. $65.
Lathen, Emma	ACCOUNTING FOR MURDER. New York: Macmillan, 1964. $65.
Lathen, Emma	DEATH SHALL OVERCOME. New York: Macmillan, 1966. $65.
Lathen, Emma	MURDER MAKES THE WHEELS GO ROUND. New York: Macmillan, 1966. $65.
Lathen, Emma	MURDER AGAINST THE GRAIN. New York: Macmillan, 1967. $65.
Lathen, Emma	A STITCH IN TIME. New York: Macmillan, 1968. $65.
Lathen, Emma	COME TO DUST. New York: Simon & Schuster, 1968. $65.
Lathen, Emma	MURDER SUNNY SIDE UP, as R. B. Dominic. New York: Abelard Schuman, 1968. $65.
Lathen, Emma	WHEN IN GREECE. New York: Simon & Schuster, 1969. $65.
Lathen, Emma	MURDER TO GO. New York: Simon & Schuster, 1969. $65.
Lathen, Emma	MURDER IN HIGH PLACE, as R. B. Dominic. New York: Doubleday, 1970. $65.
Lathen, Emma	PICK UP STICKS. New York: Simon & Schuster, 1970. $65.

AUTHOR	TITLE/EDITION INFORMATION/VALUE
Lathen, Emma	ASHES TO ASHES. New York: Simon & Schuster, 1971. $65.
Lathen, Emma	THE LONGER THE THREAD. New York: Simon & Schuster, 1971. $65.
Lathen, Emma	THERE IS NO JUSTICE, as R. B. Dominic. New York: Doubleday, 1971. $65.
Lathen, Emma	MURDER WITHOUT ICING. New York: Simon & Schuster, 1972. $65.
Lathen, Emma	SWEET AND LOW. New York: Simon & Schuster, 1974. $65.
Lathen, Emma	EPITAPH FOR A LOBBYIST, as R. B. Dominic. New York: Doubleday, 1974. $65.
Lathen, Emma	BY HOOK OR BY CROOK. New York: Simon & Schuster, 1975. $65.
Lathen, Emma	MURDER OUT OF COMMISSION, as R. B. Dominic. New York: Doubleday, 1976. $65.
Lathen, Emma	DOUBLE, DOUBLE, OIL AND TROUBLE. New York: Simon & Schuster, 1979. $65.
LeCarre, John	CALL FOR THE DEAD. New York: Walker, 1962. $225-275.
LeCarre, John	A MURDER OF QUALITY. New York: Walker, 1963. $175.
LeCarre, John	THE SPY WHO CAME IN FROM THE COLD. New York: Coward McCann, 1964. $150-200.
LeCarre, John	THE LOOKING-GLASS WAR. New York: Coward McCann, 1965. $150.
LeCarre, John	A SMALL TOWN IN GERMANY. New York: Coward McCann, 1968. $125.
LeCarre, John	TINKER, TAILOR, SOLDIER, SPY. New York: Knopf, 1974. $100.
LeCarre, John	THE HONOURABLE SCHOOLBOY. New York: Knopf, 1977. $75.
Le Fanu, Joseph Sheridan	ALL IN THE DARK. 2 vols. London, 1866, $275-350.

AUTHOR	TITLE/EDITION INFORMATION/VALUE
Le Fanu, Joseph Sheridan	CHECKMATE. 3 vols. London, 1871. $375-450.
Le Fanu, Joseph Sheridan	THE EVIL GUEST. London, (1895). $375-450.
Le Fanu, Joseph Sheridan	GHOST STORIES AND TALES OF MYSTERY. Dublin, 1851. $550-650.
Le Fanu, Joseph Sheridan	HAUNTED LIVES. 3 vols. London, 1868. $550-650.
Le Fanu, Joseph Sheridan	IN A GLASS DARKLY. 3 vols. London, 1872. $450-550.
Le Fanu, Joseph Sheridan	MADAME CROWL'S GHOST AND OTHER TALES OF MYSTERY. London, 1923. $275-325.
Le Fanu, Joseph Sheridan	THE WYVERN MYSTERY. 3 vols. London, 1869. $450-550.
Levin, Ira	A KISS BEFORE DYING. New York: Simon & Schuster, 1953. $85.
Levin, Ira	ROSEMARY'S BABY. New York: Random House, 1967. $85.
Levin, Ira	THE STEPFORD WIVES. New York: Random House, 1972. $65.
Levin, Ira	THE BOYS FROM BRAZIL. New York: Random House, 1976. $50.
Ludlum, Robert	THE SCARLATTI INHERITANCE. Cleveland: World, 1971. $35.
Ludlum, Robert	THE OSTERMAN WEEKEND. Cleveland: World, 1972. $35.
Ludlum, Robert	THE MATLOCK PAPER. New York: Dial, 1973. $35.
Ludlum, Robert	TREVAYNE, as Jonathan Ryder. New York: Delacorte, 1973. $35.
Ludlum, Robert	THE CRY OF THE HALIDON, as Jonathan Ryder. New York: Delacorte, 1974. $35.
Ludlum, Robert	THE RHINEMANN EXCHANGE. New York: Dial, 1974. $35.

AUTHOR	TITLE/EDITION INFORMATION/VALUE
Ludlum, Robert	THE ROAD TO GANDOLFO, as Michael Shepherd. New York: Dial, 1975. $35.
Ludlum, Robert	THE GEMINI CONTENDERS. New York: Dial, 1976. $35.
Ludlum, Robert	THE CHANCELLOR MANUSCRIPT. New York: Dial, 1977. $35.
Ludlum, Robert	THE MATARESE CIRCLE. New York: David Marek, 1979. $35.
McCoy, Horace	THEY SHOOT HORSES, DON'T THEY? New York: Simon & Schuster, 1935. $85-100.
McCoy, Horace	I SHOULD HAVE STAYED HOME. New York: Knopf, 1938. $75.
McCoy, Horace	NO POCKETS IN A SHROUD. New York: New American Library, 1948. $85-100.
McCoy, Horace	KISS TOMORROW GOODBYE. New York: Random House, 1948. $65.
McCoy, Horace	SCALPEL. New York: Appleton Century Crofts, 1952. $45.
McCoy, Horace	CORRUPTION CITY. New York: Dell, 1959. $25.
MacLean, Alistair Stuart	H.M.S. ULYSSES. New York: Doubleday, 1956. $125.
MacLean, Alistair Stuart	THE GUNS OF NAVARONE. New York: Doubleday, 1957. $125.
MacLean, Alistair Stuart	SOUTH BY JAVA HEAD. New York: Doubleday, 1958. $125.
MacLean, Alistair Stuart	THE LAST FRONTIER. London: Collins, 1959; as THE SECRET WAYS, New York: Doubleday, 1959. $125.
MacLean, Alistair Stuart	NIGHT WITHOUT END. New York: Doubleday, 1960. $100.
MacLean, Alistair Stuart	FEAR IS THE KEY. New York: Doubleday, 1961. $100.
MacLean, Alistair Stuart	THE SNOW ON THE BEN, as Ian Stuart. London: Ward Lock, 1961. $100.

AUTHOR	TITLE/EDITION INFORMATION/VALUE
MacLean, Alistair Stuart	THE DARK CRUSADER, as Ian Stuart. London: Collins, 1961; as THE BLACK SHRIKE. New York: Scribner, 1961. $100.
MacLean, Alistair Stuart	THE GOLDEN RENDEZVOUS. New York: Doubleday, 1962. $100.
MacLean, Alistair Stuart	THE SATAN BUG, as Ian Stuart. New York: Scribner, 1962. $100.
MacLean, Alistair Stuart	ICE STATION ZEBRA. New York: Doubleday, 1963. $85.
MacLean, Alistair Stuart	WHEN EIGHT BELLS TOLL. New York: Doubleday, 1966. $85.
MacLean, Alistair Stuart	WHERE EAGLES DARE. New York: Doubleday, 1967. $85.
MacLean, Alistair Stuart	FORCE 10 FROM NAVARONE. New York: Doubleday, 1968. $85.
MacLean, Alistair Stuart	PUPPET ON A CHAIN. New York: Doubleday, 1969. $85.
MacLean, Alistair Stuart	CARAVAN TO VACCARES. New York: Doubleday, 1970. $85.
MacLean, Alistair Stuart	BEAR ISLAND. New York: Doubleday, 1971. $85.
MacLean, Alistair Stuart	THE WAY TO DUSTY DEATH. New York, Doubleday, 1973. $85.
MacLean, Alistair Stuart	BREAKHEART PASS. New York: Doubleday, 1974. $65.
MacLean, Alistair Stuart	CIRCUS. New York: Doubleday, 1975. $65.
MacLean, Alistair Stuart	THE GOLDEN GATE. New York: Doubleday, 1976. $65.
MacLean, Alistair Stuart	DEATH FROM DISCLOSURE, as Ian Stuart. London: Hale, 1976. $65.
MacLean, Alistair Stuart	SEAWITCH. New York: Doubleday, 1977. $65.
MacLean, Alistair Stuart	GOODBYE CALIFORNIA. London: Collins, 1977; New York: Doubleday, 1978. $50.
MacLean, Alistair Stuart	FLOOD TIDE, as Ian Stuart. London: Hale, 1977. $50.

AUTHOR	TITLE/EDITION INFORMATION/VALUE
MacLean, Alistair Stuart	SAND TRAP, as Ian Stuart. London: Hale, 1977. $50.
MacLean, Alistair Stuart	FATAL SWITCH, as Ian Stuart. London: Hale, 1978. $50.
MacLean, Alistair Stuart	A WEEKEND TO KILL, as Ian Stuart. London: Hale, 1978. $50.
Marquand, John Phillips	MING YELLOW. Boston; Little, Brown, 1935. $85-125.
Marquand, John Phillips	NO HERO. Boston; Little, Brown, 1935. $75.
Marquand, John Phillips	THANK YOU, MR. MOTO. Boston: Little, Brown, 1936. $75.
Marquand, John Phillips	THINK FAST, MR. MOTO. Boston: Little, Brown, 1937. $75.
Marquand, John Phillips	MR. MOTO IS SO SORRY. Boston: Little, Brown, 1938. $75.
Marquand, John Phillips	DON'T ASK QUESTIONS. London: Hale, 1941. $75.
Marquand, John Phillips	LAST LAUGH, MR. MOTO. Boston: Little, Brown, 1942. $75.
Marquand, John Phillips	IT'S LOADED, MR. BAUER. London: Hale, 1949. $75.
Marquand, John Phillips	STOPOVER: TOKYO. Boston: Little, Brown, 1957. $75.
Maugham, William Somerset	THE CASUARINA TREE. New York: Doran, 1926. $175-225.
Maugham, William Somerset	ASHENDEN, OR THE BRITISH AGENT. New York: Doubleday, 1928. $175-225.
Maugham, William Somerset	AH KING: SIX STORIES. New York: Doubleday, 1933. $40-60.
Millar, Kenneth	THE DARK TUNNEL. New York: Dodd Mead, 1944. $225-275.
Millar, Kenneth	TROUBLE FOLLOWS ME. New York: Dodd Mead, 1944. $225.
Millar, Kenneth	BLUE CITY. New York: Knopf, 1947. $150-200.

AUTHOR	TITLE/EDITION INFORMATION/VALUE
Millar, Kenneth	THE THREE ROADS. New York: Knopf, 1948. $150-200.
Millar, Kenneth	THE MOVING TARGET, as John Macdonald. New York: Knopf, 1949. $150-200.
Millar, Kenneth	THE DROWNING POOL, as John Ross Macdonald. New York: Knopf, 1950. $150-200.
Millar, Kenneth	THE WAY SOME PEOPLE DIE, as John Ross Macdonald. New York: Knopf, 1951. $150-200.
Millar, Kenneth	THE IVORY GRIN, as John Ross Macdonald. New York: Knopf, 1952. $150-200.
Millar, Kenneth	MEET ME AT THE MORGUE, as John Ross Macdonald. New York: Knopf, 1953. $150-200.
Millar, Kenneth	FIND A VICTIM, as John Ross Macdonald. New York: Knopf, 1955. $150-200.
Millar, Kenneth	THE NAME IS ARCHER, as John Ross Macdonald. New York: Bantam, 1955. $45.
Millar, Kenneth	THE BARBAROUS COAST, as Ross Macdonald. New York: Knopf, 1956. $100.
Millar, Kenneth	THE DOOMSTERS, as Ross Macdonald. New York: Knopf, 1958. $100.
Millar, Kenneth	THE GALTON CASE, as Ross Macdonald. New York: Knopf, 1959. $135-150.
Millar, Kenneth	THE FERGUSON AFFAIR, as Ross Macdonald. New York: Knopf, 1960. $125.
Millar, Kenneth	THE WYCHERLY WOMAN, as Ross Macdonald. New York: Knopf, 1961. $125.
Millar, Kenneth	THE ZEBRA-STRIPED HEARSE, as Ross Macdonald. New York: Knopf, 1962. $135.
Millar, Kenneth	THE CHILL, as Ross Macdonald. New York: Knopf, 1964. $135-175.
Millar, Kenneth	THE FAR SIDE OF THE DOLLAR, as Ross Macdonald. New York: Knopf, 1965. $85.

AUTHOR	TITLE/EDITION INFORMATION/VALUE
Millar, Kenneth	BLACK MONEY, as Ross Macdonald. New York: Knopf, 1966. $85.
Millar, Kenneth	THE INSTANT ENEMY, as Ross Macdonald. New York: Knopf, 1968. $85.
Millar, Kenneth	THE GOODBYE LOOK, as Ross Macdonald. New York: Knopf, 1969. $85.
Millar, Kenneth	THE UNDERGROUND MAN, as Ross Macdonald. New York: Knopf, 1971. $85.
Millar, Kenneth	SLEEPING BEAUTY, as Ross Macdonald. New York: Knopf, 1973. $85.
Millar, Kenneth	THE BLUE HAMMER, as Ross Macdonald. New York: Knopf, 1976. $85.
Millar, Kenneth	LEW ARCHER, PRIVATE INVESTIGATOR. Yonkers, N.Y.: Mysterious Press, 1977. $85.
Oursler, Charles Fulton	ABOUT THE MURDER OF GERALDINE FOSTER, as Anthony Abbott. New York: Covici Friede, 1930. $85.
Oursler, Charles Fulton	ABOUT THE MURDER OF THE CLERGYMAN'S MISTRESS, as Anthony Abbott. New York: Covici Friede, 1931. $85.
Oursler, Charles Fulton	ABOUT THE MURDER OF THE NIGHT CLUB LADY, as Anthony Abbott. New York: Covici Friede, 1931. $85.
Oursler, Charles Fulton	ABOUT THE MURDER OF THE CIRCUS QUEEN, as Anthony Abbott. New York: Covici Friede, 1932. $85.
Oursler, Charles Fulton	ABOUT THE MURDER OF A STARTLED LADY, as Anthony Abbott. New York: Farrar & Rinehart, 1935. $85.
Oursler, Charles Fulton	THE PRESIDENT'S MYSTERY STORY, as Anthony Abbott, with others. New York: Farrar & Rinehart, 1935. $85.
Oursler, Charles Fulton	DARK MASQUERADE, anonymously. New York: Furman, 1936. $85.

AUTHOR	TITLE/EDITION INFORMATION/VALUE
Oursler, Charles Fulton	ABOUT THE MURDER OF A MAN AFRAID OF WOMEN, as Anthony Abbott. New York: Farrar & Rinehart, 1937. $85.
Oursler, Charles Fulton	THE CREEPS, as Anthony Abbott. New York: Farrar & Rinehart, 1939. $85.
Oursler, Charles Fulton	THE SHUDDERS, as Anthony Abbott. New York: Farrar & Rinehart, 1943. $65.
Oursler, Charles Fulton	THE WAGER, AND THE HOUSE OF FERNWOOD, as Anthony Abbott. New York: Pony, 1946. $45.
Oursler, Charles Fulton	THESE ARE STRANGE TALES, as Anthony Abbott. Philadelphia: Winston, 1948. $35.
Poe, Edgar Allan	THE PROSE ROMANCES OF EDGAR A. POE, ETC. UNIFORM SERIAL EDITION . . . NO.1 CONTAINING THE MURDERS IN THE RUE MORGUE, AND THE MAN THAT WAS USED UP. Philadelphia: 1843. Wrappers. 40 pp. At least $35,000.
Puzo, Mario	THE DARK ARENA. New York, (1955). $40-50.
Puzo, Mario	THE GODFATHER. New York, (1969). $45-60.
Queen, Ellery	THE ROMAN HAT MYSTERY. New York: Stokes, 1929. $450.
Queen, Ellery	THE FRENCH POWDER MYSTERY. New York: Stokes, 1930. $375.
Queen, Ellery	THE DUTCH SHOE MYSTERY. New York: Stokes, 1931. $90-110.
Queen, Ellery	THE EGYPTIAN CROSS MYSTERY. New York: Stokes, 1932. $90-110.
Queen, Ellery	THE AMERICAN GUN MYSTERY. New York: Stokes, 1933. $85.

AUTHOR	TITLE/EDITION INFORMATION/VALUE
Queen, Ellery	THE SIAMESE TWIN MYSTERY. New York: Stokes, 1933. $85.
Queen, Ellery	THE CHINESE ORANGE MYSTERY. New York: Stokes, 1934. $110-135.
Queen, Ellery	THE SPANISH CAPE MYSTERY. New York: Stokes, 1935. $85-100.
Queen, Ellery	HALFWAY HOUSE. New York: Stokes, 1936. $85.
Queen, Ellery	THE DEVIL TO PAY. New York: Stokes, 1938. $110-135.
Queen, Ellery, editor	THE MISADVENTURES OF SHERLOCK HOLMES. Boston, 1944. $275-325.
Rinehart, Mary Roberts	THE MAN IN LOWER TEN. Indianapolis: Bobbs Merrill, 1909. $160-175.
Rinehart, Mary Roberts	THE RED LAMP. New York: Doran, 1925. $125-175.
Rhinehart, Mary Roberts	THE BAT: A NOVEL, with Avery Hopwood. New York: Doran, 1926. $60-75.
Rohmer, Sax	THE INSIDIOUS DR. FU-MANCHU. New York: McBride, 1913. $250.
Rohmer, Sax	FU MANCHU'S BRIDE. Garden City, N.Y., 1933. $135-150.
Rohmer, Sax	THE ISLAND OF FU MANCHU. Garden City, N.Y., 1941. $150-200.
Rohmer, Sax	NUDE IN MINK. New York, 1950. Wrappers. $15-25.
Rohmer, Sax	SEVEN SINS. London, 1944. $85-100.
Rohmer, Sax	SHADOW OF FU MANCHU. Garden City, N.Y., 1948. $35-50.
Rohmer, Sax	SHE WHO SLEEPS. Garden City, N.Y., 1928. $25-35.
Sayers, Dorothy L.	GAUDY NIGHT. New York: Harcourt Brace, 1936. $110-135.

AUTHOR	TITLE/EDITION INFORMATION/VALUE
Sayers, Dorothy L.	BUSMAN'S HONEYMOON: A DETECTIVE COMEDY, with M. St. Clare Byrne. London, 1937. $225-275.
Spillane, Mickey	I, THE JURY. New York: Dutton, 1947. $100-125.
Upfield, Arthur W.	THE HOUSE OF CAIN. London, (1928). $325-375.
Van Dine, S. S.	THE BENSON MURDER CASE. New York, 1926. $225-275.
Van Dine, S. S.	THE DRAGON MURDER CASE. New York, 1933. $135-175.
Van Dine, S. S.	KENNEL MURDER CASE. New York, 1933. $40-65.
Wallace, Edgar	THE FOUR JUST MEN. London, 1905. $125-150.
Wallace, Edgar	THE MURDER BOOK OF J. G. REEDER. New York, 1929. $125-150.

13

Western Fiction Books, and Their Values

Westerns have been popular for a good many years. Few people realize how valuable many of these titles have become—or that this is also true of many of the nonwestern books by authors best known for their western novels; for example, Zane Grey, who wrote several books on big-game fishing that are now quite valuable.

The values given here are for first-edition books in very good to fine condition, and with a dust jacket if the book was originally issued with one. "Points" often need to be verified to properly identify many of these books. A librarian or rare bookseller should be consulted for verification of edition and value.

AUTHOR	TITLE/EDITION INFORMATION/VALUE
Abbey, Edward	THE BRAVE COWBOY. New York, 1956. $75-100.
Abbey, Edward	DESERT SOLITAIRE. New York, 1968. $45.
Adams, Andy	THE LOG OF A COWBOY. Boston, 1903. $85-100.
Adams, Andy	A TEXAS MATCHMAKER. Boston, 1904. $65.
Adams, Andy	THE OUTLET. Boston, 1905. $65.
Adams, Andy	CATTLE BRANDS: A COLLECTION OF WESTERN CAMP-FIRE STORIES. Boston, 1906. $65.
Adams, Clifton	THE DESPERADO. New York, 1950. $65-80.

AUTHOR	TITLE/EDITION INFORMATION/VALUE
Adams, Clifton	A NOOSE FOR THE DESPERADO. New York, 1951. $50.
Albert, Marvin H.	THE LAW AND JAKE WADE. New York, 1956. $50-65.
Albert, Marvin H.	APACHE RISING. New York, 1957. $50.
Albert, Marvin H.	THE BOUNTY KILLER. New York, 1958. $45.
Allan, Luke	THE BLUE WOLF: A TALE OF THE CYPRESS HILLS. London, 1913. $125-150.
Allan, Luke	BLUE PETE, HALF BREED: A STORY OF THE CYPRESS HILLS. New York, 1921. $75.
Allen, Hervey	WAMPUM AND OLD GOLD. New Haven, Conn., 1921. $65.
Allen, (William) Hervey	BALLADS OF THE BORDER. (El Paso, Tex.), 1916. Wrappers. $525.
Bardwell, Denver	GUN-SMOKE IN SUNSET VALLEY. New York; London, 1935. $50-65.
Bardwell, Denver	KILLERS ON THE DIAMOND A. New York, 1935. $50-65.
Beach, Rex	THE SILVER HORDE. New York, 1909. $30-45.
Beach, Rex	THE SPOILERS. New York, 1906. $75-90.
Beach, Rex	THE BARRIER. New York, 1908. $65.
Beach, Rex	THE IRON TRAIL: AN ALASKAN ROMANCE. New York, 1913. $35.
Beach, Rex	WILD PASTURES. New York, 1935. $25.
Beach, Rex	VALLEY OF THUNDER. New York, 1939. $25.
Bellah, James Warner	MASSACRE. New York, 1950. $35-50.
Bellah, James Warner	THE APACHE. New York, 1951. $35.
Bellah, James Warner	ORDEAL AT BLOOD RIVER. New York, 1959. $35.

AUTHOR	TITLE/EDITION INFORMATION/VALUE
Bellah, James Warner	THE MAN WHO SHOT LIBERTY VALANCE. New York, 1962. Wrappers. $35-50.
Bennett, Emerson	CLARA MORELAND; OR, ADVENTURES IN THE FAR SOUTH-WEST. Philadelphia, 1963. Wrappers. $275-325.
Bennett, Emerson	LENI-LEOTI; OR, ADVENTURES IN THE FAR WEST. Cincinnati, 1849. Wrappers. $550-650.
Bennett, Emerson	MIKE FINK: A LEGEND OF THE OHIO. Cincinnati, 1848. Wrappers. $575.
Bennett, Emerson	THE MYSTERIOUS MARKSMAN: OR, THE OUTLAWS OF NEW YORK. Cincinnati, ca. 1855. Wrappers. $475.
Bennett, Emerson	THE PRAIRIE FLOWER; OR, ADVENTURES IN THE FAR WEST. Cincinnati, 1849. Wrappers. $450-550.
Berger, Thomas Louis	LITTLE BIG MAN. New York, 1964. $50-65.
Brand, Max	THE UNTAMED. New York, 1919. $350.
Brand, Max	TRAILIN'. New York, 1920.
Brand, Max	THE NIGHT HORSEMAN. New York, 1920. $350.
Brand, Max	THE SEVENTH MAN. New York, 1921. $275.
Brand, Max	ALCATRAZ. New York, 1923. $275.
Brand, Max	CALL OF THE BLOOD. New York, (1934). $175-225.
Brand, Max	TIMBAL GULCH TRAIL. New York, 1934. $75-125.
Brand, Max	CALL OF THE BLOOD. New York, (1934). $175-225.
Brand, Max	THE FALSE RIDER. New York, (1947). $35-50.
Brand, Max	FLAMING IRONS. New York, (1948). $25-35.
Brand, Max	HUNTED RIDERS. New York, 1935. $140-175.

AUTHOR	TITLE/EDITION INFORMATION/VALUE
Brand, Max	MONTANA RIDES AGAIN. New York, 1934. $175-250.
Brand, Max	THE RANCHER'S REVENGE. New York, 1934. $140-175.
Brand, Max	WINE ON THE DESERT. New York, 1940. $140-175.
Brand, Max	TIMBAL GULCH TRAIL. New York, 1934. $75-125.
Caldwell, Erskine	GOD'S LITTLE ACRE. New York, 1933. $175-225.
Caldwell, Erskine	TOBACCO ROAD. New York, 1932. $225-275.
Carter, Forrest	THE REBEL OUTLAW, JOSEY WALES. Gantt, Ala., 1973. $60-75.
Castlemon, Harry	FRANK ON THE LOWER MISSISSIPPI. Cincinnati, 1867. $60-75.
Castlemon, Harry	THE SPORTSMAN'S CLUB AMONG THE TRAPPERS. Philadelphia, 1874. $60-75.
Cather, Willa	DEATH COMES FOR THE ARCHBISHOP. New York, 1927. $60-75.
Cather, Willa	A LOST LADY. New York, 1923. $60-75.
Cather, Willa	MY ANTONIA. Boston, 1918. $475-550.
Cather, Willa	O PIONEERS! Boston, 1913. $275-325.
Cather, Willa	OBSCURE DESTINIES. New York, 1932. $35-50.
Cather, Willa	ONE OF OURS. New York, 1932. $60-75.
Cather, Willa	THE PROFESSOR'S HOUSE. New York, 1925. $75-100.
Cather, Willa	THE SONG OF THE LARK. Boston, 1915. $225-275.
Cather, Willa	THE TROLL GARDEN. New York, 1905. $325-375.
Cather, Willa	YOUTH AND THE BRIGHT MEDUSA. New York, 1920. $45-60.

AUTHOR	TITLE/EDITION INFORMATION/VALUE
Cather, Willa	THE FEAR THAT WALKS BY NOON-DAY, with Dorothy Canfield. New York, 1931. Limited edition of 30. $750 or more.
Clark, Walter Van Tilburg	THE CITY OF TREMBLING LEAVES. New York, 1945. $45.
Clark, Walter Van Tilburg	THE OX-BOW INCIDENT. New York, (1940). $60-75.
Clark, Walter Van Tilburg	THE TRACK OF THE CAT. New York, 1949. $35.
Davis, Richard Harding	GALLEGHER AND OTHER STORIES. New York, 1891. Wrappers. $175-225.
Fisher, Vardis	APRIL: A FABLE OF LOVE. Caldwell, Idaho; Garden City, N.Y., 1937. $60-75.
Fisher, Vardis	CHILDREN OF GOD, AN AMERICAN EPIC. Caldwell, Idaho, 1939. $50-65.
Fisher, Vardis	CITY OF ILLLUSION. Caldwell, Idaho; New York, (1941). $45-60.
Fisher, Vardis	DARK BRIDWELL. Boston, 1931. $60-75.
Fisher, Vardis	IN TRAGIC LIFE. Caldwell, Idaho, 1932. $60-75.
Fisher, Vardis	NO VILLIAN NEED BE. Caldwell, Idaho, 1936. $60-75.
Fisher, Vardis	ODYSSEY OF A HERO. Philadelphia, 1937. $60-75.
Fisher, Vardis	PASSIONS SPIN THE PLOT. Caldwell, Idaho, 1933. $125-150.
Fisher, Vardis	WE ARE THE BETRAYED. Caldwell, Idaho, (1935). $60-75.
Garland, Hamlin	THE BOOK OF THE AMERICAN INDIAN. New York, 1923. 34 plates by Frederic Remington. $175-225.

AUTHOR	TITLE/EDITION INFORMATION/VALUE
Garland, Hamlin	CAVANAGH, FOREST RANGER. New York, 1910. $60-75.
Garland, Hamlin	JASON EDWARDS, AN AVERAGE MAN. Boston, 1892. $225.
Garland, Hamlin	A LITTLE NORSK; OR, OL' PAP'S FLAXEN. New York, 1892. $225.
Garland, Hamlin	ROSE OF DUTCHER'S COOLLY. Chicago, 1895. $175.
Garland, Hamlin	MAIN-TRAVELLED ROADS. Boston, 1891. Wrappers. $175-225.
Grey, Zane	ARIZONA AMES. New York, 1932. $175-225.
Grey, Zane	BETTY ZANE. New York, (1903). $450-525.
Grey, Zane	BOULDER DAM. New York, (1963). $100-125.
Grey, Zane	CAPTIVES OF THE DESERT. New York, (1952). $100-125.
Grey, Zane	THE DESERT OF WHEAT. New York, (1919). $150-200.
Grey, Zane	THE DUDE RANGER. New York, (1951). $200-250.
Grey, Zane	FIGHTING CARAVANS. New York, 1929. $150-200.
Grey, Zane	FORLORN RIVER. New York, 1927. $75-100.
Grey, Zane	THE HASH KNIFE OUTFIT. New York, 1933. $175-225.
Grey, Zane	HORSE HEAVEN HILL. New York, (1959). $100-150.
Grey, Zane	KNIGHTS OF THE RANGE. New York, 1939. $100-125.
Grey, Zane	LAST OF THE PLAINSMEN. New York, 1908. $275-375.
Grey, Zane	LOST PUEBLO. New York, (1954). $100-125.

AUTHOR	TITLE/EDITION INFORMATION/VALUE
Grey, Zane	THE LOST WAGON TRAIN. New York; London, 1936. $175-225.
Grey, Zane	MAJESTY'S RANCHO. London, (1942). $75-100.
Grey, Zane	THE MAVERICK QUEEN. New York, (1960). $150-175.
Grey, Zane	RAIDERS OF THE SPANISH PEAKS. New York, 1938. $175-225.
Grey, Zane	THE RAINBOW TRAIL. New York, 1915. $100-125.
Grey, Zane	THE RANGER AND OTHER STORIES. New York, (1960). $150-175.
Grey, Zane	RIDERS OF THE PURPLE SAGE. New York, 1912. $250-325.
Grey, Zane	ROBBER'S ROOST. New York; London, 1932. $30-45.
Grey, Zane	STRANGER FROM THE TONTO. New York, (1956). $50-65.
Grey, Zane	SUNSET PASS. New York; London, 1931. $35-50.
Grey, Zane	TEX THORNE COMES OUT OF THE WEST. Racine, Wis., (1937). $140-165.
Grey, Zane	THUNDERING HERD. New York, 1925. $175-225.
Grey, Zane	TO THE LAST MAN. New York, (1922). $125-175.
Grey, Zane	THE TRAIL DRIVER. New York, 1936. $275-325.
Grey, Zane	THE VANISHING AMERICAN. New York, 1925. No dust jacket. $35-45.
Grey, Zane	WANDERER OF THE WASTELAND. New York, (1923). $275-325.
Grey, Zane	WEST OF THE PECOS. New York, 1937. $275-325.
Grey, Zane	WESTERN UNION. New York, 1939. $100-125.

AUTHOR	TITLE/EDITION INFORMATION/VALUE
Grey, Zane	WILD HORSE MESA. New York, 1928. Signed. $500 or more.
Grey, Zane	WYOMING. New York, (1953). $125-150.
Gruber, Frank	FIGHTING MAN. New York, (1948). $75-100.
Gruber, Frank	OUTLAW. New York, (1941). $175-225.
Gruber, Frank	PEACE MARSHALL. New York, 1939. $275.
Gruber, Frank	GUNSIGHT. New York, 1942. $175.
Guthrie, A. B., Jr.	THE BIG SKY. New York, 1947. Trade edition. $30-40.
Guthrie, A. B., Jr.	MURDERS AT MOON DANCE. New York, 1943. $85-100.
Guthrie, A. B., Jr.	THE BIG SKY. New York, 1947. $65.
Guthrie, A. B., Jr.	THE WAY WEST. New York, 1949. $50.
Harte, Bret	CONDENSED NOVELS AND OTHER PAPERS. New York, 1867. $175-225.
Harte, Bret	THE LUCK OF ROARING CAMP AND OTHER SKETCHES. Boston, 1870. $425-475.
Henty, G. A.	IN THE HEART OF THE ROCKIES. New York, 1894. $50-60.
Henty, G. A., et al.	CAMPS AND QUARTERS. New York, 1889. Wrappers. $1,000 or more.
Hough, Emerson	THE COVERED WAGON. New York, 1922. $125-150.
Hough, Emerson	THE GIRL AT THE HALFWAY HOUSE: A STORY OF THE PLAINS. New York, 1900. $275.
Hough, Emerson	THE KING OF GEE WHIZ. Indianapolis, (1906). $165.
Hough, Emerson	THE MISSISSIPPI BUBBLE. Indianapolis, (1902). $175-225.

AUTHOR	TITLE/EDITION INFORMATION/VALUE
Hough, Emerson	THE STORY OF THE COWBOY. New York, 1897. $85.
Hough, Emerson	THE STORY OF THE OUTLAW. New York, 1907. $75.
Hough, Emerson	THE WAY TO THE WEST. Indianapolis, (1903). $85.
Jackson, Helen Hunt	RAMONA. Boston, 1884. $325-375.
James, Will	ALL IN THE DAY'S RIDING. New York, 1933. $85.
James, Will	THE AMERICA COWBOY. New York, 1902. $45-60.
James, Will	COWBOYS NORTH AND SOUTH. New York, 1924. $150.
James, Will	HOME RANCH. New York, 1935. $25-35.
James, Will	LONE COWBOY: MY LIFE STORY. New York, 1930. Trade edition. $85.
James, Will	SMOKY THE COWHORSE. New York, 1926. $150.
James, Will	THE THREE MUSTANGEERS. New York, 1933. $35-50.
Kantor, MacKinlay	THE VOICE OF BUGLE ANN. New York; London, 1935. $75-100.
Kantor, MacKinlay	SPIRIT LAKE. Cleveland, (1961). $35.
L'Amour, Louis	THE CALIFORNIANS. New York, (1974). $100-125.
L'Amour, Louis	HOPALONG CASSIDY AND THE RIDERS OF HIGH ROCK. New York, 1951. $175-225.
L'Amour, Louis	RIVERS WEST. New York, (1975). $100-125.
L'Amour, Louis	SMOKE FROM THIS ALTAR. Oklahoma City, (1939). $165.

AUTHOR	TITLE/EDITION INFORMATION/VALUE
L'Amour, Louis	TO THE FAR BLUE MOUNTAINS. New York, (1976). $100-125.
L'Amour, Louis	WESTWARD THE TIDE. Kingswood, England, 1950. $275.
London, Jack	BURNING DAYLIGHT. New York, 1910. $275-325.
London, Jack	THE CALL OF THE WILD. New York, 1903. $1,000 or more.
London, Jack	CHILDREN OF THE FROST. New York, 1902. $375-425.
London, Jack	THE CRUISE OF THE DAZZLER. New York, 1902. $1,000 or more.
London, Jack	A DAUGHTER OF THE SNOWS. Philadelphia, 1902. $375-425.
London, Jack	THE FAITH OF MEN AND OTHER STORIES. New York, 1904. $325-375.
London, Jack	THE GOD OF HIS FATHERS AND OTHER STORIES. New York, 1901. $375-425.
London, Jack	LOST FACE. New York, 1910. $450-525.
London, Jack	LOVE OF LIFE. New York, 1907. $275-325.
London, Jack	SMOKE BELLEW. New York, 1912. $225-275.
London, Jack	THE SON OF THE WOLF. Boston, 1900. $1,200 or more.
London, Jack	TALES OF THE FISH PATROL. New York, 1905. $375-425.
London, Jack	WHITE FANG. New York, 1906. $450-525.
Marryat, Frederick	THE LITTLE SAVAGE. 2 vols. London, 1848-1849. $250-325.
McCulley, Johnston	THE MARK OF ZORRO. New York, 1924. $75-100.
McCulley, Johnston	FURTHER ADVENTURES OF ZORRO. London, 1926. $50-75.

AUTHOR	TITLE/EDITION INFORMATION/VALUE
McCulley, Johnston	GOLD OF SMOKY MESA. New York, 1942. $50-75.
McGuane, Thomas Francis	THE SPORTING CLUB. New York, 1968. $75-100.
McGuane, Thomas Francis	THE BUSHWHACKED PIANO. New York, 1971. $75-100.
McMurtry, Larry	THE DESERT ROSE. New York, 1983. $40-65.
McMurtry, Larry	HORSEMAN, PASS BY. New York, (1961). $325.
McMurtry, Larry	THE LAST PICTURE SHOW. New York, (1966). $100-125.
McMurtry, Larry	THE LAST PICTURE SHOW. New York, 1966. $135.
McMurtry, Larry	LEAVING CHEYENNE. New York, (1963). $225.
Norris, Frank	A DEAL IN WHEAT AND OTHER STORIES OF THE NEW AND OLD WEST. New York, 1903. $85-110.
Norris, Frank	MC TEAGUE: A STORY OF SAN FRANCISCO. New York, 1899. $350-425.
Norris, Frank	THE OCTOPUS. New York, 1901. $125-175.
Overholser, Wayne D.	BUCKAROO'S CODE. New York, 1947. $50-65.
Overholser, Wayne D.	FABULOUS GUNMAN. New York, 1953. $35-50.
Overholser, Wayne D.	THE LONE DEPUTY. New York, 1957. $30-40.
Post, Melville Davisson	UNCLE ABNER. New York, 1918. $450-550.
Raine, William MacLeod	CATTLE BRANDS: A SKETCH OF BYGONE DAYS IN THE COW-COUNTRY. Boston, (1920). $135.

AUTHOR	TITLE/EDITION INFORMATION/VALUE
Raine, William MacLeod	A DAUGHTER OF RAASAY. New York, (1902). $175.
Raine, William MacLeod	A TEXAS RANGER. New York, 1911. $125-150.
Raine, William MacLeod	WYOMING. New York, 1908. $150-175.
Raine, William MacLeod	THE YUKON TRAIL. Boston, 1917. $100-125.
Reid, Mayne	NO QUARTER! 3 vols. London, 1888. $375-425.
Reid, Mayne	OSCEOLA THE SEMINOLE. New York, (1858). $325-375.
Reid, Mayne	THE QUADROON; OR, A LOVER'S ADVENTURES IN LOUISIANA. 3 vols. London, 1856. $550-650.
Reid, Mayne	THE WHITE CHIEF: A LEGEND OF NORTHERN MEXICO. 3 vols. London, 1855. $450-550.
Reid, Mayne	THE WILD HUNTRESS. 3 vols. London, 1861. $450-550.
Reid, Mayne	THE WOOD-RANGERS. 3 vols. London, 1860. $450-550.
Santee, Ross	COWBOY. New York, 1928. $125-150.
Santee, Ross	THE BAR X GOLF COURSE. New York, (1933). $85-100.
Santee, Ross	THE BUBBLING SPRING. New York, 1949. $75-100.
Santee, Ross	HARDROCK AND SILVER AGE. New York, 1951. $75-100.
Santee, Ross	MEN AND HORSES. New York, 1926. $175-225.
Santee, Ross	THE RUMMMY KID GOES HOME AND OTHER STORIES OF THE SOUTHWEST. New York, 1965. $50-75.
Seltzer, Charles Alden	THE COUNCIL OF THREE. New York, 1900. $60-75.

AUTHOR	TITLE/EDITION INFORMATION/VALUE
Seltzer, Charles Alden	THE BOSS OF THE LAZY Y. Chicago, 1915. $30-40.
Short, Luke	THE FEUD AT SINGLE SHOT. New York; London, 1936. $85-100.
Short, Luke	SIX GUNS OF SAN JON. New York; London, 1939. $40-50.
Short, Luke	DEAD FREIGHT FOR PIUTE. New York, 1940. $40-50.
Siringo, Charles A.	A COWBOY DETECTIVE. Chicago, 1912. $175-225.
Steinbeck, John	CANNERY ROW. New York, 1945. $125-150.
Steinbeck, John	THE GRAPES OF WRATH. New York, (1939). $425-475.
Steinbeck, John	TORTILLA FLAT. New York, (1935). $450 or more.
Stevenson, Robert Louis	THE SILVERADO SQUATTERS. $350-425.
Taylor, Robert Lewis	THE TRAVELS OF JAIMIE MC PHEETERS. New York, 1958. $65-80.
Taylor, Robert Lewis	A JOURNEY TO MATECUMBE. New York; London, 1961. $40-50.
Taylor, Robert Lewis	A ROARING IN THE WIND, BEING A HISTORY OF ALDER GULCH, MONTANA, IN ITS GREAT AND SHAMEFUL DAYS. New York, 1978. $40-50.
Tuttle, W. C.	REDDY BRANT, HIS ADVENTURES. New York, 1920. $75-100.
Tuttle, W. C.	SAD SONTAG PLAYS HIS HUNCH. New York, 1926. $50-65.
Tuttle, W. C.	HASHKNIFE OF THE DOUBLE BAR 8. London, 1927. $50-65.
Twain, Mark	THE CELEBRATED JUMPING FROG OF CALAVERAS COUNTY, AND OTHER SKETCHES. New York, 1867. $4,500 or more.

AUTHOR	TITLE/EDITION INFORMATION/VALUE
Wellman, Paul Iselin	BRONCO APACHE. New York; London, 1936. $150-175.
Wellman, Paul Iselin	THE WALLS OF JERICHO. Philadelphia, 1947. $100-125.
Wellman, Paul Iselin	THE COMANCHEROS. New York, 1952. $85-100.
Wellman, Paul Iselin	MAGNIFICENT DESTINY. New York, 1962. $85-100.
White, Stewart Edward	ARIZONA NIGHTS. New York, 1907. $125-175.
White, Stewart Edward	THE CLAIM JUMPERS. New York, 1901. Wrappers. $100-125.
White, Stewart Edward	FOLDED HILLS. Garden City, N.Y., 1934. $30-40.
White, Stewart Edward	THE FOREST. New York, 1903. Limited and signed edition. $165.
White, Stewart Edward	GOLD. New York, 1913. $50-75.
White, Stewart Edward	THE LONG RIFLE. Garden City, N.Y., 1932. $40-50.
Wilson, Mrs. Harry Leon	THE LIONS OF THE LORD: A TALE OF THE OLD WEST. Boston, 1903. $125-150.
Wilson, Mrs. Harry Leon	MERTON OF THE MOVIES. Garden City, N.Y., 1922. $90.
Wilson, Mrs. Harry Leon	RUGGLES OF RED GAP. New York, 1915. $125-150.
Wilson, Mrs. Harry Leon	ZIGZAG TALES FROM THE EAST TO THE WEST. New York, 1894. Wrappers, $125. Cloth, $65.
Wister, Owen	LIN MC LEAN. New York, 1897. $175-225.
Wister, Owen	RED MEN AND WHITE. New York, 1896. $50-75.
Wister, Owen	THE VIRGINIAN, A HORSEMAN OF THE PLAINS. New York, 1902. $125-175.

14

Children's/Juvenile Books, and Their Values

This is a very important collecting category for two reasons. One is the importance of the author, and the other is the importance of the illustrator. Scarcity of individual titles is thus dictated by those who collect the work of book illustrators, as well as those who collect children's or juvenile titles and authors.

The authors and titles presented here are those that are best known to the general public. It is reasonable to assume that all first editions by any of the authors listed here will have value, but do *not* assume that all books by the same author will have comparable values.

The values given here are for first-edition books in very good to fine condition, and with a dust jacket if the book was originally issued with one. "Points" often need to be verified to properly identify many of these books. A librarian or rare bookseller should be consulted for verification of edition and value.

AUTHOR	TITLE/EDITION INFORMATION/VALUE
(Adventures)	THE ADVENTURES OF A BROWNIE, AS TOLD TO MY CHILD [Dinah M. Craik]. London, 1872. $275-325.
Alcott, Louisa May	LITTLE MEN. Boston, 1871. $275-325.
Alcott, Louisa May	LITTLE WOMEN. 2 vols. Boston, 1868-1869, $1,700-2,000.
Alcott, Louisa May	AN OLD-FASHIONED GIRL. Boston, 1870. $85-125.

AUTHOR	TITLE/EDITION INFORMATION/VALUE
Aldrich, Thomas Bailey	THE STORY OF A BAD BOY. Boston, 1870. $450-525.
Alger, Horatio, Jr.	ABRAHAM LINCOLN, THE BACK-WOODS BOY. New York, 1883. $85-110.
Alger, Horatio, Jr.	BERTHA'S CHRISTMAS VISION: AN AUTUMN SHEAF. Boston, 1856. $375-450.
Alger, Horatio, Jr.	DAN THE DETECTIVE. New York, 1884. $350-425.
Alger, Horatio, Jr.	DEAN DUNHAM. New York, 1890. Wrappers. $110-135.
Alger, Horatio, Jr.	THE FIVE HUNDRED DOLLAR CHECK. New York, (1891). $425-475.
Alger, Horatio, Jr.	FROM CANAL BOY TO PRESIDENT. New York, 1881. $50-75.
Alger, Horatio, Jr.	GRAND'THER BALDWIN'S THANKS-GIVING. Boston, (1875). $110-135.
Alger, Horatio, Jr.	LUKE WALTON, OR THE CHICAGO NEWSBOY. Philadelphia, (1889). $60-75.
Alger, Horatio, Jr.	MARK STANTON. New York, 1890. $110-135.
Alger, Horatio, Jr.	RAGGED DICK; OR STREET LIFE IN NEW YORK WITH THE BOOT-BLACKS. Boston, (1868). $800-1,000.
Alger, Horatio, Jr.	RALPH RAYMOND'S HEIR. New York, (1892). Wrappers. $60-75.
Alger, Horatio, Jr.	ROBERT COVERDALE'S STRUGGLE. New York, (1910). $550 or more.
Alger, Horatio, Jr.	THE WESTERN BOY. (New York, 1878). $375-450.
Alger, Horatio, Jr.	THE YOUNG MINER; OR TOM NELSON IN CALIFORNIA. San Francisco, 1965. $85-100.
Alger, Horatio Jr., and O. Augusta Cheney	SEEKING HIS FORTUNE AND OTHER DIALOGUES. Boston, (1875). $575-750.
Andersen, Hans Christian	FAIRY TALES. London, (1932). Illustrated and signed by Arthur Rackham. $800-1,000.

AUTHOR	TITLE/EDITION INFORMATION/VALUE
Bannerman, Helen	THE STORY OF LITTLE BLACK SAMBO. London, 1899. $850 or more.
Barrie, Sir James M.	PETER AND WENDY. London, 1911. $135-150; New York, (1911). $60-75.
Barrie, Sir James M.	PETER PAN IN KENSINGTON GARDENS. New York, 1906. $275-350.
Baum, L. Frank	AMERICAN FAIRY TALES. Chicago, 1901. $175-225.
Baum, L. Frank	THE ARMY ALPHABET. Chicago, 1900. $800 or more.
Baum, L. Frank	THE COWARDLY LION AND THE HUNGRY TIGER. Chicago, (1913). $225-275.
Baum, L. Frank	DOROTHY AND THE WIZARD OF OZ. Chicago, (1908). $325-375.
Baum, L. Frank	THE ENCHANTED ISLAND OF YEW. Indianapolis, (1903). $275-325.
Baum, L. Frank	FATHER GOOSE'S YEAR BOOK. Chicago, (1907). $175-225.
Baum, L. Frank	THE LIFE AND ADVENTURES OF SANTA CLAUS. Indianapolis, 1902. $325-375.
Baum, L. Frank	THE MARVELOUS LAND OF OZ. Chicago, 1904. $25-475.
Baum, L. Frank	THE MASTER KEY. Indianapolis, (1901). $325-375.
Baum, L. Frank	MOTHER GOOSE IN PROSE. Chicago, (1897). Illustrated by Maxfield Parrish. $850-1,000.
Baum, L. Frank	A NEW WONDERLAND. New York, 1900. $425-475.
Baum, L. Frank	OZMA OF OZ. Chicago, (1907). $600 or more.
Baum, L. Frank	THE PATCHWORK GIRL OF OZ. Chicago, (1913). $350-425.
Baum, L. Frank	QUEEN ZIXI OF IX. New York, 1905. $325-375.

AUTHOR	TITLE/EDITION INFORMATION/VALUE
Baum, L. Frank	THE ROAD TO OZ. Chicago, (1909). $275-325.
Baum, L. Frank	THE SEA FAIRIES. Chicago, (1911). $175-225.
Baum, L. Frank	THE SONGS OF FATHER GOOSE. Chicago, 1900. $225-275.
Baum, L. Frank	THE WONDERFUL WIZARD OF OZ. Chicago; New York, 1900. $2,750 or more.
Baum, L. Frank	THE YELLOW HEN. Chicago, (1916). $175-225.
Beard, Daniel C.	AMERICAN BOY'S HANDY BOOK: WHAT TO DO AND HOW TO DO IT. New York, 1882. $85-125.
Belloc, Hilaire	THE BAD CHILD'S BOOK OF BEASTS, as H. B. Oxford, (1896). $175-225.
Belloc, Hilaire	CAUTIONARY TALES FOR CHILDREN. London, (1908). $100-125.
Browning, Robert	THE PIED PIPER OF HAMLIN. London, (1888). Illustrated by Kate Greenaway. $275-325.
Burgess, Gelett	GOOPS AND HOW TO BE THEM. New York, (1900). $275-325.
Burgess, Gelett	THE NONSENSE ALMANACK FOR 1900. New York, (1899). $125-150.
Burgess, Gelett	THE PURPLE COW! (San Francisco, 1895). 8 leaves. $325-375.
Burnett, Frances Hodgson	EDITHA'S BURGLAR. Boston, 1888. $60-75.
Burnett, Frances Hodgson	LITTLE LORD FAUNTLEROY. New York, 1886. $325-375.
Burnett, Frances Hodgson	THE SECRET GARDEN. New York, (1911). $125-150.
Burnett, Frances Hodgson	THAT LASS O LOWRIE'S. New York, 1877. $125-150.
Carroll, Lewis	ALICE'S ADVENTURES IN WONDERLAND. New York, 1866. $2,500 or more.

AUTHOR	**TITLE/EDITION INFORMATION/VALUE**
Carroll, Lewis	ALICE'S ADVENTURES UNDER GROUND. London, 1886. $175-225.
Carroll, Lewis	THE HUNTING OF THE SNARK. London, 1876. $275-325.
Carroll, Lewis	THROUGH THE LOOKING GLASS, AND WHAT ALICE FOUND THERE. London, 1872. $800 or more.
Castlemon, Harry	FRANK ON THE LOWER MISSISSIPPI. Cincinnati, 1867. $60-75.
Castlemon, Harry	GUY HARRIS, THE RUNAWAY. New York, 1887. $75-90.
Castlemon, Harry	THE SPORTSMAN'S CLUB AMONG THE TRAPPERS. Philadelphia, 1874. $60-75.
(Child's)	THE CHILD'S BOOK ABOUT WHALES. Concord, N.H., 1843. Wrappers. $140-175.
(Child's)	THE CHILD'S BOTANY [Samuel Griswold Goodrich]. Boston, 1828. $85-100.
(Cinderella)	CINDERELLA [Retold by C. S. Evans]. London, 1919. Limited edition. Illustrated and signed by Arthur Rackham. $500 or more.
Cox, Palmer	THE BROWNIES AROUND THE WORLD. New York, (1894). $150-200.
Cox, Palmer	THE BROWNIES AT HOME. New York, (1893). $75-90.
Cox, Palmer	THE BROWNIES: THEIR BOOK. New York, (1887). $550 or more.
Cox, Palmer	QUEER PEOPLE WITH WINGS AND STINGS AND THEIR KWEER KAPERS. Philadelphia, (1888). $85-125.
Cox, Palmer	QUEERIE QUEERS WITH HANDS, WINGS AND CLAWS. Buffalo, N.Y., (ca. 1887). $85-125.
Crothers, Samuel McCord	MISS MUFFET'S CHRISTMAS PARTY. St. Paul, Minn., 1892. $60-75.

AUTHOR	TITLE/EDITION INFORMATION/VALUE
De La Mare, Walter	BROOMSTICKS AND OTHER TALES. London, 1925. Signed. $85-100.
De La Mare, Walter	CROSSINGS: A FAIRY PLAY. (London, 1921). Limited edition. Boxed. $85-100.
Dickens, Charles	A CHILD'S HISTORY OF ENGLAND. 3 vols. London, 1852-1854. $450 or more.
Dickens, Charles	A CHRISTMAS CAROL. London, 1843. $1,750 or more.
Dickens, Charles	THE PERSONAL HISTORY OF DAVID COPPERFIELD. London, 1850. $350 or more.
Disney, Walt	THE ADVENTURES OF MICKEY MOUSE: BOOK I. Philadelphia, (1931). $325-375.
Disney, Walt	THE GOLDEN TOUCH. London, 1935. $175-225.
Disney, Walt	HONEST JOHN AND GIDDY. New York, (1940). $125-150.
Disney, Walt	LITTLE RED RIDING HOOD AND THE BIG BAD WOLF. Philadelphia, (1934). $135-165.
Disney, Walt	MICKEY MOUSE. Racine, Wis., (1933). Wrappers. $175-225.
Disney, Walt	MICKEY MOUSE IN KING ARTHUR'S COURT. London, (ca. 1932). $325-375.
Disney, Walt	MICKEY MOUSE STORY BOOK. Philadelphia, (1931). $175-225.
Disney, Walt	THE POP-UP MINNIE MOUSE. New York, (1933). $25-275.
Disney, Walt	STORIES FROM WALT DISNEY'S FANTASIA. New York, (1940). $175-225.
Dodge, M. E.	HANS BRINKER; OR, THE SILVER SKATES. New York, 1866. $375-425.
(Dream)	DREAM DROPS, OR STORIES FROM FAIRY LAND [Amy Lowell]. Boston, (1887). Wrappers. $1,200 or more.

AUTHOR	TITLE/EDITION INFORMATION/VALUE
Dulac, Edmund	SINBAD THE SAILOR AND OTHER STORIES FROM THE ARABIAN NIGHTS. London, (1911). Limited and signed edition. $800 or more.
(Fairy)	THE FAIRY BOOK [Dinah M. Craik]. New York, 1837. $150-175.
(Fairy)	A FAIRY GARLAND. London, (1928). Limited edition. Illustrated and signed by Edmund Dulac. $450-525.
(Faith)	FAITH GARTNEY'S GIRLHOOD [Mrs. A. D. T. Whitney]. Boston, 1863. $85-100.
(Family)	THE FAMILY ROBINSON CRUSOE, translated by Johann David Wyss. 2 vols. London, 1814. $4,250 or more.
Farquharson, Martha	ELSIE DINSMORE. New York, 1867. $2,500 or more.
Fellows-Johnston, Annie	THE LITTLE COLONEL. Boston, 1896. $85-100.
Field, Eugene	LOVE-SONGS OF CHILDHOOD. New York, 1894. Trade edition. $25-35.
Field, Eugene	POEMS OF CHILDHOOD. New York, 1904. Illustrated by Maxfield Parrish. $135-150.
Gag, Wanda	MILLIONS OF CATS. New York, 1928. $110-135.
Gilbert, W. S.	THE "BAB" BALLADS: MUCH SOUND AND LITTLE SENSE. London, 1869. $225-250.
Gilbert, W. S.	MORE "BAB" BALLADS. London, (1873). $125-150.
Goulding, F. R.	ROBERT AND HAROLD; OR, THE YOUNG MAROONERS ON THE FLORIDA COAST. Philadelphia, 1852. $225-275.

AUTHOR	TITLE/EDITION INFORMATION/VALUE
Graham, Tom	MIKE AND THE AEROPLANE. New York, (1912). $800 or more.
Grahame, Kenneth	DREAM DAYS. New York, 1899. $85-125. London; New York, 1902. Illustrated by Maxfield Parrish. $85-125.
Grahame, Kenneth	THE GOLDEN AGE. London, 1900. Illustrated by Maxfield Parrish. $110-135.
Grant, Robert	JACK HALL, OR THE SCHOOL DAYS OF AN AMERICAN BOY. Boston, 1888. $40-50.
Greenaway, Kate	A APPLE PIE. London, (1886). $175-225.
Greenaway, Kate	KATE GREENAWAY'S ALPHABET. London, (ca. 1885). $175-225.
Greenaway, Kate	KATE GREENAWAY'S BIRTHDAY BOOK FOR CHILDREN. London, (1880). $225-275.
Greenaway, Kate	KATE GREENAWAY'S BOOK OF GAMES. London, (1889). $225-275.
Greenaway, Kate	KATE GREENAWAY PICTURES. London, 1921. $175-225.
Greenaway, Kate	MARIGOLD GARDEN. (London, 1885). $225-275.
Greenaway, Kate	UNDER THE WINDOW: PICTURES AND RHYMES FOR CHILDREN. London, (1878). $450 or more.
Greenaway, Kate, illustrator	DAME WIGGINS OF LEE AND HER SEVEN WONDERFUL CATS. London, (1885). $225-275.
Greenaway, Kate, illustrator	A DAY IN A CHILD'S LIFE. London, (1881). $175-225.
Greenaway, Kate, illustrator	LANGUAGE OF FLOWERS. London, (1884). $175-225.
Greenaway, Kate, illustrator	THE "LITTLE FOLKS" PAINTING BOOK. London, (1879). $175-225.
Greenaway, Kate, illustrator	MOTHER GOOSE OR THE OLD NURSERY RHYMES. London, (1881). $275-325.

AUTHOR	**TITLE/EDITION INFORMATION/VALUE**
Grimm, Jacob L. K. and W. K.	THE FAIRY TALES OF THE BROTHERS GRIMM. London, 1909. Illustrated by Arthur Rackham. Trade edition. $350-425.
Grimm, Jacob L. K. and W. K.	HANSEL AND GRETEL AND OTHER STORIES. New York, 1925. Illustrated by Kay Nielsen. $525-575.
Grimm, Jacob L. K. and W. K.	LITTLE BROTHER AND LITTLE SISTER. London, (1917). Trade edition. $250-275.
Hale, Sarah Josepha, editor	THE GOOD LITTLE BOY'S BOOK. New York, (ca. 1848). $60-75.
(Handbook)	HANDBOOK FOR BOYS. New York: Boy Scouts of America, 1911. $125-150.
(Handbook)	HANDBOOK FOR SCOUTMASTERS: BOY SCOUTS OF AMERICA. New York: Boy Scouts of America, (1914). $85-100.
Harris, Joel Chandler	THE TAR-BABY AND OTHER RHYMES OF UNCLE REMUS. New York, 1904. $175-225.
Harris, Joel Chandler	UNCLE REMUS AND BRER RABBIT. New York, (1906). $275-325.
Harte, Bret	THE QUEEN OF THE PIRATE ISLE. London, 1886. Illustrated by Kate Greenaway. $50-550.
Hawthorne, Nathaniel	BIOGRAPHICAL STORIES FOR CHILDREN. Boston, 1842. $125-150.
Hawthorne, Nathaniel	TANGLEWOOD TALES, FOR GIRLS AND BOYS. Boston, 1853. $225-250.
Hawthorne, Nathaniel	A WONDER-BOOK FOR GIRLS AND BOYS. Boston, 1852. $650-750.
Hazel, Harry	THE WEST POINT CADET. Boston, 1845. Wrappers. $150-175.
Hearn, Lafcadio	JAPANESE FAIRY TALES. 5 vols. Tokyo, (1898-1903). Wrappers. $600-750.
Hegan, Alice Caldwell	MRS. WIGGS OF THE CABBAGE PATCH. New York, 1901. $60-75.

AUTHOR	TITLE/EDITION INFORMATION/VALUE
Henty, G. A.	ALL BUT LOST. 3 vols. London, 1869. $1,200 or more.
Henty, G. A.	IN THE HEART OF THE ROCKIES. New York, 1894. $50-60.
Henty, G. A.	A MARCH ON LONDON. London, 1898. $25-275.
Henty, G. A.	THE MARCH TO COOMASSIE. London, 1874. $375-450.
Henty, G. A.	THE QUEEN'S CUP. 3 vols. London, 1897. $1,000 or more.
Henty, G. A.	BARTHOLOMEW'S EVE. London, 1894. $175-225.
Henty, G. A.	SEARCH FOR A SECRET. 3 vols. London, 1867. $1,500 or more.
Henty, G. A.	THE TIGER OF MYSORE. London, 1896. $25-275; New York, 1895. $60-75.
Henty, G. A., et al.	BRAINS AND BRAVERY. London, 1903. Illustrated by Arthur Rackham. $225-275.
Henty, G. A., et al.	CAMPS AND QUARTERS. New York, 1889. Wrappers. $1,000 or more.
Higginson, Thomas Wentworth	THE BIRTHDAY IN FAIRY-LAND: A STORY FOR CHILDREN. Boston, 1850. Wrappers. $60-75.
Housman, Laurence	A FARM IN FAIRYLAND. London, 1894. $175-225.
Jackson, Helen Hunt	RAMONA. Boston, 1884. $325-375.
Kingsley, Charles	THE WATER-BABIES. London, 1863. $450-525.
Kingsley, Charles	WESTWARD HO! Cambridge, England, 1855. $800 or more.
Kingsley, Henry	VALENTIN: A FRENCH BOY'S STORY. 2 vols. London, 1872, $85-100.

AUTHOR	TITLE/EDITION INFORMATION/VALUE
Kipling, Rudyard	"CAPTAINS COURAGEOUS": A STORY OF THE GRAND BANKS. London, 1897. $600 or more.
Kipling, Rudyard	THE JUNGLE BOOK & THE SECOND JUNGLE BOOK. 2 vols. London, 1894-1895. $650 or more.
Kipling, Rudyard	JUST SO STORIES FOR LITTLE CHILDREN. London, 1902. $550 or more.
Kipling, Rudyard	KIM. New York, 1902. $450 or more.
Kipling, Rudyard	PUCK OF POOK'S HILL. London, 1906. $175-225.
Kipling, Rudyard	WEE WILLIE WINKIE AND OTHER CHILD STORIES. Allahabad, India, (1888). Wrappers. $800 or more.
Kneedler, H.S.	THROUGH STORYLAND TO SUNSET SEAS. Cincinnati, 1896. Wrappers. $175.
Lang, Andrew	THE BLUE FAIRY BOOK. New York, (ca. 1897). $125.
Lang, Andrew	THE GREEN FAIRY BOOK. London, 1892. Trade edition. $125.
Lang, Andrew	THE OLIVE FAIRY BOOK. New York, 1907. $125.
Lanier, Sidney	THE BOY'S MABINOGION. New York, 1881. $225.
Larcom, Lucy	CHILDHOOD SONGS. Boston, 1875. $125.
Leaf, Munro	THE STORY OF FERDINAND. New York, 1936. $675.
Lofting, Hugh	DOCTOR DOOLITTLE'S POST OFFICE. New York, 1923. $110.
Lofting, Hugh	THE STORY OF DOCTOR DOOLITTLE. New York, 1920. $275.
May, Robert L.	RUDOLPH THE RED-NOSED REINDEER. Chicago, 1939. Wrappers. $325.

AUTHOR	TITLE/EDITION INFORMATION/VALUE
Moore, Clement C.	THE NIGHT BEFORE CHRISTMAS. New York, 1902. $165.
Newell, Peter	THE HOLE BOOK. New York, 1908. $300.
Newell, Peter	THE ROCKET BOOK. New York, 1912. $100.
Percy, Stephen	ROBIN HOOD AND HIS MERRY FORESTERS. New York, 1855. $150.
Porter, Eleanor H.	POLLYANNA. Boston, 1913. $425.
Porter, Gene Stratton	LADDIE: A TRUE-BLUE STORY. New York, 1913. $175.
Potter, Beatrix	GINGER AND PICKLES. New York, 1909. $125.
Potter, Beatrix	PETER RABBIT'S ALMANAC FOR 1929. New York, 1928. $200.
Potter, Beatrix	THE TALE OF LITTLE PIG ROBINSON. Philadelphia, 1930. $200.
Pyle, Howard	THE MERRY ADVENTURES OF ROBIN HOOD. New York, 1883. $375.
Pyle, Howard	THE STORY OF THE CHAMPIONS OF THE ROUND TABLE. New York, 1905. $165.
Pyle, Howard	THE STORY OF KING ARTHUR AND HIS KNIGHTS. New York, 1903. $165.
Pyle, Howard	THE WONDER CLOCK. New York, 1888. $375.
Pyrnelle, Louise-Clarke	DIDDIE, DUMPS, AND TOT, OR PLANTATION CHILD-LIFE. New York, 1882. $450.
Rackham, Arthur	THE ARTHUR RACKHAM FAIRY BOOK. London, 1933. Limited and signed edition. $850 or more.
Ramal, Walter	SONGS OF CHILDHOOD. London, 1902. $750 or more.

AUTHOR	TITLE/EDITION INFORMATION/VALUE
Richards, Laura E.	CAPTAIN JANUARY. Boston, 1891. $150.
Richards, Laura E.	FIVE MICE IN A MOUSE-TRAP. Boston, 1881. $200.
Riley, James Whitcomb	RHYMES OF CHILDHOOD. Indianapolis, 1891. $95.
Salten, Felix	BAMBI, A LIFE IN THE WOODS. New York, 1928. $125.
Saunders, Louise	THE KNAVE OF HEARTS. New York, 1925. Illustrated by Maxfield Parrish. $850 or more. (Note: The spiral-bound edition [Racine, Wis.] is NOT the first edition.)
Seuss, Dr.	AND TO THINK I SAW IT ON MULBERRY STREET. New York, 1937. $200.
Sewell, Anna	BLACK BEAUTY. Boston, 1890. $550.
Sidney, Margaret	FIVE LITTLE PEPPERS AND HOW THEY GREW. Boston, 1880. $275.
Stevenson, Robert Louis	THE BLACK ARROW. New York, 1916. $275.
Stevenson, Robert Louis	KIDNAPPED. New York, 1913. $275.
Tarkington, Booth	PENROD. Garden City, N.Y., 1914. $1,200 or more.
Tarkington, Booth	PENROD AND SAM. Garden City, N.Y., 1916. $325.
Tarkington, Booth	SEVENTEEN. New York, 1916. $175.
Twain, Mark	ADVENTURES OF HUCKLEBERRY FINN. New York, 1885. $1,500 or more.
Twain, Mark	THE ADVENTURES OF TOM SAWYER. Hartford, Conn., 1876. $2,500 or more.
Watkins, Lucy	THE HISTORY AND ADVENTURES OF LITTLE JAMES AND MARY. Philadelphia, 1810. Wrappers. $135.

AUTHOR	TITLE/EDITION INFORMATION/VALUE
Weatherly, Frederick Edward	PUNCH AND JUDY AND SOME OF THEIR FRIENDS. London, 1885. $225.
Webster, Jean	DADDY-LONG-LEGS. New York, 1912. $150.
Wiggin, Kate Douglas	REBECCA OF SUNNYBROOK FARM. Boston, 1903. $450.

-15-

Mainstream Fiction Books, and Their Values

The authors and titles presented here are those that are best known to the general public. It is reasonable to presume that all first editions by any of the authors listed will have value, but do *not* assume that all books by the same author will have comparable values.

The values given here are for first-edition books in very good to fine condition, and with a dust jacket if the book was originally issued with one. "Points" often need to be verified to properly identify many of these books. A librarian or rare bookseller should be consuldted for verification of edition and value.

AUTHOR	TITLE/EDITION INFORMATION/VALUE
Adams, Richard	WATERSHIP DOWN. London, 1972. $175-225.
Aiken, Conrad	BLUE VOYAGE. New York, 1927. $110-135.
Ainsworth, W. Harrison	THE MISER'S DAUGHTER. 3 vols. London, 1842. $300-350.
Anderson, Sherwood	MARCHING MEN. New York, 1917. $225-275.
Anderson, Sherwood	WINDY MC PHERSON'S SON. New York, 1916. $800 or more.
Anderson, Sherwood	WINESBURG, OHIO. New York, 1919. $500 or more.
Arthur, T. S.	TEN NIGHTS IN A BAR-ROOM, AND WHAT I SAW THERE. Philadelphia, 1854. $175-225.

AUTHOR	TITLE/EDITION INFORMATION/VALUE
Atherton, Gertrude Franklin	WHAT DREAMS MAY COME, as Frank Lin. Chicago, (1888). Wrappers. $140-175.
Bacheller, Irving	EBEN HOLDEN. Boston, (1900). $125-150.
Baldwin, James	GIOVANNI'S ROOM. New York, 1956. $325-375.
Barrie, Sir James M.	THE LITTLE MINISTER. 3 vols. London, 1891. $650-750.
Barth, John	THE FLOATING OPERA. New York, (1956). $225-275.
Barth, John	THE SOT-WEED FACTOR. Garden City, N.Y., 1960. $225-275.
Barthelme, Donald	COME BACK, DR. CALIGARI. Boston, (1964). $175-200.
Bates, H. E.	THE BEAUTY OF THE DEAD AND ONE OTHER STORY. London, 1941. Limited edition. $275-325.
Bell, Currer	JANE EYRE: AN AUTOBIOGRAPHY. 3 vols. London, 1847. $5,500 or more.
Bell, Currer	THE PROFESSOR. 2 vols. London, 1857. $1,100 or more.
Bell, Ellis and Acton	WUTHERING HEIGHTS. 3 vols. London, 1847. $15,000 or more.
Bellamy, Edward	LOOKING BACKWARD, 2000-1887. Boston, 1888. $375-425.
Bellow, Saul	THE ADVENTURES OF AUGIE MARCH. New York, 1953. $135-150.
Bellow, Saul	DANGLING MAN. New York, (1944). $375-425.
Bellow, Saul	THE VICTIM. New York, (1947). $275-325.
Cabell, James Branch	JURGEN. New York, 1919. $350 or more.
Caldwell, Erskine	GOD'S LITTLE ACRE. New York, 1933. $175-225.

AUTHOR	TITLE/EDITION INFORMATION/VALUE
Caldwell, Erskine	TOBACCO ROAD. New York, 1932. $225-275.
Callaghan, Morley	STRANGE FUGITIVE. New York, 1928. $225-275.
Capote, Truman	OTHER VOICES, OTHER ROOMS. New York, (1948). $125-150.
Cather, Willa	ALEXANDER'S BRIDGE. Boston, 1912. $350-425.
Cather, Willa	APRIL TWILIGHTS. Boston, 1903. No dust jacket. $850 or more.
Cheever, John	THE WAY SOME PEOPLE LIVE. New York, (1943). $275-325.
Chesterton, G. K.	THE MAN WHO WAS THURSDAY. London, 1908. $275-325.
Clark, Walter Van Tilburg	CHRISTMAS COMES TO HJALSEN. Reno, Nev., 1930. Wrappers. $325-375.
Davis, Richard Harding	GALLEGHER AND OTHER STORIES. New York, 1891. Wrappers. $175-225.
Dickens, Charles	GREAT EXPECTATIONS. 3 vols. London, 1861. $5,000 or more.
Dickens, Charles	MASTER HUMPHREY'S CLOCK. 3 vols. London, 1840-1841. $500 or more.
Dickens, Charles	THE PERSONAL HISTORY OF DAVID COPPERFIELD. London, 1850. $350 or more.
Dickens, Charles	A TALE OF TWO CITIES. London, 1859. $1,500 or more.
Didion, Joan	RUN RIVER. New York, (1963). $110-125.
Doctorow, E. L.	WELCOME TO HARD TIMES. New York, 1960. $100-125.
Donleavy, J. P.	THE GINGER MAN. Paris, (1955). $450 or more.
Dos Passos, John	THREE SOLDIERS. New York, (1921). $450-500.

AUTHOR	TITLE/EDITION INFORMATION/VALUE
Dreiser, Theodore	JENNIE GERHARDT. New York, 1911. $225-275.
Edmonds, Walter D.	ROME HAUL. Boston, 1929. Limited edition. $175-225.
Eggleston, Edward	THE BOOK OF QUEER STORIES, AND STORIES TOLD ON A CELLAR DOOR. Chicago, 1871. $225-275.
Eggleston, Edward	THE HOOSIER SCHOOLMASTER. New York, (1871). $225-275.
Eggleston, Edward	MR. BLAKE'S WALKING-STICK. Chicago, 1870. $325-375.
Eliot, T. S.	OLD POSSUM'S BOOK OF PRACTICAL CATS. London, (1939). $175-200.
Farrell, James T.	CALICO SHOES AND OTHER STORIES. New York, (1934). $175-225.
Farrell, James T.	YOUNG LONIGAN: A BOYHOOD IN CHICAGO STREETS. New York, 1932. $225-275.
Farrell, James T.	THE YOUNG MANHOOD OF STUDS LONIGAN. New York, (1934). $175-225.
Faulkner, William	AS I LAY DYING. New York, (1930). $800 or more.
Faulkner, William	DOCTOR MARTINO AND OTHER STORIES. New York, 1934. Trade edition. $500 or more.
Faulkner, William	THE MANSION. New York, (1959). Limited and signed edition. $450 or more.
Faulkner, William	MISS ZILPHIA GANT. (Dallas Tex.), 1932. Limited edition. $1,000 or more.
Faulkner, William	MOSQUITOES. New York, 1927. $1,000 or more.
Faulkner, William	PYLON. New York, 1935. Trade edition. $275-325.

AUTHOR	TITLE/EDITION INFORMATION/VALUE
Faulkner, William	REQUIEM FOR A NUN. New York, (1951). Trade edition. $175-225.
Faulkner, William	SANCTUARY. New York, (1931). $850 or more.
Faulkner, William	SARTORIS. New York, (1929). $800 or more.
Faulkner, William	SOLDIER'S PAY. New York, 1926. $1,750 or more.
Faulkner, William	THE SOUND AND THE FURY. New York, (1929). $1,000 or more.
Ferber, Edna	DAWN O'HARA: THE GIRL WHO LAUGHED. New York, (1911). $125-150.
Fitzgerald, F. Scott	ALL THE SAD YOUNG MEN. New York, 1926. $1,000 or more.
Fitzgerald, F. Scott	THE BEAUTIFUL AND THE DAMNED. New York, 1922. $1,250 or more.
Fitzgerald, F. Scott	FLAPPERS AND PHILOSOPHERS. New York, 1920. $500 or more.
Fitzgerald, F. Scott	THE GREAT GATSBY. New York, 1925. $3,000 or more. No dust jacket, $100-150.
Fitzgerald, F. Scott	TALES OF THE JAZZ AGE. New York, 1922. $500 or more.
Fitzgerald, F. Scott	TENDER IS THE NIGHT. New York, 1934. $650-750.
Fitzgerald, F. Scott	THIS SIDE OF PARADISE. New York, 1920. $1,500 or more.
Fitzgerald, F. Scott	THE VEGETABLE. New York, 1923. $650-750.
Fitzgerald, Zelda	SAVE ME THE WALTZ. New York, 1932. $475-550.
Ford, Paul Leicester	THE HONORABLE PETER STIRLING AND WHAT PEOPLE THOUGHT OF HIM. New York, 1894. $135-160.
Forester, C. S.	THE AFRICAN QUEEN. Boston, 1935. $225-275.
Forester, C. S.	A PAWN AMONG KINGS. London, (1924). $550-650.

AUTHOR	TITLE/EDITION INFORMATION/VALUE
Forester, C. S.	PLAIN MURDER. London, (1930). $175-225.
Forster, E. M.	A ROOM WITH A VIEW. London, 1908. $250-300.
Gissing, George	THYRZA: A TALE. 3 vols. London, 1887. $450-550.
Gissing, George	WORKERS IN THE DAWN. 3 vols. London, 1880. $2,200 or more.
Golding, William	LORD OF THE FLIES. London, (1954). $500 or more.
Green, Anna Katharine	THE CIRCULAR STUDY. New York, 1900. $225-275.
Green, Anna Katharine	THE LEAVENWORTH CASE: A LAWYER'S STORY. New York, 1878. Cloth or wrappers. $1,000 or more.
Greene, Graham	THE BEAR FELL FREE. (London, 1935). Limited and signed edition. $225-275.
Grile, Dod	COBWEBS FROM AN EMPTY SKULL. London, 1874. $275-325.
Grile, Dod	THE FIEND'S DELIGHT. London, (1872). $325-375.
Hale, Lucretia	THE PETERKIN PAPERS. Boston, 1880. $225-275.
Harris, Joel Chandler	DADDY JAKE THE RUNAWAY. New York, (1889). $225-275.
Harris, Joel Chandler	TALES OF THE HOME FOLKS IN PEACE AND WAR. Boston, 1898. $175-225.
Harris, Joel Chandler	UNCLE REMUS: HIS SONGS AND HIS SAYINGS. New York, 1881. $550-650.
Harris, Joel Chandler	UNCLE REMUS RETURNS. Boston, 1918. $325-375.
Harte, Bret	CONDENSED NOVELS AND OTHER PAPERS. New York, 1867. $175-225.

AUTHOR	TITLE/EDITION INFORMATION/VALUE
Harte, Bret	GABRIEL CONROY. Hartford, Conn., 1876. $175-225.
Harte, Bret	THE LOST GALLEON AND OTHER TALES. San Francisco, 1867. $325-375.
Harte, Bret	THE LUCK OF ROARING CAMP AND OTHER SKETCHES. Boston, 1870. $425-475.
Hawthorne, Nathaniel	THE CELESTIAL RAIL-ROAD. Boston, 1843. Wrappers. $1,500 or more.
Hawthorne, Nathaniel	THE GENTLE BOY: A THRICE-TOLD TALE. Boston, 1839. Wrappers. $500 or more.
Hawthorne, Nathaniel	GRANDFATHER'S CHAIR: A HISTORY. Boston, 1841. $225-275.
Hawthorne, Nathaniel	THE HOUSE OF THE SEVEN GABLES. Boston, 1851. $650-725.
Hawthorne, Nathaniel	THE MARBLE FAUN; OR, THE ROMANCE OF MONTE BENI. 2 vols. Boston, 1860. $550 or more.
Hawthorne, Nathaniel	THE SCARLET LETTER. Boston, 1850. $900 or more.
Hawthorne, Nathaniel	TWICE-TOLD TALES. Boston, 1837. $1,500 or more.
Hemingway, Ernest	DEATH IN THE AFTERNOON. New York, 1932. $325-375.
Hemingway, Ernest	A FAREWELL TO ARMS. New York, 1929. $550 or more.
Hemingway, Ernest	THE FIFTH COLUMN AND THE FIRST FORTY-NINE STORIES. New York, 1938. $225-275.
Hemingway, Ernest	IN OUR TIME. New York, 1925. $800 or more.
Hemingway, Ernest	MEN WITHOUT WOMEN. New York, 1927. $500 or more.
Hemingway, Ernest	THE SUN ALSO RISES. New York, 1926. $1,750 or more.

AUTHOR	TITLE/EDITION INFORMATION/VALUE
Hemingway, Ernest	THREE STORIES AND AND TEN POEMS. (Paris, 1923). $4,500 or more.
Hemingway, Ernest	TO HAVE AND HAVE NOT. New York, 1937. $325-375.
Hemingway, Ernest	THE TORRENTS OF SPRING. New York, 1926. $750 or more.
Henry, O.	HEART OF THE WEST. New York, 1907. $275-325.
Henry, O.	ROADS OF DESTINY. New York, 1909. $225-275.
Henry, O.	THE VOICE OF THE CITY. New York, 1908. $275-325.
Henty, G. A.	A SEARCH FOR A SECRET. 3 vols. London, 1867. $1,500 or more.
Jackson, Shirley	THE ROAD THROUGH THE WALL. New York, (1948). $150-175.
Jewett, Sarah Orne	BETTY LEICESTER'S ENGLISH CHRISTMAS. Boston, 1894. $175-225.
Jones, James	FROM HERE TO ETERNITY. New York, 1951. $125-150.
Kesey, Ken	ONE FLEW OVER THE CUCKOO'S NEST. New York, (1962). $275-325.
Kosinski, Jerzy	THE PAINTED BIRD. Boston, (1965). $225-275.
Lardner, Ring W.	GULLIBLE'S TRAVELS. Indianapolis, (1917). $275-325.
Lardner, Ring W.	LOSE WITH A SMILE. New York, 1933. $100-125.
Lardner, Ring W.	THE LOVE NEST AND OTHER STORIES. New York, 1925. $225-275.
Lardner, Ring W.	REGULAR FELLOWS I HAVE MET. Chicago, 1919. $375-450.

AUTHOR	TITLE/EDITION INFORMATION/VALUE
Lardner, Ring W.	ROUND UP. New York, 1929. $175-225.
Lardner, Ring W.	STOP ME IF YOU'VE HEARD THIS ONE. New York, 1929. $125-150.
Lardner, Ring W.	THE STORY OF A WONDER MAN. New York, 1927. $225-275.
Lardner, Ring W.	TREAT 'EM ROUGH: LETTERS FROM JACK THE KAISER KILLER. Indianapolis, (1918). $225-275.
Lardner, Ring W.	WHAT OF IT? New York, 1925. $125-150.
Lardner, Ring W.	YOU KNOW ME AL. New York, (1916). $225-275.
Larkin, Philip	THE NORTH SHIP. London, (1945). $450-500.
Lawrence, D. H.	ENGLAND, MY ENGLAND AND OTHER STORIES. New York, 1922. $175-225.
Lawrence, D. H.	LADY CHATTERLEY'S LOVER. (Florence, Italy), 1928. Limited and signed edition. $1,000 or more.
Lawrence, D. H.	THE LOST GIRL. London, (1920). $400 or more.
Lawrence, D. H.	LOVE AMONG THE HAYSTACKS. London, 1930. Limited edition. $100-125.
Lawrence, D. H.	THE LOVELY LADY. London, 1933. $100-125.
Lawrence, D. H.	THE MAN WHO DIED. London, 1931. $135-175.
Lawrence, D. H.	THE PRUSSIAN OFFICER AND OTHER STORIES. London, (1914). $1,000 or more.
Lawrence, D. H.	THE RAINBOW. London, (1915). $2,500 or more.
Lawrence, D. H.	RAWDON'S ROOF. London, 1928. Limited and signed edition. $275-325.
Lawrence, D. H.	SONS AND LOVERS. London, (1913). $1,000 or more.
Lawrence, D. H.	THE WHITE PEACOCK. New York, 1911. $6,500 or more.

AUTHOR	TITLE/EDITION INFORMATION/VALUE
Lawrence, D. H.	WOMEN IN LOVE. New York, 1920. $175-225.
Leacock, Stephen	LITERARY LAPSES: A BOOK OF SKETCHES. Montreal, 1910. $125-150.
Leacock, Stephen	NONSENSE NOVELS. New York, 1911. $125-150.
Lee, Harper	TO KILL A MOCKINGBIRD. Philadelphia, (1960). $125-150.
Leroux, Gaston	THE PHANTOM OF THE OPERA. Indianapolis, 1911. $125-150.
Lessing, Doris	AFRICAN STORIES. London, (1964). $85-100.
Lewis, Matthew Gregory	ROMANTIC TALES. 4 vols. London, 1808. $400-500.
Lewis, Sinclair	BABBITT. New York, (1922). $140-165.
Lewis, Sinclair	DODSWORTH. New York, (1929). $110-135.
Lewis, Sinclair	FREE AIR. New York, 1919. $140-175.
Lewis, Sinclair	THE INNOCENTS. New York, (1917). $550 or more.
Lewis, Sinclair	THE JOB. New York, (1917). $350-450.
Lewis, Sinclair	MAIN STREET. New York, 1920. $450 or more.
Lewis, Sinclair	OUR MR. WRENN. New York, 1914. $425-475.
Lewis, Sinclair	THE TRAIL OF THE HAWK. New York, (1915). $425-475.
Liebling, A. J.	THE TELEPHONE BOOTH INDIAN. Garden City, N.Y., 1942. $100-125.
London, Jack	THE ABYSMAL BRUTE. New York, 1913. $350-425.
London, Jack	THE ACORN PLANTER. New York, 1916. $850 or more.
London, Jack	ADVENTURE. New York, 1911. $450-525.
London, Jack	BEFORE ADAM. New York, 1907. $275-350.

AUTHOR	TITLE/EDITION INFORMATION/VALUE
London, Jack	CHILDREN OF THE FROST. New York, 1902. $375-450.
London, Jack	THE CRUISE OF THE DAZZLER. New York, 1902. $1,100 or more.
London, Jack	A DAUGHTER OF THE SNOWS. Philadelphia, 1902. $375-450.
London, Jack	HEARTS OF THREE. New York, 1920. $125-150.
London, Jack	THE HOUSE OF PRIDE. New York, 1912. $275-325.
London, Jack	THE HUMAN DRIFT. New York, 1917. $650-750.
London, Jack	THE IRON HEEL. New York, 1908. $375-450.
London, Jack	THE JACKET. London, (1915). $275-350.
London, Jack	JOHN BARLEYCORN. New York, 1913. $700 or more.
London, Jack	THE SCARLET PLAGUE. New York, 1915. $325-375.
London, Jack	SCORN OF WOMEN. New York, 1906. $1,100 or more.
London, Jack	THE SEA-WOLF. New York, 1904. $375-425.
London, Jack	THE STAR ROVER. New York, 1915. $1,200 or more.
London, Jack	TALES OF THE FISH PATROL. New York, 1905. $375-425.
Longfellow, Henry Wadsworth	EVANGELINE: A TALE OF ACADIE. Boston, 1847. $450-500.
Longfellow, Henry Wadsworth	TALES OF A WAYSIDE INN. Boston, 1863. $175-225.
Loos, Anita	GENTLEMEN PREFER BLONDES. New York, 1925. $100-125.
Lowry, Malcolm	UNDER THE VOLCANO. New York, (1947). $550 or more.
Lucas, Victoria	THE BELL JAR. London, (1963). $450-525.

AUTHOR	TITLE/EDITION INFORMATION/VALUE
McCullers, Carson	THE HEART IS A LONELY HUNTER. Boston, 1940. $250-300.
McCullers, Carson	REFLECTIONS IN A GOLDEN EYE. (Boston), 1941. $175-225.
MacDonald, George	DEALINGS WITH THE FAIRIES. London, 1867. $375-450.
MacDonald, George	THE PRINCESS AND THE GOBLIN. London, 1897. $375-425.
MacFall, Haldane	THE WOOINGS OF JEZEBEL PETTYFER. London, 1898. $175-225.
Mailer, Norman	THE NAKED AND THE DEAD. New York, (1948). $275-325.
Malamud, Bernard	THE NATURAL. New York, (1952). $150-175.
Mann, Thomas	THE MAGIC MOUNTAIN. 2 vols. New York, 1927. Limited and signed edition. $350-425.
Mansfield, Katherine	BLISS AND OTHER STORIES. London, (1920). $175-225.
Mansfield, Katherine	IN A GERMAN PENSION. London, (1911). $450-525.
Marquand, John P.	THE UNSPEAKABLE GENTLEMAN. New York, 1922. $110-135.
Marryat, Frederick	THE LITTLE SAVAGE. 2 vols. London, 1848-1849. $250-325.
Marryat, Frederick	MASTERMAN READY. 3 vols. London, 1841-1843. $450-525.
Marryat, Frederick	POOR JACK. London, 1840. $175-225.
Masters, Edgar Lee	SPOON RIVER ANTHOLOGY. New York, 1915. $550-650.
Maugham, W. Somerset	LIZA OF LAMBETH. London, 1897. $800 or more.
Maugham, W. Somerset	THE MAKING OF A SAINT. Boston, 1898. $225-275.
Maugham, W. Somerset	A MAN OF HONOUR. London, 1903. $850 or more.

AUTHOR	TITLE/EDITION INFORMATION/VALUE
Maugham, W. Somerset	THE MERRY-GO-ROUND. London, 1904. $175-225.
Maugham, W. Somerset	OF HUMAN BONDAGE. New York, (1915). $850-1,000.
Melville, Herman	THE CONFIDENCE-MAN. New York, 1857. $1,100 or more.
Melville, Herman	ISRAEL POTTER. New York, 1855. $550-650.
Melville, Herman	MARDI: AND A VOYAGE THITHER. 2 vols. New York, 1849. $650-750.
Melville, Herman	MOBY-DICK; OR, THE WHALE. New York, 1851. $8,000 or more.
Melville, Herman	OMOO: A NARRATIVE OF ADVENTURES IN THE SOUTH SEAS. New York, 1847. Wrappers. $5,500 or more.
Melville, Herman	THE PIAZZA TALES. New York, 1856. $1,200 or more.
Melville, Herman	TYPEE: A PEEP AT POLYNESIAN LIFE. New York, 1846. $6,000—perhaps much more.
Miller, Henry	ALLER RETOUR NEW YORK. Paris, (1935). Wrappers. Limited and signed edition. $800 or more.
Miller, Henry	BLACK SPRING. Paris, (1936). Wrappers. $600 or more.
Miller, Henry	TROPIC OF CANCER. Paris, (1934). Wrappers. $5,000 or more.
Miller, Henry	TROPIC OF CAPRICORN. Paris, (1939). Wrappers. $700 or more.
Mitchell, Margaret	GONE WITH THE WIND. New York, (May) 1936. $650-750.
Mitchell, S. Weir	HUGH WYNNE, FREE QUAKER. 2 vols. New York, 1897. $175-225.
Moore, Thomas	LALLA ROOKH, AN ORIENTAL ROMANCE. London, 1817. $350-425.
Morley, Christopher	THE HAUNTED BOOKSHOP. New York, 1919. $175-225.

AUTHOR	TITLE/EDITION INFORMATION/VALUE
Morley, Christopher	PARNASSUS ON WHEELS. Garden City, N.Y., 1917. $450-525.
Nabokoff, Vladimir	LAUGHTER IN THE DARK. Indianapolis, (1938). $250-325.
Nabokov, Vladimir	BEND SINISTER. New York, 1947. $150-175.
Nabokov, Vladimir	LOLITA. 2 vols. Paris, (1955). Wrappers. $600-750.
Narmyx	UNPROFESSIONAL TALES. London, 1901. Limited edition. $325-375.
Neal, John	THE MOON-HUNTER; OR, LIFE IN THE MAINE WOODS. New York, (1864). Wrappers. $350-425.
Neal, John	RACHEL DYER: A NORTH AMERICAN STORY. Portland, Maine, 1828. $350-425.
Nin, Anais	THE HOUSE OF INCEST. Paris, (1936). Wrappers. Limited and signed edition. $425-475.
Norden, Charles	PANIC SPRING. New York, (1937). $350-425.
Norris, Frank	YVERNELLE: A LEGEND OF FEUDAL FRANCE. Philadelphia, 1892. $950 or more.
Oates, Joyce Carol	BY THE NORTH GATE. New York, (1963). $150-175.
O'Connor, Flannery	WISE BLOOD. New York, (1952). $275-325.
O'Hara, John	BUTTERFIELD 8. New York, (1935). $140-165.
Optic, Oliver	THE BOAT CLUB; OR, THE BUNKERS OF RIPPLETON. Boston, 1855. $225-275.
Orwell, George	A CLERGYMAN'S DAUGHTER. London, 1935. $450-525.
Orwell, George	KEEP THE ASPIDISTRA FLYING. London, 1936. $350-450.
Ouida	SYRLIN. 3 vols. London, 1880. $350-425.

AUTHOR	TITLE/EDITION INFORMATION/VALUE
Ouida	UNDER TWO FLAGS. 3 vols. London, 1867. $350-425.
Parley, Peter	THE TALES OF PETER PARLEY ABOUT AMERICA. Boston, 1827. $3,500 or more.
Perelman, S. J.	DAWN GINSBERGH'S REVENGE. New York, (1929). $225-275.
Poe, Edgar Allan	TALES. New York, 1845. Wrappers. $15,000—perhaps much more.
Poe, Edgar Allan	TALES OF THE GROTESQUE AND ARABESQUE. 2 vols. Philadelphia, 1840. $12,000—perhaps much more.
Porter, Eleanor H.	POLLYANNA. Boston, 1913. $350-425.
Porter, Gene Stratton	LADDIE: A TRUE-BLUE STORY. New York, 1913. $125-175.
Porter, Jane	THE SCOTTISH CHIEFS: A ROMANCE. 5 vols. London, 1810. $700-850.
Post, Melville Davisson	THE CORRECTOR OF DESTINIES. New York, (1908). $550-650.
Post, Melville Davisson	UNCLE ABNER. New York, 1918. $450-550.
Powell, Anthony	AFTERNOON MEN. London, 1931. $225-275.
Pynchon, Thomas	GRAVITY'S RAINBOW. New York, (1973). $125-150.
Pynchon, Thomas	V. Philadelphia, (1963). $325-375.
Quiller-Couch, Sir Arthur	IN POWDER AND CRINOLINE. London, (ca. 1913). Illustrated by Kay Nielsen. $500 or more.
Rand, Ayn	ATLAS SHRUGGED. New York, 1957. $125-150.
Rand, Ayn	THE FOUNTAINHEAD. Indianapolis, (1943). $175-225.
Rand, Ayn	WE THE LIVING. London, (1936). $600-750.

AUTHOR	TITLE/EDITION INFORMATION/VALUE
Reade, Charles	THE CLOISTER AND THE HEARTH. 4 vols. London, 1861. $1,200 or more.
Reid, Mayne	NO QUARTER! 3 vols. London, 1888. $375-425.
Reid, Mayne	OSCEOLA THE SEMINOLE. New York, (1858). $325-375.
Reid, Mayne	THE QUADROON; OR, A LOVER'S ADVENTURES IN LOUISIANA. 3 vols. London, 1856. $550-650.
Reid, Mayne	THE WHITE CHIEF: A LEGEND OF NORTHERN MEXICO. 3 vols. London, 1855. $450-550.
Reid, Mayne	THE WILD HUNTRESS. 3 vols. London, 1861. $450-550.
Reid, Mayne	THE WOOD-RANGERS. 3 vols. London, 1860. $450-550.
Remarque, Erich Maria	ALL QUIET ON THE WESTERN FRONT. London, (1929). $125-175.
Richter, Conrad	BROTHERS OF NO KIN AND OTHER STORIES. New York, (ca. 1924). $275-325.
Riley, James Whitcomb	THE FLYING ISLANDS OF THE NIGHT. Indianapolis, 1892. $175-225.
Robbins, Tom	ANOTHER ROADSIDE ATTRACTION. Garden City, N.Y., 1971. $175-225.
Robbins, Tom	EVEN COWGIRLS GET THE BLUES. Boston, 1976. $100-125.
Salinger, J. D.	THE CATCHER IN THE RYE. Boston, 1951. $375-450.
Salinger, J. D.	NINE STORIES. Boston, (1953). $375-425.
Salinger, J. D.	RAISE HIGH THE ROOF BEAM, CARPENTERS, AND SEYMOUR: AN INTRODUCTION. Boston, (1959). $225-275.
Saroyan, William	THE DARING YOUNG MAN ON THE FLYING TRAPEZE. New York, 1934. $125-175.

AUTHOR	TITLE/EDITION INFORMATION/VALUE
Shaw, George Bernard	PYGMALION: A ROMANCE IN FIVE ACTS. London, 1913. $700-800.
Smith, F. Hopkinson	COLONEL CARTER OF CARTERSVILLE. Boston, 1891. $110-135.
Smith, Johnston	MAGGIE: A GIRL OF THE STREETS. (New York, 1893). Wrappers. $5,500 or more.
Stapleton, Olaf	DARKNESS AND THE LIGHT. London, (1942). $175-225.
Steinbeck, John	CANNERY ROW. New York, 1945. $125-150.
Steinbeck, John	EAST OF EDEN. New York, 1952. Trade edition. $125-175.
Steinbeck, John	THE GRAPES OF WRATH. New York, (1939). $425-475.
Steinbeck, John	IN DUBIOUS BATTLE. New York, (1936). Trade edition. $250-325.
Steinbeck, John	THE MOON IS DOWN. New York, 1942. $110-135.
Steinbeck, John	OF MICE AND MEN. New York, (1937). $175-250.
Steinbeck, John	THE PASTURES OF HEAVEN. New York, 1932. $1,000 or more.
Steinbeck, John	THEIR BLOOD IS STRONG. San Francisco, 1938. Wrappers. $375-450.
Steinbeck, John	TO A GOD UNKNOWN. New York, (1933). $800 or more.
Steinbeck, John	TORTILLA FLAT. New York, (1935). $450 or more.
Stephens, James	THE CROCK OF GOLD. London, 1912. $500 or more.
Stevenson, Robert Louis	THE BLACK ARROW. New York, 1916. Illustrated by N. C. Wyeth. $275-325.
Stevenson, Robert Louis	ISLAND NIGHT'S ENTERTAINMENT. New York, 1893. $250-300.
Stevenson, Robert Louis	KIDNAPPED. New York, 1913. Illustrated by N. C. Wyeth. $275-325.

AUTHOR	TITLE/EDITION INFORMATION/VALUE
Stevenson, Robert Louis	NEW ARABIAN NIGHTS. 2 vols. London, 1882. $550-650.
Stevenson, Robert Louis	THE SILVERADO SQUATTERS. $350-425.
Stevenson, Robert Louis	TREASURE ISLAND. Boston, 1884. $800 or more.
Stockton, Frank R.	THE FLOATING PRINCE AND OTHER FAIRY TALES. New York, 1881. $175-225.
Stockton, Frank R.	THE LADY, OR THE TIGER? AND OTHER STORIES. New York, 1884. $150-175.
Stockton, Frank R.	TING-A-LING. New York, 1870. $300-375.
Stowe, Harriett Beecher	DRED: A TALE OF THE GREAT DISMAL SWAMP. 2 vols. Boston, 1856. $275-350.
Stowe, Harriett Beecher	UNCLE TOM'S CABIN. 2 vols. Boston, 1852. $5,000 or more.
Stribling, T. S.	THE CRUISE OF THE DRYDOCK. Chicago, (1917). $175-225.
Stuart, Jesse	MAN WITH A BULL-TONGUE PLOW. (New York, 1934). $275-350.
Styron, William	LIE DOWN IN DARKNESS. Indianapolis, (1951). $175-225.
Styron, William	THIS QUIET DUST. (New York, 1967). Wrappers. $350-400.
Synge, John M.	IN THE SHADOW OF THE GLEN. New York, 1904. Limited edition of 50. $1,200 or more.
Tarkington, Booth	THE GENTLEMAN FROM INDIANA. New York, 1899. $175-225.
Tarkington, Booth	PENROD. Garden City, New York, 1914. $1,100 or more.
Tarkington, Booth	PENROD AND SAM. Garden City, N.Y., 1916. $275-350.

AUTHOR	TITLE/EDITION INFORMATION/VALUE
Tarkington, Booth	SEVENTEEN. New York, (1916). $175-225.
Tarkington, Booth	THE TWO VANREVELS. New York, 1902. $250-300.

16

Literary Works/Poetry/Belles-Lettres, and Their Values

Here again I have listed the better-known writers, with emphasis on the contemporary. It is reasonable to presume that all first editions by any of the authors listed will have value, but do *not* assume that all books by the same author will have comparable values.

The values given here are for first-edition books in very good to fine condition, and with a dust jacket if the book was originally issued with one. "Points" often need to be verified to properly identify many of these books. A librarian or rare bookseler should be consulted for verification of edition and value.

AUTHOR	TITLE/EDITION INFORMATION/VALUE
Adams, Henry	THE EDUCATION OF HENRY ADAMS. Washington, D.C., 1907. Trade edition. $115.
Adams, Leonie	HIGH FALCON AND OTHER POEMS. New York, 1929. $125.
Adams, Richard	WATERSHIP DOWN. New York, 1974. $125.
Ade, George	ARTIE. Chicago, 1896. $75.
Ade, George	FABLES IN SLANG. Chicago, 1900. $75.
Agee, James	A DEATH IN THE FAMILY. New York, 1957. $150.
Agee, James	LET US NOW PRAISE FAMOUS MEN. Boston, 1941. $325.
Aiken, Conrad	BLUE VOYAGE. New York, 1927. $135.

AUTHOR	TITLE/EDITION INFORMATION/VALUE
Aiken, Conrad	EARTH TRIUMPHANT AND OTHER TALES IN VERSE. New York, 1914. $175.
Albee, Edward	THE AMERICAN DREAM. New York, 1961. $75.
Alcott, Louisa May	FLOWER FABLES. Boston, 1855. $225.
Aldington, Richard	IMAGES (1910-1915). London, 1915. Wrappers. $275.
Aldrich, Thomas Bailey	THE BALLAD OF BABIE BELL AND OTHER POEMS. New York, 1859. $125.
Aldrich, Thomas Bailey	THE STORY OF A BAD BOY. Boston, 1870. $450.
Algren, Nelson	THE MAN WITH THE GOLDEN ARM. Garden City, N.Y., 1949. $85.
Algren, Nelson	SOMEBODY IN BOOTS. New York, 1935. $425.
Allen, James Lane	FLUTE AND VIOLIN. New York, 1891. $75.
Amis, Kingsley	BRIGHT NOVEMBER. London, 1947. $175.
Anderson, Sherwood	WINDY MC PHERSON'S SON. New York, 1916. $850 or more.
Arthur, T. S.	TEN NIGHTS IN A BAR-ROOM, AND WHAT I SAW THERE. Philadelphia, 1854. $225.
Baldwin, James	GO TELL IT ON THE MOUNTAIN. New York, 1953. $375.
Bangs, John Kendrick	BIKEY THE SKICYCLE AND OTHER TALES OF JIMMIE BOY. New York, 1902. $85.
Barnes, Djuna	THE BOOK OF REPULSIVE WOMEN. New York, 1915. Gold wrappers. $450.
Barrie, Sir James M.	THE LITTLE MINISTER. New York, 1891. Wrappers. $165.
Barth, John	THE FLOATING OPERA. New York, 1956. $325.

AUTHOR	TITLE/EDITION INFORMATION/VALUE
Barth, John	THE SOT-WEED FACTOR. Garden City, N.Y., 1960. $350.
Beecher, Harriet Elizabeth	PRIZE-TALE: A NEW ENGLAND SKETCH. Lowell Mass., 1834. Wrappers. $825.
Bellamy, Edward	LOOKING BACKWARD, 2000-1887. Boston, 1888. $425.
Bellow, Saul	THE ADVENTURES OF AUGIE MARCH. New York, 1953. $150.
Bellow, Saul	HENDERSON THE RAIN KING. New York, 1959. $125.
Bemelmans, Ludwig	MADELINE. New York, 1930. $110.
Benet, Stephen Vincent	FIVE MEN AND POMPEY. Boston, 1915. $225.
Berger, Thomas	CRAZY IN BERLIN. New York, 1958. $95.
Bessie, Alvah	DWELL IN THE WILDERNESS. New York, 1935. $125.
Bierce, Ambrose	TALES OF SOLDIERS AND CIVILIANS. San Francisco, 1891. $325.
Bowen, Elizabeth	ANN LEE'S AND OTHER STORIES. New York, 1927. $85.
Boyle, Kay	PLAGUED BY THE NIGHTINGALE. New York, 1931. $135.
Cable, George W.	OLD CREOLE DAYS. New York, 1879. $275.
Cain, James M.	SERENADE. New York, 1937. $135.
Caldwell, Erskine	GOD'S LITTLE ACRE. New York, 1933. $175.
Caldwell, Erskine	TOBACCO ROAD. New York, 1932. $275.
Callaghan, Morley	STRANGE FUGITIVE. New York, 1928. $250.
Capote, Truman	BREAKFAST AT TIFFANY'S. New York, 1958. $125.

AUTHOR	TITLE/EDITION INFORMATION/VALUE
Capote, Truman	OTHER VOICES, OTHER ROOMS. New York, 1948. $165.
Caskoden, Edwin	WHEN KNIGHTHOOD WAS IN FLOWER. Indianapolis, 1898. $85.
Castaneda, Carlos	THE TEACHINGS OF DON JUAN/A YAQUI WAY OF KNOWLEDGE. Berkeley, Calif., 1968. $85.
Cather, Willa	APRIL TWILIGHTS. Boston, 1903. No dust jacket. $1,000 or more.
Cheever, John	THE ENORMOUS RADIO AND OTHER STORIES. New York, 1953. $135.
Cheever, John	THE WAPSHOT CHRONICLE. New York, 1957. $75.
Chivers, Thomas Holley	THE PATH OF SORROW. Franklin, Tenn., 1832. $475.
Collins, Wilkie	THE WOMAN IN WHITE. New York, 1860. $425.
Corelli, Marie	BARABBAS. 3 vols. London, 1893. $175.
Costain, Thomas B.	THE SILVER CHALICE. Garden City, N.Y., 1952. $20.
Cozzens, James Gould	BY LOVE POSSESSED. New York, 1957. $65.
Crane, Stephen	THE LITTLE REGIMENT AND OTHER EPISODES OF THE AMERICAN CIVIL WAR. New York, 1896. $375.
Crane, Stephen	THE RED BADGE OF COURAGE. New York, 1895. $1,000 or more.
Dahl, Roald	KISS KISS. New York, 1960. $65.
Davis, Richard Harding	GALLEGHER AND OTHER STORIES. New York, 1891. Wrappers. $225.
Dell, Floyd	WOMEN AS WORLD BUILDERS. Chicago, 1913. $125.
Deutsch, Babette	BANNERS. New York, 1919. $135.
Didion, Joan	RUN RIVER. New York, 1963. $125.

AUTHOR	TITLE/EDITION INFORMATION/VALUE
Didion, Joan	SLOUCHING TOWARD BETHLEHEM. New York, 1968. $85.
Doctorow, E. L.	RAGTIME. New York, 1966. $85.
Doctorow, E. L.	WELCOME TO HARD TIMES. New York, 1960. $125.
Dodge, M. E.	THE IRVINGTON STORIES. New York, 1965. $125.
Dos Passos, John	THE 42ND PARALLEL. New York, 1930. $135.
Dos Passos, John	THREE SOLDIERS. New York, 1921. $475.
Dreiser, Theodore	AN AMERICAN TRAGEDY. 2 vols. New York, 1925. $150.
Dreiser, Theodore	JENNIE GERHARDT. New York, 1911. $275.
Dunbar, Paul Lawrence	HOWDY, HONEY, HOWDY. New York, 1905. $225.
Dunbar, Paul Lawrence	LYRICS OF LOWLY LIFE. New York, 1908. $150.
Eddison, E. R.	THE WORM OUROBOROS. New York, 1926. $85.
Edmonds, Walter D.	DRUMS ALONG THE MOHAWK. Boston, 1936. $125.
Eggleston,Edward	THE BOOK OF QUEER STORIES, AND STORIES TOLD ON A CELLAR DOOR. Chicago, 1871. $275.
Eggleston, Edward	THE HOOSIER SCHOOLMASTER. New York, 1871. $275.
Ellison, Harlan	RUMBLE. New York, 1958. Wrappers. $75.
Ellison, Ralph	INVISIBLE MAN. New York, 1952. $135.
Farrell, James T.	CALICO SHOES AND OTHER STORIES. New York, 1934. $225.
Farrell, James T.	GAS-HOUSE MC GINTY. New York, 1933. $165.

AUTHOR	TITLE/EDITION INFORMATION/VALUE
Farrell, James T.	YOUNG LONIGAN: A BOYHOOD IN CHICAGO STREETS. New York, 1932. $250.
Faulkner, William	AS I LAY DYING. New York, 1930. $750 or more.
Faulkner, William	DOCTOR MARTINO AND OTHER STORIES. New York, 1934. Trade edition. $500.
Fearing, Kenneth	ANGEL ARMS. New York, 1929. $135.
Fearing, Kenneth	THE BIG CLOCK. New York, 1946. $75.
Ferber, Edna	DAWN O'HARA: THE GIRL WHO LAUGHED. New York, 1911. $165.
Ferber, Edna	GIANT. Garden City, N.Y., 1952. $75.
Fisher, Vardis	CHILDREN OF GOD, AN AMERICAN EPIC. Caldwell, Idaho, 1939. Trade edition. $65.
Fisher, Vardis	SONNETS TO AN IMAGINARY MADONNA. New York, 1927. $125.
Fitzgerald, F. Scott	ALL THE SAD YOUNG MEN. New York, 1926. $1,000 or more.
Fitzgerald, F. Scott	THE GREAT GATSBY. New York, 1925. $3,500 or more.
Fitzgerald, F. Scott	TENDER IS THE NIGHT. New York, 1934. $750 or more.
Fitzgerald, F. Scott	THIS SIDE OF PARADISE. New York, 1920. $1,500 or more.
Fitzgerald, Zelda	SAVE ME THE WALTZ. New York, 1932. $500.
Flanner, Janet	THE CUBICAL CITY. New York, 1926. $85.
Ford, Ford Madox	IT WAS THE NIGHTINGALE. London, 1934. $75.
Ford, Paul Leicester	THE HONORABLE PETER STIRLING AND WHAT PEOPLE THOUGHT OF HIM. New York, 1894. $165.
Forester, C. S.	THE AFRICAN QUEEN. Boston, 1935. $300.
Forester, C. S.	LIEUTENANT HORNBLOWER. Boston, 1952. $50.

AUTHOR	TITLE/EDITION INFORMATION/VALUE
Fowles, John	THE COLLECTOR. Boston, 1963. $150.
Fowles, John	THE FRENCH LIEUTENANT'S WOMAN. Boston, 1969. $85.
Gardner, John	RESURRECTION. New York, 1966. $750.
Garland, Hamlin	MAIN-TRAVELLED ROADS. Boston, 1891. $275.
Garland, Hamlin	A SON OF THE MIDDLE BORDER. New York, 1917. Trade edition. $75.
Gaskell, Elizabeth C.	SYLVIA'S LOVERS. 3 vols. London, 1893. $850.
Gershwin, George	GEORGE GERSHWIN'S SONG-BOOK. New York, 1932. Trade edition. $125.
Gibran, Kahlil	SAND AND FOAM. New York, 1926. Limited and signed edition. $250.
Glasgow, Ellen	THE FREEMAN AND OTHER POEMS. New York, 1902. $300.
Godwin, Gail	THE PERFECTIONISTS. New York, 1970. $65.
Golding, William	LORD OF THE FLIES. New York, 1954. $500 or more.
Goodman, Paul	TEN LYRIC POEMS. New York, 1934. 8 leaves. $225.
Gordon, Caroline	THE GARDEN OF ADONIS. New York, 1937. $125.
Gordon, Caroline	PENHALLY. New York, 1931. $300.
Gorey, Edward	THE BUG BOOK. New York, 1959. $125.
Gorey, Edward	THE LISTING ATTIC. New York, 1954. $165.
Grau, Shirley Ann	THE BLACK PRINCE AND OTHER STORIES. New York, 1955. $125.
Greaves, Richard	BREWSTER'S MILLIONS. Chicago, 1903. $65.
Green, Anna Katharine	THE CIRCULAR STUDY. New York, 1900. $350.

AUTHOR	**TITLE/EDITION INFORMATION/VALUE**
Green, Anna Katharine	HAND AND RING. New York, 1883. $125.
Gregory, Horace	CHELSEA ROOMING HOUSE. New York, 1930. $125.
Guthrie, A. B., Jr.	THE BIG SKY. New York, 1947. Trade edition. $35.
Hale, Lucretia P.	LAST OF THE PETERKINS. Boston, 1886. $125.
Hale, Lucretia P.	THE PETERKIN PAPERS. Boston, 1880. $275.
Hale, Sarah Josepha	NORTHWOOD: A TALE OF NEW ENGLAND. 2 vols. Boston, 1827. $125.
Hall, James Norman	KITCHENER'S MOB. Boston, 1916. $85.
Hamilton, Gail	A WOMAN'S WRONGS: A COUNTER-IRRITANT. Boston, 1868. $145.
Harris, Joel Chandler	DADDY JAKE THE RUNAWAY. New York, 1889. $325.
Harris, Joel Chandler	FREE JOE AND OTHER GEORGIAN SKETCHES. New York, 1887. $225.
Harris, Joel Chandler	THE TAR-BABY AND OTHER RHYMES OF UNCLE REMUS. New York, 1904. $225.
Harris, Joel Chandler	UNCLE REMUS: HIS SONGS AND HIS SAYINGS. New York, 1881. $650.
Harte, Bret	THE LOST GALLEON AND OTHER TALES. San Francisco, 1867. $425.
Harte, Bret	THE LUCK OF ROARING CAMP AND OTHER SKETCHES. Boston, 1870. $575.
Hawthorne, Nathaniel	THE CELESTIAL RAIL-ROAD. Boston, 1843. Wrappers. $1,750 or more.
Hawthorne, Nathaniel	THE HOUSE OF THE SEVEN GABLES. Boston, 1851. $750.
Hawthorne, Nathaniel	THE MARBLE FAUN: OR THE ROMANCE OF MONTE BENI. 2 vols. Boston, 1860. $650.

AUTHOR	TITLE/EDITION INFORMATION/VALUE
Hearn, Lafcadio	CHITA: A MEMORY OF LAST ISLAND. New York, 1889. $225.
Hearn, Lafcadio	"GOMBO ZHEBES": LITTLE DICTIONARY OF CREOLE PROVERBS. New York, 1885. $275.
Irving, John	SETTING FREE THE BEARS. New York, 1968. $225.
Irving, John	THE WORLD ACCORDING TO GARP. New York, 1978. $65.
Irving, Washington	ASTORIA, OR ANECDOTES OF AN ENTERPRISE BEYOND THE ROCKY MOUNTAINS. 2 vols. Philadelphia, 1836. $1,200 or more.
Irving, Washington	VOYAGES AND DISCOVERIES OF THE COMPANIONS OF COLUMBUS. Philadelphia, 1831. $350.
Jackson, Helen Hunt	RAMONA. Boston, 1884. $375.
Jackson, Shirley	THE LOTTERY. New York, 1949. $145.
Jackson, Shirley	THE ROAD THROUGH THE WALL. New York, 1948. $175.
James, Henry	DAISY MILLER: A STUDY. New York, 1879. Cloth or wrappers. $175.
James, Henry	A PASSIONATE PILGRIM, AND OTHER TALES. Boston, 1875. $1,000 or more.
Jarrell, Randall	BLOOD FOR A STRANGER. New York, 1942. $425.
Jarrell, Randall	THE SEVEN-LEAGUE CRUTCHES. New York, 1951. $175.
Jeffers, Robinson	CALIFORNIANS. New York, 1916. $50.
Jewett, Sarah Orne	BETTY LEICESTER'S ENGLISH CHRISTMAS. Boston, 1894. $225.
Johnson, James Weldon	GOD'S TROMBONES. New York, 1927. $145.

AUTHOR	TITLE/EDITION INFORMATION/VALUE
Jong, Erica	FRUITS AND VEGETABLES, POEMS. New York, 1971. $85.
Kantor, MacKinlay	ANDERSONVILLE. Cleveland, 1955. Trade edition. $35.
Kerouac, Jack	BIG SUR. New York, 1962. $85.
Kerouac, Jack	THE DHARMA BUMS. New York, 1958. $150.
Kesey, Ken	ONE FLEW OVER THE CUCKOO'S NEST. New York, 1962. $350.
Kilmer, Joyce	TREES AND OTHER POEMS. New York, 1914. $225.
Kosinski, Jerzy	THE PAINTED BIRD. Boston, 1965. $375.
Lanier, Sidney	TIGER-LILIES. New York, 1867. $175.
Lardner, Ring W.	BIB BALLADS. Chicago, 1915. $300 or more.
Lardner, Ring W.	GULLIBLE'S TRAVELS. Indianapolis, 1917. $375.
Lazarus, Emma	SONGS OF A SEMITE. New York, 1882. $175.
Lewis, Alfred Henry	WOLFVILLE. New York, 1897. $225.
Lewis, Sinclair	ELMER GANTRY. New York, 1927. $200.
Lewis, Sinclair	OUR MR. WRENN. New York, 1914. $500.
Liebling, A. J.	THE TELEPHONE BOOTH INDIAN. Garden City, N.Y., 1942. $125.
Lin, Frank	WHAT DREAMS MAY COME. Chicago, 1888. $450.
London, Jack	BURNING DAYLIGHT. New York, 1910. $325.
London, Jack	THE STAR ROVER. New York, 1915. $1,200 or more.
London, Jack	WHITE FANG. New York, 1906. $500 or more.

AUTHOR	**TITLE/EDITION INFORMATION/VALUE**
McCullers, Carson	THE HEART IS A LONELY HUNTER. Boston, 1940. $350.
McCutcheon, George Barr	GRAUSTARK. Chicago, 1901. $85.
McKuen, Rod	AND AUTUMN CAME. New York, 1954. $125.
McMurtry, Larry	THE LAST PICTURE SHOW. New York, 1966. $150.
McMurtry, Larry	LEAVING CHEYENNE. New York, 1963. $225.
Mailer, Norman	THE NAKED AND THE DEAD. New York, 1948. $325.
Neihardt, John G.	THE DIVINE ENCHANTMENT: A MYSTICAL POEM. New York, 1900. $275.
Nin, Anais	LADDERS TO FIRE. New York, 1946. $85.
Norris, Frank	MC TEAGUE: A STORY OF SAN FRANCISCO. New York, 1899. $450.
Norris, Frank	YVERNELLE: A LEGEND OF FUEDAL FRANCE. Philadelphia, 1892. $1,000 or more.
Oates, Joyce Carol	BY THE NORTH GATE. New York, 1963. $165.
Oates, Joyce Carol	A GARDEN OF EARTHLY DELIGHTS. New York, 1967. $150.
O'Brien, Tim	IF I DIE IN A COMBAT ZONE. New York, 1973. $325.
O'Connor, Flannery	A GOOD MAN IS HARD TO FIND. New York, 1955. $235.
O'Connor, Flannery	WISE BLOOD. New York, 1952. $325.
Odets, Clifford	GOLDEN BOY. New York, 1937. $85.
O'Hara, John	APPOINTMENT IN SAMARRA. Trade edition. $425.
O'Hara, John	BUTTERFIELD 8. New York, 1935. $165.

AUTHOR	TITLE/EDITION INFORMATION/VALUE
Olson, Charles	CALL ME ISHMAEL. New York, 1947. $200.
O'Neill, Eugene	ALL GOD'S CHILLUN GOT WINGS, AND WELDED. New York, 1924. $125.
Parker, Dorothy	LAMENTS FOR THE LIVING. New York, 1930. $125.
Peck, George Wilbur	PECK'S BAD BOY AND HIS PA. Chicago, 1883. Wrappers. $375.
Percy, Walker	LOVE IN THE RUINS. New York, 1971. $75.
Percy, Walker	DAWN GINSBERGH'S REVENGE. New York, 1929. $275.
Phylos the Tibetian	AN EARTH DWELLER'S RETURN. Milwaukee, Wis., 1940. $85.
Porter, Katherine Anne	NOON WINE. Detroit, 1937. Limited and signed edition. $225.
Porter, Katherine Anne	PALE HORSE, PALE RIDER. New York, 1939. $85.
Post, Melville Davisson	THE CORRECTOR OF DESTINIES. New York, 1908. $650.
Post, Melville Davisson	UNCLE ABNER. New York, 1918. $500 or more.
Pynchon, Thomas	THE CRYING OF LOT 49. Philadelphia, 1966. $150.
Pynchon, Thomas	GRAVITY'S RAINBOW. New York, 1973. $135.
Rand, Ayn	ATLAS SHRUGGED. New York, 1957. $150.
Rand, Ayn	THE FOUNTAINHEAD. Indianapolis, 1943. $150.
Ransom, John Crowe	POEMS ABOUT GOD. New York, 1919. $450.
Reznikoff, Charles	RHYTHMS. Brooklyn, 1918. $850 or more.
Richter, Conrad	BROTHERS OF NO KIN AND OTHER STORIES. New York, ca.1924. $325.

AUTHOR	TITLE/EDITION INFORMATION/VALUE
Riding, Laura	THE CLOSE CHAPLET. New York, 1926. $450 or more.
Riley, James Whitcomb	THE FLYING ISLANDS OF THE NIGHT. Indianapolis, 1892. $225.
Riley, James Whitcomb	RHYMES OF CHILDHOOD. Indianapolis, 1891. $100.
Robbins, Tom	ANOTHER ROADSIDE ATTRACTION. Garden City, N.Y., 1971. $225.
Robbins, Tom	EVEN COWGIRLS GET THE BLUES. Boston, 1976. $135.
Salinger, J. D.	THE CATCHER IN THE RYE. Boston, 1951. $375-450.
Salinger, J. D.	RAISE HIGH THE ROOF BEAM, CARPENTERS, AND SEYMOUR: AN INTRODUCTION. Boston, 1959. $225-275.
Saroyan, William	THE DARING YOUNG MAN ON THE FLYING TRAPEZE. New York, 1934. $175.
Sarton, May	ENCOUNTER IN APRIL. Boston, 1938. $165.
Saunders, Marshall	BEAUTIFUL JOE: AN AUTOBIOGRAPHY. Philadelphia, 1894. $175.
Schwartz, Delmore	IN DREAMS BEGIN RESPONSIBILITIES. Norfolk, Canada, 1938. $275.
Shaw, Irwin	BURY THE DEAD. New York, 1936. $90.
Simms, William Gilmore	AREYTOS; OR, SONGS OF THE SOUTH. Charleston, S.C., 1846. Wrappers. $450.
Sinclair, Upton	THE JUNGLE. New York, 1906. $125.
Sinclair, Upton	SPRINGTIME AND HARVEST. New York, 1910. $275.
Tarkington, Booth	THE GENTLEMAN FROM INDIANA. New York, 1899. $225.
Tarkington, Booth	MONSIEUR BEAUCAIRE. New York, 1900. $135.

AUTHOR	TITLE/EDITION INFORMATION/VALUE
Tate, Allen	MR. POPE AND OTHER POEMS. New York, 1928. $350.
Tate, Allen	STONEWALL JACKSON, THE GOOD SOLDIER: A NARRATIVE. New York, 1928. $275.
Teasdale, Sara	LOVE SONGS. New York, 1917. $150.
Teasdale, Sara	SONNETS TO DUSE AND OTHER POEMS. Boston, 1907. $275.
Terhune, Albert Payson	CALEB CONOVER, RAILROADER. New York, 1907. $125.
Thompson, Kay	ELOISE. New York, 1955. $125.
Thompson, Maurice	ALICE OF OLD VINCENNES. Indianapolis, 1900. $175.
Updike, John	RABBIT, RUN. New York, 1960. $165.
Updike, John	THE SAME DOOR. New York, 1959. $175.
Van Vechten, Carl	MUSIC AFTER THE GREAT WAR. New York, 1915. $150.
Van Vechten, Carl	THE TIGER IN THE HOUSE. New York, 1920. $85.
Vidal, Gore	WILLIWAW. New York, 1946. $135.
Vonnegut, Kurt, Jr.	CANARY IN A CAT HOUSE. Greenwich, Conn., 1961. $125.
Vonnegut, Kurt, Jr.	PLAYER PIANO. New York, 1952. $225.
Wakoski, Diane	COINS AND COFFINS. New York, 1962. Wrappers. $135.
Wallace, Lew	BEN HUR: A TALE OF THE CHRIST. New York, 1880. $325.
Ward, Lynd	VERTIGO: A NOVEL IN WOODCUTS. New York, 1937. $200.
Ward, Mary Jane	THE SNAKE PIT. New York, 1946. $65.

AUTHOR	TITLE/EDITION INFORMATION/VALUE
Warren, Robert Penn	JOHN BROWN: THE MAKING OF A MARTYR. New York, 1929. $450 or more.
Washington, Booker T.	THE FUTURE OF THE AMERICAN NEGRO. Boston, 1899. $275.
Weidman, Jerome	I CAN GET IT FOR YOU WHOLESALE. New York, 1937. $75.
Welty, Eudora	A CURTAIN OF GREEN. Garden City, N.Y., 1941. $350 or more.
Welty, Eudora	THE ROBBER BRIDEGROOM. Garden City, N.Y., 1942. $225.
West, Nathanael	A COOL MILLION. New York, 1934. $325.
West, Nathanael	MISS LONELYHEARTS. New York, 1933. $650 or more.
West, Rebecca	THE RETURN OF THE SOLDIER. New York, 1918. $175.
Westcott, Edward Noyes	DAVID HARUM. New York, 1898. $125.
Wharton, Edith	ETHAN FROME. New York, 1911. $375.
White, E. B.	CHARLOTTE'S WEB. New York, 1952. $175.
White, T. H.	MISTRESS MASHAM'S REPOSE. New York, 1946. $85.
Williams, Tennessee	THE GLASS MENAGERIE. New York, 1945. $185.
Williams, Tennessee	A STREETCAR NAMED DESIRE. Norfolk, Va., 1947. $325.
Wilson, Edmund	MEMOIRS OF HECATE COUNTY. Garden City, N.Y., 1946. $125.
Wilson, Edmund	THIS ROOM & THIS GIN & THESE SANDWICHES. New York, 1937. Wrappers. $275.

-17-

Science Fiction/Fantasy/Horror Books, and Their Values

The authors and titles presented here are those that are best known to the general public. It is reasonable to presume that all first editions by any of the authors listed will have value, but do *not* assume that all books by the same author will have comparable values.

The values given here are for first-edition books in very good to fine condition, and with a dust jacket if the book was originally issued with one. "Points" often need to be verified to properly identify many of these books. A librarian or rare bookseller should be consulted for verification of edition and value.

AUTHOR	TITLE/EDITION INFORMATION/VALUE
Aldiss, Brian	THE BRIGHTFOUNT DIARIES. London, (1955). $65-90.
Anderson, Poul	THE BROKEN SWORD. New York, (1954). $85-100.
Anderson, Poul	VAULTS OF THE AGES. Philadelphia, (1952). $80-100.
Asimov, Isaac	THE END OF ETERNITY. Garden City, N.Y., 1955. $80-100.
Asimov, Isaac	FOUNDATION. New York, (1951). $125-175.
Asimov, Isaac	FOUNDATION AND EMPIRE. New York, (1952). $135-160.
Asimov, Isaac	I, ROBOT. New York, (1950). $175-225.

AUTHOR	TITLE/EDITION INFORMATION/VALUE
Asimov, Isaac	PEBBLE IN THE SKY. Garden City, N.Y., 1950. $135-160.
Asimov, Isaac	SECOND FOUNDATION, (New York, 1953). $135-160.
Atterley, Joseph	A VOYAGE TO THE MOON. New York, 1827. $425-475.
Bangs, John Kendrick	A HOUSE-BOAT ON THE RIVER STYX. New York, 1896. $60-75.
Bishop, Zealia	THE CURSE OF YIG. Sauk City, Wis., 1953. $60-75.
Blackwood, Algernon	THE EMPTY HOUSE AND OTHER GHOST STORIES. London, 1906. $140-175.
Blackwood, Algernon	INCREDIBLE ADVENTURES. London, 1914. $140-165.
Blackwood, Algernon	THE LOST VALLEY. New York, 1914. $140-165.
Blavatsky, H. P.	NIGHTMARE TALES. London, 1892. $175-225.
Bradbury, Ray	THE ANTHEM SPRINTERS. New York, 1963. $85-110.
Bradbury, Ray	DANDELION WINE. Garden City, N.Y., 1957. $125-150.
Bradbury, Ray	DARK CARNIVAL. Sauk City, Wis., 1947. $425-475.
Bradbury, Ray	FAHRENHEIT 451. New York, (1953). $165-190. With wrappers, $45-60.
Bradbury, Ray	THE GOLDEN APPLES OF THE SUN. Garden City, N.Y., 1953. $60-75.
Bradbury, Ray	THE ILLUSTRATED MAN. Garden City, N.Y., 1951. $125-150.
Bradbury, Ray	THE MACHINERIES OF JOY. New York, 1964. $90-125.
Bradbury, Ray	THE MARTIAN CHRONICLES. Garden City, N.Y., 1950. $225-275.

AUTHOR	TITLE/EDITION INFORMATION/VALUE
Bradbury, Ray	A MEDICINE FOR MELANCHOLY. Garden City, N.Y., 1959. $60-75.
Bradbury, Ray	THE OCTOBER COUNTRY. New York, (1955). $135-160.
Bradbury, Ray	SWITCH ON THE NIGHT. New York, 1955. $60-75.
Burgess, Anthony	A CLOCKWORK ORANGE. London, (1962). $500 or more.
Burroughs, Edgar Rice	AT THE EARTH'S CORE. Chicago, 1922. $550-650.
Burroughs, Edgar Rice	BACK TO THE STONE AGE. Tarzana, Calif., (1937). $275-325.
Burroughs, Edgar Rice	THE CHESSMEN OF MARS. Chicago, 1922. $375-425.
Burroughs, Edgar Rice	A FIGHTING MAN OF MARS. New York, (1931). $125-150.
Burroughs, Edgar Rice	THE MASTER MIND OF MARS. Chicago, 1928. $125-175.
Burroughs, Edgar Rice	A PRINCESS OF MARS. Chicago, 1917. $550-650.
Burroughs, Edgar Rice	THUVIA, MAID OF MARS. Chicago, 1920. $400 or more.
Burroughs, Edgar Rice	THE WARLORD OF MARS. Chicago, 1919. $400 or more.
Campbell, John W.	INVADERS FROM THE INFINITE. Hicksville, N.Y., (1961). $60-85.
Clarke, Arthur C.	CHILDHOOD'S END. New York, (1953). $100-125.
Clarke, Arthur C.	EARTHLIGHT. New York, (1955). $85-100.
Clarke, Arthur C.	INTERPLANETARY FLIGHT. London, (1950). $85-100.
Cummings, Ray	THE GIRL IN THE GOLDEN ATOM. New York, 1923. $100-125.

AUTHOR	TITLE/EDITION INFORMATION/VALUE
De Camp, L. Sprague	DEMONS AND DINOSAURS. Sauk City, Wis., 1970. $60-75.
De Camp, L. Sprague, and Fletcher Pratt	LAND OF UNREASON. New York, (1942). $110-135.
Drake, Leah Bodine	A HORNBOOK FOR WITCHES. Sauk City, Wis., 1950. $650-750
Finney, Charles G.	THE CIRCUS OF DR. LAO. New York, 1935. $125-150.
Gernsback, Hugo	Ralph 124C41: A ROMANCE OF THE YEAR 2660. Boston, 1925. $550 or more.
Griffith, George	A HONEYMOON IN SPACE. London, 1901. $125-150.
Haggard, H. Rider	ALLAN QUATERMAIN. London, 1887. $175-225.
Haggard, H. Rider	ALLAN'S WIFE AND OTHER TALES. London, 1889. Trade edition. $125.
Haggard, H. Rider	AYESHA: THE RETURN OF SHE. London, 1905. $125.
Haggard, H. Rider	BLACK HEART AND WHITE HEART AND OTHER STORIES. London, 1900. $125.
Haggard, H. Rider	CETWAYO AND HIS WHITE NEIGHBOURS. London, 1882. $375.
Haggard, H. Rider	CLEOPATRA. London, 1889. Trade edition. $125.
Haggard, H. Rider	HEART OF THE WORLD. London, 1896. $150.
Haggard, H. Rider	KING SOLOMON'S MINES. London, 1885. $375.
Haggard, H. Rider	MONTEZUMA'S DAUGHTER. London, 1893. $125.

AUTHOR	TITLE/EDITION INFORMATION/VALUE
Haggard, H. Rider	PEARL MAIDEN. London, 1903. $150.
Haggard, H. Rider	SHE: A HISTORY OF ADVENTURE. New York, 1886. Wrappers. $325.
Haggard, H. Rider	STELLA FREGELIUS: A TALE OF THREE DESTINIES. New York, 1903. $160.
Heinlein, Robert	ASSIGNMENT IN ETERNITY. Reading, Pa., (1953). $100.
Heinlein, Robert	BEYOND THIS HORIZON. Reading, Pa., 1948. $125.
Heinlein, Robert	DOUBLE STAR. Garden City, N.Y., 1956. $100.
Heinlein, Robert	THE GREEN HILLS OF EARTH. Chicago, 1951. $225.
Heinlein, Robert	THE MAN WHO SOLD THE MOON. Chicago, 1950. $225.
Heinlein, Robert	REVOLT IN 2100. Chicago, 1953. $225.
Heinlein, Robert	ROCKET SHIP GALILEO. New York, 1947. $400.
Heinlein, Robert	THE ROLLING STONES. New York, 1952. $175.
Heinlein, Robert	STARMAN JONES. New York, 1953. $175.
Heinlein, Robert	STARSHIP TROOPERS. New York, 1959. $400.
Heinlein, Robert	STRANGER IN A STRANGE LAND. New York, 1961. $225.
Heinlein, Robert	TIME FOR THE STARS. New York, 1956. $175.
Hodgson, William Hope	THE HOUSE ON THE BORDERLAND AND OTHER NOVELS. Sauk City, Wis., 1946. $350.
Howard, Robert E.	ALWAYS COMES EVENING. Sauk City, Wis., 1957. $375.
Howard, Robert E.	THE COMING OF CONAN. New York, (1953). $150.

AUTHOR	TITLE/EDITION INFORMATION/VALUE
Howard, Robert E.	CONAN THE BARBARIAN. New York, (1954). $175.
Howard, Robert E.	CONAN THE CONQUEROR. New York, (1950). $225.
Howard, Robert E.	THE DARK MAN AND OTHERS. Sauk City, Wis., 1963. $275.
Howard, Robert E.	KING CONAN. New York, (1953). $150.
Howard, Robert E.	SKULL-FACE AND OTHERS. Sauk City, Wis., 1946. $425.
Howard, Robert E.	THE SWORD OF CONAN. New York, (1952). $175.
Hubbard, L. Ron	SLAVES OF SLEEP. Chicago, 1948. $175.
Hyne, C. J. Cutliffe	THE LOST CONTINENT. London, 1900. $125.
Judd, Cyril	OUTPOST MARS. New York, 1952. $65.
Kuttner, Henry, and C. L. Moore	NO BOUNDARIES. New York, 1955. $75.
Le Fanu, Joseph Sheridan	ALL IN THE DARK. 2 vols. London, 1866. $375.
Le Fanu, Joseph Sheridan	CHECKMATE. 3 vols. London, 1871. $500.
Le Fanu, Joseph Sheridan	CHRONICLES OF GOLDEN FRIARS. 3 vols. London, 1871. $450.
Le Fanu, Joseph Sheridan	THE EVIL GUEST. London, 1895. $450.
Le Fanu, Joseph Sheridan	GHOST STORIES AND TALES OF MYSTERY. Dublin, 1851. $675.
Le Fanu, Joseph Sheridan	GREEN TEA AND OTHER GHOST STORIES. Sauk City, Wis., 1945. $175.
Le Fanu, Joseph Sheridan	HAUNTED LIVES. 3 vols. London, 1868. $675.
Le Fanu, Joseph Sheridan	THE HOUSE BY THE CHURCHYARD. 3 vols. London, 1863. $600 or more.

AUTHOR	TITLE/EDITION INFORMATION/VALUE
Le Fanu, Joseph Sheridan	IN A GLASS DARKLY. 3 vols. London, 1872. $575.
Le Fanu, Joseph Sheridan	MADAME CROWL'S GHOST AND OTHER TALES OF MYSTERY. London, 1923. $275.
Le Fanu, Joseph Sheridan	THE WYVERN MYSTERY. 3 vols. London, 1869. $550.
Le Guin, Ursula	THE LEFT HAND OF DARKNESS. New York, (1969). $175.
Le Guin, Ursula	A WIZARD OF EARTHSEA. Berkeley, Calif., (1968). $175.
Leiber, Fritz	NIGHT'S BLACK AGENTS. Sauk City, Wis., 1947. $125.
Leinster, Murray	SIDEWISE IN TIME. Chicago, 1950. $125.
Lewis, Matthew Gregory	TALES OF WONDER. 2 vols. London, 1801. $550.
Long, Frank Belknap	THE HOUNDS OF TINDALOS. Sauk City, Wis., 1946. $100-125.
Lovecraft, H. P.	BEYOND THE WALL OF SLEEP. Sauk City, Wis., 1943. $600 or more.
Lovecraft, H. P.	THE CATS OF ULTHAR. Cassia, Fla., 1935. Wrappers. $175.
Lovecraft, H. P.	THE HAUNTER OF THE DARK. London, 1951. $200.
Lovecraft, H. P.	MARGINALIA. Sauk City, Wis., 1944. $250.
Lovecraft, H. P.	THE OUTSIDER AND OTHERS. Sauk City, Wis., 1939. $1,000 or more.
Lovecraft, H. P.	THE SHADOW OVER INNSMOUTH. Everett, Pa., 1936. $2,000 or more.
Lovecraft, H. P.	THE SHUNNED HOUSE. Athol, Mass., 1928. 59 pp. Unbound. $1,500 or more.
Lovecraft, H. P.	SOMETHING ABOUT CATS AND OTHER PIECES. Sauk City, Wis., 1949. $175.

AUTHOR	TITLE/EDITION INFORMATION/VALUE
McNall, Stanley	SOMETHING BREATHING. London, 1965. $85-110.
Merritt, Abraham	BURN WITCH BURN. New York, 1933. $165.
Merritt, Abraham	CREEP, SHADOW! Garden City, N.Y., 1934. $90.
Merritt, Abraham	DWELLERS IN THE MIRAGE. New York, 1932. $400.
Merritt, Abraham	THE FACE IN THE ABYSS. New York, 1931. $125.
Merritt, Abraham	THE FOX WOMAN AND OTHER STORIES. New York, (1949). $175.
Merritt, Abraham	THE MOON POOL. New York, 1919. $175.
Merritt, Abraham	THE SHIP OF ISHTAR. New York, 1926. $225.
Metcalfe, John	THE FEASTING DEAD. Sauk City, Wis., 1954. $60-75.
Moore, C. L.	NORTHWEST OF EARTH. New York, 1954. $75.
Moore, C. L.	SHAMBLEAU AND OTHERS. New York, 1953. $100.
Mundy, Talbot	C.I.D. New York, (1932). $75.
Mundy, Talbot	THE IVORY TRAIL. Indianapolis, (1919). $150.
Mundy, Talbot	JIMGRIM. New York, (1931). $125.
Mundy, Talbot	QUEEN CLEOPATRA. Indianapolis, 1929. Limited and signed edition. $125.
Mundy, Talbot	PURPLE PIRATE. New York, (1959). $45.
Mundy, Talbot	TROS OF SAMOTHRACE. New York, 1934. $225.
North, Andrew	PLAGUE SHIP. New York, 1956. $90.
Norton, Andre	STAR MAN'S SON, 2250 A.D. New York, (1952). $75.

AUTHOR	TITLE/EDITION INFORMATION/VALUE
Orwell, George	ANIMAL FARM: A FAIRY STORY. London, 1945. $500 or more.
Orwell, George	NINETEEN EIGHTY-FOUR. London, 1949. $475.
Parrish, Randall	PRISONERS OF CHANCE. Chicago, 1908. $50-75.
Parry, David M.	THE SCARLET EMPIRE. Indianapolis, 1908. $40-50.
Patlock, Robert	THE LIFE AND ADVENTURES OF PETER WILKINS, A CORNISH MAN. 2 vols. London, 1751. $800 or more.
Powers, J. F.	PRINCE OF DARKNESS AND OTHER STORIES. New York, 1947. $100-125.
Pratt, Fletcher	WELL OF THE UNICORN. New York, 1948. $50-75.
Pseudoman, Akkad	ZERO TO 80. N.p., 1937. $40-50.
Quinn, Seabury	ROADS. Sauk City, Wis., 1948. $65.
Radcliffe, Ann	THE MYSTERIES OF UDOLPHO. 4 vols. London, 1794. $650 or more.
Rohmer, Sax	SEVEN SINS. London, 1945. $125.
Roy, Lillian	THE PRINCE OF ATLANTIS. New York, (1929). $40-50.
Russell, Eric F.	DEEP SPACE. London, 1956. $50-75.
Serviss, Garrett P.	A COLUMBUS OF SPACE. New York, 1911. $175.
Serviss, Garrett P.	THE MOON METAL. New York, 1900. $275.
Shelley, Mary Wollstonecraft	FRANKENSTEIN; OR THE MODERN PROMETHEUS. 3 vols. London, 1818. $10,000 or more.

AUTHOR	TITLE/EDITION INFORMATION/VALUE
Sherriff, R. C.	THE HOPKINS MANUSCRIPT. London, 1939. $50.
Shiel, M. P.	CHILDREN OF THE WIND. London, 1923. $225.
Shiel, M. P.	THE LAST MIRACLE. London, 1906. $150.
Shiel, M. P.	PRINCE ZALESKI. London, 1895. $425.
Shiel, M. P.	THE PURPLE CLOUD. London, 1929. Limited and signed edition. $425.
Shiel, M. P.	SHAPES IN THE FIRE. London, 1896. $325.
Silverberg, Robert	STARMAN'S QUEST. New York, (1958). $45.
Simak, Clifford D.	THE CREATOR. (Los Angeles, 1946). Wrappers. $75.
Siodmak, Curt	F.P.I. DOES NOT REPLY. Boston, 1933. $45.
Smith, Clark Ashton	THE ABOMINATIONS OF YONDO. Sauk City, Wis., 1960. $90.
Smith, Clark Ashton	THE DARK CHATEAU AND OTHER POEMS. Sauk City, Wis., 1951. $325.
Smith, Clark Ashton	THE DOUBLE SHADOW AND OTHER FANTASIES. (Auburn, Calif., 1933). Wrappers. $225.
Smith, Clark Ashton	GENIUS LOCI AND OTHER TALES. Sauk City, Wis., 1948. $100.
Smith, Clark Ashton	LOST WORLDS. Sauk City, Wis., 1944. $160.
Smith, Clark Ashton	OUT OF SPACE AND TIME. Sauk City, Wis., 1942. $275.
Smith, Clark Ashton	SPELLS AND PHILTRES. Sauk City, Wis., 1958. $375.
Smith, Clark Ashton	THE STAR-TREADER AND OTHER POEMS. San Francisco, 1912. $175.
Smith, E. E.	GRAY LENSMAN. New York, n.d. $40.
Smith, E. E.	SKYLARK THREE. Philadelphia, 1948. Limited and signed edition. $110.

AUTHOR	TITLE/EDITION INFORMATION/VALUE
Smith, E. E.	SPACEHOUNDS OF IPC. Philadelphia, 1947. Limited and signed edition. $125.
Smith, George O.	NOMAD. Philadelphia, (1950). $35-50.
Smith, Jessie Wilcox	THE WATER BABIES. New York, (1916). $75-100.
Smith, Thorne	TURNABOUT. New York, 1931. $35-50.
Spencer, Edmund	THE FAERIE QUEENE. 1 or 2 vols. London, 1596. $10,000 or more.
Spielberg, Steven	CLOSE ENCOUNTERS OF THE THIRD KIND. New York, (1977). $50-75.
Spinrad, Norman	THE MEN IN THE JUNGLE. New York, 1967. $50-75.
Stevenson, Robert Louis	THE STRANGE CASE OF DR. JEKYLL AND MR. HYDE. London, 1886. Wrappers. $1,000 or more.
Stoker, Bram	DRACULA. (London), 1897. $1,000 or more.
Stoker, Bram	THE LADY OF THE SHROUD. London, 1909. $150.
Sturgeon, Theodore	MORE THAN HUMAN. New York, (1953). $275.
Sturgeon, Theodore	WITHOUT SORCERY. Philadelphia, (1948). $125.
Swift, Jonathan	A TALE OF A TUB. London, 1714. $100-125.
Swift, Jonathan	TRAVELS INTO SEVERAL REMOTE NATIONS OF THE WORLD, BY LEMUEL GULLIVER. 2 vols. London, 1724. $500 or more.
Taine, John	THE CRYSTAL HORDE. Philadelphia, 1952. Limited and signed edition. $85-110.
Taine, John	G.O.G. 606. Philadelphia, (1954). Limited and signed edition. $75-100.
Taine, John	SEEDS OF LIFE. Philadelphia, 1951. Limited and signed edition. $65-80.

AUTHOR	TITLE/EDITION INFORMATION/VALUE
Thomas, Issiah, Jr.	THE LILLIPUTIAN MASQUERADE. Worcester, Mass., 1802. Third edition. $500.
Train, Arthur, and Robert Williams Wood	THE MAN WHO ROCKED THE EARTH. New York, 1915. $125-150.
Twain, Mark	A CONNECTICUT YANKEE IN KING ARTHUR'S COURT. New York, 1889. $275-350.
Twain, Mark	THE CURIOUS REPUBLIC OF GONDOUR. New York, 1919. $175-225.
Twain, Mark	THE PRINCE AND THE PAUPER. London, 1881. $300 or more.
Vance, Jack	BIG PLANET. New York, (1957). Wrappers. $85-100.
Van Vogt, A. E.	SLAN: A STORY OF THE FUTURE. Sauk City, Wis., 1946. $225.
Van Vogt, A. E.	THE WEAPON MAKERS. Providence, R.I., (1947). $110.
Verne, Jules	FIVE WEEKS IN A BALLOON. New York, 1869. $150.
Verne, Jules	FROM THE EARTH TO THE MOON. New York, 1874. $250.
Verne, Jules	THE MYSTERIOUS ISLAND. Chicago, 1876. $125.
Verrill, A. Hyat	THE BRIDGE OF LIGHT. (Reading, Pa.), 1950. Limited and signed edition. $85-100.
Wallis, Dave	THE ONLY LOVERS LEFT ALIVE. New York, 1964. $30-40.
Walter, Elizabeth	IN THE MIST AND OTHER UNCANNY ENCOUNTERS. Sauk City, Wis., 1979. $25-35.
Wandrei, Donald	DARK ODYSSEY. St. Paul, Minn., (1931). Limited and signed edition. $135-160.

AUTHOR	TITLE/EDITION INFORMATION/VALUE
Wandrei, Donald	THE EYE AND THE FINGER. Sauk City, Wis., 1955. $100-125.
Wandrei, Donald	POEMS FOR MIDNIGHT. Sauk City, Wis., 1964. $85-110.
Wandrei, Donald	THE WEB OF EASTER ISLAND. Sauk City, Wis., 1948. $60-75.
Waterloo, Stanley	ARMAGEDDON. Chicago, (1898). $60-75.
Weinbaum, Stanley	THE RED PERIL. Reading, 1952. $35-50.
Wells, H. G.	THE ISLAND OF DR. MOREAU. New York, 1896. $150-175.
Wells, H. G.	TALES OF SPACE AND TIME. New York, 1899. $125-175.
Whitehead, Henry S.	JUMBEE AND OTHER UNCANNY TALES. Sauk City, Wis., 1944. $150.
Williamson, Jack	THE HUMANOIDS. New York, 1949. $75.
Wyndham, John	THE DAY OF THE TRIFFIDS. London, 1951. $275.

18

Miscellaneous Nonfiction Books, and Their Values

Here I am providing a sampling of the types of books that are of considerable value within each broad category. Subjects include medicine, ornithology, archaeology, business, industry, sports, architecture, ships and the sea, aviation, radio and television, publishing, science, religion, agriculture, railroads, automobiles, government, and more.

You will notice that a great many of the early nineteenth-century books were published in England, but this does not mean that they cannot be found in the United States. In those days most books were imported to this country, since our own native publishing industry was still in its infancy. So you are quite as likely to find these titles here as in Great Britain—perhaps even more likely.

The values given here are for first-edition books in very good to fine condition, and with a dust jacket if the book was originally issued with one. "Points" often need to be verified to properly identify many of these books. A librarian or rare bookseller should be consulted for verification of edition and value.

AUTHOR	TITLE/EDITION INFORMATION/VALUE
Adams, Ramon	THE RAMPAGING HERD. Norman Okla., 1959. $325.
Agassiz, Louis	LAKE SUPERIOR. Boston, 1850. $275.
Ainsworth, Ed	THE COWBOY IN ART. New York, 1968. $85.
Akerly, Lewis F.	THE GEOLOGY OF THE HUDSON RIVER. New York, 1820. $325.

AUTHOR	TITLE/EDITION INFORMATION/VALUE
Allison, William	THE BRITISH THROUGHBRED HORSE. London, 1901. $175.
Amsden, Charles A.	NAVAHO WEAVING. Santa Ana, Calif., 1934. $225.
Armitage, John	THE HISTORY OF BRAZIL. 2 vols. London, 1836. $750.
Ashley, Clifford W.	THE YANKEE WHALER. Boston, 1926. Trade edition. $275.
Ashton, John	REAL SAILOR-SONGS. London, 1891. $135.
Auscher, Ernest Simon	A HISTORY AND DESCRIPTION OF FRENCH PORCELAIN. London, 1905. $275.
Austin, Edward S.	THE HOUSEKEEPERS' MANUAL. Chicago, 1869. Wrappers. $200.
Babbitt, E. D.	THE PRINCIPLES OF LIGHT AND COLOR. New York, 1878. $185.
Babbitt, E. L.	THE ALLEGHENY PILOT. Freeport, Pa., 1855. Wrappers. $225.
Bainbridge, George C.	THE FLY-FISHER'S GUIDE. Liverpool, England, 1816. $575.
Baird, Spencer F., et al.	THE WATER BIRDS OF NORTH AMERICA. Boston, 1884. $650.
Balme, J. R.	AMERICAN STATES, CHURCHES AND SLAVERY. London, 1863. $65.
Bancroft, Hubert Howe	THE WORKS OF HUBERT HOWE BANCROFT. 39 vols. San Francisco, 1886-1890. $4,200.
Barrow, John	A CHRONOLOGICAL HISTORY OF VOYAGES INTO THE ARCTIC REGIONS. London, 1818. $425.
Bartlett, J. S., M.D.	THE PHYSICIAN'S POCKET SYNOPSIS. Boston, 1822. $110.
Barton, James L.	COMMERCE OF THE LAKES. Buffalo, N.Y., 1847. Wrappers. $135.

AUTHOR	TITLE/EDITION INFORMATION/VALUE
Barton, William P. C.	A FLORA OF NORTH AMERICA. 3 vols. Philadelphia, 1821-1823. $4,000.
Bates, H. W.	THE NATURALIST ON THE RIVER AMAZON. 2 vols. London, 1863. $525.
Beard, Daniel C.	AMERICAN BOY'S HANDY BOOK: WHAT TO DO AND HOW TO DO IT. New York, 1882. $125.
Beattie, William	SWITZERLAND ILLUSTRATED. 2 vols. London, 1836. 107 plates by W. H. Bartlett. $1,200.
Beaumont, Cyril W.	PUPPETS AND THE PUPPET STAGE. London, 1938. $135.
Beaumont, William	EXPERIMENTS AND OBSERVATIONS ON THE GASTRIC JUICE, AND THE PHYSIOLOGY OF DIGESTION. Plattsburgh, N.Y., 1833. $2,750.
Beaumont, William	THE PHYSIOLOGY OF DIGESTION. Burlington, Vt., 1847. $500.
Beebe, William	A MONOGRAPH OF THE PHEASANTS. 4 vols. London, 1918-1922. 90 color plates. 20 maps. $3,500.
Beeton, Mrs. Isabella	THE BOOK OF HOUSEHOLD MANAGEMENT. 2 vols. London, 1861. $575.
Bell, John	DISCOURSES ON THE NATURE AND CURE OF WOUNDS. Walpole, N.H., 1807. $225.
Bendire, Charles	LIFE HISTORIES OF NORTH AMERICAN BIRDS. 2 vols. Washington, D.C., 1892-1895. $275.
Benezet, Anthony A.	THE FAMILY PHYSICIAN. Cincinnati, 1826. $325.
Benjamin, Asher	THE PRACTICE OF ARCHITECTURE. Boston, 1814. $650.
Benjamin, Asher, and Daniel Reynard	THE AMERICAN BUILDER'S COMPANION. Boston, 1806. $550.
Bergman, Ray	TROUT. Philadelphia, 1938. Limited and signed edition. $750.

AUTHOR	TITLE/EDITION INFORMATION/VALUE
Bert, Edmund	TREATISE ON HAWKS AND HAWKING. London, 1891. $225.
(Cabinet)	THE CABINET OF NATURAL HISTORY AND AMERICAN RURAL SPORTS. 3 vols. Philadelphia, 1830-1833. $20,000 or more.
Carlson, Anton J.	THE CONTROL OF HUNGER IN HEALTH AND DISEASE. Chicago, 1916. $175.
Carter, Susannah	THE FRUGAL HOUSEWIFE; OR, COMPLETE WOMAN COOK. Philadelphia, 1802. $175.
Chadwick, Henry	THE GAME OF BASE BALL: HOW TO LEARN IT, HOW TO PLAY IT, AND HOW TO TEACH IT. New York, 1868. $125.
Chanute, Octave	PROGRESS IN FLYING MACHINES. New York, 1894. $275.
Chatterton, E. Keble	SHIP-MODELS. London, 1923. Limited edition. $275.
Chatterton, E. Keble	STEAMSHIP MODELS. London, 1924. Limited and signed edition. $275.
Clark, Daniel M.	THE SOUTHERN CALCULATOR, OR COMPENDIOUS ARITHMETIC. Lagrange, Ga., n.d., $135.
(Collection)	A COLLECTION OF FAMILIAR QUOTATIONS. [John Bartlett]. Cambridge, Mass., 1855. $325.
Connett, Eugene V., editor	AMERICAN BIG GAME FISHING. New York: Derrydale Press, 1935. Limited edition. Boxed. $450.
(Constitution)	CONSTITUTION AND PLAYING RULES OF THE INTERNATIONAL BASEBALL ASSOCIATION . . . AND CHAMPIONSHIP RECORD FOR 1877. Jamaica Plains, Mass., 1878. Wrappers. $175.
Cook, Frederick A.	MY ATTAINMENT OF THE POLE. New York, 1911. $85.

AUTHOR	TITLE/EDITION INFORMATION/VALUE
Cooper, J. W.	GAME FOWLS, THEIR ORIGIN AND HISTORY. West Chester, Pa., 1869. $175.
Corrill, John	A BRIEF HISTORY OF THE CHURCH OF CHRIST OF LATTER DAY SAINTS. St. Louis, 1839. Sewed. $5,000 or more.
Crowley, Aleister	MAGIC IN THEORY AND PRACTICE. London, 1929. $200.
Cushing, Luther S.	MANUAL OF PARLIAMENTARY PRACTICE. Boston, 1845. $200.
Davis, Edmund W.	SALMON-FISHING ON THE GRAND CASCAPEDIA. New York, 1904. Limited edition. $850.
Davy, Sir Humphrey	ON THE SAFETY LAMP FOR COAL MINERS. London, 1818. $500.
Dawson, William Leon	THE BIRDS OF CALIFORNIA. 4 vols. San Diego, 1923. $500.
Dawson, William Leon	THE BIRDS OF OHIO. 2 vols. Columbus, Ohio, 1903. $165.
De Gouy, L. P.	THE DERRYDALE COOK BOOK OF FISH AND GAME. 2 vols. New York, 1937. Limited edition. Boxed. $375.
Denton, Sherman F.	AS NATURE SHOWS THEM: MOTHS AND BUTTERFLIES OF THE UNITED STATES EAST OF THE ROCKY MOUNTAINS. 2 vols. Boston, 1900. Limited edition. $750.
De Vinne, Theodore L.	THE INVENTION OF PRINTING. New York, 1876. $135.
Disturnell, John	THE INFLUENCE OF CLIMATE IN NORTH AND SOUTH AMERICA. New York, 1867. $135.
(Domestic)	DOMESTIC COOKERY: THE EXPERIENCED AMERICAN HOUSEKEEPER. New York, 1823. $175.
Doring, Ernest N.	THE GUADAGNINI FAMILY OF VIOLIN MAKERS. Chicago, 1949. $525.

AUTHOR	TITLE/EDITION INFORMATION/VALUE
Dorman, Caroline	WILD FLOWERS OF LOUISIANA. New York, 1934. $100.
Dow, George Francis	THE ARTS AND CRAFTS IN NEW ENGLAND. Topsfield, Mass., 1927. $175.
Dow, George Francis	WHALE SHIPS AND WHALING. Salem, Mass., 1925. Limited edition. $150.
Downing, Andrew Jackson	THE ARCHITECTURE OF COUNTRY HOUSES. New York, 1850. $175.
Downing, Andrew Jackson	THE FRUITS AND FRUIT TREES OF AMERICA. New York, 1850. $1,000 or more.
Drake, Daniel	AN ACCOUNT OF EPIDEMIC CHOLERA, AS IT APPEARED IN CINCINNATI. Cincinnati, 1832. Wrappers. $275.
Eaton, Daniel Cady	THE FERNS OF NORTH AMERICA. 2 vols. Salem, Mass.; Boston, 1880. $425.
Edgar, Patrick Nisbett	THE AMERICAN RACE-TURF REGISTER. Vol. 1. New York, 1833. $175.
Edwards, Billy	GLADIATORS OF THE PRIZE RING, OR PUGILISTS OF AMERICA. Chicago, 1895. Folio. $225.
Elliott, D. G.	A MONOGRAPH OF THE FELIDAE, OR FAMILY OF CATS. London, 1883. 43 hand-colored plates. Folio. $15,000 or more.
Elliott, D. G.	A MONOGRAPH OF THE PITTIDAE, OR FAMILY OF ANTI-THRUSHES. New York, 1863. 31 hand-colored plates. $25,000 or more.
Elliott, D. G.	THE NEW AND HERETOFORE UNFIGURED SPECIES OF THE BIRDS OF NORTH AMERICA. 2 vols. New York, 1866-1869. 72 hand-colored plates. $22,000 or more.
Ellis, John B.	FREE LOVE AND ITS VOTARIES; OR, AMERICAN SOCIALISM UNMASKED. New York, 1870. $275.
Ellis, William	THE AMERICAN MISSION IN THE SANDWICH ISLANDS. Honolulu, 1866. $275.

AUTHOR	TITLE/EDITION INFORMATION/VALUE
Emerson, Lucy	THE NEW-ENGLAND COOKERY. Montpelier, Vt., 1808. $375.
Falconer, William	A NEW UNIVERSAL DICTIONARY OF THE MARINE. London, 1815. $425.
Feininger, Andreas	FEININGER ON PHOTOGRAPHY. New York, 1949. $85.
Feuchtwanger, Dr. Lewis	A TREATISE ON GEMS. New York, 1838. $150.
Fisher, Harry C.	THE MUTT AND JEFF CARTOONS. Boston, 1910. Folio. $150.
Fleming, Alexander	PENICILLIN. London, 1946. $165.
Flint, Timothy	LECTURES UPON NATURAL HISTORY. Boston, 1833. $225.
Forrester, Frank	THE COMPLETE MANUAL FOR YOUNG SPORTSMEN. New York, 1856. $275.
Forrester, Frank	FISHING WITH HOOK AND LINE. New York, 1858. Wrappers. $1,200 or more.
Fort, Charles	THE BOOK OF THE DAMNED. New York, 1919. $275.
Francis, Grant R.	OLD ENGLISH DRINKING GLASSES. London, 1926. $275.
Franks, David	THE NEW-YORK DIRECTORY. New York, 1786. $5,000 or more.
Freud, Sigmund	TOTEM AND TABOO. New York, 1918. $185.
Gallatin, Albert	CONSIDERATIONS ON THE CURRENCY AND BANKING SYSTEM OF THE UNITED STATES. Philadelphia, 1831. Wrappers. $165.
Gardner, Ralph D.	HORATIO ALGER; OR, THE AMERICAN HERO ERA. Mendota, Ill., 1964. $85.
Gee, Ernest R.	EARLY AMERICAN SPORTING BOOKS, 1734 TO 1846. New York: Derrydale Press, 1928. Limited edition. $325.

AUTHOR	TITLE/EDITION INFORMATION/VALUE
Genet, Edmond Charles	MEMORIAL ON THE UPWARD FORCES OF FLUIDS. Albany, N.Y., 1825. $1,500 or more.
Gesner, Abraham	A PRACTICAL TREATISE ON COAL, PETROLEUM, AND OTHER DISTILLED OILS. New York, 1861. $425.
Gilhespy, F. Brayshaw	DERBY PORCELAIN. London, 1961. $65.
Giraud, J. P., Jr.	THE BIRDS OF LONG ISLAND. New York, 1844. $450.
Glover, Mary Baker	SCIENCE AND HEALTH, WITH KEY TO THE SCRIPTURES. Boston, 1875. $1,500 or more.
Goddard, R. H.	A METHOD OF REACHING EXTREME ALTITUDES. Washington, D.C., 1919. Wrappers. $1,500 or more.
Hakewill, James	A PICTURESQUE TOUR OF THE ISLAND OF JAMAICA. London, 1825. 21 aquatint plates. $4,500 or more.
Hall, James Norman, and Charles B. Nordhoff	THE LAFAYETTE FLYING CORPS. 2 vols. Boston, 1920. $750.
Hall, Marshall	PRINCIPLES OF THE THEORY AND PRACTICE OF MEDICINE. Boston, 1839. $175.
Hall, Samuel R.	LECTURES TO FEMALE TEACHERS ON SCHOOL-KEEPING. Boston, 1832. $85.
Hammer, William J.	RADIUM, AND OTHER RADIO-ACTIVE SUBSTANCES. New York, 1903. $425.
Hannover, Emil	POTTERY AND PORCELAIN: A HANDBOOK FOR COLLECTORS. London, 1925. $475.
Hardy, John	A COLLECTION OF SACRED HYMNS, ADAPTED TO THE FAITH AND VIEWS OF THE CHURCH OF JESUS CHRIST OF LATTER DAY SAINTS. Boston, 1843. $2,500 or more.

AUTHOR	TITLE/EDITION INFORMATION/VALUE
Hargrave, Catherine Perry	A HISTORY OF PLAYING CARDS. Boston, 1930. $375.
Harlow, Alvin F.	OLD TOWPATHS. New York, 1926. $100.
Harlow, Alvin F.	OLD WAYBILLS. New York, 1934. $100.
Jackson, Mrs. F. Nevill	TOYS OF OTHER DAYS. London, 1908. Trade edition. $125.
Jackson, Helen Hunt	THE PROCESSION OF FLOWERS IN COLORADO. Boston, 1886. Limited edition. $175.
Jackson, John	THE PRACTICAL FLY-FISHER. London, 1854. $650 or more.
Jacobs, Thomas Jefferson	SCENES, INCIDENTS AND ADVENTURES IN THE PACIFIC OCEAN. New York, 1884. $575.
Jaeger, Benedict, and H. C. Preston	THE LIFE OF NORTH AMERICAN INSECTS. Providence, R.I., 1854. $85.
James, Philip	CHILDREN'S BOOKS OF YESTERDAY. London, 1933. $175.
Kant, Immanuel	CRITICK OF PURE REASON. London, 1838. $850 or more.
Kennedy, John F.	PROFILES IN COURAGE. New York, 1956. $175.
Kennedy, John F.	WHY ENGLAND SLEPT. New York, 1940. $650.
Keynes, John Maynard	THE ECONOMIC CONSEQUENCES OF THE PEACE. London, 1919. $650.
Kunz, George Frederick	THE CURIOUS LORE OF PRECIOUS STONES. Philadelphia, 1913. $325.
Lanman, Charles	ADVENTURES OF AN ANGLER IN CANADA. London, 1848. $575.

AUTHOR	TITLE/EDITION INFORMATION/VALUE
Lay, William, and Cyrus M. Hussey	A NARRATIVE OF THE MUTINY ON BOARD THE SHIP GLOBE OF NANTUCKET. New London, Conn., 1828. $750.
Lear, Edward	ILLUSTRATIONS OF THE FAMILY PSITTACIDAE, OR PARROTS. London, 1830-1832. 42 colored plates. Folio. $15,000 or more.
Loughborough, John	THE PACIFIC TELEGRAPH AND RAILWAY. St. Louis, 1849. Unbound. $650.
Lougheed, Victor	VEHICLES OF THE AIR. Chicago, 1909. $125.
Lubbock, Basil	THE LAST OF THE WINDJAMMERS. 2 vols. Boston, 1927. $225.
McClelland, Nancy	HISTORIC WALLPAPERS. Philadelphia, 1924. Trade edition. $125.
MacDonald, James, and James Sinclair	HISTORY OF HEREFORD CATTLE. London, 1886. $125.
Mackay, Charles	MEMOIRS OF EXTRAORDINARY POPULAR DELUSIONS AND THE MADNESS OF CROWDS. 3 vols. London, 1841. $350.
Mahan, A. T.	THE INFLUENCE OF SEA POWER UPON HISTORY. Boston, 1890. $450 or more.
Massie, J. Cam	A TREATISE ON THE ECLECTIC SOUTHERN PRACTICE OF MEDICINE. Philadelphia, 1854. $225.
Nightingale, Florence	NOTES ON NURSING. New York, 1869. $125.
Nutt, Frederic	THE COMPLETE CONFECTIONER. New York, 1807. $350.
Nuttall, Thomas	THE GENERA OF NORTH AMERICAN PLANTS. 2 vols. Philadelphia, 1818. $450.
Nutting, Wallace	THE CLOCK BOOK. Framingham, Mass., 1924. $85.

AUTHOR	TITLE/EDITION INFORMATION/VALUE
Offutt, Denton	THE EDUCATED HORSE. Washington, D.C., 1854. $65.
Orvis, Charles F., and A. Nelson Cheny	FISHING WITH THE FLY. Manchester, Vt., 1883. $325.
Osler, Sir William	THE PRINCIPLES AND PRACTICE OF MEDICINE. New York, 1892. $375.
Owen, Robert Dale	A BRIEF PRACTICAL TREATISE ON THE CONSTRUCTION AND MANAGEMENT OF PLANK ROADS. New Albany, Ind., 1850. $175.
Palmer, Harry	BASE BALL: THE NATIONAL GAME OF THE AMERICANS. Chicago, 1888. Wrappers. $125.
Parker, John R.	THE UNITED STATES TELEGRAPH VOCABULARY. Boston, 1832. $200.
Parmly, Levi Spear	A PRACTICAL GUIDE TO THE MANAGEMENT OF THE TEETH. Philadelphia, 1819. $225.
Paulding, Hiram	JOURNAL OF A CRUISE OF THE UNITED STATES SCHOONER DOLPHIN. New York, 1831. $1,200 or more.
Perkins, Charles Elliott	THE PINTO HORSE. Santa Barbara, Calif., 1927. $275.
Queeny, Edgar M.	PRAIRIE WINGS: PEN AND CAMERA FLIGHT STUDIES. New York, 1946. $550.
Rafinesque, C. D.	MEDICAL FLORA. 2 vols. Philadelphia, 1828-1830. $1,500 or more.
Rarey, J. S.	THE MODERN ART OF TAMING WILD HORSES. Columbus, Ohio, 1856. $500 or more.
Reynolds, J. N.	VOYAGE OF THE UNITED STATES FRIGATE POTOMAC. New York, 1835. $325.

AUTHOR	TITLE/EDITION INFORMATION/VALUE
Richards, Thomas Addison	AMERICAN SCENERY ILLUSTRATED. New York, 1854. $325.
Richtofen, Walter, Baron von	CATTLE-RAISING ON THE PLAINS OF NORTH AMERICA. New York, 1885. $525.
Saissy, Jean-Antoine	AN ESSAY ON THE DISEASES OF THE INTERNAL EAR. Baltimore, Md., 1829. $275.
Sappington, John	THE THEORY AND TREATMENT OF FEVERS. Arrow Rock, Mo., 1844. $135.
Sargent, Charles Sprague	THE SILVA OF NORTH AMERICA. 14 vols. Boston, 1890-1902. $2,500 or more.
Scammon, Charles M.	THE MARINE MAMMALS OF THE NORTH-WESTERN COAST OF NORTH AMERICA. San Francisco, 1874. $750 or more.
Schley, Frank	AMERICAN PARTRIDGE AND PHEASANT SHOOTING. Frederick, Md., 1877. $225.
Taft, Robert	PHOTOGRAPHY AND THE AMERICAN SCENE: A SOCIAL HISTORY, 1839-1889. New York, 1938. $225.
Taylor, W. F.	THE PRINCIPLES OF SCIENTIFIC MANAGEMENT. New York, 1911. $850 or more.
Thomas, Jerry	THE BAR-TENDER'S GUIDE. New York, 1862. $175.
Thompson, Hunter	HELL'S ANGELS. New York, 1967. $85.
Thompson, Maurice	THE WITCHERY OF ARCHERY. New York, 1878. $175.
Vail, Alfred	DESCRIPTION OF THE AMERICAN ELECTRO-MAGNETIC TELEGRAPH. Washington, D.C., 1845. Wrappers. $175.
Veblen, Thorstein	THE THEORY OF THE LEISURE CLASS. New York, 1899. $325.

AUTHOR	**TITLE/EDITION INFORMATION/VALUE**
Velikovsky, Immanuel	WORLDS IN COLLISION. New York, 1950. $75.
Von Oettingen, B.	HORSE BREEDING IN THEORY AND PRACTICE. London, 1909. $175.
Walcott, Mary Vaux	NORTH AMERICAN WILDFLOWERS. 5 vols. Washington, D.C., 1925-1929. Trade edition. $275.
Warren, Edward	AN EPITOME OF PRACTICAL SURGERY FOR FIELD AND HOSPITAL. Richmond, Va., 1863. $650.

– APPENDIX A –

North American Book Search Services

When using the services of these dealers, it is important to provide as complete a description as possible. All information on the title page, copyright date(s), number of pages and illustrations, approximate size, color of binding and cover, printing, and *condition.* Mention if there is a dust jacket and its condition. All of these things will affect the price you can expect to pay. If the dealer buys the book for you it will be subject to your inspection: return it if it does not meet the description you furnished.

Please note: This list is alphabetized by state, and by city within state.

ALASKA

The Observatory, POB 1770, Sitka, AK 99835

ARIZONA

Ruby D. Kaufman, 518 East Loma Vista Dr., Tempe, AZ 85282

Bookmans, 18 North Tucson Blvd., Tucson, AZ 85716

ARKANSAS

Jack Bailes-Books, POB 150, Eureka Springs, AR 72632

Yesterday's Books, 258 Whittington Ave., Box 1728, Hot Springs, AR 71901

CALIFORNIA

Book Baron, 12365 Magnolia Ave., Anaheim, CA 92804

Black Oak Books, Inc., 1491 Shattuck Ave., Berkeley, CA 94709

Regent Street Books, 2747 Regent St., Berkeley, CA 94705

Whaling Research, POB 5034, Berkeley, CA 94715

Peninsula Booksearch, POB 1305, Burlingame, CA 94010

Bookpost, 962 Greenlake Ct., Cardiff, CA 92007
Don Discher, 4830 Audrey Dr., Castro Valley, CA 94546
Shuey Book Search, 8886 Sharkey Ave., Elk Grove, CA 95624
Bookfinder, 2035 Everding St., Eureka, CA 95501
Terence M. Knaus, 21601 Foster Lane, Fort Bragg, CA 95437
Monroe Books, 809 East Olive, Fresno, CA 93728
American Book Search, POB 4448, Glendale, CA 91202
Hollywood Book Service, 1654 Cherokee Ave., Hollywood, CA 90028
Buccaneer Books, Inc., POB 518, Laguna Beach, CA 92652
Needham Book Finder, 12021 Wilshire Blvd. #13, Los Angeles, CA 90025
M. C. Wilson, 1735 Sherbourne, Los Angeles, CA 90035
Donald La Chance, 1032 Bay Oaks Dr., Los Osos, CA 93402
Health Research, 8349 Lafayette St., Box 70, Mokelumne Hill, CA 95245
This Old House Bookshop, 5399 West Holt, Montclair, CA 91763
M. R. Gildea, POB 13013, Oakland, CA 94614
Wayne Pierce, 4400 Pine Cluster, Oroville, CA 95965
Chimera Books, 405 Kipling, Palo Alto, CA 94301
Book Case Books, 461 North Lake Ave., Pasadena, CA 91101
Day's Arms & Antiques, 2163 East Main St., Quincy, CA 95971
The Silver Door, POB 3208, Redondo Beach, CA 90277
Bookie Joint, 7246 Reseda Blvd., Reseda, CA 91335
The Mermaid Books, 433 44th St., Richmond, CA 94805
'Otento' Books, 3817 Fifth Ave., San Diego, CA 92103
Academy Library, 2245 Larkin St., San Francisco, CA 94109
Antiquus Bibliopole, 4147 24th St., San Francisco, CA 94114
Califia, 2266 Union St., San Francisco, CA 94123
Louis Collins Books, 1083 Mission St., San Francisco, CA 94103
Lynn Fuller, Books, 45 Powers Ave., San Francisco, CA 94110
The Magazine, 839 Larkin St., San Francisco, CA 94109
Novel Experience, 778 Marsh St., San Luis Obispo, CA 93401
L. S. Kaiser Books, 1820 Graham Hill, Santa Cruz, CA 95060
A Change of Hobbit, 1853 Lincoln Blvd., Santa Monica, CA 90404
Concord Books, 419 Opal Cove Way, Box 725, Seal Beach, CA 90740
Lois Gereghty Books, 9521 Orion Ave., Sepulveda, CA 91343
Betsy Hook, Bookfinder, 7345 Healdsburg Ave., Sebastopol, CA 95472
B. Lynch Book Finder, 8840 Debra Ave., Sepulveda, CA 91343
Davis & Schorr Art Books, 14755 Ventura Blvd., #1-747, Sherman Oaks, CA 91403

Arnold Jacobs, 5038 Hazeltine Ave., Sherman Oaks, CA 91423
Heritage Books, 52 South Washington St., Sonora, CA 95370
Albatross II Book Shop, 100 Main St., Tiburon, CA 94920
Lois St. Clair, POB 247, Van Nuys, CA 91408
Kenneth L. Wolf, 6021 Allot Ave., Van Nuys, CA 91401
Calico Cat Bookshop, 495 East Main St., Ventura, CA 93001
Blitz Books, POB 1076, Weaverville, CA 96093
221 Books, 760 Carlisle Canyon Rd., Westlake Village, CA 91361
Ell Dee Book Finders, POB 1231, Whittier, CA 90609
J. Arthur Robinson Books, 56149 29 Palms Highway, Yucca Valley, CA 92284

COLORADO

Chinook Bookshop, 210 North Tejon, Colorado Springs, CO 80907
Steve Ballinger, 1079 Kearny St., Denver, CO 80220
Book House, 5870 South Curtice, Littleton, CO 80120
The Cache, 7157 West US 34, Loveland, CO 80537

CONNECTICUT

Bethlehem Book Co., POB 249, Bethlehem, CT 06751
Clipper Ship Book Shop, 12 North Main St., Essex, CT 06426
Bookcell Books, 90 Robinwood Rd., Hamden, CT 06517
David Howland, 99 Marshall Ridge Rd., New Canaan, CT 06840
Edgewood Books, 359 Edgewood Ave., New Haven, CT 06520
Mrs. L. M. Brew, Squash Hollow Rd., R.R. 2, New Milford, CT 06776
Elliot's Books, POB 6, Northford, CT 06472
Nutmeg Books, 354 New Litchfield St., Rte. 202, Torrington, CT 06790
Barbara Farnsworth, Route 128, West Cornwall, CT 06796
Bookerie, Simpaug Turnpike, West Redding, CT 06896

DISTRICT OF COLUMBIA

Duff & M. E. Gilfond, 1722 19th St. NW, Washington, DC 20009
Lloyd Books, 1346 Connecticut Ave. NW, Washington, DC 20036

FLORIDA

Tappin Book Mine, 705 Atlantic Blvd., Atlantic Beach, FL 32233
All Books & Prints Store, 4329 SW 8th St., Miami, FL 33134
Lucile Coleman Books, POB 610813, North Miami, FL 33261

Christopher Ackerman, 180 East Inlet Dr., Palm Beach, FL 33480
Jack Owen, 113 North Country Rd., Palm Beach, FL 33480
Brassers, 8701 Seminole Blvd., Seminole, FL 33542
Book Traders, Inc., POB 9403, Winter Haven, FL 33880

GEORGIA

James O. McMeans, POB 429352, Atlanta, GA 30342
Oxford Book Store, 2345 Peachtree Rd. NE, Atlanta, GA 30305
Book Cottage, 2403 Lawrence Highway, Decatur, GA 30033
Downs Books, 774 Mary Ann Dr. NE, Marietta, GA 30067
Margie Sachs OP Books, Route 2, Box 59, Metter, GA 30439
The Bookman of Arcady, POB 1259, Tybee Island, GA 31328

IDAHO

Boise Book Farm, 5600 Hill Rd., Boise, ID 83703
The Book Shop, Inc., 908 Main St., Boise, ID 83710
Parnassus Books, 218 North 9th St., Boise, ID 83712

ILLINOIS

Rose Lasley, 5827 Burr Oak, Berkeley, IL 60163
P. J. Henry, 4225 East, Berwyn, IL 60402
KN Enterprises, POB 87397, Chicago, IL 60680
Walter R. Schneemann, 5710 South Dorchester Ave., Chicago, IL 60637
Thomas W. Burrows, POB 400, Downers Grove, IL 60515
Bookchoice, POB A1497, Evanston, IL 60204
Chicago Book Mart, POB 418, Frankfort, IL 60423
The Book Beautiful, 228 Wentworth, Glencoe, IL 60022
Brainard Book Co., POB 444, La Grange, IL 60525
Bank Lane Books, 782 North Bank Lane, Lake Forest, IL 60045
Prairie Archives, 641 West Monroe, Springfield, IL 62704
Storeybook Antiques/Books, 1325 East State Highway 64, Sycamore, IL 60178
Bunter Books, POB 153, Winnetka, IL 60093

INDIANA

Caveat Emptor, 208 South Dunn, Bloomington, IN 47401
Used Book Place, POB 206, Dyer, IN 46311
Larry Schnell Papertique, POB 252, Elberfeld, IN 47613

Books Unlimited, 922 East Washington, Indianapolis, IN 46202
Mason's Books, 264 South Wabash, Wabash, IN 46992

KANSAS

J. Hood Booksellers, 1401 Massachusetts, Lawrence, KS 66044

KENTUCKY

The Sail Loft, 262 Cassidy Ave., Lexington, KY 40502
Carmichael's Bookstore, 1295 Bardstown Rd., Louisville, KY 40204
S-T Associates, 1317 Cherokee Rd., Louisville, KY 40204

LOUISIANA

Henry C. Hensel, 657-B Rue Perez, Belle Chasse, LA 70037
Bayou Books, 1005 Monroe St., Gretna, LA 70053
American Opinion Books, 3804 Canal St., New Orleans, LA 70119
de Ville Books, 132 Carondelet St., New Orleans, LA 70130

MAINE

Alfred Search Service, Drawer 1027, Damariscotta, ME 04534
Snowbound Books, RFD Box 620, Madison, ME 04950
The Sail Loft, Newcastle, ME 04553
G. F. Bush, POB 905, Stonington, ME 04681

MARYLAND

Dragoman Books, 680 Americana Dr. #38, Annapolis, MD 21403
Cecil Archer Rush, 1410 Northgate Rd., Baltimore, MD 21218
Quill & Brush, 7649 Old Georgetown Rd., Bethesda, MD 20814
All Edges Gilt, POB 7625, Silver Spring, MD 20907
Greetings & Readings, 809 Taylor Ave., Towson, MD 21204

MASSACHUSETTS

Jean S. McKenna Books, POB 397, Beverly, MA 01905
Xanadu Books, POB 91, Braintree, MA 02184
Smith's Book Service, Sunsmith House, Route 6-A, Brewster, MA 02631
Bohdan Zaremba, 3 Livermore Place, Cambridge, MA 02141
Atlantic Book Service, POB 218, Charlestown, MA 02129
Barrow Bookstore, 79 Main St., Concord, MA 01742
The English Bookshop, 22 Rocky Neck Ave., Gloucester, MA 01930

Jeffrey H. Weinberg, POB 2122, Lowell, MA 01851
Anthony G. Ziagos Books, POB 28, Lowell, MA 01853
The Book Collector, 375 Elliot St., Newton, MA 02164
Murray's Bookfinding Service, 115 State, Springfield, MA 01101
Barn Owl Books, POB 323, Wellesley, MA 02181
Book Store, 222 North Main St., West Bridgewater, MA 02379
Williams Bookstore, 20 Spring St., Williamstown, MA 01267

MICHIGAN

David's Books, 622 East Liberty, Ann Arbor, MI 48104
Marion the Librarian, 3668 Shimmons Circle South, Auburn Heights, MI 48057
The Necessary Press, POB 313, East Jordan, MI 49727
Curious Book Shop, 307 East Grand River, East Lansing, MI 48823
Great Lake Bookman, POB 162, Houghton, MI 49931
John C. Buckley, Searcher, 27901 Highland Park, Gull Lake, Richland, MI 49083
Barbara J. Rule Books, POB 215, Rochester, MI 48063
Treasures From the Castle, 1720 North Livernois, Rochester, MI 48064
Call Me Ishmael Books, POB 595, Saugatuck, MI 49453

MINNESOTA

Bookmailer, 2730 West Broadway, Minneapolis, MN 55411
Savran's Books, 301 Cedar Ave., Minneapolis, MN 55454
S & S Books, 80 North Wilder, St. Paul, MN 55104
Northern Lights Bookshop, 103 West Third St., Winona, MN 55987
Mary Twyce Antiques/Books, 601 East 5th St., Winona, MN 55987

MISSISSIPPI

James A. Dillon Books, Star Route, Box 23, Carlisle, MS 39049

MISSOURI

Adams Books and Hobbies, 214 North 8th St., Columbia, MO 65201
Columbia Books, POB 27, Columbia, MO 65205
Red Bridge Books, 2523 Red Bridge Terrace, Kansas City, MO 64131
Shirley's Old Book Shop, 1948 G S Glenstone, Springfield, MO 65804
Elizabeth F. Dunlap, 6063 Westminster Place, St. Louis, MO 63112
Readmore Books, 3607 Meramec, St. Louis, MO 63116

MONTANA

Bird's Nest, POB 8809, Missoula, MT 59807
Book Exchange, Holiday Village, Missoula, MT 59801

NEBRASKA

Niobrara Books, POB 2664, Lincoln, NE 68502
The Book Barn, RR1, Box 304H, South Sioux City, NE 68776

NEW HAMPSHIRE

Dartmouth Bookstore, 33 South Main St., Hanover, NH 03755
Tainters, POB 36, Temple, NH 03084

NEW JERSEY

Princeton Antiquarian Books, 2917-17 Atlantic Ave., Atlantic City, NJ 08401
Servant's Knowledge, 2915-17 Atlantic Ave., Atlantic City, NJ 08401
The People's Bookshop, 160 Main St., Flemington, NJ 08822
Jay's Booktique, 1 Canadian Woods Rd., Marlboro, NJ 07746
Wangner's Book Shop, 9 Midland Ave., Montclair, NJ 07042
Old York Books, 12 French St., New Brunswick, NJ 08903
Frank Michelli Books, 45 Halsey St., Newark, NJ 07102
Book Tracers, 869 Chamberlain Ave., Perth Amboy, NJ 08861
Book House, 218 East Front St., Plainfield, NJ 07060
Red Bank Book Store, 6 Linden Place, Red Bank, NJ 07701
Kirksco International Bookfinders, 70-212 Cedar Rd., Ringwood, NJ 07456
Rena & Merwin L. Orner, 39 North Browning Ave., Tenafly, NJ 07670
Acres of Books, 35 East State, Trenton, NJ 08608
Books On File, POB 195, Union City, NJ 07087

NEW MEXICO

Book Addict, POB 9134, Albuquerque, NM 87119
Chamisa Bookshop, 1602 Central SE, Albuquerque, NM 87106
Hummingbird Books, 2400 Hannett NE, Albuquerque, NM 87106
Taos Book Shop, POB 827, Taos, NM 87571

NEW YORK

Thomas W. Shaw, 11 Albright Ave., Albany, NY 12203
Treasures In Books, POB 53, Andes, NY 13731

Baldwin Book Service, POB 157, Baldwin, NY 11510
Books Past & Present, 428 Pearl St., Buffalo, NY 14202
Rainbow's End Books, RD3, Country Route 84, Central Square, NY 13036
Seabook Search, Clinton Corners, NY 12514
C. G. Fisher, 62 East Main St., Cobleskill, NY 12043
Ingeborg Quitzau, POB 5160, Edmeston, NY 13335
Leslie Poste, POB 68, Geneseo, NY 14454
The Book Finder, 471 Exchange St., Geneva, NY 14456
Alan C. Hunter Books, Harriman Heights Rd., Harriman, NY 10926
A Collector's Library, 520 North Greece Rd., Hilton, NY 14468
The Bookery, De Witt Mall, Ithaca, NY 14850
The Eight-Cent Nickel, 310 South Main St., Liberty, NY 12754
Hobby Helpers, 7369 East Main St., Lima, NY 14485
Talbothay's Books, POB 276, Lincolndale, NY 10540
Christian Bookfellowship, POB 763, Millbrook, NY 12545
Cooper Fox Farm Books, POB 763, Millbrook, NY 12545
Book Finders General, 145 East 27th St., New York, NY 10016
Book Ranger, 105 Charles St., New York, NY 10014
Dolphin, Book Shop, 2743 Broadway, New York, NY 10025
Donan Books, 235 East 53rd St., New York, NY 10022
Peter Thomas Fisher, 41 Union Square West, New York, NY 10003
Timothy Mawson, 134 West 92nd St., New York, NY 10025
999 Bookshop, 999 Madison Ave., New York, NY 10021
Paragon Book Gallery, 14 East 38th St., New York, NY 10016
Russica Book & Art Shop, 799 Broadway, New York, NY 10003
Theatrebooks, Inc., 1576 Broadway #312, New York, NY 10036
Peter Hennessey Books, POB 393, Peconic, NY 11958
Bengta Woo, 1 Sorgi Ct., Plainview, NY 11803
Cabin in the Pines, Route 2, Potsdam, NY 13676
Robert E. Underhill, 85 Underhill Rd., Poughkeepsie, NY 12603
Stan Marx, 15 Sinclair Martin Dr., Roslyn, NY 11576
The Book End, 521 Jewett Ave., Staten Island, NY 10302
Sterling Valley Antiquity, POB 14, Syracuse, NY 13215
Book Look, 51 Maple Ave., Warwick, NY 10990
Avonlea Books, POB 74, Main Station, White Plains, NY 10602
The Book Gallery, 15 Overlook Rd., White Plains, NY 10605
Albert J. Phiebig, Inc., POB 352, White Plains, NY 10602
All Photography Books, POB 429, Yonkers, NY 10702

NORTH CAROLINA

Pacificana, POB 398, Jamestown, NC 27282

OHIO

Susan Heller, 22611 Halburton Rd., Beachwood, OH 44122
Barbara Agranoff Books, POB 6501, Cincinnati, OH 45206
Ron-Dor Bookfinders, 4700 Masillon Rd., Greensburg, OH 44232
The Amblers, 1123 Hillridge, Reynoldsburg, OH 43068
Burley & Books, Inc., 848 Franklin Park Mall, Toledo, OH 43623

OKLAHOMA

Caravan Books, POB 861, Stillwater, OK 74074

ONTARIO, CANADA

Attic Books, 388 Clarence St., London, ON, Canada
Glooscap Study, RR1, Pefferlaw, ON L0E 1N0, Canada
Jocelyne Kidston, RR1, Tarzwell, ON P0K 1V0, Canada
Old Favorites Bookshop, 250 Adelaide West, Toronto, ON M5H 1X8, Canada

OREGON

McLaughlin's Books, POB 753, Cottage Grove, OR 97424
Joy A. Wheeler Books, Route 1, Box 49K, Elgin, OR 97827
J. Michaels Books, 376 East 11th Ave., Eugene, OR 97401
Cameron's Books, 336 SW Third Ave., Portland, OR 97204
Midvale Books, 155 SW Midvale Rd., Portland, OR 97218
The Manuscript, 223 High St. NE, Salem, OR 97301

PENNSYLVANIA

Margaret L. Tyrrell, 117 North 40th St., Allentown, PA 18104
College Hill Books, 306 Cattell St., Easton, PA 18042
The Gateway, Ferndale, PA 18921
Helen B. Leech, 7944 Slepian St., Harrisburg, PA 17112
Hobson's Choice, 511 Runnymede Ave., Jenkintown, PA 19046
The Tuckers, 2236 Murray Ave., Pittsburgh, PA 15217
Terry Harper, POB 103, Rouseville, PA 16344
Booksource Ltd., POB 43, Swarthmore, PA 19081
The Hermit's Book House, 34 Mt. Zion Rd., Wyoming, PA 18644

RHODE ISLAND

Lincoln Out-of-Print Search, POB 100, Foster, RI 02825
Tyson Books, 334 Westminster Mall, Providence, RI 02903

SOUTH CAROLINA

Norm Burleson Bookseller, 104 First Ave., Spartanburg, SC 29302

TENNESSEE

Burke's Book Store, Inc., 634 Poplar Ave., Memphis, TN 38105
Ollie's Books, 3218 Boxdale St., Memphis, TN 38118
Crabtree Booksellers, 2905 Taft Highway, Box 282, Signal Mountain, TN 37377

TEXAS

State House Books, 1604 South Congress Ave., Austin, TX 78704
David Grossblatt, POB 30001, Dallas, TX 75230
The Tracery, POB 30236, Dallas, TX 75230
Colleen's Books, 6880 Telephone Rd., Houston, TX 77061
Trackside Books, 8819 Mobud Dr., Houston, TX 77036
All Points of View, POB 321, San Antonio, TX 78292
Maggie Lambeth Books, 136 Princess Pass #3, San Antonio, TX 78212
Frederick W. Armstrong, 19 North McIlhaney, Stephenville, TX 76401
Book Cellar, 2 South Main, Temple, TX 76501
Von Blon's Books, 1111 Colcord Ave., Waco, TX 76707
Clark Wright Book Dealer, 409 Royal St., Waxahachie, TX 75165

UTAH

Brennan Books, POB 9002, Salt Lake City, UT 84109
Marie Veit, 1852 East 4650 South, Salt Lake City, UT 84117

VERMONT

Bradford Books, West Rd., Bennington, VT 05201
Bygone Books, 91 College St., Burlington, VT 05401
Kneedeep in Books, POB 1314, Manchester Center, VT 05255
Lilac Hedge Bookshop, Main St., Norwich, VT 05055
The Country Bookshop, RFD2, Plainfield, VT 05667
Bear Book Shop, RFD4, Box 219, West Brattleboro, VT 05301

VIRGINIA

Irene Rouse Bookseller, 905 Duke St., Alexandria, VA 22314
B. Tauscher, 102 Norwood Dr., Bristol, VA 24201
Forest Bookshop, POB 5206, Charlottesville, VA 22905
Allbooks, 4341 Majestic Lane, Fairfax, VA 22033
Royal Oak Bookshop, 207 South Royal Ave., Front Royal, VA 22630
Givens Books, 2345 Lakeside Dr., Lynchburg, VA 24501
Ghent Bookworm, 1407 Colley Ave., Norfolk, VA 23517
Book Search, 1741 Fairfax St., Petersburg, VA 23803
Givens Books, 1641 East Main, Salem, VA 24153
The Book House, 209-B North Boundary St., Williamsburg, VA 23185

WASHINGTON

Peggatty Books, Inc., 609 Maple St., Clarkston, WA 99403
Comstock's Bindery/Books, 7903 Rainier Ave., Seattle, WA 98118

WEST VIRGINIA

Appalachia Book Shop, 1316 Pen Mar Ave., Bluefield, WV 24701
Wolf's Head Books, POB 1048, Morgantown, WV 26507

WISCONSIN

Old Delavan Book Co., 57 East Walworth, Delavan, WI 53115
Webster's Criminal Procedure, 2526 East Webster Place, Milwaukee, WI 53211
The Antiquarian Shop, 1329 Strongs Ave., Box L, Stevens Point, WI 54481

WYOMING

Backpocket Ranch Bookshop, Star Route 4, Box 27, Sundance, WY 82729

APPENDIX B

North American Specialty Booksellers Who Issue Catalogs of Collectible Books

All of these booksellers offer catalogs of scarce and rare collectible books and other forms of printed collectibles. Some are specialists in specific genres: i.e., mystery, science fiction, Americana. Many sell by mail only. Others also operate shops with regular business hours. Most also buy by mail, and a study of their catalogs will give you a good idea of what kind of material they specialize in. Some of them also provide a book search service. A post card request will usually put you on the mailing list for their next catalog. It is a courtesy to enclose postage with your request.

Please note: This list is alphabetized by state, and by city within state.

ALBERTA, CANADA

Robert C. Scace, POB 7156, Postal Station E, Calgary, AB T3C 3M1, Canada

Tom Williams Books, POB 4126, Station C, Calgary, T2T 4M9, Canada

ARIZONA

Southwest Books, POB 319, Alpine, AZ 85920

John W. Keuhn, POB 73, Bisbee, AZ 85603

Readex Book Exchange, POB 1125, Carefree, AZ 85377

Russ Todd Books, Star Route 2, Box 872F, Cave Creek, AZ 85331

ARKANSAS

The Kingfisher, Lake Watch Route 1, Box 44, Eureka Springs, AR 72632

Martin House Books, 2212 South T, Fort Smith, AR 72901

Yesterday's Books, Etc., POB 1728, Hot Springs, AR 71901

Appletree Books, Route 1, Box 361, Williford, AR 72482

BRITISH COLUMBIA, CANADA

Okanagan Bookman, 2942 Pandosy St., Kelowna, BC V1Y 2E6, Canada
Academic Books, POB 86-365, North Vancouver, BC, Canada
Bill Ellis, POB 436, Queen Charlotte City, BC V0T 1S0, Canada
Ainslie Books, 10640 Bridgeport Rd., Richmond, BC V6X 1S7, Canada

CALIFORNIA

The Ross Valley Book Co., 1407 Solano Ave., Albany, CA 94706
House of Books, 1758 Gardenaire Lane, Anaheim, CA 92804
Gail Klemm Books, POB 518, Apple Valley, CA 92307
Rare Oriental Book Co., POB 1599, Aptos, CA 95001
Diane Peterson Booklady, POB 2544, Atherton, CA 94026
Anacapa Books, 3090 Claremont Ave., Berkeley, CA 94705
Roy Bleiweiss Fine Books, 92 Northgate Ave., Berkeley, CA 94708
The Scriptorium, 427 North Canon Dr., Beverly Hills, CA 90210
Books Et Cetera, POB 3507, Chico, CA 95927
John R. Butterworth, 742 West 11th St., Claremont, CA 91711
Beaver Books, POB 974, Daly City, CA 94017
P. F. Mullins Books, 109 Beachtree Dr., Encinitas, CA 92024
Trophy Room Books, 4858 Dempsey Ave., Encino, CA 91436
Bookfinder, 2035 Everding St., Eureka, CA 95501
Symposium Books, 4458 Myrtle Ave., Long Beach, CA 90807
Art Catalogues, 625 North Almont Dr., Los Angeles, CA 90069
Bennett & Marshall, 8205 Melrose Ave., Los Angeles, CA 90046
Dawson's Book Shop, 535 North Larchmont Blvd., Los Angeles, CA 90004
Doris Harris Autographs, 5410 Wilshire Blvd., Los Angeles, CA 90036
Heritage Bookshop, 847 North La Cienega Blvd., Los Angeles, CA 90069
George Houle Rare Books, 2277 Westwood Blvd., Los Angeles, CA 90064
Icart Vendor, 7956 Beverly Blvd., Los Angeles, CA 90048
Samuel W. Katz, 10845 Lindbrook Dr. #6, Los Angeles, CA 90024
Joe Martinez, 7057 Lexington Ave., Los Angeles, CA 90038
Kurt L. Schwarz, 738 South Bristol Ave., Los Angeles, CA 90049
Sylvester & Orphanos, POB 2567, Los Angeles, CA 90078
Tolliver's Books, 1634 South Stearns Dr., Los Angeles, CA 90035
Vaughns Fine Arts, 214 Medio Dr., Los Angeles, CA 90049

West Los Angeles Book Center, 1650 Sawtelle Blvd., Los Angeles, CA 90025
Zeitlin Periodicals Co., 817 South La Brea Ave., Los Angeles, CA 90036
Zeitlin & Ver Brugge, 815 North La Cienega Blvd., Los Angeles, CA 90069
Inter-American Books, POB 4154, Malibu, CA 90265
Wessex Books & Records, 108 El Camino, Menlo Park, CA 94025
Health Research, POB 70, Mokelumne Hill, CA 95245
Sagebrush Press, POB 87, Morengo Valley, CA 92256
Archaeologia, 707 Carlston St., Oakland, CA 94610
Holmes Book Company, 274 14th St., Oakland, CA 94612
Robert Perata Books, 3170 Robinson Dr., Oakland, CA 94602
Yosemite Collections, 618 Grand Ave., Oakland, CA 94610
The Book Sail, 1186 North Tustin, Orange, CA 92667
Fain's First Editions, 693 Amalfi Dr., Pacific Palisades, CA 90272
John P. Slattery, 352 Stanford Ave., Palo Alto, CA 94306
William P. Wreden, 200 Hamilton Ave., Palo Alto, CA 94302
William J. B. Burger, POB 832, Pine Grove, CA 95665
Acoma Books, POB 4, Ramona, CA 92065
Joanna Taylor, 2461 El Pavo, Rancho Cordova, CA 95670
Libros Latino, POB 1103, Redlands, CA 92373
The Silver Door, POB 3208, Redondo Beach, CA 90277
Rails Remembered, POB 464, Rosemead, CA 91770
Chloe's Books, POB 255673, Sacramento, CA 95865
Richard L. Press, 1228 "N" St. No. 2, Sacramento, CA 95814
Atticus Books, 728 Broadway, San Diego, CA 92101
Cape Cod Clutter, 3523 Fifth Ave., San Diego, CA 92103
Golden Hill Antiquarian, 2456 Broadway, San Diego, CA 92101
J. & J. House Booksellers, 5694 Bounty St., San Diego, CA 92101
Wahrenbrock's Books, 726 Broadway, San Diego, CA 92101
Argonaut Book Shop, 786 Sutter St., San Francisco, CA 94109
Books America, POB 4006, San Francisco, CA 94101
The Bookstall, 708 Sutter St., San Francisco, CA 94109
Brick Row Book Shop, 278 Post St. #303, San Francisco, CA 94108
Drama Books, 511 Geary, San Francisco, CA 94102
Hall, McCormick & Darling, POB 4168, San Francisco, CA 94101
The Holmes Book Company, 22 Third St., San Francisco, CA 94103
John Howell Books, 434 Post St., San Francisco, CA 94102
John Scopazzi Books, 278 Post St., San Francisco, CA 94108

Sergio Old Prints, 50 Maiden Lane, San Francisco, CA 94108
Alan Wofsy Fine Arts, 4012 China Basin St., San Francisco, CA 94107
A. S. Fischler Rare Books, 604 South 15th St., San Jose, CA 95112
R. E. Lewis, Inc., POB 1108, San Rafael, CA 94915
Dave Henson Books, POB 11402, Santa Ana, CA 92711
Milton Hammer Books, 125 El Paseo, Santa Barbara, CA 93101
Joseph the Provider, 903 State St., Santa Barbara, CA 93101
Maurice F. Neville Books, 835 Laguna St., Santa Barbara, CA 93101
Pepper & Stern, POB 2711, Santa Barbara, CA 93120
Second Debut Books, POB 30268, Santa Barbara, CA 93130
L. S. Kaiser Books, 1820 Graham Hill, Santa Cruz, CA 95060
George Robert Kane, 252 Third Ave., Santa Cruz, CA 95062
Hennessey & Ingalls Inc., 1254 Santa Monica Mall, Santa Monica, CA 90401
Michael S. Hollander, 1433 Santa Monica Blvd., Santa Monica, CA 90404
Howard Karno Books, POB 431, Santa Monica, CA 90406
Rancho Books, POB 2040, Santa Monica, CA 90406
Virginia Burgman, 3198 Hidden Valley Dr., Santa Rosa, CA 95404
Eclectic Gallery, POB 1581, Sausalito, CA 94965
Concord Books, Box 275, Seal Beach, CA 90740
Davis & Schorr Art Books, 14755 Ventura Blvd., #1-747, Sherman Oaks, CA 91403
B. & L. Rootenberg, POB 5049, Sherman Oaks, CA 91403
Heritage Books, 52 South Washington St., Sonora, CA 95370
Bay Side Books, POB 57, Soquel, CA 95073
Maxwell's Books, 2103 Pacific Ave., Stockton, CA 95204
Norman T. Hopper, 1142 Plymouth Dr., Sunnyvale, CA 94087
Len Unger Rare Books, 1575 El Dorado Dr., Thousand Oaks, CA 91362
Air Age Book Company, POB 40, Tollhouse, CA 93667
Book Buddy, 1328 Sartori Ave., Torrance, CA 90501
Books In Transit, 2830 Case Way, Turlock, CA 95380
Lois St. Clair, POB 247, Van Nuys, CA 91408
Kenneth L. Wolf, 6021 Allott Ave., Van Nuys, CA 91401
Mari Cyphers Rare Books, 1367 North Broadway, Walnut Creek, CA 94596
Hooked On Books, 1366 North Main St., Walnut Creek, CA 94596
Blitz Books, POB 1076, Weaverville, CA 96093
221 Books, 760 Carlisle Canyon Rd., Westlake Village, CA 91361
J. E. Reynolds, 3801 Ridgewood Rd., Willits, CA 95490
Natural History Books, 5239 Tendilla Ave., Woodland Hills, CA 91364

Robert Ross & Company, 6101 El Escorpion Rd., Woodland Hills, CA 91367
Geoscience Books, 13057 California St., Yucaipa, CA 92399

COLORADO

The King's Market, 1021 Pearl St., Suite D, Boulder, CO 80302
Rue Morgue Bookshop, 956 Pearl, Boulder, CO 80302
Snatarasa Books, 937 Broadway, Boulder, CO 80302
Book Home Inc., POB 825, Colorado Springs, CO 80901
Hermitage Antiquarian Books, 2817 East Third Ave., Denver, CO 80206
W. J. Bookhunter, POB 2795, Denver, CO 80201
William Allen Bookseller, POB 315, Englewood, CO 80151
E. Fithian Books, 1538 Ingalls St., Lakewood, CO 80214
RGS Books, 14266 Greenway Dr., Sterling, CO 80751

CONNECTICUT

Whitlock Farm Booksellers, 20 Sperry Rd., Bethany, CT 06525
Branford Rare Books, 221 Montowese St., Branford, CT 06405
Chimney Smoke Books, 74 Waller Rd., Bridgeport, CT 06606
Bob Cowell Book Seller, 15 Pearsall Way, Bridgeport, CT 06605
Stone of Scone Books, RFD 1, Box 262, Canterbury, CT 06331
Attic Books & Records, POB 53, Colebrook, CT 06021
Colebrook Book Barn, Route 183, Box 108, Colebrook, CT 06021
Rinehart Galleries, Upper Grey, Colebrook, CT 06021
Laurence Golder, POB 144, Collinsville, CT 06022
The Book Block, 8 Loughlin Ave., Cos Cob, CT 06807
Harrington's, 333 Cognewaug Rd., Cos Cob, CT 06807
John Woods, Main St., Coventry, CT 06238
Extensive Search Service, Squaw Rock Rd., Danielson, CT 06239
Clipper Ship Book Shop, 12 North Main St., Essex, CT 06426
Warren Blake Bookseller, 131 Sigwin Dr., Fairfield, CT 06430
Museum Gallery Book Shop, 360 Mine Hill Rd., Fairfield, CT 06430
R. & D. Emerson, The Old Church, Main St., Falls Village, CT 06031
Wolfgang Schiefer, 23 Church St., Georgetown, CT 06829
Anglers & Shooters Books, Goshen, CT 06576
William & Lois Pinkney, 240 North Granby Rd., Granby, CT 06035
American Worlds Books, POB 6162, Hamden, CT 06517
Antique Books, 3651 Whitney Ave., Hamden, CT 06518

DELAWARE

Oak Knoll Books, 414 Delaware St., New Castle, DE 19720
Horseshoe Lane Books, 436 New London Rd., Newark, DE 19711
Hollyoak Book Shop, 306 West 7th St., Wilmington, DE 19801

DISTRICT OF COLUMBIA

Bickerstaff & Barclay, POB 28452, Washington, DC 20005
East-West Feature Service, POB 8867, Washington, DC 20003
Folger Shakespeare Books, 201 East Capitol St. SE, Washington, DC 20003
William F. Hale Books, 1222 31st St. NW, Washington, DC 20007
Jean C. Jones Books, 3701 Massachusetts Ave. NW, Washington, DC 20016
Lambda Rising Inc., 2012 "S" St., Washington, DC 20009
Latin American Books, POB 39090, Washington, DC 20016
Lloyd Books, 3145 Dumbarton St. NW, Washington, DC 20007
Thomas T. Moebs, 407 "A" St. NE, Washington, DC 20002
Old Print Gallery, 1220 31st St. NW, Washington, DC 20007
Willis Van Devanter, POB 32426, Washington, DC 20007

FLORIDA

Jean Cohen, POB 654, Bonita Springs, FL 33923
Mickler's Floridiana, Box 38, Chuluota, FL 32766
Frank Guarino, POB 89, De Bary, FL 32713
Raintree Books, 432 North Eustis St., Eustis, FL 32726
Tracy Catledge, POB 583, Fern Park, FL 32730
Wake-Brook House, 990 NW 53rd St., Fort Lauderdale, FL 33309
McQuerry Orchid Books, 5700 Solerno Rd. West, Jacksonville, FL 32244
San Marco Bookstore, 1971 San Marci Blvd., Jacksonville, FL 32207
All Books & Prints Store, 4329 SW 8th St., Miami, FL 33134
Al Fogel Books, 2770 NW 32nd Ave., Miami, FL 33142
The Bookfinders, POB 2021, Miami Beach, FL 33140
The Book Trader, 170 10th St. North, Naples, FL 33940
Mycophile Books, 1166 Royal Palm, Naples, FL 33940
D. E. Whalen Samadhi, POB 729, Newberry, FL 32669
Dick Hazlett, POB 1935, West Palm Beach, FL 33402

GEORGIA

The Book Studio, POB 13335, Atlanta, GA 30324

Julian Burnett Books, POB 229, Atlanta, GA 30301
James O. McMeans, Box 420352, Atlanta, GA 30342
Old New York Book, 1069 Juniper St. NE, Atlanta, GA 30309
Oxford Book Store, 2345 Peachtree Rd. NE, Atlanta, GA 30305
Book Search Service, 36 Kensington Rd., Avondale Estates, GA 30002
Hound Dog Press Book Shop, 4285 Memorial Dr., Decatur, GA 30032
Robert Murphy Bookseller, 3113 Bunker Hill Rd., Marietta, GA 30062
Margie Sachs OP Books, Route 2, Box 59, Metter, GA 30439
Coosa Valley Book Shop, 15 East Third Ave., Rome, GA 30161
Lonnie E. Evans, 414 Bull St., Savannah, GA 31401
Jacqueline Levine, 107 East Oglethorpe Ave., Savannah, GA 31401
P. R. Rieber, Box 2202, Thomasville, GA 31792
Promenade Books, 1715 Norman Dr., Valdosta, GA 31601

HAWAII

Aldamar World of Books, 409 North King St., Honolulu, HI 96817
Prints Pacific, R.R.1, Box 276, Wailuku, Maui, HI 96763

ILLINOIS

Rose Lasley, 5827 Burr Oak, Berkeley, IL 60163
P. J. Henry, 4225 East, Berwyn, IL 60402
Abraham Lincoln Book Shop, 18 East Chestnut St., Chicago, IL 60611
Articles of War Ltd., 7101 North Ashland Ave., Chicago, IL 60626
Beasley Books, 1533 West Oakdale, Chicago, IL 60657
James M. W. Borg, 8 South Michigan Ave., Chicago, IL 60603
Richard Cady Rare Books, 1927 North Hudson Ave., Chicago, IL 60614
Gerald J. Cielec, 2248 North Kedvale Ave., Chicago, IL 60639
N. Fagin Books, 17 North State St. #1366, Chicago, IL 60602
Joseph J. Gasior, 4814 South Pulaski Rd., Chicago, IL 60632
The Globe, POB A3398, Chicago, IL 60690
Elinor Jaksto, 4104 Archer Ave., Chicago, IL 60632
Thomas J. Joyce & Company, 431 South Dearborn, Chicago, IL 60603
N. L. Laird Bookseller, 1240 West Jarvis, Chicago, IL 60626
Larry Laws, 831 Cornelia, Chicago, IL 60657
Magic, Inc., 5082 North Lincoln Ave., Chicago, IL 60625
G. B. Manasek Inc., 5805 South Dorchester, Chicago, IL 60637
Kenneth Nebenzahl Inc., 333 North Michigan Ave., Chicago, IL 60601

Nelson-Hall Booksellers, 111 North Canal St., Chicago, IL 60606
Ralph Geoffrey Newman Inc., 175 East Delaware Place, Chicago, IL 60611
A. & A. Prosser Books, 3118 North Keating Ave., Chicago, IL 60641
J. Dowd, 38 West 281, Tom's Trail, St. Charles, IL 60174
Seven Oaks Press, 405 South 7th St., St. Charles, IL 60174
The Gamebag, 973 North Princeton Ct., Vernon Hills, IL 60061
Yellowstone Books, POB 69, Villa Park, IL 60181
Richard Owen Roberts, 205 East Kehoe Blvd., Wheaton, IL 60187
Leekley Book Search, Box 337, Winthrop Harbor, IL 60096

INDIANA

Almagre Books, 3271 Spring Branch Rd., Bloomington, IN 47401
Rick Grunder Books, 915 Maxwell Terrace, Bloomington, IN 47401
Kathleen Rais, 612 North Dunn, Bloomington, IN 47401
G. J. Rausch, POB 2346, Bloomington, IN 47402
Gary Steigerwald, 1500 Maxwell Lane, Bloomington, IN 47401
G. B. Manasek Inc., POB 909, Chesterton, IN 46304
Bookstack, 112 West Lexington Ave., Elkhart, IN 46516
Campfire Books, 7218 Hogue Rd., Evansville, IN 47712
Ft. Wayne Forest Park Books, 1412 Delaware Ave., Fort Wayne, IN 46805
Back Tracts Inc., POB 30008, Indianapolis, IN 46230
Hoosier Schoolmaster's, 1228 Michigan Ave., La Porte, IN 46350
Mason's Books, 264 South Wabash, Wabash, IN 46992
Lion Enterprises, R.R.3, Box 127, Walkerton, IN 46574

IOWA

Mike Maddigan, POB 824, Cedar Rapids, IA 52406
Petersen Book Company, POB 966, Davenport, IA 52805
Pauline Millen Books, 3325 Crescent Dr., Des Moines, IA 50312
Checker Book World, 3520 Hillcrest, Dubuque, IA 52001
William A. Graf Books, 717 Clark St., Iowa City, IA 52240
Prairie Lights, 15 South Dubuque St., Iowa City, IA 52240
Gerald Pettinger Arms Books, Route 2, Russell, IA 50238

KANSAS

Forsyth Travel Library, Box 2975, Shawnee Mission, KS 66201
S. Jacobs, R.R.6, Box 264, Topeka, KS 66608

Dickey Books, 107 North Clifton, Wichita, KS 67208

KENTUCKY

T & B Books, Box 14077, Covington, KY 41014
Eagle Books, POB 12010, Lexington, KY 40579
Glover's Books, 862 South Broadway, Lexington, KY 40504
Don Grayson, 2600 Meadow Dr., Louisville, KY 40220
Donald S. Mull, 1706 Girard Dr., Louisville, KY 40222
Old Louisville Books, 426 West Oak St., Louisville, KY 40203
Vernon Owen Books, 1621 Phyliss Ave., Louisville, KY 40215
Philatelic Bibliopole, POB 36006, Louisville, KY 40233
Don Smith, 3930 Rankin St., Louisville, KY 40214
S-T Associates, 1317 Cherokee Rd., Louisville, KY 40204
The Mt. Sterling Rebel, Box 481, Mount Sterling, KY 40353

LOUISIANA

Taylor Clark, 2623 Government St., Baton Rouge, LA 70806
Henry C. Hensel, 657-B Rue Perez, Belle Chasse, LA 70037
Bayou Books, 1005 Monroe St., Gretna, LA 70053
Charles F. Hamsa, 612 Alonda Dr., Lafayette, LA 70503
Books-In-A-Bag, POB 9460, Metairie, LA 70055
American Opinion Books, 3804 Canal St., New Orleans, LA 70119
Red River Books, POB 3606, Shreveport, LA 71103

MAINE

Robert Canney Rare Books, POB 350, Alfred, ME 04002
Bill Lippincott Books, 547 Hammond St., Bangor, ME 04401
Medical Book Service, POB 447, Brewer, ME 04412
Cross Hill Books, POB 798, Brunswick, ME 04011
Leroy Cross, 21 Columbia Ave., Brunswick, ME 04011
Patricia Ledlie Books, POB 46, Buckfield, ME 04220
J. Bernard Reynolds, 12 Main St., Burnham, ME 04922
Varney's Volumes, Quaker Ridge Rd., Casco, ME 04015
Alfred Search Service, Drawer 1027, Damariscotta, ME 04534
Skeans & Clifford, POB 85, Deer Isle, ME 04627
Books and Autographs, 287 Goodwin Rd., Eliot, ME 03903
George E. Milkey, 50-A Brixham Rd., Eliot, ME 03903

MacDonald's Military, Coburn Gore, Eustis, ME 04936
Bunkhouse Books, Route 5A, Box 148, Gardiner, ME 04345
River Oak Books, RFD2, Box 5505, Jay, ME 04239
J. & J. Hanrahan, c/o Post Road Associates, Route 1, Kittery, ME 03909
Deborah Isaacson, Box 932, Lewiston, ME 04240
Maurice E. Owen, RFD2, Bowdoin Center Rd., Litchfield, ME 04350
Charles Robinson Books, Pond Rd., Box 299, Manchester, ME 04351
Sumner & Stillman, POB 225, Yarmouth, ME 04096

MARYLAND

Dragoman Books, 680 Americana Dr., #38, Annapolis, MD 21403
Artcraft Books, 6701 Cherry Hill Rd., Baldwin, MD 21013
The Chirurgical Bookshop, 1211 Cathedral St., Baltimore, MD 21201
Inscribulus Books, 857 North Howard St., Baltimore, MD 21201
Key Books, 2 West Montgomery St., Baltimore, MD 21230
Cecil Archer Rush, 1410 Northgate Rd., Baltimore, MD 21218
Sherlock Book Detective, POB 1174, Baltimore, MD 21203
B & K, POB 415, Bowie, MD 20715
Heritage Books, 3602 Maureen, Bowie, MD 20715
Old Hickory Bookshop, 20225 New Hampshire Ave., Brinklow, MD 20862
Wharf House Books, POB 57, Centreville, MD 21617
Mary Chapman Bookseller, POB 304, College Park, MD 20740
Jeff Dykes Western Books, POB 38, College Park, MD 20740
John Gach Books, 5620 Waterloo Rd., Columbia, MD 21045
Firstborn Books, 1007 East Benning Rd., Galesville, MD 20765
E. Don Bullian, 7-D Ridge Rd., Greenbelt, MD 20770
John C. Rather, POB 273, Kensington, MD 20895
Drusilla's Books, POB 16, Lutherville, MD 21093
Old Quenzel Store, POB 326, Port Tobacco, MD 20677
Harris Books, 12000 Old Georgetown Rd. #N805, Rockville, MD 20852
Moers Main Auction, 11910 Lafayette Dr., Wheaton, MD 20902

MASSACHUSETTS

Francis G. Walett, 369 High St., Abington, MA 02351
Andover Antiquarian Books, 68 Park St., Andover, MA 01810
Goodspeed's 2, 2 Milk St., Boston, MA 02108
Daniel F. Kelleher Co., 40 Broad St., Boston, MA 02109

Ralph Kristiansen, POB 524, Boston, MA 02215
Geoffrey H. Mahfuz, POB 289, Boston, MA 02199
Edward Morrill & Son, 25 Kingston St., Boston, MA 02111
David L. O'Neal, 308 Commonwealth Ave., Boston, MA 02115
Ivan Stormgart, POB 1232, Boston, MA 02205
E. Wharton & Co., 36 Hancock St., Boston, MA 02114
Organ Literature Foundation, 45 Norfolk St., Braintree, MA 02184
Xanadu Books, POB 91, Braintree, MA 02184
Smith's Book Service, Sunsmith House, Route 6A, Brewster, MA 02631
Thomas G. Boss, 80 Monmouth St., Brookline, MA 02146
Brookline Village Books, 23 Harvard St., Brookline, MA 02146
Dan Miranda, POB 145, Brookline, MA 02146
Asian Books, 12 Arrow St., Cambridge, MA 02138
Blue Rider Books, 1640 Massachusetts Ave., Cambridge, MA 02138
Grolier Book Shop, 6 Pylmpton St., Cambridge, MA 02138
In Our Time, POB 386, Cambridge, MA 02139
H. L. Mendelsohn, 1640 Massachusetts Ave., Cambridge, MA 02138
Pepper & Stern, POB 160, Sharon, MA 02067
Howard S. Mott, South Main St., Sheffield, MA 01257
Webb Dordick, 15 Ash Ave., Somerville, MA 02145
Elmcress Books, 161 Bay Rd., Route 1A, South Hamilton, MA 01982
J. & J. Lubrano, POB 127, South Lee, MA 01260
T. Small Books, POB 457, South Yarmouth, MA 02664
Sterling Bookstore, Route 12, Sterling, MA 01564

MICHIGAN

James Babcock, 5055 Point Tremble Rd., M29, Algonac, MI 48001
The Bookseller, POB 8163, Ann Arbor, MI 48107
Hartfield Fine & Rare Books, 117 Dixboro Rd., Ann Arbor, MI 48105
Keramos, POB 7500, Ann Arbor, MI 48107
Leaves of Grass, 2433 Whitmore Lake Rd., Ann Arbor, MI 48103
West Side Book Shop, 113 West Liberty, Ann Arbor, MI 48104
Wine & Food Library, 1207 West Madison St., Ann Arbor, MI 48103
Gunnerman Books, POB 4292, Auburn Heights, MI 48057
Mayflower Bookshop, 2645 West 12 Mile Rd., Berkley, MI 48072
Ceyx, POB 73, Dearborn, MI 48121
Else Fine Books, POB 43, Dearborn, MI 48121

Cellar Book Shop, 18090 Wyoming, Detroit, MI 48221
Grub Street, A Bookery, 17194 East Warren, Detroit, MI 48224
John K. King Books, Box 363, Detroit, MI 48232
Curious Book Shop, 307 East Grand River, East Lansing, MI 48823
Joseph L. Lepczyk, POB 751, East Lansing, MI 48823
Albert G. Clegg, 312 West Broad St., Eaton Rapids, MI 48827
Crabtree's Collection, 2236 Canal Rd., Eaton Rapids, MI 48827
Kregel's Bookstore, Box 2607, Grand Rapids, MI 49501
Sportsman's Outdoor Enterprises, POB 192, Grawn, MI 49637
J. E. Sheldon Fine Books, 645 West Green, Hastings, MI 49058
John B. Doukas, 3203 Bronson Blvd., Kalamazoo, MI 49008

MINNESOTA

J. & J. O'Donoghue Books, 1926 Second Ave. South, Anoka, MN 55303
ATC Books, 321 East Superior St., Duluth, MN 55802
Walter Chadde Books, Star Route 3, Box 629, Grand Marais, MN 55604
Arch Books, 5916 Drew Ave. South, Minneapolis, MN 55410
Bookmailer, 2730 West Broadway, Minneapolis, MN 55411
Thomas Dady, 2223 Sixth St. NE, Minneapolis, MN 55418
Dinkytown Antiquarian Books, 1316 SE 4th St., Minneapolis, MN 55414
Old Theology Book House, POB 12232, Minneapolis, MN 55412
Rulon-Miller Books, 716 North First St., Minneapolis, MN 55401
Scientia, POB 14254, Minneapolis, MN 55414
Page One, Highway 53, Orr, MN 55771
Bookdales, 46 West 66th St., Richfield, MN 55423
Five Quail Books, POB 278, Spring Grove, MN 55974

MISSISSIPPI

James A. Dillon Books, Star Route, Box 23, Carlisle, MS 39049
Choctaw Books, 406 Manship St., Jackson, MS 39202
Nouveau Rare Books, 5005 Meadow Oaks Park, Jackson, MS 39211
William M. Hutter, Route 3, Box 123, Ocean Springs, MS 39564

MISSOURI

Leroy Thompson, 3471 Highway A, Festus, MO 63028
Boyce E. McCaslin, POB 1580, Ironton, MO 63650
William J. Cassidy, 109 East 65th St., Kansas City, MO 64113
Cramer Book Store, POB 7235, Kansas City, MO 64113

Glenn Books, 1227 Baltimore, Kansas City, MO 64105
Klaus Grunewald Books, 807 West 87th Terrace, Kansas City, MO 64114
Smoky Hill Booksellers, POB 2, Kansas City, MO 64141
Hooked On Books, 2756 South Campbell, Springfield, MO 65807
Reginald P. Dunaway, 6138 Delmar Blvd., St. Louis, MO 63112
Elizabeth F. Dunlap, 6063 Westminster Place, St. Louis, MO 63112
Swiss Village Books, 711 North First St., St. Louis, MO 63102

MONTANA

Bay Books & Prints, Grand & Lake Sts., Bigfork, MT 59911
Thomas Minckler, 111 North 30th, Suite 221, Billings, MT 59101
Jane Graham, Box 1624, Bozeman, MT 59715
Blacktail Mountain Books, 42 First Ave. West, Kalispell, MT 59901
Douglas C. Johns, PO Drawer K, Lakeside, MT 59922
Bird's Nest, Box 8809, Missoula, MT 59807
David A. Lawyer Books, Route 2, Box 95, Plains, MT 59859

NEBRASKA

J. & L. Lee Booksellers, POB 5575, Lincon, NE 68505
Niobrara Books, POB 2664, Lincoln, NE 68502
D. N. Dupley, 9118 Pauline St., Omaha, NE 68124
Mostly Books, 1025 South 10th St., Omaha, NE 68108
1023 Booksellers, POB 3668, Omaha, NE 68103
Wordsmith Stores, POB O, Syracuse, NE 68446

NEVADA

Kalman Appel, 1412 South 16th St., Las Vegas, NV 89104
Gambler's Book Club, 630 South 11th St., Las Vegas, NV 89101

NEW BRUNSWICK, CANADA

Artican Books, Box 691, Fredericton, NB, Canada
P. J. FitzPatrick Books, Spencer St., Route 4, Fredericton, NB, Canada

NEWFOUNDLAND, CANADA

Maps & Books, 34 Kingsbridge Rd., St. Johns, NF A1C 3R6, Canada

NEW HAMPSHIRE

Kalonbooks, POB 16, Bradford, NH 03221

The Ha'Penny, RFD2, Route 121, Chester, NH 03036

Bert Babcock Bookseller, Box 1140, Derry, NH 03038

Colophon Book Shop, POB E, Epping, NH 03042

John F. Hendsey, Burley Homestead, Epping, NH 03042

Landscape Books, POB 483, Exeter, NH 03833

Jenny Watson, POB 915, Exeter, NH 03833

The Typographeum Bookshop, The Stone Cottage, Bennington Rd., Francestown, NH 03043

Louise Frazier Books, RFD6, Box 477, Gilford, NH 03246

Sacred and Profane, POB 321, Goffstown, NH 03045

Carry Back Books, Route 10, Dartmouth College Highway, Haverhill, NH 03765

Book Farm, POB 515, Henniker, NH 03242

Old Number Six Book Depot, POB 525, Henniker, NH 03242

Paul Henderson, 50 Berkeley St., Nashua, NH 03060

Burpee Hill Books, Burpee Hill Rd., New London, NH 03257

Sykes & Flanders, POB 86, North Weare Village, NH 03281

NEW JERSEY

Antic Hay Books, POB 2185, Asbury Park, NJ 07712

Bauman Rare Books, 14 South La Clede Place, Atlantic City, NJ 08401

Deskins & Greene Antiques, POB 1092, Atlantic City, NJ 08404

Richard W. Spellman, 610 Monticello Dr., Brick Town, NJ 08723

Edison Hall Books, 5 Ventnor Dr., Edison, NJ 08520

Ruth Woods Oriental Books, 266 Arch Rd., Englewood, NJ 07631

Junius Book Distributors, POB 85, Fairview, NJ 07022

The People's Bookshop, 160 Main St., Flemington, NJ 08822

Ppbk Book Co., 2200 North Central Rd., Fort Lee, NJ 07024

Rare Book Co., POB 957, Freehold, NJ 07728

Artifacts, 368 Grove St., Glen Rock, NJ 07450

J. M. Winters Books, 680 Summit Ave., Hackensack, NJ 07601

Old Cookbooks, POB 462, Haddonfield, NJ 08033

Elisabeth Woodburn, Booknoll Farm, Hopewell, NJ 08525

Edenite Society, Imlaystown, NJ 08526

James R. Zimmerman, 32 Terrace Place, Kearny, NJ 07032

DeVictor's Books, 3 Dov Place, Kendall Park, NJ 08824

Oz & Ends Book Shoppe, 14 Dorset Dr., Kenilworth, NJ 07033

The Dictionary, POB 130, Leeds Point, NJ 08220

Stephen Viederman, 108 High St., Leonia, NJ 07605
Acres of Books, 35 East State, Trenton, NJ 08608
Wilsey Rare Books, 80 Watchung Ave., Upper Montclair, NJ 07043
Stephen Koschal, POB 201, Verona, NJ 07044
H. Nestler, 13 Pennington Ave., Waldwick, NJ 07463
Albert Saifer, POB 51, West Orange, NJ 07052

NEW MEXICO

Chamisa Bookshop, 1602 Central SE, Albuquerque, NM 87106
Hummingbird Books, 2400 Hannett NE, Albuquerque, NM 87106
Jack D. Rittenhouse, POB 4422, Albuquerque, NM 87196
Robert R. White, POB 101, Albuquerque, NM 87103
Jane Zwisohn, 524 Solano Dr. NE, Albuquerque, NM 87108
Abacus Books, POB 5555, Santa Fe, NM 87502
Ancient City Book Shop, POB 1986, Santa Fe, NM 87501
Ancient City Press, POB 5401, Santa Fe, NM 87502
Richard Fitch—Old Maps, 2324 Calle Halcon, Santa Fe, NM 87505
Parker Books of the West, 300 Lomita, Santa Fe, NM 87501
Ean Richards Books, POB 9141, Santa Fe, NM 87501
Taos Book Shop, 114 Kit Carson Rd., Taos, NM 87571

NEW YORK

Joseph Geraci Rare Books, RD1, Box 258, Accord, NY 12404
John Hawley Books, POB 2061, Albany, NY 12208
Kevin T. Ransom Books, POB 176, Amherst, NY 14226
Kenneth Lang, 105 Avon Place, Amityville, NY 11701
Oan-Oceanie-Afrique Noire, POB 85, Ancram, NY 12502
Treasures in Books, POB 53, Andes, NY 13731
Autobooks East, POB 1, Babylon, NY 11702
Baldwin Book Service, POB 157, Baldwin, NY 11510
Bayshore Books, 31 West Main St., Bayshore, NY 11706
Judith Bowman Books, Pound Ridge Rd., Bedford, NY 10506

NORTH CAROLINA

Captain's Bookshelf, 26 1/2 Battery Park Ave., Ashville, NC 28801
Andrew Cahan, POB 882, Chapel Hill, NC 27514
Keith & Martin Books, 310 West Franklin St., Chapel Hill, NC 27514

Carolina Bookshop, 1601 East Independence Blvd., Charlotte, NC 28205
Little Hundred Gallery, 6028 Bentway Dr., Charlotte, NC 28226
B. L. Means, 5935 Creola Rd., Charlotte, NC 28226
Book House, Brightleaf Square, Durham, NC 27707
Book Trader, POB 603, Fairmont, NC 28304
Albemarle Books, POB 587, Gatesville, NC 27938
Pacificana, POB 398, Jamestown, NC 27282

NOVA SCOTIA, CANADA

Nautica Booksellers, 1579 Dresden Row, Halifax, NS B3J 2K4, Canada
Schooner Books, 5378 Inglis St., Halifax, NS B3H 1J5, Canada
D. A. Butcher, 87 McLean St., Trurd, NS B2N 4W2, Canada
The Odd Book, 8 Front St., Wolfville, NS, Canada

OHIO

The Bookseller Inc., 521 West Exchange St., Akron, OH 44302
The Odyssey, 1743 South Union, Alliance, OH 44601
Croissant & Company, POB 282, Athens, OH 45701
D. Gratz, Route 2, Box 89, Bluffton, OH 45817
De Anima, 122 East Evers, Bowling Green, OH 43402
Barbara Agranoff Books, POB 6501, Cincinnati, OH 45106
Old Erie Street Bookstore, 2128 East 9th St., Cleveland, OH 44115

OKLAHOMA

Ron Bever, Route 3, Box 243-B, Edmond, OK 73034
The Book Sheet, POB 1461, Lawton, OK 73502
Arcane Books, 3120 Harvey Parkway, Oklahoma City, OK 73118
Melvin Marcher, 6204 North Vermont, Oklahoma City, OK 73112
Caravan Books, Box 861, Stillwater, OK 74074
Oklahoma Bookman, 1107 Foreman Rd. NE, Yukon, OK 73099

ONTARIO, CANADA

Huronia-Canadiana, POB 685, Alliston, ON, Canada
Madonna House Bookshop, Combermer, ON, Canada K0J 1L
The House of Antique Books, 130 Shaftersbury St., Downsview, ON, Canada M3H 5M1
D. W. Goudy, 10 Douglas St., Guelph, ON, Canada N1H 2S9
Rising Trout Sporting Books, POB 1719, Guelph, ON, Canada N1H 6Z9

OREGON

McLaughlin's Books, POB 753, Cottage Grove, OR 97424
Authors of the West, 191 Dogwood Dr., Dundee, OR 97115
Backstage Books, POB 3676, Eugene, OR 97403
B. L. Bibby Books, 1225 Sardine Creek Rd., Gold Hill, OR 97525
Ernest L. Sackett, 100 Waverly Dr., Grants Pass, OR 97526

PENNSYLVANIA

Philip G. LeVan, 2443 Liberty St., Allentown, PA 18104
Margaret L. Tyrrell, 117 North 40th St., Allentown, PA 18104
Hive of Industry, POB 602, Easton, PA 18042
James S. Jaffe, POB 496, Haverford, PA 19041
Medical Manor Books, Benjamin Fox Pavilion, Box 647, Jenkintown, PA 19046

PUERTO RICO

Poe Book Shop, Bzn.119, Barrio Mani, Mayaguez, PR 00708

QUEBEC, CANADA

J. A. Benoit, 3465 Sherbrooke East, #1, Montreal, Quebec, Canada H1W 1C9
Bibliography of the Dog, 4170 Decarie Blvd., Montreal, Quebec, Canada 4H4 3K2
Mme. Lucie Javitch, 1589 Dr. Penfield Ave., Montreal, Quebec, Canada H3G 1C6
Helen R. Kahn, POB 323, Victoria Station, Montreal, Quebec, Canada H3Z 2V8
Jean Gagnon, 402-764 St. Joseph St., Bp.653 H-V, Quebec, Canada G1R 4S2

RHODE ISLAND

Jack Clinton, POB 1098, Hope Vallet, RI 02832
Anchor & Dolphin Books, POB 823, Newport, RI 02840
Armchair Sailor Bookstore, Lee's Wharf, Newport, RI 02840
Sign of the Unicorn, POB 297, Peacedale, RI 02883
Cornerstone Books, 163 Brook St., Providence, RI 02906

SASKETCHEWAN, CANADA

Northland Books, 813 Broadway Ave., Saskatoon, SK, Canada S7N 1B5

SOUTH CAROLINA

Harpagon Associates, 369 King St., Charleston, SC 29401
Noah's Ark Book Attic, Stony Point, Route 2, Greenwood, SC 29646
The Attic, Inc., POB 123, Hodges, SC 29653

The Book Shoppe, 9900 Kings Highway North, Myrtle Beach, SC 29577
Hampton Books, Route 1, Box 202, Newberry, SC 29108

UTAH

Bekker Antiquarian Books, 903 South 10th St. East, Salt Lake City, UT 84105
Cosmic Aeroplane Books, 258 East First St. South, Salt Lake City, UT 84111
Scallawagiana Books, POB 2441, Salt Lake City, UT 84110
Ute-or-Ida Books, POB 279, West Jordan, UT 84084

VERMONT

Aislinn Books, POB 589, Bennington, VT 05201
New Englandia, POB 589, Bennington, VT 05201
Kenneth Leach, POB 78, Brattleboro, VT 05301
Tuttle Antiquarian Books, 28 South Main St., Rutland, VT 05701
Weston Books, RD1, Box 90, Landgrove Rd., Weston, VT 05161

VIRGINIA

Irene Rouse, Bookseller, 905 Duke St., Alexandria, VA 22314
Virginia Book Company, POB 431, Berryville, VA 22611
B. Tauscher, 102 Norwood Dr., Bristol, VA 24210
Heartwood Books, 9 Elliewood, Charlottesville, VA 22903
Louis Ginsberg, POB 1502, Petersburg, VA 23805

VIRGIN ISLANDS

Rulon-Miller Books, Red Hook, Box 41, St. Thomas, VI 00802

WASHINGTON

Tolstoi's Ink, Third & State Sts., Marysville, WA 98270
Aero Literature, POB 1441, Olympia, WA 98507
Bainbridge Books, 322 Boylston St., Seattle, WA 98102
Bibelots & Books, 112 East Lynn, Seattle, WA 98102
Catweasel Books, POB 20695, Seattle, WA 98102

WEST VIRGINIA

Book Store, 104 South Jefferson St., Lewisburg, WV 24901
Wooden Porch Books, Route 1, Box 262, Middlebourne, WV 26149
Wolf's Head Books, POB 1048, Morgantown, WV 26507
Sebert's Books, Route 3, Box 325, Mount Nebo, WV 26679

The Bishop of Books, 117 15th St., Wheeling, WV 26003

WISCONSIN

Old Delavan Book Company, 57 East Walworth, Delavan, WI 53115
W. Bruce Fye, 1607 North Wood Ave., Marshfield, WI 54449
Constant Reader Bookshop, 1901 North Prospect Ave., Milwaukee, WI 53202
Littlwoods Book House, 200 East Park Ave., Waukesha, WI 53186

WYOMING

Backpocket Ranch Bookshop, Star Route 4, Box 27, Sundance, WY 82729

APPENDIX C

A Selected Reading List of Books About Books

Your local library may have a copy of these books. If not, your local bookstore should be able to tell you if any particular title is still in print and what the cost is, and order it for you if you wish. If the book is out of print, check your nearest used-book or antiquarian-bookseller. They may be able to locate a copy for you if they operate a search service. Or you can advertise for it yourself in the *Antique Trader Weekly, Collector's News,* or *AB, The Antiquarian Bookman,* for a copy.

AB BOOKMAN'S YEARBOOK. Annual.

Adams, Ramon F. MORE BURS UNDER THE SADDLE: BOOKS AND HISTORIES OF THE WEST. 1979.

Aldiss, Brian. BILLION YEAR SPREE: A HISTORY OF SCIENCE FICTION. 1973.

Aldiss, Brian, and Harry Harrison. HELL'S CARTOGRAPHERS: SOME PERSONAL HISTORIES OF SCIENCE FICTION WRITERS. 1975.

AMERICAN BOOK PRICES CURRENT. Annual.

Amis, Kingsley. THE JAMES BOND DOSSIER. 1965.

Ash, Brian. WHO'S WHO IN SCIENCE FICTION. 1976.

Atteberry, Brian. THE FANTASY TRADITION IN AMERICAN LITERATURE. 1980.

Bain, Robert, editor. SOUTHERN WRITERS: A BIOGRAPHICAL DICTIONARY. 1979.

Baron, Herman. AUTHOR INDEX TO ESQUIRE, 1933-1973. 1976.

Barron, Neil. ANATOMY OF WONDER: A CRITICAL GUIDE TO SCIENCE FICTION. 1981.

Baym, Nina. WOMAN'S FICTION: A GUIDE TO NOVELS BY AND ABOUT WOMEN IN AMERICA, 1820-1870. 1978.

Baynton-Williams, Roger. INVESTING IN MAPS. 1969.

Bleiler, Everett F. THE CHECKLIST OF SCIENCE FICTION AND SUPERNATURAL FICTION. 1979.

Bleiler, Everett F. THE GUIDE TO SUPERNATURAL FICTION. 1982.

Blum, Eleanor. BASIC BOOKS IN THE MASS MEDIA: AN ANNOTATED SELECTED BOOKLIST. 1980.

Bradley, Van Allen. THE BOOK COLLECTOR'S HANDBOOK OF VALUES. Latest edition.

Brandes, George Morris Cohen. MAIN CURRENTS IN NINETEENTH-CENTURY LITERATURE. 6 vols. 1972.

Breen, Jon L. WHAT ABOUT MURDER? A GUIDE TO BOOKS ABOUT MYSTERY AND DETECTIVE FICTION. 1981.

Bruccoli, Matthew, et al. DICTIONARY OF LITERARY BIOGRAPHY. 19 vols. 1978-1982.

Bruccoli, Matthew, et al. FIRST PRINTINGS OF AMERICAN AUTHORS. 4 vols. 1977-1978.

Bruccoli, Matthew, and C. E. Frazer Clark, Jr. PAGES: INSIDE THE WORLD OF BOOKS, WRITERS, AND WRITING. 1976.

Bruns, Hank F. ANGLING BOOKS OF THE AMERICAS. 1983.

Burke, W. J., and W. D. Howe. AMERICAN AUTHORS AND BOOKS. 1972. Latest edition.

Clareson, Thomas D. SCIENCE FICTION CRITICISM: AN ANNOTATED CHECKLIST. 1972.

Clarie, Thomas C. OCCULT BIBLIOGRAPHY: AN ANNOTATED LIST OF BOOKS PUBLISHED IN ENGLISH, 1971-1975. 1978.

Clark, Joseph D. BEASTLY FOLKLORE. 1968.

Cohen, Norman. LONG STEEL RAIL: THE RAILROAD IN AMERICAN FOLKLORE. 1981.

Cohen, Sarah Blacher, editor. COMIC RELIEF: HUMOR IN CONTEMPORARY AMERICAN LITERATURE. 1978.

Commire, Anne. YESTERDAYS AUTHORS OF BOOKS FOR CHILDREN. 1976.

Conningham, Frederick A. CURRIER & IVES PRINTS: AN ILLUSTRATED CHECK LIST. 1970.

CONTEMPORARY DRAMATISTS. 1982.

Cook, Michael L. DIME NOVEL ROUND-UP: AN ANNOTATED INDEX, 1931-1981. 1982.

Cook, Michael L. MYSTERY FANFARE: A COMPOSITE ANNOTATED INDEX TO MYSTERY AND RELATED FANZINES, 1963-1981. 1982.

Cook, Michael L. MURDER BY MAIL: INSIDE THE MYSTERY BOOK CLUBS, WITH COMPLETE CHECKLISTS. 1979.

Coven, Brenda. AMERICAN WOMEN DRAMATISTS OF THE TWENTIETH CENTURY: A BIBLIOGRAPHY. 1982.

Cowart, David, and Thomas L. Wymer. TWENTIETH-CENTURY AMERICAN SCIENCE FICTION WRITERS. 2 vols. 1981.

Cunningham, Eugene. TRIGGERNOMETRY. Latest printing.

Currey, L. W. SCIENCE FICTION AND FANTASY AUTHORS: A BIBLIOGRAPHY OF FIRST PRINTINGS. 1979.

Dahl, Svend. HISTORY OF THE BOOK. 1968.

Davis, David Brion. HOMICIDE IN AMERICAN FICTION, 1798-1860: A STUDY IN SOCIAL VALUES. 1968.

Day, A. Grove. BOOKS ABOUT HAWAII: FIFTY BASIC AUTHORS. 1977.

Day, A. Grove. PACIFIC ISLANDS LITERATURE: ONE HUNDRED BASIC BOOKS. 1971.

Debo, Angie. A HISTORY OF THE INDIANS OF THE UNITED STATES. 1979.

Derleth, August. A PRAED STREET DOSIER. 1968.

De Vinne, Theodore L. THE PRACTICE OF TYPOGRAPHY: A TREATISE ON TITLE PAGES. 1968.

De Waal, Ronald B. THE WORLD BIBLIOGRAPHY OF SHERLOCK HOLMES AND DR. WATSON. 1975.

Dinan, John A. THE PULP WESTERN: A POPULAR HISTORY OF THE WESTERN FICTION MAGAZINE IN AMERICA. 1981.

Dobyns, Henry F., and Robert C. Euler. INDIANS OF THE SOUTHWEST: A CRITICAL BIBLIOGRAPHY. 1981.

Dow, George Francis. SLAVE SHIPS AND SLAVING. 1968.

Drazan, Joseph G. THE PACIFIC NORTHWEST: AN INDEX TO PEOPLE AND PLACES IN BOOKS. 1979.

Duff, E. Gordon. EARLY PRINTED BOOKS. 1968.

Duffy, John. THE HEALERS: A HISTORY OF AMERICAN MEDICINE. 1979.

Earle, Alice M. STAGE-COACH AND TAVERN DAYS. 1968.

Eastman, Mary H. INDEX TO FAIRY TALES, MYTHS AND LEGENDS. 3 vols. 1926, 1937, 1952.

Eisenstein, Elizabeth. THE PRINTING PRESS AS AN AGENT OF CHANGE. 2 vols. 1979.

ELLERY QUEEN'S BOOK OF FIRST APPEARANCES. 1982.

Eppink, Norman R. 101 PRINTS: THE HISTORY AND TECHNIQUES OF PRINTMAKING. 1971.

Fairbanks, Carol, and Eugene A. Engeldinger. BLACK AMERICAN FICTION: A BIBLIOGRAPHY. 1978.

Faunce, Patricia S. WOMEN AND AMBITION: A BIBLIOGRAPHY. 1980.

Faye, Christopher U. FIFTEENTH-CENTURY PRINTED BOOKS AT THE UNIVERSITY OF ILLINOIS. 1949.

Feiffer, Jules. THE GREAT COMIC BOOK HEROES. 1965.

Fisher, Vardis, and Opal Laurel Holmes. GOLD RUSHES AND MINING CAMPS OF THE EARLY AMERICAN WEST.

Flanagan, Cathleen C., and John T. AMERICAN FOLKLORE: A BIBLIOGRAPHY, 1950-1974. 1977.

Foster, Thomas Henry. BEADLES, BIBLES AND BIBLIOPHILES. 1948.

Franklin V, Benjamin. BOSTON PRINTERS, PUBLISHERS AND BOOKSELLERS, 1640-1800. 1980.

Franklin, Linda C. ANTIQUES AND COLLECTIBLES: A BIBLIOGRAPHY OF WORKS IN ENGLISH, 16TH CENTURY TO 1976. 1978.

Gee, Ernest Richard. EARLY AMERICAN SPORTING BOOKS, 1734-1844. 1975.

Georges, Robert A., and Stephen Stern. AMERICAN IMMIGRANT AND ETHNIC FOLKLORE: AN ANNOTATED BIBLIOGRAPHY. 1982.

Glover, Dorothy, and Graham Greene. VICTORIAN DETECTIVE FICTION: A CATALOGUE. 1966.

Goodwater, Leanne. WOMEN IN ANTIQUITY: AN ANNOTATED BIBLIOGRAPHY. 1975.

Goulart, Ron. CHEAP THRILLS: AN INFORMAL HISTORY OF THE PULP MAGAZINES. 1972.

Goulart, Ron. THE HARDBOILED DICKS: AN ANTHOLOGY AND STUDY OF PULP DETECTIVE FICTION. 1965.

Greiner, Donald, editor. AMERICAN POETS SINCE WORLD WAR II. 2 vols. 1980.

Gribbin, Lenore S. WHO'S WHODUNIT: A LIST OF 3,218 DETECTIVE STORY WRITERS AND THEIR 1,100 PSEUDONYMS. 1968.

Grimes, Janet, and Diva Daims. NOVELS IN ENGLISH BY WOMEN, 1891-1920: A PRELIMINARY CHECKLIST. 1979.

Grobani, Anton. GUIDE TO BASEBALL LITERATURE. 1975.

Grobani, Anton. GUIDE TO FOOTBALL LITERATURE. 1975.

Gruber, Frank. THE PULP JUNGLE. 1967.

Grumet, Robert Steven. NATIVE AMERICANS OF THE NORTHWEST COAST: A CRITICAL BIBLIOGRAPHY. 1980.

Gunn, Drewey W. MEXICO IN AMERICAN AND BRITISH LETTERS: A BIBLIOGRAPHY OF FICTION AND TRAVEL BOOKS. 1974.

Hancer, K. THE PAPERBACK PRICE GUIDE. Annual.

Heard, J. Norman. BOOKMAN'S GUIDE TO AMERICANA. Most recent editions.

Hubin, Allen J. THE BIBLIOGRAPHY OF CRIME FICTION, 1749-1975. 1979.

Hudgeons, Thomas E. OFFICIAL PRICE GUIDE TO OLD BOOKS & AUTOGRAPHS. Latest edition.

Kirkpatrick, Daniel, editor. TWENTIETH-CENTURY CHILDREN'S WRITERS. 1978.

LeFontaine, Joseph Raymond. THE BOOK OF BOOKS.

LeFontaine, Joseph Raymond. INTERNATIONAL BOOK COLLECTORS DIRECTORY, 1983.

LeFontaine, Joseph Raymond. TURNING PAPER TO GOLD, 1987.

Lowery, Lawrence F. THE COLLECTOR'S GUIDE TO BIG LITTLE BOOKS AND SIMILAR BOOKS. Latest edition.

Matthews, Jack. COLLECTING RARE BOOKS FOR FUN AND PROFIT. 1981. (In my opinion the best book on the subject ever written for the neophyte.)

McGrath, Daniel F., editor. BOOKMAN'S PRICE INDEX. Latest edition.

Molnor, John E. AUTHOR-TITLE INDEX TO JOSEPH SABIN'S DICTIONARY OF BOOKS RELATING TO AMERICA. 3 vols. 1974.

Mossman, Jennifer, editor. PSEUDONYMS AND NICKNAMES DICTIONARY. 3 vols. 1982.

Peters, Jean. BOOK COLLECTING: A MODERN GUIDE. 1977.

Raymond, Joseph. INTERNATIONAL BOOK COLLECTORS DIRECTORY. Latest edition.

Reilly, John M., editor. TWENTIETH-CENTURY CRIME AND MYSTERY WRITERS. 1980.

Sabin, Joseph. A DICTIONARY OF BOOKS RELATING TO AMERICA. 2 vols. Latest edition.

Sampson, George, editor. THE CONCISE CAMBRIDGE HISTORY OF ENGLISH LITERATURE. Latest edition.

Sharp, Harold S. HANDBOOK OF PSEUDONYMS AND PERSONAL NICKNAMES. 5 vols. 1972-1982.

Smith, Curtis, editor. TWENTIETH-CENTURY SCIENCE FICTION WRITERS. 1981.

Tebbell, J. A. HISTORY OF BOOK PUBLISHING IN THE UNITED STATES, 1630-1980. 4 vols. 1972-1981.

Vinson, James, et al. TWENTIETH-CENTURY ROMANCE AND GOTHIC WRITERS. 1982.

Vinson, James. TWENTIETH-CENTURY WESTERN WRITERS. 1982.

Vinson, James, and D. L. Kirkpatrick, editors. CONTEMPORARY NOVELISTS. Latest edition.

Wolff, R. L. NINETEENTH-CENTURY FICTION: A BIBLIOGRAPHIC CATALOGUE. 2 vols. 1980.

APPENDIX D

Dictionary of Foreign Words and Phrases

F = French; L = Latin; G = Greek; I = Italian

à bon marché (F), Cheap
a die (L), From that day
à la bonne heure (F), Well-timed; in good time; favorably
à la carte (F), By the card
à la mode (F), In the fashion
a priori (L), From what goes before; from cause to effect
à propos (F), To the point
à volonté (F), At pleasure
à votre santé (F), To your health
ab incunabilis (L), From the cradle
ab initio (L), From the beginning
ad hominem (L), Personal; to the individual
ad nauseam (L), So as to disgust or nauseate
ad vivum (L), Like life; to the life
affaire d'amour (F), Love affair
alons (F), Come on
amour propre (F), Vanity; self-love
annus mirabilis (L), A year of wonders
ante bellum (L), Before the war
avant propos (F), Preface; introductory matter

bête noire (F), Black beast; a bugbear
billet doux (F), Love letter
bon ton (F), High fashion; first-class society
bona fide (L), In good faith
bonhomie (F), Good-natured simplicity

carte blanche (F), Full power
causa belli (L), A cause justifying war
causa sine qua non (L), An indispensable cause
chanson (F), Song
château (F), Castle
chèr amie (F), Dear (female) friend; a lover
conditio sine qua non (L), An indispensable condition
contretemps (F), Awkward mishap
coup (F), Decisive stroke
cui bono? (L), For whose advantage?; What is the good of it?

de die in diem (L), From day to day
de jure (L), By the law; by right
de profundis (L), Out of the depths
début (F), First appearance
décolleté (F), Open-breasted

demi-tasse (F), Small cup
dénouement (F), Unraveling or winding up
Deo gratias (L), Thanks be to God
Deo volente (L), God willing
Dominus vobiscum (L), The Lord be with you
double entendre (F), Double meaning

e pluribus unum (L), One out of, or composed of, many
ecce homo (L), Behold the man
éclat (F), Splendor, brilliancy
e.g. (exempli gratia) (L), For example
ennui (F), Weariness
en rapport (F), In harmony, relation, or agreement
en déshabille (F), In undress; in one's true colors
entourage (F), Surroundings
entre nous (F), Between ourselves; in confidence
esprit de corps (F), The animating spirit of a collective body of persons
ex curia (L), Out of court
ex delicto (L), From the crime
ex facto jus oritur (L), The law arises from the fact
ex officio (L), By virtue of office
ex parte (L), On one part or side
ex post facto (L), After the deed is done
ex tempore (L), Off hand; without preparation

fac simile (L), An exact imitation
faeces populi (L), The scum of the population
fait accompli (F), Accomplished fact
faux pas (F), False step; an act of indiscretion
fête (F), Feast, festival; holiday
fide et amore (L), By faith and love
fin de siècle (F), End of the century
fleur de lis (F), The flower of the lily
furor loquendi (L), A rage for speaking
furor poeticus (L), Poetical fire
furor scribendi (L), A rage for writing

gens de lettres (F), Literary men
gratia placendi (L), For the sake of pleasing
gratis dictum (L), Mere assertion

hoi polloi (L), The many, the common people
hors de combat (F), Disabled; unfit to continue a contest
hors-d'oeuvre (F), Out of course; out of accustomed place

i.e. (id est) (L), That is
impedimenta (L), Luggage; the baggage of an army
imperium in imperio (L), A government existing within another
implicite (L), By implication
in articulo mortis (L), At the point of death
in camera (L), In the judge's chambers; in secret
in extremis (L), In very bad circumstances; at the point of death
in flagrante delicto (L), In the commission of the crime; in the very act
in loco parentis (L), In the place of a parent
in pace (L), In peace
in perpetuum (L), For ever
in pleno (L), In full
in situ (L), In its proper position

in statu quo (L), In its former state
in vino veritas (L), In wine there is truth
ipso facto (L), By the fact itself
ita est (L), It is so

je ne sais quoi (F), I know not what
jure divino (L), By divine law
jure humano (L), By human law
jus divinum (L), The divine law

lagniappe (F), Thrown in as a bonus
laissez faire (F), To let alone
lapsus calami (L), A slip of the pen
le mot juste (F), Exactly the right word
le tout ensemble (F), The whole taken together
lie pendente (L), During the trial
litterateur (F), A literary man
locus criminis (L), The scene of the crime

ma chèrie (F), My dear (feminine)
mademoiselle (F), Young unmarried lady
magnum opus (L), A great undertaking
mal de mer (F), Sea-sickness
mala fide (L), With bad faith; treacherously
mardi gras (F), Shrove Tuesday (literally, Fat Tuesday)
mirabile dictu (L), Wonderful to relate
mirabile visu (L), Wonderful to see
modus operandi (L), The manner of working

n.b. (nota bene) (L), Mark well
ne plus ultra (L), Nothing further; the uttermost point; perfection
necessitas non habet legem (L), Necessity knows no law
née (F), Born
noblesse obligé (F), Nobility imposes obligations; much is expected from persons of good position
nom de guerre (F), War-name; an assumed name; a pseudonym
non sequitur (L), It does not follow; an unwarranted conclusion
nouvelles (F), News
nouvellette (F), Short tale or novel
nulli secundus (L), Second to none

obiter dictum (L), A thing said incidentally; an unofficial expression of opinion
ora pro nobis (L), Pray for us

parvenue (F), Upstart
pas à pas (F), Step by step
passé (F), Worn out
pâté de foie gras (F), Pie made from the livers of geese
pater familias (L), The father of the family
pax vobiscum (L), Peace be with you
penchant (F), Inclination; liking
per interim (L), In the meantime
per se (L), In itself; for its own sake
petit (F), Small
pied à terre (F), Resting-place; temporary lodging
pommes de terre (F), Potatoes (apples of the earth)
pot-pourri (F), Medley
prima donna (I), Leading lady singer in an opera
prima facie (L), At first glance
pro forma (L), As a matter of form
protégé (F), One protected by another
purée (F), Thick soup

qui non proficit, deficit (L), He who does not advance, loses ground

qui vive? (F), Who goes there?

quid nunc? (L), What now? What news?

quid pro quo (L), One thing for another; an equivalent

raison d'état (F), State reason

requiescat in pace (L), May he rest in peace

res gestae (L), Things done; exploits

résumé (F), Summing up

salvo jure (L), Without prejudice

sans souci (F), Free from care

savant (F), A man of science

savoir faire (F), Tact

semper fidelis (L), Always faithful

sic transit gloria mundi (L), So the glory of this world passes away

sine qua non (L), Without which, not; an indispensable condition

soirée (F), Evening party

spes sibi quisque (L), Let each man's hope be in himself; let him trust to his own resources

speude bradeos (G), Make haste slowly

status quo (L), The state in which

sub poena (L), Under a penalty

sub rosa (L), Under the rose; secretly

sub specie (L), Under the appearance of

sui generis (L), Of its own kind; unique

table d'hôte (F), Chef's special

tant pis (F), So much the worse

tempus fugit (L), Time flies

terra cotta (I), Baked clay

terra firma (L), Firm land

terra incognita (L), An unknown land

tête-à-tête (F), Conversation between two parties

tour de force (F), Feat of strength or skill

tout de suite (F), Immediately

vade in pace (L), Go in peace

veni, vidi, vici (L), I came, I saw, I conquered

via media (L), A middle course

vis à vis (F), Face to face

vita hominis sine literis mors est (L), The life of man without literature is death

voilà (F), See there; there is; there are

vox populi, vox Dei (L), The voice of the people is the voice of God

– APPENDIX E –

Ready Reckoner Value Guide

How to use the Ready Reckoner

You must have a value for a book in a specific condition to start with. From that, you can determine the value for a book in any other condition.

Examples

You have a book in *fine* condition and have determined that this same book in *good* condition is worth $38. Find $38 in the *good* column. Read across to the *fine* column—the value is $85.

You have two copies of the same book. One is *mint,* the other is *good.* You have determined that the price for the one in *good* condition should be $20. Read across to the *mint* column—the price should be $54.

For values not listed, find the nearest lower and higher value and average them.

MINT	FINE	VERY GOOD	GOOD
$ 12......	$ 10......	$ 8......	$ 4......
24......	20......	16......	9......
30......	25......	21......	11......
54......	45......	37......	20......
78......	65......	54......	29......
102......	85......	71......	38......
120......	100......	83......	44......
150......	125......	105......	55......
180......	150......	125......	65......
210......	175......	145......	80......
240......	200......	165......	90......
300......	250......	210......	110......
360......	300......	250......	135......

MINT	FINE	VERY GOOD	GOOD
$ 420	$ 350	$ 290	$155 . . . . . .
480	400	335	180 . . . . . .
540	450	375	200 . . . . . .
600	500	415	220 . . . . . .
720	600	500	265 . . . . . .
840	700	585	310 . . . . . .
960	800	665	355 . . . . . .
1080	900	750	400 . . . . . .
1200	1000	835	445 . . . . . .
1440	1200	1000	535 . . . . . .
1800	1500	1250	665 . . . . . .
2400	2000	1665	890 . . . . . .

Cautions

All values listed are for books with dust jackets (if originally issued with a dust jacket) in the same condition as the book and generally for first editions. If, however, you find a recorded price for a later edition that can be matched in any of the columns, you could use the other columns with some downgrading of the prices since the value spread will be much smaller.

Collectors should buy books in fair or poor condition as "reading copies" only, and then only if it is a scarce title.